The **Rough Guide** to

Florida

written and researched by

Mark Ellwood, Todd Obolsky, and Ross Velton

ROUGH GUIDES

NEW YORK • LONDON • DELHI

www.roughguides.com

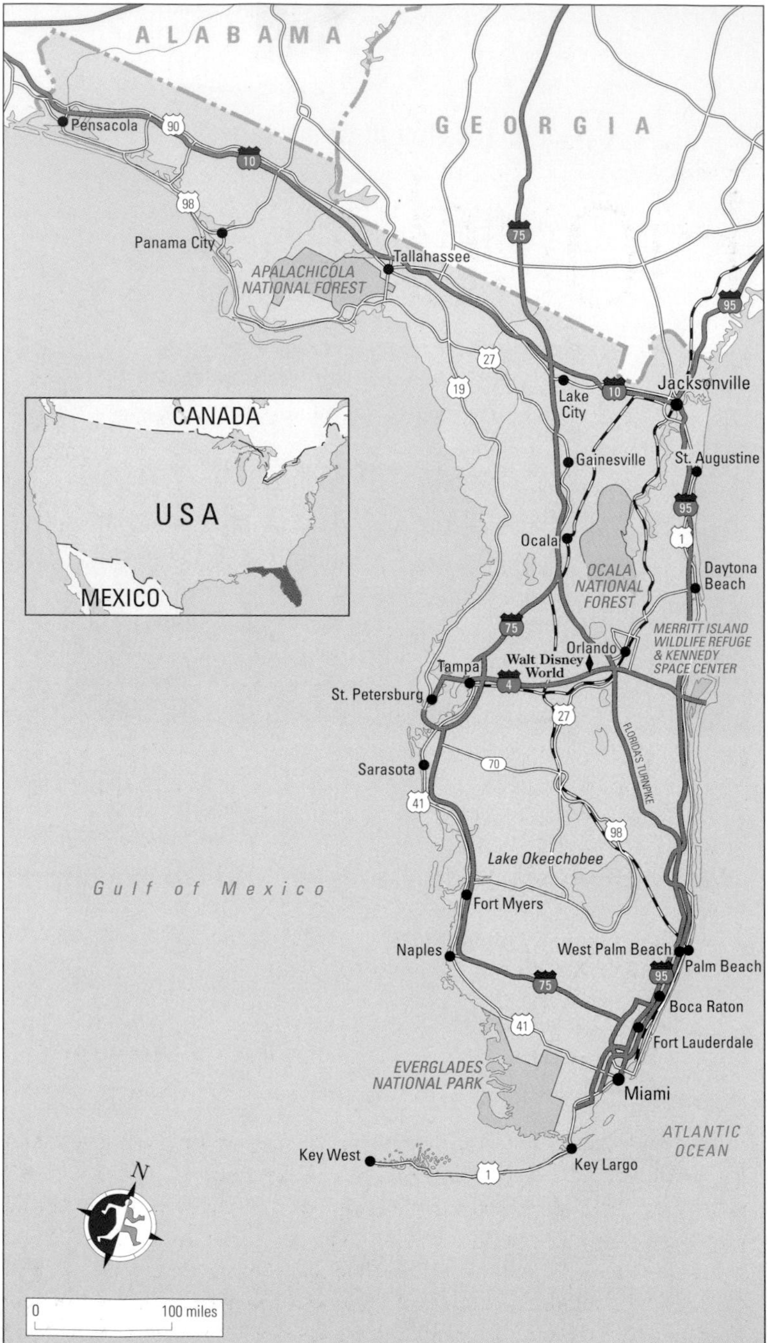
ALABAMA
GEORGIA
Pensacola
Panama City
Tallahassee
APALACHICOLA NATIONAL FOREST
Jacksonville
Lake City
Gainesville
St. Augustine
Ocala
OCALA NATIONAL FOREST
Daytona Beach
MERRITT ISLAND WILDLIFE REFUGE & KENNEDY SPACE CENTER
Orlando
Walt Disney World
Tampa
St. Petersburg
Sarasota
FLORIDA'S TURNPIKE
Lake Okeechobee
Gulf of Mexico
Fort Myers
Naples
West Palm Beach
Palm Beach
Boca Raton
Fort Lauderdale
EVERGLADES NATIONAL PARK
Miami
ATLANTIC OCEAN
Key West
Key Largo
CANADA
USA
MEXICO
N
0
100 miles
90
10
98
75
95
27
19
1
4
70
41

Introduction to Florida

The cut-rate package trips and photos of tanning flesh and Mickey Mouse that fill the pages of glossy holiday brochures ensure that everyone has an image of Florida – but seldom one that's either accurate or complete. Pulling in nearly sixty million visitors each year to its beaches and theme parks, the aptly nicknamed "Sunshine State" is devoted to the tourist trade, yet it's also among the least-understood parts of the US, with a history, character, and diversity of landscape unmatched by any other region. Beyond the palm-fringed sands, hiking and canoeing trails wind through little-known forests and rivers, and the famed beaches themselves can vary wildly over a short distance – hordes of copper-toned revelers are often just a Frisbee's throw from a deserted, pristine strand coveted by wildlife-watchers. Variations continue inland, where busy, modern cities are rarely more than a few miles away from steamy, primeval swamps.

In many respects, Florida is still evolving. Socially and politically, it hasn't stayed still since the earliest days of US settlement: stimulating growth has always been the paramount concern, and with an average of a thousand people a day moving to the booming state, it's currently the fourth most populous place in the nation. The changing demographics have helped overturn the common notion that Florida is dominated by retirees (though, coincidentally, the state song is a venerable spiritual entitled "Old

Fact file

- Spanish explorers named this territory after Pascua Florida, the "feast of flowers" celebrated at Easter; it was during this festival in 1513 that Ponce de León and crew landed on Florida's shores.
- Florida's 447-mile-long peninsula stretches between the Gulf of Mexico and the Atlantic Ocean and features 663 miles of beaches and about 4500 individual islands of ten acres or more.
- Five flags have been flown here: the French (1564), Spanish (1565–1763 and 1783–1821), British (1763–83), Confederate (1861–65), and US (1821–61 and from 1865 to the present). It was admitted as the 27th state in the Union in 1845; the capital is Tallahassee.
- Though 22nd in total area with 58,560 square miles, Florida is the fourth most populous state in the US, with more than sixteen million people.
- The two major industries are tourism and agriculture; in fact, Florida produces more citrus, tomatoes, green peppers, watermelon, sweet corn, and sugar than any other state.
- There are more golf courses in Florida than any other US state (some 1370), with the greatest concentration found in Palm Beach, which has more courses than any other county.

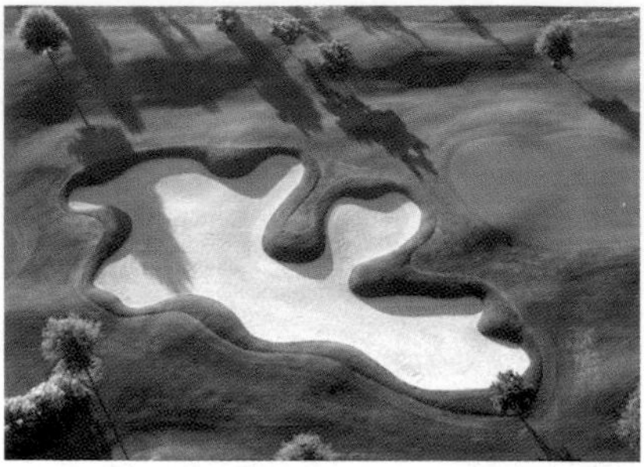

Folks at Home") or is part of the conservative Deep South, even if elements certainly do remain. The new Floridians tend to be a younger breed, taking advantage of the economic development along the US Highway 4 corridor in the center of the state – and Florida's lack of a state income tax. Immigration from outside the country has also been on the increase, with Spanish- and French-Creole-speaking enclaves providing a reminder of geographic and economic ties to Latin America and the Caribbean. These links proved almost as influential in raising the state's material wealth in the 1990s as the arrival of huge domestic and international businesses, and despite a sluggish US economy in recent years, Florida has remained on the upswing.

Not all is rosy: the state served as a major political battleground for the contested presidential election in 2000, rarely putting its best face forward as legal eagles and demonstrative protesters descended here en masse for the messy

Hordes of copper-toned revelers are often just a Frisbee's throw from a deserted, pristine strand coveted by wildlife-watchers.

proceedings. Slightly more behind the scenes, Florida is engaged in a struggle to provide enough houses, schools, and roads for its growing population; levels of poverty in the rural areas can be severe; and in an increasingly multi-ethnic society, racial tensions frequently surface. Expanding towns without jeopardizing the environment is another hot issue; uncontrolled development is posing serious ecological problems – not least to the Everglades. Nevertheless, large amounts of land are under state or federal

The Florida sun

Any visitor with sensitive skin should bear in mind that Florida shares a latitude with the Sahara Desert; the power of the Florida **sun** should never be underestimated.

Time spent outdoors should be planned carefully at first, especially between 11am and 2pm, when the sun is at its strongest. A powerful **sunscreen** is essential; anything with an SPF of less than 25 is unlikely to offer the necessary protection. Make sure to apply sunscreen liberally about thirty minutes before venturing outdoors (so that your skin has a chance to absorb it) and re-apply every two hours or if you've been in the water, regardless of whether the sunscreen is labeled "waterproof." Light-colored, loose-fitting, lightweight clothes should protect any parts of your body not accustomed to direct sunlight. Wear a hat with a wide brim as well as sunglasses with UV protection, and keep to the shaded side of the street. Drink plenty of **fluids** (but not alcohol) to prevent dehydration – public drinking-water fountains are provided for this purpose; iced tea and lemonade are the best drinks for cooling off in a restaurant.

protection, and there are signs that the conservation lobby is gaining the upper hand. For the most party, however, these factors will remain unfelt by visitors to Florida, who are likely to find its relentlessly sunny disposition and natural splendor difficult to resist.

Where to go

Heat-induced lethargy is no excuse not to get out and explore the different facets of Florida, as the state is compact enough to be toured easily and quickly. The essential stop is **Miami**, whose addictive, cosmopolitan vibe is enriched by its large Hispanic population, and where the much-photographed Art Deco district of **Miami Beach** provides an unmistakeable backdrop for the state's liveliest nightclubs.

From Miami, a simple journey south brings you to the **Florida Keys**, a hundred-mile string of islands of which each

The essential stop is Miami, whose cosmopolitan vibe is enriched by its large Hispanic population

Cuban heritage

Nowhere is evidence of Florida's **Cuban heritage** more pronounced than in Miami (see p.57). Cubans began fleeing the Batista and Castro regimes in the Fifties and Sixties, heading for the closest major city on US shores; many more were boatlifted there a few decades later. The influx has gradually reshaped the city, making it in essence a bilingual one; Hispanics, mostly of Cuban descent, now account for the majority of Miami's population, and their influence is felt in everything from the *nuevo cubano* cuisine in haute South Beach restaurants to local politics. Dominating the latter, the expatriate Cuban community here is largely composed of middle-class professionals, a staunchly conservative group that funds powerful lobbying at both state and federal levels.

Though the Cuban influence in **Key West** and **Tampa** may be less felt these days, it's no less crucial. Both places benefited enormously from the presence of the Cuban cigar industry, which left its mark in Key West in dozens of Cuban-style cottages that housed tobacco merchants who regularly commuted between factories in Key West and plantations in Havana. When Key West's fortunes failed in the 1880s, the Cuban workers decamped to Tampa further up the coast – then a small, nondescript settlement – and helped turn it into "The Cigar Capital of the World," a title the city would enjoy for forty years. With the mass arrival of the workers – as well as the railroad – the town was transformed into the commercial hub it remains today.

has something to call its own, be it sport fishing, coral-reef diving, or a unique species of dwarf deer. The single road spanning the Keys comes to a halt at **Key West**, a blob of land that's legendary for its sunsets and anything-goes attitude. North from Miami, much of the **southeast coast** is a disappointingly urbanized strip – commuter territory better suited for

living in than visiting. Alongside the busy towns, however, beaches flow for many unbroken miles and finally escape the residential stranglehold along the **northeast coast**, where communities are often subservient to the sands that flank them.

When you tire of beach life and ocean views, make a short hop inland to Florida's central portion, whose verdant terrain features cattle farms, grassy hillsides, and isolated villages beside expansive lakes. The sole but rather dramatic disruption to this rural idyll are the theme parks around Orlando, notably **Walt Disney World**, which practices tourism on the scale of the infinite. If you're in the mood, you can indulge in its ingenious fix of escapist fun; if not, the upfront commercialism may well encourage you to skip

The coral reef

Along with the Everglades, the best evidence of Florida's natural splendor lies in its extensive **coral reef**, the only living one in the continental United States. Just offshore of the Florida Keys, a string of small islands trailing from the southeastern corner of the state, the reef is made up of billions of tiny polyps – actually varieties of sea animals – that secrete limestone, which forms intricately shaped and vibrantly colored coral castles over many hundreds of years. These coral colonies are host to a stunning array of starfish, sponges, sand dollars, and angelfish, among hundreds of other species of exotic marine life. While they are well worth seeking out, the impact of millions of visitors each year has taken a toll on these delicate ecosystems, as has pollution. To minimise damage to the reefs, do not touch coral in any way – which is dangerously sharp as it is – lay your anchor on it, or remove pieces of it (which is illegal). For more about the reef, and how best to explore it, see "The Florida Keys," p.123, and in "Natural Florida," p.475.

Theme parks

Florida's most trumpeted attractions, its grandiose theme parks, offer prefabricated entertainment to millions of visitors – and locals – annually. When Walt Disney began secretly purchasing nearly thirty thousand acres of land in central Florida during the late Sixties, few could have guessed the impending seismic shift in the state's fortunes. The vast and lucrative vacation complex that resulted opened the floodgates to a number of imitators, including nearby Universal Orlando and SeaWorld Orlando, as well as Busch Gardens just outside Tampa; still, Disney remains king and constantly tries to one-up itself with each simulated safari and futuristic video display. Though the commercialism never ceases, if approached with a bit of forethought and a willingness to give in to the frenzied spirit, it may have you whooping just as loudly as the kids.

north to the deep forests of the **Panhandle**, Florida's link with the Deep South – or to the art-rich towns and sunset-kissed beaches of the **northwest and southwest coasts**. Explore these at your leisure as you progress steadily south to **the Everglades**, a massive, alligator-filled swathe of sawgrass plain, mangrove islands, and cypress swamp, which provides as definitive a statement of Florida's natural beauty as you'll encounter.

When to go

You'll have to take into account Florida's climate – and, of course, what your goals are – when deciding on the best time for a visit. Florida is split into **two climatic zones**: subtropical in the south and warm temperate – like the rest of the southeastern US – in the north. These two zones determine the state's tourist seasons and can affect costs accordingly.

Anywhere **south of Orlando** experiences very mild winters (Nov to April), with pleasantly warm temperatures and a low level of humidity. This is the peak period for tourist activity, with prices at their highest and crowds at their thickest. It also marks the best time to visit the inland parks and swamps. The southern summer (May to Oct) seems hotter than it really is (New York is often warmer) because of the extremely high humidity, relieved only by afternoon thunderstorms and sometimes even hurricanes (though the chances of being there during one are remote); at this time of year you'll be lucky to see a blue sky. Lower prices and fewer tourists are the rewards for braving the mugginess, though mosquitoes can render the natural areas off-limits.

Winter is the off-peak period **north of Orlando**; in all probability, the only chill you'll detect is a slight nip in the evening air, though it's worth bearing in mind that at this time of year the sea is really too cold for swimming, and snow has been known to fall in the Panhandle. The northern Florida summer is when the crowds arrive, and when the days – and the nights – can be almost as hot and sticky as southern Florida.

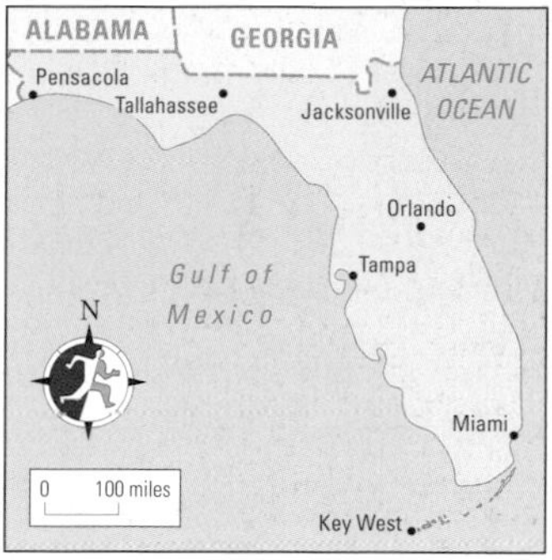

Average temperatures (°F/°C)

Jan	Feb	Mar	April	May	June	July	Aug	Sept	Oct	Nov	Dec
Jacksonville											
53/12	55/13	62/17	68/20	74/23	80/27	82/28	82/28	78/26	70/21	62/17	56/13
Key West											
70/21	70/21	74/23	77/25	81/27	83/28	85/29	84/29	83/28	80/27	76/24	72/22
Miami											
67/19	68/20	72/22	75/24	79/26	81/27	83/28	83/28	82/28	78/26	73/23	69/21
Orlando											
61/16	61/16	67/19	73/23	78/26	81/27	83/28	83/28	81/27	75/24	67/19	62/17
Pensacola											
51/11	54/12	60/16	67/19	75/24	80/27	82/28	82/28	78/26	69/21	61/16	54/12
Tallahassee											
51/11	53/12	60/16	66/19	74/23	80/27	81/27	81/27	78/26	68/20	60/16	53/12
Tampa											
60/16	61/16	67/19	71/22	77/25	81/27	82/28	82/28	81/27	75/24	68/20	62/22

29

things not to miss

It's not possible to see everything that Florida has to offer in one trip – and we don't suggest you try. What follows is a selective taste of the state's highlights: great beaches, outstanding national parks, spectacular wildlife – even good things to eat and drink. It's arranged in five color-coded categories, so that you can browse through to find the very best things to see, do, and experience. All highlights have a page reference to take you straight into the guide, where you can find out more.

01 Alligator encounters Page **174** • The "keepers of the Everglades," alligators are visible throughout the national park, particularly along the Anhinga Trail.

02 Apalachicola National Forest Page 429 • One of Florida's largest and most pristine national forests, Apalachicola offers endless opportunities for outdoor enthusiasts, like the thirty-mile Apalachicola Trail.

03 Miami Art Deco Page 77 • The colorful pastel architecture of South Beach is the reason many visitors make a beeline for the area.

04 Disney World Page **338** • Still the last word in theme park engineering and hospitality.

05 Boca Raton Resort Page **200** • Adam Mizner's eccentric architectural vision is most stunningly realized at this resort-cum-spectacle.

06 Beachcombing Page **250** • Whether you want to view suntanned bodies, collect shells, or just bum around in isolation, the beaches along the Atlantic and Gulf coasts run the gamut, including those on Sanibel Island.

07 Canoeing in the Everglades Page **180** • Florida has innumerable creeks and swamps for canoeing, the most impressive of which are in the Everglades.

08 Celebration Page **363** • Planned down to the smallest detail, Disney's own township is a fascinating example of an idealized American community.

09 Back to the Future, Universal Studios Page **355** • The rides at Universal Studios trump those of the other Orlando theme parks, perhaps none more so than the mind-bending Back to the Future.

10

Mount Dora Page **365** • Take a break from the Orlando theme parks to visit this charming Victorian-era village.

11

Sea turtle viewing Page **380** • Florida's Atlantic and Gulf coasts have abundant wildlife, like numerous varieties of sea turtles, best seen when nesting in June.

12

Cedar Key Page **304** • This remote island off Florida's northwest coast makes an enchanting getaway, with tumble-down shacks lending an atmospheric touch.

13 **Ybor City nightlife** Page **277** • The best that the Tampa Bay area has to offer, including restaurants, like the venerable *Columbia*, featuring live entertainment.

14 **Captain Tony's Saloon** Page **161** • Relax in this rustic hangout, which Ernest Hemingway made his own during his ten raucous yet productive years in Key West.

15 **The Venetian Pool** Page **92** • Lounge by the poolside or take a refreshing dip at this fanciful creation in Miami's Coral Gables.

16 Corkscrew Swamp Sanctuary Page 256 • The preserve's desolate landscape is home to the country's largest population of wood storks.

17 Bahamian Village Page 157 • The spirit of old Key West lives on in this laid-back neighborhood with Bahamian and Afro-Cuban roots.

18 Fantasy Fest Page **149** • Every October, outrageous partygoers parade in outrageous costumes along Key West's Duval Street during this gay-oriented celebration.

19 Fishing Page **42** • The waters of both Florida coasts, especially the Atlantic side, teem with every fish imaginable, including deep-sea giants like marlin and tuna; hire a boat and try your luck.

20 Manatees Page **302** • You'll most likely spot these gentle creatures at aquariums, but you can still get close to them in the waters around Crystal River in the northeast.

21 **Miami Art Museum** Page **73** • Engaging displays of art from the Forties to the present make this Miami institution the top stop for art-lovers.

22 **Hanging out on Ocean Drive** Page **77** • On weekend nights, the neon illuminations along Miami's Ocean Drive shine over a bumper-to-bumper street party.

23 Ponce Inlet Lighthouse Page **386** • The views of Daytona and New Smyrna beaches from the top of the Ponce Inlet Lighthouse are well worth the 175-foot climb.

24 Splendid China Page **361** • Take in the theatrical shows and meticulously crafted miniature replicas of Chinese landmarks at this unusual Orlando theme park.

25 Chalet Suzanne Page **297** • Some of Florida's most exquisite French meals are served amid the whimsical, vaguely Swiss-Arabic architecture of *Chalet Suzanne*, near Lake Wales.

26 **Cà d'Zan** Page **233** • John Ringling's palatial Sarasota home and stunning art collection attest to the circus owner's enormous wealth and discriminating taste.

27 **Kennedy Space Center** Page **373** • Everything you ever wanted to know about the history of the US space program, within sight of the launchpads on nearby Merritt Island.

28 St Augustine's Old Town Page **391** • Its narrow streets, preserved houses, and centuries-old fortress help St Augustine stake its claim as America's oldest city.

29
Key West delicacies
Page **160** • Gorge yourself on Key lime pie and conch, a sort of giant freshwater sea snail that is delicious both raw or deep-fried as fritters.

Contents

Using this Rough Guide

We've tried to make this Rough Guide a good read and easy to use. The book is divided into five main sections, and you should be able to find whatever you want in one of them.

Color section

The front color section offers a quick tour of Florida. The **introduction** aims to give you a feel for the place, with suggestions on where to go. We also tell you what the weather is like and include a basic country fact file. Next, our authors round up their favorite aspects of Florida in the **things not to miss** section – whether it's great food, amazing sights, or a special hotel. Right after this comes a full **contents** list.

Basics

The Basics section covers all the **pre-departure** nitty-gritty to help you plan your trip. This is where to find out which airlines fly to your destination, what paperwork you'll need, what to do about money and insurance, about Internet access, food, security, public transport, car rental – in fact just about every piece of **general practical information** you might need.

Guide

This is the heart of the Rough Guide, divided into user-friendly chapters, each of which covers a specific region. Every chapter starts with a list of **highlights** and an **introduction** that helps you to decide where to go, depending on your time and budget. Likewise, introductions to the various towns and smaller regions within each chapter should help you plan your itinerary. We start most town accounts with information on arrival and accommodation, followed by a tour of the sights, and finally reviews of places to eat and drink and details of nightlife. Longer accounts also have a directory of practical listings. Each chapter concludes with **public transport** details for that region.

Contexts

Read Contexts to get a deeper understanding of what makes Florida tick. We include a brief **history**, articles about **wildlife** and **environmental issues**, and a detailed section that reviews dozens of **books** and **films** relating to the state.

Index + small print

Apart from a **full index**, which includes maps as well as places, this section covers publishing information, credits, and acknowledgments, and also has our contact details in case you want to send in updates and corrections to the book – or suggestions as to how we might improve it.

Map and chapter list

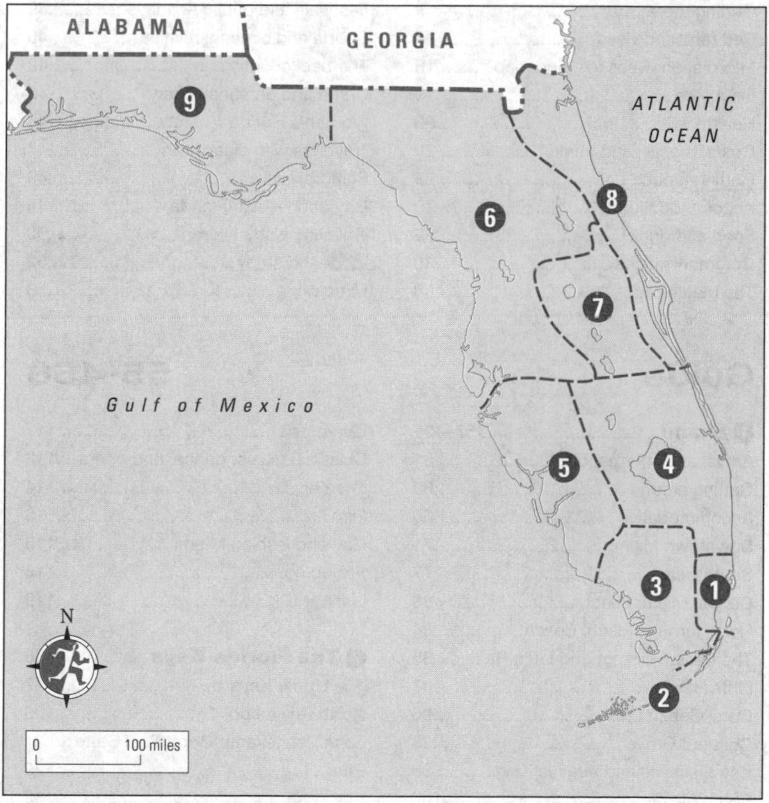

Contents

Color section i–xxiv

Basics 7–54

Guide 55–458

Contexts 459–496

Index and small print 503–512

Map symbols

maps are listed in the full index using colored text

Interstate	Monastery
US highway	Memorial
State highway	Historic house
Secondary state highway	Public gardens
Footpath/trail	Lighthouse
Railway	Marina
Ferry route	Marshland
State border	Information centre
Chapter division boundary	Post office
General point of interest	Hospital
Metro station	Wall
Airport	Stadium
Air base	Building
Campsite	Church
Picnic area	Cemetery
Battlefield	Park/preserve/refuge/forest
Castle	Indian reservation
Museum	Beach

Basics

Basics

Getting there

While Florida has beckoned visitors since the Spanish *conquistadores* made forays in the early sixteenth century, it has never been as easily accessible as now. Both Miami and Orlando have major international airports; Fort Lauderdale, Jacksonville, Tampa/St Petersburg, and Daytona Beach airports receive substantial foreign and domestic traffic; and Palm Beach, Tallahassee, Gainesville, Fort Myers, and Sarasota also have airports. Easily reachable by car, Florida lies at the end of three major interstate highways: I-95, which runs up the East Coast to Maine; I-75, which winds through the South on the way to Ohio and Michigan; and I-10, which stretches west across Texas and finally halts at Los Angeles.

In planning your vacation, remember that airfares depend on the **season**, and Florida is split into two climatic zones (see "Introduction," p.x). Note also that flying on weekends is typically more expensive; price ranges quoted below assume midweek travel. You can often cut costs by going through a **specialist flight agent** – either a consolidator, who buys up blocks of tickets from the airlines and sells them at a discount, or a **discount agent**, who in addition to dealing with discounted flights may also offer special student and youth fares and a range of other travel-related services such as travel insurance, rail passes, car rentals, tours, and the like. Some agents specialize in **charter flights**, which may be cheaper than any available scheduled flight, but again departure dates are fixed and withdrawal penalties are high. For some of the more popular destinations, you may even find it cheaper to pick up a bargain **package deal** from one of the tour operators listed below and then find your own accommodation when you get there. A further possibility is to see if you can arrange a courier flight, although you'll need a flexible schedule, and preferably be traveling alone with very little luggage. In return for shepherding a parcel through customs, you can expect to get a deeply discounted ticket. You'll probably also be restricted in the duration of your stay.

Booking flights online

Many airlines and discount travel websites offer you the opportunity to book your tickets **online**, cutting out the costs of agents and middlemen. Good deals can often be found through discount or auction sites, as well as through the airlines' own websites.

Online booking agents and general travel sites

Ⓦ **www.cheapflights.co.uk** (in UK & Ireland), Ⓦ **www.cheapflights.com** (in US), Ⓦ **www.cheapflights.ca** (in Canada), Ⓦ **www.cheapflights.au** (in Australia) Flight deals, travel agents, plus links to other travel sites.

Ⓦ **www.cheaptickets.com** Discount flight specialists.

Ⓦ **www.etn.nl/discount.htm** A hub of consolidator and discount agent Web links, maintained by the nonprofit European Travel Network.

Ⓦ **www.expedia.ca** (In Canada), Ⓦ **www.expedia.com** (in US), Ⓦ **www.expedia.co.uk** (in UK) Discount airfares, all-airline search engine, and daily deals.

Ⓦ **www.flyaow.com** Online air travel info and reservations site.

Ⓦ **www.gaytravel.com** Gay online travel agent, offering accommodation, cruises, tours, and more.

Ⓦ **www.hotwire.com** Bookings from the US only. Last-minute savings of up to 40 percent on regular published fares. Travelers must be at least 18 and there are no refunds, transfers, or changes allowed. Log-in required.

Ⓦ **www.lastminute.com** (in UK), Ⓦ **www.lastminute.au** (in Australia), Ⓦ **www.lastminute.nz** (in New Zealand) Offers good last-minute holiday package and flight-only deals.

Ⓦ **www.priceline.co.uk** (in UK), Ⓦ **www.priceline.com** (in US) Name-your-own-

price website that has deals at around 40 percent off standard fares. You cannot specify flight times (although you do specify dates) and the tickets are nonrefundable, nontransferable and nonchangeable.
Ⓦ **www.skyauction.com** Bookings from the US only. Auctions tickets and travel packages using a "second bid" scheme. The best strategy is to bid the maximum you're willing to pay, since if you win you'll pay just enough to beat the runner-up regardless of your maximum bid.
Ⓦ **www.smilinjack.com/airlines.htm** Has an up-to-date compilation of airline website addresses.
Ⓦ **www.travelocity.co.uk** (in UK), Ⓦ **www.travelocity.com** (in US), Ⓦ **www.travelocity.ca** (in Canada), Ⓦ **www.travelocity.au** (in Australia) Destination guides, hot fares, and great deals for car rental, accommodation, and lodging.
Ⓦ **www.travelshop.com.au** Australian site offering discounted flights, packages, insurance, and online bookings. Also on Ⓣ 1800/108 108.

From the US and Canada

Getting to Florida from anywhere else in North America is never a problem, as the region is well serviced by air, rail, and road networks. Every major and most minor US airlines **fly to Florida**, where Miami is the main hub, closely followed by Orlando and Tampa. Flying remains the quickest but most expensive way to travel; taking the **train** is a close second; traveling by **bus** is much less costly but also the slowest and least comfortable mode of transport.

By air

Of the **major carriers**, Delta and American Airlines have the best links with the state's many smaller regional airports. Flying into any of the major airports, you can expect to pay in the region of $250 from New York or from Chicago. From LA the lowest fare will be around $300, but be prepared to spend more. One of the better smaller airlines to check with (especially for one-way flights) is JetBlue, which runs flights to Orlando, Fort Lauderdale, Fort Myers, Tampa, and West Palm Beach; they often run Web-only specials, so be sure to check their site before making a final purchase. Also try Air Tran Airways, based in Atlanta, which has flights to Fort Lauderdale, Fort Myers, Miami, Orlando, West Palm Beach, Jacksonville, Tallahassee, Pensacola, and Tampa from a number of southern, midwestern, and East Coast cities.

From **Canada**, Air Canada flies direct from Toronto to Miami, Jacksonville, and Tampa, as well as Fort Lauderdale and Fort Myers in winter only; from Montréal the company has direct flights to Fort Lauderdale and Miami; and from Vancouver, they offer direct flights to Miami only. From Toronto and Montréal, expect to pay a minimum of Can$350 for a flight to Miami; Can$450 from Vancouver. American Airlines often offers competitive fares, with flights from Toronto to Miami, Orlando, and Fort Lauderdale plus several other Florida cities. They also fly to Miami from Vancouver (with a connection in Dallas).

Again, the place to find the lowest-priced fares is a **discount travel company**. If your plans are very flexible, scanning the travel pages of your local newspaper may turn up some bargains, but be sure to read the small print – many seemingly attractive deals have restrictive rules.

Airlines

Air Canada Ⓣ 1-888/247-2262, Ⓦ www.aircanada.ca
Air Tran Airways Ⓣ 1-800/AIR-TRAN, Ⓦ www.airtran.com
America West Airlines Ⓣ 1-800/235-9292, Ⓦ www.americawest.com
American Airlines Ⓣ 1-800/433-7300, Ⓦ www.aa.com
American Trans Air Ⓣ 1-800/225-2995, Ⓦ www.ata.com
Continental Airlines US Ⓣ 1-800/523-3273, Ⓦ www.continental.com
Delta Air Lines US Ⓣ 1-800/221-1212, Canada Ⓣ 1-800/241-4141, Ⓦ www.delta.com
Frontier Airlines Ⓣ 1-800/432-1359, Ⓦ www.flyfrontier.com
JetBlue Ⓣ 1-800/538-2583, Ⓦ www.jetblue.com
Northwest/KLM US Ⓣ 1-800/225-2525, Canada Ⓣ 1-800/447-4747, Ⓦ www.nwa.com
Southwest Airlines Ⓣ 1-800/435-9792, Ⓦ www.southwest.com
United Airlines US Ⓣ 1-800/241-6522, Canada Ⓣ 1-800/538-2929, Ⓦ www.ual.com
US Airways Ⓣ 1-800/428-4322, Ⓦ www.usair.com

Discount travel companies

Airtech ⓣ 212/219-7000, ⓦ www.airtech.com. Standby seat broker; also deals in consolidator fares and courier flights.
Council Travel ⓣ 1-800/226-8624, ⓦ www.counciltravel.com. Nationwide organization that mostly, but by no means exclusively, specializes in student/budget travel. Flights within US only.
Educational Travel Center ⓣ 1-800/747-5551 or 608/256 5551, ⓦ www.edtrav.com. Student/youth discount agent.
Skylink US ⓣ 1-800/AIR-ONLY or 212/573-8980, Canada ⓣ 1-800/SKY-LINK, ⓦ www.skylinkus.com. Consolidator.
STA Travel US ⓣ 1-800/781-4040, Canada 1-888/427-5639, ⓦ www.sta-travel.com. Worldwide specialists in independent travel; also student IDs, travel insurance, car rental, rail passes, and more.
Student Flights ⓣ 1-800/255-8000 or 480/951-1177, ⓦ www.isecard.com. Student/youth fares, student IDs.
Travac ⓣ 1-800/872-8800, ⓦ www.thetravelsite.com. Consolidator and charter broker, with offices in New York City and Orlando.
Travel Avenue ⓣ 1-800/333-3335, ⓦ www.travelavenue.com. Full-service travel agent that offers discounts in the form of rebates.
Travel Cuts Canada ⓣ 1-800/667-2887, US ⓣ 1-866/246-9726, ⓦ www.travelcuts.com. Canadian student-travel organization.
Travelers Advantage ⓣ 1-877/259-2691, ⓦ www.travelersadvantage.com. Discount travel club; annual membership fee required (currently $1 for three months' trial).

Tour operators

American Adventures ⓣ 1-800/873-5872, ⓦ www.americanadventures.com. Small-group camping adventure trips throughout the US, including a long-distance tour that takes in everything between Miami and Boston.
Contiki Tours ⓣ 1-888/CONTIKI, ⓦ www.contiki.com. Trips for the 18- to 35-year-old crowd, including the "Southern Adventure," which runs between Orlando and Los Angeles.
Cosmos ⓣ 1-800/276-1241, ⓦ www.cosmosvacations.com. Planned vacation packages with an independent focus.
Delta Vacations ⓣ 1-800/654-6559, ⓦ www.deltavacations.com. Good for package tours to Orlando, Miami, Daytona Beach, and more.
Elderhostel ⓣ 1-877/426-8056, ⓦ www.elderhostel.org. Specialists in educational and activity programs, cruises, and homestays for senior travelers.
Suntrek ⓣ 1-800/SUN-TREK, ⓦ www.suntrek.com. Group travel tours, including the $500-range "Florida Sunshine" trip, which takes in the sights from Orlando down through the Keys.

By car

How feasible it is to **drive** to Florida naturally depends on where you live and how much time you have. If you're aiming for the bustling, tourist hot spots like Orlando and Miami, you may enjoy the option of being able to spend a few days driving around the relaxing scenery of the southeast during your trip. From both New York City and Chicago, reckon on around 20 hours of actual driving to get to Miami; from Los Angeles you'll probably need around 45 hours behind the wheel.

Renting a car is the usual story of phoning your local branch of one of the majors (Avis, Hertz, Budget, Thrifty, etc – listed on pp.24–26), of which Thrifty tends to be the cheapest. Most have offices at destination airports, and addresses and phone numbers are comprehensively documented in the Yellow Pages.

Also worth considering are **fly-drive deals**, which give cut-rate (and sometimes free) car rental when buying your air ticket. They usually work out cheaper than renting on the spot and are especially good value if you intend to do a lot of driving.

By train

A few years ago, the deregulation of the airline industry helped make domestic air travel as cheap as train travel. In an effort to win back business, **Amtrak** (ⓣ 1-800/USA-RAIL, ⓦ www.amtrak.com) has sharpened up its act all around: raising comfort levels, offering better food, introducing "Thruway" buses to link with its trains, and launching new services. Consequently, traveling to Florida by train can be enjoyable and relaxing, if not particularly inexpensive.

From **New York**, the *Silver Meteor* and the *Silver Star* traverse the eastern seaboard daily to Miami via Orlando, while the *Palmetto* takes a detour at Jacksonville and continues to Miami via Tampa. Fares range from specials as low as $150 to around

$400 for a round-trip ticket, and the journey from New York takes between 26 and 29 hours. From **Los Angeles** to Orlando, the *Sunset Limited* crosses the southerly reaches of the US in a three-day journey. The lowest discounted round-trip fare varies according to season from $300 to $500.

If you really can't bear to be parted from your car and you live within driving distance of Lorton, Virginia (just south of Washington DC), the **Florida Auto Train** will carry you and your vehicle to Sanford, near Orlando. The journey time is 16 to 17 hours and passenger fares range from $75 to $190 each way; depending on the time of year and availability of space, your vehicle will cost an additional $140–280 each way.

All the above involve overnight travel. To spare yourself a restless night, Amtrak offers various types of **sleeping accommodation**, which includes meals, small toilets and showers, and will set you back an extra couple of hundred bucks per night.

By bus

Long-distance travel on **Greyhound** buses (Ⓣ1-800/231-2222, Ⓦwww.greyhound.com) can be an endurance test but is at least the cheapest form of public transport to the Sunshine State. Also, if you have the time and inclination to include a few stopovers on the way, you'll find that Greyhound operates a more comprehensive service than do planes or trains (they reach all but the smallest Florida towns). Scan your local newspaper or call your local Greyhound station for special fares, which are offered periodically, and remember that midweek travel is marginally cheaper than traveling on weekends.

Otherwise, the lowest round-trip fare from either Chicago or New York to Miami is around $125 – no refunds allowed. A more flexible ticket (allowing an 85 percent refund) costs $215. From LA to Miami the cheaper fare is, once again, around $125 and the more flexible one $50–60 more.

From the UK and Ireland

Although you can fly to the US from many of Britain's regional airports, the only nonstop scheduled flights to Florida are from London, and all of these land either at Miami or, less often, Orlando. The flight time is around eight hours, leaving London around midday and arriving during the afternoon (local time). The return journey is slightly shorter, leaving in the early evening and flying through the night to arrive in London around breakfast time. A basic round-trip economy-class ticket will cost £200–300 for a midweek flight in low season and £500–600 for a weekend flight in high season.

Travel agents (see opposite) can offer cut-price seats on direct **charter flights**. These are particularly good value if you're traveling from a British city other than London, though they tend to be limited to the summer season, be restricted to so-called "holiday destinations," and have fixed departure and return dates. Brochures are available in most high-street travel agents, or contact the specialists direct.

Many more routings use direct **one-stop** flights to Florida (a flight may be called "direct" even if it stops on the way, provided it keeps the same flight number throughout its journey). Obviously, these take a few hours longer than nonstop flights but can be more convenient (and sometimes cheaper) if you're not aiming specifically for Miami or Orlando. All the state's cities and large towns have airports – the other major one is Tampa – with good links from other US cities. Alternatively, you could take a flight to New York or **another city** on the northern East Coast and travel on from there – this won't save any money overall but is an option if you want to see more of the country before reaching Florida. Again, travel agents have the cheapest offers.

Airlines

Alitalia UK Ⓣ0870/544 8259, Republic of Ireland Ⓣ01/677 5171, Ⓦwww.alitalia.co.uk
American Airlines UK Ⓣ0845/7789 789 or 020/8572 5555, Republic of Ireland Ⓣ01/602 0550, Ⓦwww.aa.com
British Airways UK Ⓣ0845/77 333 77, Republic of Ireland Ⓣ1800/626 747, Ⓦwww.ba.com
Continental UK Ⓣ0800/776 464, Republic of Ireland Ⓣ1890/925 252, Ⓦwww.continental.com
Delta UK Ⓣ0800/414 767, Republic of Ireland Ⓣ01/407 3165, Ⓦwww.delta.com
United Airlines Ⓣ0845/8444 777, Ⓦwww.unitedairlines.co.uk

Virgin Atlantic Airways ⓣ01293/747 747, ⓦwww.virgin-atlantic.com

Flight and travel agents

Apex Travel Republic of Ireland ⓣ01/241 8000, ⓦwww.apextravel.ie. Specialists in flights to Australia, Africa, Far East, US, and Canada.
Bridge the World UK ⓣ0870/444 7474, ⓦwww.bridgetheworld.com. Specializing in round-the-world tickets, with good deals aimed at the backpacker market.
CIE Tours International Republic of Ireland ⓣ01/703 1888, ⓦwww.cietours.ie. General flight and tour agent.
Co-op Travel Care UK ⓣ0870/112 0099, ⓦwww.travelcareonline.com. Flights and holidays around the world.
Destination Group UK ⓣ020/7400 7045, ⓦwww.destination-group.com. Good discount airfares, as well as US inclusive packages.
Flightbookers UK ⓣ0870/010 7000, ⓦwww.ebookers.com. Low fares on an extensive selection of scheduled flights.
Joe Walsh Tours Republic of Ireland ⓣ01/676 0991, ⓦwww.joewalshtours.ie. General budget fares agent.
Lee Travel Republic of Ireland ⓣ021/277 111, ⓦwww.leetravel.ie. Flights and holidays worldwide.
North South Travel UK ⓣ & ⓕ01245/608 291, ⓦwww.northsouthtravel.co.uk. Friendly, competitive travel agency, offering discounted fares worldwide – profits are used to support projects in the developing world, especially the promotion of sustainable tourism.
Premier Travel Northern Ireland ⓣ028/7126 3333, ⓦwww.premiertravel.uk.com. Discount flight specialists.
Quest Travel ⓣ0870/442 3542, ⓦwww.questtravel.com. Specialists in round-the-world fares.
STA Travel UK ⓣ0870/1600 599, ⓦwww.statravel.co.uk. Worldwide specialists in low-cost flights and tours for students and under-26s, though other customers welcome.
Trailfinders UK ⓣ020/7628 7628, ⓦwww.trailfinders.co.uk, Republic of Ireland ⓣ01/677 7888, ⓦwww.trailfinders.ie. One of the best-informed and most efficient agents for independent travelers; produce a very useful quarterly magazine worth scrutinizing for round-the-world routes.
Travel Bag UK ⓣ0870/890 1456, ⓦwww.travelbag.co.uk. Discount flights to US; official Qantas agent.
Travel Cuts UK ⓣ020/7255 2082, ⓦwww.travelcuts.co.uk. Canadian company specializing in budget, student, and youth travel and round-the-world tickets.
USIT Now Republic of Ireland ⓣ01/602 1600, Northern Ireland ⓣ028/9032 7111, ⓦwww.usitnow.ie. Student and youth specialists for flights and trains.

Tour operators

Airtours UK ⓣ0870/238 7788, ⓦwww.uk.mytravel.com. Large tour company offering trips worldwide.
American Adventures UK ⓣ01295/756 200, ⓦwww.americanadventures.com. Small-group camping adventure trips throughout the US, including a long-distance tour that takes in everything between Miami and Boston.
British Airways Holidays UK ⓣ0870/442 3820, ⓦwww.baholidays.co.uk. Packages, city breaks, coach tours, cruises, and tailor-mades.
Thomas Cook UK ⓣ0870/5666 222, ⓦwww.thomascook.co.uk. Long-established one-stop 24-hour travel agency for package holidays or scheduled flights, with bureaux de change issuing Thomas Cook travelers' checks, and providing travel insurance and car rental.
Virgin Holidays ⓦwww.virginholidays.co.uk. Flights, fly-drive deals, tailor-mades, and packages to almost anywhere in Florida.

From Australia and New Zealand

Because of the enormous distance, there are **no direct flights** to Florida from Australia or New Zealand. Travelers should fly to Los Angeles or San Francisco – the main points of entry to the US – and make their way from there. Of the airlines, United Airlines, Air New Zealand, and Qantas are the best at arranging trouble-free connecting services through to Miami.

A basic round-trip **economy-class ticket** on these airlines out of Sydney or Melbourne will cost around Aus$1700 during the low season, Aus$2800 high season, while from Auckland (to Los Angeles) it will be NZ$2300/3000; add NZ$100 for departures from Christchurch or Wellington. Once in the States, you'll be looking at another US$350 or so to get to Miami. Various coupon deals, valid within the continental US, are available with your main ticket.

If you intend to take in Florida as part of a world trip, a **round-the-world** (RTW) ticket offers the greatest flexibility. In recent years, many of the major international airlines have allied themselves with one of two globe-spanning networks: the "Star Alliance," which links Air New Zealand, United, Lufthansa, Thai, SAS, Varig, and Air Canada; and "One World," which combines routes run by American Airlines, British Airways, AerLingus, Cathay Pacific, Iberia, LAN Chile, and Qantas. Both networks offer RTW deals with three stopovers in each continental sector you visit, with the option of adding additional sectors relatively cheaply. Fares depend on the number of sectors required, but start at around Aus$2200 (low season) for a US–Europe–Asia and home itinerary. If this is more flexibility than you need, you can save Aus$200–300 by going with an individual airline (in concert with code-share partners) and accepting fewer stops.

Airlines

Air Canada Australia ⓣ1300/655 747 or 02/9286 8900, New Zealand ⓣ09/379 3371, ⓦwww.aircanada.com
Air New Zealand Australia ⓣ13 24 76, New Zealand ⓣ0800/737 000, ⓦwww.airnz.co.nz
American Airlines Australia ⓣ1300/130 757, New Zealand ⓣ09/309 9159, ⓦwww.aa.com
Continental Airlines Australia ⓣ1300/361 400, New Zealand ⓣ09/308 3350, ⓦwww.flycontinental.com
Delta Air Lines Australia ⓣ02/9251 3211, New Zealand ⓣ09/379 3370, ⓦwww.delta.com
EVA Australia ⓣ02/9221 7055, New Zealand ⓣ09/358 8300, ⓦwww.evaair.com
Japan Airlines (JAL) Australia ⓣ02/9272 1111, New Zealand ⓣ09/379 9906, ⓦwww.japanair.com
KLM/Northwest Airlines Australia ⓣ1300/303 747, New Zealand ⓣ09/309 1782, ⓦwww.klm.com
Korean Air Australia ⓣ02/9262 6000, New Zealand ⓣ09/914 2000, ⓦwww.koreanair.com.au
Malaysia Airlines Australia ⓣ13 26 27, New Zealand ⓣ0800/777 747, ⓦwww.malaysiaairlines.com.my
Qantas Australia ⓣ13/13 13, ⓦwww.qantas.com.au; New Zealand ⓣ0800/808 767, ⓦwww.qantas.co.nz
Singapore Airlines Australia ⓣ13/10 11, New Zealand ⓣ0800/808 909, ⓦwww.singaporeair.com
United Airlines Australia ⓣ13/17 77, New Zealand ⓣ09/379 3800, ⓦwww.ual.com
Virgin Atlantic Airways Australia ⓣ02/9244 2747, New Zealand ⓣ09/308 3377, ⓦwww.virgin-atlantic.com

Travel agents

Flight Centre Australia ⓣ13/31 33, ⓦwww.flightcentre.com.au; New Zealand ⓣ0800/243 544 or 09/358 4310, ⓦwww.flightcentre.co.nz
Holiday Shoppe New Zealand ⓣ0800/808 480, ⓦwww.holidayshoppe.co.nz
New Zealand Destinations Unlimited New Zealand ⓣ09/414 1685
Northern Gateway Australia ⓣ1800/174 800, ⓦwww.northerngateway.com.au
STA Travel Australia ⓣ1300/733 035, ⓦwww.statravel.com.au; New Zealand ⓣ0508/782 872, ⓦwww.statravel.co.nz
Student Uni Travel Australia ⓣ02/9232 8444, ⓦwww.sut.com.au; New Zealand ⓣ09/379 4224, ⓦwww.sut.co.nz
Trailfinders Australia ⓣ02/9247 7666, ⓦwww.trailfinders.com.au

Specialist agents and tour operators

Australian Pacific Tours Australia ⓣ03/9277 8555 or 1800/675 222, New Zealand ⓣ09/279 6077, ⓦwww.aptours.com. Package tours and independent travel to the US.
Creative Holidays Australia ⓣ02/9386 2111, ⓦwww.creativeholidays.com.au. Packages to Miami and Orlando (including Disney World).
Journeys Worldwide Australia ⓣ07/3221 4788, ⓦwww.journeysworldwide.com.au. All aspects of travel to the US.
Sydney Travel ⓣ02/9220 9230, ⓦwww.sydneytravel.com. Can help with US flights, accommodation, city stays, car rental, and more.

Red tape and visas

Citizens of Australia, Britain, Ireland, New Zealand, and most European countries do not require visas for trips to the United States of less than ninety days. Instead, they need only a full passport and a visa waiver form, which is provided either by your travel agent or by the airline during check-in or on the plane, and must be presented to immigration on arrival. The same form covers entry across the land borders with Canada and Mexico as well as by air. However, those eligible for the scheme must apply for a visa if they intend to work, study, or stay in the country for more than ninety days.

Prospective visitors from parts of the world not mentioned above must have a valid passport and a **nonimmigrant visitor's visa**. How you'll obtain a visa depends on what country you're in and your status when you apply, so telephone the nearest US embassy or consulate (listed below). Further information can be found as well at Ⓦwww.travel.state.gov/visa_services.

Whatever your nationality, visas are not issued to convicted felons.

US embassies and consulates abroad

Australia

Sydney MLC Centre, 19-29 Martin Place ⓉO2/9373 9200, Ⓦusembassy-australia.state.gov

Denmark

Copenhagen Dag Hammarskjölds Allé 24, 2100 Ⓣ35 55 31 44, Ⓦwww.usembassy.dk

Ireland

Dublin 42 Elgin St, Ballsbridge Ⓣ01/668 8777, Ⓦwww.usembassy.ie

Netherlands

The Hague Lange Voorhout 102, 2514 EJ Ⓣ70/310 9209, Ⓦthehague.usembassy.gov

New Zealand

Wellington 29 Fitzherbert Terrace, Thorndon Ⓣ644/462 6000, Ⓦusembassy.org.nz

Norway

Oslo Drammensveien 18 Ⓣ471/22 44 85 50, Ⓦwww.usa.no

Spain

Madrid Serrano 75, 28006 Ⓣ91587-2200, Ⓦwww.embusa.es

Sweden

Stockholm Dag Hammarskjölds Väg 31, SE-11589 Ⓣ08/783 5300, Ⓦstockholm.usembassy.gov

UK

London 24 Grosvenor Square W1A 1AE Ⓣ020/7499 9000, Ⓦwww.usembassy.org.uk
Edinburgh 3 Regent Terrace EH7 5BW Ⓣ0131/556 8315
Belfast Queens House, 14 Queen St BT1 6EQ Ⓣ028/9032 8239

Immigration controls

During the flight, you'll be handed an **immigration form** (and a customs declaration: see p.16), which must be filled out and, after landing, given up at immigration control. Part of the form will be attached to your passport, where it must stay until you leave, when an immigration or airline official will detach it.

On the form you must cite your proposed length of stay and list an address, at least for your first night. Previously "touring" was satisfactory, but since the events of **September 11**, 2001, controls have become more stringent and they require a verifiable address. If you have no accommodation arranged for your first night, pick a plausible-sounding hotel from the appropriate section of the Guide and list that.

You should also be able to prove that you have a return air ticket (if flying in) and enough **money** to support yourself while in the US; anyone revealing the slightest intention of working while in the country is likely to be refused admission. Around $300–400 a week is usually considered sufficient – waving a credit card or two may do the trick. You may also experience difficulties if you admit to being HIV-positive or having TB.

Customs

Customs officers will relieve you of your customs declaration form and ask if you have any fresh foods. You'll also be asked if you've visited a farm in the last month: if you have, your shoes may well be taken away for inspection.

The **duty-free allowance** if you're over 17 is 200 cigarettes and 100 cigars, and, if you're over 21, a liter of spirits, wine, or beer.

As well as foods and anything agricultural, it's also **prohibited** to carry into the country any articles from North Korea, Cuba, Iran, Iraq, or Libya, obscene publications, lottery tickets, chocolate liqueurs, or pre-Columbian artifacts. Anyone caught carrying drugs into the country will not only face prosecution but be entered in the records as an undesirable and probably denied entry for all time. If you take prescription medicines, it may be a good idea to carry a letter from a doctor stating the exact nature of the pills you are carrying and/or your prescription, in order to ease your passage through Customs. There are more details on the US Customs and Border Protection website at Ⓦwww.cbp.gov/xp/cgov/travel.

Extensions and leaving

The date stamped on the form in your passport is the latest you're legally entitled to stay. Leaving a few days after may not matter, especially if you're heading home, but more than a week or so can result in a protracted – and generally unpleasant – interrogation from officials, which may cause you to miss your flight and be denied entry to the US in the future and your American hosts and/or employer to face legal proceedings.

Alternatively, you can do things the official way and get an **extension** before your time is up. The process can take a while, so it should be started as early as possible, but in no case later than your "leave by" date. This can be done by mailing form I-539 (and the $140 filing fee) to the nearest **US Bureau of Citizenship and Immigration Services (BCIS)** service center (for Florida, the address is: BCIS TSC, PO Box 851182, Mesquite, TX 75185-1182; info at Ⓦwww.bcis.gov). You may need to provide evidence of ample finances and, if possible, an upstanding American citizen to vouch for your worthiness. Obviously you'll also have to explain why you didn't plan for the extra time initially.

Information, websites, and maps

Florida's official tourism website (Ⓦwww.flausa.com) is a reasonable starting point for advance information. Once you've arrived in the state, you'll find that most large towns have at least a Convention and Visitors Bureau ("CVB," usually open Mon–Fri 9am–5pm, Sat 9am–1pm), offering detailed information on the local area and discount coupons for food and accommodation, but are unable to book accommodation.

In addition there are **Chambers of Commerce** almost everywhere; these are designed to promote local business interests, but are more than happy to provide travelers with local maps and information. Most communities have local free newspapers (see "The media," p.38) carrying news of events and entertainment – the most useful of which we've detailed in the Guide.

Drivers entering Florida will find **Welcome Centers**, fully stocked with information leaflets and discount booklets, at two points: on Hwy-231 at Campbellton, near the Florida–Alabama border, and off I-75 near Jennings, just south of the Florida–Georgia line. More convenient for arrivals on I-10 are the visitor information centers at Pensacola and Tallahassee (detailed in the Guide) and for I-95 drivers, there's one near Yulee as well.

Websites

Though we've listed relevant **websites** throughout the Guide for hotels, organizations, major sights, and so on, the following might help you pursue a few special areas of interest in preparation for your visit.

Dave Barry's Columns ⓦwww.miami.com/mld/miamiherald/news/columnists. A direct link to the latest humorous writings of Pulitzer Prize–winning *Miami Herald* columnist Dave Barry, whose topics run the gamut from politics to toxic fruitcakes.

Everglades National Park ⓦwww.nps.gov/ever. The national park's homepage contains all the information you'll need to visit, including directions, activities, wildfire updates, and more.

Florida Scuba Connection ⓦwww.florida-scuba.com. Comprehensive site dedicated to scuba diving in and around Florida; includes hundreds of links to local dive operators.

Great Outdoor Recreation Page ⓦwww.gorp.com. Highly recommended outdoors site, with a list of the state's best cycling spots, a birding guide, and the best paddling through the Everglades.

Hidden Mickeys of Disney ⓦwww.hiddenmickeys.org. Obsessive fan site that points out hundreds of the hidden Mickey Mouse carvings throughout Disney World (and Disneyland Anaheim, Disneyland Paris, etc).

MetroGuide Miami ⓦwww.miami.metroguide.net. A comprehensive listings site for Miami, with extensive dining, nightlife, and local event links.

Miami Herald ⓦwww.miami.com. For information on both local and national news, weather updates, sports scores, and entertainment happenings. Miami's daily newspaper also publishes a Spanish-language edition (ⓦwww.miami.com/mld/elnuevo).

Orlando Tourist Info ⓦwww.orlandotouristinformationbureau.com. Detailed site packed with information on Orlando's best eating, drinking, and entertainment spots.

South Florida Board Sailing Association ⓦwww.sfbsa.com. The homepage for the SFBS, a nonprofit organization dedicated to windsurfing issues throughout southern Florida; includes downloadable newsletters and driving directions to the best sailing spots.

Visit Florida ⓦwww.flausa.com. Florida's official tourism site. One of the most useful areas is their suggested driving tours, including routes focused on both Cuban and Native-American history.

Maps

General-purpose road maps from publishers like the American Automobile Association (AAA), Rand McNally, and Universal Maps concentrate on providing information for drivers, although they may also include some tourist information or street plans. Maps aimed more at the tourist market (Insight Flexi, National Geographic Society, Globetrotter) will highlight places of interest, include several plans of main cities and most visited attractions such as Disney World, and provide holiday tips as well. Some publishers (ITMB, Rand McNally, MapEasy) also do sectional maps just for the Gold Coast, Florida Keys, central Florida, and so on. **A word of warning**: the numbering of highway exits has been changed recently and some maps still show the old numbers – if in doubt, compare your map with Rand McNally or the AAA.

The best commercially available **city plans** are published by Rand McNally (see list overleaf), who produce plans of all the main cities and towns in the state. For traveling around more of the US, the *Rand McNally Road Atlas* ($11.95) is a good investment, covering the whole country plus Canada and Mexico.

If you're planning to **drive or cycle** (see "Getting around," p.23–28) through rural areas, use DeLorme's highly detailed 120-page *Florida Atlas & Gazetteer* ($19.95), which also contains a wealth of information on outdoor recreation. Local **hiking maps** are available at ranger stations in state and national parks either free or for $1–2, and some camping shops carry a supply. Trails Illustrated also publishes a GPS-compatible map of the Everglades useful for hiking or canoeing.

In Florida, **CVBs and Chambers of Commerce** give away an excellent free map of the whole state (though the Official Transportation Map does not, as its name suggests, detail public transport routes).

Members of the AAA and its overseas affiliates (such as both the AA and the RAC in Britain) can also benefit from this organisation's maps and general assistance. The AAA is based at 1000 AAA Drive, Heathrow, FL 32746-5063 (ⓣ407/444-4240, ⓦwww.aaa.com); further offices all across the state are listed in local phone books or on the association's website.

Map outlets

In the US and Canada

Adventurous Traveler Bookstore PO Box 64769, Burlington, VT 05406 ⓣ1-800/282-3963, ⓦwww.AdventurousTraveler.com
Book Passage 51 Tamal Vista Blvd, Corte Madera, CA 94925 ⓣ1-800/999-7909, ⓦwww.bookpassage.com
Distant Lands 56 S Raymond Ave, Pasadena, CA 91105 ⓣ1-800/310-3220, ⓦwww.distantlands.com
Elliot Bay Book Company 101 S Main St, Seattle, WA 98104 ⓣ1-800/962-5311, ⓦwww.elliotbaybook.com
Globe Corner Bookstore 28 Church St, Cambridge, MA 02138 ⓣ1-800/358-6013, ⓦwww.globecorner.com
Map Link Inc 30 S La Patera Lane, Unit 5, Santa Barbara, CA 93117 ⓣ800/962-1394, ⓦwww.maplink.com
Rand McNally ⓣ1-800/333-0136, ⓦwww.randmcnally.com. Around thirty stores across the US – dial ext 2111 or check the website for the nearest location.
The Travel Bug Bookstore 2667 W Broadway, Vancouver, BC V6K 2G2 ⓣ604/737-1122, ⓦwww.swifty.com/tbug
World of Maps 1235 Wellington St, Ottawa, ON K1Y 3A3 ⓣ1-800/214-8524, ⓦwww.worldofmaps.com

In the UK and Ireland

Stanfords 12–14 Long Acre, London WC2E 9LP ⓣ020/7836 1321; 29 Corn St, Bristol BS1 1HT ⓣ0117/929 9966; 39 Spring Gardens, Manchester M2 2BG ⓣ0161/831 0250; ⓦwww.stanfords.co.uk, ⓔsales@stanfords.co.uk
Blackwell's Map and Travel Shop 53 Broad St, Oxford OX1 3BQ ⓣ01865/793 550, ⓦmaps.blackwell.co.uk
Easons Bookshop 40 O'Connell St, Dublin 1 ⓣ01/858 3881, ⓦwww.eason.ie
Heffers Map and Travel 20 Trinity St, Cambridge CB2 1TJ ⓣ01865/333 536, ⓦwww.heffers.co.uk
Hodges Figgis Bookshop 56–58 Dawson St, Dublin 2 ⓣ01/677 4754
The Map Shop 30a Belvoir St, Leicester LE1 6QH ⓣ0116/247 1400, ⓦwww.mapshopleicester.co.uk
National Map Centre 22–24 Caxton St, London SW1H 0QU ⓣ020/7222 2466, ⓦwww.mapsnmc.co.uk
Newcastle Map Centre 55 Grey St, Newcastle-upon-Tyne NE1 6EF ⓣ0191/261 5622
Scotland's Map Centre 50 Couper St, Glasgow G4 0DL ⓣ0141/552 4394, ⓦwww.johnsmith.co.uk/smc/index.htm
The Travel Bookshop 13–15 Blenheim Crescent, London W11 2EE ⓣ020/7229 5260, ⓦwww.thetravelbookshop.co.uk

In Australia and New Zealand

The Map Shop 6 Peel St, Adelaide, SA 5000 ⓣ08/8231 2033, ⓦwww.mapshop.net.au
Mapland 372 Little Bourke St, Melbourne, Victoria 3000 ⓣ03/9670 4383, ⓦwww.mapland.com.au
Mapworld 173 Gloucester St, Christchurch ⓣ0800/627 967 or 03/374 5399, ⓦwww.mapworld.co.nz
Perth Map Centre 900 Hay St, Perth, WA 6000 ⓣ08/9322 5733, ⓦwww.perthmap.com.au
Specialty Maps 46 Albert St, Auckland 1001 ⓣ09/307 2217, ⓦwww.specialtymaps.co.nz

Insurance

Getting travel insurance is highly recommended, especially if you're coming from abroad and are at all concrned about your health – prices for medical attention in the US can be exorbitant. Before paying for a new policy, however, it's worth checking whether you are already covered: some all-risks home insurance policies may cover your possessions when overseas, and many private medical schemes include cover when abroad. In Canada, provincial health plans usually provide partial cover for medical mishaps in the US, while holders of official student/teacher/youth cards in Canada and the US are entitled to meager accident coverage and hospital in-patient benefits. Students will often find that their student health coverage extends during the vacations and for one term beyond the date of last enrollment.

After exhausting the possibilities above, you might want to contact a specialist travel insurance company, or consider the travel insurance deal we offer (see box below). A typical travel insurance policy usually provides cover for the loss of baggage, tickets, and – up to a certain limit – cash or checks, as well as cancellation or curtailment of your journey. Most of them exclude so-called **high-risk activities** unless an extra premium is paid: in Florida, this can mean scuba diving and windsurfing. Many policies can be chopped and changed to exclude coverage you don't need – for example, sickness and accident benefits can often be excluded or included at will. If you do take medical coverage, ascertain whether benefits will be paid as treatment proceeds or only after return home, and whether there is a 24-hour medical emergency number. When securing baggage cover, make sure that the per-article limit will cover your most valuable possession. If you need to make a claim, you should keep receipts for medicines and medical treatment, and in the event you have anything stolen, you must obtain an official theft report from the police.

Rough Guides travel insurance

Rough Guides Ltd offers a low-cost travel insurance policy, especially customized for our statistically low-risk readers by a leading British broker, provided by the American International Group (AIG), and registered with the British regulatory body, GISC (the General Insurance Standards Council).

There are five main Rough Guides insurance plans: **No Frills** for the bare minimum for secure travel; **Essential**, which provides decent all-round cover; **Premier** for comprehensive cover with a wide range of benefits; **Extended Stay** for cover lasting four months to a year; and **Annual Multi-Trip**, a cost-effective way of getting Premier cover if you travel more than once a year. Premier, Extended Stay, and Annual Multi-Trip policies can be supplemented by a "Hazardous Pursuits Extension" if you plan to indulge in sports considered dangerous, such as scuba diving or trekking. For a **policy quote**, call the Rough Guide Insurance Line: toll-free in the UK ⓣ0800/015 09 06 or ⓣ+44 1392 314 665 from elsewhere. Alternatively, get an online quote at ⓦwww.roughguides.com/insurance.

Health

If you have a serious accident while in Florida, emergency medical services will get to you quickly and charge you later. For emergencies or ambulances, dial ☎911 (or whatever variant may be on the information plate of the pay phone). If you have an accident but don't require an ambulance, most hospitals will have a walk-in emergency room (ER): for the nearest hospital, check with your hotel or dial information at ☎411. We've also listed ERs in the Guide, along with dental offices.

Should you need to see a doctor, lists can be found in the Yellow Pages under "Clinics" or "Physicians and Surgeons." A basic consultation fee is about $100, payable in advance. Medication isn't cheap either – keep receipts for all you spend and claim it back on your insurance policy when you return (see "Insurance," p.19 for more).

The most common minor ailments you'll encounter in Florida are **sunburn** and **mosquito bites**. To avoid painful – and potentially dangerous – sunburn, apply liberal amounts of sunscreen whenever outside. Those with fair skin should wear a wide-brimmed hat and consider staying out of the sun entirely during its brightest period (11am–3pm). For more on mosquitoes, see p.44 of "The backcountry."

Costs, money, and banks

To help with planning your Florida vacation, this book contains detailed price information for lodging and eating throughout the region. Unless otherwise stated, the hotel price codes given (explained on p.29) are for the cheapest double room through most of the year, exclusive of any local taxes that may apply, while meal prices include food only and not drinks or tip. Naturally, costs will increase slightly overall during the life of this edition, but the relative comparisons should remain valid.

If you're coming from elsewhere in the States, you'll likely not find Florida any more or less expensive, save in the resorts and big cities. For foreign visitors, even when the **exchange rate** is at its least advantageous (see box p.22), you'll find virtually everything – accommodation, food, gas, cameras, clothes, and more – to be better value in the US than it is at home.

Costs

Accommodation is likely to be your biggest single expense. Few hotel or motel rooms in cities cost under $40 – around $65 is more usual for a halfway decent room – and rates in rural areas are little cheaper. Although hostels offering dorm beds – usually for $15–25 – exist, they are not widespread and in any case represent only a very small saving for two or more people traveling together. Camping, of course, is cheap (anywhere from free to perhaps $20 per night), but is rarely practical in or around the big cities.

As for **food**, $15 a day is enough to get you an adequate life-support diet, while for a daily budget of around $25 you can dine pretty well. Beyond this, everything hinges on how much sightseeing, taxi-taking, drinking, and socializing you do. Much of any of these – especially in the major cities – and you're likely to go through upward of $70 a day.

The rates for **traveling around** on buses, trains, and even planes, may look cheap on paper, but the distances involved mean that costs soon mount up. For a group of two or more, **renting a car** can be a very good investment (see "Getting around," p.23), not least because it enables you to stay in the ubiquitous budget motels along the interstate highways instead of relying on expensive downtown hotels.

Remember that a **sales tax** of 6.5 percent is added to virtually everything you buy in shops, except for groceries, but it isn't part of the marked price.

Cash and travelers' checks

US dollar travelers' checks are the best way to carry money, for both American and foreign visitors; they offer the great security of knowing that lost or stolen checks will be replaced. You should have no problem using the better-known checks, such as American Express and Visa, in shops, restaurants, and gas stations (don't be put off by "no checks" signs, which only refer to personal checks). Be sure to have plenty of the $10 and $20 denominations for everyday transactions.

Major Florida **banks** – such as Bank of America, Barnett, First Florida, Southeast, and Sun – will (with considerable fuss) change travelers' checks in other currencies and foreign currency. Commission rates tend to be lower at **exchange bureaux** like Deak-Perera and Thomas Cook; airport exchange offices can also be reasonable. Rarely, if ever, do hotels change foreign currency.

Banking hours in Florida are generally 10am until 3pm Monday to Thursday and 10am to 5pm on Fridays.

The **usual fee** for travelers' check sales is one or two percent, though this fee may be waived if you buy the checks through a bank where you have an account. Make sure to keep the purchase agreement and a record of check serial numbers safe and separate from the checks themselves. In the event that checks are lost or stolen, the issuing company will expect you to report the loss forthwith to their offices (most companies claim to replace lost or stolen checks within 24 hours); see p.46 for more on what to do if your travelers' checks are lost or stolen.

Credit and debit cards

If you don't already have a **credit card**, you should think seriously about getting one before you set off. For many services, it's simply taken for granted that you'll be paying with plastic. When renting a car (or even a bike) or checking into a hotel, you may well be asked to show a credit card to establish your credit-worthiness – even if you intend to settle the bill in cash – or as security, or both. Visa, MasterCard, Diners Club, American Express, and Discover are the most widely used.

With most cards it is also possible to **withdraw cash** at any bank displaying relevant stickers, or from appropriate automatic teller machines (**ATMs**) – though remember that all cash advances are treated as loans, with interest accruing daily from the date of withdrawal; there may be a transaction fee on top of this.

You may be able to make withdrawals from ATMs using your **debit card**, which is not liable to interest payments, and the flat transaction fee is usually quite small – your bank will be able to advise on this. Foreign travelers can also use their ATM cards, as long as they're linked to international networks such as **Cirrus** and **Plus** – though it's important to check the latest details with your bank before departing, as otherwise the machine may simply gobble up your card.

A compromise between travelers' checks and plastic is **Visa TravelMoney**, a disposable prepaid debit card with a PIN which works in all ATMs that take Visa cards. You load up your account with funds before leaving home, and when they run out, you simply throw the card away. You can buy up to nine cards to access the same funds – useful for couples or families traveling together – and it's a good idea to buy at least one extra as a back-up in case of loss or theft. There is also a 24-hour toll-free customer assistance number (Ⓣ1-877/394-2247). The card is available in most countries through

Travelex/Interpayment, and also AAA. For more information, check the Visa TravelMoney website at Wusa.visa.com/personal/cards/visa_travel_money.html.

Overseas visitors should also bear in mind that fluctuating **exchange rates** may result in spending more (or less) than expected when the item eventually shows up on a statement.

Wiring money

Having money **wired** from home using one of the companies listed below is never convenient or cheap, and should be considered a last resort. It's also possible to have money wired directly from a bank in your home country to a bank in Florida, although this is somewhat less reliable because it involves two separate institutions. If you go this route, your home bank will need the address of the branch bank where you want to pick up the money and the address and routing number of the bank's state head office, which will act as the clearing house; money wired this way normally takes two working days to arrive, and costs around $40 per transaction.

Money-wiring companies

Thomas Cook US ⓣ1-800/287-7362, Canada ⓣ1-888/823-4732, Great Britain ⓣ01733/318 922, Northern Ireland ⓣ028/9055 0030, Republic of Ireland ⓣ01/677 1721, ⓦwww.thomascook.com
Travelers Express MoneyGram US ⓣ1-800/955-7777, Canada ⓣ1-800/933-3278, UK ⓣ0800/018 0104, Republic of Ireland ⓣ1850/205 800, Australia ⓣ1800/230 100, New Zealand ⓣ0800/262 263, ⓦwww.moneygram.com
Western Union US and Canada ⓣ1-800/325-6000, Australia ⓣ1800/501 500, New Zealand ⓣ0800/270 000, UK ⓣ0800/833 833, Republic of Ireland ⓣ1800/395 395, ⓦwww.westernunion.com

Youth and student discounts

Once obtained, various official and quasi-official youth/student **ID cards** soon pay for themselves in savings. Full-time students are eligible for the **International Student ID Card** (ISIC, ⓦwww.isiccard.com in the UK, or go to ⓦwww.istc.org for more information), which entitles the bearer to special air, rail, and bus fares and discounts at museums, theaters, and other attractions. For Americans there's also a health benefit, providing up to $3000 in emergency medical coverage and $100 a day for sixty days in a hospital, plus a 24-hour hotline to call in the event of a medical, legal, or financial emergency. The card costs $22 for Americans; Can$16 for Canadians; Aus$16.50 for Australians; NZ$21 for New Zealanders; £6 in the UK; and €12.70 in the Republic of Ireland.

You only have to be 26 or younger to qualify for the **International Youth Travel Card**, which costs US$22 and carries the same benefits. Teachers qualify for the **International Teacher Card**, offering similar

Money: a note for foreign travelers

Regular upheaval in the world's money markets causes the relative value of the US dollar against the currencies of the rest of the world to vary considerably. Generally speaking, one pound sterling will buy between $1.45 and $1.70; one Canadian dollar is worth between 76¢ and 85¢; one Australian dollar is worth between 67¢ and 88¢; and one New Zealand dollar is worth between 55¢ and 72¢.

US currency comes in notes worth $1, $5, $10, $20, $50, and $100, plus various larger (and rarer) denominations. Confusingly, all are the same size and same green color, making it necessary to check each note carefully. The dollar is made up of 100 cents (¢) in coins of 1 cent (known as a penny), 5 cents (a nickel), 10 cents (a dime), and 25 cents (a quarter). Look out for the new golden **Sacagawea dollar coin**, named after the Native American woman who assisted Lewis and Clark on their expeditions through the uncharted West. Very occasionally, you might come across the **JFK half-dollars** (50¢), **Susan B. Anthony dollar coins**, or, very rarely, a **two-dollar bill**. Change (quarters are the most useful) is needed for buses, vending machines, and telephones, so always carry plenty.

discounts and costing US$22, Can$16, Aus$16.50, and NZ$21. All these cards are available from student-oriented travel agents in North America, Europe, Australia, and New Zealand. Several other organizations and accommodation groups also sell their own cards, good for various discounts.

A university photo ID might open some doors, but is not as easily recognizable as the ISIC cards, although the latter are often not accepted as valid proof of age, for example in bars or liquor stores.

Getting around

Travel in the surprisingly compact state of Florida is rarely difficult or time-consuming. Crossing between the east and west coasts, for example, takes only a couple of hours and even the longest possible trip – between the western extremity of the Panhandle and Miami – can just about be accomplished in a day. With a car you'll have no problems, but traveling by public transport requires adroit planning: cities and larger towns have bus links – and, in some cases, an infrequent train service – but many rural areas and some of the most enjoyable coastal sections are much harder to reach.

By car

As a major vacation destination, Florida is one of the cheapest places in the US in which to **rent a car**, thanks to a very competitive market. Drivers are supposed to have held their licenses for at least one year (though this is rarely checked), and people under 25 may very well encounter problems or restrictions when renting, usually having to pay an extra $10–25 a day. If you are under 25, always call ahead. If you are under 21 you will not be able to rent a car, period.

Car rental companies will also expect you to have a **credit card**; if you don't have one they may let you leave a hefty deposit (at least $300–500) but don't count on it. The likeliest tactic for getting a good deal is to phone the major firms' toll-free 800 numbers for their best rates – most will try to beat the offers of their competitors, so it's worth haggling. Booking through your credit card is also another way of getting good deals as many have arrangements with car rental companies, so give them a call as well.

In general, the **lowest rates** are available at the airport branches. Always be sure to get free unlimited mileage and be aware that leaving the car in a different city than the one in which you rent it may incur a drop-off charge of as much as $200 – though most firms do not charge drop-off fees within Florida.

When you rent a car, read the small print carefully for details on **Collision Damage Waiver** (CDW), a form of insurance that often isn't included in the initial rental charge but is well worth considering. This specifically covers the car that you are driving yourself – you are in any case insured for damage to other vehicles. At $12 to $20 a day, it can add substantially to the total cost, but without it you're liable for every scratch to the car – even those that aren't your fault. Some credit card companies offer automatic CDW coverage to anyone using their card to pay in full for the rental; read the fine print beforehand in any case. You'll also be charged a Florida surcharge of $2.05 per day. Be warned that many airport branches of car companies levy additional charges of up to ten percent onto the rental price – Miami doesn't, but most other Florida airports do.

You should also check your **third-party liability**. The standard policy often only covers you for the first $10,000 of the third party's liability claim against you (plus an additional $10,000 for property damage), a paltry sum in litigation-conscious America. Companies strongly advise taking out third-party insurance, which costs a further $10–16 a day but indemnifies the driver for up to $1,000,000.

If you **break down** in a rented car, call the emergency number pinned to the dashboard. If there isn't one, you should sit tight and wait for the Highway Patrol or State Police, who cruise by regularly. Raising the hood of your car is recognized as a call for assistance, though women traveling alone should, obviously, be wary of doing this. Another tip, for women especially, is to rent a **cell phone** from the car rental agency – you often have to pay only a nominal amount until you actually use it, but having a phone can be reassuring at least, and a potential life-saver should something go horribly wrong.

Major car rental agencies

In North America

Alamo ⓣ1-800/522-9696, ⓦwww.alamo.com
Auto Europe US ⓣ1-800/223-5555, Canada ⓣ1-888/223-5555, ⓦwww.autoeurope.com
Avis US ⓣ1-800/331-1084, Canada ⓣ1-800/

Driving for foreign visitors

UK, Canadian, Australian, and New Zealand nationals can **drive** in the US provided they have a full driving license from their home country (International Driving Permits are not always regarded as sufficient). Fly-drive deals are good value if you want to rent a car (see p.11), though you can save up to sixty percent simply by booking in advance with a major firm or booking through your credit card company. You can choose not to pay until you arrive, but make sure you take a written confirmation of the quoted price with you. Remember that it's safer not to rent a car straight off a long transatlantic flight; and that standard rental cars have automatic transmissions.

It's also easier and cheaper to book **RVs** (see p.26) in advance from abroad. Most travel agents who specialize in the US can arrange RV rental, and usually do it cheaper if you book a flight through them as well. A price of £550–650 for a five-berth van for a fortnight is fairly typical.

Roads

The best roads for covering long distances quickly are the wide, straight, and fast interstate highways, usually at least six lanes wide and always prefixed by "I" (for example I-95) – marked on maps by a red, white, and blue shield bearing the number. Even-numbered interstates usually run east–west and those with odd numbers north–south.

A grade down are the **state highways** (eg Hwy-1) and the **US highways** (eg US-1), sometimes divided into scenic off-shoots such as Hwy-A1A, which runs parallel to US-1 along Florida's east coast. There are a number of toll roads, by far the longest being the 318-mile Florida's Turnpike; tolls range from 25¢ to $6 and are usually graded according to length of journey – you're given a distance marker when you enter the toll road and pay the appropriate amount when you leave. You'll also come across toll bridges, charging sometimes as much as $3 to cross. Some major roads in cities are technically state or US highways but are better known by their local names. Part of US-1 in Miami, for instance, is more familiarly known as Biscayne Boulevard. Rural areas also have much smaller **county roads**, which are known as routes (eg Route 78 near Lake Okeechobee); their number is preceded by a letter denoting their county.

Rules of the road

Although the law says that drivers must keep up with the flow of traffic, which is often hurtling along at 70mph, the official speed limit in Florida is 55mph (70mph on some interstate stretches), with lower signposted limits – usually around

272-5871, Ⓦ www.avis.com
Budget Ⓣ 1-800/527-0700, Ⓦ www.budgetrentacar.com
Dollar Ⓣ 1-800/800-4000, Ⓦ www.dollar.com
Enterprise Rent-a-Car Ⓣ 1-800/325-8007, Ⓦ www.enterprise.com
Hertz US Ⓣ 1-800/654-3001, Canada Ⓣ 1-800/263-0600, Ⓦ www.hertz.com
National Ⓣ 1-800/227-7368, Ⓦ www.nationalcar.com
Thrifty Ⓣ 1-800/367-2277, Ⓦ www.thrifty.com

In the UK

Avis Ⓣ 0870/606 0100, Ⓦ www.avis.co.uk; Northern Ireland Ⓣ 028/9024 3333
Budget Ⓣ 0800/181 181, Ⓦ www.budget.co.uk
Europcar Ⓣ 0845/722 2525, Ⓦ www.europcar.co.uk
Hertz Ⓣ 0870/844 8844, Ⓦ www.hertz.co.uk
Holiday Autos Ⓣ 0870/400 0099, Ⓦ www.holidayautos.co.uk
National Ⓣ 0870/536 5365, Ⓦ www.nationalcar.co.uk
Suncars Ⓣ 0870/500 5566, Ⓦ www.suncars.com
Thrifty Ⓣ 01494/751 600, Ⓦ www.thrifty.co.uk

In Ireland

Avis Ⓣ 01/605 7500, Ⓦ www.avis.ie
Budget Ⓣ 0903/277 11, Ⓦ www.budget.ie

30–35mph – in built-up areas. A minimum speed limit of 40mph also applies on many interstates and highways. If you get a ticket for speeding, your case will go to court and the size of the fine will be at the discretion of the judge; $75 is a rough minimum. If the **police** flag you down, don't get out of the car and don't reach into the glove compartment as the officers may think you have a gun. Simply sit still with your hands on the wheel and turn on the inside light if it's dark; when questioned, be polite and don't attempt to make jokes.

Apart from the obvious fact that Americans drive on the **right**, various rules may be unfamiliar to foreign drivers. US law requires that any **alcohol** be carried unopened in the trunk of the car; it's illegal to make a U-turn on an interstate or anywhere where a single unbroken line runs along the middle of the road; it's also illegal to park on a highway, and for front-seat passengers to ride without fastened seatbelts. At intersections, you can **turn right on a red light** if there is no traffic approaching from the left; and some junctions are four-way stops: a crossroads where all traffic must stop before proceeding in order of arrival.

It can't be stressed too strongly that **driving under the influence** (DUI) is a very serious offence. If a police officer smells alcohol on your breath, he/she is entitled to administer a breath, saliva, or urine test. If you fail, they'll lock you up with other inebriates in the "drunk tank" of the nearest jail until you sober up – and, controversially, in some parts of the state they're empowered to suspend your driving license immediately. Your case will later be heard by a judge, who can fine you $200 or, in extreme (or repeat) cases, imprison you for thirty days.

Parking

Once at your destination, you'll find in cities at least that **parking meters** are commonplace. Charges for an hour range from 25¢ to $1. **Car parks** (US "parking lots") generally charge $2–3 an hour, $6–10 per day. If you park in the wrong place (such as within ten feet of a fire hydrant) your car is likely to be towed away, or **wheel-clamped** – a sticker on the windscreen will tell you where to pay the fine ($30–45). Watch out for signs indicating the **street cleaning** schedule, as you mustn't park overnight before an early-morning clean. **Validated parking**, where your fee for parking in, say, a shopping mall's lot is waived if one of the stores has stamped your parking stub (just ask), is common, as is **valet parking** at even quite modest restaurants, for which a small tip is expected.

Whenever possible, park in the **shade**; if you don't, you might find the car too hot to touch when you return to it – temperatures inside cars parked in the full force of the Florida sun can reach 140°F (60°C).

Hertz ⓣ01/676 7476, ⓦwww.hertz.ie
Holiday Autos ⓣ01/872 9366, ⓦwww.holidayautos.ie

In Australia

Avis ⓣ13 63 33, ⓦwww.avis.com.au
Budget ⓣ1300/362 848, ⓦwww.budget.com
Dollar ⓣ02/9223 1444, ⓦwww.dollarcar.com.au
Europcar ⓣ1300/131 390, ⓦwww.deltaeuropcar.com.au
Hertz ⓣ1800/550 067, ⓦwww.hertz.com
Holiday Autos ⓣ1300/554 432, ⓦwww.holidayautos.com.au
National ⓣ13 10 45, ⓦwww.nationalcar.com.au
Thrifty ⓣ1300/367 227, ⓦwww.thrifty.com.au

In New Zealand

Avis ⓣ09/526 2847 or 0800/655 111, ⓦwww.avis.co.nz
Budget ⓣ09/976 2222, ⓦwww.budget.co.nz
Hertz ⓣ0800/654 321, ⓦwww.hertz.com
National ⓣ0800/800 115, ⓦwww.nationalcar.co.nz
Thrifty ⓣ09/309 0111, ⓦwww.thrifty.co.nz

Renting an RV

Besides cars, Recreational Vehicles (or **RVs**) – those huge juggernauts that rumble down the highway complete with multiple bedrooms, bathrooms, and kitchens – can be rented from around $350 per week for a basic camper on the back of a pickup truck. These are good for groups or families traveling together, but they can be quite unwieldy on the road.

Rental outlets are not as common as you might expect, as people tend to own their own RVs. On top of the rental fees you have to take into account mileage charges, the cost of gas (some RVs do twelve miles to the gallon or less), and any drop-off charges. In addition, it is rarely legal simply to pull up in an RV and spend the night at the roadside; you are expected to stay in designated RV parks – some of which charge $35–50 per night.

The Recreational Vehicle Rental Association (ⓣ703/591-7130, ⓦwww.rvra.org) publishes a newsletter and a directory of rental firms. Another larger company offering RV rentals is Cruise America (ⓣ480/464-7300, ⓦwww.cruiseamerica.com).

Motoring organizations

In North America

American Automobile Association (AAA) ⓣ1-800/AAA-HELP, ⓦwww.aaa.com. Each state has its own club – check the phone book or call for local address and phone number.
Canadian Automobile Association (CAA) ⓣ613/247-0117, ⓦwww.caa.ca. Each region has its own club – check the phone book or call for local address and phone number.

In the UK and Ireland

AA Ireland Dublin ⓣ01/617 9988, ⓦwww.aaireland.ie
AA UK ⓣ0870/600 0371, ⓦwww.theaa.com
RAC UK ⓣ0800/550 055, ⓦwww.rac.co.uk

In Australia and New Zealand

AAA Australia ⓣ02/6247 7311, ⓦwww.aaa.asn.au
New Zealand AA ⓣ09/377 4660, ⓦwww.nzaa.co.nz

By bus

Buses are the cheapest way to travel. The only long-distance service is **Greyhound**, which links all major cities and many smaller towns. In isolated areas buses are fairly scarce, sometimes only appearing once a day, if at all – so plot your route with care. Between the big cities, buses run around the clock to a fairly full timetable, stopping only for meal breaks (almost always fast-food dives) and driver changeovers. Any sizeable community will have a Greyhound station; in smaller places the local post office or gas station doubles as the stop and ticket office. In the Florida Keys, the bus makes scheduled stops but can also be flagged down anywhere along the Overseas Highway.

Fares are relatively inexpensive – for example $32 one way between Miami and Orlando – and can be reduced by fifteen percent if you're a student or buy your ticket at least one week in advance. If you plan on doing a lot of traveling, Greyhound's **Discovery Passes** for domestic travelers are good for unlimited travel nationwide for seven days ($229 adult/$206 student or senior), fifteen days ($349/$314), thirty days ($459/$413), and sixty days

Bus, rail, and air passes

Greyhound Discovery Passes

Foreign visitors intending to travel virtually every day by bus, or to venture further around the US, can buy a **Greyhound Discovery Pass**, offering unlimited travel within a set time limit, before leaving home: most travel agents can oblige or you can order online at Ⓦwww.greyhound.com. Costs for adults/students are $219/197 (7-day), $329/296 (15-day), $439/395 (30-day), or $599/539 (60-day). Children under 12 receive a forty percent discount; seniors five percent. The first time you use your pass, it will be dated by the ticket clerk (this becomes the commencement date of the ticket), and your destination is written on a page that the driver will tear out and keep as you board the bus. Repeat this procedure for every subsequent journey.

Amtrak rail passes

Rail travel can't get you around all of Florida, but overseas travelers have a choice of two rail passes. The least expensive, the **East Rail Pass**, available in fifteen- and thirty-day forms, costs $210 ($260 during peak summer period) and $265 ($320) respectively. Alternatively, the **National Pass** entitles you to travel throughout the US, for fifteen or thirty days, for a price of $295 ($440 during peak summer period) or $385 ($550) respectively.

Passes must be bought outside the US, and trains should also be pre-reserved. On production of a passport issued outside the US or Canada and one of these passes, your tickets will be issued. In the UK, you can buy them from Amtrak's UK agent, Leisure Rail (Ⓣ0870/750 0222). In Ireland, Australia, and New Zealand, passes are available from any travel agent.

Air passes

All the main American airlines (and British Airways in conjunction with USAir) offer **air passes** for visitors who plan to fly a lot within the US: these have to be bought in advance, and in the UK are usually sold with the proviso that you cross the Atlantic with the relevant airline. All the deals are broadly similar, involving the purchase of at least three **coupons**, each valid for a one-way flight of any duration in the US. Rates are around $375–450 for three coupons, and $60–100 for each additional coupon up to a maximum of ten, all depending on season and carrier. Read the small print before you buy as some companies will count a connection flight as one coupon whereas some don't

The **Visit USA** scheme entitles foreign travelers to a thirty percent discount on any full-priced US domestic fare, provided you buy the ticket before you leave home – but this isn't a wise choice for travel within Florida, where full-priced fares are very high.

($649/$584); the reduced rates for foreign travelers are given in the box above.

Their **website** (Ⓦwww.greyhound.com) has a useful searchable timetable; otherwise, information can be obtained from local terminals. The phone numbers for the larger Greyhound stations are given in the Guide.

By train

A much less viable way of getting about is by **train** (run by Amtrak). Florida's railroads were built to service the boom towns of the Twenties and, consequently, some rural nooks have rail links as good as the modern cities. The actual trains are clean and comfortable, with most routes in the state offering two services a day. In some areas, Amtrak services are extended by buses, usable only in conjunction with the train.

Fares can be comparable to the bus – $30 one way between Miami and Orlando is not unheard of. Again student and advance

For Amtrak information: ⓣ1-800/USA RAIL, ⓦwww.amtrak.com.
For Tri-Rail information: ⓣ1-800/874-7245, ⓦwww.tri-rail.com.

purchase (one week) discounts are your best bet. For seniors the discount is fifteen percent.

The Tri-Rail

Designed to reduce road traffic along the congested Southeast coast, the elevated **Tri-Rail** system came into operation in 1989, ferrying commuters between Miami and West Palm Beach with twelve stops on the way. The single-journey fare is calculated on a zone basis, and ranges from $2 to $5; the only drawback is the fact that services tend to run around rush hours – meaning a very early start or an early evening departure. There are only six services (each way) on Saturdays and Sundays, though all-day tickets are only $4. Tickets must be bought at the station (not on the train), and those riding without them may be subject to hefty fines.

By plane

Provided your plans are flexible and you take advantage of the special cut-rate fares that are regularly offered by airlines – check your local newspaper, or go on the Web – off-peak plane travel within Florida can work out to be only slightly more expensive than taking a bus or train – and will also, obviously, get you there more quickly. Typical cut-rate one-way fares are around $69 for Miami–Orlando and $120 for Miami–Tallahassee; full fares are much higher.

For toll-free airline numbers, see p.10.

By bicycle

Cycling is seldom a good way to get around the major cities (with the exception of some sections of Miami), but many smaller towns are quiet enough to be pleasurably explored by bicycle. In addition, there are many miles of marked cycle paths along the coast, and long-distance bike trails crisscross the state's interior. Cycling is gaining popularity among Floridians, too, and a free monthly magazine, *Florida Bicyclist*, is aimed at the growing band of devoted pedalers; find it in bookshops and bike shops or on street corners.

Bikes can be **rented** for $10–25 a day, $35–70 a week, from many beach shops and college campuses, some state parks, and virtually any place where cycling is a good idea; outlets are listed in the Guide.

The best cycling areas are in north central Florida, the Panhandle, and in parts of the Northeast coast. By contrast, the southeast coastal strip is heavily congested and many south Florida inland roads are narrow and dangerous. Wherever you cycle, avoid the heaviest traffic – and the midday heat – by doing most of your pedaling before noon.

For free biking **information** and detailed **maps** ($2–15) of cycling routes, write to the State Bicycle Program, Florida Department of Transportation, 605 Suwannee St, Tallahassee, FL 32399-0450 (ⓣ805/414-4100, ⓦwww.dot.state.fl.us). You can get the same maps from most youth hostels.

Hitching

Where it's legal, **hitching** may be the cheapest way to get around but it is also the most unpredictable and potentially very dangerous, especially for women traveling alone. Moreover, hitching is **illegal** in Miami and on the outskirts of many other cities and in whole counties. The usual advice given to hitchhikers is that they should use their common sense; in fact, common sense should tell anyone that hitchhiking in the US is a **bad idea**. We do not recommend it.

Accommodation

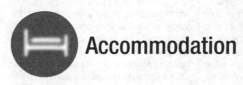

Accommodation costs inevitably account for a significant proportion of the expenses for any traveler in Florida, though you often get good value for what you pay. If you're on your own, it's possible to pare costs by sleeping in dormitory-style hostels, where a bed can cost from $15 to $25. Youth hostels in Florida, however, are few and far between, with just two affiliated to the IYHA (International Youth Hostel Association), in St Petersburg and Clearwater, for the whole west coast; there's also one just outside the Everglades in Florida City.

Groups of two or more will find it little more expensive to stay in the plentiful motels and hotels, where basic rooms away from the major cities typically cost anything upwards of $40 a night. Many hotels will set up a third single bed for around $5–10 on top of the regular price, reducing costs for three people sharing. By contrast, the lone traveler will have a hard time of it: "singles" are usually double rooms at a slightly reduced rate. Prices quoted by hotels and motels are almost always for the actual room rather than for each person using it.

Motels are abundant on the main approach roads to cities, around beaches, and by the main road junctions in country areas. High-rise **hotels** predominate along the popular sections of the coast and are sometimes the only accommodation in city centers. In major cities **campgrounds** tend to be on the outskirts, if they exist at all.

At most of the smaller hotels and during busy periods, you may be expected to **pay in advance**, at least for the first night and perhaps for further nights too. Payment can be in cash or in dollar travelers' checks, though it's more common to give your credit card number and sign for everything when you leave. **Reservations** are only held until 5pm or 6pm unless you've told the hotel you'll be arriving late. Most of the larger chains have an advance booking form in their brochures and will make reservations at another of their premises for you – in any case, you should book ahead wherever possible, especially in big cities and popular stretches of coast.

Hotels and motels

While motels and hotels essentially offer the same things – double rooms with bathroom, TV, and phone – motels are often one-off affairs run by their owners and tend to be

Accommodation price codes

It's a fact of Florida resort life that the plain and simple motel room, which costs $30 on a weekday in low season, is liable to cost two or three times that amount on a weekend in high season. To further complicate matters, high and low season vary depending on whether you're in north or south Florida, and some establishments that depend on business travelers for their trade (such as those in downtown areas, distanced from the nearest beach) will actually be cheaper on weekends than on weekdays. Local events – such as a Space Shuttle launch on the Space Coast, or Spring Break in Panama City Beach – can also cause prices to increase dramatically.

Throughout the book, we've graded accommodation prices according to the cost of the least expensive double room throughout most of the year – but do allow for the fluctuations outlined above.

❶ up to $40	❸ $60–80	❺ $100–130	❼ $175–250
❷ $40–60	❹ $80–100	❻ $130–175	❽ $250+

cheaper (typically $40–55) than hotels ($55–75), which are likely to be part of a nationwide chain. All but the cheapest motels and hotels have pools for guests' use and many offer cable TV and free local phone calls. Under $60, rooms tend to be similar in quality and features; spend $60–70 in rural areas or $80–100 in the cities and you get more luxury – a larger room and often additional facilities such as a tennis court, gym, and golf course. Paying over $150 brings all the above, plus likely an ocean view and some upmarket trappings.

Alternatively, there are a number of unexciting but dependable **budget-priced chain hotels**, which, depending on location, cost around $40–60; the cheapest are *Days Inn*, *Econo Lodge*, *Hampton Inns*, *Knights Inns*, and *Red Carpet Inns*. Higher up the scale are mid-range chains like *Best Western*, *Howard Johnson's* (now usually abbreviated to *HoJo's*), *TraveLodge*, and *La Quinta* – though if you can afford their prices (usually $75–125), there's normally somewhere nicer to stay.

On your travels you'll also come across **resorts**, which are motels or hotels equipped with a restaurant, bar, and private beach – on average these cost $70–110; and efficiencies, which are motel rooms adapted to offer cooking facilities – ranging from a stove squeezed into a corner to a fully equipped kitchen – usually for $10–15 above the basic room rate.

There are of course – especially in cities – plenty of **high-end establishments**, which can cost just about any amount of money, depending on the luxury – we've pointed out which ones are atmospheric and worthwhile in the Guide. Bear in mind that the most upscale establishments have all manner of services that may appear to be free but for which you'll be expected to **tip** in a style commensurate with the hotel's status – ie big.

Since inexpensive diners are everywhere, very few hotels or motels bother to offer **breakfast**, though there's a trend toward providing free coffee (from paper cups) and sticky buns on a self-service basis from the lobby.

Discount options

During **off-peak periods** many motels and hotels struggle to fill their rooms, and it's worth **haggling** to get a few dollars off the asking price. Staying in the same place for more than one night may bring further reductions. In addition, pick up the many discount coupons that fill tourist information offices and welcome centers (see p.17), and look out for the free *Traveler Discount Guide*. Read the small print, though: what appears to be an amazingly cheap room rate sometimes turns out to be a per-person charge for two people sharing and limited to midweek.

Bed and breakfasts

Typically, bed and breakfast inns, or "**B&Bs**," as they're usually known, are restored buildings in the smaller cities and more rural areas. If you're a fan, be aware that they are often not mentioned by visitor centers (especially if they lack the amenities of more modern and more mundane motels), so you'll need to specifically ask for bed and breakfast listings. Most towns throughout Florida have a so-called historic section, and it is worth driving around to discover bed and breakfasts in the most serene surroundings. Even the larger establishments tend to have fewer than ten rooms, sometimes without TV and phone but usually with flowers, stuffed cushions, and an almost contrived home-like atmosphere; others may just be a couple of furnished rooms in someone's home.

While always including a huge and wholesome breakfast (five courses are not unheard of), prices vary greatly: anything from $50 to $200 depending on location and season; most cost between $60 and $90 per night for a double. Bear in mind, too, that most are booked well in advance, making it sensible to contact the inn directly (details are given throughout the Guide) at least a month ahead – longer in high season.

Hostels

At around $14–20 (a few dollars more for nonmembers) per night per person, **hostels** are clearly the cheapest accommodation option other than camping. There are three main kinds of hostel-like accommodation in the US: YMCA/YWCA hostels (known as "Ys"), offering accommodation for both sexes or, in a few cases, women only; the internationally affiliated HI-AYH hostels; and a growing number of independent hostels variously aligned under assorted umbrella organizations. Although there are no YMCA/YWCA in Florida, you will find a smattering of **independent hostels**, as well as **HI-AYH youth hostels** in Miami Beach, St Augustine, Key West, Florida City, Clearwater Beach and St Petersburg. You can make reservations at HI-AYH-affiliated hostels through the International Booking Network (IBN), and for a small booking fee the Hostelling International association in your home country can reserve accommodation before leaving home (see below for contact information). This has the advantage of putting a confirmation slip in your hand, which you won't have if telephone-booking long distance once you are in the United States.

Particularly if you're traveling in high season, it's advisable to **book ahead** through one of the specialist travel agents or international youth hostel offices. Some hostels will allow you to use a sleeping bag, though officially they should (and many do) insist on a sheet sleeping bag, which can usually be rented at the hostel. The maximum stay at each hostel is technically three days, though this is again a rule that is often ignored if there's space. Few hostels provide meals, but most have cooking facilities, and there's sometimes a curfew of around midnight: alcohol, smoking, and, of course, drugs are banned.

The informative *USA Hostel Directory* ($3) is available from hostels in the US, or direct from the HI-AYH national office (see below). For overseas hostelers, the *International Youth Hostel Handbook* provides a full list of hostels. In Britain it's available from the Youth Hostel Association headquarters (see below). Handbooks and membership are also available from the YHA shops – look up the nearest outlet at Ⓦ www.yhaadventure.com.

Youth hostel associations

Australia

Australia Youth Hostels Association Ⓣ 02/9261 1111, Ⓦ www.yha.com.au. Adult membership rate Aus$52 (under-18s, Aus$16) for the first twelve months and then Aus$32 each year thereafter.

Canada

Hostelling International Canada Room 400, 205 Catherine St, Ottawa, Ontario K2P 1C3 Ⓣ 613/237-7884 or 1-800/663-5777, Ⓦ www.hihostels.ca. Rather than sell the traditional one- or two-year memberships, the association now sells one Individual adult membership with a 16- to 28-month term. The length of the term depends on when the membership is sold, but a member can receive up to 28 months of membership for just $35. Membership is free for under-18s and you can become a lifetime member for $175.

England and Wales

Youth Hostel Association Ⓣ 0870/770 8868, Ⓦ www.yha.org.uk. Annual membership £13; under-18s £6.50; lifetime £190 (or five annual payments of £40).

Ireland

Irish Youth Hostel Association Ⓣ 01/830 4555, Ⓦ www.irelandyha.org. Adult (and single parent) membership €15; family €31.50; under-18s €7.50; lifetime €75.

Hostelling International Northern Ireland Ⓣ 028/9032 4733, Ⓦ www.hini.org.uk. Adult membership £10; under-18s £6; family £20; lifetime £75.

New Zealand

YHA New Zealand Ⓣ 03/379 9970 or 0800/278 299, Ⓦ www.yha.co.nz. Adult membership NZ$40 for one year, NZ$60 for two, and NZ$80 for three.

Scotland

Scottish Youth Hostel Association Ⓣ 0870/155 3255, Ⓦ www.syha.org.uk. Annual membership £6, for under-18s £2.50.

US

Hostelling International-USA (HI-AYH) 8401 Colesville Rd, Suite 600, Silver Spring, MD 20910

IBN booking centers

Australia (Sydney) Ⓣ 02/9261 1111
Canada (Ontario) Ⓣ 1-800/663-5777
UK (London) Ⓣ 020/7836 1036
New Zealand (Auckland) Ⓣ 09/309 2802

ⓣ301/495-1240, ⓦwww.hiayh.org. Annual membership for adults (18–54) is $28, for seniors (55 or over) is $18, and free for under-18s. Lifetime memberships are $250.

Camping

Florida **campgrounds** range from the primitive (a flat piece of ground that may or may not have a water tap) to others that are more like open-air hotels with shops, restaurants, and washing facilities. Naturally, prices vary according to amenities, ranging from nothing at all for the most basic plots to up to $35 a night for something comparatively luxurious. There are plenty of campgrounds but often plenty of people intending to use them: take special care over plotting your route if you're camping during public holidays or weekends, when many sites will be either full or very crowded. By contrast, some of the more basic campgrounds in state and national parks will often be completely empty midweek. For camping in the wilderness, there's a nightly charge of $3 or so payable at the area's administrative office.

Privately run campgrounds are everywhere, their prices ranging from $8 to $35, and the best are listed throughout the Guide; for a fuller list, write for the free *Florida Camping Directory* to the Florida Campground Association, 1340 Vickers Drive, Tallahassee, FL 32303-3041 (ⓣ850/562-7151, www.floridacamping.com). State parks – there are over 300 in Florida – are often excellent places to camp; sites cost $5–20 for up to four people sharing. Never more than half the space is reserved, the rest goes on a first-come first-served basis (bear in mind that park offices close at sunset; you won't be able to camp there if you arrive later). Reservations can be made within two months of arrival by phone only, and stays are limited to fourteen days. Reservations won't be held after 5pm unless previously arranged. If you're doing a lot of camping in state parks, get the two free leaflets, *Florida State Parks Camping Reservations Procedures* and *Florida State Parks Fees Schedule*, from any state park office or by writing to the Department of Natural Resources, Division of Recreation and Parks, 3900 Commonwealth Blvd, Mail Station 535, Tallahassee, FL 32399 (ⓣ850/488-6131). In addition, you can save your space at any of Florida's state parks by contacting Reserve America (ⓣ1-800/326-3521, ⓦwww.reserveamerica.com).

Similarly priced campgrounds exist in **national parks and national forests** – see the details throughout the Guide. You may contact the National Park Service, PO Box 2416, Tallahassee, FL 32316 (ⓣ850/580-3011, ⓦwww.nps.gov), or for the Apalachicola, Ocala, or Osceola National Forests at the US Forest Service (Forest Supervisors Office), 325 John Knox Rd, Suite F-100, Tallahassee, FL 32303 (ⓣ850/523-8500, ⓦwww.southernregion.fs.fed.us/florid).

However desolate it may look, much of undeveloped Florida is, in fact, private land, so rough camping is illegal. For **permitted rough camping**, see "The backcountry," p.42.

Food and drink

Florida has a mass of restaurants, fast-food outlets, cafés, and coffee shops on every main street, all trying to outdo one another with their cut-price daily specials. In every town mentioned in this book you'll find reviews of the full range of eating options.

Fresh fish and **seafood** are abundant all over Florida, as is the high-quality produce of the state's cattle farms – served as ribs, steaks, and burgers – and junk food is as common as anywhere else in the country. But the choice of what to eat is influenced

Service and tipping

Foreign travelers should note to top up the bill in restaurants by 15–20 percent; a little less perhaps at a bar.

by where you are. In the northern half of the state, the accent is on hearty cooking – traditional Southern dishes such as grits (a hot cereal), cornbread, and fried chicken. As you head south through Florida, this gives way to the most diverse and inexpensive gathering of Latin American and Caribbean cuisines to be found anywhere in the US – you can feast on anything from curried goat to mashed plantains and yucca.

Breakfast

For the price (on average $4–6) breakfast makes a good-value, very filling start to the day. Go to a diner, café, or coffee shop, all of which are very similar and usually serve breakfast until at least 11am (some continue all day) – though there are special deals at earlier times, say 6–8am, when the price may be even less.

Lunches and snacks

Between 11.30am and 1.30pm, look for excellent-value **set menus** and **all-you-can-eat specials**. Most Cuban restaurants and fishcamps (see "Dining Out," p.34) are exceptionally well priced all the time and you can get a good-sized lunch in one for $4–5. **Buffet restaurants** – most of which also serve breakfast and dinner – are found in most cities and towns; $6–8 lets you pig out as much as you can from a wide variety of hot dishes.

As you'd expect, there's also **pizza**; count on paying $7–12 for a basic two-person pizza at national chains and local outlets. If it's a warm day and you can't face hot food, delis usually serve a broad range of salads for about $3 a pound. Frozen yogurt or ice cream may be all you feel like eating in the midday heat: look for exotic versions made with mango and guava sold by Cuban vendors.

Snacks

For **quick snacks**, many **supermarket deli** counters do ready-cooked meals for $4–6, as well as a range of salads and sandwiches. Bagels are also common: thick, chewy rolls with a hole in the middle, spread with almost anything you fancy but generally cream cheese is the standard. **Street stands** sell hot dogs, burgers, or a slice of pizza for around $1–2; in Miami, Cuban fast-food stands serve crispy pork sandwiches and other spicy snacks for $2–3, and most shopping malls have ethnic fast-food stalls, often pricier than street stands but usually with edible and filling fare. Bags of fresh oranges, grapefruit, and watermelons are often sold from the roadside in rural areas, as are boiled peanuts – a dollar buys a steaming bagful. Southern fast-food chains like *Popeye's Famous Fried Chicken* and *Sonny's Real Pit Bar-B-Q* will satisfy your hunger for $3–4, but are only marginally better than the inevitable burger chains. Coffee shops appear all through Florida, providing a huge array of basic cooking in relaxed surroundings.

Free food and brunch

Some **bars** are used as much by diners as drinkers, who fill up on the free **hors d'oeuvres** laid out by a lot of city bars between 5pm and 7pm Monday to Friday – an attempt to nab the commuting classes before they head off to the suburbs – and sometimes by beachside bars to grab beach-goers before they head elsewhere for the evening. For the price of a drink you can stuff yourself on chili, seafood, or pasta.

Brunch is another deal to look out for: indulged in on weekends between 11am and 2pm. For a set price ($8 and up) you get a light meal (or even a groaning buffet) and a variety of complimentary cocktails or champagne. We've listed the most interesting venues in the Guide.

Dining out

Even if it sometimes seems swamped by the more fashionable regional and ethnic cuisines, traditional **American cooking** is found all over Florida. Portions are big and you start with salad, eaten before the main course arrives; look out for heart of palm salad, based around the delicious vegetable at the heart of the sabal palm tree (unfortunately for the tree, once the heart is extracted, the plant dies). Main dishes tend to be dominated by enormous steaks, burgers, piles of ribs, or half a chicken, and often come with a vegetable and/or some form of potato.

Southern cooking makes its presence felt throughout the northern half of the state. Vegetables such as okra, collard greens, black-eyed peas, fried green tomatoes, and fried eggplant are added to staples such as fried chicken, roast beef, and **hogjaw** – meat from the mouth of a pig. Meat dishes are usually accompanied by cornbread to soak up the thick gravy poured over everything; with fried fish, you'll get **hush puppies** – fried corn balls with tiny bits of chopped onion. Okra is also used in gumbo soups, a feature of **Cajun** cooking, which originated in nearby Louisiana as a way of using up leftovers. A few (usually expensive) Florida restaurants specialize in Cajun food but many others offer a few Cajun items (such as red beans and rice, and hot and spicy shrimp and steak dishes).

Alligator is on many menus: most of the meat comes from alligator farms, which cull a certain number each year. The tails are deep-fried and served in a variety of styles – none of which makes much of a mark on the bland, chicken-like taste. **Frogs' legs** also crop up occasionally.

Regional **nouvelle cuisine** is largely too pretentious and expensive for the typical Floridian palate, although some restaurants in the larger cities do extraordinary and inspired things with local fish and the produce of the citrus farms, creating small but beautifully presented affairs for around $40–50 a head.

Almost wherever you eat you'll be offered **Key lime pie** as a dessert, a dish that began life in the Florida Keys, made from the small limes that grow there. The pie is similar to lemon meringue but with a sharper taste. Quality varies greatly; take local advice to find a good outlet and your tastebuds will tell you why many swear by it.

Fish and seafood

Florida excels with **fish and seafood** – which is great news for non-meat-eaters. Even the shabbiest restaurant is likely to have an excellent selection, though fish comes freshest and cheapest at **fishcamps**, rustic places right beside the river where your meal was swimming just a few hours before; a fishcamp lunch or dinner will cost around $5–9. Catfish tends to top the bill, but you'll also find grouper, dolphin (the fish, not the mammal, sometimes known by its Hawaiian name, mahimahi), mullet, tuna, and swordfish, any of which (except catfish, which is nearly always fried) may be boiled, grilled, fried, or "blackened" (rubbed with zesty spices and charcoal-grilled). Of **shellfish**, the tender claws of stone crabs, eaten dipped in butter, raise local passions during their mid-October to mid-May season; spiny (or "Florida") lobster is smaller and more succulent than its more famous Maine rival; oysters can be extremely fresh (the best come from Apalachicola) and are usually eaten raw (though best avoided during summer, when they carry a risk of food poisoning) – many restaurants have special "raw bars," where you can also consume meaty shrimp, in regular and jumbo sizes. Another popular crustacean is the very chewy **conch** (pronounced "konk"); abundant throughout the Florida Keys, they usually come deep-fried as fritters served up with various sauces, or as a chowder-like soup.

Ethnic cuisine

Florida's **ethnic cuisines** become increasingly exotic the further south you go. In Miami, **Cuban food** is extremely easy to find and can be very good value. Most Cuban dishes are meat-based: frequently pork, less often beef or chicken, always fried (including the skin, which becomes a crispy crackling) and usually heavily spiced, served with a varying combination of yellow or white rice, black beans, plantains (a sweet, banana-like

Latin American food terms

Ajiaco criollo	Meat and root vegetable stew	*Pan*	Bread
Arroz	Rice	*Pan con lechon*	Crispy pork sandwich
Arroz con leche	Rice pudding	*Piccadillo*	Minced meat, usually beef, served with peppers and olives
Bocadillo	Sandwich	*Pollo*	Chicken
Chicarones de pollo	Fried chicken crackling	*Puerca*	Pork
Frijoles	Beans	*Sopa de mariscos*	Shellfish soup
Frijoles negros	Black beans	*Sopa de plantanos*	Meaty, plantain soup
Maduros	Fried plantains	*Tostones*	Fried mashed plantains
Masitoas de puerca	Fried spiced pork	*Vaca*	Beef
Morros y Christianos	Literally "Moors and Christians," black beans and white rice		

vegetable), and yucca (cassava) – a potato-like vegetable completely devoid of taste. Seafood crops up less often, most deliciously in thick soups, such as *sopa de mariscos* – shellfish soup. Unpretentious Cuban diners serve a filling lunch or dinner for under $6, though a growing number of upmarket restaurants will charge three times as much for identical food. In busy areas, many Cuban cafés have street windows where you buy a thimble-sized cup of sweet and rich *café Cubano* – Cuban coffee – strong enough to make your hair stand on end; also available is *café con leche*, coffee with warm milk or cream, though it's strictly for the unadventurous and regarded by Cubans as a children's drink. If you want a cool drink in Miami, look out for roadside stands offering *coco frio* – coconut milk sucked through a straw directly from the coconut, for $1.

Although nowhere near as prevalent as Cuban cooking, foods from other parts of the **Caribbean** and **Latin America** are easily found around Miami: Haitian, Argentinian, Colombian, Nicaraguan, Peruvian, Jamaican, and Salvadoran restaurants also serve the city's diverse migrant populations – at very affordable prices.

Other ethnic cuisines turn up all around the state, too. **Chinese** food is everywhere and often very cheap, as is **Mexican**, though many Mexican restaurants are more popular as places to knock back margaritas than to eat in; **Japanese** is more expensive; **Italian** food is popular but can be expensive once you leave the simple pastas and explore the more gourmet-inclined Italian regional cooking in the major cities. **French** food, too, is widely available, though pricey. **Thai**, **Korean**, and **Indonesian** food is similarly city-based, though usually cheaper; Indian restaurants, on the other hand, are thin on the ground just about everywhere. More plentiful are well-priced, family-run **Greek** restaurants, and a smattering of **Minorcan** places are evidence of one of Florida's earliest groups of European settlers.

Drinking

Most **drinking** in Florida is done in restaurant or hotel lounges, at fishcamps (see opposite), or in "tiki bars" – open-sided straw-roofed huts beside a beach or hotel pool. Some beachside bars, especially in Daytona Beach and Panama City Beach, are split-level, multi-purpose affairs with discos and stages for live bands – and take great pride in being the birthplace of the infamous wet T-shirt contest (nowadays sometimes joined by G-string and "best legs" shows), an exercise in unrestrained sexism that shows no signs of declining in popularity among a predominantly late-teen and twenty-something clientele.

To buy and consume alcohol you need **to be 21 or over** and could well be asked for ID even if you look much older. Recent clampdowns have resulted in bars "carding" anyone who looks 30 and under. Licensing laws and drinking hours vary from area to area, but generally alcohol can be bought and drunk in a bar, nightclub, or restaurant any time between 10am and 2am. More cheaply, you can usually buy beer, wine, or spirits in supermarkets and, of course, liquor stores, from 9am to 11pm Monday to Saturday and from 1pm to 11pm on Sundays. Note that it is illegal to consume alcohol in a car, on most beaches, and in all state parks, with a possible fine of $100 or more.

Beer

A small band of Florida **microbreweries** (tiny, one-off operations) create interesting beers, though rarely are these sold beyond their own bar or restaurant. It's more common for discerning beer drinkers to stick to imported brews, the most widely available of which are the Mexican brands Bohemia, Corona, and Dos Equis. Don't forget that in all but the more pretentious bars, you can save money by buying a quart or half-gallon pitcher of beer. If bar prices are a problem, you can stock up with six-packs from a supermarket at $5–7 for domestic, $8–12 for imported brews.

Wine and cocktails

If **wine** is more to your taste, try to visit one of the state's fast-improving wineries: several can be toured and their products sampled for free. One of the most successful is Chautauqua Vineyards, in De Funiak Springs in the Panhandle (see p.434). In a bar or restaurant, however, beside a usually threadbare stock of European wines, you'll find a selection from Chile and California. A decent glass of wine in a bar or restaurant costs around $4–6, a bottle $15–30. Buying a bottle from a supermarket can prove cheaper still.

Cocktails are extremely popular, especially rich fruity ones consumed while gazing over the ocean or into the sunset. Varieties are innumerable, sometimes specific to a single bar or cocktail lounge, and most will cost $5–10. Cocktails and all other drinks come cheapest during **happy hours** (usually 5–7pm; sometimes much longer) when many are half-price and there might be a buffet thrown in.

Communications

It won't be hard to make contact with anyone back at home when in Florida, though the laid-back attitude prevalent in the Florida Keys may get through to the postal system there.

Mail

Post offices are usually open Monday to Friday 9am–5pm and Saturday 9am–noon, and there are blue **mail boxes** on many street corners. **Ordinary mail** within the US costs 37¢ for a letter weighing up to an ounce; addresses must include the zip code (a five-digit postal code), as well as the sender's address on the envelope. **Air mail** between Florida and Europe generally takes about four days to a week to arrive. Postcards, aerograms, and letters weighing up to an ounce (a single sheet) cost 80¢.

Letters can be sent c/o **General Delivery** (what's known elsewhere as **poste restante**) to any post office in the state, but must include the post office's zip code and will only be held for thirty days before being returned to sender – so make sure there's a return address on the envelope. If you're receiving mail at someone else's address, it should include "c/o" and the regular occupant's name, or it is likely to be returned.

Rules on sending **parcels** are very rigid: packages must be sealed according to the postal service's instructions, which are given at the start of the *Yellow Pages*. To send anything out of the country, you'll need a **customs declaration form**, available from the post office. **Postal rates** for sending a parcel airmail, weighing up to 1lb, are $16.50 to Europe, $14.50 to Australia and New Zealand – by land prices are about a third of the price but take six times as long to get there.

Telephones

Florida's telephones are run by several companies – the largest being Southern Bell – all linked to the nationwide AT&T network. **Local calls** cost a minimum of 50¢ from coin-operated public phones, which accept denominations of 5¢, 10¢, and 25¢. More expensive are **non-local calls** ("zone calls") to numbers within the same area code (commonly, vast areas are covered by a single code) and **long-distance calls** (ie to a different area code), for which you'll need plenty of change. Non-local calls and long-distance calls are far cheaper if made between 6pm and 8am. Detailed rates are listed at the front of the telephone directory (the *White Pages*). Making telephone calls from **hotel rooms** is usually more expensive than from a payphone, though some budget hotels offer free local calls from rooms – ask when you check in.

Rates are much cheaper using prepaid **phone cards** sold at convenience stores in denominations of $5, $10, and $20. You'll find a phone number and a special PIN number on the back – just dial the number, enter the PIN, then compose the number you're trying to reach.

More expensive is using a **calling card** or **telephone charge card** from your phone company back home. Using a PIN number, you can make calls that will be charged to your home account. Since most major charge cards are free to obtain, it's worth getting one at least for emergencies, but bear in mind that rates may well be more expensive than calling from a public phone.

Many government agencies, car rental firms, hotels, and other services have **toll-free numbers**, which have the prefix 1-800, 1-877, or 1-888. Within the US, you can dial any number starting with those digits free of charge, though some numbers only operate inside Florida (this won't be apparent until you try the number). Some numbers, such as the Miami Heat basketball team's info line, ⓣ1-800/777-HEAT, employ the letters on the push-button phones as part of their "number."

Phone numbers throughout this book are given with the area code followed by the local number: for local calls just dial the seven-digit local number; for calls to a different area code, dial 1 followed by the area code and local number. For international calls dial the country's access code, then 1 and the area and local numbers (see below).

Useful phone numbers and codes

Emergencies and information

Emergencies ⓣ911; ask for the appropriate emergency service: fire, police, or ambulance
Local directory information ⓣ411
Long-distance directory information ⓣ1-(area code)/555-1212
Directory enquiries for toll-free numbers ⓣ1-800/555-1212
Operator ⓣ0

International calling codes

Calling TO Florida from abroad: international access code + 1 + area code

For calls FROM Florida, the codes are as follows:
Australia: international access code + 61+ city code
Canada: 1 + area code
New Zealand: international access code + 64 + city code
Republic of Ireland: international access code + 353 + city code
UK and Northern Ireland: international access code + 44 + city code

Cell phones

US and Canadian cell phone users will likely find that their phones work fine throughout most of Florida. But before leaving home, be sure to check with your service provider to make sure that costly roaming charges don't apply. Quite often, you can change your service plan to fit your traveling needs if necessary.

If you're coming from abroad and want to use your mobile phone in Florida, you'll need to check with your phone provider whether it will work abroad, and what the call charges are. Unless you have a tri-band phone, it is unlikely that a mobile bought for use outside the US will work inside the States (and vice versa).

In the UK, for all but the very top-of-the-range packages, you'll have to inform your phone provider before going abroad to get international access switched on. You may get charged extra for this depending on your existing package and where you are traveling to. You are also likely to be charged extra for incoming calls when abroad, as the people calling you will be paying the usual rate. If you want to retrieve messages while you're away, you'll have to ask your provider for a new access code, as your home one is unlikely to work abroad.

For further information about using your phone abroad, check out ⓦwww.telecomsadvice.org.uk/features/using_your_mobile_abroad.htm.

Email

One of the best ways to keep in touch while traveling is to sign up for a **free Internet email address** that can be accessed from anywhere, for example through YahooMail or Hotmail – accessible through ⓦwww.yahoo.com and ⓦwww.hotmail.com. Once you've set up an account, you can use these sites to pick up and send mail from any Internet café or hotel with Internet access.

If you're toting along a **laptop** and want to get connected, browse ⓦwww.kropka.com, which gives details of how to plug your laptop in when abroad, phone country codes around the world, and information about electrical systems in different countries.

The media

Florida ranks among the country's more media-savvy regions, with the range of media outlets among the better ones you'll find in the US, certainly the best in the southeastern region.

Newspapers

The best-read of Florida's **newspapers** is the *Miami Herald*, providing in-depth coverage of state, national, and world events; the *Orlando Sentinel* and *Tampa Tribune* are not far behind and, naturally enough, excel at reporting their own areas. Overseas newspapers are often a preserve of specialist bookshops, though you will find them widely available in major tourist areas.

Every community of any size has at least a few **free newspapers**, found in street distribution bins or just lying around in piles. It's a good idea to pick up a full assortment: some simply cover local goings-on, others provide specialist coverage of interests ranging from long-distance cycling to getting ahead in business. Many of them are also excellent sources for bar, restaurant, and nightlife information, and we've mentioned the most useful titles in the Guide.

TV and radio

Florida **TV** is pretty much the standard network sitcom and talk-show barrage you get all over the country, with frequent interruptions for hard-sell commercials. Game shows fill up most of the morning schedule; around lunchtime you can take your pick of any of a dozen daily soaps. Slightly better are the cable networks, to which you'll have access in most hotels and which include the around-the-clock news of CNN and MTV's nonstop circuit of mainstream pop videos.

Especially in the south, Spanish-language stations provide services for the Hispanic communities.

Most of Florida's **radio stations** stick to the usual commercial format of retro-rock, classic pop, country, or easy-listening. In general, except for news and chat, the occasional fire-and-brimstone preacher, and Latin and Haitian music, stations on the AM band are best avoided in favor of the FM band, in particular the public and college stations on the air in Tallahassee, Gainesville, Orlando, Tampa, and Miami, found on the left of the dial (88–92FM). These invariably provide diverse and listenable programming, whether it be bizarre underground rock or abstruse literary discussions, and they're also good sources for local nightlife news.

Festivals and public holidays

Someone somewhere is always celebrating something in Florida, though few festivities are shared throughout the region. Instead, there is a disparate multitude of local annual events: art and craft shows, county fairs, ethnic celebrations, music festivals, rodeos, sandcastle-building competitions, and many others of every description. The most interesting of these are listed throughout the Guide and you can phone the visitor center in a particular region ahead of your arrival to ask what's coming up. For the main festivities in Miami and Miami Beach see p.116–117 and in Key West p.149.

The biggest annual event to hit Florida is **Spring Break**: a six-week invasion (late Feb through March and early April) of tens of thousands of students seeking fun in the sun before knuckling down to their summer exams. Times are changing, however: one traditional Spring Break venue, Fort Lauderdale, persuaded the students to go elsewhere; another, Daytona Beach, has had less success. Panama City Beach, though, welcomes the carousing collegiates with open arms, and Key West – despite its lack of beach – is fast becoming a favorite Spring Break location. If you are in Florida during this time, it will be hard to avoid some signs of Spring Break – a mob of scantily clad drunken students is a tell-tale sign – and at the busier coastal areas you may well find accommodation costing three times the normal price; be sure to plan ahead.

Public holidays

The biggest and most all-American of all the **public holidays** is **Independence Day** on the Fourth of July, when most of Florida grinds to a standstill as people salute the flag and take part in firework displays, marches, beauty pageants, and more, all in commemoration of the signing of the Declaration of Independence in 1776. The large amusement parks, particularly Disney World, are completely swamped during this time. More sedate is **Thanksgiving Day**, on the fourth Thursday in November, which is essentially a domestic affair, when relatives return to the familial nest to stuff themselves with roast turkey, and (supposedly) fondly recall the first harvest of the Pilgrims in Massachusetts – though in fact Thanksgiving was already a national holiday before anyone thought to make that connection.

On the national public holidays listed below, banks and offices are liable to be closed all day, and shops may reduce their hours.

National public holidays

January

1: New Year's Day

3rd Mon: Martin Luther King Jr's Birthday

February
3rd Mon: Presidents' Day
May
Last Mon: Memorial Day
July
4: Independence Day
September
1st Mon: Labor Day
October
2nd Mon: Columbus Day
November
11: Veterans Day
4th Thurs: Thanksgiving Day
December
25: Christmas Day

Sports and ocean activities

Florida is as fanatical about sports as the rest of the US, but what's more surprising is that collegiate sports are often, especially among lifelong Floridians, more popular than their professional counterparts. This is because Florida's professional teams are comparatively recent additions to the sporting scene and have none of the traditions and bedrock support that the state's college sides enjoy. In fact, seventy thousand people attending an inter-college football match is no rarity. Other sports less in evidence include soccer, volleyball, greyhound racing, and Jai Alai – the last two chiefly excuses for betting.

Baseball

Until April 1993 Florida had no professional baseball team of its own – now, the state has two. In 1997, the first Florida team to come along, the **Florida Marlins**, became the youngest expansion team in history to win the World Series, shelling out millions of dollars to attract star-quality players. After taking the championship, the team slashed its budget, lost most of its marquee names, and is now a young, developing team. The Marlins play at **Pro Player Stadium**, sixteen miles northwest of downtown Miami: tickets are available from Ticketmaster (see p.121) or direct from the box office (T 305/626-7400, W www.floridamarlins.com) – most seats are in the $5–55 range.

The Marlins, though, still generally play better ball than the bottom-of-the-barrel **Tampa Bay Devil Rays**, who joined the league in 1998 and have yet to have a winning season. The Devil Rays play at Tropicana Stadium (T 727/825-3137, tampabay.devilrays.mlb.com), which is actually located in St. Petersburg – seats are generally $5–75.

The major league **baseball season** runs from April to early October, with the league championships and the World Series, the final best-of-seven playoff, lasting through the end of the month.

Spring training

Even if the local pro team is slumping, Florida has long been the home of **spring training** (Feb and March) for a multitude of professional ball clubs – and thousands of fans plan vacations so that they can watch their sporting heroes going through practice routines and playing in the friendly matches of the Grapefruit League (the Cactus League plays out in Arizona). Much prestige is attached to being a spring training venue and the local community identifies strongly with the team that it hosts – in some cases the link goes back fifty years. Turn up at 10am to join the crowds watching the training (free); the twenty-odd sides who come to train in Florida include the following: the Boston Red Sox, City of Palms Park, Fort Myers (T 1-877/RED-SOXX); the Detroit Tigers, Joker Marchant Stadium, Lakeland

(Ⓣ863/688-7911); the LA Dodgers, Holman Stadium, Vero Beach (Ⓣ772/569-6858); the NY Mets, Thomas J. White Stadium, Port St. Lucie (Ⓣ772/871-2115); and the NY Yankees, Legends Field, Tampa (Ⓣ813/287-8844).

Football

Of the state's three **professional football teams**, the **Miami Dolphins** have been the most successful, appearing five times in the Superbowl and, in 1972, enjoying the only undefeated season in NFL history. They, like the Marlins, play at Pro Player Stadium (see opposite; Ⓦwww.miamidolphins.com; most tickets around $30–50). The **Jacksonville Jaguars**, who entered the league in 1995, have stolen a bit of the Dolphins' thunder; they've already been in the playoffs four times, twice coming within one game of the Super Bowl. They play their games at Alltel Stadium (Ⓣ904/633-2000, Ⓦwww.jaguars.com; most tickets around $30–50). The **Tampa Bay Buccaneers** have also had recent success; after spending the 1980s and most of the 1990s mired in losing seasons, they ran away with the Super Bowl in 2003. The Bucs play in Raymond James Stadium (Ⓣ813/879-BUCS or 1-800/795-2827, Ⓦwww.tampabaybucs.com; tickets $15–65).

Even greater fervor is whipped up by both the **University of Florida Gators** (in Gainesville) and the **Florida State University Seminoles** (in Tallahassee). Both play around eleven games a season, the former in the Southeast Conference, and the latter in the rival Atlantic Coast Conference (along with the popular **University of Miami Hurricanes**). Tickets to college games run upwards of $40 and can be difficult to come by for the more competitive games. Further details are given in the Guide.

The **football season** for both the professional and collegiate levels begins in late summer and lasts through January.

Basketball

The state's two **professional basketball teams** have enjoyed intermittent success in the National Basketball Association. The **Miami Heat**, who joined the NBA in 1988, play at the American Airlines Arena (Ⓣ786/777-HOOP, Ⓦwww.miamiheat.com), while the **Orlando Magic**, who joined two years later, play at the TD Waterhouse Centre (Ⓣ407/89-MAGIC, www.orlandomagic.com). Tickets for both teams are in the $14–85 range.

Top among the **college teams** are the **Florida University Gators** (Ⓣ1-800/34-GATOR, Ⓦwww.gatorzone.com) and the **Miami University Hurricanes** (Ⓣ1-800/GO-CANES, Ⓦwww.hurricanesports.com).

Ice hockey

Florida boasts two teams in the National Hockey League (NHL): the **Florida Panthers** (Ⓣ954/835-7000, Ⓦwww.flpanthers.com), who play at the Office Depot Center in Sunrise near Fort Lauderdale, and the **Tampa Bay Lightning** (Ⓣ813/301-6600, Ⓦwww.tampabaylightning.com), who play in the grandly named Ice Palace. The NHL **season** runs between October and June, and tickets for both teams are $15–75 and are available from Ticketmaster or on the spot from each team's booking office.

Watersports

Even nonswimmers can quickly learn to **snorkel**, which is the best way to see one of the state's finest natural assets: the living coral reef that curls around its southeastern corner and along the Florida Keys. Many guided snorkeling trips run to the reef, costing $25–50 – further details are given throughout the Guide. More adventurous than snorkeling is loading up with air-cylinders to go **scuba diving**. You'll need a Certified Divers Card to do this; if you don't already have one you'll be required to take a course, which can last anything from one hour to a day and costs $50–100. Get details from diving shops, always plentiful near good diving areas, which can also provide equipment, maps, and general information.

When you snorkel or dive, observing a few **underwater precautions** will increase enjoyment and safety: wear lightweight shoes to avoid treading on jellyfish, crabs, or sharp rocks; don't wear any shiny objects, as these are likely to attract hungry fish such as the otherwise harmless barracuda; never dive alone; always leave your boat by diving into the current – by doing this, the current will help glide you back to the boat later; always display the red and white "diver down" flag. And, obviously, never dive after drinking alcohol.

The same reefs that make snorkeling and diving so much fun cause **surfing** to be less common than you might expect, limiting it to a few sections of the east coast. Florida's biggest waves strike land between Sebastian Inlet and Cocoa Beach, and surfing tournaments are held in the area during April and May. Lesser breakers are found at Miami Beach's First Street Beach, Boca Raton's South Beach Park, and around the Jacksonville beaches. Surfboards can be rented from local beach shops for $10–15 a day.

If you prefer to cut a (usually) more gentle passage through water, many of the state's rivers can be effortlessly navigated by **canoe**; see "The backcountry" for more details.

Fishing

Few things excite higher passions in Florida than **fishing**: the numerous rivers and lakes and the various breeds of catfish, bass, carp, and perch that inhabit them bring eager fishermen from all over the US and beyond. Saltwater fishing is no less popular, with barely a coastal jetty in the state not creaking under the strain of weekend anglers. The most sociable way to fish, however, is from a "party boat" – a boatload of people putting to sea for a day of rod-casting and boozing; these generally cost $25–30 and are easily found in good fishing areas. Sportsfishing – heading out to deep water to do battle with marlin, tuna, and the odd shark – is much more expensive. In the prime sportsfishing areas, off the Florida Keys and off the Panhandle around Destin, you'll need at least $250 a day for a boat and a guide. To protect fish stocks, a highly complex set of rules and regulations governs where you can fish and what you can catch. For the latest facts, get the free *Florida Fishing Handbook* from the Florida Fish and Wildlife Conservation Commission, 620 South Meridian St, Tallahassee, FL 32399-1600 (T 850/488-1960, W www.state.fl.us/fwc).

The backcountry

Despite the common notion that Florida is entirely composed of theme parks and beaches, much of the state is undeveloped land containing everything from scrubland and swamps to shady hardwood hammocks and dense forests streaked by gushing rivers. Hiking and canoe trails make the wilderness accessible and rewarding – miss it and you're missing Florida.

The US's **protected backcountry** areas fall into several potentially confusing categories. **State parks** are the responsibility of individual states and usually focus on sites of natural or historical significance. **National parks** are federally controlled, preserving areas of great natural beauty or ecological importance. Florida's three **national forests** are also federally administered but enjoy much less protection than national parks.

Hiking

Almost all state parks have undemanding nature trails intended for a pleasant hour's ramble; anything called a **hiking** or **backpacking trail** – plentiful in state and national parks, national forests, and threading some unprotected land as part of the Florida National Scenic Trail – requires more thought and planning.

Many hiking trails can easily be completed

in a day, the longer ones have rough camping sites at regular intervals (see "Camping," below), and most periodically pass through fully equipped camping areas – giving the option of sleeping in comparative comfort. The best time to hike is from late fall to early spring: this avoids the exhausting heat of the summer and the worst of the mosquitoes (see "Wildlife", p.44) and reveals a greater variety of animals. While hiking, be extremely wary of the **poisonwood tree** (ask a park ranger how to identify it); any contact between your skin and its bark can leave you needing hospital treatment – and avoid being splashed by rainwater dripping from its branches. Be sure to carry plenty of drinking water, as well as the obvious hiking prerequisites.

In some areas you'll need a **wilderness permit** (free or $1) from the local park ranger's or wilderness area administration office, where you should call anyway for maps, general information on the hike, and a weather forecast – sudden rains can flood trails in swampy areas. Many state parks run organized hiking trips, details of which are given throughout the Guide. For general hiking information, write to or check the website of the Florida Department of Natural Resources, Office of Greenways and Trails, 3900 Commonwealth Blvd, MS 795, Tallahassee, FL 32399 (Ⓣ850/245-2052, Ⓦwww.floridadep.org) or the Florida Trail Association (FTA), 5415 SW 13th St, Gainesville, FL 32608 (Ⓣ1-877/HIKE-FLA, Ⓦwww.florida-trail.org). The website of the FTA gives details of most trails and is constantly updated. Two useful online hiking resources are Ⓦwww.trailmonkey.com/fahike1.htm, which focuses on trails near the national parks and seashores, and Ⓦwww.trails.com, a subscription service ($5 per month) that lets members download topographic maps and full trail descriptions.

At the time of writing, the 1300-mile **Florida National Scenic Trail** stretching the length of the state was about 85 percent completed. This loosely connected footpath extends from the Gulf Islands National Seashore in the Northwest down to Big Cypress National Preserve in the Everglades. Those wanting to hike the trail end to end ("through-hike") must join the Florida Trail Association (see above for contact details), which arranges permissions and permits on hikers' behalf as some trail sections fall on private property.

Canoeing

One way to enjoy natural Florida without getting blisters on your feet is by **canoeing**. Canoes can be rented for around $20–30 a day wherever conditions are right: the best of Florida's rivers and streams are found in north central Florida and the Panhandle. Many state and national parks have canoe runs, too; the **Florida Canoe Trails System** comprises 36 marked routes along rivers and creeks, covering a combined distance of nearly a thousand miles.

Before setting off, get a canoeing **map** (you'll need to know the locations of access points and any rough camping sites) and check **weather conditions** and the river's **water level**: a low level can expose logs, rocks, and other obstacles; a flooded river is dangerous and shouldn't be canoed; coastal rivers are affected by tides. Don't leave the canoe to walk on the bank, as this will cause damage and is likely to be trespassing. When a **motorboat** approaches, keep to the right and turn your bow into the wake. If you're **camping**, do so on a sandbar unless there are designated rough camping areas beside the river. Besides food, carry plenty of drinking water, a first-aid kit, insect repellent, and sunscreen.

Several small companies run canoe trips ranging from half a day to a week; they supply the canoe and take you from the end of the route back to where you started. Details are given throughout the Guide; or look out for the free *Canoe Florida* leaflet, available from most state parks and some local tourist information offices. For more on the Florida Canoe Trails System, pick up the free *Florida Recreational Trails System Canoe Trails* (available from the **Department of Natural Resources**, address above).

Camping

All hiking trails have areas designated for **rough camping**, with either very limited facilities (a handpump for water, sometimes a primitive toilet) or none at all. Traveling by canoe (see "Canoeing" above), you'll often pass sandbars, which can make excellent overnight stops. It's preferable to cook by stove, but otherwise start fires only in permitted areas – indicated by signs – and use deadwood. Where there are no toilets, bury human waste at least four inches in the ground and a hundred feet from the nearest water supply and campground. Burn rubbish carefully, and what you can't burn, carry away. Never drink from rivers and streams, however clear and inviting they may look (you never know what unspeakable acts people – or animals – further upstream have performed in them), or from the state's many natural springs; water that isn't from taps should be boiled for at least five minutes or cleansed with an iodine-based purifier before you drink it. Always get advice, maps, and a weather forecast from the park ranger's or wilderness area administration office – often you'll need to fill in a wilderness permit, too, and pay a small nightly camping fee.

Wildlife

Florida's location on the north-south bird migration route means that the opportunities for birdwatching here are very good, and visitors are likely to spot many unfamiliar species in greater numbers than they would elsewhere. Commonly sighted species include the **snowy egret** (entirely white, with bright yellow feet), the **brown pelican** (grayish-brown body with a white head and neck), and the **cormorant** and **anhinga** (both sleek black fish-catchers), and though you stand a better chance of seeing them in the winter months, some species are present year-round.

Casual and experienced birders alike can take advantage of the **Great Florida Birding Trail** (Ⓣ850/922-0664, Ⓦwww.floridabirdingtrail.com), which links clusters of existing birding sites (such as parks, conservation areas, and sanctuaries) via highways throughout the state using special highway signs and detailed maps. Overseen by the state's Fish and Wildlife Conservation Commission, the trail presently covers the east (from the Jacksonville area south to Ft Pierce) and west (the west coast as far south as Sarasota), and the rest of the trail is scheduled to follow by 2006.

Though you're likely to meet many kinds of wildlife on your travels, only mosquitoes and, to a much lesser extent, alligators and snakes are likely to cause any problems. From mid-May to November, **mosquitoes** are a tremendous nuisance and virtually unavoidable in any area close to fresh water. During these months, insect repellent (available for a few dollars in most camping shops and supermarkets) is essential, as is wearing long-sleeved shirts and long pants. It's rare for mosquitoes to carry diseases here, though during 2001 and 2002 Florida was hit by an outbreak of West Nile virus, a mosquito-borne flu-like disease that can cause death, the elderly being especially vulnerable. As each generation of mosquitoes dies out during the winter, it's unlikely that this will be repeated – at least not for many years.

The biggest surprises among Florida's wildlife may be the apparent docility of **alligators** – almost always they will back away if approached by a human (though this is not something you should put to the test) – and the fact that they now turn up everywhere, despite being decimated by decades of uncontrolled hunting. These days, not only is it unlawful to kill alligators (without a license), but feeding one can get you two months in prison and a hefty fine: an alligator fed by a human not only loses its natural fear of people but comes to associate them with food – and lacks the brainpower to distinguish between food and feeder. The only truly dangerous type of alligator is a mother guarding her nest or tending her young. Even then, she'll give you plenty of warning, by showing her teeth and hissing, before attacking.

Like alligators, Florida's **snakes** don't go looking for trouble, but several species will retaliate if provoked – which you're most likely to do by standing on one. Two species are potentially deadly: the coral snake, which has a black nose and bright yellow and red rings covering its body, and usually spends the daylight hours under piles of rotting vegetation; and the cottonmouth moccasin (sometimes called the water moccasin), dark-colored with a small head, which lives around rivers and lakes. Less harmful, but still to be avoided, are two types of rattlesnake: the easily identified diamond-back, whose thick body is covered in a diamond pattern, and which turns up in dry, sandy areas and hammocks; and the gray-colored pygmy, so small it's almost impossible to spot until it's too late. You're unlikely to see a snake in the wild and snake attacks are even rarer, but if bitten you should contact a ranger or a doctor immediately. It's a wise precaution to carry a snakebite kit, available for a couple of dollars from most camping shops.

For more on Florida's wildlife and its habitats, see "Natural Florida" in Contexts, p.475.

Crime and personal safety

No one could pretend that Florida is trouble-free, though outside of the urban centers crime is often remarkably low-key. Even the lawless reputation of Miami is in excess of the truth, though several clearly defined areas are strictly off limits. At night you should always be cautious – though not unduly so – wherever you are. All the major tourist and nightlife areas in cities are invariably brightly lit and well policed. By being careful, planning ahead, and taking good care of your possessions, you should, generally speaking, have few real problems.

Car crime

When **driving**, under no circumstances stop in any unlit or seemingly deserted urban area – and especially not if someone is waving you down and suggesting that there is something wrong with your car. Similarly, if you are "accidentally" rammed by the driver behind, do not stop immediately but drive on to the nearest well-lit, busy, and secure area (such as a hotel, toll booth, or gas station) and phone the emergency number (☎**911**) for assistance. Keep your doors locked and windows never more than slightly open (as you'll probably be using air-conditioning, you'll want to keep them fully closed anyway). Do not open your door or window if someone approaches your car on the pretext of asking directions. Even if the person doing this looks harmless, they may well have an accomplice ready to attack you from behind. Hide any valuables out of sight, preferably locked in the trunk or in the glove compartment (any valuables you don't need for your journey should be left in your hotel safe).

Always take care when planning your route, particularly through urban areas, and be sure to use a **reliable map** such as the ones we've recommended on p.17. Particularly in Miami, local authorities are making efforts to add directions to tourist sights and attractions to road signs, thereby reducing the possibility of visitors unwittingly driving into dangerous areas. Aside from these problem areas, however, there is an easygoing and essentially safe atmosphere on roads throughout the state.

Street crime and hotel burglaries

After car crime, the biggest problem for most travelers in Florida is the threat of **mugging**. It's impossible to give hard-and-fast rules about what to do if you're confronted by a mugger. Whether to run, scream, or fight depends on the situation – but most locals would just hand over their money.

Of course, the best thing is simply to avoid being mugged, and there are a few **basic rules** worth remembering: don't flash money around; don't peer at your map (or this book) at every street corner, thereby announcing you're a lost stranger; even if you're terrified or drunk (or both), don't appear so; avoid dark streets and never start to walk down one that you can't see the end of; and in the early hours stick to the roadside edge of the sidewalk so it's easier to run into the road to attract attention.

If the worst happens and your assailant is toting a gun or (more likely) a knife, try to stay calm: remember that he (for this is generally a male pursuit) is probably scared, too. Keep still, don't make any sudden movements – and hand over your money. When he's gone, you should, despite your shock, try to find a phone and dial ☎**911**, or head to the nearest police station. Here, report the theft and get a reference number on the report to claim insurance and travelers' check refunds. If you're in a big city, ring the local Travelers Aid (their numbers are listed in the phone book) for sympathy and practical advice.

Another potential source of trouble is having your hotel room burglarized. Some Orlando area hotels are notorious for this and many such break-ins appear to be inside jobs. Always store valuables in the hotel safe when you go out; when inside, keep your door locked and don't open it to anyone you don't trust; if they claim to be hotel staff and you don't believe them, call reception to check.

Stolen travelers' checks and credit cards

Keep a record of the numbers of your **travelers' checks** separately from the actual checks; if you lose them, ring the issuing company on the toll-free number below. They'll ask you for the check numbers, the place where you bought them, when and how you lost them, and whether it's been reported to the police. All being well, you should get the missing checks reissued within a couple of days – and perhaps an emergency advance to tide you over.

To report stolen travelers' checks and credit cards, call:

American Express checks ☎1-800/221-7282
American Express cards ☎1-800/528-4800
Diners Club ☎1-800/234-6377
MasterCard ☎1-800/MC-ASSIST
Thomas Cook ☎1-800/223-7373
Visa checks ☎1-800/227-6811
Visa cards ☎1-800/336-8472

Women's Florida

Though this is the state that invented the wet T-shirt contest and that still promotes itself with photos of bikini-clad models draping themselves around palm trees, practically speaking, a woman traveling alone in Florida is not usually made to feel conspicuous or liable to attract unwelcome attention. Outside of Miami and the seedier sections of the other major cities, much of the state can feel surprisingly safe. But as with anywhere, particular care has to be taken at night. Use common sense at all times: walking through unlit, empty streets is never a good idea; take a cab if you've got any qualms.

In the major urban centers, provided you listen to advice and stick to the better parts of town, going into bars and clubs alone should pose few problems. Gay and lesbian bars are usually a trouble-free and welcoming alternative.

More serious than the odd offensive comment, rape has a high incidence in the US, and it goes without saying that you should never hitch alone – this is widely interpreted as an invitation for trouble and there's no shortage of weirdos to give it. Similarly, be wary of picking someone up for a ride. Avoid traveling at night by public transport – deserted bus stations, if not actually threatening, will do little to make you feel secure – and where possible you should team up with a fellow traveler. There really is security in numbers. On buses, make a point of sitting as near to the front – and the driver – as possible. Should disaster strike, all major towns have some kind of rape counseling service; if not, the local sheriff's office will make adequate arrangements for you to get help, counseling, and, if necessary, get you home.

If your **vehicle breaks down** in a country area, walk to the nearest house or town for help; on interstate highways or heavily traveled roads, wait in the car for a police or highway patrol car to arrive. One increasingly available – and handy – option is to rent a cellular phone with your car, for a small additional charge.

Specific **women's contacts** are listed in the city sections of the Guide, but for detailed country-wide info, read the annual *Index/Directory of Women's Media* (published by the Women's Institute for the Freedom of the Press, 1940 Calvert St NW, Washington, DC 20009-1052; ⓣ202/265-6707, ⓦwww.wifp.org), which lists women's publishers, bookshops, theater groups, news services and media organizations, and more throughout the country.

Travelers with disabilities

Travelers with mobility problems or other physical disabilities are likely to find Florida to be in tune with their needs. All public buildings must be wheelchair-accessible and have suitable toilets, most city street corners have dropped curbs, and most city buses are able to "kneel" to make access easier and are built with space and handgrips for wheelchair users.

When organizing your holiday, read your **travel insurance** small print carefully to make sure that people with a pre-existing medical condition are not excluded. A **medical certificate** of your fitness to travel, provided by your doctor, is also extremely useful; some airlines or insurance companies may insist on it. Make sure that you have extra supplies of **prescription drugs** – carried with you if you fly – and a prescription including the generic name in case of emergency. Carry spares of any clothing or equipment that might be hard to find; if there's an association representing people with your disability, contact them early in the planning process.

Use your **travel agent** to make your journey simpler: airline or bus companies can cope better if they are expecting you. With at least a day's notice, domestic airlines, and most transatlantic airlines, can do much to ease a disabled person's journey; wheelchairs can be provided at airports, staff primed to help, and, if necessary, a helper will usually be permitted free travel.

On the ground, the **major car rental firms** can, given sufficient notice, provide vehicles with hand controls (though these are usually only available on the more expensive makes of vehicle); **Amtrak** will provide wheelchair assistance at its train stations, adapted seating on board, and a fifteen percent discount on the regular fare, provided they have 72 hours notice; **Greyhound** buses, despite the fact that they lack designated wheelchair space, will allow a necessary helper to travel free.

Many of Florida's **hotels and motels** have been built recently, and disabled access has been a major consideration in their construction. Rarely will any part of the property be difficult for a disabled person to reach, and often several rooms are specifically designed to meet the requirements of disabled guests.

The state's **major theme parks** are also built with disabled access in mind, and attendants are always on hand to ensure that a disabled person gets all the necessary assistance and derives maximum enjoyment from their visit. Even in the Florida wilds, facilities are good: most **state parks** arrange programs for disabled visitors; the Apalachicola National Forest has a lakeside nature trail set aside for the exclusive use of disabled visitors and their guests; and, in Everglades National Park, all the walking trails are wheelchair-accessible, as is one of the backcountry camping sites.

Useful resources are *Travel for the Disabled*, *Wheelchair Vagabond*, and *Directory for Travel Agencies for the Disabled*, all produced by **Twin Peaks Press** PO Box 129, Vancouver, WA 98666 (ⓣ360/694-2462 or 1-800/637-2256).

Contacts and resources

In the US and Canada

Access-Able ⓦwww.access-able.com. Online resource for travelers with disabilities.

Directions Unlimited 123 Green Lane, Bedford Hills, NY 10507 ⓣ914/241-1700 or 1-800/533-5343. Tour operator specializing in custom tours for people with disabilities.

Mobility International USA 451 Broadway, Eugene, OR 97401 ⓣ541/343-1284 (voice and TDD), ⓦwww.miusa.org. Information and referral services, access guides, tours, and exchange programs. Annual membership $35 (includes quarterly newsletter).

Society for the Advancement of Travelers with Handicaps (SATH) 347 Fifth Ave, New York, NY 10016 ⓣ212/447-7284, ⓦwww.sath.org. Nonprofit educational organization that has actively represented travelers with disabilities since 1976.

Wheels Up! ⓣ1-888/38-WHEELS, ⓦwww.wheelsup.com. Provides discounted airfare, tour, and cruise prices for disabled travelers, also publishes a free monthly newsletter and has a comprehensive website.

In the UK and Ireland

Access Travel 6 The Hillock, Astley, Lancashire M29 7GW ⓣ01942/888 844, ⓦwww.access-travel.co.uk. Tour operator that can arrange flights, transfers, and accommodation. This is a small business, personally checking out places before recommendation. They can guarantee accommodation standards in Florida.

Holiday Care 2nd floor, Imperial Building, Victoria Rd, Horley, Surrey RH6 7PZ ⓣ0845/124 9971, Minicom ⓣ0845/124 9976, ⓦwww.holidaycare.org.uk. Provides free lists of accessible accommodation abroad.

Irish Wheelchair Association Blackheath Drive, Clontarf, Dublin 3 ⓣ01/818 6400, ⓦwww.iwa.ie. Useful information provided about traveling abroad with a wheelchair.

Tripscope Alexandra House, Albany Rd, Brentford TW8 0NE ⓣ0845/7585 641, ⓦwww.tripscope.org.uk. This registered charity provides a national telephone information service offering free advice on transport for those with a mobility problem.

In New Zealand

Disabled Persons Assembly 4/173–175 Victoria St, Wellington, New Zealand ⓣ04/801 9100 (also TTY), ⓦwww.dpa.org.nz. Resource center with lists of travel agencies and tour operators for people with disabilities.

Senior travelers

For many senior citizens, retirement brings the opportunity to explore the world in a style and at a pace that would be the envy of younger travelers. As well as the obvious advantages of being free to travel for longer periods during the quieter, more congenial, and less expensive seasons, anyone over the age of 62 can enjoy the tremendous variety of discounts available, but must produce suitable ID. Both Amtrak and Greyhound, for example, and many US airlines, offer modest reductions on fares to older passengers. Museums, art galleries, and even hotels offer small discounts as well, and since the definition of "Senior" can drop as low as 55, it is always worth asking.

Any US citizen or permanent resident aged 62 or over is entitled to free admission for life to all national parks, monuments, and historic sites using a **Golden Age Passport**, for which a once-only $10 fee is charged; it can be issued at any such site. This free entry also applies to any accompanying passengers in their car or, for those hiking or cycling, the passport-holder's immediate family. It also gives a fifty percent reduction on fees for camping, parking, and boat launching.

Contacts and resources

In the US

American Association of Retired Persons ⓣ 1-800/424-3410, membership hotline ⓣ 202/434-2277 or 1-800/515-2299, ⓦ www.aarp.org. Can provide discounts on accommodation and vehicle rental. Membership open to US and Canadian residents aged 50 or over for an annual fee of US$12.50.

Elderhostel 75 Federal St, Boston, MA 02110 ⓣ 1-877/426-8056, ⓦ www.elderhostel.org. Runs an extensive worldwide network of educational and activity programs, cruises, and homestays for people over 60 (companions may be younger). Programs generally last a week or more and costs are in line with those of commercial tours.

Saga Holidays ⓣ 1-800/343-0273, ⓦ www.sagaholidays.com. Specializes in worldwide group travel for seniors. Saga's Road Scholar coach tours have a more educational slant.

Vantage Deluxe World Travel ⓣ 1-800/322-6677, ⓦ www.vantagetravel.com. Specializes in worldwide group travel for seniors.

In the UK

Saga Holidays ⓣ 0130/377 1111, ⓦ www.holidays.saga.co.uk. The country's biggest and most established specialist in tours and holidays aimed at older people.

Gay and lesbian Florida

The biggest gay and lesbian scene in Florida is in Key West, at the very tip of the Florida Keys. The island town's live-and-let-live tradition has made it a holiday destination favored by American gays and lesbians for decades, and many arrivals simply never went home: instead, they've taken up permanent residence and opened guesthouses, restaurants, and other businesses – such as running gay and lesbian snorkeling and diving trips.

In **Miami** and **Fort Lauderdale** the networks of gay and lesbian resources, clubs, and bars are quite extensive – within certain areas – and it's not hard to pick up on the scene. There are smaller levels of activity in the other cities, and along developed sections of the coast a number of motels and hotels are specifically aimed at gay travelers – Fort Lauderdale, for example, has over thirty gay hotels. Predictably, attitudes to gay and lesbian visitors get progressively worse the further you go from the populous areas. Being open about your sexuality in the rural regions is likely to provoke an uneasy response if not open hostility. There are also active and relaxed gay scenes in **Pensacola** and, to a lesser extent, **Tallahassee.**

For a complete rundown on local resources, bars, and clubs, see the relevant headings within accounts of individual cities. Of the statewide **publications** to look out for, by far the best is the free *TWN* (*The Weekly News*; ⓣ305/757-6333), packed with news, features, and ads for Florida's gay bars and clubs. On the Internet, ⓦwww.gay-guide.com and ⓦwww.funmaps.com provide a wide range of useful information about gay and lesbian travel in Florida.

Contacts and resources

In the US and Canada

Damron Company ⓣ1-800/462-6654 or 415/255-0404, ⓦwww.damron.com. Publisher of the *Men's Travel Guide*, a pocket-sized yearbook full of listings of hotels, bars, clubs, and resources for gay men; the *Women's Traveler*, which provides similar listings for lesbians; the *Road Atlas*, which shows lodging and entertainment in major US cities; and *Damron Accommodations*, which provides detailed listings of over 1000 accommodations for gays and lesbians worldwide. All of these titles are offered at a discount on the website. No specific city guides – everything is incorporated in the yearbooks.

Gayellow Pages ⓣ212/674-0120, ⓦwww.gayellowpages.com. Useful directory of businesses in the US and Canada as well as regional directories for New England, New York, and the South.

International Gay/Lesbian Travel Association ⓣ954/776-2626 or 1-800/448-8550, ⓦwww.iglta.org. A trade group that can provide a list of gay- and lesbian-owned or friendly travel agents, accommodation, and other travel businesses.

In the UK

www.gaytravel.co.uk Online gay and lesbian travel agent, offering good deals on all types of holidays. Also lists gay- and lesbian-friendly hotels.

Dreamwaves Holidays ⓣ0870/042 2475, ⓦwwwgayholidaysdirect.com. Specializes in exclusively gay holidays, including summer sun packages.

In Australia and New Zealand

Gay and Lesbian Travel ⓦwww.galta.com.au. Directory and links for gay and lesbian travel worldwide.

Parkside Travel ⓣ08/8274 1222, ⓔparkside@herveyworld.com.au. Gay travel agent associated with local branch of Hervey World Travel; all aspects of gay and lesbian travel worldwide.

Silke's Travel ⓣ1800/807 860 or 02/8347 2000, ⓦwww.silkes.com.au. Long-established gay and lesbian travel specialist, with the emphasis on women's travel.

Traveling with children

Much of Florida is geared toward kid-friendly travel, what with the theme parks, water slides, beaches, and so on, so you're unlikely to encounter too many problems with children in tow.

Hotels and **motels** almost without exception welcome children: those in major tourist areas such as Orlando often have a games room and/or a play area, and allow children below a certain age (usually 14, sometimes 18) to stay free in their parents' room.

In all but the most formal restaurants, young diners are likely to be presented with a **kids' menu** – liberally laced with hot dogs, dinosaur burgers, and ice cream – plus crayons, drawing pads, and assorted toys.

Activities

Most large towns have at least one child-orientated **museum** with plenty of interactive educational exhibits – often sophisticated enough to keep even adults amused for hours. Virtually all museums and other tourist attractions have reduced rates for kids under a certain age.

Florida's **theme parks** may seem the ultimate in kids' entertainment but in fact are much more geared toward entertaining adults than most people expect. Only Walt Disney World's Magic Kingdom is tailor-made for young kids (though even here, parents are warned that some rides may frighten the very young); adolescents (and adults) are likely to prefer Disney-MGM Studios or Universal Studios.

Away from the major tourist stops, **natural Florida** has much to stimulate the young. In the many state parks and in Everglades National Park, park rangers specialize in tuning formative minds in to the wonders of nature – aided by an abundance of alligators, turtles, and all manner of brightly colored birds. A boat trip in dolphin-inhabited waters – several of these are recommended in the Guide – is another likely way to stimulate curiosity in the natural world.

On a more cautious note, adults should take great care not to allow young skin to be exposed to the Florida sun for too long: even a few minutes' unprotected exposure can cause serious **sunburn**.

No matter how you go, once you get there take special care to keep track of one another – it's no less terrifying for a child to be lost at Walt Disney World than it is for him or her to go missing at the shopping mall. Whenever possible agree on a meeting place before you get lost, and it's not a bad idea, especially for younger children, to attach some sort of wearable ID card and for toddlers to be kept on reins.

A good idea in a major theme park is to show your child how to find (or how to recognize and ask uniformed staff to take them to) the **"Lost Kids Area."** This designated space not only makes lost kids easy to locate but provides supervision plus toys and games to keep them amused until you show up. Elsewhere, tell your kids to stay where they are and not to wander; if you get lost, you'll have a much easier time finding each other if you're not all running around anxiously.

Getting around

Children under 2 years old **fly** for free – though that doesn't mean they get a seat – and when aged from 2 to 12 they are usually entitled to half-price tickets.

Most families choose to travel by car, and while this is the least problematic mode of transport, it's worth planning ahead to assure a pleasant trip. Don't set yourself unrealistic targets if you're hoping to enjoy a driving vacation with your kids. Pack plenty of sensible snacks and drinks; plan stops every couple of hours; arrive at your destination well before sunset; and if you're passing through big cities, avoid traveling during rush hour. Also, it can be a good idea to give an older child some responsibility for route-finding – having someone "play navigator" is good fun, educational, and often a real help to the driver. If you're doing a fly-drive vacation, note that car rental companies can usually provide kids' car seats for around $5 a day. You would, however, be advised to take your own, as they are not always available.

Contacts and resources

Rascals in Paradise Ⓣ415/921-7000, Ⓦwww.rascalsinparadise.com. Can arrange scheduled and customized itineraries built around activities for kids.

Travel With Your Children Ⓣ1-888/822-4388 or 212/477-5524. Publishes a regular newsletter, Family Travel Times (Ⓦwww.familytraveltimes.com), as well as a series of books on travel with children, including Great Adventure Vacations with Your Kids.

Work and study

Far from being the land of the "newly wed and the nearly dead" as many comedians have described the state, Florida's immaculate climate has persuaded people from all over the US and the rest of the world to arrive in search of a subtropical paradise. The following suggestions for finding work are basic and, if you're not a US citizen, represent the limits of what you can do without the all-important Social Security number (without which, legally, you can't work at all).

Finding work

Since the federal government introduced **fines** of up to $10,000 for illegal employees, employers have become understandably choosy about whom they hire. Even the usual **casual jobs** – catering, restaurant, and bar work – have tightened up for those without a **Social Security number**. If you do find work it's likely to be of the less visible, poorly paid kind – as washer-up rather than waiter. **Agricultural work** is always available on central Florida farms during the October to May citrus harvest; check with the nearest university or college, where noticeboards detail what's available. There are usually no problems with papers in this kind of work, though it often entails working miles from major centers and is wearying "stoop" (continually bending over) labor in blistering heat. If you can stick it out, the pay is often good and comes with basic board and accommodation. House-cleaning and baby-sitting are also feasible, if not very well-paid options.

Publications and websites

Another pre-planning strategy for working abroad is to get hold of *Overseas Jobs Express* (ⓣ01273/699 611, ⓦwww.overseasjobs.com), a fortnightly publication with a range of job vacancies, available by subscription only. Vacation Work also publishes books on summer jobs abroad and how to work your way around the world; call ⓣ01865/241 978 or visit ⓦwww.vacationwork.co.uk for their catalogue. Travel magazines like the reliable *Wanderlust* (every two months; £2.80) have a Job Shop section that often advertises job opportunities with tour companies.

Study and work programs

From the UK and Ireland

British Council ⓣ020/7930 8466. Produces a free leaflet that details study opportunities abroad. The Council's Central Management Direct Teaching (ⓣ020/7389 4931) recruits TEFL teachers for posts worldwide (check ⓦwww.britishcouncil.org/work/jobs.htm for a current list of vacancies), and its Central Bureau for International Educational and Training (ⓣ020/7389 4004, ⓦwww.centralbureau.org.uk) enables those who already work as educators to find out about teacher development programs abroad. It also publishes a book, *Year Between*, aimed principally at gap-year students detailing

Opportunities for foreign students

Foreign students wishing to **study in Florida** can either try the long shot of arranging a year abroad through their own university, or apply directly to a Florida university (being prepared to stump up the painfully expensive fees). The Student Exchange Visitor Program, for which participants are given a J-1 visa enabling them to take a job arranged in advance through the program, is not much use since almost all the jobs are at American summer camps – of which the state has none. If you're interested anyway, organizations to contact in the UK include BUNAC; see opposite for details.

volunteer programs and schemes abroad.
BUNAC (British Universities' North America Club) Ⓣ020/7251 3472, Ⓦwww.bunac.co.uk. Organizes working holidays in the US for students, typically at summer camps or training placements with companies.
Council Exchange Ⓣ020/7478 2000 Ⓦwww.councilexchanges.org.uk. International study and work programs for students and recent graduates.

From Australia and New Zealand

Australians Studying Abroad Ⓣ03/9509 1955, Ⓦwww.asatravinfo.com.au. Study tours focusing on art and culture.
Council on International Educational Exchange Ⓣ1300/135 331 or 02/8235 7000, Ⓦwww.councilexchanges.org.au. International student exchange programs.

Directory

Addresses Generally speaking, roads in built-up areas are laid out to a grid system, creating "blocks": addresses of buildings refer to the block, which will be numbered in sequence from a central point usually somewhere downtown; for example, 620 S Cedar will be six blocks south of this downtown point. In small towns and parts of larger cities, "streets" and "avenues" often run north–south and east–west respectively; streets are usually named (sometimes alphabetically), avenues generally numbered.
Cigarettes and smoking Smoking is universally forbidden on public transport and flights, and restaurants are typically divided into smoking and nonsmoking sections.
Departure tax None: airport tax is included in the price of your ticket.
Donations Many museums request donations rather than an admission fee; usually you'll be expected to put $2–3 or so into the collection as you enter. If you don't, you won't be turned away but will suffer the indignity of being considered a complete cheapskate.
Electricity 110V AC. All plugs are two-pronged and rather insubstantial. Some travel plug adapters don't fit American sockets. British-made equipment won't work unless it has a voltage-switching provision.
Flea markets Beside almost any major road junction, you'll find something touting itself as "Florida's Biggest Fleamarket." The genuinely big ones usually take place on Fridays and weekends, with hundreds of booths selling furniture, household appliances, ornaments, clothes – often hideous and always cheap.
Hurricanes Despite the much publicized onslaught of Hurricane Andrew in August 1992, statistically it's highly improbable (an average of five will hit the US coast in a three-year period) that a hurricane will affect your visit, and even if it does there will be plenty of warning – accurate tracking of potential hurricanes brewing around the Gulf of Mexico and the Caribbean from June to November (regarded as the hurricane season) being a feature of every TV weather bulletin. Local services are well equipped, most buildings are (supposedly) hurricane-proof, evacuation routes are signposted, and even phone books carry tips on how to survive – and, as shown by mass evacuations prior to the near-miss of Hurricane Floyd in 1999, Floridians have become much less blasé in their attitude to hurricanes. A more likely source of danger is thunderstorms; see p.54.
ID Should be carried at all times. Two pieces should suffice, one of which should have a photo: a passport and credit card(s) are your best bets.
Laundry All but the most basic hotels will wash laundry for you, but it'll be a lot cheaper for a wash (about $1.50–2) and tumble dry ($1–1.50) in the laundromats found all over; take plenty of quarters.
Measurements and sizes The US has yet to go metric, so measurements are in inches, feet, yards, and miles; weight in ounces, pounds, and tons. Liquid measurements differ, too: American pints and gallons are about

four-fifths of British ones. US clothing sizes can be calculated by subtracting two from British sizes; thus, a British women's size 12 is a US size 10. Shoe sizes are one and a half more than the equivalent British size.

Public toilets They don't exist as such in most areas. Bars, restaurants, and fast-food outlets are the places to go, though technically you should be a customer.

Tax Be warned that 6.5 percent sales tax is added to virtually everything you buy in a shop.

Thunderstorms Subtropical southern Florida has frequent, very localized thunderstorms throughout the summer. Obviously, if possible you should shelter inside a building to avoid being struck by lightning (which, on average, kills eleven people a year). If you're caught in the open, stay away from metallic objects and don't make a dash for your car – most people who are struck are doing this. On the plus side, the air after a storm is refreshingly free of humidity.

Tickets For music, theater, and sports matches, use Ticketmaster (Ⓦwww.ticketmaster.com), whose plentiful offices are listed in the phone book – you can buy tickets over the phone with your credit card.

Time Most of Florida runs on Eastern Standard Time; the section of the Panhandle west of the Apalachicola River, however, is on Central Standard Time – one hour behind the rest of Florida.

Tipping You shouldn't depart a bar or restaurant without leaving a tip of at least 15 percent (unless the service is utterly disgusting). About the same amount should be added to taxi fares – and round them up to the nearest 50¢ or dollar. A hotel porter should get roughly $1 per item for carrying your baggage to your room. When paying by credit or charge card, you're expected to add the tip to the total bill before filling in the amount and signing.

Videos The standard format used for video cassettes in the US is different from that used in Britain. You cannot buy videos in the US compatible with a video camera bought in Britain.

Florida terms

Barrier island A long, narrow island of the kind protecting much of Florida's mainland from coastal erosion, comprising sandy beach and mangrove forest – often blighted by condos (see below).

Condo Short for "condominium," a tall and usually ugly block of (normally) expensive apartments.

Cracker Nickname given to Florida farmers from the 1800s, stemming from the sound made by the whip used in cattle round-ups (or possibly from the cracking of corn to make grits – a hot cereal). These days it's also a disparaging term for the state's conservative ruralites.

Crackerbox Colloquial architectural term for the simple wooden cottage lived in by early Crackers (see above), ingeniously designed to allow the lightest breeze to cool the whole dwelling.

Florida ice Potentially hazardous mix of oil and water on a road surface following a thunderstorm.

Hammocks Not open-air sleeping places but patches of trees. In the south, and especially in the Everglades, hammocks often appear as "tree islands" above the flat wetlands. In the north, hammocks are larger and occur on elevations between wetlands and pinewoods. All hammocks make excellent wildlife habitats and those in the south are composed of tropical trees rarely seen elsewhere in the US.

Intracoastal Waterway To strengthen coastal defenses during World War II, the natural waterways dividing the mainland from the barrier islands (see above) were deepened and extended. The full length, along the east and southwest coasts, is termed the "Intracoastal Waterway."

Key Derived from the word "cay" – an island or bank composed of coral fragments.

No see'ums Tiny, mosquito-like insects; near-impossible to spot until they've already bitten you.

Snowbird Term applied to a visitor from the northern US coming to Florida during the winter to escape sub-zero temperatures – usually recognized by their sunburn.

Guide

Guide

1

Miami

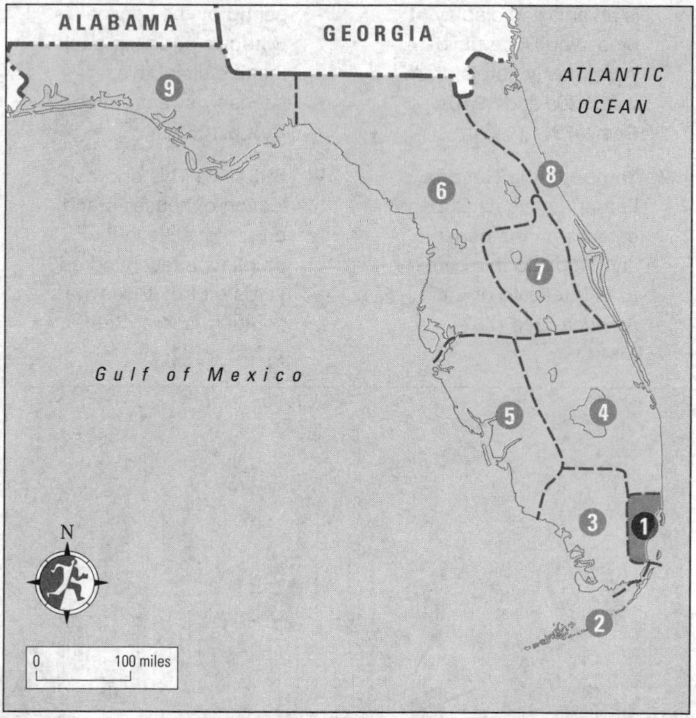
ALABAMA
GEORGIA
ATLANTIC OCEAN
Gulf of Mexico
9
8
6
7
5
4
3
1
2
N
0
100 miles

CHAPTER 1

Highlights

* **Ocean Drive** Amble along here at dawn, before the tourist hordes arrive, and the morning light shows this attractive street at its best. See p.77

* **Art Deco architecture** The core of South Beach is an amazing display of preserved Deco buildings, mostly hotels, from the 1930s and 1940s. See p.79

* **Yambo, Little Havana** Forget the ersatz Cuban eateries on the beach and step into this café for a true taste of Latin America. See p.87

* **Venetian Pool, Coral Gables** Coral Gables' civic amenities don't come better than this – a converted quarry that's both inviting and historic. See p.92

* **Café Cubano at David's Café** Join the locals lingering by the service windows and gulp back thimblefuls of this intensely sweet coffee. See p.105

* **Stiltsville** This odd collection of houses stand on top of stilts in the mudflats a few hundred yards off Key Biscayne's southern shore. See p.100

△ Miami Beach

1 Miami

By far the best-known city in Florida, **MIAMI** is a gorgeous gaudy city, part tropical paradise, part throbbing urban hub, resting on the edge of the Caribbean. It lives up to every cliché of the holiday brochures: the bodies on the beach are buff and tanned as you'd imagine, the nightlife raucous and raunchy, and the Art Deco hotels stylish. There are palm trees everywhere, and the temperature rarely dips below balmy. And though the climate and landscape may be near-perfect, it's the people that give Miami its depth and diversity. In direct contrast to the traditional Anglo-American-dominated US metropolis, two-thirds of Miami's over two million population is of Hispanic origin, of which the majority are Cubans. They form easily the most visible – and powerful – ethnic group in a city that's home to dozens from all over Latin America and the Caribbean. Spanish is the main language in most areas, and news from Havana, Caracas, or Bogotá frequently gets more attention than the latest word from Washington. The city is no melting pot, however, and ethnic divisions and tensions are often all too evident – there's friction between Hispanic, Anglo, and African-American groups, though a casual visitor is unlikely to encounter either racism or racial violence.

Miami has cleaned itself up considerably since the Eighties, when it was plagued by the highest murder rate in America: the local morgue was forced to rent portable coolers to cope with the influx of corpses. The city has also grown rich as a key gateway for US-Latin American trade, to which the glut of expensively designed banks and financial institutions bears witness. Strangely enough, another factor in Miami's revival was the mid-Eighties cop show *Miami Vice*, which was less about crime than designer clothes and subtropical scenery; set in Miami Beach's **Art Deco** district, the series helped make this a popular location for fashion shoots.

Little has been recorded of the area's indigenous inhabitants: the Tequesta people were virtually wiped out by the Spanish *conquistadores* led by **Juan Ponce de León**, who arrived in 1513. The new invaders had no interest in developing southern Florida, being far more concerned with Cuba, and built only a few small settlements along the Miami River and around Biscayne Bay. The whole of the region was finally sold by Spain to the British in 1763, and until a century ago Miami was a swampy outpost where some one thousand mosquito-tormented settlers commuted by boat between a trading post and a couple of coconut plantations.

The first mention of the **"Village of Miami"** comes after the Second Seminole War ended in 1842, when a William English re-established a plantation once owned by his uncle and started selling plots of land. The construction by Henry Flagler of the railroad in 1896 (though only after being given

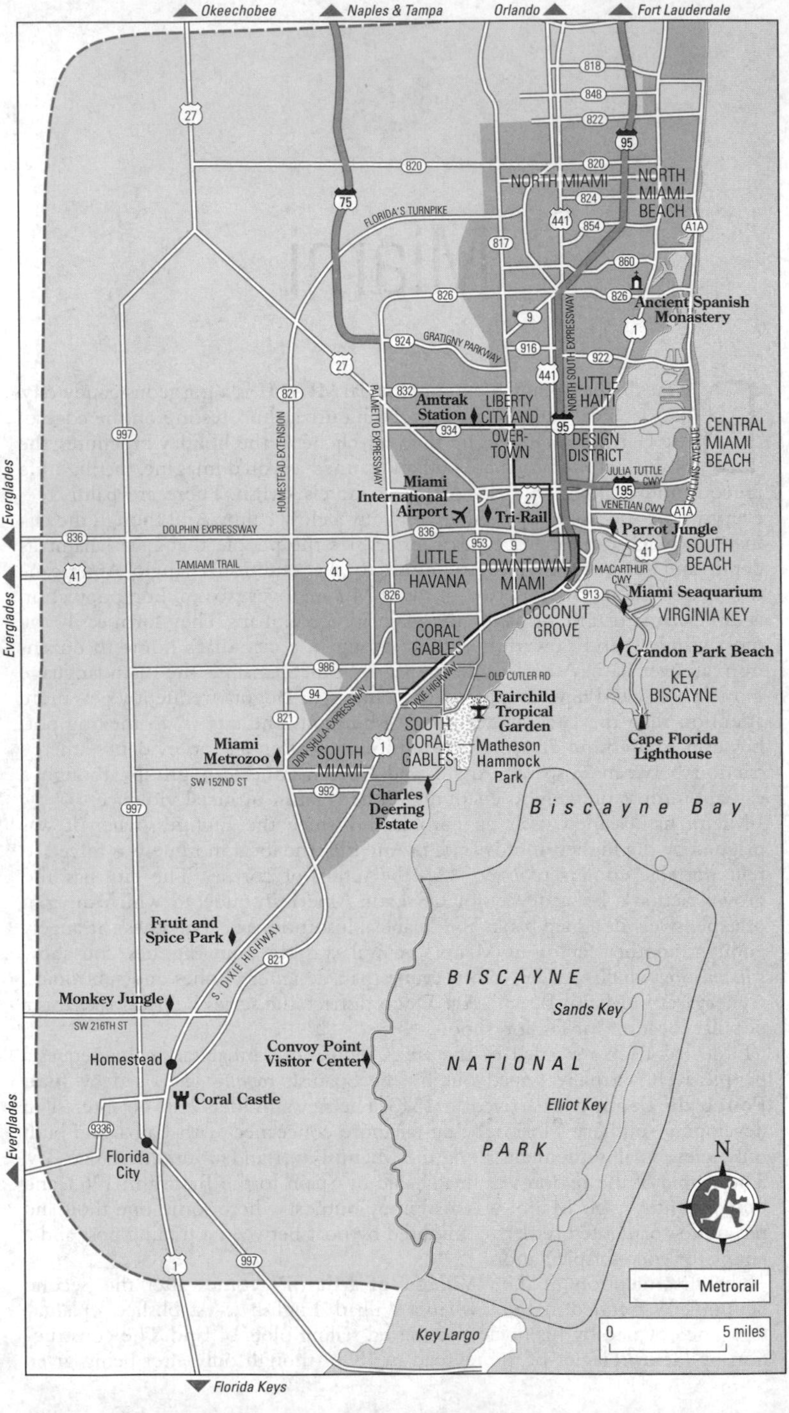
Okeechobee
Naples & Tampa
Orlando
Fort Lauderdale
Everglades
Everglades
Everglades
Everglades
Florida Keys
NORTH MIAMI
NORTH MIAMI BEACH
Ancient Spanish Monastery
FLORIDA'S TURNPIKE
GRATIGNY PARKWAY
PALMETTO EXPRESSWAY
HOMESTEAD EXTENSION
NORTH SOUTH EXPRESSWAY
LITTLE HAITI
Amtrak Station
LIBERTY CITY AND OVER-TOWN
DESIGN DISTRICT
CENTRAL MIAMI BEACH
COLLINS AVENUE
JULIA TUTTLE CWY
VENETIAN CWY
Miami International Airport
Tri-Rail
Parrot Jungle
SOUTH BEACH
DOLPHIN EXPRESSWAY
TAMIAMI TRAIL
LITTLE HAVANA
DOWNTOWN MIAMI
MACARTHUR CWY
Miami Seaquarium
VIRGINIA KEY
COCONUT GROVE
CORAL GABLES
Crandon Park Beach
KEY BISCAYNE
OLD CUTLER RD
DIXIE HIGHWAY
Fairchild Tropical Garden
DON SHULA EXPRESSWAY
SOUTH CORAL GABLES
Matheson Hammock Park
Cape Florida Lighthouse
Miami Metrozoo
SOUTH MIAMI
SW 152ND ST
Charles Deering Estate
Biscayne Bay
Fruit and Spice Park
S. DIXIE HIGHWAY
BISCAYNE NATIONAL PARK
Monkey Jungle
SW 216TH ST
Sands Key
Homestead
Convoy Point Visitor Center
Coral Castle
Elliot Key
Florida City
N
Metrorail
Key Largo
0
5 miles
818
848
822
95
820
75
824
441
854
A1A
817
860
826
9
1
924
916
922
27
441
821
832
934
997
195
836
953
41
913
826
986
94
821
992
997
821
9336
1
997

vast swathes of land in the city) gave Miami its first fixed land link with the rest of the country, and literally cleared the way for the 1920s property boom. Entire communities, such as George Merrick's **Coral Gables**, sprang up almost overnight and formed the basis of the city that stands today; the land here was relentlessly shilled to sun-seeking northerners who swarmed down to enjoy Florida's climate (and with luck make a fast buck on the turf they bought).

During the 1950s, **Miami Beach** established itself as a celebrity-filled resort, while at the same time – and with much less fanfare – thousands of Cubans fleeing the successive Batista and Castro regimes began arriving on mainland Miami. The 1960s and 1970s brought decline, as Miami Beach's celebrity cachet waned and it became a haven for retirees. The city's tourist industry was damaged still further by the Liberty City Riot of 1980, which marked a low-point in Miami's black-white relations.

Since then, with the strengthening of Latin American economic links and a younger, more cosmopolitan breed of visitor energizing Miami Beach – notably the fashionable district of **South Beach** – the city is enjoying a surge of affluence and optimism.

Arrival and information

However and whenever you arrive in Miami, you will not have difficulty getting your bearings. All points of entry are within a few miles of the center, and public transportation links are generally reliable. Numerous offices around the city dispense general tourist information and advice.

By air

All passenger **flights** land at Miami International Airport (Ⓣ305/876-7000, Ⓦwww.miami-airport.com), a chaotic complex six miles west of downtown Miami. Once through the gate, it's a simple matter to get across the city.

Some of the main **car rental firms** (see "Driving and car rental," p.63) have desks close to the baggage claim area and provide free transport to collect a vehicle. Otherwise, you have to grab your luggage, leave the terminal, and flag down a bus belonging to your rental company. **Local buses** depart from several points beside the airport's concourse; take #7 ($1.25 exact change only; every 40min; Mon–Fri 5.30am–8.30pm, Sat & Sun 7am–7pm) to downtown Miami (40–50min), or the #J bus ($1.25 plus 25¢ surcharge to beach; every 30min; daily 5.30am–11.30pm) for the slightly longer journey to Miami Beach. If you arrive late at night, there's an Airport Owl shuttle that runs on an infrequent but reliable route looping through South Beach, downtown, and back to the airport (hourly 11.50pm–5.50am). City Bus and Tri-Rail Shuttle signs opposite the airport's E departure gates indicate the bus stop. A short **taxi** ride from the airport will deliver you to the Miami West Greyhound station, which has links to other parts of Miami (see overleaf) and beyond.

Quicker, if more expensive, than public transportation, the blue and yellow **SuperShuttle** minivans (Ⓣ305/871-2000, Ⓦwww.supershuttle.com) run around the clock and will deliver you to any address in or around Miami, with per-person rates ranging from $9 to $15, depending on the destination. Their representatives are easy to spot as you leave the baggage claim area. Taxis are in plentiful supply outside the airport building and there are flat rates from the airport: $18 to downtown, $24 to South Beach, $41 to northern Miami Beach.

By bus

Of several **Greyhound** (Ⓣ305/374-6160 or 24-hour info line Ⓣ1-800/231-2222, Ⓦwww.greyhound.com) stations in Miami, the busiest is **Miami West**, near the airport, at 4111 NW 27th Street. Most Greyhound buses, however, including those to and from Key West, also stop at the **Downtown** station, 100 NW 6th Street. This is the nearest stop to downtown Miami and South Beach (take the Metrorail from the adjacent Overtown station to Government Center and change to a bus for either) – it's worth noting that Overtown is not a pleasant place to arrive in during the day, let alone after dark. Local bus services are detailed on p.65.

By train and Tri-Rail

The **train** station, 8303 NW 37th Ave (Ⓣ1-800/872-7245, Ⓦwww.tri-rail.com), is seven miles northwest of downtown Miami, and there is an adjacent **Metrorail** stop that provides access to downtown Miami and beyond; bus #L stops here on its way to Central Miami Beach. The Tri-Rail (Ⓣ1-800/TRIRAIL), the cheap commuter service running between Miami and West Palm Beach (see Basics, p.28), links directly with the Metrorail at 1149 E 21st St, also seven miles northwest of downtown Miami. Fares range from $3.50 to $9.25 return; make sure to buy tickets before you board the train. For more information on the Metrorail, see p.64.

By car

Most of the major **roads** into Miami take the form of elevated expressways that – accidents and rush hours permitting – make getting into the city simple and quick, though potentially hair-raising. From the north, **I-95** (also called the **North-South Expressway**) streaks over the downtown streets before joining **US-1** (also called **South Dixie 1**), an ordinary road that continues on through South Miami. Crossing the Everglades from the west coast, **US-41** (also called the **Tamiami Trail**) enters Miami along SW 8th Street, and you'll save time by turning off north along Florida's Turnpike (coming from the north and skirting the city's western periphery) to reach the **Dolphin Expressway (Hwy-836)**, which meets I-95 just south of downtown Miami. US-27, the main artery from central Florida, becomes the **Robert Frost Expressway** close to the airport and intersects with I-95 just north of the downtown area. The slower, scenic coastal route, **Hwy-A1A**, enters the city at the northern tip of Miami Beach.

Information

There's no official tourist information center at Miami airport, and the downtown office of the Miami Convention & Visitors Bureau, 701 Brickell Ave, Suite 2700 (Mon–Fri 8.30am–6pm; Ⓣ305/539-3000, Ⓦwww.gmcvb.com) isn't geared to handle drop-ins. On the mainland, you're best off visiting the unofficial stand at the entrance to Bayside Marketplace downtown and the Downtown Welcome Center in the lobby of the Gusman Theater, 174 E Flagler St (Mon noon–6pm, Tues–Sat 10am–6pm; ⓣ305/379-7070, ⓦwww.downtownmiami.net); otherwise, try the Miami Beach Chamber of Commerce, 1920 Meridian Ave (Mon–Fri 9am–6pm, Sat & Sun 10am–4pm; ⓣ305/672-1270, ⓦwww.miamibeachchamber.com), which is cramped but packed with leaflets and staffed by helpful locals.

Also at Miami Beach is the Art Deco Welcome Center, 1001 Ocean Drive, where the **Miami Design Preservation League** provides information on South Beach's historic Art Deco district and organizes tours (Mon–Fri 10am–5pm; ⓣ305/672-2014, ⓦwww.mdpl.org). Useful **chambers of commerce** in other districts are detailed throughout the Guide. If you're spending time in Homestead, the Everglades, or just passing through, be sure to stop at the area's excellent Tropical Everglades Visitor Information Center, 160 US-1 (Mon–Sat 8am–5pm, Sun 10am–2pm; ⓣ1-800/388-9669, ⓦwww.tropicaleverglades.com).

Getting around

While designed for the car, Miami is an easily navigable city boasting a comprehensive public transit system that provides a sound alternative for daytime travel.

Driving and car rental

Driving around Miami is practical and reasonably easy. Traffic in and out of Miami can be heavy, but the city's **expressways** (see "Arrival and information" above) will carry you swiftly from one area to another. Driving between Miami and Miami Beach is straightforward using one of six causeways; each is well marked and quickly accessed from the main arteries.

There is plenty of provision for **street parking** in Miami, though actually finding an empty space can prove difficult, particularly at night in Coconut Grove and South Beach. Parking meters are everywhere and usually cost 25¢

Miami addresses and orientation

Miami's **street naming and numbering system** may seem confusing at first but won't take long to get used to. On the mainland, the city splits into quadrants (northeast, southeast, northwest, and southwest), divided by Flagler Street and Miami Avenue, which intersect downtown; numbers rise as you move away from this intersection in any direction. Meanwhile, within a quarter, Roads, Avenues, Courts, and Places run north-south, while everything else runs east-west.

In some areas the pattern varies, most obviously in Coral Gables, where streets have names instead of numbers and avenues are numbered in sequence from Douglas Avenue. In Miami Beach, most avenues run north-south and streets run east-west.

per twenty minutes; save every quarter you get as you'll need vast quantities. Parking at public **parks and beaches** normally costs $4–5 per day; **parking lots** are pricier – the best deal on South Beach is the municipal lot on 13th Street between Ocean Drive and Collins Avenue, which costs a maximum of $8 for any 24-hour period. In the downtown shopping district the best option is the reasonably priced parking lot on NE Second Street between First and Second avenues, which costs a maximum of $5 Monday through Friday from 7am to 9pm and Saturday from 7am to 7pm. Note that parking in a marked residential area will incur a ticket.

Most of the major **car rental** companies have booking desks at the airport and provide free transportation from the terminals to their offices, where your car will be waiting. Many companies also have offices along Collins Avenue in South Beach: Alamo, 2401 Collins Ave (ⓣ1-800/327-9633, ⓦwww.goalamo.com); Avis, 8330 S Dixie Highway & 2318 Collins Ave (ⓣ1-800/831-2847, ⓦwww.avis.com); Budget, 3655 Coral Way (ⓣ305/871-2722, ⓦwww.budget.com); Hertz, 354 SE 1st St (ⓣ305/871-0300, ⓦwww.hertz.com); and Thrifty, 400 SE 2nd Ave & 1520 Collins Ave (ⓣ1-800/367-2277, ⓦwww.thrifty.com). Charges – including taxes – are around $40–50 a day or $150–300 a week for an economy car, with an insurance premium of $20–30 depending on the type of cover.

Public transportation

An integrated **public transportation** network of buses, trains, and a monorail run by Metro-Dade Transit covers Miami (ⓣ305/770-3131, ⓦwww.co.miami-dade.fl.us/transit), making the city easy – if time-consuming – to get around by day. Night travel is much harder, especially away from South Beach.

Bus routes cover the entire city, most emanating from downtown Miami, and run from 4am to 2.30am daily. The flat-rate one-way **bus fare** is $1.25, payable on board by dropping the exact amount in change or notes into a machine beside the driver. If you need to transfer to another bus, say so when you get on; for an additional 25¢, the driver will give you a **transfer** ticket, which you hand over to the driver of the next bus. Transfer tickets are route- and time-stamped to prevent you lingering too long between connections or taking scenic detours (if you do so, you'll be charged the full fare again). One way to get around South Beach is via the **Electrowave** – an air-conditioned shuttle that runs solely on electricity. One route loops along Washington Avenue and Lincoln Road; another circles the northern end of Collins Avenue and the Convention Center (every 10–15min; Mon–Wed 8am–2am, Thurs–Sat 8am–4am, Sun & holidays 10am–2am; 25¢, exact change only).

On the mainland there are two further options: the first, **Metrorail**, is an elevated monorail that links the northern suburbs with South Miami. Trains run every five to twenty minutes between 6am and midnight. Useful stops are Government Center (for downtown), Vizcaya, Coconut Grove, and Douglas Road or University (for Coral Gables). Stations do, however, tend to be awkwardly situated, and you'll often need to use Metrorail services in conjunction with a bus. One-way **Metrorail fares** are $1.25; buy a token from the machines (insert five quarters) at the station and use it to get through the turnstile. Transfers between buses and Metrorail cost 25¢ from the bus driver or a Metrorail station transfer machine.

Downtown Miami is ringed by the **Metromover** (sometimes called the "People Mover"), a monorail loop that is fast and clean, if a little limited – but a great way to get your bearings on arrival (daily 5.30am–midnight, later during major events at American Airlines arena; free; ⓣ305/770-3131).

Major Miami bus routes

Metro-Dade Transit, from downtown Miami to:
Coconut Grove #48
Coral Gables #24
Key Biscayne #B
Little Haiti and the Design District #3
Little Havana #8
Miami Beach #C, #K (along Washington Ave) or #S (along Alton Rd)
Miami International Airport #7

Greyhound within Miami, from downtown Miami to:
Homestead (3 daily; 1hr 15min)
Miami Beach (18 daily; 25–45min)
Miami West (18 daily; 15–45min)
North Miami Beach (18 daily; 20–45min)

If you're sticking around for a while, consider a **Metropass**, which gives unlimited rides on all services for a calendar month. The Metropass costs $60 from any shop displaying the Metro-Dade Transit sign and is on sale from the 20th of each month.

For **free route maps and timetables**, go to the Transit Service Center inside the Metro-Dade Center in downtown, 101 NW 1st St (Mon–Fri 8am–6pm).

Taxis

Taxis are abundant and often the only way to get around at night without a car. **Fares** are $1.50 for the first quarter mile and $2 a mile after that. From downtown Miami you'll pay around $12 to Coconut Grove and $16 to Miami Beach. An empty cab will stop if the driver sees you waving, but if you want to prebook, try one of the following: Central Cab (ⓣ305/532-5555), Metro Taxi (ⓣ305/888-8888), and Yellow (ⓣ305/444-4444) are all fairly reliable.

Cycling and rollerblading

Although you won't be able to see all of Miami by **cycling**, Coral Gables and Key Biscayne are perfectly suited to bike trips, and there's a fifteen-mile cycle path through Coconut Grove and into South Miami. For details, get hold of the free leaflet *Miami on Two Wheels* from the Greater Miami Convention and Visitors Bureau (see "Information," p.62).

You can **rent a bike** for $10–20 per day from several outlets including: in Key Biscayne, Mangrove Cycles, The Square, 260 Crandon Blvd (ⓣ305/361-5555); and in Miami Beach, the Miami Beach Bicycle Center, 601 5th St, (ⓣ305/674-0150). Helmets are usually included in the price, though you may have to pay an extra $1 per day for the lock; the Miami Beach Bicycle Center also offers weekly rates ($70).

Otherwise, you can try **rollerblading**, particularly popular in South Beach; see "Listings," p.120, for rental (or sales) details.

Tours

For an informative and entertaining stroll, take one of **Dr Paul George's Walking Tours** (no tours July & Aug; $15 and up; ⓣ305/375-1621, ⓦwww.historical-museum.org), which are offered in conjunction with the

Miami media

Miami has only one daily **newspaper,** the 100-year old *Miami Herald* (35¢ weekdays, $1 Sunday): it's disappointingly bland, and the best day to pick up a copy is Friday when a free and informative entertainment supplement is bundled with the paper. Otherwise, try the *Florida Sun-Sentinel* (35¢ weekdays, $1 Sunday) – less good on local news, but with more in-depth national reporting; or better still, try either *New Times* or *Street Miami*, pithy weekly freesheets with copious entertainment listings. The following are the best sources of up-to-date entertainment and arts listings; most can be picked up free around town and at hotels.

Lincoln Road ⓣ305/695-8484, ⓦwww.lincolnroadmagazine.com. Upstart social magazine and rival to the established *Ocean Drive* (see below).

New Times ⓣ305/372-0004, ⓦwww.newtimes.com. The best weekly listings paper in Miami covers food, drink, entertainment, and, to a lesser extent, the arts. Published Thursdays.

Ocean Drive ⓣ305/532-2544, ⓦwww.oceandrive.com. Glossy freesheet available in every hotel that follows the Beautiful People on the local scene.

Street Miami ⓣ305/523-7878, ⓦwww.streetmiami.com. Reasonable listings and editorials; not as in-depth as *New Times* but not as unwieldy either.

Historical Museum of Southern Florida and take in a number of areas, including downtown Miami, Coconut Grove, Coral Gables, Little Havana, South Beach, and the Miami Cemetery. There are 25 different itineraries, each lasting around 2–3 hours. For less-visited parts of the city, try David Brown, who specializes in Miami's black neighborhoods, including Liberty City and Little Haiti (ⓣ1-866/663-4455, ⓔdb3227@aol.com). The often-overlooked old buildings in downtown are highlighted by the Downtown Miami Partnership, which produces a self-guided walking tour of downtown's architectural highlights that's available from most tourist offices (the latter run guided tours, too).

In South Beach, you shouldn't miss the ninety-minute **Art Deco Walking Tour**. A perfect introduction to the area's phenomenal architecture, the tour begins each Saturday at 10.30am and Thursday at 6.30pm from the Art Deco Welcome Center, 1001 Ocean Drive ($15; ⓣ305/672-2014, ⓦwww.mdpl.org).

Accommodation

Finding a place to stay in Miami is only a problem over New Year's and important holiday weekends such as Memorial Day and Labor Day. The city is small enough that you can stay just about anywhere and not feel isolated, though the lion's share of **hotels** and **motels** are on **Miami Beach**: an ideal base for nightlife, beachlife, and seeing the city. Prices vary from $35 to $300, but you can anticipate spending at least $40–75 during the summer and $60–100 during the winter (or upwards of $200 per night in the ultra-chic South Beach hotels).

For most visitors, there's little reason not to stay on the beach, though we've provided a pick of the best of the rest. While there are pleasant enough places in Coconut Grove and Coral Gables, there's no compelling reason to stay in either place for the casual visitor. Otherwise, downtown is clogged with expensive chains, and Key Biscayne's luxury pads are out of most people's budgets; conversely, the cheap motels that line Biscayne Boulevard close to Little Haiti and the Design District are mostly flophouses or worse. The **airport** area hotels should only be considered if you're catching a plane at an unearthly hour or arriving late and want to avoid driving into Miami after dark.

During the winter you'd be well advised to **reserve ahead**, either directly or through an agent. Between May and November, however, you'll save by going for the best deals on the spot (though you may want to arrange your first night in advance). Don't be afraid to **bargain**, as this can result in more than a few dollars being lopped off the advertised rate – especially if you're staying for more than a few days, though **single** rooms are rarely cheaper than **doubles**.

Prices below are for low season – in other words, summer; expect higher rates December to April, especially at weekends.

Downtown Miami and around

Holiday Inn Marina Park 340 Biscayne Blvd ⓣ305/371-4400 or 1-800/526-5655, ⓦwww.holiday-inn.com/marinapark. A bland exterior shields a much warmer, more welcoming interior. One of the better mainland options, with views across the Port of Miami and the neighboring parks. ❸

Inter-Continental Miami 100 Chopin Plaza ⓣ305/577-1000, ⓦwww.intercontinental.com. The pick of the upscale chains in downtown for its breathtaking views across Biscayne Bay and the Port of Miami – ask for a room on one of the upper floors. The rooms themselves are plush but nondescript. ❻

Miami River Inn 118 SW South River Drive, Little Havana ⓣ305/325-0045, ⓦwww.miamiriverinn.com. Most of the buildings making up the inn date to 1908 and provide comfortable accommodation clustered around a tree-shaded pool. There's free breakfast and friendly staff – but it's off the beaten track and only really an option if you have a car. ❸

Miami Sun Hotel 226 NE First Ave ⓣ305/375-0786. The rooms at this budget motel are far more attractive than the lobby, with its fake leather sofas and forlorn disco ball, might suggest. They're clean, with bright floral bedspreads, and have fridges: the four-person suites are a steal for $55. ❷

South Beach

Albion Hotel 1650 James Ave ⓣ305/913-1000 or 1-877/RUBELLS, ⓦwww.rubellhotels.com. A sensitive conversion of a classic Nautical Deco building, this is one of the best-value hotels on the beach. Rooms are stylishly simple, while the raised pool – with portholes cut into its sides – is also a big draw. ❻

Aqua 1530 Collins Ave ⓣ305/538-4361. Funky, industrial chic rooms, with concrete floors and poppy, citrus, and blue fixtures set around a shady inner courtyard. ❹

Brigham Gardens Guesthouse 1411 Collins Ave ⓣ305/531-1331, ⓦwww.brighamgardens.com. Large rooms with either basic or fully equipped kitchens. A tropical garden patio and friendly atmosphere help make this one of the most pleasant places to stay in South Beach. Ten percent discount for stays of seven days or more. ❸

Clay Hotel Hostel-Miami Beach International Youth Hostel 406 Española Way ⓣ305/534-2988, ⓦwww.clayhotel.com. The location's great, and this hotel-hostel hybrid is a terrific place to meet other travelers – just make sure to see a room before you commit, since some are cleaner and more welcoming than others. Private rooms with bath $57, without bath $47; dorm rooms $16 IYH members, $18 others.

Clinton Hotel 825 Washington Ave ⓣ305/938-4040, ⓦwww.clintonsouthbeach.com. One of the newest hotels in town, where rooms have a vague bondage theme with corset-inspired chairs and mirrors. The bedrooms are equipped with CD players, and the massive bathrooms have luxurious two-person showers. ❺

Delano 1685 Collins Ave ⓣ305/672-2000, ⓦwww.ianschragerhotels.com. One of South Beach's chicest lodgings mixes Art Deco with minimalist modernism (eg, lots of white) and all-round luxury. Gauzy white curtains billow in the lobby – a shame the staff are so sniffy. ❼

The Hotel 801 Collins Ave ⓣ305/531-2222, ⓦwww.thehotelofsouthbeach.com. Designer Todd Oldham oversaw every element in the renovation of this hotel, and his colorful yet thoughtful makeover makes it one of the best luxury options on the beach. Don't miss the rooftop pool, shaped like a gemstone in honor of the hotel's original name, preserved in the "Tiffany" sign on the turret. ❼

The Kent 1131 Collins Ave ⓣ305/604-5068 or 1-800/OUT-POST, ⓦwww.islandoutpost.com. Famed 1960s fashion designer Barbara Hulanicki has created a crazy lavender-and-lucite trip in this renovated Deco hotel – there's lots of brushed steel in the rooms, too, which are cosy if a little dark. ❺

Ninth Street Hostel 236 9th St ⓣ305/534-0268, ⓦwww.sobehostel.com. Friendly hostel with beds in four-person dorms starting at $13 ($15 for non-IYHA-members), as well as private singles and doubles (from $36), centrally positioned in South Beach. Offers Internet facilities, kitchen, laundry, a comfortable movie-lounge, and also books tours.

Park Central 640 Ocean Drive ⓣ305/538-1611, ⓦwww.theparkcentral.com. One of the first hotels to be reborn during the South Beach renaissance of the early 1990s. The colonial safari look of the wicker-crammed rooms is a little outdated, but the reasonable prices make this an attractive option nonetheless. ❺

Pelican 826 Ocean Drive ⓣ305/673-3373 or 1-800/7-PELICAN, ⓦwww.pelicanhotel.com. Irreverent Italian jeanswear company Diesel owns this hotel, so the quirky, campy decor of the rooms should come as no surprise. Each is individually themed and named – try the lush red bordello known as the "Best Little Whorehouse" room. ❻

Raleigh 1775 Collins Ave ⓣ305/534-6300 or 1-800/848-1775, ⓦwww.raleighhotel.com. Recently refurbished, this fusty gem has retained signature touches like the curvy pool – where many 1920s synchronized swimming movies were shot – and the dark, wood-paneled bar. The rooms, though, have been jazzed up, with orthopedic beds and sumptuous linens. ❼

Sagamore 1671 Collins Ave ⓣ305/535-8088, ⓦwww.sagamorehotel.com. A low-key luxury hotel, with enormous rooms decorated in muted shades of chocolate and taupe. There's a beachfront pool, where you can swim a few laps then climb out straight onto the sands. Don't miss the stunning modern art collection dotted around the public areas. ❼

The Shore Club 1901 Collins Ave ⓣ305/895-3100, ⓦwww.shoreclub.com. Ian Schrager swooped in to save this high end hotel when it floundered only months after opening – and thanks to his magic touch, it's now *the* place to stay on the beach. Rooms are minimalist in style, but decorated in splashy colors, but you won't spend long inside when you can be lounging with the beautiful people in the poolside *Sky Bar* (see box, p.110). ❽

Townhouse 150 20th St ⓣ305/534-3800 or 1-877/534-3800, ⓦwww.townhousehotel.com. From the small but beautifully designed white rooms to the chatty, cheerful staff and the relaxing roofdeck filled with squishy waterbeds, this boutique hotel aims to please – and the prices are surprisingly low, too. Highly recommended. ❹

The Tropics Hotel and Hostel 1550 Collins Ave ⓣ305/531-0361, ⓦwww.tropicshotel.com. Housed in a stylish Art Deco building, this is more of a hotel than a hostel and more genteel than either of the above. Spotless and comfortable four-person dorms start at $75 per room, with doubles also available for $50. A clean kitchen, swimming pool, laundry facilities, and airport shuttle are all available. Attracts a more mature crowd.

Villa Paradiso 1415 Collins Ave ⓣ305/532-0616, ⓕ673-5874. Fully equipped studios and one-bedroom apartments with kitchens, just one block away from the beach: the spaciousness of the rooms make up for the dated *Miami Vice*–inspired decor. ❸

The Wave 350 Ocean Drive ⓣ305/673-0401 or 1-800/501-0401, ⓦwww.wavehotel.com. Nestled in the newly hip area south of 5th Street (blossoming thanks to a new bar opening nearby), this hotel has small but fully equipped rooms, each with a mood machine so you can drift off to sleep to the sound of crashing waves. The huge free breakfasts are a major plus. ❺

The Whitelaw 808 Collins Ave ⓣ305/398-7000, ⓦwww.whitelawhotel.com. This budget boutique hotel has all-white rooms with CD players and fridges, but best of all are the copious freebies, from airport pick-up to lavish breakfasts and a happy hour every evening in the lobby. A real find. ❺

Central Miami Beach and north

Beach House Bal Harbour 9449 Collins Ave, Surfside ⓣ305/535-8600 or 1-877/RUBELLS, ⓦwww.rubellhotels.com. A dash of the Hamptons in Florida, this preppy hotel is plush and comfy, from a common area where you can dawdle in the overstuffed armchairs and flick through magazines to the cushion-strewn beds. ❻

Best Western Thunderbird Resort 18401 Collins Ave, Sunny Isles Beach ⓣ305/931-1700 or 1-800/327-2044, for info ⓦwww.dezerhotels.com, for booking ⓦwww.bestwestern.com. No frills, but handy for both Miami and Fort Lauderdale. As in most hotels around here, you can step straight out of your room into the pool or onto the beach. ❹

Eden Roc Resort & Spa 4525 Collins Ave, Miami Beach ⓣ305/531-0000 or 1-800/327-8337, ⓦwww.edenrocresort.com. A landmark on the Miami Beach since the 1950s, *Eden Roc* has been refurbished to the last detail – a shame, perhaps, since the rather garish rooms are now stripped of any period detail. The lobby, though, is stunning and injects a touch of Fifties glamour. ❻

Fontainebleau Hilton 4441 Collins Ave, Miami Beach ⓣ305/538-2000, ⓦwww.fontainebleau.hilton.com. Once the last word in glamour, it's now a family favorite thanks to its kid-friendly facilities. Rooms are fine enough, but bland. ❼

The Golden Sands 6910 Collins Ave, North Beach ⓣ305/866-8734, ⓦwww.goldensands.com. Nothing flashy and mostly filled by Europeans on package tours, but likely to turn up some of the cheapest accommodation with a pool in this pricey area. ❷

Howard Johnson Bayshore 4000 Alton Rd, Miami Beach ⓣ305/532-4411 or 1-800/532-4411, ⓦwww.hojo.com. Off the beaten track, this large motel at the western end of 41st Street is a terrific option whenever the other, more central hotels are full: the rooms are clean, bright, and furnished with the standard amenities. ❸

Roney Palace 2399 Collins Ave, Miami Beach ⓣ305/604-1000 or 1-800/432-4317, ⓦwww.roney-palace.com. The one major plus at this hotel, popular with conventioneers, is the huge apartment-style rooms. On the minus side are all the extra costs, from a daily resort fee (whether you use the pool or not) to exorbitant phone charges. ❽

Coral Gables and Coconut Grove

Biltmore 1200 Anastasia Ave, Coral Gables ⓣ305/445-1926 or 1-800/727-1926, ⓦwww.biltmorehotel.com. A landmark, Mediterranean-style hotel that has been pampering the rich and famous since 1926. The rooms, furnished in peach and cream tones, will bring to mind a villa on a Spanish island, but it's the massive chevron-shaped pool that proves to be the main draw. ❼

Doubletree Hotel Coconut Grove 2649 S Bayshore Drive, Coconut Grove ⓣ305/858-2500 or 1-800/222-TREE, ⓦwww.doubletree.com. Elegant high-rise hotel surrounded by banyan trees, with cozy rooms and great views – just a quarter of an hour's walk from the area's cafés and bars. ❹

Gables Inn 730 S Dixie Hwy, Coral Gables ⓣ305/661-7999, ⓔthegablesinn@aol.com. Coral Gables' version of a motel – so it's slightly fancier than most, with its Mediterranean Revival architecture. Note that it's located right on the S Dixie Highway, so it can be noisy. ❸

Hampton Inn 2800 SW 28th St, Coconut Grove ⓣ305/448-2800 or 1-800/HAMPTON, ⓦwww.hamptoninns-florida.com. Basic but bright accommodation, geared to the business traveler – but the free local calls, free breakfast, and onsite coin laundry make this an attractive option for those on a budget. ❹

Place St Michel 162 Alcazar Ave, Coral Gables ⓣ305/444-1666 or 1-800/848-HOTEL, ⓦwww.hotelplacestmichel.com. A small, romantic hotel just off the Miracle Mile, with modernized rooms, Laura Ashley decor, and copious European antiques. Rates include continental breakfast. ❺

Key Biscayne

Silver Sands Oceanfront Motel 301 Ocean Drive ⓣ305/361-5441, ⓕ361-5477, ⓦwww.silversandsmiami.com. Fairly standard rooms unexceptional for the price, but you get to watch the marine iguanas who have colonized their botanical garden and occasionally swim in the pool. ❻

Sonesta Beach 350 Ocean Drive ⓣ1-800/SONESTA or 305/361-2021, ⓦwww.sonesta.com. High-rise resort with luxurious rooms, sports facilities, bars, and a prime stretch of private beach. ❼

South of Miami

Best Western Gateway to the Keys 411 S Krome Ave, Florida City ⓣ305/246-5100, ⓦwww.bestwestern.com. One of the most comfortable places to stay hereabouts, and usefully located between the Keys, Miami, and the Everglades. All rooms are nonsmoking. ❸

Grove Inn Country Guesthouse 22540 SW Krome Ave, Redland ⓣ305/247-6572 or 1-877/247-6572, ⓦwww.groveinn.com. A former fruit farm, this comfortable B&B is a secluded getaway, made ever more attractive by its friendly, helpful owners. ❸

Redland Hotel 5 S Flagler Ave, Homestead ⓣ305/246-1904 or 1-800/595-1904, ⓦwww.redlandhotel.com. An historic inn, where each room is named for a local pioneer family. The rooms are floral and chintzy, but comfortable. ❹

At the airport

Hampton Inn-Miami Airport 777 NW 57th Ave ⓣ305-262-5400 or 1-800/HAMPTON, ⓕ305/262-5488, ⓦwww.hamptoninns-florida.com. Branch of a good-value hotel chain two miles from the airport, offering some of the best rates in the area. Twenty-four-hour courtesy bus available to airport. ❻

MIA Miami International Airport ⓣ305/871-4100 or 1-800/327-1276, ⓕ305/871-0800, ⓦwww.miahotel.com. There's no excuse for missing your plane if you stay here; this fully equipped, if bland, hotel is located inside the airport, but you'll pay for the convenience. ❻

Miami Airways Motel, 5001 36th St ⓣ305/883-4700. Recently renovated modern rooms offer the cheapest deal in the area. ❷

The City

Miami is a wildly varied place, filled with diverse districts jigsawed into a vast city. Distances between its neighborhoods can be large, so if you're planning on exploring the whole city, it's worth hiring a car. If you're sticking to the most popular areas downtown and on Miami Beach, though, you can zip around easily by bus and on foot. Either way, it pays to remember that, though the crime-spattered Miami of the 1980s is a distant memory, there are still some rough urban areas where visitors should exercise caution – we've noted them in the text.

The obvious starting point for any visit is **downtown Miami**, the small, bustling nerve center of the city. Its streets are lined by low-slung, garishly decorated shops, and most of the conversation you'll hear on the street will be in Spanish – it's easy to imagine you're not even in America at all standing by one of the roadside cafés slugging back a *café Cubano*. Downtown is sandwiched between two areas at opposite ends of Miami's economic ladder: **Brickell**, across the river to the south, home to dozens of international banks and upscale condos; and **Overtown** to the north, an impoverished, largely African-American district with a history of racial unrest. East of Overtown, the largely residential Biscayne Corridor is notable for two districts worth seeking out: the trendy **Design District**, packed with furniture showrooms, and the authentic immigrant neighborhood known as **Little Haiti**.

Commanding the most attention, however, is the small island of **Miami Beach**. Three miles offshore, sheltering Biscayne Bay from the Atlantic Ocean, Miami Beach was an ailing fruit farm in the 1910s when its Quaker owner, John Collins, formed an unlikely partnership with a flashy entrepreneur named Carl Fisher. With Fisher's money, Biscayne Bay was dredged, and the muck raised from its murky bed provided the landfill that transformed the island into the sculptured landscape of palm trees, hotels, and tennis courts that – by and large – it is today.

In varying degrees, all twelve miles of Miami Beach are worth seeing – and its firm, crushed-coral-rock beaches offer excellent sunbathing and swimming opportunities, but most people spend their time in **South Beach**, a fairly small area at the southern end, where many of Florida's leading art galleries, trend-setting restaurants, and much of its boisterous club scene are found. Heading north, **Central Miami Beach** was where Fifties screen stars had fun in the sun and helped cement Miami's international reputation as a glamorous vacation spot. Oddly enough, it's the monolithic hotels remaining from these times that give the area a modicum of appeal, with their playful, Miami Modernist architecture. Further on, as you reach the areas known as **North Beach, Surfside,** and **Bal Harbour**, there's less action; in some ways, though, it's only here that a visitor can see the real life behind the raucous partying that overruns South Beach – many of the workers who staff the attractions further south live in the condos here. This strip is a scenic back route if you're heading north from Miami toward Fort Lauderdale.

The first of Miami's Cubans settled southwest of downtown, just across the Miami River, in (what became) **Little Havana**. This is still one of the more intriguing parts of the city, rich with Latin American looks and sounds, though it's less solidly Cuban than it used to be. Immediately south, Little Havana's street grid gives way to the spacious boulevards of **Coral Gables**. This ersatz-

European fantasy of broad lawns, massive houses, and ornate public buildings was the brainchild of one man, George Merrick, who decided to replicate a chunk of Spain in southern Florida. South of the downtown area is **Coconut Grove**, the oldest settlement in the area and once an arty, bohemian place, but nowadays known for its malls and cafés. The large island visible off the coast of Coconut Grove is **Key Biscayne**, linked to the mainland via the massive Rickenbacker Causeway. This classy, secluded island community offers exquisite beaches, only five miles from downtown.

Beyond Coconut Grove and Coral Gables, **South Miami** is a lackluster residential sprawl with little of note, fading into farming territory toward **Homestead** on Miami's southern edge, and into the barren expanse of the Everglades to the west.

Downtown Miami and around

DOWNTOWN MIAMI is not a place in which to relax: humanity storms down its short streets, rippling the gaudy awnings of countless cut-price electronics, clothes, and jewelry stores, easing up only to buy imported newspapers or to gulp down a spicy snack and a mango juice from a fast-food stand. Since the early Sixties, when newly released Cuban Bay of Pigs veterans came here to spend their US Government back pay, the predominantly Spanish-speaking businesses of the downtown square mile have reaped the benefits of any boost in South or Central American incomes. Affluent Latinos pour into Miami International Airport and move downtown in droves, seeking the goods they can't find at home. Minorities in this throng include dazed-looking European tourists, clean-cut Anglo-Americans with local government jobs, and street people of indeterminate origin dragging their worldly possessions with them. Only some solid US public architecture and whistle-blowing traffic cops remind you that you're still in Florida and not on the main drag of a busy, slightly chaotic Latin American capital. All in all, it's a thrilling, chaotic experience.

Though it's often neglected on sightseeing itineraries, downtown is one of Miami's most compact and manageable districts; the nerve-jangling streets and the feeling they induce of being at the crossroads of the Americas are reason enough to spend half a day wandering around here, but added attractions like the **Historical Museum of Southern Florida** and the stunning modern art round-up at the **Miami Art Museum** make downtown a must.

Flagler Street and the Metro-Dade Cultural Center

Nowhere gives a better first taste of downtown Miami than **Flagler Street**, by far the loudest, brightest, busiest strip, and long the area's main attraction. Start at the eastern end by glancing inside the 1938 **Alfred DuPont Building**, no. 169 E, which currently houses the Florida National Bank (whose first floor is open to the public), to find fanciful wrought-iron screens, bulky brass fittings, and frescoes of Florida scenes epitomizing the decorative style popular with US architects at the end of the Depression. Nearby, the even less restrained **Gusman Center for the Performing Arts**, no. 174 E (Ⓣ305/374-2444, Ⓦwww.gusmancenter.org) began life in the Twenties as a vaudeville theater, and displays all the exquisitely kitsch trappings you'd expect inside a million-

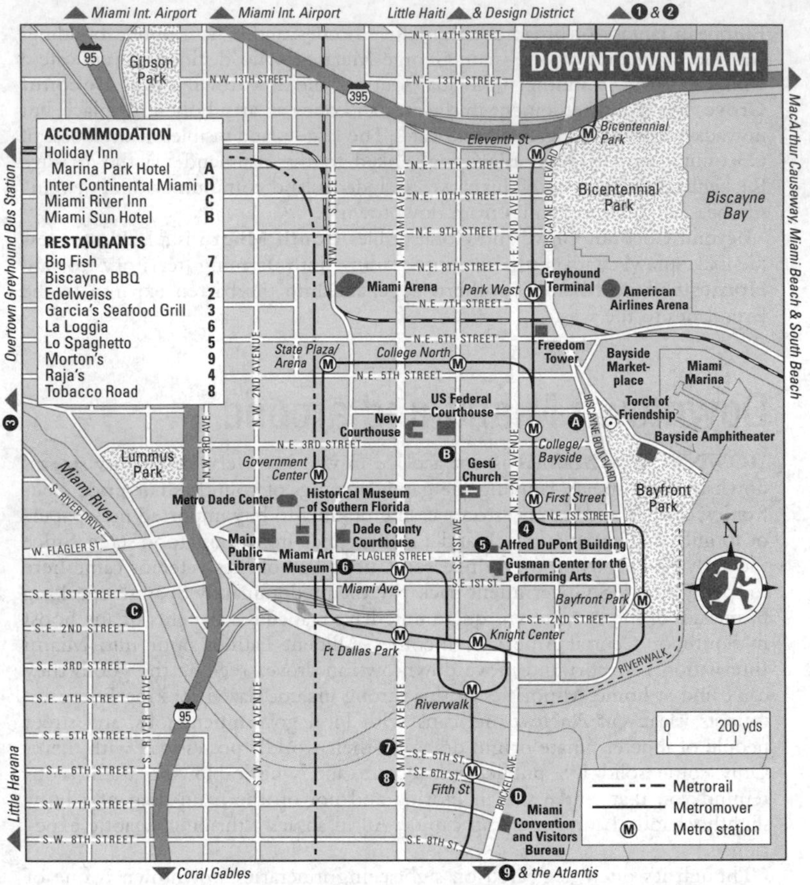

dollar building designed to resemble a Moorish palace. The turrets, towers, and intricately detailed columns remain (having escaped demolition in 1972), and a crescent moon still flits across the star-filled ceiling of the auditorium – the latter viewable only with a ticket to a performance. Further along the street, at no. 73 W, four forbidding Doric columns mark the entrance to the **Dade County Courthouse**. Built in 1926 on the site of an earlier courthouse – where public hangings used to take place – this was Miami's tallest building for fifty years (until it was dwarfed by the 55-story First Union Financial Center on South Biscayne Boulevard), and its night lights showed off a distinctive stepped pyramid peak that beamed out a symbolic warning to wrongdoers all over the city.

The Metro-Dade Cultural Center

Little inside the courthouse is worth passing the security check for (the juiciest cases are tried in the New Courthouse; see p.74). Instead, you should cross SW First Avenue toward the giant, air-raid shelter-like building of the **Metro-Dade Cultural Center**, entered via a ramp off Flagler Street. This was an ambitious attempt by renowned architect Philip Johnson to create a postmodern Mediterranean-style piazza, a congenial gathering place where Miami could display its cultural side. The theory almost worked: superb art shows, historical collections, and a major library frame the courtyard, but Johnson forgot the power of the south Florida sun. Rather than pausing to rest and gossip, most people scamper across the open space toward the nearest shade.

Looming above the plaza's western flank, the **Historical Museum of Southern Florida** (Mon–Wed, Fri & Sat 10am–5pm, Thurs 10am–9pm, Sun noon–5pm, third Thursday of each month 10am–9pm; $5; ⓣ305/375-1492, ⓦwww.historical-museum.org) offers a comprehensive look at South Florida's past. The exhibits on Native American inhabitants are patchy, since so little is known about their way of life: better to skip to the early European settlers, and especially the surprisingly accurate maps of Florida dating back to the late eighteenth century. Also well chronicled are the fluctuating fortunes of Miami Beach, from its early days as a celebrity vacation spot – with amusing photos of Twenties Hollywood greats – through to the renovation of the Art Deco district. The exhibition ends with a look at the arrival of Cuban and Haitian immigrants, including two genuine refugee rafts, shockingly small given their passenger load. Standing in sharp contrast is the jaunty model of airborne luxury nearby, a miniature version of a Pan-Am jet from the 1960s.

A few yards away at the plaza's eastern edge, the **Miami Art Museum** (Tues–Fri 10am–5pm, Sat & Sun noon–5pm, third Thursday of each month 10am–9pm; $5, free Sundays; ⓣ305/375-1700, ⓦwww.miamiartmuseum.org) has a stunning and intelligently curated permanent collection. Its display is refreshed four times yearly, though highlights are likely to include brightly colored canvases by Damien Hirst, photographs of Ku Klux Klansmen by Andres Serrano, and sketches by Christo. Don't miss the gorgeous works by the late Cuban-American conceptual artist Felix Gonzalez-Torres: the museum has several of his organic pieces, designed to change through viewing – for example a pile of candy stacked in a stark white corner that dwindles as passersby help themselves to it. Plans are afoot to relocate the museum to a waterfront space known as Museum Park Miami late in 2004 – call for the latest information or check ⓦwww.sciencecenteroftheamericas.org. Directly opposite the art museum is the **Main Public Library** (Mon–Sat 9am–6pm, Sun mid-Oct to mid-May only 1–5pm; ⓣ305/375-2665, ⓦwww.mdpls.org), which, besides the usual lending sections, has temporary exhibitions on art and literary themes as well as a massive collection of Florida magazines and books.

Adjoining the Cultural Center, the **Metro-Dade Center** (also called the Government Center) chiefly comprises county government offices, but useful bus and train timetables can be gathered from the **Transit Service Center** (daily 7am–6pm; ⓣ305/770-3131) by the Metrorail entrance at the eastern side of the building.

North of Flagler Street

The tempo drops and storefronts become less brash as you head **north of Flagler Street**. Look out for the 1925 Catholic **Gesú Church**, 118 NE Second St (ⓣ305/379-1424), its painted exterior the color of peach sherbet with foamy lemon meringue touches. The interior is nothing special, a stout, darkish sanctum that usually hums with private prayers. Continue north along First Avenue and you'll reach the **US Federal Courthouse**, no. 300 NE (Mon–Fri 8.30am–5pm; ⓣ305/523-5100), with its Neoclassical design and Corinthian columns, sheltering behind enormous palm trees. Finished in 1931, the building first functioned as a post office; Miami's then negligible crime rate required just one room on the second floor for judicial purposes. The room did acquire a monumental **mural**, however: *Law Guides Florida's Progress*, by Denman Fink (for more of his work, see p.92, Coral Gables), a 25-foot-long depiction of Florida's evolution from swampy backwoods to modern state. The mural's usually accessible to visitors, provided there's no closed-door court case in session – call in advance to check and make sure to bring photo ID. In 1985, fresco artist David Novros was commissioned to decorate the building's medieval-style inner **courtyard**, to which his bold, colorful daubs make a lively addition.

By the late Sixties, Miami's crime levels became too much for the old courthouse to handle, and the building of the $22 million **New Courthouse** was started next door (main entrance on N Miami Ave; Mon–Fri 8.30am–5pm), a gruesome creation of concrete and glass. The major advantage of the new courthouse – other than size – is that jurors can pass in and out unobserved: "Getting them out without getting them dead," as one judge commented. Now, even this courthouse is to be superseded by a soaring new structure a few blocks away, set to open in 2004.

Bayside Marketplace and the Torch of Friendship

Typical Miamian consumerism is on display at the **Bayside Marketplace**, 401 N Biscayne Blvd (Mon–Thurs 10am–10pm, Fri & Sat 10am–11pm, Sun 11am–9pm; Ⓣ305/577-3344, Ⓦwww.baysidemarketplace.com), a large, pink shopping mall providing pleasant waterfront views from its terraces. The views – and the handy unofficial tourist information stand at its western entrance by NE 5th Street – are really the only reason to stop by; otherwise, the mall's crammed with the usual upscale chain stores and trinket stalls. The mall caps the northern end of Bayfront Park, a pleasant enough greenspace that is home to the perpetual flame of the John F. Kennedy Memorial **Torch of Friendship**. It was designed to symbolize good relations between the US and its southern neighbors, with a pointed space left for the Cuban national emblem among the alphabetically sorted crests of each country. Sadly, it's so neglected now that there are several missing emblems, which means Cuba's omission no longer stands out.

South of the Miami River

Fifteen minutes' walk south from Flagler Street, the **Miami River** marks the southern limit of downtown. If your crossing is delayed by the drawbridge being raised to allow a ship through, glance westwards to the concrete modernity of the *DuPont Plaza Hotel* (earmarked for demolition) at the river's mouth: it was built on the site where Henry Flagler's *Royal Palm Hotel* stood at the turn of the century. At the behest of Miami's biggest landowners, Flagler – a millionaire oil baron whose railroad opened up Florida's east coast and brought wealthy wintering socialites to his string of smart hotels – extended the rail line here from Palm Beach. His luxury hotel and subsequent dredging of Biscayne Bay to accommodate cruise ships did much to put Miami on the map. Meanwhile, as you cross the bridge, glance across to the tip of the southern bank, the site of a few mysterious old stones known as the **Miami Circle.** The developer who bought this land for a condo complex in the mid-1990s was shocked when the archaeologists hired to clear the area for construction unearthed this coral rock circle, carbon-dated to be at least 10,000 years old. No-one knows much about its true purpose, and as yet it isn't open to the public. The developer, meanwhile, was able to resell the land back to the city for more than three times his original purchase price of $8 million.

Brickell and the Atlantis

One landowner, William Brickell, ran a trading post on the south side of the river, in an area now known as **BRICKELL** (rhymes with pickle). Beginning immediately across the SE Second Avenue Bridge and running to Coconut Grove (see p.95), its main thoroughfare, Brickell Avenue, was *the* address in 1910s Miami, easily justifying its "millionaires row" nickname. While the original grand homes have largely disappeared, money is still Brickell Avenue's most obvious asset: over the bridge begins a half-mile parade of banks, the largest group of international **banks** in the US, whose imposing forms are softened by forecourts filled with sculptures, fountains, and palm trees. Far from being places to change travelers' checks, these institutions are bastions of international high finance. From the late Seventies, Miami emerged as a corporate banking center, cashing in on political instability in South and Central America by offering a secure home for Latin American money, some of which needed laundering.

The sudden rise of the Brickell banks was matched by new condominiums of breathtaking proportions but little architectural merit a few blocks further along. In their pastel-shaded midst, these astronomically priced abodes include the most stunning modern building in Miami: the **Atlantis**, at no. 2025. First sketched on a napkin in a Cuban restaurant and finished in 1983, the Atlantis crowned several years of innovative construction by a small architectural firm called Arquitectonica, whose style – variously termed "beach-blanket Bauhaus" and "ecstatic modernism" – fused postmodern thought with a strong sense of Miami's eclectic architectural heritage. (Arquitectonica has since gone on to become one of the biggest and most successful architecture firms in Miami.) The building's focal point is a gaping square hole through its middle where a palm tree, a Jacuzzi, and a red-painted spiral staircase tease the eye. You won't be allowed inside unless you know someone who lives there, which might be just as well: even its designers admit the interior doesn't live up to the exuberance of the exterior, and claim the building to be "architecture for 55mph" – in other words, seen to best effect from a passing car.

North of downtown

North of downtown, sights thin out considerably and neighborhoods grow rougher. Before you reach the derelict warehouses, however, there's one stunning attraction on Biscayne Boulevard: the **FREEDOM TOWER** (Ⓣ305/592-7768, Ⓦwww.canf.org), originally home to the now defunct *Miami News*. It earned its current name by housing the Cuban Refugee Center, which began operations in 1962. Most of those who left Cuba on the "freedom flights" got their first taste of US bureaucracy here: between 1965 and 1972, ten empty planes left Miami each week to collect Cubans allowed to leave the island by Fidel Castro. The 1925 building isn't the only one in Miami that was modeled on the Giralda bell tower in Seville, Spain; so were the now-demolished Roney Plaza on Miami Beach and the *Biltmore Hotel* in Coral Gables (see p.94). The building's odd shape made it hard to lease over the years, but recently, the Cuban-American National Foundation began a major renovation to transform the building into a Cuban museum (call for up-to-date information).

Beyond the Freedom Tower, there's little more to see within walking distance, and you're on the fringe of some of the city's most impoverished – and dangerous – neighborhoods. You might venture a few blocks further to the **City of Miami Cemetery**, on the corner of North Miami Avenue and NE 18th Street, though this should only be undertaken with a **walking tour** (Ⓣ305/375-1621, Ⓦwww.historical-museum.org for schedules). There are historical stories aplenty here, such as Julia Tuttle's, whose claim to fame as "mother of the city" is that she and the Brickell family bribed Henry Flagler to bring the railway to Miami. Alas, many of the graves are littered with used syringes, anything valuable has been stolen, and the family vaults of early Miami bigwigs have had their doors torn off by the homeless seeking shelter. You're better off heading to the Woodlawn Cemetery in Little Havana, which has richer, safer pickings.

Overtown

From the earliest days, Coloredtown, as **OVERTOWN** was previously known, was divided by train tracks from the white folks of downtown Miami: safely cordoned off from the rest of the population, the black community here thrived – during the Thirties, jazz clubs crammed NW 2nd Avenue between 6th and 10th streets (then known as Little Broadway), thrilling multiracial audiences. By World War II, though, the area was in decline, accelerated rapidly in the Sixties by the construction of the I-95 freeway through the neighborhood, which displaced some 20,000 residents and isolated it from local amenities. Overtown came to be synonymous with Miami's every ill, from drugs to violence, and though today it's clawing its way back to economic health, this is still a dangerous place for visitors even during the daytime. If you're curious to visit this historic part of Miami, make sure to do so on an organized tour (see p.66) – preferably one that includes the **Overtown Historic District.** Though it's now dirty and rubbish-strewn, there are a few remnants of Overtown's glory days still standing here, notably the **D.A. Dorsey House** at 250 NW 9th St.

The riots of Liberty City

Aside from Overtown, the other overwhelmingly African-American area in Miami is **Liberty City**, a public housing development that opened in the Thirties and has been the site of numerous black expressions of rage at racial injustice. In December 1979, after a prolonged sequence of unpunished assaults by white police officers on members of the African-American community, a respectable black citizen, Arthur MacDuffie, was dragged off his motorbike in Liberty City and beaten to death by a group of four white officers. Five months later, an all-white jury acquitted the accused officers, sparking off what became known as the **Liberty City Riot.** On May 18, 1980, the night after the trial, the whole of Miami was ablaze from Carol City in the far north to Homestead in the south. The violence began on Sunday, roadblocks sealed off African-American neighborhoods until Wednesday, and a citywide curfew lasted until Friday. In the final tally, eighteen were dead, 400 injured, and damage to property was estimated at over $200 million. Reports of shooting, stone throwing, and whites being dragged from their cars and attacked or even burned alive, were rife in the press, though the majority of the victims were actually African-Americans killed by police and National Guardsmen. Racial rumblings have continued there ever since, and despite the best efforts of beautification, there isn't much for a casual tourist to see in Liberty City, and it's certainly a no-go area come nightfall.

This white, two-story clapboard home was built in 1914 by the first African-American millionaire in Miami. Close by, on a deserted strip, is the regal **Lyric Theater**, 819 NW 2nd Ave, which after a $1.5 million restoration is showcasing local theater and arts performances.

South Beach

Undoubtedly, Miami Beach's most exciting area is **SOUTH BEACH**, which occupies the southernmost three miles. Filled with pastel-colored Art Deco buildings, up-and-coming art galleries, modish diners, and suntanned beach addicts, it's been celebrated as one of the hippest places in the world. For a time in the Nineties, South Beach attracted multinational swarms of fashion photographers, who cherished the affordable scenic backdrops and spectacular early-morning light, though as Miami's prices rose they've moved on to cheaper locations elsewhere.

Socially, South Beach still has an unbeatable buzz. Here, Latin, black and white cultures happily collide, gay and straight tourists soak up the sun together, and Cuban cafés and chic boutiques sit side by side. Though elsewhere Miami's cultural schizophrenia may cause friction, here it's at its riotous, cocktail-clinking best.

Although South Beach suffered through tough economic times in the Eighties, there's little remaining of that edgy, dangerous time. More than anywhere else in the city, you can wander safely in South Beach day or night. The only time the streets are empty is early morning, when most of Miami Beach is still sleeping off the excesses of the night before. This is also the perfect time to grasp South Beach's allure for photographers and see the sheer beauty of its Art Deco buildings; make sure to turn in early one night and wake at dawn for an early morning stroll – the lucid white light and wave-lapped tranquillity are astonishing.

The Art Deco District

As much as the beach and the wild nightlife, it's the Art Deco architecture that has defined Miami in the minds of most. The neat row of Art Deco hotels along Ocean Drive has become one of the most clichéd images of the city, but even so, the 1,200 or so buildings that make up the **Miami Beach Art Deco Historic District**, between 5th and 20th streets and Ocean Drive and Lenox Avenue, more than live up to every photograph.

Ocean Drive

Painstaking restoration notwithstanding, little of the Art Deco district looks today quite like it did in the Thirties. Nowhere is this more apparent than in the colors – "a palette of Post Modern cake-icing pastels now associated with *Miami Vice*," in the words of disgruntled Florida architecture chronicler Hap Hatton – that appeared in 1980 when local designer Leonard Horowitz started adorning the buildings. Furthermore, the details of restoration reflect the tastes of the buildings' owners more than historical accuracy – but Miami Beach Art Deco of the new millennium is a sight to behold in its own right.

Examples of the Art Deco style are too numerous to list (or view) in full; just stroll around and keep your eyes open. If you want a more structured stroll round the area's architectural highlights, don't miss the **walking tour** from the Art Deco Welcome Center (see p.66), a fun way to see the key buildings and hear the colorful stories behind their construction and preservation.

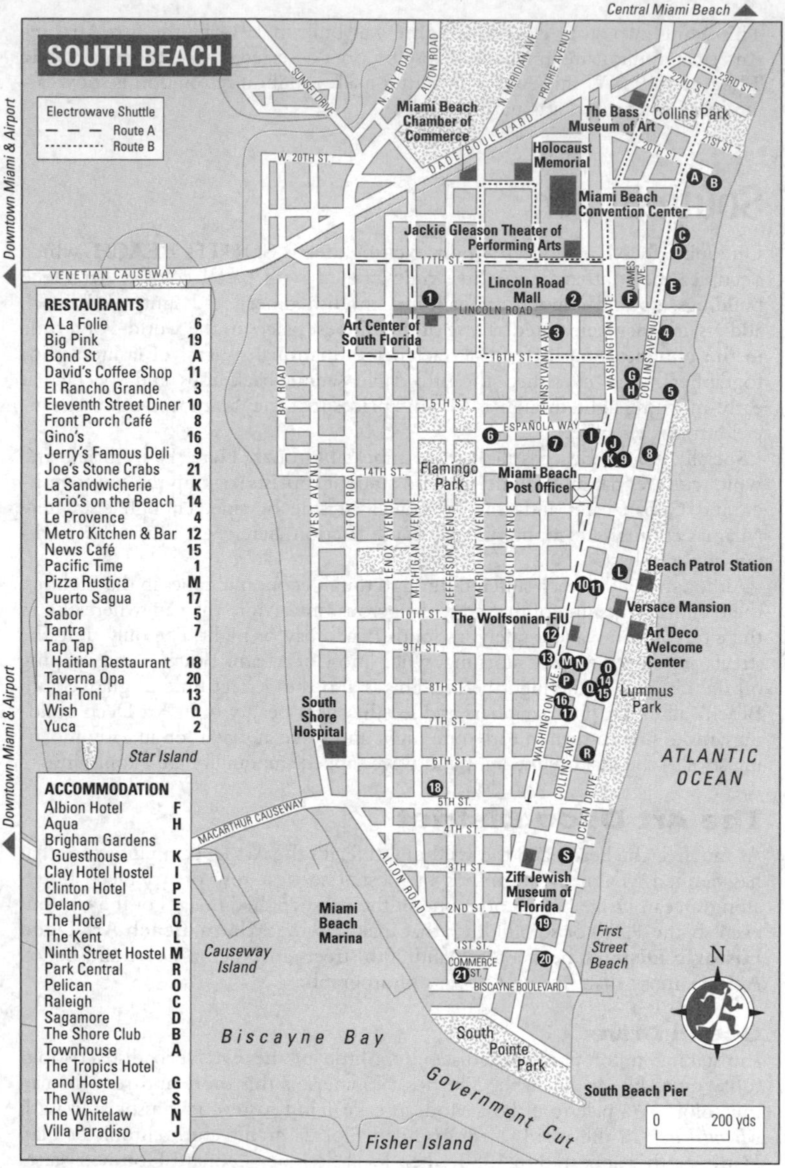

The best place to start is Ocean Drive, the main drag that hugs the glorious wide beach and is home to dozens of stunning Deco buildings. One of the earliest renovations was the **Park Central**, at no. 640: it's a geometric *tour de force*, with octagonal windows, sharp vertical columns, and a wrought-iron decorated stairway leading up to the mezzanine level, which displays monochrome photos of Miami Beach in the Twenties. Across the street in Lummus Park (the grassy patch that separates Ocean Drive from the beach), and more honestly redolent of the old days, stands the boat-shaped **Beach Patrol Station**, unmistakeable for its vintage oversized date and temperature sign, and still the base of the local lifeguards.

Oddly, one of the best known buildings on Ocean Drive is a Mediterranean Revival monolith at no. 1114: it's officially known as Casa Casuarina, but everyone calls it the **Versace Mansion**. It was originally built as an apartment complex in 1930; the designer Gianni Versace bought the place in 1992 and lived here until his murder on the front steps five years later. The mansion's pool was built on the former site of another architectural gem, the *Revere Hotel*, which Versace bought and demolished in a brazen act of architectural vandalism just before a preservation order could be enacted. The mansion is now owned by telecommunications magnate Peter Loftin, who paid a cool $19 million for it, with plans to turn it into a fashion museum. For now, you'll have to be content to stare through the hedges at the pool and pose on the front steps.

Decoding Art Deco

Miami became a haven for **Art Deco** in large part due to the wrecking power of South Florida's hurricanes. In 1926, the city was leveled by a devastating storm, and its wooden buildings were replaced with concrete structures in the newly modish Art Deco style. Cheap and sleek, it was ideal for developers anxious to throw up fresh hotels as quickly as possible – although shoddy construction methods doomed some treasured buildings to demolition less than fifty years later.

Art Deco in the city can be split into three main periods, which are easily identifiable by their signature features. The earliest phase, **Tropical or Miami Deco** (most popular in the Twenties and Thirties), is the base style from which all the other Deco types spring: look for "eyebrows" above the windows that provided shade as well as decoration and reliefs featuring palm trees and flamingos. This style gave way to the simpler **Depression Moderne**, which surfaced at the onset of the Depression; it was less ostentatious and ornamental than its predecessor, and money was spent subtly on interior spaces, like murals and ironwork. The last phase is known as **Streamline Deco** (1930s–1940s), which bridges the simplicity of early Deco and the playfulness of Miami Modern or MiMo. As in many MiMo designs, all elements of Streamline buildings are designed to give a feeling of movement, and the hard edges are rounded off.

Though Deco dominated building in Miami for more than twenty years, there was a contemporary alternative, known as **Mediterranean Revival**, whose asymmetry and ramshackle design were intended to give the impression of age. Many at the time sniffed that this was how gangsters and movie stars – ie, those with more money than taste – liked to commission houses; even so, almost one third of the structures in the so-called Art Deco Historic District are classified under this style.

It's a sobering thought that Miami Beach almost lost all of these significant structures, which fell into decline from the late Fifties and were sought after by property developers wishing to replace them with anonymous high-rise condominiums. In the mid-Seventies, the **Miami Design Preservation League** (see "Information," p.63) – whose first meeting drew just six people – was born with the aim of saving the buildings and raising awareness of their architectural and historical importance. The league's success has been dramatic – a major turning point was convincing the buck-hungry developers of the earning potential of such a unique area. The driving force of the movement was the late Barbara Capitman, but it was her preservation partner, interior designer Leonard Horowitz, who came up with the now-trademark palette of sherbet yellows, pinks, and blues. Originally, most Deco buildings were painted white with their features picked out in navy or dark brown – a rare surviving example of this color scheme is the City Hall in Coconut Grove (see p.97).

Washington and Collins avenues

South Beach has two main commercial thoroughfares, which run parallel to Ocean Drive. **Collins Avenue**, one block west, is lined with mid-range hotels, and includes a swanky shopping strip between 5th and 7th streets; it runs along the coast all the way to Fort Lauderdale (see p.188). One block further west is the district's heart, **Washington Avenue**, where small, Cuban-run supermarkets stand alongside local boutiques and nightclubs, and its grubbiness is pleasantly refreshing after the plucked-and-tweezed perfection closer to the beach. It also holds two of South Beach's most noteworthy buildings: the **Wolfsonian-FIU** and the local **Post Office**.

The Wolfsonian-FIU and the United States Post Office

Some 70,000 late-nineteenth century and twentieth century decorative arts and crafts from Europe and the Americas have been assembled in an imposing Mediterranean-Revival building by Mitchell Wolfson Jr at the **Wolfsonian-FIU**, 1001 Washington Ave (Tues–Wed, Fri & Sat 11am–6pm, Thurs 11am–9pm, Sun noon–5pm; $5; ⓣ305/531-1001, ⓦwww.wolfsonian.fiu.edu). Anyone with a passing interest in decorative, architectural, or politically inspired art ought to be able to find something of interest in the galleries, though it's confusingly curated and many of the exhibits blur into one another. The gems here are often the high-profile, traveling exhibitions. A few blocks north is the strikingly simple **Miami Beach Post Office**, 1300 Washington Ave (lobby Mon–Fri 6am–6pm, Sat 6am–4pm), a squat turret built in the Depression Moderne style – duck into the rotunda to see its flashy geometric murals.

Española Way

At the northern end of Washington Avenue, sandwiched between 14th Place and 15th Street stands **Española Way**, a pedestrian strip built by Carl Fisher, who disliked the prevalent Art Deco style and made this Mediterranean-Revival development his pet project. Completed in 1925, it was grandly envisaged as an artists' colony, but only the rumba dance craze of the Thirties – said to have started here, stirred up by Cuban bandleader Desi Arnaz – came close to fitting the bill. Following South Beach's social rise in the Eighties, however, a group of commercial art galleries, trinket stores, and a haphazard market have moved in, but it's not a place to linger long.

Lincoln Road Mall and the Art Center of South Florida

A short walk further north, between 16th and 17th streets, the pedestrianized **Lincoln Road Mall** was considered the flashiest shopping precinct outside of New York during the Fifties, its jewelry and clothes stores earning it the label "Fifth Avenue of the South." Store dresser-turned-architect Morris Lapidus (see p.83) was the genius behind its pedestrianization – then a revolutionary idea – and also designed the space-age structures that serve as sunshades. Though its fortunes plummeted alongside the rest of South Beach in the Seventies and Eighties, now it's a sparkling shopping strip lined with groovy brand name stores and dozens of sidewalk cafés; the Sunday afternoon stroll here is a ritual not to be missed. It's worth stopping by the **Art Center of South Florida** at no. 810 (gallery space open Mon–Wed 1–10pm, Thurs-Sun 1–11pm; ⓣ305/674-8278; ⓦwww.artcentersf.org), an artists' collective that has been here since the early 1980s, to see the work of more than fifty local painters, sculptors, and photographers.

The Jackie Gleason Theater and the Miami Beach Convention Center

The first of two public buildings immediately north of Lincoln Road Mall, the 3000-seat **Jackie Gleason Theater of Performing Arts** at 1700 Washington Ave, fronted by Pop artist Roy Lichtenstein's expressive *Mermaid* sculpture, stages Broadway shows and classical concerts (see p.114). However, it is best known to middle-aged Americans as the home of exuberant entertainer Jackie Gleason's immensely popular TV show, *The Honeymooners*, which began in the Fifties and ran for twenty years.

On the far side of the theater, sunlight bounces off the white exterior of the massive **Miami Beach Convention Center**, which occupies a curious niche in US political history. At the Republican Convention held here in August 1968, Richard Nixon won the nomination that would take him to the White House. Nixon counted his votes oblivious to the fact that the first of Miami's Liberty City riots had just erupted (see "Overtown" and box on Liberty City, p.76).

The Holocaust Memorial

It's impossible not to be moved by Kenneth Treister's **Holocaust Memorial**, 1933–1945 Meridian Ave (daily 9am–9pm; $2 donation for brochure; ⓣ305/538-1663, ⓦwww.holocaustmmb.org), completed in 1990 and dedicated to Elie Wiesel, depicting a 42-foot-high bronze arm tattooed with an Auschwitz number reaching toward the sky. Life-sized figures of emaciated, tormented people attempt to climb this wrenching and sculpture. The black marble walls around it are etched with the names of the dead as well as some shockingly graphic photographs of Nazi atrocities.

The Bass Museum of Art

A little further north stands the **Bass Museum of Art**, 2121 Park Ave (Tues & Wed, Fri & Sat 10am–5pm, Thurs 10am–9pm, Sun 11–5pm; $6; ⓣ305/673-7530,

Watson Island

The small island just off the coast of downtown that you pass while driving along the Macarthur Causeway is known as **WATSON ISLAND.** For many years, it was a seaplane landing area and haven for local vagrants, which was an embarrassing eyesore for the city's government. That's all changed since the arrival of **Parrot Jungle** (daily 10am–6pm; $25.50, parking $5; ⓣ305-2-JUNGLE, ⓦwww.parrotjungle.com), a park that abandoned its charming, if old-fashioned, site in South Miami and opened a multimillion-dollar facility here. Many of its signature attractions have been retained, including the flamingo park and reptile area, all hidden within a lushly landscaped jungle habitat. Don't underestimate the charm of the chatty parrots; the squawking, gaudy birds that sit in cages beside the trails are oddly enchanting. The best areas to dawdle are the Manu encounter, modeled on Peru, where you can wander among free-flying macaws; and the nursery, where trainers raise young birds. The **Japanese Gardens** that once stood on this site will be reinstated in a one-acre project next to the main parking lot. (Call the park for the latest details.) Opposite Parrot Jungle, the newest attraction is the new **Miami Children's Museum** (daily 10am-6pm; $8; ⓣ305/373-5437, ⓦwww.miamichildrensmuseum.org), housed in a jagged building designed by Arquitectonica (see p.75). It's a quirky place, ideal to amuse restive children for an afternoon or so: among other interactive exhibits, there's a mini supermarket and television studio, though the Meet Miami section, which explores the architecture and history of the city, is especially fun.

There's plentiful, if pricey, parking on the island if you're coming by car; otherwise, you can catch bus #S, #K, or #C from either downtown or South Beach.

Ⓦwww.bassmuseum.org). The only fine art museum on Miami Beach, the Bass is housed in a squat, white 1930s building designed by Russell Pancoast, the architect son-in-law of beach pioneer John Collins. What began as the local public library became a museum to house the private collection of local socialites John and Johanna Bass, which was donated to the city in 1963. After years of delays, the museum's much-heralded expansion by Japanese architect Arata Isozaki has finally been completed, the white box he grafted onto the original building along Park Avenue tripling its exhibition space. There are some gems in the collection, notably the stunning Flemish tapestry known as *The Tournament*, but many of the big names here, such as Rubens and Botticelli, are represented by minor works.

South of 5th Street

The last chunk of South Beach to undergo gentrification lies south of 5th Street, where bars and restaurants are slowly spreading downward and bringing the tourist crowds with them. This area was originally the Jewish ghetto on the beach, since 5th Street marked the northernmost point where Jews could buy housing. By the 1980s, though, the area had collapsed into a shabby, crime-ridden, no-go area, spurred by the arrival of undesirables in the wake of the Mariel boatlift. The most obvious sign of the current upswing is an influx of new residents, drawn to what local realtors have taken to calling "SoFi" (Souht of Fifth), especially at the southern tip known as **South Pointe**. The high-rises here – like the luxury 26-story South Pointe Towers that leap skyward from South Pointe Park (see below) – dwarf the older houses, a sad legacy of the city's once lax zoning laws.

Ziff Jewish Museum of Florida

During the Twenties and Thirties, South Beach became a major destination for Jewish tourists escaping the harsh northeastern winters. In response, many of the hotels placed "Gentiles Only" notices at their reception desks, and the slogan "Always a view, never a Jew" appeared in many a hotel brochure. Despite this, by the 1940s South Beach had a largely Jewish population and for a time it was home to the second largest community of Holocaust survivors in the country. The **Ziff Jewish Museum of Florida**, 301 Washington Ave (Tues–Sun 10am–5pm; $5, free Sat; Ⓣ305/672-5044, Ⓦwww.jewishmuseum.com), bears testimony to Jewish life not only in Miami Beach, but in all of Florida, since the earliest days of European settlement. The permanent collection is exhaustive, and there are visiting exhibitions on Jewish life in general – make sure to chat with one of the docents when wandering around as they're both enthusiastic and knowledgeable. The museum itself is housed in an elegant 1936 Art Deco building – now lavishly restored – that served as an Orthodox synagogue for Miami Beach's first Jewish congregation.

South Pointe

The best route through **South Pointe** is the mile-long shorefront boardwalk, beginning near the southern end of Lummus Park and finishing by the 300-foot-long jetty lined with people fishing off First Street Beach, the only surfing beach in Miami and alive with tanned, athletic bodies even when the waves are calm. You can swim and snorkel here, too, but bear in mind that the big cruise ships frequently pass close by and stir up the current.

On its inland side, the boardwalk skirts **South Pointe Park** (daily 8am–sunset), whose handsome lawns and tree-shaded picnic tables offer a respite from the packed beaches. The park is a good place to be on Friday evenings when its open-air stage is the venue for enjoyable free **music events** (details are posted up around South Beach).

Seats on the southern edge of the park give you a view of **Government Cut**, a waterway first dredged by Henry Flagler at the turn of the century and now, substantially deepened, the route for large cruise ships beginning their journeys to the Bahamas and Caribbean. You might also witness an impounded drug-running vessel being towed along by the authorities. Don't be surprised, either, to hear the neighing of horses: Miami Beach's police horses are stabled on the eastern side of the park.

Central Miami Beach and north

Art Deco gems give way to massive tower blocks as South Beach settles into the more sedate area known as **CENTRAL MIAMI BEACH**. Collins Avenue charts a five-mile course through the area, between Indian Creek – across which are the golf courses, country clubs, and secluded palatial homes of Miami Beach's seriously rich – and the once-swanky hotels around which the Miami Beach high life revolved during the glamorous Fifties. These often madly ostentatious establishments are the main attraction of Central Miami Beach; the strand itself is largely the preserve of families and older folk, and is backed by a long and lovely boardwalk that stretches over a mile from 21st Street.

Along Collins Avenue

The southern edge of Central Miami Beach is defined by the garbage-clogged **Collins Canal**, cut in the 1910s to speed the movement of farm produce through the mangrove trees that then lined Biscayne Bay. The canal is a dismal sight, but improves as it flows into the luxury-yacht-lined **Indian Creek**, and along Collins Avenue you'll see the first of the sleek condos and hotels that characterize the area. Unlike their smaller Art Deco counterparts in South Beach, the later **hotels** of Central Miami Beach are massive monuments to the Fifties. When big was beautiful, these state-of-the-art pleasure palaces drew the international jet set by offering much more than mere accommodation: a price that few could afford also bought access to exclusive bars, restaurants, and lounges where film and TV stars cavorted to the envy of the rest of the country. Yet the good times were short-lived. As everyone tried to cash in, cheap imitations of the pace-setting hotels formed an ugly wall of concrete along **Collins Avenue**; quality sank, service deteriorated, and the big names moved on. By the Seventies, many of the hotels looked like what they really were: monsters from another age. The Eighties saw Miami's social star re-emerge, and a revival was soon under way. Many of the polished-up hotels are now occupied by well-heeled Latin American tourists – along with gray-haired swingers from the US for whom Miami Beach never lost its cachet.

The Fontainebleau Hilton

Before Central Miami Beach became a celebrities' playground, the nation's rich and powerful built rambling shorefront mansions here. One of them, the winter home of tire-baron Harvey Firestone, was demolished in 1953 to make room for the **Fontainebleau Hilton**, 4441 Collins Ave (Ⓣ305/538-2000, Ⓦwww.hilton.com), a dreamland of kitsch and consumerism cooked up by architect Morris Lapidus that defined the Miami Beach of the late Fifties and Sixties. Gossip-column perennials, such as Joan Crawford, Joe DiMaggio, Lana Turner, and Bing Crosby, were Fontainebleau regulars, as was crooner Frank

Sinatra who, besides starting a scrambled-egg fight in the coffee shop, shot many scenes here as the private-eye hero of the Sixties film *Tony Rome*. Little of interest remains inside the building, since it's been brutally remodeled several times; at least Lapidus' trademark bowties have survived in the terrazzo floor pattern of the main lobby.

North through Miami Beach and inland

Collins Avenue continues for seven uninspiring miles through **North Beach**, a run-down, working-class enclave that's slowly being revitalized, though the few restaurants along 71st Street and the pleasant oceanfront parks won't detain you for long. The low-rise buildings of the next neighborhood, **Surfside**, retain a rather appealing old-fashioned ambience; the neighborhood's **beach**, between 91st and 95th streets, is the main reason most people spend an afternoon here.

Directly north, **Bal Harbour** – its aspirations of "Olde Worlde" elegance reflected in its anglicized name – is similar in size to Surfside but entirely different in character: an upmarket area filled with the carefully guarded homes of some of the nation's wealthiest people. The exclusive Bal Harbour Shops, 9700 Collins Ave (Ⓣ305/886-0311, Ⓦwww.balharbourshops.com), packed with outrageously expensive designer stores, sets the tone for the area; ironically, given its upscale aspirations, the town's origins lie in a soldiers' training camp that once stood here during World War II.

The most notorious local attraction, though, is further north, in **Haulover Beach Park**. This is Miami's only nude beach, but the furore around the fad for clothing-free bathing eclipses its other upsides – the sands are wide enough to never feel crowded, there are ample picnic tables, showers, and bathrooms, and it's only a twenty-minute drive from South Beach. To get there take buses #H, #K, or #S up Collins Avenue and get off at the coastguard station, where there are also parking facilities ($4). From here turn right for the regular beach or left for the "clothing optional" one, which starts at beach watch-station 24 and ends at watch-station 29, predominantly a gay area. With a new school being planned nearby, the days of nude sunbathing here may be numbered – call Ⓣ305/944-3040 to find out if you'll need to bring your bikini.

Sunny Isles Beach and Golden Beach

Beyond Haulover Park, the resort of **Sunny Isles Beach** is clogged with mainly European package tourists and the condo-hotels and chain restaurants that cater to them. Founded in the 1950s, Sunny Isles Beach was a blatant Las Vegas rip-off and a few of the architecturally excessive hotels erected then still linger. Along Collins Avenue, watch out for the camels and sheikhs guarding the now-shuttered *Sahara*, no. 18335; the crescent-moon-holding maidens of the *Blue Mist*, no. 19111; and the kitschy Deco and Moorish confection of the *Marco Polo*, no. 19200. The main draw here is the still-sumptuous beaches, which to combat erosion are regularly replenished by sand dredged from the ocean floor. By the time you reach **Golden Beach**, the northernmost community of Miami Beach, much of the traffic pounding Collins Avenue has turned inland on the Lehman Causeway (192nd Street), and the anachronistic hotels have given way to quiet shorefront homes. Public beach access here is virtually nonexistent, and unless you're intending to leave Miami altogether (Collins Avenue, as Hwy-A1A, continues north to Fort Lauderdale), it's better to head directly inland.

North to Fort Lauderdale

The coastal route, Hwy-A1A (Collins Avenue), and the mainland US-1 (Biscayne Boulevard), both continue into Hollywood, at the southern edge of the Fort Lauderdale area, fully described in Chapter 4, "The southeast."

Inland: the Ancient Spanish Monastery

The Sunny Isles Causeway (163rd Street, Dixie Highway) leads across to North Miami Beach, on the mainland. Despite its confusing name, this area is a continuation of the depressed suburbs north of downtown Miami, and not a place to linger unless you're visiting the **Ancient Spanish Monastery**, at 16711 West Dixie Hwy (Mon–Sat 10am–5pm, Sun 1.30–5pm; $5; Ⓣ305/945-1461, Ⓦwww.spanishmonastery.com), an unremarkable medieval building from Spain whose checkered history is far more interesting than the surprisingly diminutive structure itself.

The monastery's drawn-out relocation began in 1925 when newspaper magnate William Randolph Hearst purchased the place while visiting Europe, and then had it dismantled and shipped to America, planning to incorporate the building into his Hearst Castle in California – itself stitched together from other such souvenirs he had collected.

However, upon arrival in New York, the disassembled monastery was quarantined by customs, due to an outbreak of foot-and-mouth disease in Spain, and never made it to the West Coast, as Hearst's financial troubles set in soon after. After being sold at auction in 1952, the pieces were brought here and reassembled as a tourist attraction by its new owners. The job took a year and a half, and was done largely by trial and error thanks to incorrect repackaging of the pieces.

Today, the monastery is a working Episcopal church with a tiny chapel that was formerly the monks' refectory, while the cloisters themselves are small and rather frayed around the edges. Getting there is difficult without a car; however, if you're determined, bus #3 from downtown and #H, #E, and #V from the beaches drop off at the corner of 163rd and West Dixie Highway. Call ahead to check whether it's open, especially at weekends, as hours can be erratic.

The Design District and Little Haiti

On Miami's run-down north side, between north Miami and downtown, lie two neighborhoods that have only recently appeared on visitors' itineraries: the trendy **Design District** and the immigrant enclave of **Little Haiti**. Although sights are few and far between in both areas, it's worth spending an afternoon browsing the stylish housewares stores and sampling the Caribbean ice cream.

The Design District

The **Design District**, hemmed in by 36th Street and 41st Street between Miami Avenue and Biscayne Boulevard, was originally a pineapple plantation owned by Theodore Moore, the "Pineapple King of Florida." On a whim, he opened a furniture showroom on NE 40th Street, and had soon created what became known as **Decorators' Row**. During Miami's Art Deco building boom of the Twenties and Thirties, this was the center of the city's design scene, filled with wholesale interiors stores selling furniture and flooring: look for the Designers' Walk of Fame along 40th Street, where stars embedded into the sidewalk honor design luminaries of that time.

By the early 1990s, though, the factory-filled district was deserted and crime-ridden, with only a handful of interiors shops holding out despite the lure of the gleaming new Design Center of the Americas building in Fort Lauderdale, a specially constructed mall for showrooms. Savvy developer Craig Robins, one of the masterminds behind the gentrification of South Beach, spotted the potential here and started buying buildings, enticing high-end showrooms like Knoll and Kartell. He's overseen the regeneration of this area with plans to revive the Design District, including an emphasis on public art and sculpture: one of his best known projects is the whimsical **Living Room Building**, 4000 N Miami Ave. The entranceway to this squat office block has been turned inside out, and features a giant pink concrete sofa and standard lamp, as well as bright orange walls – in other words, a witty, irresistible photo opportunity.

Just south of the Design District proper, the **Rubell Collection**, 95 NW 29th St (Thurs–Sat, call for hours; ☎305/573-6090), is a massive modern art collection housed in an old warehouse once used by the Drug Enforcement Agency for storing evidence. An exhaustive survey of the last thirty years in modern art, the collection sets acknowledged masterpieces alongside lesser-known, more experimental work, included early photography from Cindy Sherman, post-modern sculpture from Jeff Koons, and even graffiti canvases by the late Keith Haring. The gallery is scheduled to move to a bigger site in North Miami soon, so call to check the current location and hours before heading over.

Little Haiti

About 200,000 Haitians live in Miami, forming one of the city's major ethnic groups – albeit it far smaller than the Cuban population – and roughly a third of them live in **LITTLE HAITI**, a district running along the bay from 40th to 85th streets. There are few specific sights in Little Haiti, so it's best to wander along the main drag, NE 2nd Avenue, and enjoy the Caribbean colors, music, and smells. Almost all Miami's Haitians speak English as a third language after Creole and French, so look out for the tri-lingual signage. It's easy enough to spot one of the area's landmarks, the **Caribbean Marketplace** at 5927 NE 2nd Ave, with its brightly colored ironwork modeled after that of a similar bazaar in Port-au-Prince, Haiti, though it's looking rather forlorn now. The market was designed as an urban renewal project to showcase Caribbean crafts while drawing tourist dollars to the area, but poor management forced the bank to foreclose on the venture, and the future of the building remains up in the air.

At the southeast corner of NE 2nd Avenue and 62nd Street sits one of the oldest buildings in the area. Built in 1902 in what was once the heart of Lemon City, the now-derelict **Dupuis Building** served as a pharmacy and a post office before being abandoned several decades ago. Plans are afoot to transform the building into a welcome center-cum-tourist office, though they are still in the early stages.

If you're in the area, be sure to make a detour down **54th Street**, the heart of Miami's *voudou* and Santería culture, which is lined with several *botanicas*, where believers can purchase ritual potions, candles, and statuettes. Almost all will permit a casual visitor to browse their merchandise but it goes without saying that photographing the racks of gaudy statuary and glass jars packed with herbs is both rude and foolish.

Santería: Saints and sacrifices

Estimated numbers of those practicing the Caribbean religion of **Santería** worldwide vary wildly, anywhere from 60,000 up to 5 million; regardless, it has a hidden but influential role in Miami society, as many people are at least part-time believers. A secretive religion with an oral tradition, Santería was one of the many spiritual hybrids created under colonial rule. Slaves, many of them Yoruba from West Africa, were forcibly baptized and converted to Christianity, but this conversion proved to be largely cosmetic: to preserve their own religions, gods or *orishas* in the African pantheon were "translated" into Christian saints, so that they could be worshipped without fear of being caught. In fact, the name Santería itself began as slang, when colonial Spaniards noticed how greatly their African slaves venerated the saints rather than Christ.

Much like the gods in Ancient Greece, *orishas* have flaws and favorites: each is identified with a given color, food, and number, and requires animal sacrifices and human praise for nourishment. Altars in Santería temples are covered with offerings of cigarettes or designer perfume – the *orishas* are all too human in their vulnerability to flattery and expensive gifts. Religious services, conducted in secret by a priest or priestess, involve channeling the gods through dance and trance. Its practitioners can get *orishas* to give magical aid and guidance through plant, food, or animal sacrifices offered during chants and dancing initiations.

Wandering around Miami, you'll see signs of Santería activity if you look hard enough – streetside offerings, usually nailed to holy kapok trees, are common in Little Havana and Haiti. There is also much sensationalist reporting when Santería offerings are discovered near local courthouses, supposedly attempts by family members to invoke the *orishas*' help during trials. Despite opposition to the religion – much of it from animal-rights activists – a court case in Miami's Hialeah district in 1993 confirmed the constitutional rights of adherents to practice their religion.

Little Havana

The impact of **Cubans** – unquestionably the largest ethnic group in Miami – on the city over the last four decades has been incalculable. Unlike most Latino immigrants to the US, who trade one form of poverty for another, Miami's first Cuban arrivals in the late Fifties had already tasted affluence. They rose quickly through the social strata and nowadays wield considerable clout in the running of the city, and indeed the state.

The first Miami Cubans settled a few miles west of downtown Miami in what became known as **LITTLE HAVANA**, a quiet district of sherbet-colored houses where you're more likely to see newspaper boxes selling *El Nuevo Herald* rather than the English-language *Miami Herald*, and statues of Cuba's patron saint, the Virgin Mary, in front gardens. Only the neighborhood's main strip, SW 8th Street, or **Calle Ocho**, offers more than houses: tiny cups of sweet Cuban coffee are sold from street-side counters, the odors of cigars being rolled and bread being baked waft across the sidewalk, shops sell Santería (see box above) ephemera beside six-foot-high models of Catholic saints, and you'll spot the only branch of Dunkin' Donuts to sell guava-filled doughnuts. Though there are few official sights, most people come here to gorge themselves on the delicious, gut-busting Cuban food in one of the local eateries and to wander around the monuments on Memorial Boulevard (see p.89).

The Cuban question

Proximity to the Caribbean island has long made Florida a place of refuge for Cuban activists and economic migrants. A raft ride from Cuba's northern shore, propelled by prevailing currents, can take four days to arrive in South Florida. From José Martí in the 1890s to Fidel Castro in the early Fifties, the country's radicals arrived to campaign and raise funds, and numerous deposed Cuban politicians have whiled away their exile in Florida. However, until comparatively recent times, New York, not Miami, was the center of Cuban émigré life in the US.

During the mid-Fifties, when opposition to the Batista dictatorship in Cuba – and the country's subservient role to the US – began to assert itself, a trickle of Cubans started arriving in the predominantly Jewish section of Miami called Riverside, moving into low-rent properties vacated as the extant community grew wealthier and moved out. The trickle became a flood when Castro came to power, and as Cuban businesses sprang up on SW 8th Street and Cubans began making their mark on Miami life, the area began to be known as **Little Havana**.

Those who left Cuba derived largely from the affluent middle classes who stood to lose the most under communism. Many regarded themselves as the entrepreneurial sophisticates of the Caribbean, and stories are plentiful of formerly high-flying Cuban capitalists who arrived penniless in Little Havana, took menial jobs and, over the course of two decades – and aided by a formidable network of old ex-pats – toiled, wheeled, and dealed their way steadily upwards to positions of power and influence (and not just locally – leading Miami Cubans also have considerable influence over the US government's policy toward Cuba) with their 800,000 votes and hefty campaign contributions.

The second great Cuban influx into Miami was of a quite different social nature and racial composition: the **Mariel boatlift** in May 1980 brought 125,000 predominantly black islanders from the Cuban port of Mariel to Miami. Unlike their more worldly predecessors, these arrivals were largely poor and uneducated, and a fifth of them were fresh from Cuban jails – incarcerated for criminal rather than political crimes. Bluntly put, Castro had dumped his criminals and misfits on Miami. Only a few of them wound up in Little Havana: most "Marielitos" settled in South Beach, where they proceeded to terrorize the local community, thereby becoming a source of embarrassment to Miami's longer-established and determinedly respectable (and white) Cubans.

Yet local division gives way to fervent agreement when the subject turns to Fidel Castro: he's universally detested. Fueled by a mix of machismo and hero-worship of early Cuban independence fighters, passions run high, and action – usually violent – has been prized more than words. In Miami, Cubans even *suspected* of advocating dialogue with Castro have been killed; one man had his legs blown off in the Eighties for suggesting violence on the streets was counterproductive, and the Cuban Museum of the Americas was bombed for displaying the work of Castro-approved artists. No doubt the biggest test lies ahead, after Castro's death, when the Cuban-exile leadership will eventually be able to return to the island, and the armchair politicians from Miami face the daunting task of governing a very different country from the one they left behind.

For all the memorials marking the area's fierce connection to Cuba, Little Havana is increasingly a misnomer: as the successful Cuban community decamps to wealthier neighborhoods like Coral Gables, they're gradually replaced by Latin American immigrants from Honduras, Colombia, and Nicaragua.

Along Calle Ocho

The most vivid introduction to Little Havana is **Cuban Memorial Boulevard,** between 12th and 13th avenues just south of Calle Ocho. There's a cluster of monuments here, of which the **Brigade 2506 Memorial** is the best known. Inscribed with the brigade crest, and topped by the Cuban flag and an eternal flame, this simple stone remembers those who died at the Bay of Pigs on April 17, 1961, during the attempt by a group of US-trained Cuban exiles to invade the island and wrest control from Castro. Depending on who tells the story, the outcome was the result of either ill-conceived plans, or the US's lack of commitment to Cuba (JFK withheld air support that may have changed the battle's outcome) – to this day, sections of the Cuban community hate Kennedy only slightly less than Fidel Castro. Every anniversary, veterans clad in combat fatigues and carrying assault rifles gather here to make pledges of patriotism throughout the night.

Close by, there's also a statue of Jose Martí, hero of the first Cuban war of independence, and one of the Virgin Mary holding a decapitated baby Jesus, whose state of disrepair underscores the brooding isolation of the monuments.

A less emotionally charged gathering place is **Máximo Gómez Domino Park** (daily 8am–6pm), a few yards away on a corner of 14th Avenue; access to its open-air tables is (quite illegally) restricted to men over 55, and this is one place where you really will see old men in *guayaberas* playing dominoes. Be aware that the men don't take kindly to snapshot-happy tourists.

Further west, the peaceful greenery of **Woodlawn Cemetery**, 3260 SW 8th St (daily sunrise–dusk), belies the scheming and skulduggery that some of its occupants indulged in during their lifetimes. Two former Cuban heads of state are buried here: Gerardo Machado, ousted from office in 1933, is in the mausoleum, while one of the protagonists in his downfall, Carlos Prío Socarras, president from 1948 to 1952, lies just outside. Also interred in the mausoleum (and marked only by his initials) is **Anastasio Somoza**, dictator of Nicaragua until overthrown by the Sandinistas in 1979, and later killed in Paraguay, as well as George Merrick, founder of Coral Gables (see p.90).

Around Calle Ocho

There's little of interest for visitors beyond Calle Ocho, which is sandwiched between low-income housing to the north and modest Spanish Revival Twenties bungalows to the south. One possible detour is **La Esquina de Tejas restaurant**, 101 SW 12th Ave (☎305/545-0337), where you can mull over the signed photos of Ronald Reagan. It was in this otherwise ordinary Cuban eatery that the president, seeking re-election, took a well-publicized lunch in 1983 in an effort to harness the powerful Cuban vote in Miami. Four years later, George Bush called by for a swift *café Cubano* and a drawn-out photo op. Aside from his right-wing domestic policies, Reagan gained immense popularity among Miami Cubans for his support of the Nicaraguan Contras, viewed as kindred spirits in the guerrilla struggle against communism. (It's widely acknowledged that the Contras ran their anti-Sandinista operation from offices in Miami and trained for combat in the Everglades.) The community's affection was demonstrated by the renaming of 12th Avenue as Ronald Reagan Boulevard.

There's no point in actually going there (except for a sports event; see "Listings", p.120), but from here you can see the rising hump of the 70,000-seat **Orange Bowl** stadium, about ten blocks north. This is home to the University of Miami's football team, the Hurricanes, but is best remembered by older Cubans as the place where, on a December night in 1962, John Kennedy took the Brigade 2506 flag and vainly promised to return it "in a free Havana."

Coral Gables

Though all of Miami's constituent cities are quick to assert their individuality, none has a greater case than **CORAL GABLES**, south of Little Havana. Encompassing twelve square miles of broad boulevards and leafy streets lined by elaborate Spanish- and Italian-style architecture, the city was the pet project of one man, **George Merrick**. Whereas Miami's other early property developers built cheap and fast in search of a quick buck, Merrick was as much of an aesthete as an entrepreneur. Taking Mediterranean Europe as his inspiration, he envisaged a lavish Venetian settlement (albeit with Spanish street names) steeped in old world grandeur to inspire civic pride among its residents. He enlisted his artist uncle, Denman Fink, and architect Phineas Paist to plan the plazas, fountains, and carefully aged stucco-fronted buildings that would sit on the 3000 acres of citrus groves and pineland he inherited from his father.

Merrick's true flair, however, was in publicity, and he staged countless stunts to attract attention and residents – including sending fleets of coral-colored buses across Florida to ferry potential customers down to the site. Of the $150 million he made in the five years following the first sale in 1921, he funneled one third into publicity and advertising. The layout and buildings of Coral Gables quickly took shape, but the sudden end of Florida's property boom in 1926 (see Contexts, p.470, for the full account) wiped Merrick out. He ran a fishing camp in the Florida Keys until that was destroyed by a hurricane, and wound up as Miami's postmaster until his death in 1942.

Coral Gables: Entrances and villages

To make a strong first impression on visitors to Coral Gables, founder George Merrick (see above) planned eight grand **entrances** on the main access roads, of which only four were completed before he went bust. The three most impressive are along a two-and-a-half-mile stretch of SW 8th Street, and well worth seeking out.

The million-dollar **Douglas Entrance** (junction with Douglas Road) was the most ambitious, consisting of a gateway and tower with two expansive wings of shops, offices, and artists' studios. During the Sixties it was almost bulldozed to make room for a supermarket, but survived to become a well-scrubbed business area, still upholding Merrick's Mediterranean themes in its architecture. Further west, the sixty-foot-high vine-covered **Granada Entrance** (junction with Granada Boulevard) is based on the entrance to the city of Granada in Spain. A better appetizer for Coral Gables is the **Country Club Prado Entrance** (junction with Country Club Prado), the expensive re-creation of a formal Italian garden bordered by freestanding stucco-and-brick pillars topped by ornamental urns and lamps with wrought-iron brackets.

To revive the flagging housing market, which began to soften in the 1920s, Merrick hit on another architectural gimmick, the so-called **International Villages**, which were clusters of houses around town, each built in a different style. Though fourteen were planned, only seven were built before Merrick ran out of money. The most eye-popping of these is the **Chinese Village**, just south of US-1 on Riviera Drive: its red and yellow chinoiserie, complete with carved balconies and dragons, is gaudy and irresistible. There's also the brown and white timber-beamed cottages of the **French Normandy Village**, on the 400 block of Vizcaya Avenue at Le Jeune Road, and the **French City Village**, on the 1000 block of Hardee Road, where the front gardens of the neat townhouses are boxed in by high walls.

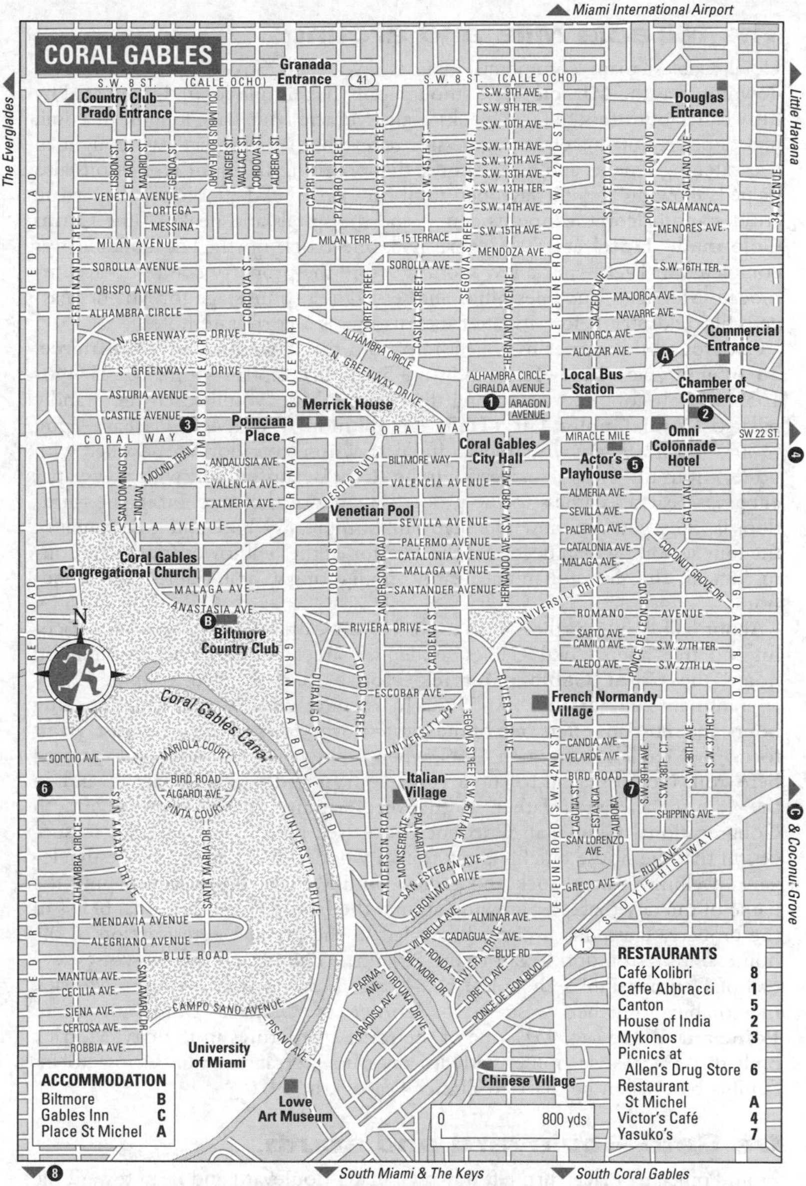

Coral Gables, however, was built with longevity as well as beauty in mind. Despite successive economic crises, it has never lost its good looks, and these days, boosted equally by a host of multi-national companies in the renovated office buildings and by its very image-conscious population, it's as well to do and well kept as ever.

The Miracle Mile and around

Coral Gables' main commercial drag is SW 22nd Street, which is known downtown as the **Miracle Mile** (though only half a mile long). Dominated by fusty ladies' outfitters, the five blocks of the Miracle Mile have long been a dull, lifeless place. Fortunately, an aggressive redevelopment project has brought in eye-catching tenants and busier stores; the loosening of liquor restrictions also helped, allowing bars to stay open until 2am on weekdays. Notice the ornate arcades and balconies along its course and the spirals and peaks of the **Omni Colonnade Hotel** at 180 Aragorn Ave, one block north. The building was completed in 1926 – just a few months before the property crash – to accommodate Merrick's land sales office and served as a soundstage for Miami's nascent film industry before its latest incarnation as a corporate hotel.

Cut around the corner to collect info from the **Chamber of Commerce**, 50 Aragon Ave (Mon–Thurs 8.30am–5pm, Fri 8.30am-4pm; ⓣ305/446-1657). If you continue west along the Miracle Mile, you'll reach the grandly pillared **Coral Gables City Hall**, 405 Biltmore Way (Mon–Fri 8am–5pm; ⓣ305/460-5217, ⓦwww.citybeautiful.net), whose corridors are adorned with posters from the Twenties advertising the "City Beautiful" and with newspaper clippings bearing witness to the property mania of the time. From the third-floor landing you can view Denman Fink's impressive blue and gold mural of the four seasons, which decorates the interior of the bell tower (not to be confused with the dreadful mural nearby spotlighting Coral Gables' key attractions).

About half a mile further west, at no. 907 on Coral Way – a typically peaceful and tree-lined Coral Gables residential street – is Merrick's childhood home, the **Coral Gables Merrick House** (Sun & Wed 1–4pm; $2, by appointment only; ⓣ305/460-5361). In keeping with its restrictive opening hours, the museum offers one of the pithiest overviews of the area's past, via its focus on Merrick's family. In 1899, when George was 12, his family arrived here from New England to run a 160-acre fruit and vegetable farm – and, in the case of George's father, to deliver sermons at the local Plymouth Congregational Church in Coconut Grove (see p.96). The farm was so successful that the house quickly grew from a wooden shack into a modestly elegant dwelling of coral rock and gabled windows (the inspiration behind the name of the city that later grew up around the family farm). The dual blows of the property crash and a citrus blight led to the gradual deterioration of the house, until restoration began in the Seventies. The place now showcases several of Denman Fink's chocolate box-like canvases as well as quirky Merrick memorabilia. Further west at the corner of Granada Boulevard stands **Poinciana Place** (no. 937), one of the earliest structures in the city: Merrick built this ranch-style home, with its low-slung terracotta tiling, close to his family's base when he married Eunice Peacock in 1916.

De Soto Boulevard and south

From Poinciana Place, turn left down Granada Boulevard and head toward the opulent **De Soto Fountain**, named for the conquistador Hernando de Soto, who led an expedition to Florida from Cuba in 1539. Near here, De Soto Boulevard curls southward past three of Merrick's grandest achievements. While his property-developing contemporaries left ugly scars across the city after digging up the local limestone, Merrick had the foresight – and the help of Denman Fink – to turn his biggest quarry into a sumptuous swimming pool. **The Venetian Pool**, 2701 De Soto Blvd (June–Aug Mon–Fri

△ Biscayne Bay

11am–7.30pm, Sept & Oct, April & May Tues–Fri 11am–5.30pm; Nov–March Tues–Sun 10am–4.30pm; year-round Sat & Sun 10am-4.30pm; nonresident adults $8.50; ⓣ305/460-5356, ⓦwww.venetianpool.com), an elaborate conglomeration of palm-studded paths, Venetian-style bridges, and coral-rock caves, was opened in 1924. Despite its ornamentation, the pool was never designed with the social elite in mind; admission was cheap and open to all, and even today, local residents get a special discount.

A few minutes' walk further south, on land donated by Merrick, stands the **Coral Gables Congregational Church**, 3010 De Soto Blvd (Mon–Fri 8am–4pm; ⓣ305/448-7421, ⓦwww.coralgablescongregational.org), a Spanish Revival flurry topped by a barrel-tiled roof and enhanced by Baroque features. Though somewhat dark inside, the building has excellent interior acoustics that make it a popular venue for jazz and classical **concerts**; ask for details at the church office, just inside the entrance.

The Biltmore Hotel

Merrick's crowning achievement – aesthetically if not financially – was the **Biltmore Hotel**, 1200 Anastasia Ave (ⓣ305/445-1926 or 1-800/727-1926, ⓦwww.biltmorehotel.com). The hotel's 26-story tower can be seen across much of low-lying Miami: if it seems similar to the Freedom Tower (see p.75), it's because they're both modeled on the Giralda bell tower of Seville Cathedral in Spain. The *Biltmore* was hawked as "the last word in the evolution of civilization," and everything about it was outrageous: 25-foot-high frescoed walls, vaulted ceilings, a wealth of imported marble and tiles, immense fireplaces, and custom-loomed rugs. To mark the opening in January 1926, VIP guests were brought in on chartered, long-distance trains, fed on pheasant and trout, and given the run of the casino. The following day, they could fox-hunt, play polo or swim in the US's largest pool – whose first swimming instructor was Johnny Weissmuller, future Olympic champion and the original screen Tarzan.

Although high-profile celebrities, such as Bing Crosby, Judy Garland, and Ginger Rogers, kept the *Biltmore* on their itineraries, the end of the Florida land boom and the start of the Depression meant that the hotel was never the success it might have been. In the Forties, many of the finer furnishings were lost when the hotel became a military hospital, and decades of decline followed. The future looked rosier in 1986, when $55 million was lavished on a restoration program, but the company hired went bust, and the great building remained closed. Only in 1993 did it finally reopen, after another multi-million dollar refit. Now once again it is functioning as a hotel; you can step inside to admire the elaborate architecture or take afternoon tea in the lobby for $15. There are also free historical tours beginning at 1.30pm, 2.30pm, and 3.30pm every Sunday in the main hall, plus a free "ghost history" tour every Thurs at 7pm, but these both tend to be hit and miss – the best way to absorb the hotel's grandeur is just to amble through its spacious common areas.

The neighboring **Biltmore Country Club**, also open to the public, has fared better. You can poke your head inside for a closer look at its painstakingly renovated Beaux Arts features, but most people turn up to knock a ball along the lush fairways of the **Biltmore Golf Course**, which, in the glory days of the hotel, hosted the highest-paying golf tournament in the world.

The Lowe Art Museum

One of the few parts of Coral Gables where Mediterranean-style architecture doesn't prevail is on the campus of the **University of Miami**, whose dismal, box-like buildings about two miles south of the *Biltmore* are disappointingly

South Coral Gables

Exploring the southern reaches of Coral Gables is impractical without a **car**, and the sights there are more conveniently seen with those of South Miami. To read about attractions in south Coral Gables, including the Charles Deering Estate, see "South Miami," p.101.

bland. Merrick donated the land for the university, figuring that a world-class city needed a top-notch seat of learning, but today UM is best known for its sports teams, like the perennially successful Hurricanes. The campus' star attraction is the rather overrated **Lowe Art Museum**, 1301 Stanford Drive (Tues & Wed, Fri & Sat 10am–5pm, Thurs noon–7pm, Sun noon–5pm; $5; ⓣ305/284-3535, ⓦwww.loweartmuseum.org). Established in 1950, the Lowe underwent major renovation and extension work in 1995 and is now one of the largest museums in Florida. Its holdings zigzag from Old Master paintings to pre-Columbian, African, and East Asian artefacts; it also absorbed the collection of the controversial Cuban Museum of the Americas, which was finally shuttered in 1999 after one too many firebomb attacks. Sadly, the European pictures are mostly shabby small canvases and the non-Western artefacts are largely ephemera; the few standouts are in the museum's modern art collection, including the freakishly life-like football player sculpted in fiberglass by Duane Hanson.

Coconut Grove

A stomping ground of down-at-heel artists, writers, and lefties throughout the Sixties and Seventies, **COCONUT GROVE** is better known these days for two large malls and a slew of expensive condo towers with stunning waterfront views. Though it may have lost its counter-culture edge, Coconut Grove has retained its ornery character: many locals still treat it as distinct from the rest of Miami, which annexed it in the late nineteenth century. It owes its character in part to the strange mix of settlers who first called it home: Bahamian immigrant laborers lived alongside New England intellectuals who came here searching for spiritual fulfilment, and together created a fiercely independent community. The distance between Coconut Grove and the rest of Miami is still very much apparent: cleaner and richer than ever, but continuing to fan the flames of liberalism – indeed, the local populace has tried several times to secede from the city, to no avail.

Central Coconut Grove and around

Central Coconut Grove is compact and walkable, filled with shops and restaurants – including two of the city's best-known malls – and plentiful parking. Open-air **CocoWalk** at 3000 Grand Avenue is the middle-brow one, a major force for revitalization when it was first built in the Nineties. It's filled with restaurants, bars, and a movie theater (see "Film", p.115). The more upscale **Streets of Mayfair** at the corner of MacFarlane Road and Grand Avenue, was less successful; its zigzagging walkways – decorated by fountains, copper sculptures, climbing vines, and Romanesque concrete doodles – are almost always empty, and there are dozens of vacant store spaces, making it an oddly lifeless place to browse.

Heading south down Main Highway you'll come across the beige and white, Mediterranean Revival **Coconut Grove Playhouse**, at no. 3500 (see "Theater," p.114). Opened in 1926 as a lavish movie house (it cost a then-staggering $400,000 to build), it's still going strong as a playhouse on a steady diet of broad comedies and Broadway blockbusters. The theater's greatest claim to fame, though, is that Samuel Beckett's *Waiting for Godot* had its US premiere here in 1956.

The Barnacle

Across Main Highway from the Coconut Grove Playhouse, a short, tree-shaded track leads to the tranquil bayside garden and century-old house known as the **Barnacle** (Fri–Mon, 9am–4pm, tours depart at 10am, 11.30am, 1pm, 2.30pm from the porch; $1; ⓣ305/448-9445), built by "Commodore" Ralph Middelton Munroe: sailor, brilliant yacht-designer, and a devotee of the Transcendentalist Movement (which advocated self-reliance, a love of nature, and a simple lifestyle). The pagoda-like Barnacle was ingeniously put together in 1891 with local materials and tricks learned from nautical design. Raising the structure eight feet off the ground in 1908 improved air circulation and prevented flooding, a covered veranda enabled windows to be opened during rainstorms, and a skylight allowed air to be drawn through the house – all major innovations that alleviated some of the discomforts of living all year in the heat and humidity of south Florida. More inventive still, when Munroe needed more space for his family he simply jacked up the single-story structure and added a new floor underneath. Only with the guided tour can you see inside the house, where many original furnishings remain alongside some of Munroe's intriguing photos of pioneering Coconut Grovers. The grounds, however, you are free to explore on your own. The lawn extends to the shore of Biscayne Bay, while behind the house are the last remnants of the tropical hardwood hammock that extended throughout the Miami area.

Charles Avenue and Black Coconut Grove

The Bahamian settlers of the late 1800s, who later provided the labor that went into building Coconut Grove and nearby areas, mostly lived in an area known as Kebo, along what became **Charles Avenue** (off Main Highway, close to the playhouse), in simple wooden houses similar to the "conch houses" that fill Key West's Old Town (see "The Florida Keys," p.157). You'll find a trio of these still standing on the "3200" block, though be warned that they are on the edge of **Black Coconut Grove** (not a name you'll find on maps, but one which everyone uses), a run-down area stretching westwards to the borders of Coral Gables. The fact that such a derelict district exists within half a mile of one of the city's most fashionably upmarket areas provides a stark reminder of the divisions between Miami's haves and have-nots.

On the southern edge of Black Coconut Grove, the 1917 **Plymouth Congregational Church** (Mon–Fri 8.30am-4.30pm; ⓣ305/444-6521, ⓦwww.plymouthmiami.com), on the corner of Devon Road and the Main Highway, has a striking, vine-covered, coral-rock facade; remarkably, this finely crafted exterior was the work of just one man. Note, too, the 375-year-old main door, hand-carved in walnut, which looks none the worse for its journey from an early seventeenth-century monastery in the Spanish Pyrenees. At one time, George Merrick's father was a minister here, back when this was the home of the Union Congregational Church. The interior is unremarkable, but if you're determined to look inside, call ahead to make an appointment with the church office.

Bayshore Drive and around

Heading northeast from downtown Coconut Grove, you'll encounter the most upscale enclaves in Coconut Grove, notably the "1600" to "2100" blocks of Bayshore Drive, an area known as Silver Bluff. This limestone ridge is where the earliest Coconut Grove settlers built their homes, on one of the highest and safest points in the flood-prone city. Down by the water is **Miami City Hall**, 3400 Pan American Drive (Ⓣ305/250-5300), the small and unlikely seat of local government far removed from the business hub downtown. The blue-and-white-trimmed Art Deco building used to be an airline terminal: in the Thirties, passengers checked in here for the Pan American Airways seaplane service to Latin America, and the sight of the lumbering craft taking off used to draw thousands to the waterfront. Today, there's no public access to the building's interior, though the small plaque out front records that this was where the veterans of the Bay of Pigs invasion stepped ashore after their release from Cuba in 1962.

Close by is an historic sight of a different ilk, nestled next to Dinner Key. Though it's now known as the **Coconut Grove Exhibition Center**, this was once the Dinner Key Auditorium where in 1969 the rock legend Jim Morrison, singer with the Doors, dropped his leather pants to expose himself during the band's first – and last – Florida show; this caused Miami's police to clamp down on local rock clubs, and increased the band's fame and notoriety a hundredfold. **Peacock Park**, at the end of Bayshore Drive beside MacFarlane Road, was an infamous hippie haunt at the time of Morrison's misdemeanor in Coconut Grove. More recently it's been cleaned up to fit the area's present smart, sophisticated image, and now features tennis courts and some peculiar abstract rock sculptures. The **Coconut Grove Chamber of Commerce**, 2820 MacFarlane Rd (Mon–Fri 9am–5pm; Ⓣ305/444-7270, Ⓦwww.coconutgrove.com), on a corner of the park, has copious selections of free leaflets and maps of the area.

Villa Vizcaya

In 1914, farm-machinery mogul James Deering followed his brother, Charles (of Charles Deering Estate fame; see "South Miami," p.101), to south Florida and blew $15 million recreating a sixteenth-century Italian villa within the belt of vegetation between Miami and Coconut Grove. A thousand-strong work-force – ten percent of Miami's population at the time – was hired to complete his **Villa Vizcaya**, 3251 S Miami Ave (daily 9.30am–4.30pm; gardens open until 5.30pm, free house tours begin every 10min; $10; Ⓣ305/250-9133, Ⓦwww.vizcayamuseum.org), in just two years. Taken individually, the rooms here are appealing, but en masse they can be overwhelming. The lasting impression of the grandiose structure is that both Deering and his designer (the crazed Paul Chalfin, who was hell-bent on becoming an architectural legend) were driven more by the need to acquire than any sense of taste. Deering's madly eclectic art collection and his belief that the villa should appear to have been inhabited for 400 years, resulted in a thunderous clash of Baroque, Renaissance, Rococo, and Neoclassical fixtures and furnishings, and even the landscaped **gardens**, with their fountains and sculptures, weren't spared his grand pretensions. Even so, Villa Vizcaya is one of Miami's unmissable sights, showcasing yet again Miami's obsession with the watery old world grandeur of Venice, especially in its waterfront plaza. Wandering around the grounds, you're likely to spot teenage girls, festooned in meringue-like gowns, being photographed for their *quince* – the Cuban version of a Sweet Sixteen.

Museum of Science and Space Transit Planetarium

Straight across South Miami Avenue from Villa Vizcaya is the **Museum of Science and Space Transit Planetarium**, at no. 3280 (daily 10am–6pm; last admission 5pm; $10; ⓣ305/854-4200, ⓦwww.miamisci.org). Its interactive exhibits provide a good two-hour family diversion, though a stronger reason to visit is the collection of wildlife at the museum's rear. Vultures and owls are among a number of injured birds seeing out their days here, a variety of snakes can be viewed at disturbingly close quarters, and the resident tarantula is happy to be handled. The adjoining **planetarium** (shows hourly on the hour) has the usual trips-around-the-cosmos shows. Details are available by phone or from the ticket office inside the museum. The museum is scheduled to relocate downtown, in a specially constructed complex known as Museum Park Miami, which it will share with the Miami Art Museum; the move is expected to be completed in late 2004, but call for the latest information or check ⓦwww.sciencecenteroftheamericas.org.

Church of Ermita de la Caridad del Cobre

Five minutes' walk along the road, look for signs down a winding side road to the **Church of Ermita de la Caridad del Cobre**, 3609 S Miami Ave (daily 8am–9pm; ⓣ305/854-2404), which is perched on the waterfront in the shadows of the massive Mercy Hospital. Looking like a large, angular meringue half-dipped in chocolate, the modernist church was built on 10¢ donations from Miami Cubans. It's the religious heart of expat Cuban life and its architecture and design are highly symbolic: the six columns represent the six traditional provinces of Cuba, while beneath the altar there's Cuban soil, sand, and rock salvaged from a refugee boat. There's also a patchy sepia mural behind the altar tracing the island's history.

Key Biscayne and Virginia Key

A compact, immaculately manicured community five miles off the Miami shore, **Key Biscayne** is a great place to live – if you can afford it. Seeking relaxation and creature comforts away from life in the fast lane, the moneyed of Miami fill the island's upmarket homes and condos: even Richard Nixon had his presidential winter house here, and singer Sting has recuperated between tour dates in one of the luxury shorefront hotels. This elite enclave got its start in the decades after World War I, when the Matheson family – who made millions supplying mustard gas to the government – moved in; their wealthy friends soon followed and the island came to be known as a place where the rich could live undisturbed. More recently, many wealthy Latin Americans have bought second homes here, and it's now estimated that two thirds of Key Biscayne's population is Hispanic. For visitors, Key Biscayne (and the smaller island to the north known as **Virginia Key**) offers a couple of inviting beaches, a third inside a state park, and a fabulous cycling path running the full length of the island, but cheap eats and lodgings are in predictably short supply.

Virginia Key

Without a private yacht, the only way onto Key Biscayne is via **Rickenbacker Causeway**, a four-mile-long continuation of SW 26th Road just south of downtown Miami; it soars high above Biscayne Bay, allowing shipping to glide underneath, and provides a breathtaking view of the Brickell Avenue skyline (see p.75). Drivers have to pay a $1 toll; otherwise you can cross the causeway by bus (#B), bike, or even on foot.

The first land you'll hit is the unexceptional and sparsely populated **VIRGINIA KEY**. Its main point of interest is **Virginia Beach** (daily 8am–sunset; cars $2; ⓣ305/361-2749), reached by a two-mile lane that winds through a cluster of woodland. During the years of segregation, this was set aside for Miami's black community (chosen, cynics might say, for its proximity to a large sewage works). Today, it's best known as the location of local institution *Jimbo's* (see review, p.111), a place that's part-bar, part-junkyard. In contrast, on the right of the main road, the **Miami Seaquarium** marine park (daily 9.30am–6pm, box office closes 4.30pm; adults $24, children 9 and under $19; parking costs extra; ⓣ305/365-2525, ⓦwww.miamiseaquarium.com) is a bustling place where you can while away three or four hours watching the usual roster of performing seals and dolphins. Be sure not to miss Lolita, the 8000-pound star of the spectacular killer-whale show (daily, noon). The park's most important work – undertaking breeding programs to preserve Florida's endangered sea life and serving as a halfway house for injured manatees and other sea creatures – goes on behind the scenes. Though the park, which served as the backdrop for the *Flipper* TV series, is enjoyable, remember that there are plenty more marine parks in Florida, such as Orlando's SeaWorld, and much more in Miami on which to spend your time and money.

Key Biscayne

Not content with living in one of the best natural settings in Miami, the people of **KEY BISCAYNE** also possess one of the finest landscaped beaches in the city – **Crandon Park Beach** (8am–sunset; cars $4; ⓣ305/361-5421), a mile along Crandon Boulevard (the continuation of the main road from the causeway). Three miles of golden beach fringe the park, and you can wade out in knee-deep water to a sandbar far from the shore. Filled by the sounds of boisterous kids and sizzling barbecues on weekends, the park at any other time is disturbed only by the occasional jogger or holidaymaker straying from the private beaches of the expensive hotels nearby. Relax beside the lapping ocean waters and keep a look out for manatees and dolphins, which are both known to swim by.

Besides its very green, manicured looks, **residential Key Biscayne**, beginning with an abrupt wall of apartment buildings at the southern edge of Crandon Park Beach, has little to offer visitors. You'll need to pass through, however, on the way to the much more rewarding Bill Baggs Cape Florida State Recreation Area (see below), and while doing so should pick up information on the area at the very friendly and informative **Chamber of Commerce** at 87 West McIntyre St (Mon–Fri 9am–5pm; ⓣ305/361-5207, ⓦwww.keybiscaynechamber.org). Afterwards, loop along **Harbor Drive**, where at no. 485 W stands the former home of ex-president Richard Nixon, who picked up his *Miami Herald* here one morning in 1972 to read of a break-in at the Watergate Complex in Washington; the seemingly insignificant event (only featured by the paper because two Miami Cubans were involved) led to Nixon's resignation two years later.

Crandon Boulevard terminates at the entrance to the 400-acre **Bill Baggs Cape Florida State Recreation Area** (daily 8am–sunset; cars $4, pedestrians and cyclists $1; ⓣ305/361-5811), which covers the southern extremity of Key Biscayne. An excellent swimming **beach** lines the Atlantic-facing side of the park, and a boardwalk cuts around the wind-bitten sand dunes toward the **Cape Florida Lighthouse**, an 1845 replica of the original structure from the 1820s which was destroyed during the first Seminole War. Ranger-led tours limited to the first ten people to arrive (daily 10am & 1pm; free) are the only way can you climb through the 95-foot-high structure, which offers fantastic views of the whole island and the last few remaining huts of Stiltsville (see below). The lighthouse remained in use until 1878, and now serves as a navigation beacon.

Stiltsville

Looking out from the park across the bay, you'll spy the grouping of fragile-looking houses known as **Stiltsville**. Held above water by stilts, these wooden dwellings were built and occupied by fishermen in the Forties and Fifties, and enraged the authorities by being outside the jurisdiction of tax collectors. Stiltsville's demise has more or less been assured by a recent law forbidding repair work on the ramshackle structures, whose state of disarray was compounded by the destruction wrought by Hurricane Andrew in 1992; only seven of the fourteen original houses are still standing, used largely for parties or Boy Scout trips. Locals are now trying to preserve the area, and more info can be found at Ⓦwww.stiltsville.org.

South Miami

South of Coral Gables and Coconut Grove, monotonous middle-class suburbs consume almost all of **SOUTH MIAMI**, an expanse of cozy family homes reaching to the edge of the Everglades, interrupted only by golf courses and a few contrived tourist attractions. Mini-malls, gas stations, cut-price waterbed outlets, and bumper-to-bumper traffic are the star features of its primary thoroughfare, US-1. You can't avoid this route entirely, but from South Coral Gables a better course is Old Cutler Road, which makes a pleasing meander from Coconut Grove through a thick belt of woodland (see also Matheson Hammock Park and Fairchild Tropical Garden, below) between Biscayne Bay and the suburban sprawl. Cutting inland from US-1 is unrewarding (and unthinkable without a car), since there are no stops of any major importance.

South Coral Gables

Much as his Venetian Pool was a cleverly converted quarry, Merrick turned the construction ditches that ringed the infant Coral Gables into a network of canals, calling them the "Miami Riviera" and floating gondolas on them. Although the idea never really took off, the placid waterways remain, running between the university campus and a secluded residential area on Biscayne Bay. Dividing Coconut Grove and South Miami, the **Matheson Hammock Park**, 9601 Old Cutler Rd (6am–sunset; $4 per car; Ⓣ305/665-5475), was a coconut plantation before becoming a public park in 1930. On the weekends, thousands flock here to picnic, use the marina, and take a dip in the artificial lagoon, great for small children but with little to offer adults; the rest of the sizeable park is much less crowded, and you can easily while away a few hours strolling around the wading pond – popular with people catching crabs – or along the winding trails above the mangrove swamps.

Virtually next door, the **Fairchild Tropical Garden**, 10901 Old Cutler Rd (daily 9.30am–4.30pm; $8; Ⓣ305/667-1651, Ⓦwww.fairchildgarden.org), turns the same rugged terrain into lawns, flowerbeds, and gardens decorated by artificial lakes. A good way to begin exploring the 83-acre site – the largest tropical botanical gardens in the continental United States – is to hitch a ride on the free tram (departing hourly, on the hour, from inside the garden's entrance) for a forty-minute trip along the trails, with a live commentary on the various plants.

The tropical habitats reproduced here – some more successfully than others – range from desert to rainforest, though there's relatively little space devoted to fauna endemic to southern Florida. As a research institution, Fairchild works with scientists all over the world to preserve the diversity of the tropical environment; many of the plant species here, such as Cape Sable Whiteweed and Alvaradoa, are extinct in their original environments, and efforts have been made to re-establish them in their places of origin. Don't miss the Windows to the Tropics, a hothouse filled with the most delicate, exotic plants, as well as the *amorphophallus titanium*, nicknamed "Mr Stinky," whose rare blooms are renowned for their rotting-flesh smell.

Food can be brought into the gardens to be consumed in a special picnic area, though you'll need to stock up before entry as there are no shops nearby. Otherwise, there's only a small **café** (9.30am–4.30pm) serving overpriced sandwiches and snacks.

The Charles Deering Estate

Long before modern highways scythed through the city, **Old Cutler Road** was the sole road between Coconut Grove and Cutler, a small town that went into terminal decline in the 1910s after being bypassed by the new Flagler railroad. A wealthy industrialist and amateur botanist, Charles Deering (brother of James, the owner of Villa Vizcaya; see "Coconut Grove," p.97), was so taken with the natural beauty of the area that he purchased all of Cutler and, with one exception, razed its buildings to make way for the **Charles Deering Estate**, 16701 SW 72nd Ave (10am–5pm, last ticket sold at 4pm; $6; ⓣ305/235-1668, ⓦwww.deeringestate.com), completed in 1922. The one building that Deering preserved was Richmond Cottage, Cutler's only hotel, which he turned into his own living and dining quarters. Its pleasant wooden form now stands in marked contrast to the limestone mansion he erected alongside, whose interior – echoing halls, dusty chandeliers, and checker-board-tile floors – is Mediterranean in style but carries a Gothic spookiness. Sadly, there's little to see inside as Deering's daughters sold off much of the opulent furnishings after his death. Better to more spend time ambling around the tranquil, 420-acre grounds; signs of human habitation dating back 10,000 years have been found amid the pine woods, mangrove forests, and tropical hardwood hammocks. The ticket price includes a free one-hour historical tour of the interior and a half-hour tour of the grounds, led by one of the extremely knowledgeable rangers – make sure not to miss out.

Visitor information

While in this vicinity, you should take advantage of the excellent **Tropical Everglades Visitor Information Center** (Mon–Sat 8am–5pm, Sun 10am–2pm; ⓣ305/245-9180 or 1-800/388-9669, ⓦwww.tropicaleverglades.com), located at 160 US-1, close to the junction with Hwy-9336 (344th Street); it offers a wealth of information on attractions around South Miami, but is particularly strong on the Everglades.

Metrozoo

An extensive display of wildlife is on view at the **Metrozoo**, 12400 SW 152nd St (daily 9.30am–5.30pm; adults $12, children $7; ⓣ305/251-0401, ⓦwww.miamimetrozoo.com). This vast compound organizes animals by continent, and mixes in unusual creatures like anoa (which resemble small buffalo) alongside the giraffes and lions. Thoughtfully designed, the zoo uses moats and other natural barriers rather than cages, and the educational plaques flagging each species are highly informative. Make sure to come early in the day, though, as the baking noonday sun makes most of the animals sluggish. The zoo's prize white Bengal tigers – only one of which, oddly, is actually white – are fed at 11am.

Fruit and Spice Park and Monkey Jungle

The subtle fragrances of the fauna in **Fruit and Spice Park**, 24801 SW 187th Ave (daily 10am–5pm; $4; ⓣ305/247-5727, ⓦwww.co.miami-dade.fl.us/parks/Parks/fruit_spice.htm), tickle your nostrils as soon as you enter. Star fruit and the aptly named Panama candle tree are the highlights of a host of tropical curiosities, which are grouped together by species or by theme (look for the bizarre banana plantation where dozens of misshapen varieties are grown together). Labeling at the park is spotty at best, however, so unless you're an avid gardener you're unlikely to be able to identify or learn about much here.

Continuing south toward Homestead, at 14805 SW 216th St, **Monkey Jungle** (daily 9.30am–5pm; last admission 4pm; adults $16, children 3–9 $10; ⓣ305/235-1611, ⓦwww.monkeyjungle.com) is one of the few preserves in the US for endangered primates. Covered walkways keep visitors in closer confinement than the monkeys and lead through a steamy hammock where baboons, orangutans, gorillas, and 35 species of monkeys move through the vegetation. Despite initial impressions, plenty of the monkeys *are* in cages and signage is infrequent, making it far from the eco-utopia its owners claim. However, it's a fun place to visit – make sure to bring plenty of quarters to buy nuts to feed the monkeys, who've devised ingenious ways of accessing food dishes.

Homestead and around

Suburbia yields to agriculture as you leave South Miami along US-1, where broad, fertile fields grow fruit and vegetables for the nation's northern states. Aside from offering as good a taste of Florida farm life – the region produces the bulk of America's winter tomatoes – as you're likely to find so close to its major city, the district can be a money-saving stop (see "Accommodation," p.69) en route to the Florida Keys or the Everglades National Park.

HOMESTEAD is the agricultural area's main town and the least galvanizing section of Miami. Krome Avenue, just west of US-1, slices through the center, but besides a few restored 1910s–1930s buildings (such as the Old City Hall, no. 43 N), there's little to detain you other than the **Florida Pioneer Museum**, no. 826 (Wed & Sat 1–5pm, Fri 5.30–8pm; free; ⓣ305/245-9180). Thanks to the enthusiastic efforts of locals, the museum has finally reopened after a ten-year hiatus caused by Hurricane Andrew. You'll find mostly a collection of nineteenth-century artefacts, including sewing machines, pots and pans, as well as photos and objects from Homestead's formative years, especially train-related memorabilia: this end-of-the-line town was planned by Flagler's railroad engineers in 1904.

Around Homestead

Time is better spent around Homestead than actually in it, with plenty of diversions just a few minutes' drive from the town. You can also gather your own dinner in this area; keep an eye out for **"pick your own"** signs, where, for a few dollars, you can take to the fields and load up with peas, tomatoes, and a variety of other crops.

The Coral Castle

The one essential stop in these parts is the **Coral Castle**, 28655 S Dixie Hwy (daily 7am–9pm; adults $10, children 7–12 $5; ⓣ305/248-6345, ⓦwww.coral-castle.com), whose bulky coral-rock sculptures can be found about six miles northeast of Homestead, beside US-1, at the junction with 286th Street. Remarkably, these fantastic creations, whose delicate finish belies their imposing size, are the work of just one man – the enigmatic **Edward Leedskalnin**. Jilted in 1913 by his 16-year-old fiancée in Latvia, Leedskalnin spent seven years working his way across Europe, Canada, and the US before buying an acre of land just south of Homestead. Using a profound – and self-taught – knowledge of weights and balances, he raised enormous hunks of coral rock from the ground, then used a workbench made from car running boards and handmade tools fashioned from scrap to refine the blocks into chairs, tables, and beds. It is thought the castle was intended as a love nest to woo back his errant sweetheart. Leedskalnin died here in 1951.

You can wander around the slabs, sit on the hard but surprisingly comfortable chairs, swivel a nine-ton gate with your pinkie, and admire the numerous coral representations of the moon and planets that reflect Leedskalnin's interest in astronomy and astrology; also on display is his twenty-foot-high telescope. But you won't be able to explain how the sculptures were made. No one ever saw the secretive Leedskalnin at work, or knows how, alone, he could have loaded 1100 tons of rock onto the rail-mounted truck that brought the pieces here in 1936.

Biscayne National Park

If you're not going to the Florida Keys, make a point of visiting **Biscayne National Park**, at the end of Canal Drive (328th Street), east of US-1 (underwater portion open 24hr, Convoy Point daily 7am–5.30pm, except Christmas; ⓣ305/230-7275, ⓦww.nps.gov/bisc). The bulk of the park lies beneath the clear ocean waters, where stunning formations of living coral provide a habitat for shoals of brightly colored fish and numerous other creatures too delicate to survive on their own. For a full description of the wondrous world of the living coral reef, see John Pennekamp Coral Reef State Park, in "The Florida Keys", p.129.

The lazy way to view it is on the three-hour **glass-bottomed boat** trip from the National Park Service (NPS) concession near the entrance at Convoy Point (daily at 10am; $25; reservations ⓣ305/230-1100, ⓔdive970@aol.com), but for a fuller encounter you should embark on one of their three-hour snorkel tours (daily 1.30pm; $35 including all equipment). The concession also rents out canoes ($9/hr) and two-person kayaks ($16/hr). Maps and information about the park are available at the **visitor center** next door (8.30am–5pm). For tours and dives, phone at least a day ahead to make reservations; the schedules are subject to change, so make sure to confirm departure times.

Another option is to visit the Park's **barrier islands**, seven miles out. A tour boat leaves for **Elliot Key** from Convoy Point at 1.30pm on Sundays between December and May – tickets ($20 return) can be bought from

NPS. Once ashore, besides calling at the **visitor center** (Sat & Sun 10am–4pm) and contemplating the easy six-mile hiking trail along the island's forested spine, there's nothing to do on Elliot Key except sunbathe in solitude.

Eating

Miami's cosmopolitan character is best displayed in its **food**, a realm in which the city's cobbled-together history fuses the flavours and traditions of Haiti, Cuba, the US, and elsewhere. Recent years have seen the development of a hybrid style of cooking known as **New Floridian** (also **Floribbean**), which successfully combines nouvelle cuisine methods and presentation with Caribbean ingredients, such as tropical fruit and fish. **Seafood**, every bit as plentiful and good as you would expect so close to fish-laden tropical waters, is a common feature among the city's myriad of cuisines drawn from every corner of the Americas – and beyond. Much of what is out there is fairly affordable, at least by American big-city standards, so you'll rarely need an expense account to dine out on a giant mess of stone-crab claws – a regional specialty – or fresh-picked lobsters. More than five hundred species of fish thrive offshore, both run-of-the-mill and exotic; basically, if you can't find it on your plate somewhere, it hasn't evolved yet.

Miami offers ethnic cuisines from every continent, though of course **Cuban** food is a staple. The price of a sizeable lunch or dinner in one of the innumerable small, family-run Cuban diners (always pleased to show off their culinary skills to non-Spanish-speaking customers) will normally be less than $10. **Haitian** cooking is slowly gaining popularity in Miami, and the restaurants in Little Haiti, just north of downtown Miami, are just some of the places in which to sample it. **Argentine**, **Jamaican**, and **Peruvian** eateries bear witness to the city's strong Caribbean and Latin American elements, though aside from Cuban food, for sheer quality and value for money it's hard to better the many **Japanese** outlets, most north of downtown Miami and a few in South Miami – all much cheaper than their European counterparts – while in South Beach, expensive but good-quality sushi is the current rage. Chinese and Thai places are abundant, too, as are **Italian**. By contrast, **Mexican** food is far less common than in most other parts of the US, though there are a few choice outlets. All of the restaurants listed below are open for lunch and dinner unless otherwise noted, while most Cuban restaurants also have a limited breakfast service (including coffee and snacks). Always check your bill when you get it, especially around the South Beach tourist drags – and remember they'll often automatically add a fifteen percent gratuity that you can cross off if you're not happy with the service.

Downtown and around

Big Fish 55 SW Miami Ave ⓣ305/373-1770. Lively spot on the Miami River, with folding chairs, benches, and picnic tables. Menu includes home-cooked fish dishes and vegetarian options – try the delicious signature crab cakes. Fairly pricey, but the main dishes can easily feed two.

Biscayne Bar-B-Q 2041 Biscayne Blvd ⓣ305/438-1520. Laid-back takeout joint that serves smoky, pulled chicken sandwiches and juicy pork ribs at rock-bottom prices.

Edelweiss 2655 Biscayne Blvd ⓣ305/573-4421. Hearty German and Swiss food with traditional schnitzel, bratwurst, and excellent strudel desserts.

Garcia's Seafood Grille 398 NW N River Drive ⓣ305/375-0765. Charming waterfront café with ramshackle wooden benches and superb, fresh fish dishes for around $11 (breakfast and lunch only); there's also an onsite fish market. Highly recommended.

La Loggia 68 W Flagler St ⓣ305/373-4800. Somewhat upscale Italian wine bar–restaurant serving simple pasta dishes for around $10. One of the few restaurants that's open for dinner in central downtown.

Lo Spaghetto inside the DuPont Building, 169 E Flagler St ☎305/379-2000. If you stop by to admire the building's interior, there's an Italian café serving delicious pasta, panini, and coffee from 7.30am to 3.30pm.

Mike Gordon's Seafood Restaurant 1201 NE 79th St ☎305/751-4429. A local favorite, this mid-range seafood eatery is just as good as the famed *Joe's Stone Crabs* in South Beach (see below), but much cheaper, too.

Morton's Steakhouse 1200 Brickell Ave, Brickell ☎305/400-9990. Clubby old world steakhouse in the midst of skyscraping banks, serving juicy slabs of aged beef to an upscale clientele – try the Porterhouse or double filet mignon. One of the few places in downtown to remain lively during the evening.

Raja's 33 NE 2nd Ave ☎305/539-9551. This no-nonsense restaurant serves South Indian staples like a *masala dosa* (potato pancake), accompanied by tangy *sambhar* (hot and sour soup). Prices hover around $6 per dish, and the portions are generous. Lunch only.

Tobacco Road 638 S Miami Ave ☎305/381-8970. The restaurant section of this bar (see "Drinking," p.110 and "Live music," p.113) offers hamburgers, fries, and sandwiches, which are consumed by relaxing yuppies and the occasional biker.

South Beach

A La Folie 516 Espanola Way ☎305/538-4484. This authentic French *crêperie* is a welcome respite from the tourist traps found elsewhere on Espanola Way. Settle down with a copy of *Le Monde* while sipping your *café* – it also serves gooey *croque monsieurs*.

Big Pink 157 Collins Ave ☎305/532-4700. Futuristic diner decked out in pink Lucite and aluminium that serves massive portions of all-American favorites – try the novel TV dinners presented on old-fashioned trays or the lush red-velvet cake. The long tables are good for getting to know your fellow diners.

Bond St basement of the *Townhouse Hotel*, 150 20th St ☎305/398-1806. The Miami outpost of the chic New York sushi bar is similarly hip, with white banquettes and dark corners for snacking *a deux*. For all the hype, the food's not bad either, especially the vegetarian rolls with sundried tomato and avocado or the signature "saketini" cocktail.

David's Coffee Shop 1058 Collins Ave ☎305/534-8736. Locals will tell you that this is *the* Cuban restaurant on the beach. Eat deep-fried delicacies at the counter, wedged between businessmen and teens, or grab a *cafecito* at the take-out window. There's dining room-style seating at the second branch, 1654 Meridian Ave, just off Lincoln Road.

El Rancho Grande 1626 Pennsylvania Ave ☎305/673-0480. Low-cost, authentic Mexican food is served with a smile in this cozy, colorfully painted restaurant, handily placed just off Lincoln Road. Open 24hr.

Eleventh Street Diner 1065 Washington Ave ☎305/534-6373. All-American fare served around the clock in a converted silver railroad car, with good happy hour specials on food and drink Mon–Fri 5–7pm and 10pm–midnight.

Front Porch Café 1418 Ocean Drive ☎305/531-8300. This local hangout is refreshingly low-key given its touristy location: the delicious, dinner plate–sized pancakes will double as both breakfast and lunch, as will the chunky, doorstop-sized sandwiches.

Gino's 731 Washington Ave ☎305/673-2837. Open 24 hours a day, this pizzeria prides itself on staying open whatever the weather. Each slice of the thin, New York-style pizza comes with a free, buttery garlic knot.

Jerry's Famous Deli 1450 Collins Ave ☎305/532-8030. This 24-hour deli, housed in a converted cafeteria, offers a menu so vast that you'll find almost anything you're craving (try the salad served in a pizza crust – it's better than it sounds). It may be a little overpriced, but it's convenient.

Joe's Stone Crabs 11 Washington Ave ☎305/673-0365. Only open from October to May when Florida stone crabs are in season; expect long lines of tourists waiting (usually a couple of hours) to pay $20 for a succulent plateful.

La Sandwicherie 229 W 14th St ☎305/532-8934. Open until 5am, this outdoor café serves sandwiches stuffed with gourmet ingredients that make others look miniature in comparison – all for around $7.

Lario's on the Beach 820 Ocean Drive ☎305/532-9577. The reason to come to singer Gloria Estefan's Nuevo Cuban restaurant is the *mojitos*, the signature concoction of crushed mint and rum – most people concede that *Lario's* serves the best on the beach. The food itself is average at best.

Le Provence 1627 Collins Ave ☎305/538-2406. This French bakery close to the beach is a terrific place to stock up on baguettes and brioches before a day on the sands. The croissants are outstanding. Daily 7am–8pm.

Metro Kitchen & Bar inside the *Astor Hotel*, 956 Washington Ave ⓣ305/531-8081. One of the hottest eateries at the beach, thanks to its celebrity clientele, this sunken restaurant boasts a fine garden, simple but delicious Italian-inflected food, and killer cocktails – with the attendant celebrities and local hipsters.

News Café 800 Ocean Drive ⓣ305/538-NEWS. Sidewalk café with an extensive mid-price breakfast, lunch, and dinner menu, and front-row seating for the South Beach promenade. Not the scene it once was, but still a local favorite. Open 24hr.

Pacific Time 915 Lincoln Rd ⓣ305/534-5979. The first upscale eatery to open on then up-and-coming Lincoln Road ten years ago, *Pacific Time* serves excellent Modern American cooking with strong East Asian influences. Worth the splurge. Dinner only.

Pizza Rustica 863 Washington Ave ⓣ305/674-8244. Mouthwateringly fresh gourmet pizza, with slab-like slices costing around $4. Try the signature "rustica," which comes with lashings of artichoke, prosciutto, sun-dried tomato, and olives. Highly recommended.

Puerto Sagua 700 Collins Ave ⓣ305/673-1115. Where local Cubans meet gringos over espresso coffee, beans, and rice. Cheap, filling breakfasts, lunches, and dinners.

Sabor 1501 Ocean Drive ⓣ305/608-9282. Located inside the Billboardlive complex, this upscale restaurant features a good pan-Mediterreanean menu, but most people come to spot celebrities in the dining room's darker corners.

Tantra 1445 Pennsylvania Ave ⓣ305/672-4765. The sensual French/Mediterranean flavors offered up here are no mistake – the restaurant's theme, enhanced by muted lighting, is based on Tantric philosophies and aphrodisiac ingredients. Fun, if a little hokey, the restaurant even has belly dancers during dinner.

Tap Tap Haitian Restaurant 819 5th St ⓣ305/672-2898. The tastiest and most attractively presented Haitian food in Miami, at very reasonable prices. Wander around the restaurant to admire the Haitian murals, and visit the upstairs gallery where exhibits on worthy Haitian themes are held. Highly recommended. Dinner only.

Taverna Opa 36-40 Ocean Drive ⓣ305/673-6730. This massive Greek restaurant – with its frantic table-dancing, loud music, and Mediterranean-themed decor – might at first seem like a tourist trap, but it's an absolute gem. Skip the forced bonhomie inside and grab a table on the patio outback; the food is delicious, authentic, and well priced – the tapas-style *meze* dishes run $3–5.

Thai Toni 890 Washington Ave ⓣ305/538-8424. Tasty Thai food at moderate prices in this bamboo-themed fashionable hangout. Dinner only.

Wish inside *The Hotel,* 801 Collins Ave ⓣ305/531-2222. Sumptuous Floribbean food (think fish and fruit combos) with unexpected but delicious touches like chili-soaked slabs of watermelon in a lush, fountain-side setting. You'll pay for the privilege, but it's worth a splurge.

Yuca 501 Lincoln Rd ⓣ305/532-9822. Serving some of Miami's best Nuevo Cubano cuisine, this gourmet restaurant is a high-priced, high-style experience. The cooking's still impressive even if it's no longer the white-hot place it once was.

Central Miami Beach, and north

Arnie & Richie's Deli 525 41st St ⓣ305/531-7691. Authentic deli in the middle of the main Jewish drag at the beach, where you can stock up on pickles, chicken soup, and pastrami on rye while chatting with the local old ladies who stop in regularly.

Café Prima Pasta 414 71st St ⓣ305/867-0106. One of Miami's best pasta restaurants, and reasonably priced. The place is tiny, so arrive early: there's also a small terrace in front where a lucky few can dine al fresco. Cash only. Mon–Sat lunch and dinner, Sun dinner only.

Chef Allen's 19088 NE 29th Ave ⓣ305/935-2900. Outstanding "New Floridian" cuisine, such as yellowtail smothered in a coconut-milk-and-curry sauce and Caribbean antipasto, is created here by Allen Susser, widely rated as one of America's greatest chefs. Only dine here if money's not a problem.

The Forge 432 41st St ⓣ305/538-8533. Dining at this Miami Beach institution is an unmissable experience, not for the staggeringly huge wine cellar (available for tours if you ask nicely), the hearty and traditional food, or the kitschy gilt decor, but rather for the vibrant scene, where you'll find hip locals eating alongside sixty-something old school Miami Beachers.

Nina 74th St and Ocean Terrace ⓣ305/861-5333. An airy waterfront café with minimalist decor and patio seating. American food with an Asian twist (such as sesame chicken or filet mignon) for around $15 per entree. Closed Mon.

Rascal House 17190 Collins Ave ⓣ305/947-4581. Largest, loudest, and most authentic New York deli in town; huge portions and waitresses who look like they've worked here since its heyday in the Fifties. Highly recommended.

Little Haiti and the Design District

190 190 NE 46th St, Design District ☎305/576-9779. Bohemian-style café, booming with loud, laidback music and filled with thrift store furniture that spills out onto a small front patio. The best time to stop by is during the All You Can Eat Sunday brunches ($15), when you can choose from a range of traditional waffles and pancakes as well as quiches and salads.

Dogma 7030 Biscayne Blvd, Little Haiti ☎305/759-3433. Hipsters make pilgrimages to this stylish hot dog stand on a sketchy part of Biscayne Blvd. Sit at red and white tables and munch on cheap, filling dogs – try the traditional bacon chili cheese or more exotic inventions like the Athens, topped with feta, oregano, and cucumbers (both under $4).

Grass 28 NE 40th St, Design District ☎305/573-3355. This outdoor restaurant-lounge with a French-Polynesian theme has tiki hut–style touches throughout (each booth has its own straw roof), offset by dark-wood furniture and brocade upholstery. The food's fine enough, but most people come to sip and sashay around the large bar. Lunch Mon–Fri, dinner daily.

Piccadilly Garden 35 NE 40th St, Design District ☎305/573-8221. Granddaddy of the groovy hangouts around here, the *Piccadilly Garden* has been open for decades. Dine in the lush, wicker-furnished courtyard or the dark-wood eating area inside. Prices hover around $13 per entree for an American steak or chicken dish.

The Secret Sandwich 3918 N Miami Ave, Design District ☎305/571-9990. Spy-themed café, with a massive world map spread across one wall, serving hearty sandwiches for around $7: try the flavorful Mata Hari (lime-marinated chicken with caramelized onions) and the deliciously creamy flan.

Soyka 5556 Biscayne Blvd, Little Haiti ☎305/759-3117. This upscale restaurant, among the first of its kind to open in the area, serves tasty, Italian-inflected dishes in a raw concrete space.

Little Havana

Ayestaran 706 SW 27th Ave ☎305/649-4982. Long a favorite Cuban restaurant among those in the know, especially good value for its $5–8 daily specials.

Casa Juancho 2436 SW 8th St ☎305/642-2452. Generally pricey, but the Castilian tapas are good value at $6–8, and there's a convivial mood as strolling Spanish musicians serenade the wealthy Cuban clientele. Don't be put off by the faux chalet exterior – the restaurant has a truly impressive Spanish wine cellar.

Casa Panza 1620 SW 8th St ☎305/643-5343. Less formal and more Iberian than many of the other Spanish restaurants hereabouts, with authentic tapas, *raciones*, and main dishes prepared in a mainly *madrileño* (Madrid) style. Above-average prices, but you get to watch free flamenco on Tues and Thurs–Sat from 8pm onwards.

Covadonga 6480 SW 8th St ☎305/261-2406. Fairly pricey Cuban seafood specialties abound in this nautical-themed restaurant frequented by a local clientele.

El Padrinito 3494 SW 8th St ☎305/442-4510. Excellent Dominican entrees like grouper steak smothered in coconut sauce served in a home-style setting. Lunch and dinner.

El Palacio de los Jugos 5721 W Flagler Ave ☎305/264-1503. A handful of tables at the back of a Cuban produce market, where the pork sandwiches and shellfish soup from the takeout stand are the tastiest for miles. Be sure to try one of the namesake *jugos* (juices) – orange-carrot and *guanabana* are both outstanding.

Exquisito 1510 SW 8th St ☎305/643-0227. Inexpensive family-run Cuban dive serving tasty Creole-Cubana dishes to locals.

Hy-Vong 3458 SW 8th St ☎305/446-3674. Tiny, dinner-only Vietnamese restaurant. No frills, slow service, and long waits, but excellent food. Tues–Sun, dinner only.

Islas Canarias 285 NW 27th Ave ☎305/649-0440. Tucked away inside a drab shopping mall. Gargantuan piles of fine, unpretentious Cuban food at unbeatable prices.

La Carreta 3632 SW 8th St ☎305/444-7501. Look for the real sugar cane growing around the wagon wheel outside this chain Cuban restaurant. The food can feel a little mass produced, but portions are huge and prices reasonable.

La Esquina de Tejas 101 SW 12th Ave ☎305/545-0337. Where Reagan and Bush Senior both courted the Hispanic vote. A dependable address for Cuban lunches and dinners.

Los Pinarenos 1334 SW 8th St ☎305/285-1135 Enormous *fruteria* sprawling along the southern side of Little Havana's main drag: for $2 you'll snag a flagon of juice squeezed to order. Even better, you'll rub elbows with the old timers from the neighborhood who hang out here during the day. Breakfast and lunch only.

Versailles 3555 SW 8th St ☎305/444-0240. Gorge on inexpensive, authentic Cuban food amid chandeliers, mirrored walls, and a buzzing neighborhood atmosphere.

Yambo 1643 SW 1st St ☎305/649-0203. For less than $5 a plate you can gorge on Nicaraguan specialties like *puerca asada* (grilled pork), but the

24-hour eats

The five below, all in South Beach, are places where you can get reasonably priced food all night. See the South Beach listings for full details.
David's Coffee Shop 1058 Collins Ave ☎305/534-8736
Eleventh Street Diner 1065 Washington Ave ☎305/534-6373
Gino's Pizzeria 731 Washington Ave ☎305/673-2837
Jerry's Famous Deli 1450 Collins Ave ☎305/532-8030
News Café 800 Ocean Drive ☎305/538-NEWS

real draw is the atmosphere: a slice of Central America, with mosaic-encrusted tables, Spanish-language radio blaring from the kitchen, and passersby peddling CDs at your table.

Coral Gables

Café Kolibri 6901 Red Rd ☎305/665-9051. Bakery with gourmet, low-fat, and vegan entrees. Also doubles as a restaurant with delicious Tuscan specialties.
Caffe Abbracci 318 Aragon Ave ☎305/441-0700. Original dishes like pumpkin ravioli hold the attention of a fashionable crowd as they sip their vintage wine.
Canton 2614 Ponce de León Blvd ☎305/448-3736. Hub of Eastern flavors of Cantonese, Mandarin, and Szechuan, known for huge portions of honey garlic chicken. Good sushi bar as well.
House of India 22 Merrick Way ☎305/444-2348. Quality catch-all Indian food including some excellently priced lunch buffets ($7 weekdays, $8 weekends). Not the chicest place, perhaps, but terrific value.
Mykonos 1201 Coral Way ☎305/856-3140. Greek food in an unassuming atmosphere. *Spinakopita*, lemon chicken soup, *gyros*, *souvlaki*, and huge Greek salads are among the offerings, along with good vegetarian options.
Picnics at Allen's Drug Store 4000 Red Rd ☎305/665-6964. Low-priced, home-style cooking, such as freshly made burgers, in an old-fashioned drugstore complete with a jukebox that blasts golden oldies.
Restaurant Saint Michel in *Hotel Place Saint Michel*, 2135 Ponce de León Blvd ☎305/446-6572. Outstanding French and Mediterranean cuisine amid antiques and flowers. Not cheap, but very alluring.
Yasuko's 4041 Ponce de León Blvd ☎305/444-6622. Intimate mid-price Japanese restaurant with an outstanding sushi bar and usually packed with students from the nearby University of Miami. Dinner only.

Coconut Grove

Bacio 3462 Main Hwy ☎305/442-4233. Glorious sorbets and ice creams are sold at this modernist *gelateria*, staffed by Italians who give the place a laidback European feel.
Le Bouchon du Grove 3430 Main Hwy ☎305/448-6060. Don't let the chi-chi name fool you. Here you'll find unpretentious award-winning French food, with fabulous Kir Royales and freshly prepared desserts at reasonable prices. Great place for coffee and a croissant in the morning too.
Chrysanthemum 2911 Grand Ave ☎305/443-6789. Superb Peking and Szechuan cooking at fairly moderate prices; a surprise in a city not known for quality Chinese food.
Daily Bread Marketplace 2400 SW 27th St ☎305/856-5893. This is a Middle Eastern grocery store that's great for a quick sandwich filled with aromatic, exotic ingredients. Also worth trying are the spinach pie and the sticky pistachio baklava.
Greenstreet Café 3468 Main Hwy ☎305/444-0244. Quaint sidewalk café with an eclectic assortment of low- to mid-priced cuisine ranging from Middle Eastern to Jamaican. The terrific, hearty egg breakfasts make this café a real scene at weekends.
Paulo Luigi's 3324 Virginia St ☎305/445-9000. Supposedly the favorite haunt of local NBA players who come for the deliciously inventive (and relatively inexpensive) home-style pasta and meat dishes. Meat and poultry tend to be a better bet than the seafood dishes.
Scotty's Landing 3381 Pan American Drive ☎305/854-2626. Tasty, inexpensive seafood and fish 'n' chips served at marina-side picnic tables in a simple setting. Somewhat hard to find as it's tucked away on the water by City Hall – ask for directions.
Señor Frog's 3480 Main Hwy ☎305/448-0999. Broad selection of reasonably priced Mexican food, but most people come to gulp down the $8 margaritas.

Key Biscayne

Donut Gallery 83 Harbour Drive ☎305/361-9985. With its red vinyl stools and faded formica tables, this old-time diner (open at 5.30am for breakfast) is a great place to indulge a craving for sugar-dusted donuts.

Rusty Pelican 3201 Rickenbacker Causeway ☎305/361-3818. The American, Italian, and seafood dishes are only OK, but you'll mainly want to come here for the absolutely breathtaking views of the bay as you dine.

Sundays on the Bay 5420 Crandon Blvd ☎305/361-6777. Marina seafood eatery catering to the boats and beer set. Very casual.

South Miami

Akashi 5830 S Dixie Hwy, South Miami ☎305/665-6261. Generous sushi boats make this restaurant trip worthwhile. The cooked food isn't bad either – try the tender chicken teriyaki or the *ton katsu* (a Japanese fried pork chop).

El Toro Taco 1 S Krome Ave, Homestead ☎305/245-8182. Excellent family-run Mexican restaurant serving generous portions at a great price. A gem in the center of Homestead that makes a good place to stop en route to the Keys.

Robert Is Here 19200 SW 344th St, Florida City ☎305/246-1592. Legendary local fruit stand, serving creamy smoothies blended with whatever fruits are in season. Close to the eastern entrance to the Everglades National Park (see p.169).

Rosita's Restaurante 199 W Palm Drive, Florida City ☎305/246-3114. Delicious Mexican dishes each accompanied by creamy refried beans and tongue-lashing salsa. The decor's nothing fancy, but the real atmosphere comes from the radio blaring Spanish-language news and music.

Sakura 8225 SW 124th St, South Miami ☎305/238-8462. Tiny, good-value sushi bar and restaurant that's always packed. Lunch Mon–Fri; dinner daily.

Sango Jamaican and Chinese Restaurant 9485 SW 160th St, South Miami ☎305/252-0279. Somewhat of an offbeat combination, and the Caribbean food is far better than the Chinese confections, but it's still a worthwhile stop, especially given its low prices. Try the curried goat and jerk chicken. Mainly a takeout joint, but there are a few tables if you want to linger.

Shorty's Bar-B-Q 9200 S Dixie Hwy, South Miami ☎305/670-7732. Sit at a picnic table, tuck a napkin in your shirt, and graze on barbecued ribs, chicken, and corn on the cob – pausing only to gaze at the cowboy memorabilia on the walls.

Drinking

For a city renowned for its nightlife, Miami is not a hard **drinking** town. This is a place of upscale lounges and louche bars where you can linger all evening over a cocktail or two; most restaurants will also have a small bar area, as will the hipper hotels (in fact, the hotel bars here are often the trendiest pit stops). There are also a few old-time dive bars left where anyone determined to drink to oblivion can happily – and more cheaply – do so.

Not surprisingly, **South Beach** has the largest selection of drinking spots, though you'll find a few places worth a detour scattered around the city. Most places where you can drink don't really get going until at least 10pm – before then, there's little atmosphere anywhere – and they keep serving until at least 2am. It's also worth remembering that most bars will be buzzing every night of the week, and it's often best to avoid the hippest places at weekends, when they'll be choked with suburbanites, sniffily nicknamed the Causeway Crowds by South Beach locals.

Bear in mind that the dividing lines between bars, restaurants, and clubs can be blurry, so check the "Nightlife" listings on pp.111–112 for additional suggestions.

Downtown and north

Churchill's Hideaway 5501 NE 2nd Ave, Little Haiti ☎305/757-1807. A British enclave within Little Haiti, with big-screen live soccer matches and UK beers on tap. Look out for the enormous Union Jack emblazoned on the side of the building. See also "Live music," p.113.

Grass 28 NE 40th St, Design District ☎305/573-3355. This restaurant-bar is currently blazing hot, luring hipsters from South Beach with its Polynesian-themed open-air bar, which is specially popular on Monday nights.

Magnum Lounge 709 NE 79th St Causeway, Little Haiti ☎305/757-3368. This out-of-the-way

South Beach hotel bars

The Raleigh Bar *Raleigh Hotel*, 1775 Collins Ave ☎305/534-6300. Grab a cocktail at this classic hotel bar and settle in for an evening of elegant drinking.

Rose Bar *Delano Hotel*, 1685 Collins Ave ☎305/672-2000. This bar spills out onto the hotel's white gauze-draped lobby: a little past its prime, but still fun.

Sky Bar *Shore Club*, 1901 Collins Ave ☎786/276-6771. Sprawling outdoor bar arranged around the hotel pool, with giant overstuffed square seats. Check out the smaller *Sand Bar* attached to it, with fine views of the beach and ocean.

Studio *Shelborne Beach Resort*, 1801 Collins Ave ☎305/695-1770. Hardly hip, but this raucous karaoke bar is a great alternative to the achingly cool places around it – the best time to stop by is early in the morning, when the drunken singers are at their most confident.

Tides Bar *Tides Hotel,* 1220 Ocean Drive ☎305/604-5130. Terrific, tiny bar in the center of the *Tides Hotel*'s noted restaurant. Known for its cocktails (try a *mojito)*, the bar also serves light snacks like conch hush puppies.

restaurant-bar feels more like a bordello or a speakeasy, with its lush red banquettes and hidden entrance. The food's so-so, but the campy sing-alongs around the piano and stiff cocktails make it a fun detour for a drink or two.

Tobacco Road 626 S Miami Ave, downtown ☎305/374-1198. Gloriously gritty dive bar, which snagged the city's first liquor license in 1912 and has been pouring drinks ever since; it's also a venue for lively R&B (see "Live music," p.113).

South Beach

The Abbey Brewing Company 1115 16th St ☎305/538-8110. Small, unpretentious, pub-like microbrewery serving the best beers on SoBe. Acclaimed for their creamy Oatmeal Stout, with $1 off all beers during the happy hour (Mon–Fri 1–7pm). Open daily until 5am.

Club Deuce Bar & Grill 222 14th St ☎305/531-6200. Raucous neighborhood bar open until 5am, with a CD jukebox, pool table, and a clientele that includes cops, transvestites, artists, and models. Its low prices are a major plus.

Nikki Beach 1 Ocean Drive ☎305/538-1231. Beachfront bar where you can grab a drink and wander onto the sand, or even relax in one of its oceanside teepees.

Privé 136 Collins Ave ☎305/674-8630. This hidden lounge, attached to the *Opium Garden* nightclub, is tucked away in a back alley. The door policy is one of the tightest around, especially on Friday nights, so make sure to sashay like a VIP if you want to sip with the A-list behind the silk curtains.

Purdy Lounge 1811 Purdy Ave ☎305/531-4622. A little-known beachside gem, this large neighborhood bar sees a mixed crowd of Beautiful People and locals, all enjoying cheap drinks in a vaguely Arabian setting.

The Room 100 Collins Ave ☎305/531-6061. Miami outpost of the minimalist New York bar, with raw concrete floors, industrial metal tables, and low lighting.

Ted's Hideaway South 124 Second St ☎305/532-9869. Laidback local sports bar with two happy hours (noon–7pm & 1–3am) for $2 bottles of beer. Daily noon–5am.

Wet Willie's 760 Ocean Drive ☎305/532-5650. There's something irresistibly uncool about this fratboy-packed bar: chug one of the frozen drinks, served from washing machine-sized mixers, on its upstairs terrace.

Coral Gables

John Martin's 253 Miracle Mile ☎305/445-3777. Irish pub and restaurant with occasional folk singers and harpists accompanying a good batch of imported brews. See "Live music," p.113.

Titanic Brewing Company 5818 Ponce de León Blvd ☎305/667-2537. The latest addition to the microbrewery craze, serving six types of stouts and ales brewed on the premises. Very popular with students and has live rock music at the weekends.

Coconut Grove

Monty's Bayshore Restaurant 2550 S Bayshore Drive ☎305/858-1431. Drinkers often outnumber the diners at this tiki-style bar, drawn here by the gregarious mood and the views across the bay. The reggae music can be overpoweringly loud though.

Oxygen Lounge 2911 Grand Ave, in the *Streets of*

Mayfair shopping complex, Coconut Grove ⓣ305/476-0202, ⓦwww.oxygenlounge.biz. Enormous lounge where the futuristic decor helps makes up for its unprepossessing mall location– try and snag one of the comfy cubbyholes, where you can lounge on sofas as you sip.

Tavern in the Grove 3416 Main Hwy ⓣ305/447-3884. Down-to-earth locals' haunt with a bouncy jukebox and easy-going mood. The real draw, however, is the rock-bottom drinks prices.

Key Biscayne

Jimbo's inside the park at Virginia Key Beach, Virginia Key ⓣ305/361-7026. Renowned ramshackle bar where you can help yourself to a beer from a wheelbarrow filled with ice and chat with the old-timers here.

Rusty Pelican 3201 Rickenbacker Causeway ⓣ305/361-3818. The views of Miami's skyline from the terrace here are superb: settle back with a drink and enjoy the sunset.

Nightlife

Miami is a city with a flexible concept of what makes a club or a restaurant or a bar: you could end up dancing almost anywhere, since aside from a few megaplexes (listed below) almost every dance floor is attached to a bar or eatery. And while Miami's **nightlife** scene may have sobered up slightly since its debauched and celebrity-studded heyday of the early Nineties, there's still plenty of choice and – especially away from the beach – some intriguing options. Many of the major clubs (like *Space*) are located in **Park West**, a warehouse district just north of downtown and the latest hot spot, though so far there's little to do here other than dance. Earlier in the evening, you're better off sticking to South Beach and one of the better bars for dancing like *Mynt*. Otherwise, if you're feeling adventurous, skip the hard house and techno beats, and check out one of the city's **salsa** or **merengue** (slinky dance music from the Caribbean) clubs, hosted by Spanish-speaking DJs.

Most places open at 10pm, but don't even think of turning up before midnight as they only hit a peak between then and 2am – although some continue until 7am or 8am. However, Miami Beach's liquor laws prohibit drinks from being served there after 5am – past this you'll need to head to the mainland, where there's no such proscription on partying.

Expect a **cover charge** of around $20, and a **minimum age of 21** (it's normal for ID to be checked). In a city as VIP-conscious as Miami, its also pays to remember that the unstylish and the downright scruffy will be turned away at almost every door.

Many of the clubs below present gay nights during the week; for gay- and lesbian-specific clubs, see p.115. As ever, the best places for up-to-date listings are the freesheets *New Times* and *Street Miami*.

Mainland

Cafe Nostalgia 66 SW 6th St, Little Havana ⓣ305/358-1999, ⓦwww.cafenostalgia.com. After a few years bouncing between venues, this legendary Cuban club has finally found a home on the banks of the Miami River: there's a massive dance floor as well as a landscaped garden and rooftop bar.

Club Tipico Dominicano 1344 NW 36th St, Little Havana ⓣ305/634-7819. Top merengue DJs host sessions Fri–Sun; $5 cover.

El Palenque 981 SW 8th St, Little Havana ⓣ305/644-7376. Restaurant-nightclub serving inexpensive Mexican and Salvadorian cuisine during the day, and Latin grooves at night – including occasional *bachata*, the rhythmic music of Santo Domingo. Daily 11am–6pm & 9pm–5am; usually no cover.

Space 34 NE 11th Street, Park West, information ⓣ305/375-0001, VIP reservations ⓣ786/256-5732, ⓦwww.clubspace.com. Formerly known as *Club Space*, this downtown pioneer has moved to an even bigger warehouse space, but retained its rough decor and illicit ambience. Most people migrate here when the other venues shut down. Fri 10pm–Sat 10am, Sat 10pm–Sun 10am.

Miami Beach

Club Tropigala 4441 Collins Ave, in the *Fontainebleau Hilton*, Miami Beach ⓣ305/672-7469. Fabulously camp Vegas-meets-Miami throwback, a flashy, sequinned affair with live acts and an orchestra; the best option, though, is to dress to the nines and be ready to salsa the night away after the showstoppers. Shows Wed–Sat 8.30pm, Sun 8pm.

Crobar 1445 Washington Ave, South Beach ⓣ305/531-8225, ⓦwww.crobarmiami.com. The hardest partying club on the beach, with heavy-hitting house DJs most nights. Expect a fairly large gay crowd, especially on Sundays. Wed–Mon 10pm–5am; cover varies, usually around $15.

Level 1235 Washington Ave, South Beach ⓣ305/532-1525, ⓦwww.levelnightclub.com. Largest club in South Beach featuring progressive house on the cavernous main dance floor, with two smaller ones playing Ibiza sounds and hip-hop. The second floor balcony is the best place to take a break from boogie-ing, but skip the $6 bottles of water. Daily 10pm–5am.

Mynt Ultra Lounge 1921 Collins Ave ⓣ786/276-6132. Lounge/danceclub washed in green light, with an enormous bar and large, black leather sofas. It's *the* place to be on Friday, but expect a tough door policy any night of the week.

Nerve Lounge 247 23rd St, South Beach ⓣ305/695-8697 Legendary nightclub impresario Rudolph, who took over the space (formerly *Lola*), plans to redecorate it entirely every two months. The music is standard house and trance.

Opium Garden 136 Collins Ave ⓣ305/531-5535. Massive open-air space with a vaguely Asian theme and an enormous central dance floor.

Live music

In a city that still goes crazy over the studio-based Latin-pop of local girl Gloria Estefan, you might not expect to find a **live music** scene at all. However, a large number of locales – many of them poky clubs or the back-rooms of restaurants or hotels – host bands throughout the week, though it's often a matter of quantity over quality.

If you're imagining you might be able to catch some good **Cuban music**, forget it. None of the native Cuban musicians can come here, and local talent is rather thin on the ground.

Be they glam, goth, indie, or metal, the city's **rock bands** tend to be pale imitations of the better-known US and European groups that periodically add Miami to their tour schedules. **Jazz** fans fare slightly better, and there's a trustworthy **R&B** scene plus a very minor **folk** one. It's **reggae**, however, that's most worth seeking out; aside from acts flying in from Jamaica, the musicians among Miami's sizeable Jamaican population appear regularly at several small spots.

Other than for megastar performers (see below), to see a band you've heard of, expect to pay $20 upwards; for a local act, admission will be $5–10 or free. Most places open up at 8pm or 9pm, with the main band going onstage around 11pm or midnight.

Miami also gets its share of **big performances**, as the venues listed in the box opposite – none of which has much atmosphere – attract top names in rock, soul, jazz, reggae, and funk; tickets are $20–35 from Ticketmaster (see "Listings," p.121), over the phone, or on the Internet by credit card. Check *Street Miami* and *New Times* for weekly gig listings.

Latin, Caribbean, and reggae

Bayside Hut 3501 Rickenbacker Causeway, Virginia Key ⓣ305/361-0808. Free bayside open-air reggae jams on Fri and Sat at 8pm; don't bother with the mediocre food – just come to drink and dance.

Club Mystique inside the *Hilton*, 5101 Blue Lagoon Drive, Miami Airport ⓣ305/265-3900, ⓦwww.clubmystique.com. Though it's inside a nondescript airport hotel, the music and dancing here are for serious salsa fans. This is one of the best places to catch big-name performers at the weekends, or to take free lessons every Thursday. Thurs, Sun 9pm–4am, Fri 5pm–5am, Sat 9pm–5am.

Big performance venues

American Airlines Arena 601 Biscayne Blvd, downtown ⓣ786/777-1000, ⓦwww.aaarena.com

James L. Knight Center 400 SE 2nd Ave, downtown Miami ⓣ305/372-4633, ⓦwww.jlknightcenter.com

Miami Arena 701 Arena Blvd, downtown Miami ⓣ305/673-3330, ⓦwww.miamiarena.com

Pro Player Stadium 2269 Dan Marino Blvd, 16 miles northwest of downtown Miami – take bus #27. ⓣ305/623-6100, ⓦwww.proplayerstadium.com

Hoy Como Ayer 2212 SW 8th St, Little Havana ⓣ305/541-2631, ⓦwww.hoycomoayer.net. About the only place to hear decent Cuban music in Miami, this dark, smoky joint is plastered with black-and-white photos of Cuban crooners past. It's best known for its Thursday night Latin fusion party *¡Fuácata!* – still hopping (and hip) despite all the media coverage. Wed–Sat 9am–3am; cover varies, usually around $10.

Mango's 900 Ocean Drive, South Beach ⓣ305/673-4422. Shamelessly tacky and gloriously over-the-top, with mainstream, Latin-inflected music spilling out onto the sidewalk. Best on weekdays when the crowd's more local. Cover $5–10.

Tap Tap 819 5th St, South Beach ⓣ305/672-2898. Best known for its excellent restaurant (see "Eating," p.106), interesting gallery, and regular live Haitian music – phone ahead for details.

Rock, jazz, and R&B

Churchill's Hideaway 5501 NE 2nd Ave, Little Haiti ⓣ305/757-1807, ⓦwww.churchillspub.com. Good place to hear local hopeful rock and indie bands. Cover $10–15. See "Drinking," p.109.

Jazid 1432 Washington Ave, South Beach ⓣ305/673-9372, ⓦwww.jazid.net. An alternative to the relentless house heard on South Beach's main clubbing drag, *Jazid* showcases decent jazz – nothing adventurous, but it's easy to spend an evening here. Daily 9pm–3am; $5 cover after 10pm.

John Martin's 253 Miracle Mile, Coral Gables ⓣ305/445-3777. Spacious Irish bar (see "Drinking," p.110) and restaurant with Irish folk music several evenings a week; free.

Luna Star Café 775 NE 125th St, North Miami ⓣ305/892-8522. There's an open-mic night on Saturday, poetry readings during the week, and occasional folk concerts at this largely vegetarian café. Phone before you go as it has erratic opening hours. No cover.

Tobacco Road 626 S Miami Ave, downtown Miami ⓣ305/374-1198. This rather grotty downtown bar is known for its two stages, where nightly live acts perform. Mon–Sat 11.30am–2am, Sun noon–midnight. Cover usually around $7.

The Van Dyke Café 846 Lincoln Road, South Beach ⓣ305/534-3600, ⓦwww.thevandyke.com/jazz. For serious jazz fans only – don't expect to chatter during the performance at this upstairs venue, or you'll get glowers from other patrons. $5 cover.

Classical music, dance, and opera

To find out **what's on**, read the listings in the free *New Times* (published on Thursdays). The Miami-based New World Symphony Orchestra, 541 Lincoln Rd (ⓣ305/673-3331, ⓦwww.nws.org), offers concert experience to some of the finest graduate **classical** musicians in the US, so the quality of performances is usually high. Its season runs from October to May with most performances at the Lincoln Theater; ticket prices start at only $12. For better-known names, look out for top-flight soloists guesting with the Miami Chamber Symphony (ⓣ305/858-3500) at the Gusman Concert Hall at the University of Miami; tickets $12–30.

The city's major professional **dance** company is the Miami City Ballet, 2200 Liberty Ave, South Beach (ⓣ305/929-7010, ⓦwww.miamicityballet.org),

Centers for classical music and performing arts

Colony Theater 1040 Lincoln Rd, Miami Beach ⓣ305/674-1026

Gusman Center for the Performing Arts 174 E Flagler St, downtown Miami ⓣ305/372-0925, ⓦwww.gusmancenter.org

Gusman Concert Hall 1314 Miller Drive, University of Miami ⓣ305/284-6477, ⓦwww.music.miami.edu.

Jackie Gleason Theater of the Performing Arts 1700 Washington Ave, South Beach ⓣ305/673-7300, ⓦwww.gleasontheater.com

Lincoln Theater 541 Lincoln Rd, South Beach ⓣ305/673-3331

Miami-Dade County Auditorium 2901 W Flagler St, near 27th Ave ⓣ305/547-5414

which performs roughly once every two months at the Jackie Gleason Theater; otherwise, you can stop by rehearsals at its studio. An alternative to the classical rigors of this company is the Ballet Flamenco La Rosa, 555 17th St (ⓣ305/899-7729), devoted to exploring new and avant garde styles based on traditional Flamenco and Latin dance; call for schedules and prices.

Opera is the poor relation of classical music and dance in Miami despite the efforts of the Florida Grand Opera (ⓣ305/854-1643, ⓦwww.fgo.org), which brings impressive names to a varied repertoire at the Miami-Dade County Auditorium as well as performing in Fort Lauderdale at the Broward Center for the Performing Arts (see p.195); tickets $21–135.

The **Miami Performing Arts Center**, which will serve as the permanent home of the Florida Grand Opera, Miami City Ballet, New World Symphony, and Florida Philharmonic Orchestra, is set to open north of downtown in fall 2004. Check ⓦwww.pacmiami.com for updates.

Theater

Miami's **theater** scene is lively, if mainstream, though Spanish speakers should make a point of visiting one of the city's **Spanish-language theaters**, whose programs are listed in *El Nuevo Herald* (the Spanish-language version of the *Miami Herald* newspaper): try Bellas Artes, 2173 SW 8th Street (ⓣ305/325-0515) for plays and musicals, and Teatro Trail, 3717 SW 8th Street (ⓣ305/448-0592) for comedies.

Major and alternative theaters

Actors Playhouse at Miracle Theater 280 Miracle Mile, Coral Gables ⓣ305/444-9293, ⓦwww.actorsplayhouse.org. There are two stages here – the 300-seat Balcony Theater and the main stage, which is twice the size. Often part of the Off-Broadway tryout circuit for major new shows. $32–40.

Coconut Grove Playhouse 3500 Main Hwy, Coconut Grove ⓣ305/442-2662, ⓦwww.cgplayhouse.com. Comfortable and well-established mainstream theater that bucks up its schedule with many interesting experimental efforts; $20–45.

Gusman Center 174 E Flagler Street ⓣ305/372-0925. Classical and contemporary plays, music, and dance are staged here from October to June. The only way to check out the elaborate interior is by taking in a show. $15–30.

New Theater 4120 Laguna St, Coral Gables ⓣ305/443-5909, ⓦwww.new-theatre.com. Sitting neatly between mainstream and alternative, this intimate, 100-seat space often produces the best theater in the city. $10–20.

Film

The choice of movies in Miami is vibrant and wide-ranging. For one, there's the **Miami Film Festival** (T 305/377-FILM, W www.miamifilmfestival.com), ten days and nights of new films from far and wide in February held at various locations across the city. There's also a strong **Gay & Lesbian Film Festival** in April (see p.116). In fact, at one point in American history, Florida might have rivaled Hollywood as the film capital of the world (see the *Colonnade Hotel* in Coral Gables, p.92, and "Contexts," p.483). There are plenty of multi-screen **cinemas** inside shopping malls showing first-run American features: check the "Weekend" section of the Friday *Miami Herald* for complete listings, or call the Movie Hotline (T 305/888-FILM). The main theater locations are the Regal South Beach 18, 1100 Lincoln Rd, South Beach (T 305/673-6766); the eight-screen AMC inside CocoWalk, 3015 Grand Ave, Coconut Grove (T 305/466-0450); and the massive AMC Sunset Place 24, in the Sunset Place mall, 5701 Sunset Drive, South Miami (T 305/466-0450). Expect to pay $8–10 per ticket.

For **arthouse** films try the Absinthe House Cinematique, 235 Alcazar Ave, Coral Gables (T 305/446-7144), and the Bill Cosford Cinema on the University of Miami campus, Coral Gables (T 305/284-4861), for indie and academic movies. You'll find quirky mainstream fare at the Mercury Theatre, 5580 NE 4th Court, near the Design District (T 305/759-8809).

Gay and lesbian Miami

Miami has long been viewed as a prime destination by **gay and lesbian** tourists – a welcoming place with an "anything goes" Caribbean vibe that only grew stronger during South Beach's glory days of the early Nineties. Now, though, the pace has slowed somewhat as mainstream tourism has taken over the beach and pushed gay and lesbian locals further up the coast to Fort Lauderdale (see p.188). Even as the population shifts, there's little evidence of discrimination or discomfort with gay and lesbian tourists anywhere in the city, though it's only in South Beach that same-sex couples are likely to stroll hand-in-hand. The one time of year when gay culture utterly subsumes straight culture is during the White Party (contact Care Resource, T 305/667-9296 or 574-5411) at Thanksgiving (see "Miami festivals" box on pp.116–117).

Resources

Miami Herald W www.miami.com. Unusual among newspapers in having a beat reporter assigned to cover gay and lesbian issues.

Out in Miami W www.outinmiami.com. Smart, informative web-only resource– one of the best available.

Outlook T 954/567-1306, W www.outlook.com. Covers the whole of the state, with a heavy focus on the party scene; better for men's information than for women's.

South Beach Business Guild T 305/534-3336 or 1-888/893-5595. This gay chamber of commerce can advise on accommodation, amenities, and all aspects of local gay life.

TWN The Weekly News T 305/757-6333, W www.twnonline.org. Weekly gay and lesbian freesheet available everywhere.

Wire T 305/588-0000, W www.thewireonline.com. South Beach–centric weekly freesheet that's good for club and other nightlife listings.

Bars, clubs, and discos

Cactus 2041 Biscayne Blvd T 305/438-0662, W www.thecactus.com. Happy hours aplenty (daily 4–9pm) and daily tropical-drinks specials at its tiki bar make this one of the liveliest gay bars in the area.

Miami festivals

The precise dates of the festivals listed below vary from year to year; check the details at any tourist information office or Chamber of Commerce, or online at ⓦwww.festivalsmiami.com.

January

1 *Orange Bowl Parade*: The best known of the New Year's bashes all over the city, with floats, marching bands, and the crowning of the Orange Bowl Queen at the Orange Bowl (ⓣ305/371-4600).

Mid *Art Deco Weekend*: Talks and free events focusing on South Beach architecture. On Ocean Drive (ⓣ305/672-2014, ⓦwww.mdpl.org).

Taste of the Grove: Pig out on food and free music in Coconut Grove's Peacock Park (ⓣ305/444-7270, ⓦwww.coconutgrove.com).

Late *Key Biscayne Art Festival*: Enjoy music, arts and crafts, and fresh seafood along Crandon Boulevard (ⓣ305/361-0049, ⓦwww.key-biscayne.com).

February

Early *Homestead Championship Rodeo*: Professional rodeo cowboys compete in steer-wrestling, bull-riding, calf-roping, and bareback riding (ⓣ305/247-3515, ⓦwww.homesteadrodeo.com).

Miami Film Festival: Arthouse and mainstream films from the US and overseas are shown at the Colony and Regal theaters on South Beach and the Gusman Center in downtown Miami (ⓣ305/377-3456, ⓦwww.miamifilmfestival.com).

Mid *Coconut Grove Arts Festival*: Hundreds of (mostly) talented unknowns display their works in Coconut Grove's Peacock Park and on nearby streets (ⓣ305/447-0401, ⓦwww.coconutgroveartsfest.com).

March

Early *Carnival Miami*: A nine-day celebration of Latin culture, with Hispanic-themed events across the city culminating in a parade at the Orange Bowl on the first Saturday of the month (ⓣ305/644-8888, ⓦwww.carnaval-miami.org).

Mid *Lipton Open*: Men and women compete in the world's largest tennis tournament held at the Crandon Park Tennis Center in Key Biscayne (ⓣ305/446-2200 for information; ⓣ305/442-3367 for tickets).

Late *Winter Music Conference*: This convention brings together music promoters, producers and managers, as well as well-known DJs who perform at local clubs. (ⓣ954/563-4444. ⓦwww.wmcon.com).

April

Early *Miami Gay and Lesbian Film Festival*: Amateur and professional submissions are shown at the Colony Theater in South Beach (ⓣ305/534-9924, ⓦwww.miami-gayandlesbianfilm.com).

May

Early *The Great Sunrise Balloon Race & Festival*: held at Kendall-Tamiami airport (ⓣ305/275-3317, ⓦwww.sunrisegroup.org).

Club Boi 726 NW 79th St, Little Haiti ⓣ305/836-8995. A refreshing change from the circuit boy scene on South Beach, this largely black club plays hip-hop, house, and old school R&B every Friday and Saturday night.

Laundry Bar 721 N Lincoln Lane ⓣ305/531-7700. Relaxed lesbian/gay/straight bar with low lighting and an un-cruisey scene. Hosts DJ's at the weekends and yes, you can do your laundry here. Open daily 10am–5am.

Miami's Concorde Supper Club 2301 SW 32nd Ave, Coral Gables ⓣ305/441-6974. One of the few lesbian-dominated places in town, this club is raucous fun and has a roomy dance floor for its varied DJ selections.

June

Early *Goombay Festival*: a spirited bash in honor of Bahamian culture, in and around Coconut Grove's Peacock Park (Ⓣ305/372-9966).

July

4 *America's Birthday Bash*: music, fireworks, and a laser-light show celebrate the occasion at Bayfront Park in downtown Miami (Ⓣ305/358-7550).
Tropical Agricultural Fiesta: enjoy fresh mangoes along with exotic fruits and ethnic foods at the Fruit and Spice Park (Ⓣ305/278-4185, Ⓦwww.tropicalag.org).

August

Early *Miami Reggae Festival*: celebration on the first Sunday of the month of Jamaican Independence Day with dozens of top Jamaican bands playing around the city (Ⓣ305/891-2944).

September

Mid *Festival Miami*: three weeks of performing and visual arts events organized by the University of Miami, mostly taking place in Coral Gables (Ⓣ305/284-4940, Ⓦwww.music.miami.edu).

October

1–31 *Hispanic Heritage Festival*: lasts all month and features innumerable events linked to Latin American history and culture (Ⓣ305/541-5023).
Mid *Columbus Day Regatta*: Florida's largest watersports event is a race commemorating Columbus's historic voyage. At Key Biscayne (Ⓣ305/858-3320).

November

Mid *Miami Book Fair International*: a wealth of volumes from across the world spread across the campus of Miami-Dade Community College in downtown Miami (Ⓣ305/237-3258, Ⓦwww.miamibookfair.com).
Harvest Festival: a celebration of southern Florida's agricultural traditions, including homemade crafts, music, and pioneer re-enactments at the Fair/Expo Center on Coral Way (Ⓣ305/375-1492, Ⓦwww.historical-museum.org).
Late *The White Party*: Huge HIV/AID fundraiser held over the Thanksgiving weekend, with parties held across the city culminating in the outrageous White Party costumed ball at Villa Vizcaya (Ⓦwww.whiteparty.net).

December

Late *Indian Arts Festival*: Native American artisans from all over the country gather at the Miccosukee Village – 27 miles west of Miami – to display their work (Ⓣ305/223-8380).
30 *King Mango Strut*: a very alternative New Year's Eve celebration, with part-time cross-dressers and clowns parading through Coconut Grove (Ⓣ305/401-1171).

Pump 841 Washington Ave, South Beach Ⓣ305/538-7867. A cruisey after-hours club, open 3am–9am, with a soundtrack heavy on Hi-NRG. $15 cover.

Score 727 Lincoln Rd, South Beach Ⓣ305/535-1111. This video bar on the Lincoln Road main drag attracts a dressed-up, mostly male crowd. There's a popular tea dance every Sunday. No cover.

Twist 1057 Washington Ave Ⓣ305/538-9478, Ⓦwww.twistsobe.com. Longest-running gay bar on SoBe and a bit of an institution. Now featuring six different environments with comfy lounges, an outdoor terrace and two packed techno dance-floors. Go-go boys perform every Friday, Saturday, and Sunday in the garden bar. No cover and daily two-for-one happy hour 1–9pm.

Shopping

Shopping for the sake of it isn't the big deal in Miami that it is in some American cities, though there's plenty of opportunity for eager consumers to exercise their credit cards. The big disappointment in Miami's retail landscape is the dearth of bookstores – Miami Beach, for instance, has only one small outlet. There are, however, plenty of options for music buffs, especially anyone interested in club or Cuban culture, and while Miami has few home-grown designers, South Beach does have some appealing clothes shops. Most stores in the city stay open late, so you can browse well into the evening, often until 9 or 10pm, especially in South Beach.

The most eclectic collection of shops is in South Beach, along Collins and Washington avenues, and Lincoln Road. Away from the beach, you're better off sticking to the **malls** – sterile, perhaps, but they do have the widest selection. Coral Gables is working to spruce up the offerings along its Miracle Mile and, for the most part, succeeding, although there aren't many shops worth seeking out yet, aside from a huge outpost of Barnes & Noble.

Unless you're existing on a shoestring budget – or are preparing a picnic – you won't need to shop for **food and drink** at all, although supermarkets are plentiful and usually open until 10pm: alcohol is sold there, too, as well as in the many **liquor stores**.

Books

Books & Books 296 Aragon Ave, Coral Gables (☎305/442-4408) and a small branch at 933 Lincoln Rd, South Beach (☎305/532-3222). Excellent stock of general titles but especially strong on Floridian art and design, travel, and new fiction; also has author signings and talks. Call ☎305/444-9044 for the latest events. Daily 10am–11pm.

Downtown Book Center 247 SE 1st St, downtown Miami ☎305/377-9939. Tiny downtown bookstore, strong on popular fiction, thrillers, and romances. Also stocks European newspapers and magazines. Mon–Fri 9am–5.30pm, Sat 9am–2pm.

Fifteenth Street Books 296 Aragon Ave, Coral Gables ☎305/442-2344. Run by the original founder of Books & Books, this highly browsable secondhand store is strong on art books and old hardcovers in prime condition.

Kafka's Kafe 1464 Washington Ave, South Beach ☎305/673-9669. Rather ratty selection of used books – only good for budget-priced beach reading.

Murder on Miami Beach 16850 Collins Ave, Sunny Isles Beach ☎305/956-7770. Not surprisingly, a store specializing in murder and mystery books – a wide selection, whether you're looking for Hammett or Hiaasen.

Clothes and thrift stores

Banana Republic 1100 Lincoln Rd, South Beach ☎305/534-4706. There are branches of this chain everywhere, but whether you like the clothes or not, be sure to stop in and see the sensitive conversion of an old bank here, where the vaults are now changing rooms.

Base 939 Lincoln Rd, South Beach ☎305/531-4982. Funky urban clothes for men and women, designed by choreographer-turned-fashion designer Stephen Giles, plus a tiny collection of homewares.

Douglas Gardens Thrift Store 5713 NW 27th St, Liberty City ☎305/638-1900. One of several vast warehouses of secondhand clothes clustered together, where you'll find outrageous bargains, but be sure to drive as it's a sketchy area.

Miami Twice 6562 SW 40th St, Coral Gables ☎305/666-0127. Department store–sized vintage clothing store that's good for mid-twentieth century furniture and jewelry.

Recycled Blues 1507 Washington Ave, South Beach ☎305/538-0656. Largest selection of vintagewear (especially denim) on South Beach: a great selection, but not cheap.

Department stores and malls

Aventura Mall 19501 Biscayne Blvd, Aventura ☎305/935-1110. One of the largest enclosed malls in the state, boasting virtually every major department store: Macys, Sears, J C Penney. Pick up a map on entry or you'll never find your way out.

Bal Harbour Shops 9700 Collins Ave, Miami Beach ☎305/866-0311, Ⓦwww.balharbourshops.com. Packed with designer names like Gucci and Prada, this upscale mall is always crowded, but great fun to browse in.

Bayside Marketplace anchored at 400 Biscayne Blvd, downtown Miami ⓣ305/577-3344, ⓦwww.baysidemarketplace.com. Squarely aimed at tourists, but with a good blend of diverse stores – selling everything from Art Deco ashtrays to bubblegum – beside the bay, with some excellent food stands.
Burdines 22 E Flagler St, downtown Miami ⓣ305/577-2312, ⓦwww.burdines.com. "Florida's department store" offers a selection of clothes tailored to the heat and humidity of the climate – expect plenty of pastel colors and lightweight wools. The landmark building is one of downtown's first skyscrapers.
CocoWalk 3015 Grand Ave, Coconut Grove ⓣ305/444-0777, ⓦwww.cocowalk.com. In the heart of Coconut Grove, this open-air complex has a relatively small range of stores, some good places to eat, and a decent sixteen-screen multiplex cinema.
The Falls US-1 and SW 136th St, South Miami ⓣ305/255-4570. Sit inside a gazebo and contemplate the waterfalls and the rainforest that prettify suburban Miami's classiest set of shops.
Prime Outlets 250 E Palm Drive, Florida City ⓣ305/248-4727. Located where the Florida Turnpike meets US-1 and conveniently located for people traveling to the Keys or Everglades. Dedicated shoppers will find huge savings on name brands.
Streets of Mayfair 2911 Grand Ave, Coconut Grove ⓣ305/448-1700, ⓦwww.streetofmayfair.com. Rather forlorn mall that's usually empty – the one draw is a huge branch of the Borders bookstore.
Village of Merrick Park Ponce de León and Highway 1, Coral Gables ⓣ305/529-0200, ⓦwww.villageofmerrickpark.com. Recent upscale rival to long-established Bal Harbour Shops: amid the open-air walkways, you'll find a branch of the sumptuous Elemis Spa, as well as fashions from Burberry, Diane von Furstenberg, and Jimmy Choo.

Music

Grooveman Music 1543 Washington Ave, South Beach ⓣ305/535-6257. A DJ's dream, stocking an ample selection of house and trance.
Les Cousins 7858 NE 2nd Ave, Little Haiti ⓣ305/754-8452. Smallish store specializing in Caribbean music, terrific if you're looking for authentic sounds.
Lily's Records 1260 SW 8th St, Little Havana ⓣ305/856-0536. Unsurpassed stock of salsa, merengue, and other Latin sounds.
Spec's Music 501 Collins Ave, South Beach ⓣ305/534-3667. Mainstream record store with an adequate selection of well-known music of all genres. The place to pick up another CD to listen to on the beach – just don't go looking for anything too obscure.

Specialty goods

Botanica Esperanza 901 SW 27th Ave at SW 9th St, Little Havana ⓣ305/642-2488. Santería supplies, like religious candles, bead necklaces, animal skins, and Mexican good-luck charms.
La Casa de las Guyaberas 5840 SW 8th St, Little Havana ⓣ305/266-9683. Pick up one of the billowy Cuban shirts known as *guyaberas* here; the cheapest cost around $20, while a custom-made design starts at $200.
El Credito Cigar Factory 1106 SW 8th St, Little Havana ⓣ305/858-4162. One of the best-known smokeshops in the city, with rows of *tabaqueros* (cigar rollers) to be seen working here.

Listings

Airlines Air Canada ⓣ1-888/247-2262, ⓦwww.aircanada.ca; American Airlines ⓣ1-800/433-7300, ⓦwww.aa.com; British Airways ⓣ1-800/247-9297, ⓦwww.british-airways.com; Continental ⓣ1-800/523-3273, ⓦwww.continental.com; Delta ⓣ1-800/221-1212, ⓦwww.delta.com; Northwest Airlines/KLM ⓣ1-800/225-2525, ⓦwww.nwa.com; United ⓣ1-800/241-6522, ⓦwww.ual.com; US Airways ⓣ1-800/428-4322, ⓦwww.usair.com; Virgin Atlantic ⓣ1-800/862-8621, ⓦwww.virgin-atlantic.com.
Airport Miami International, six miles west of downtown Miami (ⓣ305/876-7000, ⓦwww.miamiairport.com). Take local bus #7 from downtown Miami (around 30–45min) or local bus #J from Miami Beach (around 40–50min). There are also privately run SuperShuttle minivans (ⓣ305/871-2000). More details on p.61
American Express Main hotline ⓣ1-800/325-1218. Offices around the city: in downtown Miami, 100 N Biscayne Blvd ⓣ305/358-7350; in Coral Gables, 32 Miracle Mile ⓣ305/446-3381; in Miami Beach, at Bal Harbour Shops, 9700 Collins Ave ⓣ305/865-5959.
Amtrak 8303 NW 37th Ave ⓣ1-800/USA-RAIL, ⓦwww.amtrak.com.

Banks See "Money exchange," below.

Bike rental See p.65.

Boat rental Skim over Biscayne Bay in a motor boat. Such vessels can be rented for 2–8hr – rates start at $89 for two hours – from Beach Boat Rentals, 2400 Collins Ave, Miami Beach (☎305/534-4307).

Coastguard ☎305/535-4313.

Consulates Canada, 200 S Biscayne Blvd, Suite 1600, downtown Miami ☎305/579-1600; Denmark, PH 1D, 2655 Le Jeune Rd, Coral Gables ☎305/446-0020; France, 1 Biscayne Tower, Suite 1710, downtown Miami ☎305/372-9799; Germany, Suite 2200, 100 N Biscayne Blvd, downtown Miami ☎305/358-0290; Netherlands, 800 Brickell Ave, Suite 918, downtown Miami ☎305/789-6646; UK, 1001 Brickell Bay Drive, Suite 2800 918, downtown Miami ☎305/374-1522.

Dentists To be referred to a dentist: ☎305/667-3647 or 1-800/336-8478.

Doctor To find a physician: ☎305/324-8717.

Emergencies Dial ☎911 and ask for relevant emergency service.

Greyhound ☎1-800/231-2222, ⓦwww.greyhound.com.

Helplines Crisis Counseling Hotline, ☎305/538-4357.

Hospitals with emergency rooms. In Miami: Jackson Memorial Medical Center, 1611 NW 12th Ave ☎305/585-1111; Mercy Hospital, 3663 S Miami Ave ☎305/854-4400. In Miami Beach: Mt Sinai Medical Center, 4300 Alton Rd ☎305/674-2121; South Shore Hospital, 630 Alton Rd ☎305/672-2100.

Internet cafés Available all over Miami and South Beach in particular. Prices are generally $7–9 per hour, or $1 for five minutes. The best places to surf are at the public library (see below), which offers 45 minutes free, or the no-charge access at the Museum of Science (see p.98). Otherwise try these South Beach locations: Kafka's Kafe, 1464 Washington Ave (daily 8.30am–midnight; ☎305/673-9669), or Cybr Caffe, 1574 Washington Ave (Mon–Fri 10am–12.30am, Sat & Sun 11am–12.30am; ☎305/534-0057).

Laundromats Many hotels will have some kind of laundry service. You can also try the Wash Club of South Beach, 510 Washington Ave (6am–midnight; ☎305/534-4298) or Clean Machine, 226 12th St (open 24hr; ☎305/534-9429). If you fancy a drink while you wash, try the *Laundry Bar* (see "Gay and lesbian Miami," p.116).

Library The biggest is Miami-Dade County Public Library, 101 W Flagler St (Mon–Sat 9am–6pm, Thurs until 9pm; Oct–May also Sun 1–5pm; ☎305/375-2665, ⓦwww.mdpls.org) – see p.73.

Lost and found For items lost on Metro-Dade Transit, call ☎305/375-3366 (Mon–Fri 8.30am–4.30pm). Otherwise contact the police (☎305/673-7960).

Money exchange Using your bank/credit card at an ATM is the easiest and safest way. Alternatively, bring US dollar travelers' checks or cash, but if you need to change money, facilities are available at the airport, at American Express offices, and the following locations in downtown Miami: Bank of America, 100 SE 2nd St (☎1-800/299-2265) and 1 SE 3rd Ave (☎305/350-6350); SunTrust Bank, 777 Brickell Ave (☎305/591-6000).

Parking The fine for an expired meter is $18, for parking in a residential area $23 – both increasing to $45 if not paid within thirty days. You'll find the addresses where you can pay on the back of the ticket (☎305/673-PARK).

Pharmacies Usually open from 8am or 9am until 9pm or midnight. Pharmacies open 24 hours include Eckerd, 200 Lincoln Rd, South Beach (☎305/673-9502) and Walgreens, 5731 Bird Rd, Coral Gables (☎305/666-0757).

Police Nonemergency: ☎305/673-7900; emergency: ☎911. If you are robbed anywhere on Miami Beach, report it at the station at 1100 Washington Ave and the report (for insurance purposes) can usually be collected within 3 to 5 days (records office Tues–Fri 8am–3pm; ☎305/673-7100).

Post offices In Miami Beach, 1300 Washington Ave (☎305/538-2708); in downtown Miami, 500 NW 2nd Ave (☎305/373-7562); in Coral Gables, 251 Valencia Ave (☎305/443-2532); in Coconut Grove, 3191 Grand Ave (☎305/529-6700); in Homestead, 739 Washington Ave (☎305/247-1556). All open Mon–Fri 8.30am–5pm, Sat 8.30am–12.30pm, or longer hours.

Rape hotline ☎305/585-7273.

Road conditions ☎305/470-5277.

Rollerblading Hugely popular in Miami, especially in South Beach. Fritz Skate & Bikes, at 730 Lincoln Rd (Daily 10am–10pm; ☎305/532-1954), both sells and rents out rollerblades and safety gear. Rental costs around $7.50 per hour, $22 per day; bike rentals are also available at the same rates.

Sports The Miami Dolphins (☎305/573-8326, ⓦwww.miamidolphins.com) and the Florida Marlins (☎305/623-6100, ⓦwww.flamarlins.com) play at Pro Player Stadium, 2269 Dan Marino Blvd (named for the retired quarterback), sixteen miles northwest of downtown Miami. Tickets are available from TicketMaster (see below) or the box office at Gate G (Mon–Fri 8.30am–5.30pm, Sat 10am–4pm) – seats are $27–47 for football and

$4–55 for baseball. The football season lasts August through December, and the baseball season April through September. The Miami Heat basketball team plays NBA games in downtown Miami at the American Airline Arena, 601 Biscayne Blvd (ⓣ786/777-4328 for tickets, ⓦwww.heat.com); tickets $8–200 from TicketMaster or the box office (Mon–Fri 10am–5pm). The basketball season lasts November through April. The University of Miami's famed football, basketball, and baseball teams are all called the Miami Hurricanes: game and ticket (usually $5–99) info Mon–Fri 8am–6pm on ⓣ305/284-2263 or ⓦwww.hurricanesports.com. The football team plays at the Orange Bowl, 1400 NW 4th St, Little Havana.

TicketMaster Tickets for arts and sports events, payable by credit card: ⓣ305/358-5885, ⓦwww.ticketmaster.com.

Weather information ⓣ305/229-4522.

Western Union Offices all over the city; call ⓣ1-800/325-6000 to find the nearest branch.

Women's Resources Miami Women's Healthcenter, at North Shore Medical Center, 1100 NW 95th St (ⓣ305/835-6165), offers education information, support and discussion groups, physician referrals, mammograms, seminars, and workshops. Planned Parenthood of Greater Miami (ⓦwww.ppgm.org), which has branches at 681 NE 125th St, North Miami (ⓣ305/895-7756) and 1699 SW 27th Ave (ⓣ305/285-5535), provides economical health care for both men and women, including birth control supplies, pregnancy testing, treatment of sexually transmitted diseases, and counseling. 24hr info-line ⓣ305/285-2061.

Travel details

Trains (Amtrak)

Miami to: New York (3 daily; 26hr 25min–28hr 40min); Ocala (1 daily; 7hr 39min); Sebring (3 daily; 3hr 15min); Orlando (2 daily; 5hr 15min); St Petersburg (1 daily; leaves 10.35am for Orlando, from where buses leave for St Petersburg at 4.30pm; total journey time 8hr 45min); Tampa (1 daily at 5pm; 5hr 15min); Washington DC (3 daily; 22hr 7min–24hr 34min); Winter Haven (3 daily; 4hr).

Tri-Rail (5–15 daily)

Miami to: Boca Raton (1hr); Delray Beach (1hr 7min); Fort Lauderdale (31min); Hollywood (16min); West Palm Beach (1hr 34min).

Buses

Miami to: Daytona Beach (3 daily; 7hr 5min–7hr 55min); Fort Lauderdale (hourly; 55min); Fort Myers (4 daily; 4hr–4hr 45min); Fort Pierce (8–9 daily; 3hr–3hr 30min); Jacksonville (8 daily; 7hr 30min–8hr); Key West (3–4 daily; 4hr 40min); Orlando (7 daily; 6hr); Sarasota (4 daily; 6hr 30min–7hr); St. Petersburg (7 daily; 7–8hr); Tampa (5 daily; 7–9hr); West Palm Beach (7–8 daily; 2hr).

2

The Florida Keys

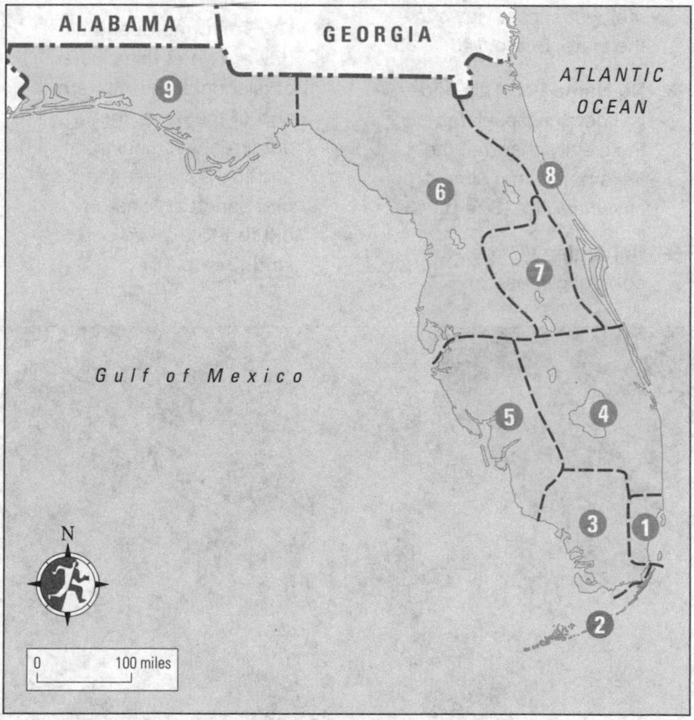

CHAPTER 2

Highlights

* **Indian Key** The ruins of the settlement that once thrived here are spooky and evocative, overrun by untamed greenery. See p.136

* **Seven Mile Bridge** Just south of Marathon, this bridge affords some of the best sunset views in the state. See p.140

* **No Name Pub** This oddball gem encapsulates the cranky charm of the Keys better than almost anywhere else. See p.143

* **Bahamian Village** A colorful glimpse of Caribbean culture amid the hubbub of Key West. See p.157

* **Key lime pie and conch fritters** Two fine local specialties worth seeking out; Key West's restaurants are your best bet. See p.160–161

* **Dry Tortugas** Spend a day or two at this cluster of islands at the western end of the Keys: the coral reef is stunning, and there's a teeming bird sanctuary and an old fort to explore on land. See p.164

△ Key Largo

2

The Florida Keys

Trailing from Florida's southern tip, the **FLORIDA KEYS** are a string of over ten thousand small islands of which fewer than fifty are inhabited, the hundred-mile long arc petering out to within ninety miles of Cuba. The Keys (so named from the Spanish word "cayo," meaning small islet or coral bank) are most known for the **Florida Reef**, a great band of living coral just a few miles offshore whose range of color and dazzling array of ocean life – including dolphins and loggerhead turtles – are exceptional sights. Throughout the Keys, and especially for the first sixty-odd miles, fishing, snorkeling, and diving dominate – and are ruthlessly hawked at every opportunity – and if you're not planning to indulge in watersports, you'll be hard-pressed to find much else to fill your time. Here and there, houses built around the turn of the nineteenth century by Bahamian settlers and seedy waterside bars run by refugees from points north hint at the islands' history. And while there are some stunning natural areas and worthwhile ecology tours, the whole stretch is primarily a build-up to **Key West**, the real pearl on this island strand.

Heading down the chain from the mainland, the first place to visit the reef is the **John Pennekamp State Park**, one of the few interesting features of **Key Largo** on the **Upper Keys**. Like **Islamorada**, further south, Key Largo is rapidly being populated by suburban Miamians, drawn by the sailing and fishing but unable to survive without shopping malls. Islamorada is the best base for fishing, and also has some natural and historical points of note – as does the next major settlement, **Marathon**, which is at the center of the **Middle Keys** and thus makes a useful short-term base. Thirty miles on, the **Lower Keys** get fewer visitors and less publicity than their neighbors, but in many ways they're the most unusual and appealing of the chain. Covered with dense forests, they are home to a tiny and endangered species of Key deer as well as mud turtle, mangrove terrapin, and mole slink, and, at **Looe Key**, offer a tremendous departure point for trips to the Florida Reef. **Key West**, the final dot of the North American continent before a thousand miles of ocean, is the end of the road in every sense: shot through with an intoxicating aura of abandonment, but it's also a small but immensely vibrant place. The only part of the Keys with a real sense of history, Key West was once – unbelievably – the richest town in the US and the largest settlement in Florida. There are old homes and museums to explore and plenty of bars in which to while away the hours. Key West also has a couple of small **beaches**, which are rarely found elsewhere in the island chain owing to the reef. The meager sand and surf, though, are easily made up for by the Keys' spectacular **sunsets**: as the nineteenth-century ornithologist John James Audubon once rhapsodized: "a blaze of refulgent glory streams through the portals of the west, and the masses of vapor assume the semblance of mountains of molten gold."

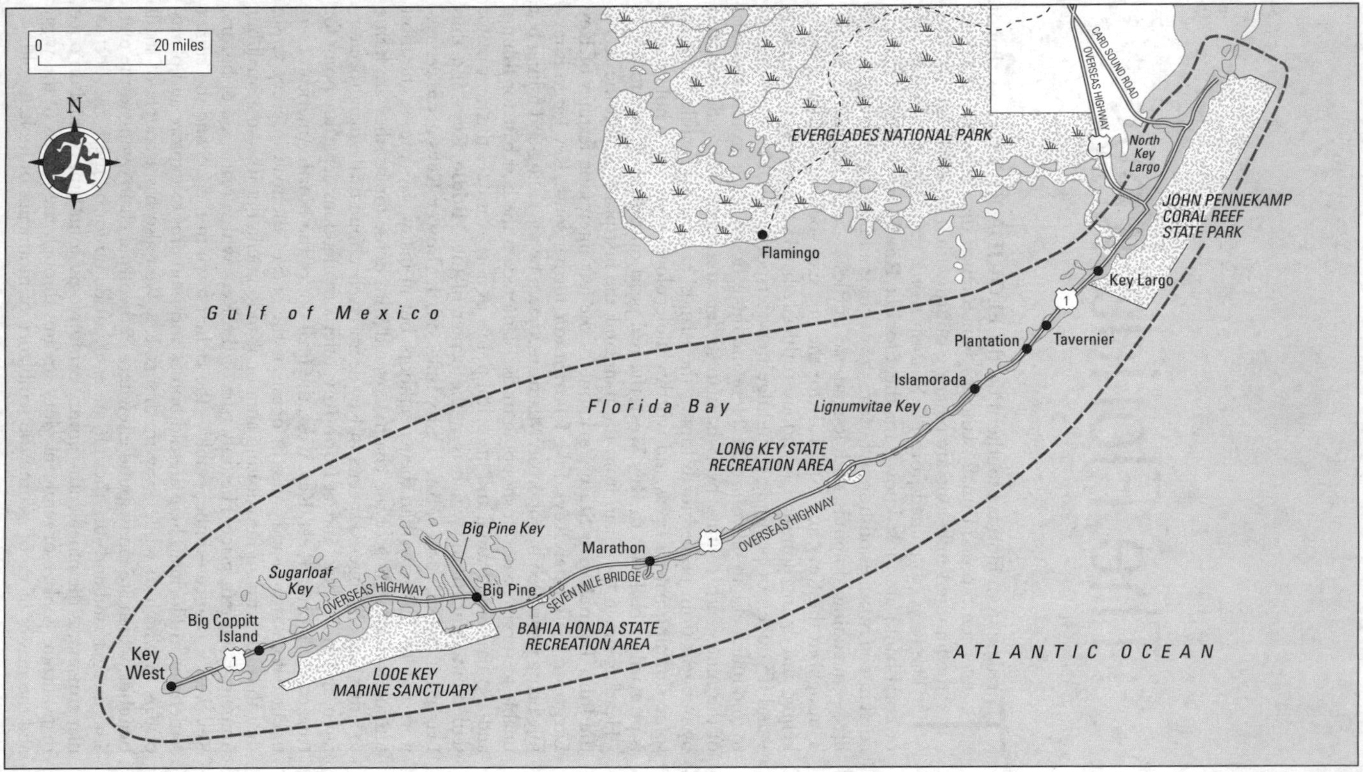
0
20 miles
N
Miami
CARD SOUND ROAD
OVERSEAS HIGHWAY
EVERGLADES NATIONAL PARK
North Key Largo
JOHN PENNEKAMP CORAL REEF STATE PARK
Flamingo
Key Largo
Gulf of Mexico
Plantation
Tavernier
Islamorada
Florida Bay
Lignumvitae Key
LONG KEY STATE RECREATION AREA
OVERSEAS HIGHWAY
Big Pine Key
Marathon
Sugarloaf Key
OVERSEAS HIGHWAY
Big Pine
SEVEN MILE BRIDGE
Big Coppitt Island
BAHIA HONDA STATE RECREATION AREA
ATLANTIC OCEAN
Key West
LOOE KEY MARINE SANCTUARY

Practicalities

Traveling through the Keys could hardly be easier as there's just one route all the way through to Key West: the **Overseas Highway (US-1)**. This is punctuated by **mile markers (MM)** – posts on which mileage is marked, starting with MM127, just south of Homestead (see p.102), and finishing with MM0, in Key West at the junction of Fleming and Whitehead streets. Almost all places of business use mile markers as an address, and throughout this chapter they are tagged with an "MM" (for example, "the *Holiday Inn*, at MM100"). The only islands large enough to require street addresses are Key Largo and Big Pine Key. We've also followed the local convention of indicating whether buildings sit north (Bayside) or south (Oceanside) of the freeway.

Traveling from Miami presents two options. Either take the I-95 south to US-1 or, for a shorter route, take the Florida's Turnpike Extension toll route south and pick up US-1 at Florida City. Most motels and restaurants are strung along the highway, often using the mile markers as addresses. Public transportation consists of three daily Greyhound **buses** between Miami and Key West (see "Travel details" at the end of the chapter) and a skeletal local bus service in Key West.

Accommodation is abundant but more expensive than on the mainland. During high season, November to April, budget for *at least* $50–85 a night, and $35–55 the rest of the year. **Camping** is considerably less expensive and is well catered for throughout the Keys.

Visitor centers in the Upper, Middle, and Lower keys, and also Key West, are listed at the beginning of the relevant section. Be aware that these official visitors offices will be signposted by a blue sign with white writing at the roadside – all others that you'll pass, however smart-looking, are privately run concerns that are not guaranteed to provide the best impartial advice.

Note that throughout this chapter only the most basic **diving information** is given. Always take local advice before venturing into the water. (See "The backcountry" on p.42 for information on outdoor safety).

The Upper Keys

The northernmost portion of the Florida Keys, the **UPPER KEYS** are roughly made up of three major communities – Key Largo, Tavernier, and Islamorada – between which lies a scattering of small islands, most of which

Upper Keys information

If you don't stop at the well-stocked Tropical Everglades Visitor Information Center near Homestead (see "Miami," p.101), pull up at the highly informative **Key Largo Chamber of Commerce**, MM106-Bayside (daily 9am–6pm; ⓣ305/451-1414 or 1-800/822-1088). The Colonial-style center has piles of brochures, discount vouchers, and hotel booking information. Otherwise, try the small **Islamorada Visitors Center**, MM82.5-Bayside (Mon–Fri 9am–5pm, Sat 9am–4pm, Sun 9am–3pm), housed in a natty red caboose on the roadside and staffed by friendly locals.

Swimming with dolphins

Long before the Sixties TV show *Flipper* brought about a surge in their popularity, **dolphins** – marine mammals smaller than whales and differentiated from porpoises by their beak-like snout – were the subject of centuries of speculation and mythology. According to the wildest theories, dolphins once lived on land but became so disenchanted by the course of civilization during ancient times that they took to the sea, vowing to bide their time until humankind was ready to receive their wisdom. Whatever the truth, there's no disputing that dolphins are extremely intelligent, with brains similar in size to those of humans. They communicate in a **language** of clicks and whistles, and use a sonar technique called echolocation to detect food in dark waters and, perhaps, to create "sound pictures" for one another.

The world's dolphin population has been reduced by several factors, including the nets of tuna fishermen, but they are a common sight around the Florida Keys and are the star attraction of the state's many marine parks – though watching them perform somersaults in response to human commands gives just an inkling of their potential. However, there is some attempt at preservation, and the **Dolphin Research Center** (details below) rescues and rehabilitates sick or wounded dolphins and other sea mammals found around the Keys – using these opportunities to further expand their ongoing sea-mammal research. At the center, dolphins are used in therapy programs for cancer sufferers and mentally handicapped children; the exceptional patience and gentleness displayed by the dolphins (all of which are free to swim out to sea whenever they want) in this work suggest that their sonar system may allow them to make an X-ray-like scan of a body to detect abnormalities and perhaps even to "see" emotions. Take a **tour** (daily 9am–4pm every half hour; $17.50, age 4–12 $11.50) of the research center to become better informed on these remarkable – and still barely understood – mammals. The Dolphin Research Center is also one of four places in the Florida Keys where you can **swim with dolphins** ($155 for around twenty minutes); call at least a month ahead (six weeks in high season) to book a session. Averaging seven feet in length, dolphins look disconcertingly large at close quarters – and will lose interest in you long before you tire of their company – but if you do get the opportunity to join them, it's an unforgettable experience.

In Key Largo: **Dolphins Plus**, MM100-Oceanside (Ⓣ305/451-1993, Ⓦwww.dolphinsplus.com) and **Dolphin Cove**, MM102-Bayside (Ⓣ305/451-4060, Ⓦwww.dolphinscove.com).

In Islamorada**: Theater of the Sea**, MM84.5-Oceanside (see p.135 for contact info).

In Marathon: **Dolphin Research Center**, MM59-Bayside (Ⓣ305/289-1121, Ⓦwww.dolphins.org).

are accessible only by boat. **Key Largo** is the biggest, though not the prettiest, of the Keys and boasts the **John Pennekamp Coral Reef State Park** as its main attraction. Further on, the little town of **Tavernier** is really a place to pass through on the way to bigger and livelier **Islamorada**, which is mostly made up of a string of state parks.

North Key Largo

The best way to arrive in the Keys **by car** is on Card Sound Road (Hwy-905A; $1 toll), which branches off US-1 a few miles south of Homestead. Doing so avoids the bulk of the tourist traffic and, after passing through the desolate southeastern section of the Everglades, gives soaring views of the mangrove-dotted waters of Florida Bay (where a long wait and a lot of luck might be rewarded with a the sight of a rare American crocodile) – and a glimpse of the Keys as they would all have looked long ago before commercialism took hold.

The bulk of **North Key Largo**, where Hwy-905 touches ground, is free of development, and human habitation is marked only by the odd shack amid a rich endowment of trees. Despite elaborate plans to turn the area into a city called Port Bougainvillea, with high-rise blocks and a monorail (a plan mercifully dashed by sudden bankruptcy), much of the land here is now owned and protected by the state. Horror stories about drug smugglers and practitioners of the voodoo-like Santería seem designed to ward off visitors, but in reality, although it goes on, there's probably no more drug smuggling here than anywhere else in the Keys, and magic merchants come not to sacrifice innocent tourists but to gather weird and wonderful herbs for use in rituals. There's probably more danger from the exclusive *Ocean Reef Club*, whose golf course you'll spot after a few miles if you turn left where Hwy-905 splits; it's regarded by the FBI as the country's most secure retreat for such very important people as Colin Powell – watch out for nervous, armed men in dark suits. If you want to explore North Key Largo at length, you'll have to eat and sleep in Key Largo or Tavernier (see pp.133–134).

Further south, Hwy-905 merges with US-1 near MM109. Known from here on as the **Overseas Highway**, US-1 is the only road all the way to Key West.

John Pennekamp Coral Reef State Park

The one essential stop as you approach Key Largo is the **John Pennekamp Coral Reef State Park**, at MM102.5-Oceanside (daily 8am–sunset; $2.50 per car and driver, plus $2.50 for first passenger, 50¢ for each additional passenger, pedestrians and cyclists $1.50; info line ⓣ305/451-1202, ⓦwww.floridastateparks.org). At its heart is a protected 78-square-mile section of living coral reef, part of the reef chain that runs from here to the Dry Tortugas, five miles off of Key West (see p.164). Just a few decades ago, great sections of the reef were dynamited or hauled up by crane to be broken up and sold as souvenirs. These days, collecting Florida coral is illegal, and any samples displayed in tourist shops have most likely been imported from the Philippines. Despite the damage wrought by ecologically unsound tourism, experts still rate this as one of the most beautiful reef systems in the world. Whether you opt to visit the reef here or elsewhere in the Keys (such as Looe Key, see "The Lower Keys," p.143), make sure you do visit it – the eulogistic descriptions you'll hear are rarely exaggerations.

Seeing the reef: practicalities

Since most of the park lies underwater, the best way to see it is with a **snorkeling tour** (9am, noon, & 3pm; 1hr 30min; adults $26.95, plus $6 for equipment; ⓣ305/451-1621, ⓦwww.pennekamppark.com) or, if you're qualified, a **guided scuba dive** (9.30am & 1.30pm; 1hr 30min; $41; diver's certificate required; ⓣ305/451-6322). If you prefer to stay dry, a remarkable amount of the reef can be enjoyed on the park's two-and-a-half-hour **glass-bottomed boat tour** (9.15am, 12.15pm, & 3pm; $20; ⓣ305/451-1621). You can also rent a boat, ranging from a single-person kayak to a 22-foot power boat –

canoes cost $10 per hour ($30 per half-day) and power boats $30 or $40 per hour (Ⓣ305/451-6325). Note that only during the summer are you likely to get a place on these tours or obtain a boat without booking ahead. To be sure, call to make a reservation, or drop into Sundiver Station, MM103-Bayside (Ⓣ305/451-2220). If there's no room, try one of the numerous local diving shops, like Ocean Divers, MM106-Bayside (Ⓣ305/451-0037, Ⓦwww.oceandivers.com), which operate their own trips out to the reef – and cover a larger area than park tours – at around the same rates.

At the reef

Only when you're at the reef does its role in providing a sheltered environment for a multitude of crazy-colored fish and exotic sea life become apparent. Even from the glass-bottomed boat you're virtually guaranteed to spot lobsters, angelfish, eels, and wispy jellyfish shimmering through the current, as well as shoals of minnows stalked by angry-faced barracudas, and many more less easily identified aquatic curiosities.

Despite looking like a big lump of rock, the **reef** itself is a delicate living thing, composed of millions of minute coral polyps that extract calcium from the seawater and grow from one to sixteen feet every 1000 years. Coral takes many shapes and forms, resembling anything from staghorns to a bucket, and comes in a paint-box variety of colors due to the plants, zooxanthellae, living within the coral tissues. Sadly, it's far easier to spot signs of death rather than life on the reef: white patches show where a carelessly dropped anchor or a diver's hand have scraped away the protective mucus layer and left the coral susceptible to lethal disease.

This destruction got so bad at the horseshoe-shaped **Molasses Reef**, about seven miles out, that the authorities sank two obsolete coastguard cutters nearby to create an alternative attraction for divers. In as much as the destruction has slowed, this plan worked and today you'll enjoy some great snorkeling around the reef and the cutters. If you prefer diving amid older wrecks, head for **the Elbow**, a section of the reef a few miles northeast of Molasses, where a number of intriguing, barnacle-encrusted nineteenth-century specimens lie; like most of the Keys' diveable wrecks, these were deliberately brought here to bolster tourism in the Seventies, which lessens their allure somewhat and means you definitely won't find any treasure.

By far the strangest thing at the reef is the **Christ of the Deep**, a nine-foot bronze statue of Christ intended as a memorial to perished sailors. The algae-coated creation, twenty feet down at Key Largo Dry Rocks, is a replica of Guido Galletti's *Christ of the Abyss*, similarly submerged off the coast of Genoa, Italy – and is surely the final word in Florida's long-time fixation with Mediterranean art and architecture. Glass-bottomed boat trips, by the way, don't visit the Elbow or the statue.

Back on land: the visitor center

Provided you visit the reef early, there'll be plenty of time left to enjoy the terrestrial portion of the park. The ecological displays at the **visitor center** (daily 8am–5pm) provide an inspiring introduction to the flora and fauna of the Keys and will give you a practical insight into the region's transitional zones: the vegetation changes dramatically within an elevation of a few feet. The park's fine tropical **hardwood hammock** – a pocket of woodland able to flourish where the ground elevation rises a few feet above the surrounding wetlands (see "Natural Florida" in Contexts for further information) meanders through

△ Ernest Hemingway Home

red mangroves, pepper trees, and graceful frangipani. Raccoon, heron, and fiddler crab tracks are everywhere, and hairy-legged, golden orb spiders dangle from many a branch. The park also boasts some fine artificial beaches (you won't find any more – artificial or not – until Key West), but note that the coral is very unforgiving to bare feet. Another option for exploring the park is to rent a canoe (single $10 per hour, double $15 per hour; $50/$75 per day) and glide around the mangrove-fringed inner waterways.

Key Largo

Thanks to the 1948 film in which Humphrey Bogart and Lauren Bacall grappled with what were then Florida's best-known features – crime and hurricanes – almost everybody has heard of **KEY LARGO**. Ironically, the film's title was chosen for no other reason than it suggested somewhere warm and exotic, and, though set here, the film was almost entirely shot in Hollywood – hoodwinking countless millions into thinking that paradise was a town in the Florida Keys.

Recognizing a potential tourist bonanza, business people here soon changed the name of their community from Rock Harbor to Key Largo (a title that until then had applied to the whole island, derived from *Cayo Largo* – Long Island – the name given to it by early Spanish explorers), and tenuous links with Hollywood are maintained even today. The steam-powered boat that was used in *The African Queen* is moored (when not on promotional tours) in the marina of the *Holiday Inn*, MM100-Oceanside, and the hotel's lobby displays a selection of stills of Bogart and co-star Katharine Hepburn acting their hearts out – in England and Africa.

Clinging to an image based more in movies than reality, Key Largo proper is really a jumble of filling stations, shopping plazas, and fast-food outlets. There are one or two low-key attractions, and the offshore islands may persuade you to stay for a night or two. If you're in more of a hurry and are here in the early evening, at least make time to hop off the Overseas Highway to enjoy the sunset.

There are two places on the key where you can swim with dolphins. The first is **Dolphins Plus**, just south of MM100-Oceanside (daily 9am–5pm; Ⓣ305/451-1993, Ⓦwww.dolphinsplus.com), a dolphin education and research facility where you can indulge in a "dolphin encounter" with one of twelve friendly creatures. The price of a "structured" half-hour swim with them is $160 (8.30am, 12.45pm, and 3pm; to observe only $10, under-15s $5), and there is also an "unstructured" swim with wild dolphins that is $125 – though with the latter, contact is not guaranteed (9.30am & 1.30pm). The other venue is **Dolphin Cove**, a five-acre marine environment research center at MM102-Bayside (daily 8am–5pm; Ⓣ305/451-4060, Ⓦwww.dolphinscove.com). If you have a swimsuit, a towel, and $160, you can join sessions run daily at 8.30am, 12.30pm, and 3.30pm (weekends only March to mid-Dec) – plan to book around four weeks in advance: the dolphins here live in a small inlet that opens directly onto the sea, so the experience is a little more authentic than swimming laps in a pool. There's also a natural swim, where you snorkel alongside the dolphins but aren't guaranteed contact, for $125 (9.45am & 1.45pm). If you can't afford a close encounter, $20 (under-16s $15) gets you in as a non-swimming observer. Dolphin Cove is also the departure point for Captain Sterling's Eco-Tours (Mon–Fri 9.30am, 11am, & 1.30pm, Sat & Sun 11am & 4pm; $39.95; Ⓣ1-888/224-6044, Ⓦwww.captainsterling.com; reservation required), one of the more knowledgeable backcountry tours in the area.

Accommodation

In addition to beds, plenty of **motels** offer diving packages. Look for signs or try *Economy Efficiency* (also known as *Ed & Ellen's*), MM103.5-Oceanside (Ⓣ305/451-9949 or 1-888/333-5536, Ⓦwww.ed-ellens-lodgings.com; ❷), which is basic but clean; *Largo Lodge*, MM101.5-Bayside (Ⓣ305/451-0424 or 1-800/INTHESUN, Ⓦwww.largolodge.com; ❹), offers comfortable apartments in a lovely garden setting right on the beach, though children aren't allowed; and though not plush, *Seafarer*, MM98-Bayside (Ⓣ305/852-5349 or 1-800/599/7112, Ⓦwww.keylargoparadise.com; ❷), has spotless cottages and daily diving tours to the local marine sanctuaries. Next door, prices go up at the *Kona Kai Resort*, MM97.8-Bayside (Ⓣ305/852-4629 or 1-800/365-7829, Ⓦwww.konakairesort.com; ❺), but the chalets are huge and stylish, a dozen strains of banana grow in the garden, and the hotel has its own art gallery. Very costly but one of a kind, *Jules' Undersea Lodge*, at 51 Shoreland Drive (Ⓣ305/451-2353 or 1-800/858-7119, Ⓦwww.jul.com; ❽), is a tiny "hotel" thirty feet below the ocean's surface. It's more theme park than a place to stay and is always booked well in advance; the two-bedroom accommodations are perfectly safe and are linked to land by an intercom system. The overnight, two-person luxury option ($1200) comes with such amenities as caviar and flowers. Just remember your diver's certificate – otherwise you'll have to take the hotel's three-hour crash course ($95) before you'll be allowed to unpack.

Of the many **campgrounds** in and around Key Largo, the cleanest and cheapest is the John Pennekamp Coral Reef State Park, MM102.5-Oceanside (Ⓣ305/451-1202; see above), though for high season you'll need to book several months ahead. *The Key Largo Kampground*, MM101.5-Oceanside (Ⓣ305/451-1431), is a reasonable alternative but has no grass pitches.

Eating and drinking

Far enough south for fine Caribbean cuisine, but close enough to the Everglades for a taste of 'gator, Key Largo is a fine place for **eating**. The best breakfasts are found at *Ballyhoo's Grill and Grog*, MM98 in the median (Ⓣ305/852-0822), opposite the *Seafarer* hotel (see above). Opened 25 years ago by a couple of fishermen, it features pancakes, omelettes, croissants dipped in orange juice and egg, and a wide selection of grilled food and drinks. *Ganim's Restaurant*, MM99-Bayside (Ⓣ305/451-2895), has cheap breakfasts and lunches; try the "Sealegs Supreme" salad of crabmeat, tuna, and fruit in honey mustard, and the huge portions of sweet pies. If you've got a hankering for alligator, a good spot is *Snappers Raw Bar*, MM94.5-Oceanside at 139

Islands off Key Largo

The tiny, uninhabited **islands** just off Key Largo make glorious forays, and there's no better way of exploring them than hiring a boat or catamaran. Signs abound for **boat rentals**, but the most reliable and user-friendly option is Robbie's Marina at MM77.5-Bayside (Ⓣ1-877/664-8498, Ⓦwww.robbies.com). A rugged, Hemingway-esque personality, Captain Tim (everyone goes by their first name in the Keys) will take good care of you whether you rent a boat to explore Indian Key or to snorkel in Alligator Reef with Captain Keith, a self-styled "jellyfish warrior." They can take you out, but if you decide to go it alone, do heed their advice about the varying shades of shallow waters to avoid grounding your boat. If a **glass-bottomed boat tour** is more up your alley, head to the *Holiday Inn* docks at MM100-Oceanside (Ⓣ305/451-4655), where the *Key Largo Princess* makes two-hour cruises at 10am, 1pm, and 4pm ($18).

Seaside Ave (Ⓣ305/852-5956). Enjoy the waterside, candlelit setting with an alligator starter, or swing by for the Sunday champagne jazz brunch (10am–2pm). The best place for a splash-out seafood meal is *The Fish House Restaurant and Seafood Market*, MM102.5-Oceanside (Ⓣ305/451-4665), a must for all seafood lovers.

If you are undaunted by bikers in leather jackets and tropical shorts, check out the *Caribbean Club*, MM104-Bayside (Ⓣ305/451-4466), for a lively **drink** (it also offers cheap jet-ski rentals during the day). For a mellower crowd, visit *Coconuts,* the bar at the *Marina del Mar Resort*, MM100-Oceanside (Ⓣ305/451-4107). And if you'd like to relax with some good conch fritters and a beer, head up to *Alabama Jack's*, just north of the toll booth on the Card Sound Road (Hwy-905A).

Tavernier

Just ten miles south of Key Largo on the Overseas Highway is **TAVERNIER**, a small, homely town that was once the first stop on the Flagler railway (the Keys' first link to the mainland; see "The Seven Mile Bridge" p.140). There's not a whole lot here, but Tavernier's historic buildings and decent *café Cubano* (see "Practicalities" below) make it worth a short stop.

Just before crossing into Tavernier, at MM93.6-Bayside, is the **Florida Keys Wild Bird Rehabilitation Center** (daily 8.30am–5.30pm; $5 suggested donation; Ⓣ305/852-5339, Ⓦflorida-keys.fl.us/keyswildbird.htm), an inspirational place where volunteers rescue and rehabilitate birds that have been orphaned or have met with other common catastrophes like colliding with cars or power lines. A wooden walkway is lined with huge enclosures, and signs detail the birds' histories.

If you drop into **Harry Harris Park**, MM 93.5-Oceanside at the end of windy Burton Drive (nonresidents $5; Ⓣ305/852-7161), on a weekend, you could well find an impromptu party and live music – locals sometimes drop by with instruments and station themselves on picnic tables for jam sessions. Otherwise, during the week, it's a fine place to lounge since there's a wide, sandy beach.

A rarity in the Keys outside of Key West, the old buildings of the **historic district**, between MM91 and MM92, deserve stopping for. In addition to the plank walls and tin roofs of the turn-of-the-twentieth-century Methodist Church (now functioning as a small visitor center) and post office, you'll see some of the Red Cross buildings erected after the 1935 Labor Day hurricane, which laid waste to a good chunk of the Keys. Built of foot-thick walls of concrete and steel, the new buildings were supposedly invincible to nature's fiercest poundings. Unfortunately, the use of seawater in the construction caused the walls to crumble, leaving only rusting steel frames. To find the historic center, turn down the side of the *Tavernier Hotel*, and then take the first right up Atlantic Circle Drive. More quaint than spectacular, it's the sort of place where the Waltons might have had a retreat.

Practicalities

Despite its dismal exterior, the *Sunshine Supermarket*, at MM91.8-Oceanside (no phone and no English spoken), is really a hidden gem: inside, at its small café, you can get a top-notch *cafecito* for $1 and piled-high plates of Cuban food; rice and beans is only $4. Close by, *The Copper Kettle* is a chintzy English-style tearoom that features candlelit dinners of honey Cajun shrimp and other regional delights. The restaurant is owned by the 18-room *Tavernier Hotel* next door, MM91.8-Oceanside (Ⓣ305/852-4131, Ⓦwww.tavernierhotel.com; ❷). This old-fashioned hotel, painted bubblegum pink, began life as an open-air theater, but was quickly converted into accommodation; the homey rooms each have fridges and there's an onsite coin laundry as well.

Islamorada

Once over Tavernier Creek, you're at the start of a twenty-mile strip of islands: Plantation, Windley, and Upper and Lower Matecumbe, which are collectively known as **ISLAMORADA** (pronounced "eye-lah-more-RAH-da"). More than any other section of the Keys, fishing is headline news here. Tales of monstrous tarpon and blue marlin captured off the coast are legendary, and there's no end to the smaller prey routinely hooked by total novices. (Even former president George H.W. Bush successfully cast a line or two in these waters.)

If you'd like to head out to sea, you'll be well provided for. There's no problem renting fishing boats, or, for much less, joining a fishing party boat from any of the local marinas. The biggest docks are at the Holiday Isle, MM84.5-Oceanside (Ⓣ305/664-2321, ext 641), and Bud 'n' Mary's Marina and Dive Center, MM80-Oceanside (Ⓣ1-800/742-7945).

There's notable **snorkeling** and **diving** in the area, too. Crocker and Alligator reefs, a few miles offshore, both have near-vertical sides, whose cracks and crevices provide homes for a lively variety of crabs, shrimp, and other small creatures that in turn attract bigger fish looking for a meal. Nearby, the wrecks of the *Eagle* and the *Cannabis Cruiser* provide a home for families of gargantuan amberjack and grouper. Get full snorkeling and diving details from the marinas (see above) or any dive shop on the Overseas Highway – expect to pay $40 for a half-day of snorkeling.

Back on dry land, you might want to pass a couple of hours at the **Theater of the Sea**, MM84.5-Oceanside (daily 9.30am–4pm; adults $18.50, under-13s $11.50; Ⓣ305/664-2431, Ⓦwww.theaterofthesea.com), but only if you're not planning to visit any of the other marine parks in Florida, which are better. Here, you'll find the usual dolphin and sea lion shows that can be seen at any water park, the one advantage being that the arena is smaller and more intimate, so there's a likelier chance of getting close to the animals themselves. There are also sea horse, turtle, and nurse shark exhibits, but overall the park is unappealing and overwhelmingly commercial.

For nonfishing folk, there's little in Islamorada to warrant an extended stay. Half a mile further south at MM82-Oceanside, the Art Deco **Hurricane Monument** marks the grave of the 1935 Labor Day hurricane's 425 victims, killed when a tidal wave hit the train that was attempting to evacuate them. Officially tagged the Florida Keys Memorial, it's recently been spruced up after decades of disrepair – look for the sparkling mosaic showing a map of the Middle Keys and the stone relief of coconut palm trees bending ominously in the wind.

Islamorada's state parks

Indian Key, **Lignumvitae Key**, and **Long Key** – three state parks at the southern end of Islamorada – offer a broader perspective of the area than just fishing and diving. The **guided tours** to Indian Key and Lignumvitae Key are particularly enchanting, and the former reveals a near-forgotten chapter of the Florida Keys' history, the latter a virgin forest. The Indian Key tour (Thurs–Mon 9am & 1pm) departs from Robbie's Marina, MM77.5-Bayside ($15, children $10; ⓣ305/664-9814, ⓦwww.robbies.com), as does the Lignumvitae Tour (10am & 2pm; $15, children $10). A tour of both keys is available for $25.

Indian Key

You'd never guess from the highway that **Indian Key**, one of many small, mangrove-skirted islands off Lower Matecumbe Key, was once a busy trading center, given short-lived prosperity – and notoriety – by a nineteenth-century New Yorker named Jacob Houseman. After stealing one of his father's ships, Houseman sailed to Key West looking for a piece of the lucrative wrecking (or salvaging) business. Ostracized by the close-knit Key West community, he retreated to Indian Key, which he bought as a base for his own wrecking operation in 1831. In the first year, Houseman made $30,000 and furnished the eleven-acre island with streets, a store, warehouses, a hotel, and a population of around fifty. However, much of his income was not honestly gained: He was frequently accused of deliberately running ships aground on the reef using misleading lanterns on the island's shore, and eventually lost his license for salvaging from an anchored boat. In 1838, Indian Key was sold to plant-mad doctor Henry Perrine, who had been cultivating tropical plants here with an eye to their commercial potential. A Seminole attack in 1840 burnt every building to the ground and ended the island's habitation. Though Perrine was killed, his plants still thrive, and the island is now choked with agave cacti, as well as sisal, coffee, tea, and mango plants. The trip here is well worth it for the ruins, which are an evocative, if crumbling, reminder of early settler life in the Keys – especially the grassy paddock that was once the town square – and the observation tower's spectacular views across the island's lush and jumbled foliage. Look, too, for Houseman's grave – his body was brought here after he died working on a wreck off Key West.

Lignumvitae Key

By the time you finish the three-hour tour of **Lignumvitae Key**, you'll know a strangler fig from a gumbo limbo and will instantly be able to recognize many more of the hundred or so species of tropical trees – "lignumvitae" is Latin for "wood of life" – in this two-hundred-acre hammock. Further treats are the sizeable spiders, such as the golden orb, whose silvery web regularly spans the pathway. The trail through the forest was laid out by a wealthy Miamian, W.J. Matheson, who made millions supplying mustard gas to the government during World War I, and purchased the island for only $1. His 1919 limestone **house** is the island's only sign of habitation and shows the deprivations of early island living – even for the well-off; the house actually blew away in the 1935 hurricane, but was found and brought back.

Now a state park, Lignumvitae Key is considered the best remaining example of Florida Keys tropical hammock and is used primarily as a research facility by the University of Miami and other institutions. The island is ravaged by mosquitoes, though, so make sure to bring long-sleeved shirts and long pants – plus plenty of repellent.

Long Key State Recreation Area

Many of the tree species found on Lignumvitae Key can be spotted at **Long Key State Botanical Site**, MM67.5-Oceanside (daily 8am–sunset; cars $3.25

The backcountry

If you've access to a boat or sufficient money (at least $200 a day) to rent one with a guide, Islamorada makes a good base for exploring the fish-laden waters and bird-filled skies of the **backcountry**. This is the term for the countless small, uninhabited islands that fill Florida Bay, beginning about eighteen miles west and constituting the edge of Everglades National Park – more fully described in "The Everglades," p.169. Ask at any Islamorada marina for more details.

plus 50¢ per person; ⓣ305/664-4815, ⓦwww.floridastateparks.org). There's a nature trail that takes you along the beach and on a boardwalk over a mangrove-lined lagoon, and guided tours to take you around (info on ⓣ305/664-9814). Or, better still, you can rent a canoe ($4 per hour) and follow the simple **canoe trail** through the tidal lagoons in the company of mildly curious wading birds. **Camping** in the park costs $24.69 (ⓣ1-800/326-3521, ⓦwww.reserveamerica.com).

Practicalities

You're unlikely to find **accommodation** in Islamorada for under $70 a night, although price wars among the bigger hotels can reveal occasional finds. The popular *Holiday Isle Beach Resort*, MM84-Oceanside (ⓣ305/664-2321 or 1-800/327-7070, ⓦwww.holidayisle.com; ❸), is a psychedelic trip: vivid citrus-colored plastics and tiki huts fill this vacation village. The atmosphere is young and friendly and the hotel itself is very comfortable. Otherwise, the best bets are *Drop Anchor*, MM85-Oceanside (ⓣ305/664-4863 or 1-888/664-4863; ❷) and the *Key Lantern/Blue Fin*, MM82 Bayside (ⓣ305/664-4572, ⓦwww.keylantern.com; ❷) – ask for a room at the *Blue Fin* if you can, since these were more recently renovated. If you have a tent, use either Long Key State Recreation Area (see above) or the RV-dominated *KOA* campground on Fiesta Key, MM70-Bayside (ⓣ305/664-4922 or 1-800/562-7730, ⓦwww.koa.com/where/fl/09250.htm).

Provided you avoid the obvious tourist traps, you can **eat** well and fairly cheaply. Best of all is the excellent-value fare at *Islamorada Fish Company*, MM81.5-Bayside (ⓣ1-800/258-2559), whose fresh seafood is exported all over the world. Despite a constant full house (try to get here before 6pm), the staff are particularly friendly. *Manny & Isa's*, MM81.5-Oceanside (ⓣ305/664-5019), serves high-quality, mid-price Cuban food; *Whale Harbor Inn*, MM83.5-Oceanside (ⓣ305/664-4959), offers massive seafood buffets to devil-may-care gluttons; the ramshackle but justifiably pricey *Green Turtle Inn*, MM81.5-Oceanside (ⓣ305/664-9031; closed Mon), has glorious chowders; and the *Hungry Tarpon*, at MM77.5-Bayside, Lower Matecumbe Key (ⓣ305/664-0535), serves superb fish from local recipes in a converted 1940s bait shop. For more elegant surroundings, try the seafood and Italian dishes at *Little Italy Restaurant*, MM68.5-Bayside (ⓣ305/664-4472); open for breakfast, lunch, and dinner, it offers main courses for $13–15.

When it comes to **nightlife**, many people get no further than the huge tiki bar at *Holiday Isle Beach Resort* (see above), which always throbs on weekends to the sound of insipid rock bands. Alternatively, investigate the nightly drink specials at *Lor-e-lei's*, MM82-Bayside (ⓣ305/664-4656), where nightly sunset celebrations reel in the crowds. For raunchy blues and boozing, visit the much less touristy *Woody's*, MM82-Bayside (ⓣ305/664-4335; closed Mon), which picks up steam after 11pm.

The Middle Keys

The Long Key Bridge (alongside the old Long Key Viaduct) points south from Long Key and leads to the **Middle Keys**, which stretch from Duck Key to Bahia Honda Key. The largest of these islands is Key Vaca – once a shantytown of railway workers – which holds the area's major settlement, **MARATHON**, an appealingly blue-collar town said to be named for the back-breaking shifts that workers endured as they raced to finish the Seven Mile Bridge (see p.140).

Marathon

If you didn't get your fill of tropical trees at Lignumvitae Key (see "Islamorada," p.136), turn right onto 55th Street at MM50.5-Bayside (opposite the K-Mart), which leads to 63 steamy acres of subtropical forest at **Tropical Crane Point Hammock** (Mon–Sat 9am–5pm, Sun noon–5pm; $7.50; ⓣ305/743-9100, ⓔTrpcranept@aol.com). A free booklet gives details of the trees you'll find along the one-mile **nature trail**, and you'll also pass one of the last examples of Bahamian architecture in the US: **Adderley House**, built in 1903 by Bahamian immigrants, gives a vivid impression of what life was like for them, with its simple construction and bare-bones amenities.

The hammock's excellent **Museum of Natural History of the Florida Keys** (same hours and admission) offers a thought-provoking rundown of the area's history – starting with the Caloosa Indians (who had a settlement on this site until they were wiped out by disease brought by European settlers in the 1700s) and continuing with the story of early Bahamian and American settlers. Not to be missed is the motley collection of artifacts near the museum shop, including a raft made of inner tubes that carried four Cuban refugees across ninety miles of ocean in the early 1990s.

A large section of the museum features interactive displays designed to introduce kids to the wonders of the Keys' subtropical ecosystems, including the hardwood hammocks and reefs. Much the same ground is covered at the adjoining **Florida Keys Children's Museum** (same hours and admission), which houses a tropical aquarium, a terrarium, and an artificial saltwater lagoon where you can feed the fish. The hammock's resident mosquitoes are a painful nuisance, so consider buying bug spray at the pharmacy directly opposite.

If you have more leisurely activities in mind, spend the day at **Sombrero Beach** (daily 7.30am–dusk). Follow the signs for Sombrero Beach Road off the Overseas Highway near MM50-Oceanside: at the promontory, there's a slender, well-kept strip of sand, with full facilities including showers and picnic tables, and ample shade from lush palms.

Just east of Marathon is the **Dolphin Research Center**, MM59-Bayside

Middle Keys information

For one-stop information on the Middle Keys area and accommodation, head to the **Middle Keys Visitor Center** at MM53.5-Bayside (daily 9am–5pm; ⓣ305/743-5417 or 1-800/262-7284, ⓦwww.floridakeysmarathon.com).

(Wed–Sun, 9am–4pm; ⓣ305/289-1121, ⓦwww.dolphins.org), which offers dolphin encounters – for details, see the box on p.128.

Accommodation

There's decent mid-range accommodation around Marathon. The only **campground** permitting tents (others are designed for motor homes and trailers only) is *Knights Key Park*, MM47-Oceanside (ⓣ305/743-4343 or 1-800/348-2267, ⓦwww.keysdirectory.com/knightskeycampground).

Banana Bay MM49.5-Bayside ⓣ305/743-3500 or 1-800/226-2621, ⓦwww.bananabay.com. Good-value beachside resort, with well-equipped rooms and a freshwater swimming pool – with the requisite tiki bar – surrounded by palm trees. ❹

Best Western Marathon MM48-Bayside ⓣ305/743-3855. This resort, with pool, tiki bar, large clean rooms, and free breakfasts is a well-priced option, if a little lacking in Keys character. ❸

Flamingo Inn MM59-Bayside ⓣ305/289-1478 or 1-800/439-1478, ⓦwww.flamingoinnflakeys.com. Very comfortable beds, big clean rooms, and a pool – and everything's painted pink. ❷

Sea Dell MM50-Bayside ⓣ305/743-5161 or 1-800/648-3854, ⓦwww.seadellmotel.com. The bright white and turquoise rooms are simply furnished but spotlessly clean, making the *Sea Dell* one of the best budget options in the Keys. It's also well located for local nightlife and has a freshwater heated pool. ❷

Seaward MM50-Oceanside ⓣ305/743-5711. Another basic but clean motel option, with fair prices and a large pool. ❷

Snorkeling, diving, fishing, and sailing

The choice locale for the pursuits of **snorkeling** and **scuba diving** is around **Sombrero Reef**, marked by a 142-foot-high nineteenth-century lighthouse, whose nooks and crannies provide a safe haven for thousands of darting, brightly colored tropical fish. The best time to go out is early evening when the reef is most active, since the majority of its creatures are nocturnal. The pick of local dive shops is Hall's Diving and Snorkeling Center (ⓣ305/743-5929 or 1-800/331-4255, ⓦwww.hallsdiving.com), at MM48.5-Bayside. Day-long introductory diving courses cost $150, while night diving, wreck diving, and Instructor's Certificate courses are available to the experienced. Once certified, you can rent equipment and join a dive trip (9am & 1pm): snorkel trips start at $25, dive trips $45 and up.

Around Marathon, **spearfishing** is permitted a mile offshore (there's a three-mile limit elsewhere), and the town hosts four major **fishing tournaments** each year: in early May (for tarpon); late May (dolphin, the fish not the mammal); early October (bonefish); and early November (sailfish). Precise dates are available from the **Middle Keys Visitor Center** (see opposite). You may fancy your chances, but entering costs several hundred dollars and only the very top anglers participate. Just being around during a tournament, however, will give you an insight into the Big Time Fishing mentality, and if you feel inspired to put to sea yourself, wander along one of the marinas and ask about chartering a boat. Boats take out up to six people and charge between $400 and $850 for a full day's fishing (7am–4pm), including bait and equipment. If you can't get a group together, join one of the countless group boats for about $40 per person for a full day's fishing – remember, though, that it's easier to catch fish with fewer people aboard. Reliable options for **fishing charters** include Richard Stancyzk (ⓣ1-800/742-7945, ⓦwww.budnmarys.com), who specializes in deep-sea sport fishing in the Upper Keys at Islamorada; Jim Sharpe (ⓣ305/745-1530, ⓔseaboots5@aol.com), another deep-sea specialist, based on Summerland Key further south; and Tina Brown in Marathon (ⓣ305/942-3806, ⓔtina824us@yahoo.com), who is a good choice for novices.

Although most of the boats at the local marinas are large power vessels designed for anglers, Marathon is also a major **sailboat** base, offering vessels for charter – with or without a captain – as well as sailing courses. A reliable source of both is the Faro Blanco Marina Resort, MM48.5 Bayside ⓣ305/743-9018 or ⓣ1-800-759-3276.

Eating

Marathon will definitely be your base for **eating** in this stretch of the Middle Keys, and it's not a bad one at that. It does go to sleep early, though; the only place with a hint of nightlife is the tiki bar of *Shuckers Raw Bar and Grill*, MM50.5-Bayside at 725 11th St (℡305/743-8686), which is also a prime vantage point for sipping a drink as the sun goes down.

Castaway 15th St, near MM47.5-Oceanside ℡305/743-6247. No-nonsense local restaurant with plastic chairs, tables, and cloths plus a screened-in patio; it's known for its beer-steamed shrimp and doughy honey-drenched buns.

Don Pedro Restaurant MM53-Oceanside ℡305/743-5247. Good Cuban fare at reasonable prices, and one of the best value places around. Though the decor's nothing to rave over, the food's cheap, filling, and authentic.

The Hurricane Grille MM49.5-Bayside ℡305/743-2220. Classic roadside American bar with nightly live music on a small stage at the back. This is an early stop on the nightly pub-crawl that concludes around 4am in the *Brass Monkey*, MM50-Oceanside in nearby K-Mart Plaza.

Porky's BBQ MM47.5-Bayside ℡305/289-2065. This thatched-roof shack by the marina serves inexpensive if average food – the BBQ platters are among the better options. Notable for being one of the few cheap options in the area.

The Seven Mile Grill MM47.5-Bayside ℡305/743-4481. Locals flock here for fine conch chowders and shrimp steamed in beer. The empty cans seem to have been used as decoration.

Village Café at the Gulf-side Village Plaza, MM50-Bayside ℡305/743-9090. Quality Italian dishes served in a simple setting.

The Seven Mile Bridge and Pigeon Key

In 1905, Henry Flagler, whose railway opened up Florida's east coast (see Contexts, p.468), undertook the extension of its tracks to Key West. The Overseas Railroad, as it became known (though many called it "Flagler's folly"), was a monumental task that took seven years to complete and was marked by the appalling treatment of the railworkers.

Bridging the Middle Keys gave Flagler's engineers some of their biggest headaches. North of Marathon, the two-mile-long Long Key Viaduct, a still-elegant structure of nearly two hundred individually cast arches, was Flagler's personal favorite and was widely pictured in advertising campaigns. Yet a greater technical accomplishment was the **Seven Mile Bridge** (built from 1908 to 1912) to the south, linking Marathon to the Lower Keys. At one point, every US-flagged freighter on the Atlantic was hired to bring in materials – including German concrete impervious to salt water seepage – while floating cranes, dredges, and scores of other craft set about a job that eventually cost the lives of 700 laborers. When the trains eventually started rolling, passengers were treated to an incredible panorama: a broad sweep of sea and sky, sometimes streaked by luscious red sunsets or darkened by storm clouds.

The Flagler bridges were strong enough to withstand everything that the Keys' volatile weather could throw at them, except for the calamitous 1935 Labor Day hurricane, which tore up the railway. The bridges were subsequently adapted to accommodate a road: the original Overseas Highway. Tales of hair-raising bridge crossings (the road was only 22 feet wide), endless tailbacks as the drawbridges jammed – and the roadside parties that ensued – are part of Keys folklore. The later bridges, such as the $45-million new **Seven Mile Bridge** between Key Vaca and Bahia Honda Key that opened in the early Eighties, certainly improved traffic flow but also ended the mystique of traveling the old road – and its walls are just high enough to hide the fabulous view.

The old bridge, intact but for the mid-sectional cuts to allow shipping to pass, now make extraordinarily long fishing piers and jogging strips. A section of the former Seven Mile Bridge also provides the only land access to **Pigeon Key**, which served as a railway work camp from 1908 to 1935, and until recently was used by the University of Miami for marine science classes. Its seven original wooden buildings have been restored as **Historic Pigeon Key** (daily 10am–4pm, last train leaves at 2.50pm; $8.50 including shuttle price; ⓣ305/289-0025, ⓦwww.pigeonkey.org), whose museum reveals the hardships routinely suffered by the workers. Cars are not permitted access to Pigeon Key, which contributes to the serene atmosphere of the place. A shuttle bus leaves hourly on the hour (10am–4pm) from the visitor's center on Knight's Key at MM47-Oceanside.

The Lower Keys

Starkly different from their northerly neighbors, the **LOWER KEYS** are quiet, heavily wooded, and predominantly residential. Aligned north-south (rather than east-west) and resting on a base of limestone (rather than a coral reef), these islands have flora and fauna that are very much their own. Species like the Key deer, the Lower Keys cotton rat, and the Cudjoe Key rice rat – all of which are endangered – live here, though mainly tucked away miles from the Overseas Highway. Most visitors speed through the area on the way to Key West, just forty miles further, but the area's lack of rampant tourism and easily found seclusion make this a good place to linger for a day or two.

Bahia Honda State Recreation Area

While not officially part of the Lower Keys, the first place of consequence you'll hit after crossing the Seven Mile Bridge is the 300-acre **Bahia Honda State Recreation Area**, MM37-Oceanside (daily 8am–sunset; cars $4 with 50¢ for each additional person; pedestrians and cyclists $1; ⓣ305/872-2353, ⓦwww.floridastateparks.org), one of the Keys' prettiest spots. The northeasterly section of the park rings a lagoon that has a natural beach and inviting, two-tone ocean waters. Closest to the park entrance, delightful Sandspur Beach has all the usual amenities and scattered plants growing in the sand, while Calusa and Loggerhead beaches at the western tip are more family-friendly, each with

Lower Keys information

The **Lower Keys Visitor Center**, at MM31-Oceanside in the main settlement of Big Pine (Mon–Fri 9am–5pm, Sat 9am–3pm, ⓣ305/872-2411 or 1-800/872-3722), is packed with information on the area.

a specially marked swimming area and marina, though the ripe ocean smells and sea grass debris may be off-putting to some.

While here, you should ramble on the **nature trail**, which loops from the shoreline through a hammock of silver palms, geiger, and yellow satinwood trees, passing rare plants, such as dwarf morning glory and spiny catesbaea. Though it's pleasant enough, the hammock isn't as developed as, say, Tropical Crane Point further north (see p.138), since most trees are only around six feet tall. Keep a lookout for white-crowned pigeons, great white herons, roseate spoonbills, and giant ospreys (whose bulky nests are plentiful throughout the Lower Keys, often atop telegraph poles). Of the ranger-run programs offered every day, the **nature walk** every Tuesday at 11am is by far the best, but it's all pleasant enough without a guide.

For solitary sunbathing, pick your way through the undergrowth toward the two-story **Flagler Bridge**, immediately south of which lies a gloriously isolated strip of golden sand. The waters here are good for swimming (beware, though, that currents here can be very swift), as well as for snorkeling, diving, and especially windsurfing – rent equipment from the Bahia Honda marina's dive shop. The unusually deep waters here (Bahia Honda is Spanish for "deep bay") made this the toughest of the old railway bridges to construct, and widening it for the road proved impossible: the solution was to put the highway on a higher tier. It's actually far safer than it looks, and there's a fine view from the top of the bridge over the Bahia Honda channel toward the forest-coated Lower Keys.

Facilities in the park include a campground and cabins, a snack bar, and a dive shop offering reef snorkeling trips (daily 9.30am and 1.30pm; $27.95; ⓣ305/872-3210, ⓦwww.bahiahondapark.com), scuba trips, and kayak rental (single $10/hr, $30/half day; double $18/hr, $54/half day).

Big Pine Key and around

The eponymous trees on **Big Pine Key** are less of a draw than its **Key deer**, delightfully tame creatures that enjoy the freedom of the island; don't feed them (it's illegal), and be cautious when driving – signs alongside the road state the number of road-kills to date during the year. The deer, no bigger than large dogs, are related to the white-tailed deer and arrived long ago when the Keys were still joined to the mainland; they provided food for sailors and Key West residents for many years, but hunting and the destruction of their natural habitat led to near-extinction by the late Forties. The **National Key Deer Refuge** was set up here in 1954 to safeguard the animals – one refuge manager went so far as to burn the cars and sink the boats of poachers – and their population has now stabilized between 250 and 300.

Pick up factual information on the deer from the **refuge headquarters** (Mon–Fri 8am–5pm, park open daily sunrise–sunset; ⓣ305/872-2239, ⓦwww.nationalkeydeer.fws.gov), at the western end of Watson Boulevard, off Key Deer Boulevard. To see the creatures, drive along Key Deer Boulevard or turn east onto No Name Key. You should spot a few; they often amuse themselves in domestic gardens. The best time to spot them is at sunrise or sunset, when the deer come out to forage. Also on Key Deer Boulevard, the **Blue Hole** is a freshwater lake with a healthy population of soft-shelled turtles and at least one alligator, which now and then emerges from the cool depths to sun itself – parts of the lakeside path may be closed if it has staked out a patch for the day. Should the alligator get your adrenalin pumping, take a calming stroll along the short **nature trail**, a quarter of a mile further south along Key Deer Boulevard.

Nearby **No Name Key** is home to a few settlers living off solar power and septic tanks, but it's better known as the staging ground for the Bay of Pigs invasion (see p.472). Cuban patriots practiced here before their disastrous attempt to dislodge Castro, and you can still make out the decaying airstrip in a clearing to the south of the key. No Name Key's main attraction, however, is the rollicking **No Name Pub**, MM30-Bayside (Ⓣ305/872-9115), which is well worth the rather circuitous detour for a sight of the rather unusual wallpaper: dollar bills covering every inch of wall and ceiling inside, worth some $60,000 by the owners' account. If you fancy adding a bill or two, just ask the staff for the house staple gun.

To find the pub, turn right at the only stoplight in Big Pine (MM30) and follow the right-hand fork when the road splits. Continue for 100 yards or so to another stop sign, and turn left; take the curving road for two miles through a residential neighborhood until the pub appears on the left, just before the bridge that leads to No Name Key.

The rest of the Lower Keys

An even more peaceful atmosphere prevails on the Lower Keys south of Big Pine Key, despite the efforts of property developers. **The Torch Keys**, so-named for their forests of torchwood – used for kindling by early settlers, since it burns even when green – can be swiftly bypassed on the way to **Ramrod Key**, where Looe Key Marine Sanctuary is a terrific place for viewing the coral reef (see below).

Perhaps the most expensive thing you'll see anywhere in the Keys, if not in all of Florida, is the balloon-like "aerostat" hovering 10,000 feet above **Cudjoe Key**. With an annual budget of over $23 million, it is used by the US government to beam TV images and radio broadcasts of American-style freedom – "unbiased news," sitcoms, and soap operas – to Cuba. Called TV Martí and Radio Martí, the aerostat's stations were named after the late-nineteenth-century Cuban independence fighter, José Martí, and are under the control of the US Broadcasting Board of Governors. Castro and the Cuban government allegedly expend a lot of effort trying to jam the TV signal.

Looe Key Marine Sanctuary

Keen underwater explorers should head for **Looe Key Marine Sanctuary**, clearly signposted from the Overseas Highway on Ramrod Key. Named after *HMS Looe*, a British frigate that sank here in 1744, this five-square-mile area of protected reef is in every part the equal of the John Pennekamp Coral Reef State Park (see p.129). The crystal-clear waters and reef formations create an unforgettable spectacle: showy elkhorn and star coral, as well as rays, octopus, and a multitude of gaily colored fish flit between tall coral pillars. The water, which ranges 8 to 35 feet deep, will appeal to novice and experienced snorkelers alike, but anyone wanting to catch sight of the *HMS Looe* will be disappointed as it has long since disintegrated.

The **sanctuary office** (Mon–Fri 8am–5pm; Ⓣ305/292-0311, Ⓦwww.fknms.nos.noaa.gov) can provide free maps and information. You can only visit the reef on a trip organized by one of the many diving shops throughout the Keys; the nearest is the neighboring Looe Key Dive Center (snorkel and diving trips start at $25; Ⓣ1-800/942-5397, Ⓦwww.diveflakeys.com).

If you're here around the second Saturday in July, you may want to don your flippers and check out the annual **Lower Keys Underwater Music Festival**. The music is broadcast via special speakers suspended beneath boats positioned above the reef. The music ranges from the Beatles' *Yellow Submarine* to Handel's *Water Music*, and there's quite a carnival atmosphere, with many people dressing up before they go down. There's no actual charge, though you'll have to pay for the boat and diving equipment at the sanctuary office. For more info call ⓣ305/872-9100.

Perky's Bat Tower

On Sugarloaf Key, fifteen miles from Ramrod Key, the 35-foot **Perky's Bat Tower** stands as testimony to one man's misguided belief in the mosquito-killing powers of bats. A get-rich-quick book of the Twenties, *Bats, Mosquitoes, and Dollars*, led Richter C. Perky, a property speculator who had recently purchased the island, into thinking that bats would be the solution to the Keys' mosquito problem. With much hullabaloo, he erected this brown cypress lath tower in 1929 and dutifully sent away for the costly "bat bait," which he was told would lure an army of bats to the tower. It didn't work: no bat ever showed up, the mosquitoes stayed healthy, and Perky went bust soon after. The background story is far more interesting than the actual tower, but if the tale tickles your fancy, drive down the bumpy road between the air strip and the sprawling *Sugarloaf Lodge*, at MM17-Bayside.

Practicalities

For what they offer, **motels** in the Lower Keys are expensive. *Looe Key Reef Resort*, MM27.5-Oceanside (ⓣ305/872-2215 or 1-800/942-5397, ⓦwww.divelooekey.com; ❸), is convenient for visiting the marine sanctuary, or there's *Parmer's Resort*, off MM28.5-Bayside at 565 Barry Ave (ⓣ305/872-2157; ❸). For a real splurge, stay at the idyllic *Little Palm Island*, MM28.5-Oceanside, Little Torch Key (ⓣ305/872-2524 or 1-800/343-8567, ⓦwww.littlepalmisland.com; no children; ❽), whose thatched cottages are set in lush gardens a few feet from the beach on the private islet. They also have a fantastic and truly expensive fish restaurant. **Campgrounds** are plentiful; try the Bahia Honda State Recreation Area's *Big Pine Key Fishing Lodge*, MM33-Oceanside (ⓣ305/872-2351; ❶), *Sea Horse*, MM31-Bayside (ⓣ305/872-2443; ❶), and *Sugar Loaf Key KOA*, MM20-Oceanside (ⓣ305/745-3549 or 1-800/562-7731, ⓦwww.koa.com; ❶). Three **bed and breakfast inns** on Big Pine Key make cozy alternatives, but book early: *Deer Run B&B*, 1985 Long Beach Drive, MM33-Oceanside (ⓣ305/872-2015, ⓦwww.floridakeys.net/deer; ❹); *Barnacle*, 1557 Long Beach Drive, MM33-Oceanside (ⓣ305/872-3298 or 1-800/465-9100, ⓦwww.thebarnacle.net; ❹); and the adult-only *Casa Grande*, 1619 Long Beach Drive, MM33-Oceanside (ⓣ305/872-2878, ⓦwww.floridakeys.net/casagrande; ❹).

Aside from the *No Name Pub* (see p.143), which serves knockout pizzas, the other good option in the Lower Keys is *Mangrove Mama's*, at MM20-Bayside (ⓣ305/745-3030; closed Sept), for its rustic atmosphere, great seafood, and home-baked bread. A real locals' joint is *Big Pine Coffee Shop*, MM30-Bayside (ⓣ305/872-2790), where you can sit at formica tables and gorge on crab salads and steamed shrimp by the half-pound. For breakfast, *Baby's Coffee*, MM15-Oceanside (ⓣ1-800/523-2326, ⓦwww.babyscoffee) is unbeatable, serving delicious home-roasted blends also sold by the pound. Otherwise, try *Bobalu's Southern Café*, MM10-Bayside (ⓣ305/296-1664), for good, cholesterol-rich Southern cooking fare for breakfast, lunch, and dinner. **Nightlife** is not a strong suit since locals who want to live it up head for Key West. Try the *No Name Pub* or the *Looe Key Reef Resort* (see opposite) for weekend drinking.

Key West

Much closer to Cuba than mainland Florida, **KEY WEST** can often seem very far removed from the rest of the US. Famed for their tolerant attitudes and laidback lifestyles, its 30,000 islanders seem adrift in a great expanse of sea and sky. Despite the million tourists who arrive each year, the place resonates with an anarchic and individualist spirit that hits you the instant you arrive. Long-term residents here are known as Conchs, named after the giant sea snails eaten by early settlers (Freshwater Conchs are new arrivals), and ride bicycles, shoot the breeze on street corners, and smile at complete strangers.

Yet as wild as it may at first appear, Key West today is far from being the misfits' paradise that it was just a decade or so ago. Much of the sleaziness has been gradually brushed away through rather cutesy restoration and revitalization – it takes a lot of money to buy a house here now – paving the way for a sizeable vacation industry that at times seems to revolve around party boats and heavy drinking. Not that Key West is near to losing its special identity; it's still nonconformist, and don't dare suggest otherwise. The liberal attitudes have attracted a large influx of gay people, estimated at two in five of the population, who take an essential role in running the place and sink thousands of dollars into its future.

The sense of isolation from the mainland – much stronger here than on the other Keys – and the camaraderie of the locals are best appreciated by adjusting to the mellow pace and joining in. Amble through the side streets, make meals last for hours, and pause regularly for refreshment in the numerous bars. Key West's knack for tourism can be gaudy, but it's quite easy to bypass the commercial traps and discover an island as unique for its present-day society as for its remarkable past.

The tourist epicenter is on **Duval Street**, whose northern end is marked by **Mallory Square**, a historic landmark that is now home to a brash chain of bars that entirely ignores the whimsical, freethinking spirit of the island. But just a few steps east of here is the historic section, a network of streets teeming with rich foliage and brilliant blooms draped over curious architecture. This area boasts many of the best guesthouses, many eateries, and wacky galleries – not to mention the streets themselves, which are peopled with characters straight out of the wildest of imaginations.

To the west of Duval Street, just off Whitehead Street, lies Bahamian Village, an area of dusty lanes where cockerels wander and birds screech into the night. This unique enclave boasts some of the best-hidden restaurants on the island, although developers are already speculating on the area's future.

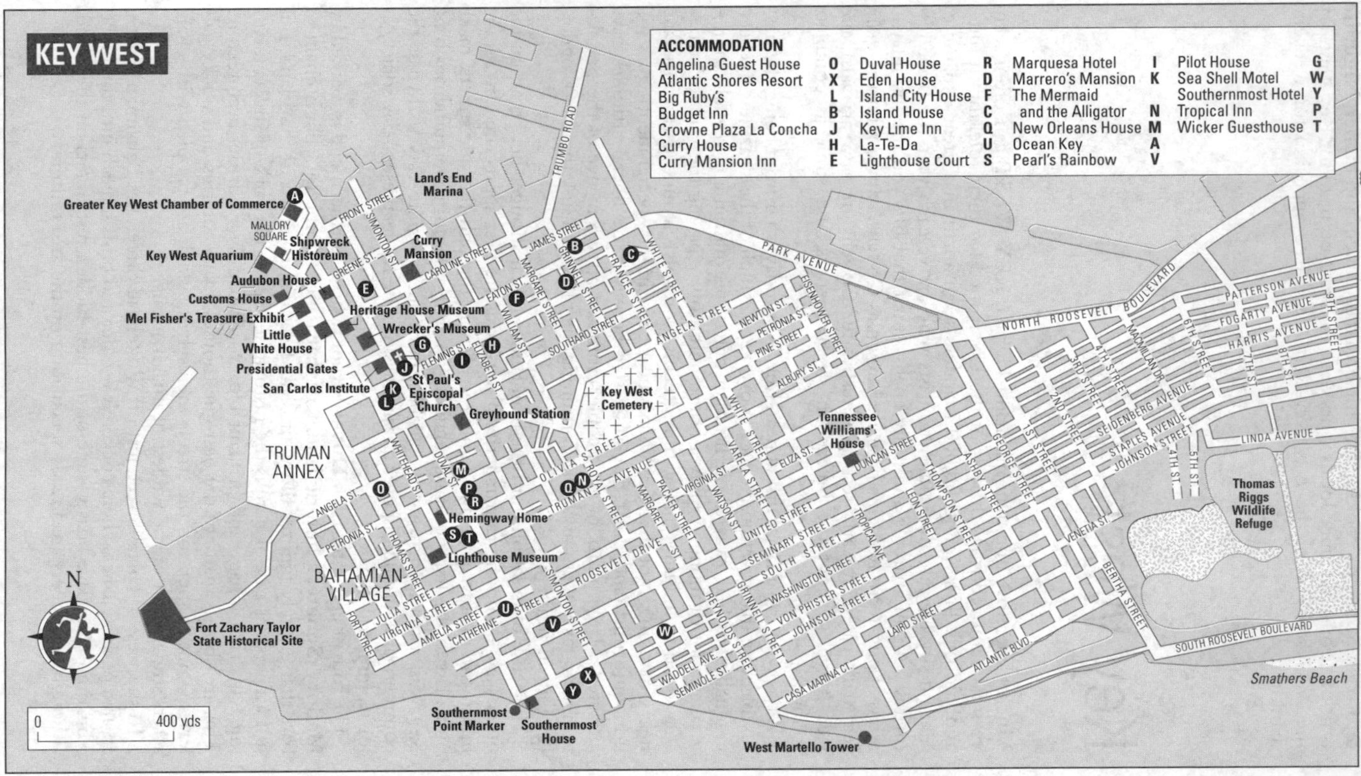
KEY WEST
ACCOMMODATION
Angelina Guest House O
Atlantic Shores Resort X
Big Ruby's L
Budget Inn B
Crowne Plaza La Concha J
Curry House H
Curry Mansion Inn E
Duval House R
Eden House D
Island City House F
Island House C
Key Lime Inn Q
La-Te-Da U
Lighthouse Court S
Marquesa Hotel I
Marrero's Mansion K
The Mermaid and the Alligator N
New Orleans House M
Ocean Key A
Pearl's Rainbow V
Pilot House G
Sea Shell Motel W
Southernmost Hotel Y
Tropical Inn P
Wicker Guesthouse T
Greater Key West Chamber of Commerce
Mallory Square
Key West Aquarium
Shipwreck Historeum
Audubon House
Customs House
Mel Fisher's Treasure Exhibit
Little White House
Presidential Gates
San Carlos Institute
Heritage House Museum
Wrecker's Museum
St Paul's Episcopal Church
Curry Mansion
Land's End Marina
Greyhound Station
Key West Cemetery
Truman Annex
Hemingway Home
Lighthouse Museum
Bahamian Village
Fort Zachary Taylor State Historical Site
Southernmost Point Marker
Southernmost House
Tennessee Williams' House
West Martello Tower
Thomas Riggs Wildlife Refuge
Smathers Beach
Airport and East Martello Tower
Front Street
Simonton St.
Greene St.
Caroline Street
James Street
Grinnell Street
Frances Street
White Street
Eaton St.
Margaret Street
William St.
Southard Street
Fleming St.
Elizabeth St.
Angela Street
Newton St.
Petronia St.
Pine Street
Albury St.
Eisenhower Street
Park Avenue
Trumbo Road
North Roosevelt Boulevard
Whitehead St.
Duval St.
Olivia Street
Truman Avenue
Royal Street
Packer Street
Virginia St.
Watson St.
Varela Street
Eliza St.
Duncan Street
United Street
Seminary Street
South Street
Washington Street
Von Phister Street
Johnson Street
Laird Street
Leon Street
Thompson Street
Tropical Ave.
Ashby Street
George Street
1st Street
2nd Street
3rd Street
4th Street
MacMillan Dr.
6th Street
7th St.
8th St.
9th Street
Patterson Avenue
Fogarty Avenue
Harris Avenue
Seidenberg Avenue
Staples Avenue
Johnson Street
Linda Avenue
4th St.
5th St.
Venetia St.
Bertha Street
Atlantic Blvd
Casa Marina Ct.
Reynolds Street
Waddell Ave.
Seminole St.
Roosevelt Drive
Simonton Street
Catherine Street
Amelia Street
Virginia Street
Julia Street
Fort Street
Thomas Street
Petronia St.
Angela St.
South Roosevelt Boulevard
0
400 yds
N

Some history

Piracy was the main activity around Key West – first settled in 1822 – before Florida joined the US and the navy established a base here. This cleared the way for a substantial **wrecking industry**. Millions of dollars were earned by lifting people and cargo off shipwrecks along the Florida reef, and by the mid-nineteenth century, Key West was the wealthiest city in the US. Key West also played a crucial role in the Civil War, as, along with Fort Jefferson (see p.164), it was a Union port while the rest of Florida hewed to the Confederacy. Its decision to side with the North wasn't wholly voluntary – Key West port was being blockaded into submission, since the Union wanted to be able to liquidate the Confederate ships it captured at Key West's lucrative wreckers' auctions.

The building of reef lighthouses sounded the death knell for the wrecking business by the end of the nineteenth century, but Key West continued to prosper even so. Many **Cubans** arrived bringing cigar-making skills, and migrant **Greeks** established a lucrative sponge enterprise (the highly absorbent sea sponges, formed from the skeletons of tiny marine creatures, were the forerunners of today's synthetic sponges). Industrial unrest and a sponge-blight drove these businesses north to Tampa and Tarpon Springs and left Key West ill prepared to face the **Depression**. Diehard Conchs, living on fish and coconuts, defied any suggestion that they move to the mainland, but by the summer of 1934 they were finally driven into bankruptcy. Under Franklin Roosevelt's New Deal, Key West was tidied up and readied for tourism, yet the 1935 Labor Day hurricane blew away the Flagler railway – Key West's only land link to the outside world. Luckily, the bridges were used for the construction of the Overseas Highway, which first saw use in 1938.

An injection of naval dollars during World War II eventually saved Key West by providing the backbone for its economy, while the island's geographical

The Conch Republic

The story behind Key West's nickname, the "**Conch Republic**," offers a telling example of the town's political savvy and its sense of humor. In April 1982, the US Border Patrol set up a roadblock on US Highway 1 at the *Last Chance Saloon* in Florida City, ostensibly to prevent illegal aliens from entering the US mainland; while local residents were suspected of smuggling Cuban refugees, drugs were also thought to be a target. The roadblock effectively cut off the Florida Keys at the confluence of the only two roads out to the mainland, leading to seventeen-mile tailbacks and a sudden, sharp decline in tourist numbers – as well as causing massive disruption to basic services. The mayor of Key West (with the backing of other community leaders), after failing to remove the checkpoint through legal means, formed the "Conch Republic" and seceded from the US in Mallory Square on April 23 – and declared war on Washington for good measure. The first shots fired were of stale Cuban bread broken over the head of a man dressed in an admiral's uniform – though some claim there were more concrete targets in the form of Federal spies who had quickly descended upon the town. The new prime minister then surrendered to the US navy – and demanded US foreign aid and war reparations of one billion dollars. Washington didn't respond directly (at least with an aid package), though it did quietly remove the offending checkpoint. A publicity stunt for sure, but one that worked, and the event is now celebrated annually at the Conch Republic Independence Celebration (see p.149), a great excuse for making a week-long party as well as a humorous but serious political point: the community – already separated geographically from the mainland – will always strive to maintain a social distance as well.

location made it an ideal vantage point from which to survey communist Cuba in the Sixties. **Tourists** started arriving in force during the Eighties, just as a taste for independence was rising among the locals and a strange chain of events led to the formation of the "**Conch Republic**" (see box, p.147).

Arrival, information, and getting around

Four miles east of town is the **Key West International Airport** (ⓣ305/296-5439), whose name belies its services – it only handles flights from Miami and other Florida cities. There are no buses from the airport to town, and a taxi costs around $10. Greyhound **buses** stop only once in town (at the junction of Simonton and Virginia streets) before carrying on to the airport.

The Overseas Highway, the only road into Key West, runs through the bland eastern section of the island to the infinitely more interesting Old Town. On the way you'll pass the useful, if unofficial, **Welcome Center** (Mon–Sat 9am–7.30pm, Sun 9am–6pm; ⓣ305/292-8962, ⓦwww.keywestwelcomecenter.com) at 3840 North Roosevelt Blvd. If you don't feel like stopping here, press on and use the **Greater Key West Chamber of Commerce**, next to Mallory Square at 402 Wall St (Mon–Fri 8.30am–6.30pm, Sat & Sun 8.30am–5pm; ⓣ305/294-2587 or 1-800/527-8539, ⓦwww.keywestchamber.org), for free tourist pamphlets and discount vouchers.

For **getting around** the narrow, pedestrian-filled streets of the Old Town, you're far better off walking or cycling than driving. If street signs appear curiously absent, you'll find them painted vertically on the base of each junction lamppost, though many are peeling off. If you're planning to venture further afield, **rent a bike** ($7–10 per day) or moped ($25–30 per day) from one of two Adventure Scooter & Bicycle Rentals locations: 708 and 925 Duval St, or the *Key West International Hostel* (see "Accommodation," p.150). Remarkably, there is a **bus service** (ⓣ305/292-8164) in Key West: two routes, clockwise and counterclockwise, loop around the tiny island roughly every fifteen minutes between 7am and 9am, and 2.30pm and 5.30pm. You'll also notice the **cycle-rickshaws** that are pedaled around (in their highest gear) and charge $1 a minute – that's about $20 from one end of Duval Street to the other. Otherwise, if you're feeling flush or lazy, try one of the nifty mini electric cars that can be rented from sites where Duval Street meets Caroline Street or Truman Avenue (two-seaters from $58 for 2hrs, four-seaters from $78 for 2hrs; ⓣ305/294-4724 or 1-888/800-8802, ⓦwww.keywestcruisers.com).

The oft-plugged, ninety-minute guided tours of the island's main sights are a fair option, but only if you're really pushed for time and won't be able to explore on your own. The **Conch Tour Train** (Mallory Square; every 20–30min, 9am–4pm; $20; ⓣ305/294-5161, ⓦwww.conchtourtrain.com) or the **Old Town Trolley** (board at any of the marked stops around the Old Town; every 30min, 9am–4.30pm; $20; ⓣ305/296-6688, ⓦwww.oldtowntrolley.com) dole out loud-speakered information, but the tours don't really foster an appreciation of the island's atmosphere.

A number of easily found **free publications** list current events: *Solares Hill* (monthly) is the most informative, but look out also for *Island Life* (weekly) and *The Conch Republic* (monthly).

Key West festivals

January

Early *Key West Literary Festival:* Four-day celebration of the island's famous four – Tennessee Williams, Ernest Hemingway, Robert Frost, and Thornton Wilder. Includes seminars, discussions, and readings with well-known living authors as well as special tours (Ⓣ1-888/293-9291).

February

Late *Old Island Days*: Tours, talks, concerts, flower shows, and art festivals celebrating Key West's history (Ⓣ305/294-1241).

April

Late *Conch Republic Independence Celebration*: A party in Mallory Square with a symbolic raising of the Conch Republic flag, commemorating the declaration of the Keys' independence from the US in 1982 (see box on p.147; Ⓣ305/296-0213, Ⓦwww.conchrepublic.com).

June

Mid *Cuban-American Heritage Festival*: A celebration of all things Cuban-American, including a street fiesta as well as more serious discussions at a symposium (Ⓣ305/295-9665, Ⓦwww.cubanfest.com).

July

Mid *Hemingway Days*: Literary seminars, writers' workshops, daft trivia competitions, arm-wrestling, and look-alike contests commemorate Ernest Hemingway, Key West's best-known writer (Ⓣ305/294-5717, Ⓦwww.hemingwaydays.com).

September

Early *WomenFest:* Key West's only dedicated lesbian-orientated event, with art shows, theater, and other assorted happenings (Ⓣ305/296-2491, Ⓦwww.women-fest.net).

October

Late *Goombay Festival*: Caribbean street party in Bahamian Village (Ⓣ305/294-9024).

Late *Fantasy Fest*: A gay-dominated version of Mardi Gras, with outrageous costumes paraded throughout the night along Duval Street – if you want a room at this time you'll need to book well in advance and expect significant rate hikes (Ⓣ305/296-1817, Ⓦwww.fantasyfest.net).

December

Mid-month *Lighted Boat Parade:* Lighted boats sail in and around Key West Harbor (Ⓣ305/292-9520).

Get **precise dates** on all of these from the Chamber of Commerce or Welcome Center (contact details opposite) or check online at the sites above.

Accommodation

Accommodation costs in Key West are always high – particularly from November to April when the simplest motel room will be in excess of $90 per night. Prices drop considerably at other times, but expect to pay at least $70 wherever you stay. Genuine **budget options** are limited to pitching a tent or renting a basic cottage at *Jabour's Trailer Court*, 223 Elizabeth St (ⓣ305/294-5723, ⓦwww.kwcamp.com) or the seaside (but out of town) *Boyd's Campground*, 6401 Maloney Ave (ⓣ305/294-1465, ⓔboydscamp@aol.com). The *Key West International Hostel*, 718 South St (ⓣ305/296-5719, ⓦwww.keywesthostel.com; members $19.50, nonmembers $22.50), has small, grubby dorms but is the only hostel on the island. Cheaper motels can be found along US-1 at the northern end of the island, but any savings you'll make on the room will be eaten up by the cost of parking in town. You're better off checking into one of the centrally located hotels or guesthouses that we've listed below. Wherever you stay, a reservation is essential from November to April, and would be a sensible precaution for weekend stays at any other time. If you arrive in October during Fantasy Fest, a hugely popular gay and lesbian Mardi Gras, expect a hike in room cost and a multi-night minimum stay.

Many of the restored villas operating as guesthouses in the historic district are gay- and lesbian-run, and while most welcome all adults, few accept young children. A handful (listed below) are exclusively gay male, while only one is for lesbians only.

Hotels and motels

Atlantic Shores Resort 510 South St ⓣ305/296-2491 or 1-800/526-3559, ⓦwww.atlanticshoresresort.com. Open to all, this Art Deco resort is popular for its "clothing optional" pool area and its onsite liquor store, while gay visitors swarm its Wednesday and Sunday "tea-dances" (see p.163). Rooms are rather shabby, though, stuck in the 1980s and painted in a gaudy palette of banana, mint green, and purple. ❸

Budget Inn 1031 Eaton St ⓣ305/294-3333 or 1-800/403-2866, ⓦwww.budgetkeywest.com. Tucked away north of the Old Town near the seaport, this is a rare find in Key West, offering low prices, pleasant rooms, and good location (though staff are rather frosty). ❸

Crowne Plaza La Concha 430 Duval St ⓣ305/296-2991 or 1-800/745-2191, ⓦwww.laconchakeywest.com. Now a link in the Crown Plaza chain, this colorful hotel first opened in 1925 and has retained some of its Twenties-style decor. Big pluses are the large swimming pool and bar overlooking the town. ❺

Ocean Key Zero Duval St ⓣ305/296-7701 or 1-800/328-9815, ⓦwww.oceankey.com. Perched by the ocean at the tip of Duval Street, this is one of the best hotels in the city, though you'll pay for the convenience and views. The lavish rooms are brightly furnished in tropical prints, and many have balconies. ❽

Sea Shell Motel 718 South St ⓣ305/296-5719, ⓦwww.keywesthostel.com. If the adjoining youth hostel is full or doesn't appeal, this place offers standard motel rooms at the lowest rates in the neighborhood. ❸

Southernmost Hotel 1319 Duval St ⓣ305/296-6577 or 1-800/354-4455, ⓦwww.oldtownresorts.com. This recently refurbished motel-turned hotel offers swankier rooms than the basic lobby might suggest – all decked in dark blues and greens, with Art Deco–like fixtures, deep bay windows, and generous bathrooms. Just ten-minute's walk to the center of town. ❻

Guesthouses

Angelina Guest House 302 Angela St ⓣ305/294-4480 or 1-888/303-4480, ⓦwww.angelinaguesthouse.com. A charming guesthouse, with a cool, Caribbean feel, tucked away in the back streets of the Bahamian Village. One of the best deals in town, with fourteen simple rooms decorated in pastel yellow, green, or blue. The small pool is a great place to enjoy the owners' cinnamon rolls at breakfast time. Shared bath ❷, private ❸

Blue Parrot Inn 916 Elizabeth St ⓣ305/296-0033 or 1-800/231-2473, ⓦwww.blueparrotinn.com. The friendly owners of this comfy 1884 house in the heart of the historic district serve excellent breakfasts in a lush, courtyard garden. No children. ❸

Curry Mansion Inn 511 Caroline St ⓣ305/294-5349 or 1-800/253-3466, ⓦwww.currymansion.com. Pricey but worth it for a night in this landmark Victorian home (see p.157). Enjoy the antiques, superb breakfasts, complimentary cocktail parties, and use of the pool and showers all day after check-out. ❻

Duval House 814 Duval St ⓣ305/294-1666, ⓕ292-1701. The lower-priced rooms are excellent value, and paying a bit more gets you a four-poster bed and a balcony overlooking the grounds.

One of the few places with ample parking. ❺
Eden House 1015 Fleming St ⓣ305/296-6868 or 1-800/533-5397, ⓦwww.edenhouse.com. Don't let the rather grotty reception put you off this place – it's a gem. Rooms (some with private bath) are decorated in the usual pastels and pale woods, though many have large, claw-foot tubs and most overlook the pool. Best of all, there's free off-street parking and a free happy hour every night 4–5pm (plus a complimentary beer at check-in). ❹
Island City House 411 William St ⓣ305/294-5702 or 1-800/634-8230, ⓦwww.islandcity-house.com. This massive mansion, built in the 1880s for a Charleston merchant family, claims to be the oldest in town (since the early 1900s). The luxurious studios and one- or two-bedroom apartments overlook the pool and tropical gardens. ❼
Key Lime Inn 725 Truman Ave ⓣ305/294-5229 or 1-800/549-4430, ⓦwww.keylimeinn.com. A cluster of cottages, near the center of Old Town, with a variety of rooms done in Key West tropical. A good buffet breakfast is served by the pool, and ample onsite parking is a major plus. Splash out on one of the bungalows for their seclusion and verandas. ❹
La-Te-Da 1125 Duval St ⓣ305/296-6706 or 1-800/528-3320, ⓦwww.lateda.com. This 1894 house has spacious rooms (though they're a little dark) with comfortable wicker furniture and floral decor, many overlooking the cozy pool area. Attached to the classy *Alice's* restaurant (see p.160 for review) and the *Crystal Room* cabaret, which offers popular drag shows (see p.163). ❹
Marquesa Hotel 600 Fleming St ⓣ305/292-1919 or 1-800/869-4631, ⓦwww.marquesa.com. A grand guesthouse (built in 1884) with a formal clientele and lush green surroundings. Pop in to view the old photographs of Key West's past, though avoid the restaurant, which borders on pompous. ❻
Marrero's Mansion 410 Fleming St ⓣ305/294-6977 or 1-800/459-6212, ⓦwww.marreros.com. Reputedly haunted, this antique-crammed old mansion is an opulent place to stay – ghost-hunters should ask for room 18, where most paranormal activity has been reported. ❹, room 18 ❻
The Mermaid & the Alligator 729 Truman Ave ⓣ305/294-1894 or 1-800/773-1894, ⓦwww.kwmermaid.com. A gem of a house with stunning interior decor. Fabulous gardens, a pool, and wine served each evening make for a deeply relaxing stay. No children under 16. ❸
Tropical Inn 812 Duval St ⓣ305/294-9977, ⓦwww.tropicalinn.com. Large, airy rooms in a charming restored conch house (see p.157) at the center of the action. Most of the rooms sleep three, and the more expensive ones have balconies. Ask about the neighboring cottages, which have hot-tubs and kitchens. No children. ❺
Wicker Guesthouse 913 Duval St ⓣ305/296-2475 or 1-800/880-4275, ⓦwww.wickerhouse-kw.com. One of the least expensive guesthouses on Key West, this complex of four restored Conch houses (see p.157) centers on a pool and communal Jacuzzi. The rooms are impressive given the price, splashily decorated with orange and red bedspreads and (naturally) white wicker furniture. Its biggest plus, though, is the chirpy staff. ❹

Exclusively gay guesthouses

Big Ruby's 409 Appelrouth Lane ⓣ305/296-2323 or 1-800/477-7829, ⓦwww.bigrubys.com. A cluster of buildings, all dotted round a lagoon pool and patio where you can lounge and listen to piped-in Motown most days. There are lots of extras, including splendid Sunday brunches (try the eggs Benedict), free drinks 6–8pm, and affable staff. ❹
Curry House 806 Fleming St ⓣ305/294-6777 or 1-800/633-7439, ⓔcurrygh@aol.com. The furniture here, though a little overwrought, is refreshingly wicker-free: each of the nine large, colonial-style rooms is filled with antiques – think monumental dressers and four-poster beds – and several have private balconies. A sumptuous breakfast is served poolside each morning. ❹
Island House 1129 Fleming St ⓣ305/294-6284 or 1-800/890-6284, ⓦwww.islandhousekeywest.com. Cruisey, men-only resort, with a sauna, video room, and large pool-cum-sundeck (in fact, guests need only wear clothes when using the exercise equipment in the gym). The surprisingly appealing rooms have overstuffed leather chairs, VCR, and crisp white linens. A day-pass to use the hotel's facilities is $25. ❹
Lighthouse Court 902 Whitehead St ⓣ305/294-9588, ⓦwww.lighthousecourt.com. Located in a gated compound opposite the Hemingway House, this sprawling, clothing-optional resort has been open for more than 25 years: its 45 rooms are housed in small, standalone houses and each is blandly decorated but clean. The big minus here is the haughty staff. ❹
New Orleans House 724 Duval St ⓣ305/293-9800 or 1-888/293-9873, ⓦwww.neworleanshousekw.com. Huge, very clean rooms come with full kitchens at this centrally located guesthouse – it's a pity the common areas are so tatty. Ask for a room at the back if you want to sleep before 3am, as the guesthouse is attached to the popular *Bourbon Street Pub*. ❺

Pearl's Rainbow 525 United St ⓣ305/292-1450 or 1-800/749-6696, ⓦwww.pearlsrainbow.com. The lone women-only guesthouse on the island, this attractive former cigar factory serves breakfast and has two pools and two Jacuzzis. There's also *Pearl's Patio*, a bar open to nonguests (Sun–Tues noon–8pm, Wed–Fri until 10pm, Sat until midnight). ❹

Pilot House 414 Simonton St ⓣ305/293-6600 or 1-800/648-3780, ⓦwww.pilothousekeywest.com. Sharing the same owners as *New Orleans House* (above), this guesthouse has contemporary suites split across two buildings, all with kitchenettes and wicker furniture. Clothing is optional, the crowd a mix of gay and straight, and there's also a small pool. The house was once owned by Joseph Otto, a prominent Prussian surgeon, who happens to have one of the oddest graves in Key West cemetery (see p.159). ❼

The Old Town

The square mile of the **Old Town** contains a good portion of what you'll want to see and is certainly the best place to absorb Key West's easygoing atmosphere, despite the throngs of tourists. Though visitors choke the main streets, only blocks away the casually hedonistic mood infects everyone, whether you've been here twenty years or twenty minutes. All of the Old Town can be seen on foot in a couple of days, but you should allow at least three – dashing won't do the place justice.

Along Duval Street

Anyone who saw Key West two decades ago would now barely recognize the main promenade, **Duval Street**, which cuts a mile-long swathe right through the Old Town, making it easy to regain bearings after exploring the side streets. Teetering precariously on the safe side of seedy for many years, much of the street has been transformed into a well-manicured strip of boutiques; plentiful beachwear and T-shirt shops cater to the vacationing middle-aged of Middle America. Yet its colorful "local characters" and round-the-clock action mean that Duval Street is still an interesting place to hang out in.

Other than shops and bars, few places on Duval Street provide a break from tramping the pavement. One, however, is the **Oldest House Museum**, also known as the **Wrecker's Museum** (daily 10am–4pm; $5; ⓣ305/294-9502), at no. 322, indeed the oldest house on the street, but it originally stood a few blocks away at the junction of Whitehead and Caroline streets. The exhibits here give some background to the wrecker industry – the salvaging of cargo and passengers from foundering vessels – on which Key West's earliest good times were based. In the days before radio and radar, wrecking crews simply put out in bad weather and sailed as close as they dared to the menacing reefs, hoping to spot a grounded craft. Judging by the choice furniture that fills the museum, Captain Watlington, the wrecker who lived here during the 1830s, did pretty well. Three quarters of the pieces are original – look for the courting lamp in the parlor, which provided amorous couples the chance to chat as long as the oil lasted, and the wonky cookhouse in the back garden, built separately from the main house to reduce risks of fire.

A few blocks on, **St Paul's Episcopal Church**, at no. 401 (ⓣ305/296-5142, ⓦwww.stpaulskw.org), is worth entering briefly for its richly colored stained-glass windows. If you have time, scoot around the corner for a look at the **Old Stone Methodist Church**, 600 Eaton St (ⓣ305/296-2392). The oldest church in Key West, it was built in 1877 and is shaded by a giant Spanish laurel tree in its front yard.

At 516 Duval St, the **San Carlos Institute** (Tues–Sun 11.30am–5pm; $3 donation; ⓣ305/294-3887) has played a leading role in Cuban exile life since it opened (albeit on nearby Anne Street) in 1871. It was here in 1892 that Cuban Revolutionary hero José Martí welded the Cuban exiles together into a force that would topple the regime ten years later. The current building, which dates from 1924, was financed by a $100,000 grant from the Cuban government after a hurricane wrecked the original wooden shack. Cuban architect Francisco Centurion designed the two-story building in the Cuban Baroque style of the period, noticeable in the wrought-iron balconies and creamy facade. The soil on its grounds is from Cuba's six provinces, and a cornerstone was taken from Martí's tomb. Following the break in diplomatic ties between the US and Cuba in 1961, the building fell on hard times – and was briefly used as a cinema, much to the annoyance of local Cubans – until it was revived by a million-dollar restoration project. Now, besides staging opera in its acoustically excellent auditorium and maintaining a well-stocked research library (including, most notably, the records of the Cuban consulate from 1886 to 1961), it has a passable permanent exhibition focusing on Martí and his men, mostly old newspaper clippings and letters. You can also pick up a free map here of the Cuban Heritage Trail, a self-guided tour of the key sights in Key West.

You'll know when you get near the southern end of Duval Street because, whether it's a motel, filling station, or a pharmacy, everything sprouts a "southernmost" epithet. The true **southernmost point** in Key West, and consequently in the continental US, is to be found at the intersection of Whitehead and South streets: it's only 90 miles from Cuba and flagged by a squat red, black, and white marker. Watch out, though, for the seemingly helpful passersby who offer to take your photograph – and then demand a tip for their troubles.

Close by, the **Southernmost House**, 1400 Duval St (daily 9am–6pm; $8 including one free drink; ⓣ305/296-3141, ⓦwww.southernmosthouse.com), offers an experience so bad it's almost good, though the fact that admission to its "museum" includes a drink at the inviting poolside bar here should tip you off that there isn't much worth paying to see. Originally built for Florida Curry, daughter of the state's first millionaire and sister of the man behind the Curry Mansion (see below), the house looks more like a rickety set for a local production of *Carmen* than the jazzy 1950s Cuban nightclub it was modeled after. Exhibits are limited to celebrity autographs and a few inexplicable trinkets, which the mandatory tour guide highlights with robot-like enthusiasm.

Mallory Square and around

In the early 1800s, thousands of dollars' worth of marine salvage was landed at the piers, stored in the warehouses, and sold at the auction houses on **Mallory Square**, just west of the northern end of Duval Street. Nowadays, thousands of cruise ship day-trippers and other tourists flock here by day for the souvenir market selling overpriced ice cream, trinkets, and T-shirts, and for the hokey sunset celebration at night, started in the 1960s by local hippies. Jugglers and fire-eaters are on hand to create a merry backdrop for the sinking of the sun, but the event's charms are rather over-rated, and even an hour amid the relentless commercial shill can be overwhelming. In fact, the sunset party's major draw – the sunset itself – is often blocked by the mammoth cruise ships anchored on the plaza's edge.

Key West Aquarium

More entertaining than the square during the day is the small gathering of sea life inside the adjacent **Key West Aquarium**, 1 Whitehead St (daily 10am–6pm; $9; ⓣ305/296-2051, ⓦwww.keywestaquarium.com), where fascinatingly ugly creatures such as porcupine fish and longspine squirrel fish leer from behind glass, and sharks (the smaller kinds such as lemon, blacktip, and bonnethead) are known to jump out of their open tanks during the half-hour **guided tours and feedings** (11am, 1pm, 3pm, & 4.30pm). If you intend to eat conch, a rubbery crustacean sold as fritter or chowder all over Key West, do so before examining the live ones here – they're not the world's prettiest crustaceans.

Mel Fisher Maritime Museum and around

Not all the ships that foundered off Key West were salvaged when they sank – some early galleons, which plied the trade route between Spain and its New World colonies during the sixteenth and seventeenth centuries, held onto their treasure until only a few decades ago when advanced technology enabled treasure hunters to locate them. You can see a lavish selection of such rescued cargo at **Mel Fisher Maritime Heritage Society Museum**, 200 Greene St (daily 9.30am–5pm; $9; Ⓣ305/294-2633, Ⓦwww.melfisher.org), among them a chunky emerald cross, a gold bar you can actually lift, and a "poison cup" said to neutralize toxins, all salvaged from two seventeenth-century wrecks. As engrossing as the collection is, the museum is really a celebration of an all-American rags-to-riches story: though he's now the high priest of Florida's many treasure-seekers, Fisher was running a surf shop in California before he arrived in the Sunshine State armed with several old Spanish sea charts and unbending optimism (his motto: "Today's the day!"). In 1985, after years of searching, he discovered the *Nuestra Señora de Atocha* and the *Santa Margarita,* both sunk during a hurricane in 1622, forty miles southeast of Key West – they yielded a haul said to be worth at least $200 million. Among matters you won't find mentioned at the exhibit is the raging dispute between Fisher and the state and federal governments over who owns what, and the ecological disturbance that uncontrolled treasure-seeking has wrought upon the Keys (reasons for the recent name change from "Treasure Exhibit" to "Heritage Museum"). The museum may be a little careworn, and its layout rather illogical, but it's well worth stopping by since it showcases arguably the best selection of wrecker's treasure in town.

At Greene and Front streets, the imposing, Romanesque **Customs House** (daily 9am–5pm; $6; Ⓣ305/295-6616, Ⓦwww.kwahs.org) was built in 1891 and used as a post office, customs office, and federal courthouse. It was long derelict, but has finally been launched as the Key West Museum of Art & History – exhibits are hit and miss, but it's worth dawdling here for an hour. Skip the hokey showcase of local pirate activity (whose highlight, oddly, is an oversized prop skeleton from the movie "Hook"); instead focus on the old newspaper cuttings detailing the dramatic impact of hurricanes and rafts of refugees or the moody watercolor evoking Key West's poorest days during the Depression. Above all, don't miss the craggy portraits of Conchs that line the upstairs corridor, especially Lee Neil, the so-called Queen of Key Lime Pies, with her veiny arms, seemingly exhausted after hours of lime squeezing.

Just a block up Wall Street from Mallory Square (in front of the waterfront Playhouse Theater) is the **Historic Sculpture Garden** (Ⓣ305/294-2587). This tiny, offbeat walled garden houses cast-iron busts of a random selection of local heroes, most of whom look as if they'd be more at home in a waxwork chamber of horrors than this supposedly stirring tribute; each sculpture is glossed with a brief rundown of the the subject's achievements. Aside from heavyweights like Hemingway, Truman, and Henry Flagler, look for the scions of several local families whose names – like Whitehead and Mallory – now grace streets and squares round town.

The Truman Annex and Fort Zachary Taylor

The old naval storehouse that contains the Fisher trove was once part of the **Truman Annex** (daily 8am–6pm; free), a decommissioned section of a naval base established in 1822 to keep a lid on piracy around what had just become US territory. Some of the buildings subsequently erected on the base, which spans a hundred acres between Whitehead Street and the sea, were – and still are – among Key West's most distinctive; the Customs House (see opposite) is a fine example. The most famous among them, however, is the comparatively plain **Harry S. Truman Little White House Museum** (daily 9am–5pm; $10, admission by guided tour only; ⓣ305/294-9911), by the junction of Caroline and Front streets. This house earned its name by being the favorite holiday spot of President Harry S. Truman (for whom the Annex was named), who first visited in 1946 and allegedly spent his vacations playing poker, cruising Key West for doughnuts, and swimming. Primitive plumbing meant that no one in the house was allowed to flush the toilet during his visits. The house is now a museum that chronicles the Truman years with an immense array of memorabilia; there's nothing especially compelling about the trinkets here, but the affable tour guides' encyclopedic knowledge enlivens the visit considerably.

In 1986, the Annex passed into the hands of a property developer who encouraged redevelopment by opening up the **Presidential Gates** on Caroline Street, which had previously only budged for heads of state, to the public – a smart move that defused much local suspicion and anxiety. The complex is now the site of some of the most luxurious homes in Key West – pick up a free map from one of the boxes dotted throughout the complex – the buildings' interiors, unfortunately, are closed to the public.

The Annex also provides access, along a curving roadway, to the **Fort Zachary Taylor State Historical Site** (daily 8am–sunset; $2.50 per car and driver, plus $2.50 for first passenger, 50¢ for each additional passenger, pedestrians and cyclists $1.50; ⓣ305/292-6713), built in 1845 and later used in the blockade of Confederate shipping during the Civil War. Yet within fifty years, the fort was made obsolete, thanks to the invention of the powerful rifled cannon, and over ensuing decades the fort simply disappeared under sand and weeds. Recent excavation work has gradually revealed much of historical worth, though it's hard to comprehend the full importance without joining the free 45-minute **guided tour** (daily at noon & 2pm). Most locals pass by the fort on the way to the best **beach** in Key West – a place yet to be discovered by tourists, just a few yards beyond, with picnic tables and plenty of trees for shade. Be aware, though, that the beach has pebbles rather than sand, and the craggy sea bottom can be tough on your feet, so bring waterproof sandals.

Whitehead Street

If the crowds on Duval Street get to be too much, head a block west to **Whitehead Street**, where it's much quieter and the mix of rich and poor homes reveals a more diverse side of Key West – and a couple of terrific museums as well.

Housed in a wooden plank building on Mallory Square is the **Shipwreck Historeum** (daily shows start at 9.45am and run every 30min until 4.45pm; $9; ⓣ305/292-8990). Enthusiastic guides throw out dozens of creaky gags while introducing an informative, if careworn, movie on the wrecking industry. On the two upper floors are several exhibits of cargo from the *Isaac Allerton*, which sank in 1856 and remained untraced until 1985: the most arresting items are feathery lace gloves, still intact after more than a century in the sea, and the pots ornamented with crusty coral. Better still is the panoramic view of Key West seen from the top of the reconstructed tower.

On the corner with Greene Street, the **Audubon House and Tropical Gardens** (daily 9.30am–5pm; $9 for audio tour, $5 for self-guided tour of gardens only; ⓣ305/294-2116, ⓦwww.audubonhouse.com) was the first of Key West's elegant Victorian-style properties to get a thorough renovation in 1958. The wealthy Wolfson family, who purchased the place to prevent its demolition, set about restoring the house to its original grandeur, using the family collection of furniture and decorative arts. Their success encouraged a host of others to follow suit and sent housing prices soaring.

The house takes its name from famed ornithologist John James Audubon, who actually had nothing to do with the place. Audubon spent a few weeks in Key West in 1832, scrambling around the mangrove swamps (now protected as the Thomas Riggs Wildlife Refuge, see p.159), looking for the birdlife he later portrayed in his highly regarded *Birds of America* portfolio. His link to the house goes no further than the lithographs that decorate the walls and staircase. The man who actually owned the property was a wrecker named John Geiger. In addition to twelve children of their own, Geiger and his wife took in many others from shipwrecks and broken marriages. Self-guided **tours** through the house require the visitor to wear a personal stereo system, which broadcasts the ghostly voices of Mrs Geiger and the children chatting to you about how life was back in their day and pointing out some of the house's fine nineteenth-century European furniture and antiques.

The Ernest Hemingway Home and Museum

It may be the biggest tourist draw in Key West, but to the chagrin of Hemingway fans, the **Ernest Hemingway Home and Museum**, 907 Whitehead St (daily 9am–5pm; $10, admission by tour only, tours leave every 10min and last approximately 30min; ⓣ305/294-1136, ⓦwww.hemingwayhome.com) deals more in fantasy than fact. Although Hemingway owned this large, vaguely Spanish Colonial–style house for thirty years, he lived in it for barely ten, and the authenticity of the furnishings – a motley bunch of tables, chairs, and beds about which the guide is rather smug – was hotly disputed by Hemingway's former secretary.

Hemingway bought the house in 1931, not with his own money but with an $8000 gift from the rich uncle of his then wife, Pauline. Originally one of the grander Key West homes, built for a wealthy nineteenth-century merchant, the dwelling was seriously run-down by the time the Hemingways arrived. It soon acquired such luxuries as an inside bathroom and a swimming pool, and was filled with an entourage of servants and housekeepers.

Hemingway produced some of his most acclaimed work in the deer-head-dominated study, located in an outhouse, which the author entered by way of a homemade rope bridge. Here he penned the short stories "The Short Happy Life of Francis Macomber" and "The Snows of Kilimanjaro"; the novella *The Old Man and the Sea* and the novels *A Farewell to Arms* and *To Have and Have Not*, the latter describing Key West life during the Depression.

To see inside the house (and the study) you have to join the half-hour **guided tour**. Among the highlights are pictures of the author's four wives and a lovely ceramic sculpture of a cat by Picasso. Hemingway's studio is a colorful affair, with a quarry-tiled floor and deer heads that look onto his old Royal typewriter. In the garden, a water trough for the cats is supposedly a urinal from *Sloppy Joe's* (see "Nightlife," p.162), where the big man downed many a pint. When Hemingway divorced Pauline in 1940, he boxed up his manuscripts and moved them to a back room at *Sloppy Joe's* before heading off to a house in Cuba with his new wife, journalist Martha Gellhorn.

After the tour, you're free to roam at leisure and play with some of the fifty-odd **cats**, several of which have paws with extra toes. The story that these are descendants from a feline family that lived in Hemingway's day is yet another dubious claim: the large colony of inbred cats once described by Hemingway was at his home in Cuba.

The Lighthouse Museum and the Bahamian Village

From the Hemingway House, you'll easily catch sight of the **Lighthouse Museum**, 938 Whitehead St (daily 9.30am–4.30pm; $8; ⓣ305/294-0012, ⓦwww.kwahs.com), simply because it is an 86-foot lighthouse – one of Florida's first, raised in 1847, and still functioning. There's a tiny collection of lighthouse junk and drawings at ground level, and it's possible (if tedious) to climb the 88 steps to the top of the tower, though the views of Key West are actually better from the top-floor bar of the Shipwreck Historeum (see p.155) or the Curry Mansion (see below). Most of the pictures taken here are not of the lighthouse but of the massive Chinese banyan tree at the base. But you can ogle the lighthouse's huge lens – a twelve-foot high, headache-inducing honeycomb of glass.

The narrow streets around the lighthouse and to the west of Whitehead Street constitute **Bahamian Village**, one of the few places that still has the feel of real Key West. Many of the small buildings – some of them former cigar factories – are a little rundown, in refreshing contrast to much of the over-elegant restoration found elsewhere in the Old Town. The Caribbean vibe here is authentic, dating back to the many Bahamians working in the salvage trade who eventually settled in Key West, and noticeable in the lilting music playing in cafés and the laidback attitude of locals. Sadly, the little tour trains are now running close by, and property developers are slowly bringing Bahamian Village up to speed with tourist traps like the **Bahama Village Market**, 318 Petronia St. For now, though, the place is still relatively untouched: locals still dress up on Sundays and file into the unusual, flaking churches, and the village teems with energy day and night. Though you may see chickens on the street everywhere in Key West, you're likely to see the largest number here. The descendants of Cuban fighting cocks, they are protected from harm by law, especially as their appetite for scorpions helps keeps the population down.

Caroline and Greene streets

At the northern end of Duval Street turn right onto **Caroline Street** or **Greene Street**, and you'll come across numerous examples of late-1800s "**conch houses**," built in a mix-and-match style that fused elements of Victorian, Colonial, and Tropical architecture. The houses were raised on coral slabs and rounded off with playful "gingerbread" wood trimming. Erected quickly and cheaply, conch houses were seldom painted, but many here are bright and colorful, evincing their recent transformation in the last fifteen years from ordinary dwellings to hundred-thousand-dollar winter homes. The reason such houses have lasted so well is that many were put up by shipwrights using boat-building techniques, so they sway in high winds and weather extremes of climate well.

In marked contrast to the tiny conch houses, the grand three-story **Curry Mansion**, 511 Caroline St (daily 8.30am–5.30pm; $5; ⓣ305/294-5349 or 1-800/253-3466, ⓦwww.currymansion.com), was first built in 1869 as the abode of William Curry, Florida's first millionaire. The current structure dates from 1886, when Curry's son Milton rebuilt the mansion after a major fire. Exhaustively restored, the house is an awkward hybrid of museum and hotel run by Al and Edith Amsterdam; inside, amid a riot of antiques and oddities, is a stash of strange and stylish fittings such as Henry James's piano and a lamp designed by Frank Lloyd Wright. The real reason to stop by, however, is the **Widow's Walk** (a tiny lookout on the roof where sailors' wives watched for their husbands' return), which affords an impressive view across the Old Town.

Heritage House Museum

A delightful hour or two can be spent at the charming **Heritage House Museum**, 410 Caroline St (Mon–Sat 10am–4pm, closed Aug & Sept except by appointment; tours begin every half hour; $5, $7 guided tour; ⓣ305/296-3573, ⓦwww.heritagehousemuseum.org). This double-veranda, Colonial-style home has been in the same family for seven generations, and the present owner, Jean Porter, lives in an annex. Jean's mother, Jessie Porter, who died in 1979, was the great-granddaughter of William Curry (see above). Miss Jessie, as she was known, was renowned as a lavish society hostess, and she used her connections to preserve the historic section of town. Among the luminaries she counted as friends were Tallulah Bankhead, who visited with Tennessee Williams, Gloria Swanson, and Thornton Wilder; their photographs are mounted in the hallway. Robert Frost also came and lived in a specially built cottage in the garden in 1940. While you can dawdle in the orchid-packed garden, the cottage itself is off-limits.

Other highlights include an enticing music room where you can play the 1865 French piano, a library of rare books, and an exotic room filled with Oriental *objets d'art* that Miss Jessie collected on her extensive travels. Don't miss the chance to chat with the knowledgeable docents on a tour, whose enthusiastic stories do much to illuminate the house and its history.

The dockside area

Between Williams and Margaret streets, the **dockside** area has been spruced up into a shopping and eating strip called **Land's End Village** (see "Nightlife," p.162), where a highlight is the restaurant-bar *Turtle Kraals*, in business as a turtle cannery until the Seventies, when harvesting turtles became illegal. There are tanks of touchable sea life inside and, just along the short pier, a grim gathering of the gory machines used to slice and mince green turtles – captured off the Nicaraguan coast – into a delicacy known as "Granday's Fine Green Turtle Soup." (The word "Kraals" comes from the Afrikaans word for corral, the pen where captured green turtles were kept before slaughter.) Apart from pleasure cruisers and shrimping boats along the docks, you might catch a fleeting glimpse of a naval hydrofoil – vessels of unbelievable speed employed on anti-drug-running missions from their base a mile or so along the coast.

Key West Cemetery

Leaving the waterfront and heading inland along Margaret Street for five blocks will take you to the **Key West Cemetery** (daily sunrise–6pm; free), which dates back to 1847, and whose residents are buried in vaults above ground (a high water table and solid coral rock prevent the traditional six-feet-under interment). There may be a lack of celebrity stiffs here, but by wandering through this massive graveyard you'll notice the impact of immigration on Key West – the cemetery is filled with people from across the country and abroad. Most visitors amble about without guides, but a far better plan is to join a tour. Local historian and preservationist **Sharon Wells** (1hr 30min; $20; Ⓣ305/294-8380, Ⓦwww.seekeywest.com) is the best-known guide, but the chatty, low-key tours run by the Historic Florida Keys Foundation are cheaper and just as enjoyable (Tues & Thurs 9.30am; $10, reservations essential; Ⓣ305/292-6718, Ⓔhfkf@bellsouth.net). If you decide to explore on your own, several plots are worth seeking out, including those of Edwina Lariz, whose stone reads "devoted fan of singer Julio Iglesias"; B.P. Roberts, who continues to carp from beyond the grave "I told you I was sick"; and Thomas Romer, a Bahamian born in 1789 who died 108 years later and was "a good citizen for 65 of them." Look out also for the fenced grave of Dr Joseph Otto, whose family home is now the Pilot House guesthouse (see p.152). Included on the plot is the grave of his pet Key deer, Elphina and three of his Yorkshire terriers, one of whom is described as being "a challenge to love."

A fifteen-minute walk from the cemetery, at 1431 Duncan St, is the modest two-story clapboard **house** kept by **Tennessee Williams**, who arrived in 1941 and died in 1985. Unlike his more flamboyant counterparts, Williams – Key West's longest residing literary figure, made famous by his steamy evocations of Deep South life in plays such as *A Streetcar Named Desire* – kept a low profile during his thirty odd years here. The house, which unfortunately isn't open to the public, is still a fine example of a Bahamian-style home, though it's only worth a pilgrimage if you're a devoted fan.

The rest of Key West

There's not much more to Key West beyond its compact Old Town. Most of the **eastern section** of the island – encircled by the north and south sections of Roosevelt Boulevard – is residential, but Key West's longest beach is located here, and there are several minor points of botanical, natural, and historical interest.

At the southern end of White Street, **West Martello Tower** is one of two Civil War lookout points complementing Fort Zachary Taylor (see p.155). Despite its original military purpose, it's now filled by the intoxicating colors and smells of a **tropical garden** (daily 9.30am–3.15pm; free; Ⓣ305/294-3210). Though it makes a nice outdoor break, a more worthwhile target is the tower's sister fort, East Martello Tower, which now incorporates a museum (see below).

From the tower, Atlantic Avenue quickly intersects with South Roosevelt Boulevard, which skirts one side of the lengthy but slender Smathers Beach – the weekend parade ground of Key West's most toned physiques and a haunt of windsurfers and parasailors – and on the other side the forlorn salt ponds of the **Thomas Riggs Wildlife Refuge**. From a platform raised above the refuge's mangrove entanglements, you should spot a variety of wading birds prowling the grass beds for crabs and shrimp. Save for the roar of planes in and out of the nearby airport, the refuge is a quiet and tranquil place; to gain admission you have to phone the Audubon House (Ⓣ305/294-2116, Ⓦwww.audubonhouse.com) to learn the combination of the locked gate.

Half a mile further, just beyond the airport, the **East Martello Museum and Gallery** (daily 9.30am–4.30pm; $6; Ⓣ305/296-3913, Ⓦwww.kwahs.com) is the second of the two Civil War lookout posts. The solid, vaulted casements now store a fascinating assemblage on local history, plus the wild junk-sculptures of legendary Key Largo scrap dealer Stanley Papio and the Key West scenes created in wood by a Cuban-primitive artist named Mario Sanchez. There are also displays on local writers and memorabilia from films shot in Key West; the island's old houses and dependable climate have made it a popular shooting location.

Eating

While there are some excellent places to thrill the palate – and despite the abundant **restaurants** and **snack stands** along the main streets – it's difficult to eat cheaply in Key West. There's no shortage of chic venues for fine French, Italian, and Asian cuisine, but if you want really good, inexpensive food and don't want to resort to fast-food chains, visit any of the **Cuban sandwich shops**, which also offer filling, tasty meals at a fraction of the price of a main-street pizza. Explore streets off the beaten path and understand that the less a place is hyped, the better the quality will normally be. Most menus, not surprisingly, feature fresh **seafood**, and you should sample **Conch fritters** – a Key West specialty – at least once.

Cafés, bakeries, and sandwich shops

Blond Giraffe 629 Duval St ☎305/293-6998. Awarded "Best Key Lime Pie" in a local bake-off a couple of years ago, this café even lets you watch them make it – and the benches are perfectly positioned for people watching. Branch at 1209 Truman Ave ☎305/293-6667.

Cole's Peace 930-A Eaton St ☎305/292-6511. Tiny, stylish bakery offering crusty bread and unfussy, wholegrain pastries – a healthy pit stop for breakfast.

Conch Shop 308 Petronia St, next to Johnson's Grocery ☎305/294-4140. Formica tables and a staff sweating over bubbling oil makes this down-to-earth "soul & sea food" eatery appear kind of gritty. Be brave – the fritters, served with potato salad and iced tea or jungle punch, are excellent and well priced. Erratic opening hours, especially on the weekend.

Dennis Pharmacy 1229 Simonton St ☎305/294-1577. Superb *café con leche* and set breakfasts served in a real drugstore. The service is no-frills, but there's plenty of local gossip to overhear while you sip. Only open until 5pm.

Dining in the Raw 800 Olivia St ☎305/295-2600. There isn't much room to sit, but the exquisite mid-priced vegetarian (mostly vegan) dishes can be ordered for takeout. Desserts are to die for and include nondairy pecan pie, raw apple cobbler, and iced herbal teas.

Five Brothers Grocery 930 Southard St ☎305/296-5205 or 1-888/646-6423. Expect long lines at this age-old grocery store, a real locals' favorite for its strong Cuban coffee and cheap Cuban sandwiches ($3.95). It's also crammed with provisions, plus pots and pans dangling from the ceiling. Opens at 6am.

Johnson's Café 801 Thomas St ☎305/292-2286. The motto at this small café is "Bust your belly" and the cheap, enormous sandwiches ($6) don't disappoint. Buy a beer from the grocery across the road and settle down on the veranda with your meal. Lunch only Tues–Thurs, lunch and dinner Fri & Sat.

Just for Loco's 517 Truman Ave ☎305/296-1177. Tiny, inexpensive café attached to a laundromat, and serving filling, authentic Cuban and Mexican dishes for around $5. Don't miss the walls where the owner has carefully created a collage from photos of bikini-clad tourists. Daily 8am–4pm.

Sandy's Café inside the M&M Laundry, 1026 White St ☎305/295-0159. A deliciously dingy shack serving terrific, cheap Cuban sandwiches: try the Cuban-mix sandwich ($3.50) and watch the locals milling round you.

Restaurants

A&B Lobster House 700 Front St ☎305/294-5880. There could hardly be a more scenic setting than this harborside restaurant for indulging in a luxury seafood dinner. If you find the prices too rich (or want to eat at lunchtime), try *Alonso's* raw bar upstairs – run by the same people at about half the price.

Alice's at La-Te-Da 1125 Duval St ☎305/296-6706. The menu here is Asian-inflected, and heavy on seafood – think pistachio-crusted grouper with mangoes – and the open-air dining room is a lovely place to spend an evening. The crowd is mixed (gay & straight) and reasonably upscale given the prices.

Antonia's 615 Duval St ☎305/294-6565. Excellent northern Italian cuisine served in a formal though friendly environment. Expensive but worth it, especially for the home-made pasta. Dinner only.

Awful Arthur's Seafood Company 628 Duval St ☎305/AWE-SOME. This fish shack offers excellent-value nightly specials, such as All You Can Eat Snow Crab for $20, crisp, tangy french fries, and bargain priced beer. Recommended, especially given its central location.

Bahama Mama's 324 Petronia St ☎305/294-3355. Brightly colored Caribbean café, with ample outdoor seating and jaunty reggae piped around the courtyard. Entrees hover around $15 – try the conch platter with plantains and hush puppies.

Blue Heaven Café corner of Thomas and Petronia streets ⓣ305/296-0867, ⓦwww.blueheavenkw.com. Sit in this dirt yard in Bahamian Village where Hemingway once refereed boxing matches and enjoy the superb food while chickens wander aimlessly around your feet. Try the mouthwatering banana bread, the lobster Benedict, or one of the sumptuous desserts. Highly recommended (though it's not cheap).

Café Marquesa 600 Fleming St ⓣ305/292-1244. Attractive small café located inside the *Marquesa Hotel*, offering an imaginative New American menu – chichi presentation and prices to match.

Camille's 1202 Simonton St ⓣ305/296-4811. Recently reopened in a huge new location, *Camille's* is known as one of the best places in town for breakfast: try one of the decadent specials like French toast with Godiva chocolate sauce or cashew nut waffles with coconut milk for around $8.

Caribe Soul 425 Grinnell St ⓣ305/296-0094. Moderately priced Caribbean dishes, well presented in laid-back surroundings – try the shrimp eggs Benedict for breakfast.

El Siboney 900 Catherine St ⓣ305/296-4184. A little out of the way, but well worth the effort for some of the best – and best-value – food on the island. Sit at canteen-style tables with red and white checkered cloths and ask the wait staff for recommendations. The pork tenderloin portion alone could feed four. Highly recommended.

Hot Tin Roof inside the *Ocean Key Resort*, Zero Duval St ⓣ305/295-7057. The food's rich and Caribbean-inflected at this upscale restaurant – try the crab cakes – and make sure to save room for the inventive desserts. The best tables are outside on the patio overlooking the water.

Mangia Mangia 900 Southard St ⓣ305/294-2469. The best-value Italian restaurant on the island, with fine fresh pasta (you can watch them making it in their front window), a nice atmosphere, and good prices.

Mango's 700 Duval St ⓣ305/292-4606. Don't be put off by its location in the middle of Duval Street's T-shirt row: the creative menu is Caribbean influenced and the shaded street front patio is a great place for a cocktail (the house special is a mango-rita) at lunchtime.

Origami Sushi Bar Duval Square shopping center, 1075 Duval St ⓣ305/294-0092. The sushi served at this tiny restaurant is tasty, fresh, and a bargain compared to many restaurants nearby: most rolls are $4.50 (try the unusual bagel roll), while sushi is $1.50–2 per piece.

Seven Fish Restaurant 632 Olivia St ⓣ305/296-2777. This little-known restaurant, easy to miss in its tiny white corner building, serves some of the best food in Key West – there are just over a dozen tables, so it pays to book. The cooking's simple and delicious and the crowd is a mix of straight and gay.

Nightlife

The carefully cultivated "anything goes" nature of Key West is exemplified by the **bars** that make up the bulk of the island's **nightlife**. Gregarious, rough-and-ready affairs they are often open until 4am and offer a cocktail of yarn-spinning locals, revved-up tourists, and (often) live blues, funk, country, folk, or rock music. The mainstream bars are grouped around the northern end of Duval Street, no more than a few minutes' stagger apart. Much of Key West's best nightlife, though, revolves around its eateries, and the best are far from Mallory Square's well-beaten path.

Bars, clubs, and live music venues

The Bull 224 Duval St ⓣ305/296-4565. This loud and rowdy bar features the best of local musicians each night – mainly playing blues and R&B. Check the list on the door to see who's playing – or just turn up to drink. Open till 4am nightly.

Captain Tony's Saloon 428 Greene St ⓣ305/294-1838. This rustic saloon was the original *Sloppy Joe's* (see p.162), a renowned hangout of Ernest Hemingway – he met his third wife, Martha Gellhorn, here. One of the better choices for live music, and a must-stop for Hemingway fans.

El Meson de Pepe, next to Mallory Square at 410 Wall St ⓣ305/295-2620. Cuban-style restaurant/bar in a converted warehouse, funkily decked out with brightly colored murals and the obligatory black-and-white photos of 1950s Havana. The faux Cuban fakery can be a little cloying, but the pleasant tiki bar in the garden makes a fair refuge from Mallory Square at sunset.

Green Parrot Inn 601 Whitehead St ⓣ305/294-6133. Grubby old-time pub that's been a landmark for more than 100 years. Drinks are cheap, the place is full of locals, and there are antique bar games alongside the pool tables. Often hosts live music at weekends on its small stage.

Hog's Breath Saloon 400 Front St ⓣ305/292-2032. Despite its central location, and the boozed-up patrons staggering out of the front door whatever the time of day, this bar's one of the best places to catch live music in town, mostly for a nominal cover. A must-see during the Key West songwriters' festival in early May.

Margaritaville 500 Duval St ⓣ305/292-1435. Owner Jimmy Buffett – a Florida legend for his rock ballads extolling a laid-back life in the sun – occasionally pops up to join the live country bands that play here nightly.

Sloppy Joe's 201 Duval St ⓣ305/294-5717. Despite the memorabilia on the walls and the hordes of tourists, this bar – with live rock or blues nightly – is not the one made famous by Ernest Hemingway's patronage. For the real thing, see *Captain Tony's Saloon*, p.161. Eminently missable and a symbol of the worst of Key West's tourist excesses.

Turtle Kraals Land's End Village, end of Margaret St ⓣ305/294-2640. A locals' hangout, offering fine views over the marina and mellow blues on Friday and Saturday nights from the second-story *Tower Bar*.

Two Friends 512 Front St ⓣ305/296-3124. A small, friendly restaurant/bar with live jazz every night but Monday.

Virgilio's on Appelrouth Lane, adjoining *La Trattoria* at 524 Duval St ⓣ305/296-1075. This martini bar has an outdoor patio, as well as small indoor bar and stage, often occupied by loud Cuban bands. Drinks are served with a flourish, as each cocktail's overflow is presented alongside your glass in a mini carafe on ice.

Wax 42 Applerouth Lane ⓣ305/296-6667. The closest Key West comes to a traditional nightclub – overstuffed red sofas and bead curtains decorate a chic, dimly lit space. Open daily 9pm–4am; there's usually no cover.

Gay and lesbian Key West

Gay life in Key West is always vibrant and attracts frolicking hordes from North America and Europe. The party atmosphere is laidback, sometimes outrageous, and there's an exceptional level of integration between the straight and gay communities. Unlike other Florida gay centers like South Beach, Key West does a fine job at keeping the catwalk-strutting at bay (though it's always lurking at poolsides in the sun). Outside the Old Town, though, it's not always a good idea to be openly gay and there have unfortunately been reports recently of gay-bashing late at night in these areas.

The tragedy of AIDS has hit Key West hard since the mid-1980s. Many of those stricken have come to soak up the temperate climate and the very evident camaraderie of the locals. A somber but important trip to the ocean at the end of White Street reveals a striking AIDS memorial, where blocks of black granite are engraved with a roll call of those in Key West who have been struck down.

Just about all the gay bars and hotels – all from Duval Street's 800 block southwards – are male-orientated, though most are welcoming to women. Also nearby is the Gay and Lesbian Community Center in unit C14, Duval Square (entrance at 1075 Duval St; ⓣ305/292-3223, ⓦwww.glcckeywest.org), which has all the latest information as well as literary seminars, gay-interest video screenings, and lesbian social events on Fridays. Otherwise, stop off at the Gay & Lesbian Information Center, 728 Duval St (Mon–Fri 9am–5pm; ⓣ305/294-4603, ⓦwww.gaykeywestfl.com). The unofficial gay beach is **Higgs Memorial Beach**, at the southern end of Reynolds Street; for a spell on the water, take one of the day or evening boat trips that depart from here

– one of the best is Tea on the Sea, run by Sebago Watersports (Tues, Sat $30 men only; Thurs $35 women only, including unlimited wine and beer; ⓣ1-800/507-9955, ⓦwww.sebagokeywest.com), which leaves at 9pm from the dock at the end of William Street. For information on what's happening pick up a copy of the free *Southern Exposure* magazine or check out *Celebrate! Key West* (ⓦwww.celebratekeywest.com), a newsier, more informative freesheet.

Bars

801 Bourbon Bar 801 Duval St ⓣ305/294-4737. Free drag shows upstairs every night at 8 & 11pm, while downstairs there's a nondescript bar with a mixed, slightly older crowd that opens on to Duval Street, so you can watch passersby. Friendly, if bland, atmosphere.

Aqua 711 Duval St ⓣ305/294-0555. Large, pumping club with a massive dance floor; the music's mainstream house and Hi-NRG. Good happy hour specials 2–8pm daily.

Atlantic Shores Beach Club 511 South St ⓣ305/296-2491. Offers a wildly popular Tea by the Sea on Sunday (7–11pm) and Wednesday (6–10pm), with great views out onto the ocean. Nonguests can also pay $3 for a deck chair and towel to spend the day by the pool: this is a "clothing optional" resort, but only a small percentage of bathers go bare.

Bourbon Street Pub 724 Duval St ⓣ305/296-1992. A huge pub with five bars, seven TV screens, and a pleasant garden out back, complete with large hot tub. There's a diverse blend of locals and tourists. There are go-go boys every night, and happy hour until 8pm.

Kwest Men 705 Duval St ⓣ305/294-5995. Small, cruisey bar on the main drag where there's a daily happy hour 3–8pm with drinks specials, and go-go boys dancing to the pumping house music from 10pm nightly.

La-Te-Da 1125 Duval St ⓣ305/296-6706 or 1-877/528-3320. The various bars and discos of this hotel complex have long been a favorite haunt of locals and visitors. The upstairs Crystal Room is one of the best known showcases for drag divas in town – during season, there are shows nightly at 8.30pm and 10.30pm ($18).

Listings

Airport Key West International airport (EYW) is four miles east of the Old Town, on South Roosevelt Blvd (ⓣ305/296-5439). No public transportation link to the Old Town; a taxi will cost around $10. American Airlines (ⓣ1-800/433-7300; from Miami, Tampa), Delta (ⓣ1-800/221-1212; from Orlando, Tampa), Continental/Gulfstream (ⓣ1-800/525-0280; from Miami, Fort Lauderdale, Tampa), and USAir (1-800/428-4322; from Miami, Tampa) fly into Key West. Flights between Key West and Miami start at around $150 return (depending on season and availability).

Bike rental From Adventure Scooter & Bicycle Rentals, at nos. 1 and 601 Duval Street (plus five other locations around the Old Town (ⓣ305/293-9933, ⓦkeywest.com/scooter.html) and the *Youth Hostel*, 718 South St (ⓣ305/296-5719).

Bookstores Compared with book-bereft Miami, Key West is a literary haven. Best of all is the Key West Island Bookstore, 513 Fleming St (daily 10am–9pm; ⓣ305/294-2904), which is packed with the works of Key West authors and Keys-related literature, and has an excellent selection of rare and secondhand books. Blue Heron at 1014 Truman Ave (Mon–Sat 10am–9pm, Sun 10am–6pm; ⓣ305/296-3508) is very knowledgeable and friendly. Specializing in gay studies and the works of local authors, it also has a good general stock. Flaming Maggies, 830 Fleming St (Mon–Sat 10am–6pm; ⓣ305/294-3931), stocks gay- and lesbian-interest books and also serves excellent coffee. Bargain Books, 1028 Truman Ave (daily 7am–10pm; ⓣ305/294-7446), has a massive stock of secondhand books, usually at half the cover price.

Buses Local information ⓣ305/292-8160, ⓦwww.keywestcity.com.

Car rental Only worth it if you're heading off to see the other Keys. All companies are based at the airport: Alamo (ⓣ305/294-6675); Dollar (ⓣ305/296-9921); Hertz (ⓣ305/294-1039).

Cigars Key West used to be a major producer of cigars, but now the traditional industry survives in only a few workshops. The best places to pick up cigar souvenirs are Conch Republic Cigar Factory, 512 Greene St (ⓣ305/292-2858, ⓦwww.conch-cigars.com), Sunset Cigar Co of Key West, 306 Front St (ⓣ305/295-0600 or 1-866-597-6653), and Tropical Republic, 112 Fitzpatrick St (ⓣ305/292-9595).

Dive shops Diving and snorkeling trips and equipment rental can be arranged all over Key West. Try the highly acclaimed Southpoint Divers, 714 Duval St (ⓣ1-800/891-DIVE, ⓦwww.southpointdivers.com). The shop runs two trips daily (8.30am for wreck and reef, 1.30pm for two reefs); snorkelers pay $45, divers $59–75. Another option is Seabreeze Reef Raider, 617 Front St (ⓣ1-800/370-7745, ⓦwww.keywestscubadive.com); snorkel boats ($35) leave at 10am, 1.30pm, and during summer 5pm for a snorkel-sunset combo, while dive boats ($65–75) leave at 9am and 2pm. (See also "Reef trips" and "Ecology tours" below.)
Ecology tours Dan McConnell, based at Mosquito Coast Island Outfitters, 310 Duval St (ⓣ305/294-7178, ⓦwww.mosquitocoast.net), runs six-hour kayak tours of backcountry mangroves ($55 per person) filled with facts on the ecology and history of the Keys; you can also snorkel during the trip, which leaves at 8.45am and returns at 3pm. To explore the reef by boat, join the informative half- or full-day tours aboard the 65-foot schooner *Reef Chief* ($40; times vary by season; ⓣ305/292-1345, ⓦwww.reefchief.com for details).
Greyhound Office at airport (ⓣ305/296-9072).
Hospitals 24-hour casualty department at Lower Florida Keys Medical Center, 5900 College Rd, Stock Island (ⓣ305/294-5531).
Internet cafés Getting connected to the Internet is not cheap in Key West, and the majority of cybercafés charge around $10 for an hour's access. However, if you do need to get online, the best options are Internet Isle, 118 Duval St (ⓣ305/293-1199); the coffee shop *Sippin' on Eaton*, 424 Eaton St (ⓣ305/293-0555); and the Monroe County Library, 700 Fleming St (ⓣ305/292-3595).
Late-night food stores Owls, 712 Caroline St, daily until 11pm; and Sunbeam Market, 500 White St, which never closes.
Library 700 Fleming St (ⓣ305/292-3595, ⓦwww.co.monroe.fl.us/pages/csd/lib.htm); book sale on the first Saturday of each winter month.
Newsagents L. Valladares & Son, 1200 Duval St (ⓣ305/296-5032), stocks British and Irish newspapers and a vast selection of magazines from the US and elsewhere.
Parking 24-hour parking is available at the corner of Caroline and Grinnell streets ($1.25/hr, $8/day; ⓣ305/293-6426).
Police Emergency ⓣ911, nonemergency ⓣ305/296-2424.
Post office 400 Whitehead St (Mon 8.30am–5pm, Tues–Fri 9.30am–5pm, Sat 9.30am–noon; ⓣ305/294-9539). Zip code is 33040.
Reef trips *The Discovery* glass-bottomed boat makes three two-hour trips a day from the northern tip of Duval Street to the Florida Reef ($30; ⓣ305/293-0099, ⓦwww.discoveryunderseatours.com). For snorkeling and diving, see "Dive shops" above.
Supermarket Fausto's Food Palace, 522 Fleming St (Mon–Sat 8am–8pm, Sun 8am–6pm) or, for big supermarkets, head for the Overseas Market between N Roosevelt Blvd and Paterson Ave.
Taxi Unlikely to be necessary except to get to the airport (see above); try Five (ⓣ305/296-6666) or Friendly Cab (ⓣ305/292-0000).
Watersports Jet-skiing, waterskiing, and parasailing are all possible, in the right conditions, using outlets set up alongside Smathers Beach. For more details phone Seabago Watersports (ⓣ1-800/507-9955, ⓦwww.sebagowatersports.com).

Beyond Key West: the Dry Tortugas

Seventy miles west of Key West in the Gulf of Mexico is a small group of islands that the sixteenth-century Spaniard Juan Ponce de León named the **Dry Tortugas** for the large numbers of turtles (*tortugas* in Spanish) he found there – the "dry" was added later to warn mariners of the islands' lack of fresh water. Comprising Garden Key and its neighboring reef islands, the entire area has been designated a wildlife sanctuary to protect the nesting grounds of the sooty tern – a black-bodied, white-hooded bird that's unusual among terns for choosing to lay its eggs in scrubby vegetation and bushes. From early January, these and a number of other winged rarities show up on Bush Key, and they are easily spied with binoculars from Fort Jefferson on Green Key.

Fort Jefferson

Green Key is the last place you'd expect to find the US's largest nineteenth-century coastal fortification, but **FORT JEFFERSON** (daily during daylight hours; ⓣ305/242-7700, ⓦwww.nps.gov/drto), which rises mirage-like in the distance as you approach, is exactly that. Started in 1846 and intended to protect US interests on the Gulf, the fort was never completed, despite thirty years of building. Instead it served as a prison, until intense heat, lack of fresh water, outbreaks of disease, and savage weather made the fort as unpopular with its guards as its inmates; in 1874, after a hurricane and the latest yellow fever outbreak, it was abandoned. Look for the change in colors of the bricks: the shift marks the outbreak of the Civil War, when the Union-loyal fort here was no longer able to buy supplies from Key West. Of course, the bricks shipped down from the north at the top of the walls have weathered the hot, humid weather less well than the local materials at the base.

Following the signposted **walk** around the fort and viewing the odds and ends in the small museum won't take more than an hour – and spare time should be allocated to **swimming** and **snorkeling**: get a free map of the best locations from the park ranger's office by the entrance.

You can **get to the fort** by air in half an hour with *Seaplane of Key West* from Sunset Marina, 5603 Junior College Rd, Stock Island ($179 half-day, $305 full day; ⓣ1-800/950-2FLY, ⓦwww.seaplanesofkeywest.com) – a beautiful trip that takes you low over the turquoise water. Less expensive and more relaxed is the Tortugas high-speed ferry, *Yankee Freedom II*, which leaves from the Key West Sea Port (daily 8am; $119 day-trip, $149 overnight; ⓣ1-800/YANKEECAT, ⓦwww.yankeefleet.com) – though sea-sickness sufferers might do better to take the plane, as the crossing can prove choppy. The price includes breakfast, lunch, guided tour, and snorkel gear. After a few leisurely hours at the fort, the ferry returns at 5.30pm. Avid birdwatchers can **camp** at Fort Jefferson for up to twenty days, though given its lack of amenities you have to come well prepared with your own supplies of water and food; only in an emergency can you count on help from the park ranger.

Travel details

Buses

Three Greyhound buses a day run between Miami and Key West. Scheduled stops are listed below, though the bus can be waved down at other stops – stand by the side of the Overseas Highway and jump about like a maniac when you see the bus coming.

Scheduled stops are in: North Key Largo (Central Plaza, 103200 Overseas Highway; ⓣ305/451-6280); Islamorada (Burger King, MM82; ⓣ305/852-4266); Marathon (6363 Overseas Highway; ⓣ305/743-3488); Big Pine Key (MM30.2; ⓣ305/872-4022); Key West (junction Duval, Simonton, and Virginia streets); and Key West International Airport (ⓣ305/296-9072). From Miami to: Big Pine Key (3hr 50min); Islamorada (2hr 20min); Key West (4hr 30min); Marathon (3hr 20min); North Key Largo (1hr 55min).

Ferries

A passenger-only ferry service operated by X-press (ⓣ1-800/650-5397, ⓦwww.xp2kw.com) will take you from Key West across to Fort Myers on the Gulf of Mexico side of mainland Florida (see "Sarasota and the Southwest" chapter). The ferry leaves from the A & B Marina on Front Street, and is a good way of getting to Florida's west coast without zigzagging back across the Keys and through the Everglades. The ferry runs daily – weather permitting – only at 5.30pm and ticket prices are $70 one way or $119 round-trip – though there's a $10 surcharge on return tickets if you don't come back the same day.

There's also a new catamaran service connecting with Miami, which allows you to bypass the often-clogged US-1. Island Rocket (ⓣ1-800/854-8121, ⓦwww.islandrocket.com) leaves Bayside Marketplace in downtown Miami at

8.30am Thurs–Sun and arrives two hours later in Islamorada; the return leg departs at 4.30pm. Tickets are $48.50 one way and $89.50 round-trip.

Planes

A more sensible option is to fly on an island hopper – Cape Air (ⓣ1-800/352-0714, ⓦwww.flycapeair.com) flies to Naples, Fort Meyers, and Fort Lauderdale from Key West daily.

3

The Everglades

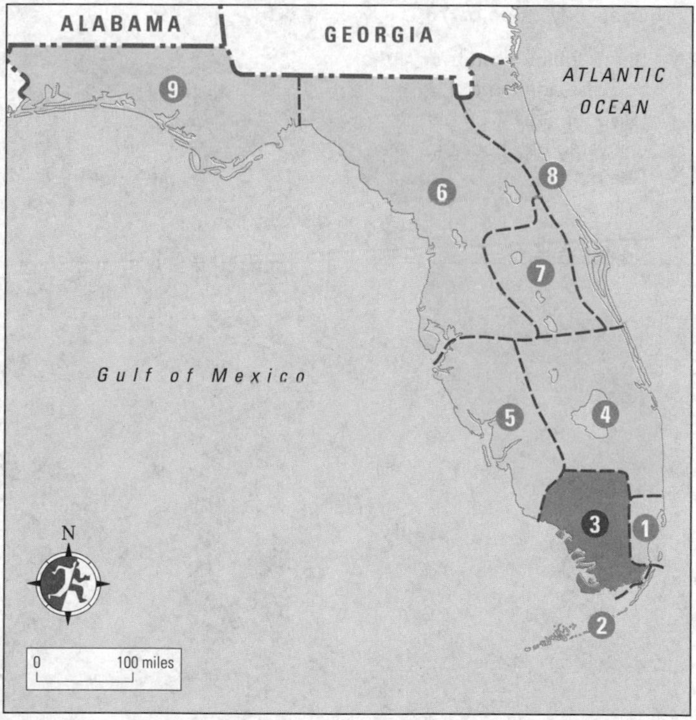

CHAPTER 3

Highlights

* **The Anhinga Trail** In season, the popular route is teeming with birds and reptiles. **See p.174**
* **Pelican Backcountry Cruise** Take a leisurely ride through tea-colored water to Whitewater and Coots bays. **See p.176**
* **Shark Valley tram tour** You'll be adrift in the "River of Grass" on an enjoyable two-hour trip. **See p.176**
* **Fakahatchee Strand** The atmospheric dwarf cypress forest should hold allure for all who visit it. **See p.179**
* **Ten Thousand Islands** Ply the waters of this unusual swampscape by boat or by canoe. **See p.180**

△ Egret

3

The Everglades

Nothing anywhere else is like them: their vast glittering openness, wider than the enormous visible round of the horizon, the racing free saltness and sweetness of their massive winds, under the dazzling blue heights of space. They are unique also in the simplicity, the diversity, the related harmony of the forms of life they enclose. The miracle of the light pours over the green and brown expanse of sawgrass and of water, shining and slow-moving below, the grass and water that is the meaning and the central fact of the Everglades of Florida. It is a river of grass.

Marjory Stoneman Douglas, *The Everglades: River of Grass*

Whatever scenic excitement you might anticipate from one of the country's more celebrated natural areas, no mountains, canyons, or even signposts herald your arrival in the **EVERGLADES**. From the straight and monotonous ninety-mile course of US-41, the most dramatic sights are small pockets of trees poking above a completely flat sawgrass plain that stretches to the horizon. It looks dead and empty; you wonder what all the fuss is about. Yet these wide-open spaces resonate with life, forming part of an immensely subtle and ever-changing ecosystem that has evolved through a unique combination of climate, vegetation, and wildlife.

Originally encompassing everything south of Lake Okeechobee, throughout the last century the Everglades' boundaries have steadily been pushed back by human demands for farmland, fresh water, and urban development. Only a comparatively small section around Florida's southern tip is under the federal protection of **Everglades National Park**. It's here, where public access is designed to inflict minimum damage, that the vital links holding the Everglades together become apparent: the all-important cycle of wet and dry seasons; the ability of alligators to discover water and dig for it with their tails; and the tree islands providing sanctuaries for animals during the flood period. None of this can be comprehended from a car window or a half-hour ride through the sawgrass on an airboat; in fact, the noisy, destructive contraptions touted all along the Tamiami Trail (US-41) are banned inside the park.

Don't expect to fathom it all: the Everglades are a constant source of surprise, even for the few hundred people who live in them. Use the visitor centers, read the free material, take the guided tours and, above all, explore slowly. It's then that the Everglades begin to reveal themselves and you'll realize you're in the middle of one of the natural world's most remarkable ecosystems.

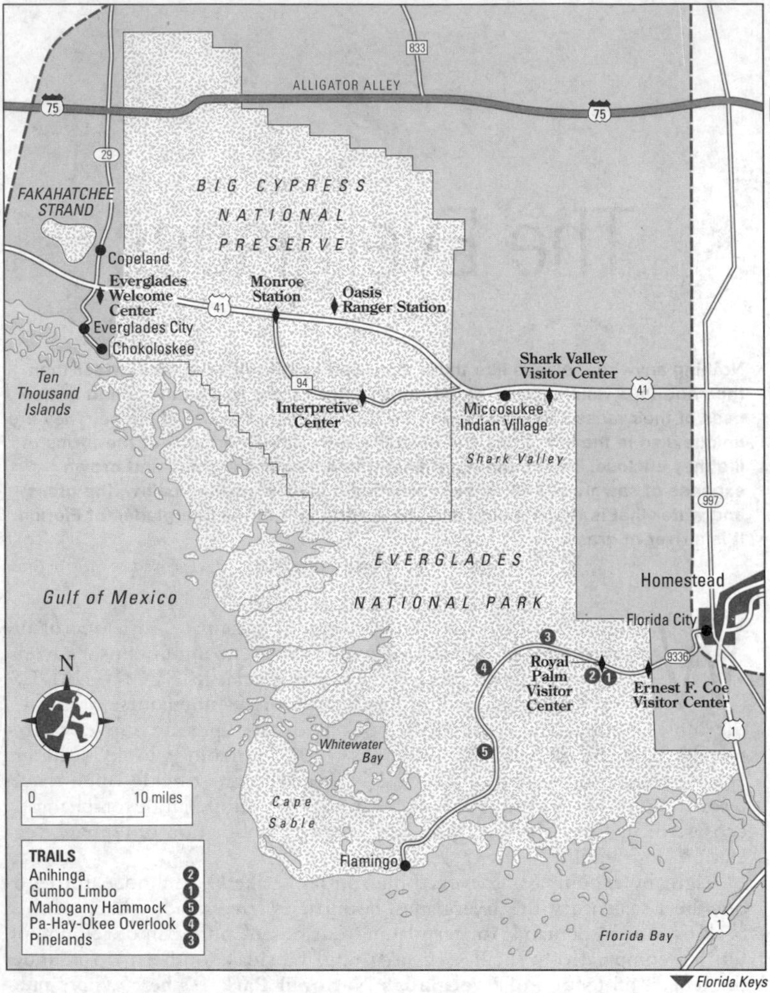

Everglades history and preservation

Appearing as flat as a tabletop, the limestone on which the Everglades stands (once part of the seabed) actually tilts very slightly – a few inches over seventy miles – toward the southwest. For thousands of years, water flowed as a sixty mile wide sheet through the Everglades, from Lake Okeechobee to the coast. This sheet flow replenishes the **sawgrass**, which grows on a thin layer of soil – or "marl" – formed by decaying vegetation on the limestone base, and gives birth to the algae at the foot of a complex food chain that sustains much larger creatures, most importantly alligators.

Alligators earn their "keepers of the Everglades" nickname during the dry winter season. After the summer floodwaters have reached the sea, drained through the bedrock, or simply evaporated, the Everglades is barren except for the water accumulated in ponds or "gator holes" – created when an alligator senses water and clears the soil covering it with its tail. Besides nourishing the alligator, the pond provides a home for other wildlife until the summer rains return.

Sawgrass covers much of the Everglades, but where natural indentations in the limestone fill with marl, tree islands – or "**hammocks**" – appear, just high enough to stand above the flood waters and fertile enough to support a variety of trees and plants. Close to hammocks, often surrounding gator holes, you'll find wispy green-leafed willows. Smaller patches of vegetation, like small green humps, are called "**bayheads**." **Pinewoods** grow in the few places where the elevation exceeds seven feet and, in the deep depressions that hold water the longest, dwarf cypress trees flourish, their treetops forming a distinctive "cypress dome" when large numbers cover an extensive area.

Human settlement and exploitation

Before dying out through contact with Europeans, several Native American tribes lived hunter-gatherer existences in the Everglades. The shell mounds they built can still be seen in sections of the park. In the nineteenth century, **Seminole Indians**, who'd fled white settlers in the north, also lived peaceably in the area (for more on them, see "Miccosukee Indian Village," p.177). By the late 1800s, a few white settlements – such as those at Everglades City and Flamingo – had sprung up, peopled by fugitives, outcasts, and loners who, unlike the Indians, looked to exploit the land rather than live in harmony with it.

As Florida's population grew, the damage caused by uncontrolled hunting, road building, and draining the Everglades for farmland gave rise to a significant conservation lobby. In 1947, a section of the Everglades was declared a national park, but unrestrained commercial use of nearby areas continued to upset the Everglades' natural cycle. The problem was acknowledged – if hardly alleviated – by the preservation in the Seventies of the **Big Cypress Swamp**, just north of the park.

As human understanding increases, so the severity of the problems faced by the Everglades becomes ever more apparent. The 1200 miles of canals built to divert the flow of water away from the Everglades toward the state's expanding cities, the poisoning caused by agricultural chemicals from the farmlands around Lake Okeechobee, and the broader changes wrought by global warming and invasion by non-native species, threaten to turn Florida's greatest natural asset into a wasteland – with wider ecological implications that can only be guessed at.

The future of the Everglades

In an attempt to increase the natural sheet flow in the Everglades, Congress authorized a thirty-year, $7.8 billion plan in 2000 to dismantle miles of levees and canals, and divert and store part of the 1.7 billion gallons of water lost each day (in the flow from Lake Okeechobee to the ocean) for later use. The plan, however, is not without its problems. One potential obstacle lies with the technology that would be used to build massive underground aquifers, which has not been tested on so large a scale; furthermore, no alternatives have been proposed should the technology fail. Another relates to the croplands near Lake

Okeechobee, which environmental groups had been eyeing for conversion into reservoirs. Government efforts to acquire the land were met with stiff resistance from local sugar growers and so far have yielded little acreage. Meanwhile, critics of the plan have predicted that without addressing the root causes of the Everglades plight, the project is bound to fail. Given the years of projects and studies that still lie ahead, and the plan's scale and complexity, it will be some time before it's clear whether all the effort will produce any, if not all, of the desired results.

Everglades practicalities

From Miami and points north, take the **Florida's Turnpike Extension**, following signs for "Homestead and the Florida Keys" to the end, where it drops you on US-1 South. Make a right at the first traffic light (onto Palm Drive, or 344th Avenue), and follow the signs for the park entrance. Beyond here is the Ernest F. Coe Visitor Center (the park's main one).

From the east or west coasts, take the busy two-lane road **US-41** (the **Tamiami Trail**). Not the scenic drive you might expect, the road runs along the northern edge of the park between Naples and Miami, providing the only land access to the park entrances at Everglades City and Shark Valley, and to Fakahatchee Strand, the Big Cypress National Preserve, and the Miccosukee Indian Village.

No public transport of any kind runs along US-41 or to any of the park entrances, though day-trips are organized by almost every tour operator in Miami and Naples as well (see p.257). Between Naples and Fort Lauderdale, Greyhound buses use "Alligator Alley," the popular title for Route 84, twenty miles north of US-41, recently converted into a section of I-75.

When to visit

Though open all year, the park changes completely between its **wet** (summer) and **dry** (winter) seasons. The best time to visit is **winter** (Nov to March), when receding floodwaters cause wildlife, including migratory birds, to congregate around gator holes and sloughs (freshwater channels). During this period, ranger-led activities – such as guided walks, canoe trips, and talks – are frequent, and the mosquitoes are bearable, but this is also when the park is at its busiest, and accommodation prices rise accordingly – rates at the lone hotel, *Flamingo Lodge*, are fifty percent higher in winter than in summer – and it is advisable to book ahead, especially on the weekends.

The picture is entirely different in **summer** (mid-May to Oct), when afternoon storms flood the sawgrass prairies and pour through the sloughs, leaving only the hammocks visible above water. Around this time, **mosquitoes** and **deerflies** become a severe annoyance, rendering the backcountry campgrounds and marshy areas almost uninhabitable – you'd best think long and hard before undertaking a visit then. In addition, organized activities are substantially reduced, most migratory birds have gone, and the park's wildlife spreads throughout the park due to a plentiful supply of food.

A clever compromise is a visit **between the seasons** (April to early May, or late Oct to early Nov), which avoids the worst of the mosquitoes and the winter tourist crowds, but at the same time reveals plenty of wildlife and the park's changing landscapes.

Entering the park

Entering the park is free at Everglades City (though you can only see it by boat or canoe). At the entrance near the Coe Visitor Center, admission is $10 per car, $5 pedestrians and cyclists. At Shark Valley, it's $8 per car, $4 pedestrians and cyclists, and this is the only entrance that closes for the night (5pm). Tickets are valid for seven days and can be used at all park entrances. (At the time of writing, access at Chekika was closed due to high water and poor road conditions; check with the park's visitor centers for updates.) With the exception of the Wilderness Waterway canoe trail between Everglades City and Flamingo, you can't travel from one section of the park into another.

Accommodation and eating

Apart from the two organized campgrounds (see p.174) and a hotel at Flamingo (see p.174), park accommodation is limited to backcountry campgrounds. In most cases these are raised wooden platforms with a roof and chemical toilet accessible by boat or canoe. To stay, you need to pick up a permit, issued free from the closest ranger station, no more than 24 hours beforehand. One backcountry site at Flamingo, Pearl Bay, is accessible to disabled visitors, with lower ground access to huts and other facilities.

Ten miles outside the park in Florida City, the *Everglades International Hostel*, 20 SW Second Ave (☎305/248-1122 or 1-800/372-3874, ⓦwww.evergladeshostel.com), offers beds for $16 a night ($13 for members), with private rooms starting at $33, and the hostel is perfectly situated for continuing on to the Florida Keys or to Miami International Airport. Bike and kayak rental is also available, and the very friendly staff will lend you racks to transport equipment on your car or give you a lift to the park entrance.

For **food**, *Rosita's*, opposite the *Everglades International Hostel* at 199 W Palm Drive (☎305/246-3114), serves excellent and reasonably priced Mexican dishes, and is even open for breakfast. Otherwise the closest restaurants are in Homestead: try *Gullotto Italian Bakery and Deli*, 243 NE 8th St (☎305/245-6949), for fine coffee, pastries, and sandwiches; or *Capri Restaurant*, 935 N Krome Ave (☎305/247-1542), a reliable option for home-cooked Italian dishes.

What to bring

In the park, wear a hat, sunglasses, and loose-fitting clothes with long sleeves and long trousers, and carry plenty of **insect repellent**. Aside from anticipating the hazards of sunburn (there's very little shade) and mosquitoes, you need take no special measures for the walking trails, many of which are short trots along raised boardwalks.

Traveling and camping in the **backcountry** requires more caution. Most exploration is done by boat or canoe along marked trails, with basic campgrounds situated on the longer routes. Take a **compass**, **maps** (available from visitor centers), and ample provisions, including at least a **gallon of water** per person per day. Supplies should be carried in **hard containers**, as raccoons can chew through soft ones. Be sure to leave a **detailed plan** of your journey and its expected duration with a park ranger. Finally, pay heed to the latest **weather forecast** and note the tidal patterns if you're canoeing in a coastal area.

Pine Island

The **Pine Island** section of the park – the entire southerly portion, containing Cape Sable and Flamingo (see opposite) – holds virtually everything that makes the Everglades tick: spend a well-planned day or two here for an introduction to its complex ecology. Just a short distance along from the **Ernest F. Coe Visitor Center** (daily 8am–5pm; ⓣ305/242-7700), the road passes through the **park entrance** (always open; cars $10, pedestrians and cyclists $5), and continues for 38 miles to the tiny coastal settlement of Flamingo, a one-time pioneer fishing colony now comprising a marina, hotel, and campground. There's nothing to compel you to drive the whole way, and the short walking trails (none longer than half a mile) along the route will keep you engaged for hours; sensibly, though, you should devote one day to walking and another to the canoe trails close to Flamingo.

There are well-equipped **campgrounds** ($14 per tent site) at Long Pine Key, near the main visitor center, and Flamingo, as well as many backcountry sites (free) on the longer walking and canoe trails. Reservations can be made up to five months in advance by calling ⓣ1-800/365-CAMP or by visiting ⓦreservations.nps.gov. Spare space at Flamingo (which invariably fills first) or Long Pine Key can be checked on the board just inside the park entrance. If there is space and the visitor center is closed, you can use the site, but should pay at the visitor center before 10am the following day. For the backcountry sites, you will, of course, need a permit. These are issued free at the visitor centers. The only **rooms** within the park are at *Flamingo Lodge* (ⓣ239/695-3101 or 1-800/600-3813, ⓦwww.flamingolodge.com; ❸), which has a full-service restaurant that's open daily in peak season – off-peak, there's a limited menu at the lodge's nondescript *Buttonwood Patio Café*. It's advisable to reserve a room months in advance if arriving between November and April.

Toward Flamingo: walking trails

A good place to gather information on the Everglades' various habitats is the **Royal Palm Visitor Center** (daily 8am–5pm), a mile from the main park entrance. Apparently unimpressed by the multitudinous forms of nature and wildlife throughout the Everglades, large numbers of park visitors simply want to see an alligator, and most are satisfied by walking the half-mile **Anhinga Trail** here; the reptiles are easily seen during the winter, often splayed near the trail, looking like plastic props. They're notoriously lazy, but give them a wide berth, as they can be extremely quick in the right circumstances. Turtles, marsh rabbits, and the odd raccoon are also likely to turn up on the route, but you

Before entering the park

It's a good idea to stop for a snack or drink before entering the park – otherwise you'll have to wait until Flamingo, 38 miles later at the end of Park Drive. Your last chance for refreshments is the unusually named fruitstand and store, **Robert Is Here**, on SW 344th Street in Homestead, directly on the way to the park (daily 8am–7pm; ⓣ305/246-1592, ⓦwww.robertishere.com). Fresh corn, tomatoes, and spinach, and unfamiliar Caribbean produce like sapodilla, black sapote (often said to taste like chocolate pudding), and mamey line the plank shelves, along with hot sauces, chutneys, preserves, syrups, and coconut candy. Pick up some sugarcane juice or a cherry–Key lime milkshake ($3) to cool your body temperature in preparation for the heat of the Everglades.

should watch for the bizarre anhinga, a black-bodied bird resembling an elongated cormorant, which, after diving for fish, spends ages drying itself on rocks and tree branches with its white-tipped wings fully spread. Beat the crowds to the Anhinga Trail and then peruse the adjacent but very different **Gumbo Limbo Trail**, a hardwood jungle hammock packed with exotic subtropical growths: strangler figs, red-barked gumbo limbos, royal palms, wild coffee, and resurrection ferns. The latter appear dead during the dry season, but "resurrect" themselves in the summer rains to form a lush collar of green. Much of the vegetation along the trail was destroyed by Hurricane Andrew in 1992 and is just now beginning to grow back.

By comparison, the **Pinelands Trail**, a few miles further, by the Long Pine Key campground (ⓣ305/242-7700), offers an undramatic half-mile ramble through a forest of slash pine, though the solitude comes as a welcome relief after the busier trails. The hammering of woodpeckers is often the loudest sound you'll hear. More birdlife – including egrets, red-shouldered hawks, and circling vultures – is viewable six miles ahead from the **Pa-hay-okee Overlook Trail**, which emerges from a stretch of dwarf cypress to face a sweeping expanse of sawgrass. Although related to California's giant redwoods, the mahogany trees of the **Mahogany Hammock Trail**, seven miles from the Overlook Trail, are disappointingly small despite being the largest of the type in the country. A greater draw is the colorful snails and golden orb spiders lurking amongst their branches. The sight of the red mangrove trees – recognizable by their above-ground roots – rising from the sawgrass is a sure indication that you're approaching the coast.

Flamingo and around

A century ago, the only way to reach **FLAMINGO** was by boat, a fact that failed to deter a small group of settlers who came here to fish, hunt, smuggle, and get paralytic on moonshine whiskey. It didn't even have a name until the opening of a post office made one necessary: "The End of the World" was favored by those who knew the place, but "Flamingo" was eventually chosen due to an abundance of roseate spoonbills – pink-plumed birds, killed for their feathers – wrongly identified by locals. The completion of the road to Homestead in 1922 was expected to bring boom times to Flamingo, but as it turned out, most people seized on this as a chance to leave. None of the old buildings remains, and present-day Flamingo does a brisk trade servicing the needs of sportsfishing fanatics. On land, the **visitor center** (Dec–April, 7.30am–5pm, rest of year intermittent hours; ⓣ239/695-2945) and the marina of the *Flamingo Lodge* (see opposite) are the activity bases.

There are several walking trails within reach of Flamingo, but more promising are the numerous **canoe trails**. Rent a canoe ($22 half day, $32 full day, $40 for 24 hours) or kayak ($27 half day, $43 full day, $50 for 24 hours) from the marina, and get maps and advice from the visitor center. Obviously, you should pick a canoe trail that suits your level of expertise. A likely one for novices (don't go it alone if you've no experience whatsoever) is the two-mile **Noble Hammock Trail**, passing through sawgrass and around mangroves, using a course pioneered by makers of bootleg booze. An alternative, the **Mud Lake Loop** (6.8 miles), travels through Buttonwood Canal, Coot's Bay, Mud Lake, and the Bear Lake Canoe Trail, with plenty of opportunities for prime bird-watching. For polished paddlers, the hundred-mile **Wilderness Waterway** to Everglades City (see p.180), lined by plentiful backcountry campgrounds, is the trip you've been waiting for.

If you lack faith in your own abilities, take one of the **guided boat trips** from the marina. The most informative, the **Pelican Backcountry Cruise** (daily; $18; reservations on ⓣ239/695-3101, ext 322), makes a two-hour foray around the mangrove-enshrouded Coot's and Whitewater bays, offering good views of **Cape Sable**, a strip of deserted beach and rough prairie hovering uncertainly between land and sea.

Shark Valley

In no other section of the park does the Everglades' "River of Grass" tag seem as appropriate as it does at **Shark Valley** (daily 8.30am–5pm; cars $8, pedestrians and cyclists $4), in the northern reaches of the park along the Tamiami Trail. From here the sawgrass plain stretches as far as the eye can see, dotted by hardwood hammocks and the smaller bayheads. It's here, too, that the damage wrought by humans on the natural cycle can sometimes be disturbingly clear. The thirst of Miami coupled with a period of drought can make Shark Valley resemble a stricken desert.

Seeing Shark Valley

Aside from a few simple walking trails close to the **visitor center** (daily: Nov–April, 8.30am–5.15pm; May–Oct, 9am–4.30pm; ⓣ305/221-8776), you can see Shark Valley only from a fifteen-mile loop road. Too lengthy and lacking in shade to be covered comfortably on foot, and off limits to cars, the loop is ideally covered by **bike** (rental costs $5.25 an hour; return by 4pm). Alternatively, a highly informative two-hour **tram tour** (at least 4 tours daily, hourly during winter; $12, children $8; reservations recommended Dec–April; ⓣ305/221-8455) will get you around and stops frequently to view wildlife, but won't allow you to linger in any particular place.

Set out as early as possible (the wildlife is most active in the cool of the morning), ride slowly and stay alert: otters, turtles, and snakes are plentiful but not always easy to spot, and the abundant alligators often keep uncannily still. During September and October you'll come across female alligators tending their young; the brightly striped babies often sun themselves on the backs of their extremely protective mothers; watch them from a safe distance. More of the same creatures – and a good selection of birdlife – can be seen from the **observation tower** overlooking a deep canal and marking the far point of the loop.

Airboat tours

Airboat tours are synonymous with the Everglades and all along US-41 operators will try and tempt you onto one of their trips. In the hands of a responsible operator they are not a problem; however, not all operators are so inclined and these tours have a damaging impact on the environment. Oil and gas from the boats pollute the rivers, and constant use of the same routes leaves scars in the environment. Many give passengers marshmallows to feed the alligators, thus ensuring you get to see one. Feeding wild animals is not the best of ideas and is strongly discouraged by the authorities as it makes animals lose their natural fear of humans and become aggressive and dangerous. If you do want to take an airboat tour, be careful which operator you choose.

Miccosukee Indian Village

Driven out of central Florida by white settlers, several hundred Seminole Indians retreated to the Everglades during the nineteenth century to avoid forced resettlement in the Midwest. They lived on hammocks in open-sided *chickee* huts built from cypress and cabbage palm, and traded, hunted, and fished across the wetlands by canoe. Descendants of the Seminoles and a related tribe, the **Miccosukee**, still live in the Everglades, though the coming of US-41 – making the land accessible to the white settlers – brought another fundamental change in their lifestyle as they set about grabbing their share of the tourist dollars.

A mile west of Shark Valley, the **Miccosukee Indian Village** (daily 9am–5pm; $5; ⓣ305/223-8380) symbolizes the tribe's uneasy compromise. In the souvenir shop good-quality traditional crafts and clothes stand side by side with blatant tat, and in the "village" men turn logs into canoes and women cook over open fires. Despite the authentic roots, it's such a contrived affair that anyone with an ounce of sensitivity can't help but feel uneasy – the arrow-shooting gallery and the awful alligator-wrestling don't help. Since it's the only chance you're likely to get to discover anything of Native American life in the Everglades, it's hard to resist taking a look, though a plateful of traditional pumpkin bread from the *Miccosukee Restaurant* (ⓣ305/894-2374) across the road and a look at the *Seminole Tribune* newspaper, describing modern concerns, might serve as a better introduction.

Big Cypress National Preserve

The completion of US-41 in 1928 led to the destruction of thousands of towering bald cypress trees – whose durable wood is highly marketable – that lined the roadside sloughs. By the Seventies, attempts to drain these acres and turn them into saleable residential plots had caused enough damage to the national park for the government to create the **Big Cypress National Preserve** – a massive chunk of protected land mostly on the northern side of US-41. Sadly, neither the bald cypress trees nor the wood storks that once flourished here are present in anything like their previous numbers (a better place to observe both is the Corkscrew Swamp Sanctuary north of Naples, see p.256). Although this stretch of the highway has frequent warning signs reminding drivers to be careful of panthers on the road, you're as likely to see one as you are to win the Florida lottery. When Miami started to grow in the late 1800s these timid cats were seen as a threat and now, due to over-hunting, it is estimated that there are only between thirty and fifty cats – the official state mammal of Florida – left alive.

Seeing the preserve

The only way to traverse the entire Big Cypress Swamp is on a very rugged 29-mile (one-way) hiking trail, beginning on US-41 at the **Oasis Ranger Station** (daily 8.30am–4.30pm; ⓣ239/695-1201). Visitors are required to pick up a free backcountry permit, for either day or overnight use. More manageable hiking routes include the five-mile **Fire Prairie Trail** (on Turner River Road, fourteen miles north of US-41); its slight elevation means it tends to be on the dry side, giving colorful prairie flowers a chance to bloom in the spring. There's also the 6.5-mile Loop Road to US-41 (see p.179), though it's often submerged in knee-deep water. More serious treks require advance planning, perseverance, and hauling all of your own water; ask the visitor centre for details.

△ Ten Thousand Islands

Near the visitor center is the **Big Cypress Gallery**, 52388 Tamiami Trail (Mon–Sun 10am–5pm; ⓣ239/695-2428 or 1-888/999-9113, ⓦwww.clydebutcher.com), which exhibits the work of Everglades photographer Clyde Butcher. His amazing pictures capture all the beauty and magic of the area. Framed pictures are on the expensive side, but they also come as smaller cards that make perfect souvenirs. There's also a convenient gator hole beside the gallery where you can take your own close-up photos of alligators. While it's not actually part of the national preserve, be sure to visit the nearby **Fakahatchee Strand**, directly north of Everglades City on Route 29. This water-holding slough sustains dwarf cypress trees (much smaller than the bald cypress; gray and spindly during the winter, draped with green needles in summer), a stately batch of royal palms, and masses of orchids and spiky-leafed air plants. If possible, see it on a **ranger-guided walk** (details on ⓣ239/695-4593).

Dragonfly Expeditions (ⓣ305/774-9019 or 1-888/9-WANDER, ⓦwww.dragonflyexpeditions.com) offer excellent backwater half-day treks in which small groups are led off the beaten track – which in summer means wading waist-deep in water – right into the heart of the Everglades. More of an adventure than a hike, these treks are led by highly informed field guides who offer loads of information on the environment and wildlife in it. A gourmet lunch under a canopy of Spanish moss is also included in the price – as are the use of water shoes and walking sticks (which you may need to pull yourself out of the mud!). Tours start at $75 per person and tour guides will either meet you at the Big Cypress Gallery (see above), or provide transport to the start of the walk. On their Miccosukee Indian Heritage Tours a Native American guide leads groups to the Miccosukee/Seminole island camp, offering the chance to learn about the wildlife and the history and culture of the Miccosukee; tours start at $55 per person.

If you're up for an off-road trek, and if your car's suspension is dependable, turn left off US-41 at Monroe Station, four miles west of the Oasis Ranger Station, onto Loop Road, a gravel road that's potholed in parts and prone to sudden flooding which winds its way through cypress stands and pinewoods. Once you reach Pinecrest, things get easier: the road becomes paved (and is now called Hwy-94) and after another twenty minutes or so, rejoins US-41 at Forty Mile Bend, just west of the Miccosukee Indian Village.

North of the preserve

Though not part of the national preserve, the Big Cypress Seminole Reservation directly to the north on I-75 has a couple of attractions that may hold your interest for an hour or two. Located between Naples and Fort Lauderdale, they aren't in the vicinity of the aforementioned sights and are more easily seen while traveling east or west long I-75. At **Billie Swamp Safari**, sixteen miles north on North Hwy-833, after exiting I-75 at exchange 49 daily 8.30am–6pm; ⓣ1-800/949-6101), swamp buggies resembling inflated army jeeps take visitors cruising over the Everglades (1hr narrated, $20), where alligators, egrets, and American buffalo are sure to be seen. An all-day pass, which includes a buggy tour, airboat ride, and an educational presentation on snakes and alligators, is $38 ($24 for children). You can also experience a traditional overnight camp-out in a native-style *chickee* (an open-sided, palm-thatched hut) and listen to ancient Seminole tales (a two-person *chickee* is $35 per night, eight-person dorm $65). About three miles down the road, at the **Ah-Tah-Thi-Ki Museum** (Tues–Sun 9am–5pm; $6; ⓣ863/902-1113), you can learn more about the Seminole people and their traditions through the displays and rare collection of clothing and implements.

Everglades City and around

Purchased and named in the Twenties by an advertising executive dreaming of a subtropical metropolis, **EVERGLADES CITY** not only serves as a good base from which to explore the Everglades, it also warrants investigating in its own right. Thirty miles from Naples and three miles south off US-41 along Route 29, the city has a population of under five hundred in summer that swells to around 1500 in winter. Despite taking a direct hit from Hurricane Donna in the Sixties, which destroyed many of its buildings, the city has lost none of its charm and sense of identity in its re-creation. Some of the properties left standing in the wake of the Hurricane Donna have been restored, offering a glimpse of life before the destruction. One such building is the **Museum of the Everglades**, 105 W Broadway (Tues–Sat 11am–4pm; $2; ⓣ239/695-0008), housed in what used to be the old laundry when it was built in the late 1920s. It now displays a small selection of artifacts and old photographs documenting the last two thousand years in the southwest Everglades. It's hard to miss the large, wooden, triangular building that houses the Everglades **Area Chamber of Commerce Welcome Center** (daily 8.30am–5pm; ⓣ239/695-3941, ⓦwww.florida-everglades.com), at the junction of Route 29 and US-41.

Many of the visitors are here for the fishing, especially around the numerous mangrove islands scattered like jigsaw-puzzle pieces along the coastline – aptly named **Ten Thousand Islands**. For a closer look at the mangroves that safeguard the Everglades from surge tides, ignore the ecologically dubious tours advertised along the roadside and take one of the park-sanctioned **boat trips**. Try Everglades National Park Boat Tours (ⓣ239/695-2591 or toll-free within Florida 1-800/445-7724), which has 95-minute excursions starting from $16, and Everglades Rentals and Eco Adventures (ⓣ239/695-4666, ⓦwww.evergladesadventures.com), located at *Ivey House Bed and Breakfast* (see "Accommodation" below), which offers a range of activities from November through April, from a three-hour paddle ($50) to full-day excursions ($75–125). Canoes and kayaks can also be rented from both outfits if you want to explore on your own, and from the dockside **Gulf Coast Visitor Center** (daily Nov–April 7.30am–5pm, May–Oct 8.30am–5pm; ⓣ239/695-3311), which provides information on the boat trips, as well as excellent ranger-led **canoe trips**. Anybody adequately skilled with the paddle, equipped with rough camping gear, and with a week to spare, should have a crack at the hundred-mile **Wilderness Waterway**, a marked trail through Whitewater Bay to Flamingo (see p.175), with numerous backcountry campgrounds en route.

Accommodation

Other than boat-accessed camping, there's no **accommodation** inside this section of the park. In Chokoloskee, five miles south of Everglades City, you can rent an RV by the night for $40–55 at *Outdoor Resorts* (ⓣ239/695-2881). Camping is available at the **Big Cypress Trail Lakes Campground**, eight miles away in Ochoppe on US-41 (ⓣ239/695-2275), where it costs $12 a night to pitch a tent. There are also basic motel rooms (and RV space) in the cheap but shabby *Barron River Resort* on Route 29 (ⓣ239/695-3591 or 1-800/535-4961; ❷). *Ivey House Bed & Breakfast*, 107 Camellia St (ⓣ239/695-3299, ⓦwww.iveyhouse.com; open Nov–April – booking advisable; ❸), is charming and clean, breakfast is included with the room rate, and evening meals are served daily at 6pm for an extra $10–15 (they also run a slightly nicer inn on the premises, where rooms come with TV, phone, and private bathroom; ❹). *The Captain's Table*, 102 E Broadway (Ⓣ239/695-4211 or 1-800/741-6430, Ⓦwww.capttable.com; ❷), has a great heated pool overlooking a lake and guests get a good discount at the *Everglades Seafood Depot* restaurant (see below). The *Rod & Gun Lodge*, 200 Riverside Drive (Ⓣ239/695-2101; ❸), used to be an exclusive club whose members included presidents, but now anyone can stay here; for an extra $10–20 you can eat at their restaurant. *The Banks of the Everglades*, located at 201 W Broadway (Ⓣ239/695-3151 or 1-888/431-1977; ❺), is an unusual B&B and day spa housed in what used to be the first bank in the county. Breakfast is served in the old walk-in vault and the whole place is crammed full of artifacts from the building's previous life.

Eating and drinking

It's no surprise that there's plenty of **seafood** to be eaten in the area. Situated in the old train depot, *The Everglades Seafood Depot*, 102 Collier Ave (Ⓣ239/695-0075), offers a good selection of Mexican and Caribbean dishes as well as seafood, and will cook any fish that you have caught (and cleaned). At the *Oyster House*, on Chokoloskee Causeway (Ⓣ239/695-2073), you can watch the sunset over the Ten Thousand Islands while you eat, and enjoy a full cocktail lounge – the "Glades Margarita" is a specialty – and entertainment on the weekends. At *Joanie's Blue Crab Café*, 39395 US-41 in Ochopee (daily 10am–5pm; Ⓣ239/695-2682), a colorful shack crammed with knickknacks, you can dine on a meal of frog legs, 'gator pieces, and Indian fry bread for $13, or choose from the usual sandwiches and seafood dishes.

4

The Southeast

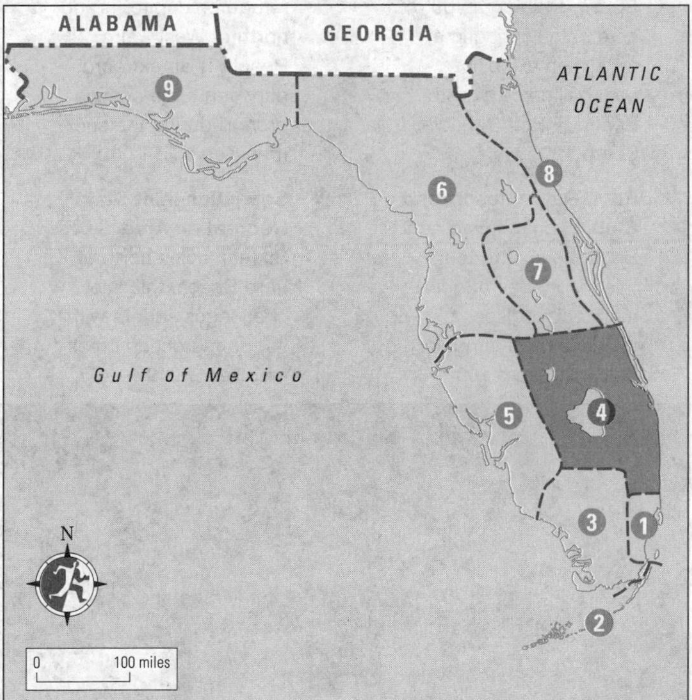

CHAPTER 4

Highlights

* **Fort Lauderdale** The town's reputation as a haven for teens and retirees has begun to diminish, and some lovely buildings and a fine museum make it an inviting destination. See p.188

* **Spring training** If you're here in the springtime, take in an exhibition baseball game at Vero Beach or Port St Lucie. See p.190

* **Boca Raton Resort and Club** If you're going near Boca, be sure to tour this resort, one of quirky architect Addison Mizner's most intriguing designs. See p.200

* **Morikami Museum and Japanese Gardens** You'll feel like you've been transported to Japan after stepping into an intricate tea ceremony here. See p.202

* **Hobe Sound National Wildlife Refuge** This refuge on Jupiter Island, north of West Palm Beach, is an extraordinary sea turtle nesting ground during the summer. See p.214

* **Sebastian Inlet State Recreation Area** Sixteen miles north of Vero Beach, this inlet challenges surfers with its roaring ocean breakers. See p.219

△ Fort Lauderdale

4

The Southeast

Comprising the better part of the **SOUTHEAST** and stretching from the fringes of northern Miami along almost half of Florida's Atlantic shoreline, the 130-mile **southeast coast** is the sun-soaked Florida of the popular imagination, with bodies bronzing on palm-dotted beaches as warm ocean waves lap idly against silky-soft sands. Roughly half the region forms one of the fastest-growing residential areas in the state, however, leaving many of the once spectacular ocean strips walled by unappealing high-rises. While you can drop your beach towel just about anywhere, don't spend all your time on the southeast coast cultivating a tan. Take the time to explore some of the towns and seek out the undeveloped, protected sections, where you'll experience the Florida coastline as nature intended it. The **Gold Coast**, the first fifty-odd miles of the southeast coast up to Palm Beach, lies deep within the sway of Miami and comprises back-to-back conurbations often with little to tell them apart. However, the first and largest, **Fort Lauderdale**, is certainly distinctive: the reputation for rowdy beach parties – stemming from its years as a student Spring Break destination – is well out of date; the town has cultivated a cleaner-cut, sophisticated, and posher image, aided by an excellent art museum and an ambitious downtown improvement project. Further north, diminutive **Boca Raton**, which possesses some of the Gold Coast's finest beaches, is renowned for its 1920s Mediterranean Revival buildings. Boca Raton was shaped by the unconventional architect Addison Mizner, but the latter is best remembered for his work in **Palm Beach**, which is now inhabited almost exclusively by multi-millionaires, yet accessible to visitors of all budgets. Less than an hour inland is **Lake Okeechobee**, markedly less brash and a prime fishing spot for big bass anglers.

North of Palm Beach, the population thins, and nature asserts itself forcefully throughout the **Treasure Coast**. Here, rarely crowded beaches flank long, pine-coated barrier islands such as Jupiter and Hutchinson islands, whose miles of untainted shoreline are quiet enough for sea turtles to come ashore and lay their eggs.

By car, the scenic route along the southeast coast is **Hwy-A1A**, which sticks wherever possible to the ocean side of the **Intracoastal Waterway**. Beloved of Florida's boat owners, this stretch was formed when the rivers dividing the mainland from the barrier islands were joined and deepened during World War II to reduce the threat of submarine attack. When necessary, Hwy-A1A turns inland and links with the much less picturesque **US-1**. The speediest road in the region, **I-95**, runs about ten miles west of the coastline, splitting the residential sprawl from the wide-open Everglades, and is only worthwhile if you're in a hurry.

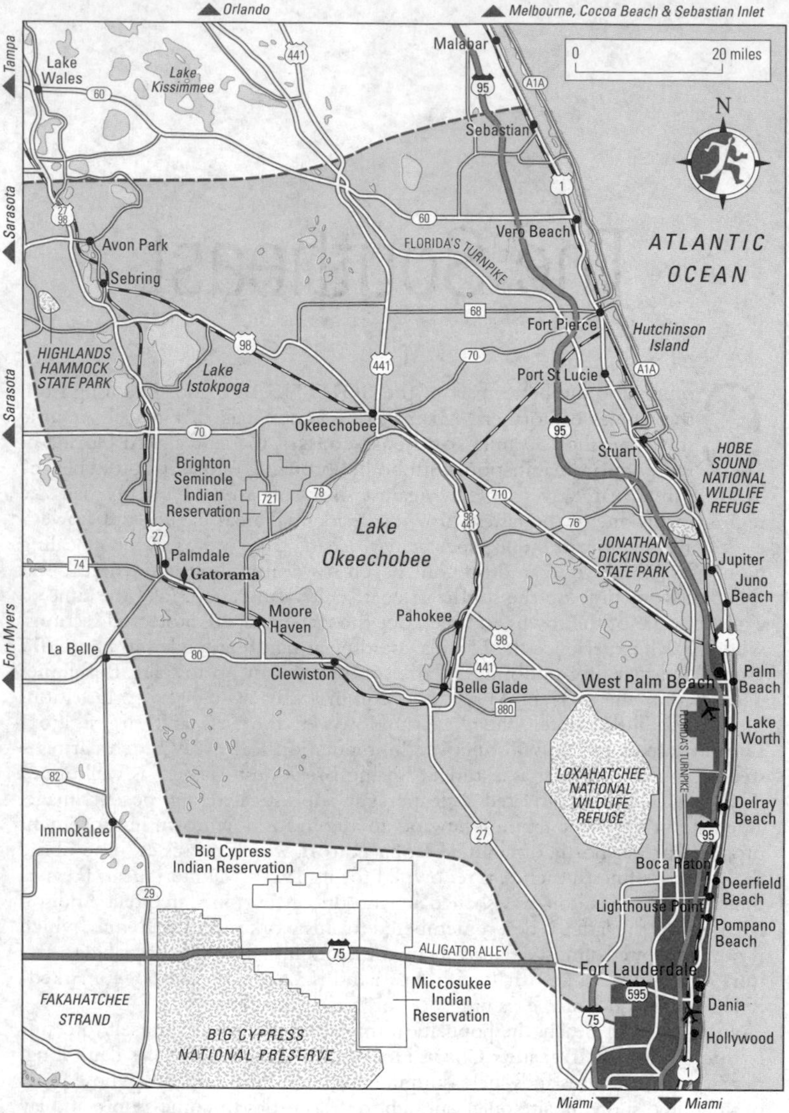

Frequent Greyhound connections link the bigger towns, and a few daily services run to the smaller communities. Local **buses**, plentiful from the edge of Miami to West Palm Beach, are nonexistent in the more rural Treasure Coast. Along the Gold Coast, there's the additional option of the dirt-cheap Tri-Rail rush-hour service, while Amtrak has two daily **trains** running as far north as West Palm Beach.

The Gold Coast

The widely admired beaches and towns occupying the fifty-mile commuter corridor north of Miami make the **GOLD COAST** – named for the booty washed ashore from sunken Spanish galleons – one of the most heavily populated and tourist-besieged parts of the state. The sands sparkle, the nightlife rocks, and many of the communities have an assertively individualistic flavor – but if you're seeking peace and seclusion, look elsewhere.

Hollywood

From Miami Beach, Hwy-A1A runs through undistinguished Hallandale before reaching **HOLLYWOOD** – founded and named by a Californian in 1924 – with a generous beach and a more cheerful persona than the better-known and much larger Fort Lauderdale, ten miles north. Allocate an hour to the 2.5-mile-long pedestrian-only **Broadwalk**, parallel to Hwy-A1A (known here as Ocean Drive), whose snack bars and skateboarders enliven a casual amble. Afterwards, drop by the **Art and Culture Center of Hollywood**, 1650 Harrison St (Tues–Sat 10am–4pm, Sun 1–4pm; $3; ⓣ954/921-3274), for a look at works by emergent Florida artists, and stroll around the surrounding **Harrison Street Art and Design District**, where small galleries, restaurants, quirky stores, and occasional street players draw modest crowds in the evening. The Downtown Hollywood Events Line (ⓣ954/921-3016, ext 19) can clue you in to what's going on around town.

Reasonably priced **motels** line Hollywood's oceanside streets. For good value try the *Manta Ray Inn*, 1715 S Surf Rd (ⓣ1-800/255-0595; ❹), or the *Tide Vacation Apartments*, 2800 N Surf Rd (ⓣ954/923-3864, ⓦwww.tideapartments.com; ❹). As usual, you'll save a few dollars by staying further inland, where the *Shell Motel*, 1201 S Federal Hwy (ⓣ954/923-8085, ⓦwww.shellmotelhollywood.com; ❷) offers good rates. At the other end of the spectrum, the beachfront *Westin Diplomat* at 3555 S Ocean Drive (ⓣ954/602-6000 or 1-888/627-7218, ⓦwww.diplomatresort.com; ❽) has replaced the celebrated *Diplomat* hotel but retained the luxury, with an enormous pool, several elegant restaurants, and spa privileges.

What it lacks in terms of sights, Hollywood more than makes up for with its restaurants, bars, and clubs, especially in the area around Harrison Street and Hollywood Boulevard, west of US-1. A cheap, intimate place to **eat** Thai food is *Try My Thai*, 2003 Harrison St (ⓣ954/926-5585), while the small and friendly luncheonette *Grace & Jack's*, 1862 N Young Circle (ⓣ954/920-9299), has tasty sandwiches and pastries (it even has Internet access at $5 for 30min). For **nightlife**, there's live blues (Thurs–Sun) and Japanese food on offer at the small and rather pricey *Sushi Blues*, 1836 S Young Circle (ⓣ954/929-9560). If you fancy a drink right on the beach, accompanied by live jazz and Caribbean food, head for *Sugar Reef Tropical Bar and Grill*, 600 N Surf Ave (ⓣ954/922-1119; closed Tues in summer), while the rotating shows of quality jazz, blues, and R&B are the main draw at *O'Hara's Jazz Café*, 1903 Hollywood Blvd (ⓣ954/925-2555), while out toward the beach, *Shenanigans Sports Bar*, 3033 Sheridan St (no cover; ⓣ954/981-9702), has live rock or blues every night except Sunday, when DJs spin. For those with the urge to dance, *Club Atlantic*, 101 N Ocean Drive (ⓣ954/926-3350), specializes in global house music.

Dania

Ocean Drive continues north into **DANIA**, whose prime asset isn't the grouping of pseudo-English antique shops along US-1 but the pine trees and sands of the **John U. Lloyd Beach State Recreational Area**, at no. 6503 (daily 8am–sunset; cars $3.25, pedestrians and cyclists $1). Situated on a peninsula jutting out into the entrance to the shipping terminal of Port Everglades, the 251-acre park provides an enjoyable, 45-minute nature trail around its mangrove, seagrape, and guava trees. If you're around during June and July, you can find out about loggerhead turtle watching; trips include a twenty-minute slide presentation and a visit to a nest (if one is available), but try to book a month or so in advance as they are immensely popular – and take plenty of insect repellent. Check with a park ranger (☎954/923-2833) for details on this and other scheduled activities.

With more time to spare, visit the **South Florida Museum of Archaeology and Natural History**, 481 S Federal Hwy (Tues–Sat 10am–4pm, Thurs until 8pm, Sun 1–4pm; $10; ☎954/925-7770), where copious Tequesta Indian artifacts that were unearthed locally highlight an excellent pre-Columbian collection, augmented by items from Africa and Egypt.

If you're in need of sustenance, the *Islamadora Fish Company,* inside Bass Pro Shops Outdoor World at 200 Gulf Stream Way, Dania Beach (☎954/927-7737), has some of the freshest (and largest) sushi imaginable alongside the usual fish dishes. When you're done, you can gawk at live fish in the massive aquarium at the center of Outdoor World.

Toward Fort Lauderdale: by boat, car, or bus

To continue north without a car you can use local **bus** #1 (which you can catch at any BCT stop on US-1), or the pricier Greyhound, 1707 Tyler St in Hollywood (☎954/922-8228). Alternatively, if you're not weighed down by luggage, call the Water Taxi (☎954/467-6677) to ferry you from the recreational area to any dockable part of Fort Lauderdale – see "Fort Lauderdale" below for more details.

Fort Lauderdale

A thinly populated riverside trading camp at the turn of the century, **FORT LAUDERDALE** came to be known as "the Venice of America" when its mangrove swamps were fashioned into slender canals during the Twenties.

From the Thirties on, intercollegiate swimming contests drew the nation's youth here, a fact seized upon by the 1960 teen-exploitation film, *Where the Boys Are*, which instantly made Fort Lauderdale the country's number one Spring Break venue. Hundreds of thousands of students congregated around the seven miles of sand for a six-week pre-exam frenzy of underage drinking and lascivious excess, earning the place a global reputation for rambunctious beach life. By the late Seventies, the students were also bringing six weeks of traffic chaos, and proving a deterrent to regular tourists. Fighting back, the local authorities began a negative advertising campaign across the country's campuses in the early Nineties, enacting strict laws to restrict boozing and wild behavior around the beach. As a result, the swell has been reduced from over 300,000 at its 1986 peak, to the current crowd of 50,000 less manic revelers.

Subsequently, Fort Lauderdale has emerged as an affluent business, historical, and cultural center dominated by a mix of wealthy retirees and affluent yuppies keen to play down the beach-party tag and play up the town's settler-period history. It's a pleasant place (with a flourishing gay scene, see "Gay and lesbian Fort Lauderdale"; p.196), and a long way from the social inferno you might have been led to expect.

Arrival, information, and getting around

Known as Federal Highway, US-1 plows through the center of **downtown Fort Lauderdale**, three miles inland from the coast. Just south of downtown, **Hwy-A1A** veers oceanward off US-1 along SE Seventeenth Street and runs through beachside Fort Lauderdale. All the long-distance public transport terminals are in or near downtown: the Greyhound **bus station** is at 515 NE Third St (Ⓣ954/764-6551), while the **train** and Tri-Rail station is two miles west at 200 SW 21st Terrace (Amtrak Ⓣ1-800/USA-RAIL, Ⓦwww.amtrak.com; Tri-Rail Ⓣ1-800-TRI-RAIL, Ⓦwww.trirail.com), linked to the center by regular bus #22.

Professional sports venues

Sports enthusiasts will find the Greater Fort Lauderdale area a hub of professional athletic activity: you can catch the spring training (in March) of baseball's **Baltimore Orioles** at Fort Lauderdale Stadium (Ⓣ954/523-3309) and, during the regular season, watch the **Florida Marlins** (Ⓣ305/626-7400, Ⓦflorida.marlins.mlb.com) at Pro Player Stadium, 2269 NW 199th St, sixteen miles northwest of downtown Miami. Mid-July to August sees the preseason training of football's **Miami Dolphins** (Ⓣ305/620-2578, Ⓦwww.miamidolphins.com) in nearby Davie at the Nova Southeastern University campus, 7500 SW 30th St; during the regular season they, too, play in Pro Player Stadium. The Office Depot Center at 2555 Panther Parkway, just west of Fort Lauderdale in Sunrise, is home to the **Florida Panthers** hockey team (Ⓣ954/835-7000, Ⓦwww.floridapanthers.com). It's also not far to the American Airlines Arena, 601 Biscayne Blvd, to see professional basketballers the Miami Heat (Ⓣ786/777-HOOP, Ⓦwww.nba.com/heat).

The **Convention and Visitors Bureau** is located inside the port administration building at 1850 Eller Drive, Suite 303 (Mon–Fri 8.30am–5pm; Ⓣ954/765-4466, Ⓦwww.sunny.org) in the Port Everglades area, which is nearly impossible to find without a car. You're better off picking up a copy of the free *CityLink* magazine or *New Times* (available throughout the city) to find out what's going on. For nightlife, dining, and shopping ideas, check the *Guest Informant* and *Great Locations* publications that are usually found in hotel rooms. Also available is a free **tourism and cultural hotline** (Ⓣ954/527-5600), staffed by operators fluent in five languages. For **Internet** access, try ENet Café, 1497 SE 17th St (Ⓣ954/332-2976).

The handiest service offered by the thorough **local bus** network (BCT Ⓣ954/357-8400, Ⓦwww.broward.org/bct) is the #11, which runs twice hourly along Las Olas Boulevard between downtown Fort Lauderdale and the beach; **timetables** are available from Governmental Center (at the corner of Andrews Avenue and Broward Boulevard), the bus terminal directly opposite, or from libraries and check cashing centers. If you are using the buses, remember to buy a **Buz Pass** ($2.50), which allows unlimited travel on the buses throughout Broward County – otherwise it's $1 a journey and there are no transfers.

More expensive than buses – but more fun – are **water taxis** (daily 10am–midnight; Ⓣ954/467-6677, Ⓦwww.watertaxi.com), a series of small boats that will pick up and deliver you almost anywhere along Fort Lauderdale's many miles of waterfront, from Broward up to Seventeenth Street Causeway. These taxis are without a doubt the best way to see the city, and an all-day pass, allowing unlimited usage, costs only $5 (single tickets are $4).

If you'd rather have a structured **water tour** of the city, two operators offer dinner cruises and riverboat tours of Millionaire's Row, the Venetian Isles, and the New River Jungles for about $15: Jungle Queen Riverboat, at Seabreeze Boulevard at Hwy-A1A (Ⓣ954/462-5596), and Riverfront Cruises, Las Olas Riverfront at 305 S Andrews (Ⓣ954/463-3440).

Accommodation

A handy free booklet, *Superior Small Lodgings Guide*, is available from the Convention and Visitors Bureau (see above) and lists reasonably priced accommodation. Options for staying in downtown Fort Lauderdale are relatively limited, but the scores of **motels** clustered between the Intracoastal Waterway and the ocean can be exceptionally good value.

If money is tight there are two **hostels** in town: *Backpacker Beach Hostel*, 2115 N Ocean Blvd (Ⓣ954/567-7275, Ⓦwww.fortlauderdalehostel.com; dorm beds $18), is clean, offers free parking, food, and snorkel gear, has a pleasant rooftop patio, and will pick you up from anywhere in Fort Lauderdale during the day; and the less central but friendly *Floyd's International Youth Hotel and Crew House*, 445 SE Sixteenth St (Ⓣ954/462-0631, Ⓦwww.floydshostel.com; dorm bed $17), which has similar amenities.

The closest **campground** is *Easterlin*, corner of 1000 NW 38th St and Tenth Avenue, Oakland Park (Ⓣ954/938-0610; $17–22 per person), three miles north of downtown.

Banyan Marina Apartments 111 Isle of Venice Ⓣ 1-800/524-4431, Ⓦwww.banyanmarina.com. These apartments (with a few double rooms) are on a waterway a short drive from the beach and close to Las Olas Boulevard. ❸

Bermudian Waterfront 315 N Birch Rd Ⓣ954/467-0467, Ⓦwww.bermudian-tropical.com. Located on the Intracoastal Waterway, this simple motel offers standard rooms, studio apartments, efficiencies, and one- or two-bed suites. ❸

Eighteenth Street Inn 712 SE Eighteenth St Ⓣ954/467-7841 or 1-888/828-4466. A real find, with seven creatively decorated rooms and suites, each with its own name, bordering a palm-fringed pool. The friendly hosts serve a superb breakfast (included in rates). ❺

La Casa Del Mar 3003 Granada Blvd Ⓣ954/467-2037. Though this attractive B&B caters mainly to a gay clientele, all are welcome to the wine and cheese afternoons by the pool. Its claim to fame is the "Judy Garland Room," where the actual Munchkins slept during a film festival. ❺

Lago Mar Resort and Club 1700 S Ocean Lane Ⓣ954/523-6511 or 1-800/LAGO MAR, Ⓦwww.lagomar.com. A luxury resort with two tropical pools, four restaurants, a complete spa, and its own private patch of sand. ❻

Pillars at New River Sound 111 N Birch Rd Ⓣ1-888/800-7666, Ⓦwww.pillarshotel.com. This quiet, relaxing British-colonial-style hotel, with plush rooms, antique furniture, and a pool, is only half a block from the ocean. ❼

Riverside Hotel 620 E Las Olas Blvd Ⓣ1-800/325-3280. Elegant, comfortable and well-placed (but slightly overpriced) downtown option. ❼

Royal Saxon Motel 551 Breakers Ave Ⓣ954/566-7424. Fresh flowers and fruit in every room, and a ten-minute walk to restaurants and shopping, help make this one of the best-value finds in Fort Lauderdale. ❹

Shell Resort at the Ocean 3030 Bayshore Drive Ⓣ954/463-1723, Ⓦwww.shellmotel.com. This cheerful, well-equipped motel is a stone's throw from the beach. ❹

Downtown Fort Lauderdale

Tall, anonymous, glass-fronted buildings make an uninspiring first impression, but **downtown Fort Lauderdale** has an outstanding modern art museum and a number of restored older buildings to usefully occupy several hours. Due to a multi-million-dollar effort to prettify the district, parks and promenades are linked by the pedestrian-only, one-and-a-half-mile **Riverwalk** along the north bank of the New River, which ends at the state-of-the-art Museum of Discovery & Science.

The Museum of Art

In a postmodern structure shaped like a slice of pie, the **Museum of Art**, 1 E Las Olas Blvd (Tues–Sat 10am–5pm, Sun noon–5pm, $7; guided tours Sat & Sun 1.30pm, free; Ⓣ954/525-5500, Ⓦwww.museumofart.org), provides ample space and light for the best art collection in the state, with an emphasis on modern painting and sculpture. The strongest exhibits are drawn from the museum's hoard of works from the **CoBrA** movement, which began in 1948 with a group of artists from Copenhagen, Brussels, and Amsterdam (hence the acronym). CoBrA's art is typified by bright expressionistic canvases combining playful innocence with deep emotional power. Important names to look for include Asger Jorn, Carl

Henning-Pedersen, and Karel Appel, though many later adherents of the movement also produced formidable works, and there are plenty of them here to admire. Another attraction is the William Glackens wing, named for the early twentieth-century American Impressionist who painted most of his pieces exhibited here while in France, and which includes a period-outfitted drawing room.

The historic district and the Stranahan House

For a quick look at Fort Lauderdale's past, walk a few blocks west from the Art Museum to the **historic district**, at the center of which is the **Hoch Heritage Center**, on Riverwalk at 219 SW Second Ave (Wed & Fri 10am–4pm, Sat noon–4pm; Ⓣ954/463-4431). Here you can pick up details on walking tours past (and, in some cases, inside) three of the oldest buildings in Fort Lauderdale, located nearby and in the process of being spruced up for the public: the 1907 **King-Cromartie House** (tours by reservation only), whose many then-futuristic fixtures include the first indoor bathroom in Fort Lauderdale; the three-story 1905 **New River Inn**, which was the first hotel here and also houses the small Fort Lauderdale Museum of History (Tues–Sun noon–5pm; $5); and the 1905 **Philomen Bryan House**, once the home of the Bryan family, who constructed many other buildings in this area. To give some perspective on the old buildings and the town's past in general, the Historical Society mounts informative displays and stocks plenty of historical books and free pamphlets in the Heritage Center.

A few minutes' walk east stands a more complete reminder of early Fort Lauderdale life: the carefully restored **Stranahan House**, 335 SE Sixth Ave (Mon–Sat 10am–5.30pm, Sun 1–5.30pm, Oct–May only; $5; Ⓣ954/524-4736, Ⓦwww.stranahanhouse.com), behind the *Cheesecake Factory* and Hyde Park Market on Las Olas Boulevard. Erected in 1901, with high ceilings, narrow windows, and wide verandas, the building is a fine example of Florida frontier style, and served as the home and trading post of a turn-of-the-twentieth-century settler, Frank Stranahan. An occasionally hokey-sounding recording tells the story of Stranahan, a prosperous dealer in otter pelts, egret plumes, and alligator hides, which he purchased from Seminole Indians trading along the river. Financially devastated by the late-Twenties Florida property crash, Stranahan drowned himself in the same waterway.

The Museum of Discovery & Science

Directly west from the historic district, and marking the end of Riverwalk, the gleaming **Museum of Discovery & Science**, 401 SW Second St (Mon–Sat 10am–5pm, Sun noon–6pm; $14; Ⓣ954/467-6637, Ⓦwww.mods.org), is among the best of Florida's many child-orientated science museums. However, childless adults shouldn't think twice about coming (though they should aim to avoid weekends and school holidays, when the place is packed) because the exhibits present the basics of science in numerous ingenious and entertaining ways. You can even pretend to be an astronaut, rising in an air-powered chair to realign an orbiting satellite or making a simulated trip to the moon. The museum also contains a towering 3-D IMAX film theater that screens daily (check admission booth for times); the regular admission price includes one IMAX film, or you can pay $9 for the film alone.

Around Las Olas Boulevard and the beach

Downtown Fort Lauderdale is linked to the beach by **Las Olas Boulevard** – on the cutting edge of fashion, art, and food (from restaurants to sidewalk cafés) – and then by the Isles, well-tended canal-side land where residents park their

△ West Palm Beach

cars on one side of their mega-buck properties and moor their luxury yachts on the other. Once across the arching Intracoastal Waterway Bridge, about two miles on, you're within sight of the ocean and the mood changes appreciably. Where Las Olas Boulevard ends, **beachside Fort Lauderdale** begins – T-shirt, sunscreen, and swimwear shops are suddenly everywhere, spilling over into the surrounding communities and punctuating over 25 miles of "Blue Wave" beaches (those certified as clean, safe, and environmentally friendly).

Along the seafront, **Fort Lauderdale Beach Boulevard** bore the brunt of Spring Break partying until the clean-up of the Eighties. The whole area has benefited from a multi-million-dollar facelift, and now only a few beachfront bars bear any trace of the carousing of the past, though the sands, flanked by graciously aging coconut palms and an attractive promenade, are by no means deserted or dull; joggers, rollerbladers, and cyclists create a stereotypical beach scene, and a small number of whooping students still turn up here each spring.

Since accommodation is easily available here, you'll have no difficulty exploring the beach, the bars, and a few other items of interest in either direction along the main strip.

South along Ocean Boulevard

A short way south of the Las Olas Boulevard Junction, the **International Swimming Hall of Fame**, 1 Hall of Fame Drive (Mon–Fri 9am–7pm, Sat–Sun 9am–5pm; $3; ⓣ954/462-6536), salutes aquatic sports with a collection even dedicated nonswimmers will enjoy. The two floors are stuffed with medals, trophies, and press cuttings pertaining to the muscle-bound heroes and heroines of swimming, diving, and many more obscure watery activities.

For a few hours of solitude, thread through the residential streets a mile further south to the placid **South Beach Park**, a restful spot at the tip of Fort Lauderdale's coastline.

North along Ocean Boulevard

At the lackluster commercial complex called **BeachPlace** just north of the Las Olas Boulevard junction, you'll find three levels of predictable shops (such as Banana Republic, Gap, Speedo) with a smattering of bars and restaurants, including *Hooters* and *Cafe Iguana*. The good thing about BeachPlace is that you can hop up from the sand to grab a bite to eat, buy souvenir paraphernalia, or go to the rest room. Otherwise it's just another overhyped mall with a spectacular waterfront location.

Further north, in the midst of the high-rise hotels and apartment blocks that dominate the beachside area, Fort Lauderdale's pre-condo landscape can be viewed in the jungle-like 35-acre grounds of **Bonnet House**, 900 N Birch Rd (Dec–April Tues–Sat 10am–4pm; May–Nov Wed–Fri 10am–3pm, Sat 10am–4pm, Sun noon–4pm; last tour 90min before closing; $10; ⓣ954/563-5393), a few minutes' walk off Fort Lauderdale Beach Boulevard. The house and its surroundings – including a swan-filled pond and resident monkeys – were designed by Chicago muralist Frank Clay Bartlett and completed in 1921. The tours of the vaguely plantation-style abode highlight Bartlett's eccentric passion for art and architecture – and for collecting ornamental animals, dozens of which fill virtually all of the thirty rooms.

Another green pocket is nearby: beside Sunrise Boulevard, the tall Australian pines of the **Hugh Taylor Birch State Recreation Area** (daily 8am–sunset; cars $3.25, pedestrians and cyclists $1) form a shady backdrop for canoeing on the park's mangrove-fringed freshwater lagoon – a good way to perk yourself up after a morning spent prostrate on the beach.

Eating

Fort Lauderdale has many affordable, enjoyable **places to eat**, featuring everything from Asian creations to home-made conch chowder. Restaurants tend to be grouped in different sections of the town, and are especially easy to find on Las Olas Boulevard and in the Riverfront District.

Bimini Boatyard 1555 SE 17th St ⓣ954/525-7400. Well-prepared and -presented salads and seafood, served in a great location on the Intracoastal Waterway. Less expensive than it looks, with lunch plates $7–13, dinner $10–21.

Café Europa 726 E Las Olas Blvd ⓣ954/763-6600. Funky, moderately priced café, always packed, with mouthwatering desserts, unusual pizza toppings, and views of the city skyline. Daily 10am–11.30pm/midnight.

Casablanca Café intersection of Alhambra and Ocean blvds, opposite the beach ⓣ954/764-3500. An American piano bar in a Moroccan setting with a good, eclectic menu and moderate prices. Expect large portions of Mediterranean standards, such as paella. Daily 11.30am–11.30pm, bar until 2am.

Ernie's BBQ Lounge 1843 S Federal Hwy ⓣ954/523-8636. The scruffy but likeable *Ernie's*, south of downtown, is a local legend for its glorious conch chowder (add sherry to taste). Daily 11am–2am.

The Floridian 1410 E Las Olas Blvd ⓣ954/463-4041. Inexpensive downtown 24-hour coffee shop with a cozy diner style, popular for its mammoth breakfasts.

Japanese Village 716 E Las Olas Blvd ⓣ954/763-8163. Good Japanese food graces this central location at reasonable prices. Daily noon–2pm & 5.30–10.30pm.

Louie Louie 1003 E Las Olas Blvd ⓣ954/524-5200. Classic and not-so-classic Italian dishes are on the menu at this brick-walled establishment, where good service accompanies the reasonable prices.

Rustic Inn 4331 Ravenswood Rd ⓣ954/584-1637. At this ultra-casual site on the water, crack open mountains of delicious steamed garlic blue crabs onto the newspaper-covered tables.

Shooters Waterfront Café 3033 NE 32nd Ave ⓣ954/566-2855. Popular beachside restaurant drawing large crowds for its generous – though fairly pricey – portions of seafood, burgers, and salads. Good place for Sunday brunch. Mon–Sat 11.30am–3am, Sun 11am–4pm.

Southport Raw Bar 1536 Cordova Rd ⓣ954/525-CLAM. This boisterous local bar offers succulent crustaceans and well-prepared fish dishes. Daily 11.30am–2am.

Taverna Opa 3051 NE 32nd St ⓣ954/567-1630. A raucous time can be had at this fun and satisfying Greek establishment, complete with flowing ouzo and crashing dishes.

Drinking

In addition to the bars listed below, some of the restaurants above, particularly *Shooters* and the *Southport Raw Bar*, are also notable drinking spots.

Bierbrunnen 425 S Fort Lauderdale Beach Blvd ⓣ954/462-1008. Reliable for a variety of German beers and bratwurst.

Elbo Room 241 S Fort Lauderdale Beach Blvd ⓣ954/463-4615. Once a Spring Break favorite, this is now the ideal place for an evening drink as the ocean breeze ruffles your hair.

Mangos 904 E Las Olas Blvd ⓣ954/523-5001. The airy outdoor area is perfect for people watching along Las Olas Boulevard, while the roaring live rock, R&B, and jazz inside keeps things lively. Decent food is available as well.

Parrot Lounge 911 Sunrise Lane ⓣ954/563-1493. This easygoing bar specializes in oversized pitchers of beer.

Samba Room 350 E Las Olas Blvd ⓣ954/468-2000. The festive atmosphere is fueled by the potent drinks from the Cuban bar and spicy Latin café food, served at lunch, dinner, and late at night.

Nightlife and entertainment

To find out who's playing where, call the free Entertainment Hotline (ⓣ954/527-5600), pick up the free *CityLink* or *New Times* magazines from newsstands, or consult the "Showtime" segment of the Friday edition of the local *Sun-Sentinel* newspaper. For high culture in town, you might check out the **Broward Center for the Performing Arts**, 201 SW Fifth Ave (ticket information (T)954/462-0222, (W)www.browardcenter.org), a modern waterfront building that hosts Broadway shows and more offbeat productions in its intimate Amaturo Theater. Otherwise a walk around the **Riverwalk Arts and Entertainment District**, at the western end of downtown's Riverwalk, will usually turn something up.

Cheers 941 E Cypress Creek Rd (T)954/771-6337. Rock and roll brings the house down until 4am (except Sun, which features jazz).

O'Hara's 722 E Las Olas Blvd (T)954/524-1764. This dark bar has live jazz and blues music every night at 9pm.

Poor House 110 SW Third Ave (T)954/522-5145. Smoky blues and the occasional swing band are featured here. No cover.

Rush Street 220 SW Second St (T)954/522-6900. The mix of techno and hip-hop (two DJs Friday and Saturday nights) puts this among the dance club favorites.

Gay and lesbian Fort Lauderdale

Fort Lauderdale has been one of **gay** America's favorite holiday haunts for years and is often referred to as San Francisco-by-the-Sea. Like the rest of Fort Lauderdale, the scene has quieted down considerably over recent years, but there's still plenty going on. For more information, contact the Gay and Lesbian Community Center at 1717 N Andrews Ave (Mon–Fri 10am–10pm, Sat & Sun noon–5pm; (T)954/463-9005, (E)glccvoice @aol.com), pick up free copies of *411* and *Hot Spots* magazines located throughout the area, or visit the Fort Lauderdale section of Columbia Fun Maps ((W)www.funmaps.com).

Accommodation

Fort Lauderdale has over thirty **guesthouses** aimed at gay men: the comfortable and friendly *Gigi's Resort by the Beach*, 3005 Alhambra St ((T)954/463-4827 or 1-800/910-2357, (W)www.gigisresort.com; 5), and the swankier *Royal Palms Resort*, 2901 Terramar St ((T)954/564-6444 or 1-800/237-PALM, (W)www .royalpalms.com; 7). Of the lodgings that do not cater exclusively to gays, try the *Oasis*, 1200 S Miami Rd ((T)954/523-3043; 3), whose inland location keeps its prices down, or *La Casa Del Mar* (see p.191).

Bars and clubs

Gay **bars** and **clubs** in Fort Lauderdale fall in and out of fashion; read the statewide free gay weekly newspaper, *The Weekly News*, or the free *CityLink* magazine for the latest hotspots. Usually among the pacesetters are *Cathode Ray*, 1305 E Las Olas Blvd ((T)954/462-8611), a video bar that steadily warms up as the evening wears on; *Copa*, 2800 S Federal Hwy ((T)954/463-1507), a long-running dance club that draws all ages; the loud, high-energy *Boom* at 2232-36 Wilton Drive ((T)954/630-3556), another spot for dancing; and *Georgie's Alibi*, 2266 Wilton Drive ((T)954/565-2526), which is currently one of the most popular. For **eating** as well as drinking, try *Bar Amici*, 1301 E Las Olas Blvd ((T)954/467-3266), which offers steaks, chops, seafood, and popular Italian dishes in a prime location; and *Chardees*, 2209 Wilton Drive ((T)954/563-1800), which has a lively piano bar and a fabulous Sunday brunch. The biggest – and some say best – **disco** is *The Coliseum*, 2520 S Miami Rd ((T)954/832-0100, (W)www.coliseumnightclub .com), which plays techno sounds and is open till late every weekend (often free until 11pm, with $12 cover after).

Inland from Fort Lauderdale: Davie and around

Away from its beach and downtown area, Fort Lauderdale lapses into dismal suburbia all the way to the Everglades. Most people only pass through to reach "Alligator Alley" – the familiar name for **I-75**, which speeds arrow-straight toward Florida's west coast a hundred miles distant (see "Sarasota and the Southwest," p.225).

An exception to the prevailing factories, housing estates, and freeway interchanges, **DAVIE** lies twenty miles from the coast on Griffin Road, surrounded by citrus groves, sugar cane, and dairy pastures. Davie's 40,000 inhabitants are besotted with the Old West: jeans, plaid shirts, and Stetsons are the order of the day, and there's even a hitching post (for tethering horses) outside the local *McDonald's*. Davie's cowboy origins go back to settlers who came here in the 1910s to herd cattle and work the fertile black soil. If you're charmed by the attire, stock up in Grif's Western, 6211 SW 45th St (Ⓣ954/587-9000), a leading purveyor of boots, hats, and saddles; otherwise simply turn up for the rodeo, held the last Saturday of the month at 8pm at the Davie Arena, on the Bergeron Rodeo Grounds, 4271 Davie Rd (Ⓣ954/384-7075, Ⓦwww.fivestarrodeo.com; $14, children $8) – look for the rearing white horse sign. The smaller Jackpot Rodeo ($4; Ⓣ954/475-9787) takes place every Wednesday evening at the same venue.

Like its counterparts elsewhere in the state, the **Seminole Okalee Indian Village and Museum** at the Seminole Reservation (daily 9am–4pm; $5 for a self-guided tour; $10 for guided tour with alligator-wrestling show; Ⓣ954/961-4519), a mile south of Davie on US-441, is a depressing place where plastic tomahawks are flogged to tourists. There is some sensitivity to be found, however, in the paintings by Guy LaBree, a local white man who spent time on Seminole reservations during his childhood and whose work is intended to pass legends and history on to younger Seminole generations. More likely, it's the bingo and gaming casino (closed Mon) near the village that attracts most white people: laws against high-stakes bingo don't apply to Indian reservations, and you can win $100,000 or more here. You can buy your fill of tax-free cigarettes, too. A more entertaining attraction on the Seminole Reservation (though on the other side of it, and somewhat of a drive) is **Billie Swamp Safari** (p.179).

Twelve miles northeast of Davie at Coconut Creek, **Butterfly World**, 3600 W Sample Rd (Mon–Sat 9am–5pm, Sun 1–5pm, last admission 4pm; $16, children $11; Ⓣ954/977-4400), stocks, as its name suggests, a massive collection of butterflies. Many are hatched here from larvae – which you'll see in the laboratory – and flap out their short lives around nectar-producing plants inside several aviaries. Exhibits include the colorful Jewels of the Sky Hummingbird Aviary and the fragrant Rose Garden. Spotting Ecuadorian metalmarks, Blue Morphos, and their equally exotic peers will keep amateur lepidopterists amused for hours.

North of Fort Lauderdale

Stay on Hwy-A1A **north from Fort Lauderdale**, a far superior route to US-1 that passes through several sedate beachside communities. One of these, **Lauderdale-by-the-Sea,** lies around four miles up the coast and is one of the best places to don scuba-diving gear and explore the reefs.

There are pleasant **B&Bs** to be found here, many along El Mar Drive. Among the best are *Blue Seas Courtyard*, 4525 El Mar Drive (T 954/772-3336; 3), with a Mexican beach-style and feel; *Courtyard Villa on the Ocean*, 4312 El Mar Drive (T 954/776-1164; 5), an attractive faux-antique European hotel, which includes a full breakfast; the homey and romantic *Best Florida Resort*, 4628 North Ocean Drive (T 954/772-2500; 3), with a tropical garden; and the excellent *A Little Inn by the Sea*, 4546 El Mar Drive (T 1-800/492-0311; 4), with luxurious linens and gourmet breakfasts. You'll soon find the best eateries, including the *Aruba Beach Café*, 1 E Commercial Blvd (T 954/776-0001), where you can tickle your tastebuds with Caribbean and New World cuisine.

Pompano and Deerfield beaches

Pompano Beach, centered on Pompano Square, is just two miles on from Lauderdale-by-the-Sea. This is one of the larger beach towns, with a moderately good ocean strip. Still, there's not too much to occupy you, unless you have a particular penchant for horses – the **Pompano Harness Track**, 1800 SW Third St (T 954/972-2000, W www.pompanopark.com), features racing from October to May.

Three miles further, Hwy-A1A crosses the Hillsboro Inlet, whose 1907 lighthouse gives its name to the posh canal-side community of **Lighthouse Point**. There's nothing to detain you here except the offshore *Cap's Place* (dinner only, booking recommended; T 954/941-0418), which can only be reached by ferry (call for directions to the dock). The food – fresh seafood from $19 to $27 – is one attraction, but the fact that the restaurant doubled as an illegal gambling den during Prohibition is another: Franklin Roosevelt, Winston Churchill, and the Duke of Windsor, remembered by fading photos, are just three notables who relaxed in the company of owner Cap Knight, a one-time rumrunner whose family presides over the restaurant.

More offbeat history is attached to **Deerfield Beach**, four miles on. As Hwy-A1A twists to the right, you'll catch a glimpse of the triangular Deerfield Island Park in the Intracoastal Waterway. During the Thirties, Al Capone considered purchasing the island, which he and his gangster colleagues frequented when gambling at the swanky *Riverview Restaurant*'s casino, underneath the Hillsboro Boulevard Causeway at 1741 Riverview Rd. Capone's property bid was thwarted by his arrest for tax evasion, and the island, untarnished by development, is occupied today by raccoons and armadillos. Its two walking trails are reachable only with the free ferry from the *Riverview* on Wednesday and Saturday mornings; call T 954/360-1320 for times.

Boca Raton and around

Directly north of Deerfield Beach, Hwy-A1A and US-1 both enter Palm Beach County, the latter becoming the Stars-and-Stripes-decorated **Blue Memorial Highway**: "a tribute to the armed forces that have served the United States of America," confirming the general conservatism of the region. You can practically smell the money as you cross into the county's southernmost town, **BOCA RATON** (literally "the mouth of the rat"), where smartly dressed valets park your car at supermarkets, and golf-mad retirees and executives from numerous hi-tech industries – most notably computer giant IBM – hibernate year-round. More noticeably, Boca Raton has an abundance of Mediterranean Revival architecture, a style prevalent here since the Twenties

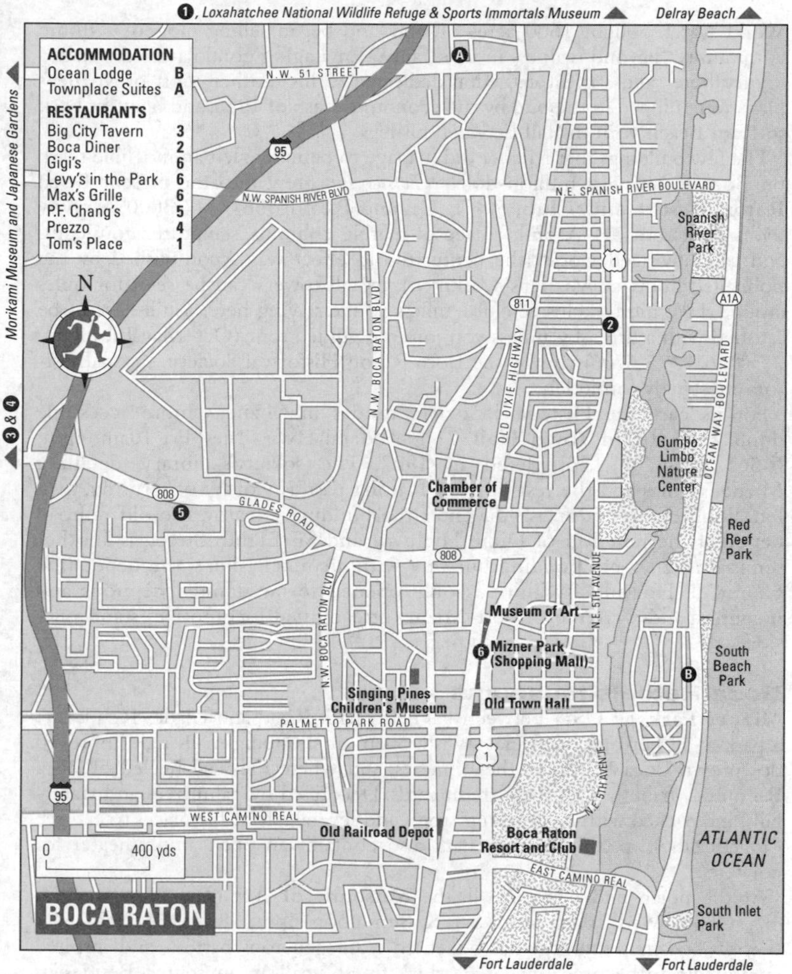

and preserved by strict building codes: the town's newer structures are obligated to incorporate arched entrance ways, fake bell towers, and red-tiled roofs whenever possible. Other than the architecture, the town features some fine under-recognized beaches and parks.

Downtown Boca Raton

The origins of Boca Raton's Mediterranean-flavored architecture, which you see all over the **downtown** area, go back to **Addison Mizner**, the "Aladdin of architects" (a nickname given because of the almost magical flare in his designs, which were influenced by the Moorish styles of southern Spain), who furnished the fantasies of Palm Beach's fabulously wealthy (see p.207) through the Twenties. Unable to give reign to his megalomaniacal desires elsewhere, Mizner swept into Boca Raton on the tide of the Florida property boom after

World War I, bought 1600 acres of land, and began selling plots of a future community "beyond realness in its ideality." Envisaging gondola-filled canals, a luxury hotel, and a great cathedral dedicated to his mother, most of Mizner's plans were nipped in the bud by the economic crash of 1926, and he went back to Palm Beach with his tail between his legs.

The few buildings that Mizner did manage to complete left an indelible mark on Boca Raton. His million-dollar *Cloister Inn* grew into the present **Boca Raton Resort and Club**, 501 E Camino Real (Ⓣ561/447-3000, Ⓦwww.bocaresort.com; ❼). A pink palace of marble columns, sculptured fountains, and carefully aged wood (the centuries-old effect was accomplished by the hobnailed boots of Mizner's workmen), its tall towers can be seen for miles around. Like most exclusive clubs, unless you're staying here, you'll have to be satisfied with a drive-by, unless you join the guided tour (Oct–May Tues 2pm; $7; Ⓣ561/395-6766) run by the Boca Raton Historical Society – casual visitors are strictly forbidden.

For its part, the Historical Society resides in Mizner's more accessible dome-topped **Old Town Hall**, 71 N Federal Hwy (Tues–Fri 10am–4pm; Ⓣ561/395-6766), completed in 1927. The society's library, detailing Mizner's times and the rest of Boca Raton's past, is worthy of scrutiny; turn left along the corridor as you enter the building. Nearby, the old railroad depot, at the junction of Dixie Highway and SE Eighth Street, is another seminal Mizner-era building but one without much allure; the depot (the Count de Hoernle Pavilion) is only opened for wedding receptions and meetings, and a couple of post-Mizner streamlined locomotives stand outside.

Boca Raton's museums

Mizner Park, off US-1 between Palmetto Park Road and Glades Road, isn't a park at all but one of several stylish, open-air shopping malls that improved downtown Boca Raton in the Nineties, and where the well-heeled of Boca Raton pay tribute with their credit cards. Decorated by palm trees and waterfalls, and packed with *haute couture* stores and several affordable places to eat (see "Practicalities," p.202), Mizner Park also contains an open amphitheater for concerts.

At the north end of the mall, the **Museum of Art** (Tues, Thurs & Fri 10am–5pm, Wed 10am–9pm, Sat & Sun noon–5pm; $8; Ⓣ561/392-2500, Ⓦwww.bocamuseum.org) has benefited from generous patrons and inspired curatorship to become one of Florida's finest small art museums. Besides its temporary exhibitions on leading Florida artists, the museum has a permanent collection that includes the Mayers Collection of drawings by modern masters – Degas, Matisse, Picasso, and Seurat are among those represented – and a formidable trove of African art.

To escape the Mizner influence altogether, head for the beaches (see opposite) or turn to the **Singing Pines Children's Museum**, 498 Crawford Blvd (Tues–Sat noon–4pm; $3; Ⓣ561/368-6875). Housed in a 1913 driftwood "cracker" cottage – the simple abode of early Florida farmers (see Contexts, p.469) – the museum stocks entertaining remnants from the pioneer days alongside exhibitions aimed at kids.

Sports fanatics, meanwhile, will revel in the **Sports Immortals Museum**, 6830 N Federal Hwy (Mon–Fri 10am–6pm, Sat 10am–5pm; $5; Ⓣ561/997-2575), which houses an overwhelming assortment of sporting mementos, from Muhammad Ali's championship belt to the baseball that killed the ballplayer Ray Chapman in 1920.

Boca Raton's beaches

All four of Boca Raton's beaches are open to the public, but they are walled in by tall rows of Australian pine, so it is unlikely that you'll stumble across them. They tend, therefore, to be the preserve of select Floridians rather than long-distance travelers.

The southernmost patch, **South Inlet Park**, at 1298 S Ocean Blvd, is the smallest and quietest of the quartet, often deserted in midweek save for a few people fishing along its short jetty. To reach it, watch for a track turning sharply right off Hwy-A1A, just beyond the Boca Raton Inlet. **South Beach Park**, a mile north, is a surfers' favorite, though the actual beach is a fairly tiny area of coarse sand. **Red Reef Park**, a mile further, is far better for sunbathing and swimming – activities that should be combined with a walk around the **Gumbo Limbo Nature Center** (Mon–Sat 9am–4pm, Sun noon–4pm; donations suggested; ⓣ561/338-1473, ⓦwww.gumbolimbo.org), directly across Hwy-A1A at 1801 N Ocean Blvd, whose wide boardwalks take you through a tropical hardwood hammock and a mangrove forest beside the Intracoastal Waterway. Keep your eyes peeled for ospreys, brown pelicans, and the occasional manatee lurking in the warm waters. Between the end of May and early July, you can join the center's scheduled tours to observe sea turtles. These can be extremely popular, however, and bookings must be made in person.

Boca Raton's most explorable beachside area, however, is **Spanish River Park** (daily 8am–sunset; cars $10 weekdays, $12 weekends & holidays, pedestrians and cyclists free), a mile north of Red Reef Park on Hwy-A1A. Here you'll find fifty acres of lush vegetation, most of which is only penetrable on secluded trails through shady thickets. Aim for the forty-foot observation tower for a view across the park and much of Boca Raton. The adjacent beach is a slender but serviceable strip, linked to the park by several nifty tunnels beneath Hwy-A1A.

Boca Raton makes a good base from which to visit Loxahatchee National Wildlife Refuge (see p.211), about ten miles north of here, just off US-441. Also available is the chance to see the Everglades from an airboat, which you can arrange at **Loxahatchee Everglades Tours**, 15490 Loxahatchee Rd, off State Road 7/US-441 (daily tours leave hourly from 10am–4pm; $25.50 per person, $12.75 children; ⓣ1-800/683-5873).

Practicalities

The nearest Greyhound **bus** terminals are in Pompano Beach, 2190 NE Fourth St (ⓣ954/946-7067) and Delray Beach, 402 SE Sixth Ave (ⓣ561/272-6447). The Tri-Rail station is near the *Embassy Suites*, off Yamato Road and I-95, at 601 NW 53rd St (ⓣ1-800/TRI-RAIL), and their shuttle buses connect with the town center. The Palm Tran bus #91 ($1.25 each way; call ⓣ561/841-4BUS for schedules) operates daily leaving once an hour from Mizner Park through downtown west to the Sandalfoot Shopping Center. The Boca Raton Historic Society runs weekly trolley tours of the city as well, for $10 (winter only, Thurs 9.15am; ⓣ561/395-6766).

The Chamber of Commerce, 1800 N Dixie Hwy (Mon–Thurs 8.30am–5pm, Fri 8.30am–4pm; ⓣ561/395-4433), supplies the usual information on area hotels and such. You can stay in relative luxury at places like the *Boca Raton Resort and Club* (see "Downtown Boca Raton" opposite); otherwise, one of the better-value **motels** near the beaches is the *Ocean Lodge*, 531 N Ocean Blvd (ⓣ561/395-7772; ❸), which also has kitchen units. During the low season you'll save money by sleeping slightly inland at the *Townplace Suites*, 5110 NW Eighth Ave (ⓣ561/994-7232; ❸).

The Morikami Museum and Japanese Gardens

South Florida might be the last place you'd expect to find a formal Japanese garden complete with a Shinto shrine, a teahouse, and a museum recording the history of a Japanese agricultural colony, but ten miles northwest of Boca Raton in Delray Beach, at the **Morikami Museum and Japanese Gardens**, 4000 Morikami Park Rd (Tues–Sun 10am–5pm; adults $7, children 6–18 $4; ⓣ561/495-0233, ⓦwww.morikami.org), you'll find all three. These are reminders of a group of Japanese farmers who came here at the turn of the twentieth century at the behest of the Florida East Coast Railway to grow tea and rice and to farm silkworms in a colony called Yamato, but wound up selling pineapples until a blight killed off the crop in 1908.

Artifacts and photographs within the Morikami's older set of buildings remember the colony. Across the beautifully landscaped grounds, the newer portion of the museum stages themed exhibitions drawn from an enormous archive of Japanese objects and art, and has user-friendly computers with information about various aspects of Japan and Japanese life. A traditional **teahouse**, assembled here by a Florida-based Japanese craftsman, is periodically used for tea ceremonies.

As for places to **eat**, there's plenty of choice. At Mizner Park in downtown, you can choose from a range of options: reasonably priced steaming brisket and matzoh balls at *Levy's in the Park*, a kosher Jewish deli at 435 Plaza Real (ⓣ561/393-3989); upscale American dishes with ethnic influences at *Max's Grille*, 404 Plaza Real (ⓣ561/368-0080); or French bistro fare at the elegantly casual *Gigi's*, 346 Plaza Real (ⓣ561/368-4488), which also features live music. North of downtown, try *Tom's Place*, at 7521 N Federal Hwy (ⓣ561/997-0920) for tasty barbecued ribs and steaks, and the *Boca Diner*, 2801 N Federal Hwy (ⓣ561/750-6744), which serves Greek and Italian standards. There's more choice further west on the N Federal Highway: *P.F. Chang's*, 1400 Glades Rd (ⓣ561/393-3722), has arresting decor and a contemporary Chinese menu, and *Prezzo*, at 7820 Glades Rd, tucked away inside the Arvida Parkway Center (ⓣ561/451-2800), features delicious homemade pastas and oak-oven pizza specialties that are worth shelling out for. Just west of I-98, *Big City Tavern*, 5250 Town Center Circle (ⓣ561/361-4551), serves tasty pub food.

North toward Palm Beach

Most of the shoulder-to-shoulder towns **north of Boca Raton** that are connected by Hwy-A1A have a nice patch of beach, and a couple are putting their modest histories on display, but none should be considered lengthy stops. If you're reliant on public transportation, you can take the local Palm Tran bus #1 (ⓣ561/841-4BUS), which runs every half-hour (limited service on Sundays) through towns between Boca Raton and West Palm Beach.

Delray Beach

Five miles north of Boca Raton, **Delray Beach** justifies at least a half-day visit: its powdery-sanded **municipal beach**, at the foot of Atlantic Avenue, is rightly popular and is one of the few in Florida to afford a view of the Gulf Stream – a cobalt-blue streak about five miles offshore.

Nipping a short way inland along Atlantic Avenue, you'll find more to pass the time. On the corner of Atlantic and Swinton avenues, an imposing schoolhouse dating from 1913 is now the **Cornell Museum of Art and History** (Tues–Sat 10.30am–4.30pm, also Sun 1–4.30pm Oct–April; $5, children $1; ⓣ561/243-7922), part of **Old School Square**, a group of buildings restored and converted into a cultural center. The spacious first floor of the former school hosts temporary art exhibitions, though a peek upstairs reveals several one-time classrooms still furnished with desks and black-painted walls used to avoid the exorbitant cost of slate blackboards. Within sight, just across NE First Street, the **Cason Cottage** (Tues–Fri 10am–3pm; free), erected in 1920 for Dr John Cason, member of an illustrious local family, warrants a look for its simple woodframe design based on pioneer-era Florida architecture.

An unusual find, in the Atlantic Antique Mall at 504 E Atlantic Ave, is the **US Military Uniform Museum** (Sun–Thurs 10am–6pm, Fri & Sat 10am–10pm; free; ⓣ561/330-6336), which has a small but engaging display of authentic, primarily Civil War and Spanish-American War uniforms and accessories.

Nature lovers, meanwhile, will enjoy the **International Orchid Center**, 16700 AOS Lane (Tues–Sun 10am–4.30pm; $7; ⓣ561/404-2000, ⓦwww.orchidweb.org), where they can linger in a steaming orchid jungle as well as formal gardens and a habitat entirely populated by native Florida plants. (Ideally, a visit here would be taken in with the tranquil Japanese gardens of the Morikami Museum; see opposite.) The nearby **Sandoway House and Nature Center**, 142 S Ocean Blvd (Tues–Sat 10am–4.30pm; $2; ⓣ561/274-7263), which looks at local history as well as marine life, is also worthwhile.

Among the reasonably priced beachside **accommodation** is the *Bermuda Inn*, 64 S Ocean Blvd (ⓣ561/276-5288; ❸). The *Colony Hotel*, 525 E Atlantic Ave (ⓣ561/276-4123; ❸), with its garnet-and-pale-yellow awning, has been a fixture since 1926. For a bit of laidback style, try the *Crane's BeachHouse*, 82 Gleason St (ⓣ561/278-1700 or 1-866/372-7263, ⓦwww.cranesbeachhouse.com; ❻), with its tropical-themed rooms, bamboo tiki huts, and miniature waterfalls.

Delray Beach makes a sensible lunch stop. At the municipal beach, *Boston's on the Beach*, 40 S Ocean Blvd (ⓣ561/278-3364), serves incredibly fresh seafood at reasonable prices, while *Caffe Luna Rosa*, next door at no. 34 (ⓣ561/274-9404), offers casual American-style fare in an attractive exposed-brick space hung with unusual portraits, and with occasional live music. Another good bet is the long-standing *Beach Dogs*, 142A SE Sixth Ave (ⓣ561/279-2824), where you can sample fifteen different varieties of franks, including the local favorite, chili cheese.

Lake Worth

If you're pressing on by car, a more inspiring option than US-1 is Hwy-A1A, which charts a picturesque course along twenty-odd miles of slender barrier islands, ocean views on one side and the Intracoastal Waterway – plied by luxury yachts and lined with opulent homes – on the other. Whichever route you take, make a quick stop at **Lake Worth** (not to be confused with the actual lake of the same name that divides Palm Beach from West Palm Beach), ten miles north of Delray Beach, for the entertaining clutter of the **Historical Museum**, in the Utilities Department Buildings at 414 Lake Ave (Tues–Fri 10am–2pm; free). Plant-filled bathtubs, artistically arranged rusting tools, and picks aplenty from bygone decades are all infectiously doted over by the museum's curator.

The main reason to stop here is the recently relocated **Palm Beach Institute of Contemporary Art**, 601 Lake Ave (Tues–Sun noon–6pm, docent tours given Sat at 2pm; $3; ⓣ561/582-0006, ⓦwww.palmbeachica.org), devoted to forward-thinking art in all media: painting, sculpture, video, and photography have all been regularly featured among its rotating exhibits.

There's not much else to hinder your progress to Palm Beach (with Hwy-A1A) or West Palm Beach (with US-1) just a few miles north.

Palm Beach

A small island town of palatial homes, pampered gardens, and streets so clean you could eat your dinner off them, **PALM BEACH** has been synonymous for nearly a century with the kind of lifestyle only limitless loot can buy. A bastion of conspicuous wealth, whose pomposity – banning clothes lines, for example – knows no bounds, Palm Beach is, for all its faults, irrefutably unique.

The nation's upper crust began wintering here in the 1890s, after Standard Oil magnate **Henry Flagler** brought his Florida East Coast Railway south from St Augustine and built two luxury hotels on this then-secluded, palm-filled island. Throughout the Twenties, **Addison Mizner** began a vogue for Mediterranean-style architecture, covering the place with arcades, courtyards, and plazas – and the first million-dollar homes. Since then, corporate tycoons, sports heroes, jet-setting aristocrats, rock stars, and CIA directors have all flocked here, eager to become part of the Palm Beach elite and enjoy its aloofness from mainland life.

Summer is very quiet and easily the least costly time to stay here. The pace heats up between November and May, with the winter months a whirl of elegant balls, fund-raising dinners, and charity galas – local residents give more to tax-deductible causes in a year than most people earn in a lifetime. Winter also brings the polo season – watching a chukka or two is the one time Palm Beach denizens show themselves in the less particular environs of West Palm Beach (on the mainland), where the games are held.

Even by walking – much the best way to view the moneyed isle – you'll get the measure of Palm Beach in a day. Either drive in along Hwy-A1A from the south, or use one of the two bridges over Lake Worth from West Palm Beach, the nearest bus and train stop.

The waters off the beach also merit investigation; artificial reefs were created here in the 1960s to protect the coastline by preventing erosion of the natural reef. These are now a spectacular draw for divers; contact the Palm Beach County Chamber of Commerce (see p.210) for further information.

Arrival and information

If you're arriving by **car** from US-1 or I-95, take Okeechobee Blvd east into Palm Beach. From the towns to the south, Hwy-A1A runs north to Palm Beach. **Public transportation** to Palm Beach is limited, and all long-distance terminals are located in West Palm Beach (see p.209). To get to Palm Beach from West Palm Beach, take any PalmTran bus ($1.25; ⓣ561/841-4BUS) terminating at Quadrille Road and transfer to the #41 or the #42 (no Sunday service)

The **Palm Beach County Convention and Visitors Bureau**, 1555 Palm Beach Lakes Blvd, Suite 800 (Mon–Fri 9am–5pm; ⓣ561/233-3000, ⓦwww.palmbeachfl.com), provides free **maps** and **information** for the entire county, which stretches from Boca Raton to Jupiter (see p.213). Definitely stop in to pick up their annual publication, *$1000 Worth of the Palm Beaches Free*, for discounts on attractions and lodging; or alternately, it can be downloaded from their website.

Accommodation

You'll need plenty of money **to stay** in Palm Beach: comfort and elegance are the key words, and prices can vary greatly depending on the time of year. To save money, your best bet is to visit between May and mid-December when prices on the island are lowest. Obviously it's far cheaper to stay outside Palm Beach and visit by day – easily done from West Palm Beach even without a car (see p.210 for more).

Brazilian Court 301 Australian Ave ⓣ561/655-7740 or 1-800/552-0335, ⓦwww.braziliancourt.com. A comfortable and quiet small hotel, comprising Spanish-style villas surrounding a courtyard. Despite a thorough renovation, the hotel has kept its 1920s flair. ❺

Chesterfield 363 Cocoanut Rd ⓣ561/659-5800 or 1-800/243-7871, ⓦwww.chesterfieldpb.com. Opulent boutique hotel, with antique-filled rooms and public areas. Serves a traditional English tea every afternoon. ❺

Colony 155 Hammon Ave ⓣ561/655-5430 or 1-800/521-5525. Steps away from chic Worth Ave, the *Colony* has hosted former presidents, sheiks, and Hollywood royalty. If you've got some cash, it's lovely and convenient. ❻

Fairfield Inn & Suites 2870 S Ocean Blvd ⓣ561/582 2581 or 1-800/347-5434. One of the cheaper options and catering to the business set, with clean, decent-sized rooms and complimentary newspaper and continental breakfast. Located about 5 miles south of Worth Ave. ❸

Heart of Palm Beach 160 Royal Palm Way ⓣ561/655-5600 or 1-800/523-5377. Casual but smart hotel, with brightly colored rooms accented by dark woods, and helpful staff. ❹

Palm Beach Bed & Breakfast 365 S County Rd ⓣ561/832-4009 or 1-800/918-9773. A friendly B&B in a very convenient locale, with some of the best rates in town, but you'll need to book early. ❹

Plaza Inn 215 Brazilian Ave ⓣ561/832-8666 or 1-800/233-2632, ⓦwww.plazainnpalmbeach.com. Choose from individually decorated (French, Italian etc) rooms, some with four-poster beds, at this boutique hotel. ❹

Approaching Palm Beach: the south of the island

Though near-neighbors like to think otherwise, the Palm Beach that conjures up images of wealth, extravagance, and exclusivity begins about five miles north of the town of Lake Worth on Hwy-A1A, by the junction with Southern Boulevard (Hwy-98). Here, the **Palm Beach Bath and Tennis Club** is the first of the community's strictly members-only watering holes; its arched windows give sweeping ocean views – passersby see just the club's guarded entrance. Likewise, for the next couple of miles along this busy two-lane highway (a bad place to cycle or walk, or even stop your car) the high-class homes are shielded from prying eyes by walls of hedges.

You should have no trouble, however, spotting the red-roofed Italianate tower topping **Mar-a-Largo**. Finished in 1926, this was the $8-million winter abode of breakfast cereal heiress Marjorie Merriweather-Post, queen of Palm Beach high society for nearly forty years. On her death in 1973, Mar-a-Largo's 118 rooms and eighteen-acre grounds were bequeathed to the US government – which couldn't afford the upkeep. Instead, what has been called "Florida's most sybaritic private residence" was sold to property tycoon Donald Trump and it remains a very private residence.

Further on, close to the Via La Selva turning, a sprawling Colonial-style property once owned by John Lennon and Yoko Ono can just be glimpsed. Hardly

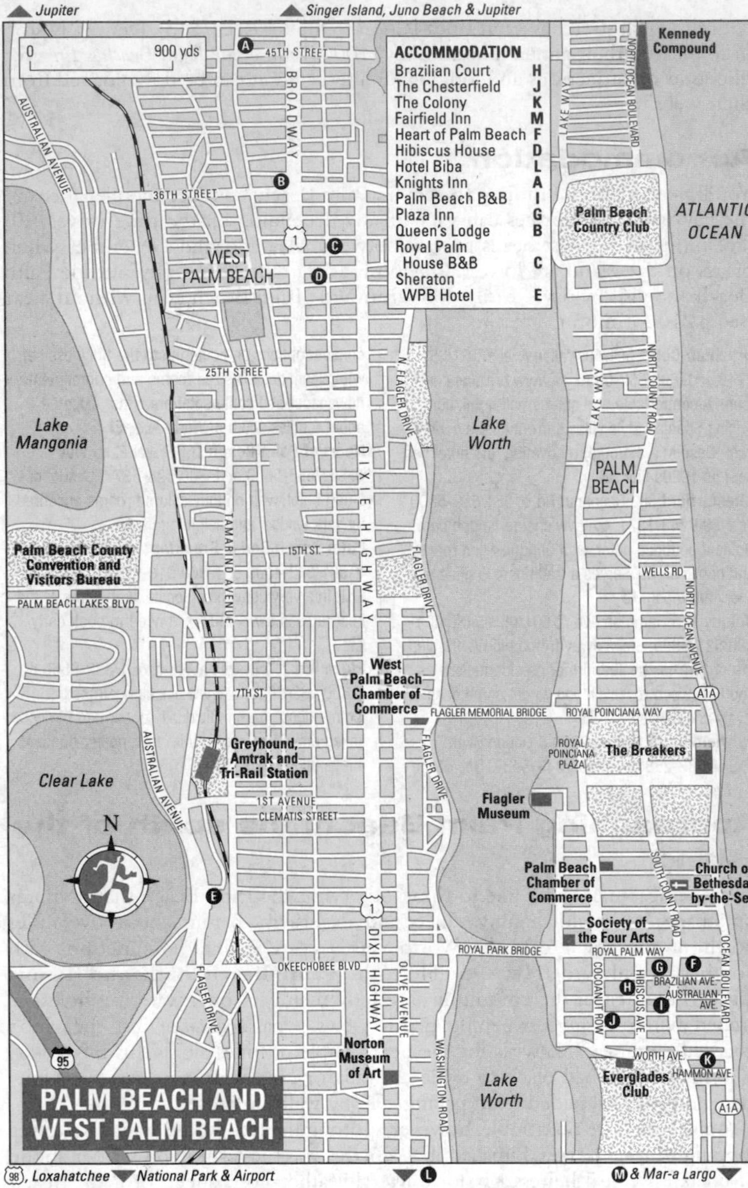

a place to enhance the ex-Beatle's anti-establishment credentials, it originally belonged to turn-of-the-century multi-millionaire Cornelius Vanderbilt. Half a mile north, Hwy-A1A becomes Ocean Boulevard as it enters the town of Palm Beach.

Palm Beach: the town

The main residential section of Palm Beach – **the town** – is where you should spend most of your time, and **Worth Avenue**, cruised by classic cars and filled with designer stores and high-class art galleries, is a good place to start your stroll, even if you can only afford to window-shop.

Other than expense-account acquisition, the most appealing aspect of the street is its architecture: stucco walls, crafted Romanesque facades, and narrow passageways leading to small courtyards where miniature bridges cross nonexistent canals and spiral staircases climb to higher levels. On the top floor of one of the courtyard buildings, Via Mizner, situated on the corner with Hibiscus Avenue, sits the former pied-à-terre of the man responsible for the Mediterranean look replicated all over Palm Beach – the flamboyant architect **Addison Mizner**. Unfortunately, it's not open to the public.

After heading up to Worth Avenue's western end to gawk at the vessels moored on Lake Worth – rows of ocean-going yachts with more living space than most people's homes – you should explore the rest of the town along Cocoanut Row or County Road.

Cocoanut Row

Four blocks north from its junction with Worth Avenue, **Cocoanut Row** crosses Royal Palm Way close to the stuccoed buildings and gardens of the **Society of the Four Arts**, at 2 Four Arts Plaza (Mon–Sat 10am–5pm, Sun 2–5pm; suggested donation $5; ⓣ561/655-7226). Aside from presenting art shows and lectures of an impressive standard between early December and mid-April, the organization also has a library worth browsing.

Half a mile further along Cocoanut Row you'll notice the white Doric columns fronting Whitehall, also known as the Henry Morrison **Flagler Museum** (Tues–Sat 10am–5pm, Sun noon–5pm; last tour leaves between 3.15pm and 3.30pm; $8; ⓣ561/655-2833, ⓦwww.flagler.org). The most

Palm Beach's architect: Addison Mizner

A former miner and prizefighter, **Addison Mizner** was an unemployed architect when he arrived in Palm Beach in 1918 from California to recuperate from the recurrence of a childhood leg injury. Inspired by the medieval buildings he'd seen around the Mediterranean, Mizner, financed by the heir to the Singer sewing machine fortune, built the **Everglades Club**, at 356 Worth Ave, which is off limits to the public. Described by Mizner as "a little bit of Seville and the Alhambra, a dash of Madeira and Algiers," the Everglades Club was the first public building in Florida in the Mediterranean Revival style, and fast became the island's most prestigious social club.

The success of the club, and the house he subsequently built for society bigwig Eva Stotesbury, won Mizner commissions all over Palm Beach as the wintering wealthy decided to swap their suites at one of Henry Flagler's hotels for a "million-dollar cottage" of their own.

Brilliant and unorthodox, Mizner's loggias and U-shaped interiors made the most of Florida's pleasant winter temperatures, while his twisting staircases to nowhere became legendary. Pursuing a medieval look, Mizner used untrained workmen to lay roof tiles crookedly, sprayed condensed milk onto walls to create an impression of centuries-old grime, and fired shotgun pellets into wood to imitate worm holes. By the mid-Twenties, Mizner had created the Palm Beach Style – which Florida architecture buff Hap Hattan called "the Old World for the new rich," and he would go on to fashion much of Boca Raton (see p.198).

overtly ostentatious home on the island, Whitehall was a $4-million wedding present from Henry Flagler to his third wife, Mary Lily Kenan, whom he married (after controversially persuading the Florida legislature to amend its divorce laws) in 1901. Like many of Florida's first luxury homes, Whitehall's interior design was created by pillaging the great buildings of Europe: among the 73 rooms are an Italian library, a French salon, a billiard room with a Swiss-style mantel, a hallway modeled on the Vatican's St Peter's, and a Louis XV ballroom. All are richly stuffed with ornamentation but – other than their mutual decadence – lack any aesthetic cohesion. Flagler was in his seventies when Whitehall was built, 37 years older than his bride and not enamored of the banquets and balls she continually hosted. He often sloped off to bed using a concealed stairway, perhaps to ponder plans to extend his railway to Key West – a display on the project fills his former office. From the 110-foot hallway, informative (but not compulsory) 45-minute **free guided tours** depart continuously and will leave you giddy with the tales – and the sights – of the earliest Palm Beach excesses. Don't miss the authentic railroad car, outside the exit to the gift shop, and the spectacular views of West Palm Beach from Flagler's enormous backyard.

Whitehall was built beside Flagler's first Palm Beach resort, the *Royal Poinciana Hotel*: a six-story, Colonial-style structure of 2000 rooms, which became the world's largest wooden building on its completion in 1894. A small plaque marks the spot, but only the remains of a grand ballroom are left of the hotel, whose hundred-acre grounds spread to what's now Royal Poinciana Way.

County Road

In terms of things to see, **County Road** is the poor relation of Cocoanut Row – to which it runs parallel – but is still worth a stroll. Along it, two blocks north of Worth Avenue, Mizner's Mediterranean Revival themes are displayed in Palm Beach's very tidy local administration offices and bank buildings. By contrast, the 1926 **Church of Bethesda-by-the-Sea**, a fifteen-minute walk further north to no.141 S County Road, is a handsome imitation-Gothic pile replacing the island's first church (see opposite): the large stained-glass windows depict Christianity around the world, but ignore them and walk instead through the echoing cloisters to the **Cluett Memorial Gardens** (daily 9am–5pm; free), a peaceful spot in which to take a stone pew and tuck into a picnic lunch.

A little further north, County Road is straddled by the golf course of *The Breakers* (Ⓣ1-888/BREAKERS; ❽), a castle-like hotel erected in 1926 and the last of Palm Beach's ultra-swanky resorts. Though security is tighter than in the past, you can still catch a glimpse of the ornate lobby on a trip to the hotel's high-end shops or restaurants. If you're here on Wednesdays, local historian Mr Ponce leads guided tours of the premises at 3pm (free for guests, $15 for the public; info on Ⓣ561/655-6611, ext 7691).

The north of the island

The limited points of interest beyond Royal Poinciana Way are best viewed from the three-mile **Lake Trail**, a bicycle and pedestrian path skirting the edge of Lake Worth, almost to the northern limit of the island. A bicycle is the ideal mode of transportation here: rent one from Palm Beach Bicycle Trail Shop, 223 Sunrise Ave (Ⓣ561/659-4583), for $26 a day.

Most locals use the trail as a jogging strip, and certainly there's little other than exercise and fine views across the lake to make it worthwhile. Keep an eye out, though, for "Duck's Nest," the oldest remaining home in Palm Beach, built

Thrift stores

Amazingly high-class threads, some of them discarded after only a single use, turn up in Palm Beach's thrift stores, though the prices are above normal thrift-store levels. Worth perusing are The Church Mouse, 374 S County Rd (☎561/659-2154; open Oct–May only); Goodwill Embassy Boutique, 210 Sunset Ave (☎561/832-8199); or Deja Vu, 219 Royal Poinciana Way (☎561/833-6624). Be warned, though, that many shops in Palm Beach close for the summer or operate on reduced hours – call before you go.

in 1891, and the **original Church of Bethesda-by-the-Sea**, at Barton Avenue and South County Road, which dates from 1889. Serving a congregation of early homesteaders across a 125-mile stretch of coast, all of whom had to get here by boat, the shingled church is now a private house, but easily spotted by the clockface hanging from its short tower.

The Lake Trail ends a few minutes' pedal south of the Lake Worth Inlet, a narrow cut separating Palm Beach from the high-rise-dominated Singer Island. To get to the inlet – for a sight of the neighboring island and a modest sense of achievement – weave your way through the short residential streets. For variation, cycle back to central Palm Beach along Ocean Drive (take care as there's no marked cycle path), which passes the two-acre former **Kennedy Compound**, at 1095 N Ocean Blvd, bought by Joe Kennedy – father of John, Robert, and Edward – in 1933. The Kennedys never fully integrated into ultra-conservative Palm Beach life, and it's said that few Palm Beach tears were shed in 1963 when John was assassinated. In April 1991, Palm Beach was rocked by the arrest here of William Kennedy Smith, nephew of Senator Edward Kennedy, on charges of sexual battery (Florida's legal term for rape). He was later acquitted.

Eating

Though it may be difficult to land affordable accommodation in Palm Beach, it's still possible to **eat** relatively cheaply here. Options are more abundant in West Palm Beach, however; for restaurants in the latter, see p.211.

Café L'Europe 150 Worth Ave ☎561/655-4020. If money's no object (you'll spend at least $50 a head) and you're dressed to kill, make for this super-elegant French restaurant.

Charley's Crab 456 S Ocean Blvd ☎561/659-1500. Serves up a mean shrimp cocktail among other scrumptious seafood offerings (and a killer Sunday brunch, too), in a location overlooking the dunes. Entrees $10–20.

Echo 230A Sunrise Ave ☎561/802-4222. If you're feeling especially flush, this is the place for imaginatively presented pan-Asian cuisine, served amid dramatic surrounding. Entrees $25–50. Dinner only, closed Mon.

Hamburger Heaven 314 S County Rd ☎561/655-5277. Dispensing delicious ground-beef burgers since 1945.

Michael's 250 Worth Ave ☎561/655-9996. A rarity in the Worth Ave area: a casual café serving smoothies, fresh juices, and sandwiches. Open Mon–Sat 9am–7pm, Sun noon–5pm.

Renato's 87 Via Mizner ☎561/655-9752. Comfortable Italian restaurant in lovely setting, hidden among the courtyards of Via Mizner. Entrees $24–34.

Testa's 221 Royal Poinciana Way ☎561/832-0992. Moderately priced ($16–25) option for exquisite seafood and pasta.

West Palm Beach and around

Founded to house the workforce of Flagler's Palm Beach resorts, **WEST PALM BEACH** has long been in the shadow of its glamorous neighbor across the lake. Only during the last two decades has the town gained a life of its own, with smart new office buildings, a scenic lakeside footpath – and less seemly industrial growth sprouting up on its western edge. Above all, West Palm Beach holds the promise of accommodation and food at a more reasonable price than in Palm Beach, and is the closest you'll get to the island using public transportation – PalmTran buses from Boca Raton and Greyhound services stop here, leaving a few minutes' walk to Palm Beach over one of the Lake Worth bridges.

Arrival, information, and accommodation

The West Palm Beach Amtrak (Ⓣ1-800/USA-RAIL), Tri-Rail (Ⓣ1-800/TRI-RAIL), and Greyhound (Ⓣ561/833-8536) stations are all located at 205 S Tamarind Ave, and linked by regular shuttle buses to the downtown area. Most local PalmTran (Ⓣ561/841-4BUS) bus routes converge at Quadrille Road.

The **Chamber of Commerce**, 401 N Flagler Drive, at the corner of Fourth Street (Mon–Fri 8.30am–5pm; Ⓣ561/833-3711, Ⓦwww.palmbeaches.com), has stacks of free leaflets and can answer questions on the whole Palm Beach County area. You can also stop by the Palm Beach County CVB (see p.204).

For **places to stay**, West Palm Beach offers a wider selection than Palm Beach and includes a number of lower-priced options. The best deals are to be found at *Queens Lodge*, 3712 Broadway (Ⓣ561/842-1108; ❷), a simple budget option by the highway; *Hotel Biba*, 320 Belvedere Rd (Ⓣ561/832-0094, Ⓦwww.hotelbiba.com; ❸), where the spare, uncluttered rooms have a subtle Eastern feel; and *Knights Inn*, 2200 45th St (Ⓣ561/478-1554 or 1-877/309-5225, Ⓦwww.knightsinn.com; ❸), which has quick highway access and limited noise. For a real treat that won't cost an arm and a leg, try *Hibiscus House*, 501 30th St, off Flagler Street (Ⓣ561/863-5633 or 1-800/203-4927; ❹). Loaded with beautiful antiques – including a baby grand piano – it offers color-themed rooms with four-poster beds. The owner, a virtual encyclopedia of Palm Beach, is usually more than happy to impart his knowledge. Nearby, the Twenties-style B&B *Royal Palm House Bed & Breakfast*, 3215 Spruce Ave (Ⓣ561/863-9836 or 1-800/655-3196; ❹), has comfy rooms equipped with fans and/or A/C, and a tropical garden in the back where you can enjoy free refreshments. Closer to downtown there's the reliable *Sheraton West Palm Beach Hotel at CityPlace*, 630 Clearwater Park Rd (Ⓣ561/833-1234 or 1-888/627-7081, Ⓦwww.pb-sheraton.com; ❺), close to many shops and restaurants.

Downtown West Palm Beach

Other than tending to basic needs, one of the few reasons to linger in **downtown West Palm Beach** is the fine collections of the **Norton Museum of Art**, 1451 S Olive Ave (Mon–Sat 10am–5pm, Sun 1–5pm, closed Mon May–Oct; $8, children 13–21 $3; docent tours given daily at 2pm Ⓣ561/832-5196, Ⓦwww.norton.org), a mile south of the downtown area. Together with some distinctive European paintings and drawings by Braque, de Chirico, Degas, Picasso, and others, the museum boasts a solid grouping of twentieth-century American works: Duane Hanson's soft sculpture *Young Worker* (you'll just about swear he's breathing) and Roger Brown's dark *Guilty without Trial: Protected by the Bill of Rights* are among the most impressive. There's also a sparkling roomful of Far Eastern pieces including seventh-century sculpted Buddhas, absorbingly complex amber carvings, and a collection of tomb jades dating from 1500–500 BC. The museum also hosts temporary exhibits ranging from contemporary glassware to Japanese anime.

In the late Fifties the boom of shopping malls in Palm Beach practically shut down the small boutiques and cafés on **Clematis Street**, turning it into another bland area of downtown West Palm Beach. Today, thanks to a major renovation project during the late Nineties, Clematis Street is once again home to a diverse mix of restaurants, shops, galleries, and a busy schedule of cultural activities. Daytime lunch concerts, the Thursday evening "Clematis by Night" events, and a continual parade of food and arts-and-crafts vendors have brought the area to life. The second Tuesday of the month heralds "Clematis Backstage," which can range from concerts to holiday celebrations in the spacious outdoor Meyer Amphitheater, and on Saturday mornings the street turns green with a farmer's market. Colorfully landscaped, Clematis Street stretches from the Intracoastal Waterway to the heart of downtown, culminating with the **fountain** in Centennial Square, which shoots jets of water into the air amidst dripping and squealing adults and children.

Eating

The majority of good **places to eat** can be found on Clematis Street in downtown, though there are plenty of options among the faux-European plazas at CityPlace, 700 S Rosemary Ave (Ⓣ561/366-1000, Ⓦwww.cityplace.com) and other shopping centers. For something on the lighter side, try *Robinson's Pastry Shop*, 215 Clematis St (Ⓣ561/833-4259), which sells delicious freshly baked snacks and sandwiches throughout the day.

Brewzzi 700 S Rosemary Ave, at CityPlace Ⓣ561/366-9753. The homemade microbrews (from light to red to dark) add gusto to this classy but casual Italian-American restaurant/pub, with a wide selection of pizzas ($12–20).

Cabana 118 Clematis St Ⓣ561/833-4773. Try the mouthwatering *chuletas do cerdo* (pork chops) and *pollo asado* at this inexpensive and not strictly Cuban restaurant (they serve *paellas* and Brazilian *churrasco* as well).

City Cellar Wine Bar and Grill 700 S Rosemary Ave, at CityPlace Ⓣ561/366-0071. Choose from subtly flavoured appetizers (such as spinach salad with spiced pears, gorgonzola, and hazelnuts) and hearty fish and meat main dishes, then wash it all down with something from the extensive wine list.

Dax Key West Grill 300 Clematis St Ⓣ561/833-0449. This Caribbean-themed restaurant serves tasty sandwiches and grilled or fried fish for around $10 or less, and you have your pick of fifteen colorful daiquiris.

Roxy's 319 Clematis St Ⓣ561/833-2402. The sandwiches and burgers are under $8 (entrees $10–18) at this long-standing homey grill.

Drinking and nightlife

Some of the restaurants listed above, such as *Dax Key West* (with its fifteen daiquiri varieties) and *Brewzzi*, are also known as **drinking** establishments. In addition, the *Blue Martini*, 550 S Rosemary Ave, at CityPlace (Ⓣ561/835-8601), has over twenty versions of the cocktail on the menu, along with tapas dishes and cool jazz. The **nightlife** options lacking in Palm Beach proper can be found in West Palm Beach. The *Respectable Street Café*, at 518 Clematis St (Wed–Sat Ⓣ561/832-9999) carries dance music only, sometimes live, from 11pm until very late. You can also cut loose at *Liquid Room* no. 313 (Ⓣ561/655-2332) and *Monkey Club*, no. 219 (Ⓣ561/833-6500), which has drink specials and events like quick-dating and (mechanical) bull-riding.

Inland from West Palm Beach

West Palm Beach makes a good stepping-off point for the **Loxahatchee National Wildlife Refuge**, 10216 Lee Rd in Boynton Beach (daily sunrise–sunset; cars $5, pedestrians and cyclists $1; visitor center open Wed–Sun 9am–4pm; Ⓣ561/732-3684, Ⓦloxahatchee.fws.gov). The 200 square miles of sawgrass marshes – the northerly extension of the Everglades (see p.167) – are only marginally penetrable on two easy walking trails from the **visitor center** (daily 9am–4pm, closed Mon & Tues May to mid-Oct). One trail (0.8 miles) leads around the marshes to an observation tower, and the other is a boardwalk that meanders through a cypress hammock. On both, you'll probably see a few snakes and local birds and get a firm impression of what undeveloped inland Florida is like – and how incredibly flat it is. It's also possible to go on guided canoe trails, airboat rides, bird walks, and "night prowls"; check with the visitor center for details. The less-accessible areas of the refuge had a starring role in the 2002 movie "Adaptation".

African and Asian wildlife is the star attraction of **Lion Country Safari** (daily 9.30am–5.30pm; last vehicles admitted 4.30pm; $17, children under 9 $13, plus parking fee of $3; ⓣ561/793-1084, ⓦwww.lioncountrysafari.com), on Hwy-80/Southern Boulevard (sixteen miles west of I-95 and before the junction of Hwy-98 and US-441). Lions, elephants, giraffes, chimpanzees, zebras, and ostriches are among the creatures roaming a 500-acre plot in which human visitors are confined to their cars. It's awkward to reach and perhaps overly expensive to visit, but if you can't leave Florida without photographing a flamingo, Lion Country Safari could well be for you.

Venturing further inland to the Lake Okeechobee area (see p.220), Hwy-80 from Lion Country Safari runs the twenty miles to the lakeside town of Belle Glade.

The Treasure Coast

West Palm Beach marks the northern limit of Miami's hinterland and the end of the southeast coast's heavily touristed sections. Aside from some small and uninspiring towns, the next eighty miles – dubbed the **TREASURE COAST** simply to distinguish it from the Gold Coast – missed out entirely on the expansion seen to the south and to the north, leaving wide open spaces and some magnificent swathes of quiet beach that attract Florida's nature lovers and a small band of well-informed tan-seekers.

Singer Island and Juno Beach

North of West Palm Beach, Hwy-A1A swings back to the coast at **SINGER ISLAND**, which gets its name from the sewing-machine heir Paris Singer. The beaches are perfectly adequate but the place lacks life and is predominantly residential. If you find the need **to stay**, the *Days Inn Oceanfront Resort*, 2700 N Ocean Drive (ⓣ561/848-8661; ❹), is a decent budget option, while for a bit more luxury your best bet is the *Crowne Plaza*, 3200 N Ocean Drive (ⓣ561/842-6171 or 1-800/327-0522; ❻), worth checking for their off-season Internet specials.

Continuing northward up Hwy-A1A, the **John D. MacArthur Beach State Park** (daily 8am–sunset; visitor center open Wed–Mon 9am–5pm; cars

$3.25, pedestrians and cyclists $1; ⓣ561/624-6950, ⓦwww.macarthurbeach.org) is one of the few beach state parks with more to offer than just sun and sand. A 1600-foot boardwalk (with a tram service along it during the day) leads across the estuary to a picturesque beach bordered by sea grape trees. From the boardwalk's end, some worthwhile nature trails lead off through the park, and there are also ranger-led kayak tours ($20) as well as evening concerts (mostly free) and summertime turtle walks.

The next few miles are mostly golf courses and planned retirement communities, but one good stop is **JUNO BEACH**, where Hwy-A1A follows a high coastal bluff from which it's relatively easy to find one of the unmarked paths down to the uncrowded sands.

On the other hand, you can set your sights on Loggerhead Park, also the site of the **Marine Life Center** (on Hwy-A1A, Tues–Sat 10am–3pm; donation; ⓣ561/627-8280, ⓦwww.marinelife.org), intended for kids but good for adults wanting to brush up on their knowledge of marine life in general and sea turtles in particular. There's a turtle hatchery here and displays on their life cycles, and this is also one of several places along the Treasure Coast where you can take expeditions to watch the turtles as they steal ashore to lay eggs under cover of darkness (the only time they give up the security of the ocean is between June and July). Reservations are essential and taken from May onwards; the center can provide you with further details.

Jupiter and Jupiter Island

Splitting into several colorless districts around the wide mouth of the Tequesta River, **JUPITER**, about six miles north of Juno Beach, was a rumrunners' haven during the Prohibition era; these days it's better known as the hometown of Florida's favorite son, actor Burt Reynolds. Most symbols of "Burt-ness" have gone under, such as his restaurant, the museum on his ranch, and the Jupiter Theater. Burt Reynolds Park, beside US-1 near the town center, is a nice enough park that carries the man's name, but only the most zealous fan need seek it out.

The newest attraction in the area has nothing to do with Burt – the recently relocated **Hibel Museum of Art**, 5353 Parkside Drive (Tues–Sat 11am–5pm, Sun 1–5pm; free; ⓣ561/622-5560, ⓦwww.hibel.org). Forget Warhol and Rothko, the most commercially successful artist in the US is Edna Hibel, an octagenarian resident of Singer Island (just north of West Palm Beach; see opposite), whose works fill this deep-carpeted museum. Inspired by "love," Hibel has been churning out coy, sentimental portraits, usually of serene Asian and Mexican women, since the late Thirties, often working seven days a week to meet demand. Pay a visit, though, if only to admire the unflappable devotion of the guides, and to figure out why Hibel originals change hands for $50,000.

A visit to the **Loxahatchee River Historical Museum**, 805 N US-1 (Tues–Fri 10am–5pm, Sat & Sun 1–5pm; $5; ⓣ561/747-6639), describes pioneer life on and around the Tequesta River long before Burt's time. To gain more insight into how the pioneers lived, you can walk through the **Dubois Pioneer Home**, a house dating to 1898 located in nearby Dubois Park (Wed & Sun 1–4pm; $2). Also worth your time is the red-brick **Jupiter Lighthouse** on the north bank of the Jupiter Inlet (Sun–Wed 10am–4pm, last tour 3.15pm; $6; ⓣ561/747-8380), built in 1860 – making it the oldest building in Palm Beach County – with a small museum devoted to nineteenth-century nautical paraphernalia. The lighthouse can be seen from Beach Road, the route Hwy-A1A takes back to the coast after looping through the town. This route skirts the Jupiter Inlet Colony – a wealthy community whose roads are guarded by photo-electric beams, enabling police to check any suspicious traffic cruising the dead-end streets – before heading north along Jupiter Island.

Jupiter Island

Two miles into **Jupiter Island** on Hwy-A1A, pull up at the **Blowing Rocks Nature Preserve** (daily 9am–4.30pm; $3; ⓣ561/747-3113, ⓦwww.tnc.florida.org), where a limestone outcrop covers much of the beach and powerful incoming tides are known to drive through the rocks' hollows, emerging as gusts of spray further on. At low tide, it's sometimes possible to walk around the outcrop and peer into the rock's sea-drilled cavities. Guided nature walks are available, though if you fancy a swim, note that no lifeguards are present.

Seven miles further north, the shell-strewn Hobe Sound Beach marks the edge of the 960-acre **Hobe Sound National Wildlife Refuge** (daily sunrise–sunset; $5), which occupies the remainder of the island. Having achieved spectacular success as a nesting ground for sea turtles during the summer (turtle hikes available May–July Tues, Thurs & Fri evenings; ⓣ561/546-2067), the refuge is also rich in birdsong, with scrub jays among its tuneful inhabitants. To find out more about the refuge's flora and fauna, visit the small **nature center** (Mon–Fri 9am–3pm; ⓣ561/546-2067, ⓦwww.hobesoundnaturecenter.org) on the mainland on US-1.

The northern end of Jupiter Island comprises **St Lucie Inlet State Preserve** (daily 8am–sunset; cars $3.25, pedestrians and cyclists $1; ⓣ561/744-7603), whose 928 acres include mangrove-lined creeks and over two miles of beach accessible by boat ($2) from Hobe Sound Beach. It's occasionally possible to see manatees feeding in the grass beds north of the dock, though the boardwalk is notable primarily for the skunk-like aroma emitted by the white stopper, a tropical tree.

Inland: the Jonathan Dickinson State Park

Two miles south of the Hobe Sound interpretive center on US-1, the **Jonathan Dickinson State Park** (daily 8am–sunset; cars $3.25, pedestrians and cyclists $1; ⓣ561/546-2771, ⓦwww.dep.state.fl.us/parks) preserves a natural landscape quite different from what you'll see at the coast. Step up to the observation platform atop **Hobe Mountain**, an 86-foot-high sand dune, and survey the pines, palmetto (a stumpy, tropical palm fan) flatlands, and the mangrove-flanked course of the winding Loxahatchee River. The intrepid can obtain hiking maps from the entrance office and set off along the nine-mile Kitchen Creek Trail, which starts from the park's entrance and finishes in a cypress hammock at some basic campgrounds; beware that campground space must be booked in advance (tents for one to four people May–Oct $14, Nov–April $17; cabins $65–85 a night for a minimum of two nights; ⓣ561/746-1466).

Anyone more adventurous should rent a canoe ($10 for 2 hrs, $4 for each additional hr) from the people who rent out the cabins (see above) and paddle along the Loxahatchee River – don't be put off by the preponderance of alligators – to the **Trapper Nelson Interpretive Center**, named for a Quaker washed ashore near here in 1697. A less strenuous way to get there is by taking the two-hour cruise aboard the *Loxahatchee Queen II* (four daily at 9am, 11am, 1pm, and 3pm; $12, children $7; reservations ⓣ561/746-1466), which leaves from the park's pier.

Stuart and Hutchinson Island

HUTCHINSON ISLAND, another long barrier island, lies immediately north of Jupiter Island. To reach it (with either US-1 or Hwy-A1A), you'll first pass through **STUART**, a neat and tidy, but rather uninteresting, town on the south bank of the St Lucie River. Stuart has a number of century-old wooden buildings proudly preserved on and around Flagler Avenue – pick up a free walking guide from the **Chamber of Commerce** at 1650 S Kanner Hwy (Mon–Fri 8.30am–5pm; ⓣ772/287-1088, ⓦwww.goodnature.org) – but not much else to keep you engaged. For a bite to **eat** in downtown Stuart, try the *Riverwalk Café*, 201 SW St Lucie Ave (ⓣ772/221-1511), or the good but somewhat expensive *Flagler Grill*, 47 SW Flagler Ave (dinner only; ⓣ772/221-9517).

Hutchinson Island

Largely hidden behind thickly grouped Australian pines, several beautiful beaches line the twenty-mile-long **Hutchinson Island**, located to the east of Stuart along Hwy-A1A (also known as Ocean Boulevard). Keep your eyes peeled for the public access points. It would be hard, however, to miss **Stuart Beach**: facing Hwy-A1A, it is a low-key stretch of brown sand where tourists are heavily outnumbered by locals – a fine venue for a few hours of ray absorption.

Close by, at 825 NE Ocean Blvd, the **Elliott Museum** (Mon–Sat 10am–4pm, Sun 1–4pm; $6, children $2; ⓣ772/225-1961) exhibits a sizeable hodgepodge of mechanical objects and ornaments, few of which seem to be the work of Sterling Elliott, whom the place is intended to commemorate. A talented inventor active during the 1870s, Elliott's creations displayed here include an automatic knot-tier and the first addressing machine, while his quadricycle – a four-wheeled bicycle – solved many of the technical problems that hindered the development of the car. It's hard, therefore, to fathom why much of the museum is given over to reconstructed turn-of-the-century shops, Victorian fashion accessories, and a hangar full of vintage cars, autographed memorabilia of Baseball Hall of Famers, and various Seminole artifacts.

A mile south at 301 SE MacArthur Blvd, **Gilbert's Bar House of Refuge** (Mon–Sat 10am–4pm, Sun 1–4pm; $4, children $2; ⓣ772/225-1875) is a better stop: a convincingly restored refuge for shipwrecked sailors that was one of ten erected along Florida's east coast during 1875. Furnished in a Victorian style, the rooms of the refuge are best understood with the free guided tours (every day except Saturday). There's more evidence of the refuge's importance in the entrance area – lifeboat equipment, ship's logs, and a modern weather station – along with reminders of the building's more recent function as a sea turtle hatchery.

Pushing on north, roughly halfway along the island, **Jensen Beach** has the only road to the mainland between Stuart and Fort Pierce, as well as a small but pleasant beach. Jensen Beach also marks the start of a cycle path, which continues – passing Florida Power & Light (FPL), one of Florida's two nuclear power stations (which has a visitor center with interactive exhibits; Sun–Fri 10am–4pm; free; ⓣ772/468-4111) – to the Fort Pierce Inlet that divides Hutchinson Island in two. (You can **rent bikes** at Jensen Beach from Mac's Bike and Fitness Shop, 3472 NE Savannah Rd ⓣ772/334-4343.) To reach the northern half of the island (known as North Hutchinson Island), you'll need to pass through the area's biggest town, Fort Pierce.

Fort Pierce

A number of rustic motels, bars, and restaurants grouped along Hwy-A1A beside a more than adequate beach make the first taste of **FORT PIERCE** a favorable one. The bulk of the town (looped through by Hwy-A1A) lies two miles away across the Intracoastal Waterway, where tourism plays second fiddle to processing and transporting the produce of Florida's citrus farms. The convivial coastal section makes an amenable base for island exploration, but the mainland town has only a few features likely to detain you for long. Scuba diving (see "Practicalities," p.218) off the coast is, however, an entirely different prospect, giving you a chance to explore reefs and wrecks dating back to the

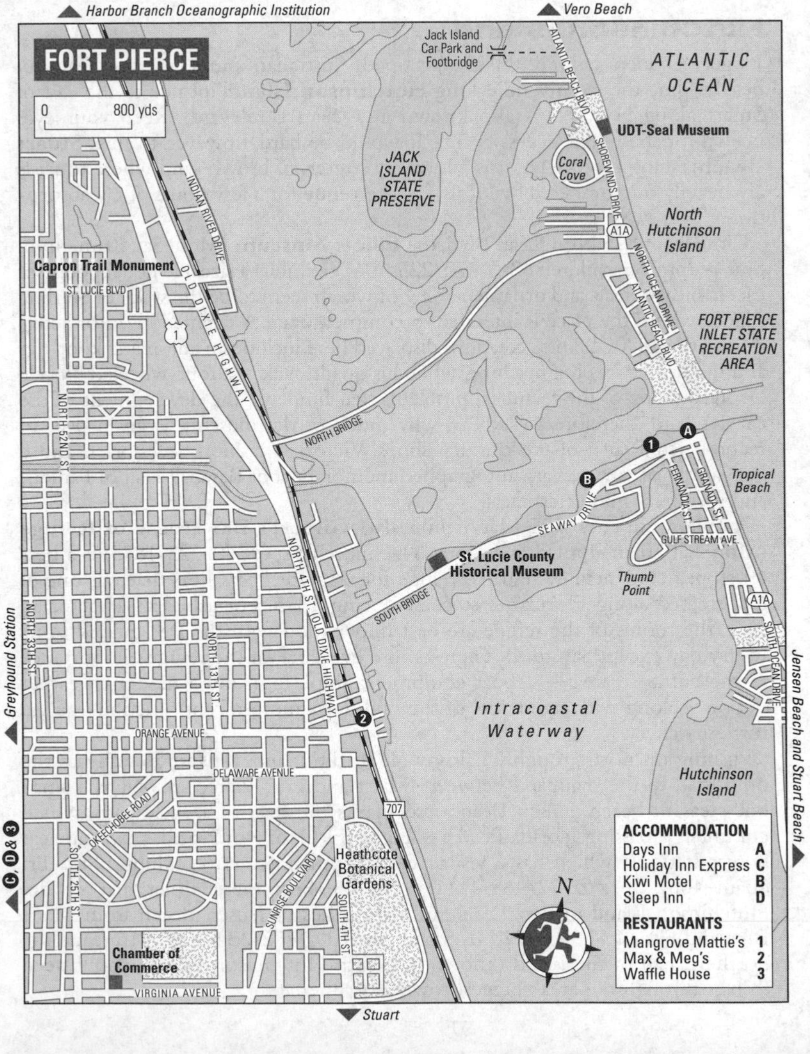

time of the Spanish galleons. If you're visiting between mid-November and early April, you might catch sight of manatees in the Indian River Lagoon – try the viewing area at Moore's Creek at the marina, where Avenue C and North Indian River Drive meet.

Close to the Intracoastal Waterway bridge at 414 Seaway Drive, the **St Lucie County Historical Museum** (Tues–Sat 10am–4pm, Sun noon–4pm; $2; ⓣ772/462-1795) keeps a cogent assembly of relics. Among them are a full-sized Seminole Indian *chickee* (a palm-thatched hut) and a solid account of the Seminole Wars, including the 1838 fort from which Fort Pierce took its name, and a re-creation of P.P. Cobb's general store, the hub of the turn-of-the-century town. Outside the museum at **Gardner House**, a 1907 "cracker" cottage, note the tall ceilings and many windows that allowed the muggy Florida air to circulate in the days before air-conditioning. The museum also contains an exhibition gallery and a fully restored 1919 fire engine.

Downtown Fort Pierce and around

Entering **downtown Fort Pierce** along US-1, your gaze is assaulted by a sewage treatment works and the towers of a cement factory, which provide a stark contrast to Hutchinson Island's raging vegetation. If you've time, however, Hwy-A1A quickly escapes oceanwards to North Hutchinson Island (see p.218). Don't bother with the downtown area, but make an excursion a few miles north along US-1, where several sites can easily occupy a few hours.

The Capron Trail Monument and Indian River Drive

A couple of miles north of downtown Fort Pierce, US-1 crosses St Lucie Boulevard, and a left turn along here leads to a memorial (by the junction with 25th St) recalling the nineteenth-century soldiers who inched their way from here toward Fort Brooke – the site of present-day Tampa. Their machetes hacked out the **Capron Trail**, one of the first east–west cross-Florida routes. Driving back, stay on St Lucie Boulevard as it crosses US-1 and turn left along **Indian River Drive**, where gracious, rambling wooden homes dating from the early 1900s line the Intracoastal Waterway.

The Heathcote Botanical Gardens

At 210 Savanna Rd, off US-1 and north of Jefferson Plaza, the **Heathcote Botanical Gardens** (Tues–Sat 9am–5pm; also Nov–April Sun 1–5pm; $4; ⓣ772/464-4672) is an oasis in an otherwise gray setting, providing a relaxing and surprisingly cool place to while away a couple of hours amidst a well-laid-out display of tropical flowers and trees as well as a small Japanese garden.

The Harbor Branch Oceanographic Institution

Five miles north of St-Lucie Boulevard, the **Harbor Branch Oceanographic Institution**, 5600 N US-1 (ⓣ772/465-2400, ⓦwww.hboi.org), is a phenomenally well-equipped deep-sea research and education center. The highly informative tours (Mon–Sat: land tours at noon & 2pm, $12 adults, $6 children; boat tours at 1pm & 3pm, $17 adults, $12 children) depart from the visitor center and cover such highlights as full-scale models of research submersibles and an "Aquaculture" exhibit featuring interactive displays and videos to show you how seafood can be specially cultured for human consumption and thus help to satisfy our increasing demand on the seas. You'll also get the chance to eat in the research center's canteen: a good deal for $7 – try the meatloaf or, of course, the seafood.

Practicalities

The Fort Pierce Greyhound **bus station** (☎772/461-3299) is six miles from downtown at 7150 Okeechobee Rd, near the junction of Hwy-70 and Florida's Turnpike. A taxi ride from here to the beach will cost $15–20; try Checker Cab (☎772/878-1234). You can get general **information** from the **Chamber of Commerce**, 2200 Virginia Ave (Mon–Fri 8.30am–5pm; ☎772/595-9999, Ⓦwww.stluciechamber.org).

A group of ordinary but inexpensive **accommodation** options are available close to the I-95. For rooms, try *Holiday Inn Express*, 7151 Okeechobee Rd (☎772/464-5000; ❸), or the *Sleep Inn*, 2715 Cross Rd Parkway (☎1-866/833-9330; ❸).

Otherwise, sleeping (with the exception of camping) and dining are best done close to the beach, two miles east of downtown Fort Pierce. Most motels are geared up for stays of several nights and many rooms include cooking facilities. Try the *Days Inn*, 1920 Seaway Drive (☎772/461-8737, Ⓦwww.daysinn.com; ❹), which features a pool and cable TV, or join the fishing folk at the more basic *Kiwi Motel*, 1240 Seaway Drive (☎772/461-6645; ❹), whose rooms do come with kitchens. There are additional choices along Seaway Drive and the northern part of Ocean Drive; ask on the spot for the best deals. For **camping**, head inland and seven miles south of downtown Fort Pierce along Route 707 to *Savannah's* (☎772/464-7855), a sizeable square of reclaimed marshland beside the Intracoastal Waterway where you can pitch a tent for $14. To explore this unspoiled landscape, take one of the nature trails or hire a canoe.

Eating options in Fort Pierce include lots of seafood options, with *Max & Megs*, 122 N Second St (☎772/467-0065), being one of the less expensive ones. If you're feeling flush, you can always visit the more refined *Mangrove Matties*, 1640 Seaway Drive (☎772/466-1044), which offers such dishes as coconut shrimp and conch chowder and has a great waterside location. Family-style food is available at the *Waffle House*, next to the bus station, at 7147 Okeechobee Rd (☎772/461-8444).

The Fort Pierce area is also known for some of the best **diving** in the US. Try Dive Odyssea, 621 N Second St (☎772/460-1771), and Blue Planet, 1317B NW St Lucie West Blvd, in nearby Port St Lucie (☎772/871-9122), both of which conduct local diving trips for around $115 (including equipment and a wetsuit).

Port St Lucie

Adjacent to and merging with southern Fort Pierce lies **Port St Lucie**. The chief attractions here are the marina and the St Lucie County Sport Complex, at 527 NW Peacock Loop (☎772/871-2115), where the **New York Mets** baseball team holds its spring training – if you're around in February or March it's worth checking out the goings-on. It's also the regular home of the St Lucie Mets, a Florida State League baseball team, whose season opens in April.

North Hutchinson Island

Covering 340 acres at the southern tip of North Hutchinson Island, **Fort Pierce Inlet State Recreation Area** (daily 8am–sunset; cars $3.25, pedestrians and cyclists $1; ☎772/468-3985), at 905 Shorewinds Drive, off Hwy-A1A, overlooks the Fort Pierce Inlet and the community's beach. Its location makes it a scenic setting for a picnic, as well as a launch site for local surfers. A mile north, on Hwy-A1A, a footbridge from the parking lot of the **Jack Island State Preserve** (same times and fees as above) leads onto the mile-long Marsh Rabbit Run, a boardwalk trail cutting through a thick mangrove swamp to an observation tower on the edge of the Indian River. Keep alert to spot the great blue herons and ospreys nesting in the area.

Concern for the environment is not something shared by the **UDT-SEAL Museum** (Tues–Sat 10am–4pm, Sun noon–4pm; $5; ⓣ772/595-5845), at 3300 N Hwy-A1A between the recreation area and the wildlife refuge, dedicated to the US Navy's frogman demolition teams who've been exploding sea-mines and maintaining beach defenses since the Normandy landings. During World War II, the UDTs (Underwater Demolition Teams) trained on Hutchinson Island – like most of Florida's barrier islands, it was off limits to civilians at the time. The more elite SEALs (Sea Air Land) came into being later during the Sixties. The museum covers the technicalities of establishing beach-heads, though jingoism is predictably apparent – anyone who can't keep doubts over US foreign policy to themselves should steer clear.

Vero Beach and around

For the next fourteen miles north, Australian pines mar Hwy-A1A's ocean view until North Hutchinson Island imperceptibly becomes **Orchid Island** and you reach **VERO BEACH**, the area's sole community of substance and one with a pronounced upmarket image. It makes an enjoyable hideaway, however, with a fine group of beaches around Ocean Drive, parallel to Hwy-A1A. There's little to tempt you from the sands, but it's worth taking the trouble to view the *Driftwood Resort*, 3150 Ocean Drive (ⓣ772/231-0550; ❹), a Thirties hotel, now fully equipped apartments, erected from a jumble of driftwood, bells, religious statuary, mosaics, flea-market finds, and pieces of demolished Palm Beach mansions.

Good-value **eateries** include *Waldo's*, part of the *Driftwood Resort* (ⓣ772/231-7091), which serves items like beer-battered dolphin fingers, salads, and cheesesteak sandwiches (around $10 for lunch) and more substantial dinner selections; and *Tangos*, 3001 Ocean Drive (ⓣ772/231-1550), which is renowned for both its baked crab, brie, and artichoke dip and its lobster quesadilla entrees.

North of Vero Beach: Sebastian Inlet

Tiny beachside communities dot the rest of the island, but you'll find most activity – and campgrounds ($17 Dec–April, $13 May–Nov) – around the **Sebastian Inlet State Recreation Area**, 9700 S Hwy-A1A (open 24hr; cars $3.25, pedestrians and cyclists $1; ⓣ321/984-4852), sixteen miles north of Vero Beach. Roaring ocean breakers lure surfers here, particularly over Easter when contests are held, and anglers cram the jetties for the east coast's finest fishing. Without a board or a rod, you can amuse yourself by keeping an eye out for the endangered birdlife making sorties from nearby Pelican Island, the oldest wildlife refuge in the country (established by Teddy Roosevelt in 1903). The island itself is off limits to humans, though an entire industry is devoted to plying the surrounding waters. For a bit of dolphin and manatee watching, the *Inlet Explorer* (located inside Inlet Marina; $17, children under 12, $11; ⓣ1-

800/952-1126) offers two-hour tours of the Indian River Lagoon. Similar tours are offered by Sebastian River Boat Tours (leaving from *Hurricane Harbor* restaurant, 1542 Indian River Drive; ⓣ772/589-1115), and River Queen Cruises (at *Captain Hiram's* restaurant, 1606 Indian River Drive; ⓣ1-888/755-6161). If you'd prefer to paddle about under your own steam, try Kayaks, Etc (ⓣ1-888/652-9257, ⓦwww.kayaksetc.com), which runs excursions on the Indian River with lunch for around $35; $20 if you bring your own kayak.

Beyond Sebastian Inlet you reach the outskirts of the **Space Coast**, which is covered in "The Northeast" chapter, starting on p.371. Alternatively, heading inland from the coast will bring you to the slow-paced towns of south central Florida, which offer plenty of relaxed diversions in their lake-filled vicinity.

South central Florida

Trapped in the triangle between the beaches of the Palm Beach and Tampa Bay areas and the vacation haunts of Orlando, the main towns of **SOUTH CENTRAL FLORIDA** haven't been done any favors by decades of phosphate mining, which have left their surrounds pockmarked with craters. However, matters are gradually being improved. Many of the unsightly holes have been turned into artificial lakes (joining a large number of natural ones), and the prospect of boating, waterskiing, and fishing on them attracts visitors from the grip of Orlando. More interestingly, several of the region's small towns were formerly big towns around the turn of the twentieth century and are keen to flaunt their pasts – and near them can be found several refreshingly under-hyped attractions, which were bringing tourists into the state when Walt Disney was still in short trousers.

Venturing inland from either West Palm Beach (seventy miles on Hwy-710) or Fort Pierce (forty miles on Hwy-70) brings you to **Lake Okeechobee**, the second largest freshwater lake in the US.

Lake Okeechobee and around

For many years, one of the best-kept secrets in Florida was the outstanding natural beauty of **Lake Okeechobee**. The former preserve of sugarcane, beef, and dairy farmers, as well as fishermen in search of catfish or large-mouthed bass, the lake started to draw tourists only in the last decade, a result of both a statewide push and the area's abundance of plants and **wildlife**. Birds feature strongly: over 120 varieties have been spotted, and this is one of the few places in the world where you can still sight a snail kite. Other inhabitants include bobcats, alligators, turtles, otters, snakes, and, occasionally, manatees.

For centuries, the lake was home exclusively to Native Americans (who named the lake "Big Water" in their Seminole language). The area's first farming settlers began arriving in 1910, encouraged by the work carried out by wealthy Philadelphian Hamilton Disston, who, in the nineteenth century, started dredging canals and draining the land for agriculture. Next came the railroads, extending around three-quarters of the lake by the late Twenties and providing easy access to the rest of the state. Today the area is also served by three **highways**, which join to encircle the lake and allow access to the towns dotted around its shores (see below). Staying a day or two in one of them is ideal for exploring Lake Okeechobee and its environs at your leisure.

Lake Okeechobee

Covering 730 square miles and ranging from ten to fourteen feet in depth, **Lake Okeechobee** is fed by several rivers, creeks, and canals, and has always played an important role not only in the lives of communities close to its shores but also in the life cycle of the Everglades. After a devastating hurricane in 1928, a retaining wall encircling the lake was built, and the lake has since served as both a flood-control safety valve during the hurricane season and as a freshwater storage reservoir. Traditionally, the lake's waters have drained slowly south to nourish the Everglades after the summer rains, but the disruption caused by extensive "reclaiming" of land for farming is one of the hottest environmental issues in Florida.

The lake itself is best enjoyed by **boat** or by **walking/cycling trails** (there is a 110-mile trail that runs along the top of the Hoover Dike). For more information on the trails, call the Florida Trail Association (Ⓣ1-877/HIKE-FLA, Ⓦwww.florida-trail.org).

Okeechobee town

The lakeside community of **OKEECHOBEE** offers a base from which to explore and provides the most alternatives for accommodation, food, and entertainment. The town was designed by the ubiquitous Henry M. Flagler (see "Palm Beach," p.204), whose grandiose plan demanded wide streets and wooden-framed buildings, some of which remain.

The town has a few places worthy of a visit for an hour or two, should the weather prevent you from more active pursuits; you might try the **Historical Museum**, 1850 Hwy-98 N (in the Historical Park; Thurs only 9am–1pm; free) and the 1926 **County Court House** at 304 NW 2nd Street, a pretty example of Mediterranean Revival architecture, a style much favored by Flagler. Details on these and other places of interest, as well as local events, can be found at the **Chamber of Commerce** at the intersection of routes 70 and US-441 at 55 S Parrott Avenue (Mon–Fri 9am–4pm; Ⓣ863/763-6464).

If you're interested in **fishing**, still a primary activity in the area, go to Garrard's Tackle Shop, 4259 US-441 S (Ⓣ863/763-3416). They will supply all the gear and a guide to help ensure you catch something.

Practicalities

Although the town is easy to get to – Greyhound stops at the *Wendy's* restaurant at 502 NE Park St, and Amtrak has a depot at 801 N Parrot Ave (Ⓣ1-800/872-7245) – there is no local public transportation system, and taxis stop running at 9pm. This means that if you don't have a car you'll be pretty much tied to the town in the evenings and may therefore want to limit your time to one or two nights. Of the places to **stay**, the quiet and unassuming *Wanta Linga Motel*, 3225 SE US-441 (Ⓣ863/763-1020 or 1-800/754-0428; ❷), offers reasonably priced rooms with microwaves and mini fridges. The *Motel Pier II*, 2200 SE US-441 (Ⓣ863/763-8003 or 1-800/874-3744; ❸), offers standard, clean, and comfortable accommodation, plus a pool, a five-story viewing tower, and access to a fishing pier with a lounge. The 43-room *Holiday Inn*, 3975 US-441

S (☎863/357-3529; ❸), offers a bit more comfort and includes a free breakfast bar. For **camping**, you'll find the largest *KOA* campground in North America just outside the town as you're heading toward the lake on US-441 S (☎863/763-0231 or 1-800/562-7748). A tent site costs $35, an RV site $45, and a one-room cabin (sleeping up to four) is around $60. A nine-hole golf course is on the premises, and there's miniature golf, tennis courts, and a restaurant and lounge as well.

For **eating**, *Lightsey's Fish Co*, 10435 Hwy-78 W (☎863/763-4276), serves a selection of fresh fish and home-style food at reasonable prices. Alternatively, try *The Clock*, 1111 S Parrott Ave (☎863/467-2224), a good choice for American-style breakfasts, lunches, and dinners, or the steak and seafood at *Michael's Restaurant*, 1001 S Parrott Ave (☎863/763-2069). The *Angus Restaurant*, 2054 Hwy-70 W at junction 98 (☎863/763-2040; closed Sun), specializes in steak and prime rib, for which they're famous, plus a wide selection of seafood. They also run the *Club Angus*, which has live music on Friday nights and a DJ the rest of the week.

Brighton Seminole Indian Reservation

Leaving Okeechobee via US-441, follow Route 78, which charts a 34-mile course along the west side of the lake, passing through Fisheating Creek and continuing into the treeless expanse of Indian Prairie, part of the 35,000-acre **Brighton Seminole Indian Reservation**.

The Seminole Indians migrated here in the eighteenth century from Georgia and Alabama, replacing the already decimated original Native American population. After they, too, became the target of aggression, a small number managed to establish themselves here on the western side of the lake, where about 450 remain, as successful cattle farmers. Although they live in houses rather than traditional Seminole *chickees*, or thatched huts, the current residents have remained faithful to long-held beliefs, and while handicrafts may be offered from the roadside, you won't find any of the tacky souvenir shops common to reservations in more populous areas. The tribe does, however, run a casino (follow the signs on Hwy-70 west to Route 721 south; ☎1-866/2-CASINO), which is open from 10am (closed Mon) and features video gaming, poker, and "high stakes" bingo (call for schedule).

On this side of the lake, **accommodation** is limited to several well-equipped **campgrounds**, the best of which is *Twin Palms Resort* (☎863/946-0977), located twenty miles from the town of Okeechobee. This RV park offers self-contained cottages for $50 and tent sites for $18.50 per night.

Clewiston and Belle Glade

Continue south on Route 78 to its junction with US-27, which is walled by many miles of sugar cane – half of all the sugar grown in the US, in fact – harvested between November and March by Jamaican laborers who are flown in, housed in hostels, and notoriously underpaid for their physically demanding and even dangerous work. Many in Florida, particularly the 43,000 locally employed in the sugar industry, seem content to turn a blind eye to the scandalous treatment of the migrants. Their plight is not a subject wisely brought up in **CLEWISTON**, fourteen miles further south, which is dominated by the US Sugar Corporation and the company's multi-million-dollar profits. The two notable attractions are the **Clewiston Museum**, 114 S Commercio St (Mon–Fri 1–5pm, closed July; free; ☎561/983-2870), which provides an interesting rundown of the agricultural and cultural history of the area; and the entertaining **Sugarland Tour**, run by the **Chamber of Commerce**, 544 W Sugarland Hwy (Ⓣ863/983-7979, Ⓦwww.clewiston.org), a half-day tour (Oct–April) that takes in a sugar cane farm, a sugar factory, and an insect lab where mites beneficial to the sugar industry are bred. You must reserve in advance, and the $27.50 fee includes lunch at the *Clewiston Inn* (see below).

The small town of **BELLE GLADE** has the biggest sugar mill in the country, as well as numerous trailer parks aimed largely at attracting fishermen. In its otherwise quiet history, one event stands out: the loss of 2000 lives when the lake was whipped up by a hurricane in 1928. The Belle Glade **Chamber of Commerce** is at 540 S Main St (Mon–Fri 9am–3pm; Ⓣ561/996-2745).

Accommodation is relatively plentiful in these towns, though squarely aimed at fishing folk – if that's not your scene you may as well stay away. In Clewiston, *Roland Martin's Lakeside Resort*, 920 E Del Monte Ave (Ⓣ1-800/473-6766 or 863/963-3151; ❸), has RV hookups ($30), along with an outfitter shop, restaurant, and tiki bar. For something a little nicer, try the *Clewiston Inn*, 108 Royal Palm Ave (Ⓣ863/983-8151 or 1-800/749-4466; ❹), notable for its Southern-style hospitality, simple yet comfortable rooms, and a 360-degree mural of local wildlife in its "Everglades Lounge." In Belle Glade, the *Budget Inn* on 1075 S Main St (Ⓣ561/992-8600; ❷) has decent lodging, while two miles west of Belle Glade on Route 717, you can camp on Torrey Island at *The City of Belle Glade's Marina Campground* (Ⓣ561/996-6322), which has lots of campervan space and a tent area ($20 a night), plus a miniature golf course. There's also a marina and a campground (Ⓣ561/924-7832) with waterside tent sites ($25 for RVs, $21 for tents) in nearby Pahokee.

North of Lake Okeechobee

The section of US-27 that runs **north from Lake Okeechobee** is among Florida's least eventful roads: a four-lane snake through a landscape of gentle hills, lakes, citrus groves, and sleepy communities dominated by retirees. Busy with farm trucks, the highway itself is far from peaceful, but provides an interesting course off the beaten track if you're making for either coast.

Sebring and Avon Park

An hours' drive from Lake Okeechobee, US-27 traces a ten-mile path around a series of lakes to **SEBRING**, where the unusual semicircular street plan was devised by its founder, George Sebring. He planted an oak tree here in 1912 to symbolize the sun, and declared that all the town's streets would radiate out from it. There's been no sign of the oak tree for decades, but Route 17 passes the small circular park, now sporting a commemorative plaque, just before reconnecting with US-27.

As quiet as can be for eleven months of the year, Sebring's tranquillity is shattered each March when tens of thousands of motor-racing fans pack its motels and restaurants, arriving for a twelve-hour endurance contest known as the **12 Hours of Sebring**, held at a race track about ten miles east – if you're passing through around this time, plan accordingly. Otherwise, if you decide to **stay**, for the area's lakes, unspoilt landscape, or the race track, the historic *Kenilworth Lodge*, 836 SE Lakeview Drive (Ⓣ863/385-0111 or 1-800/423-5939, Ⓦwww.kenlodge.com; ❸), is a mammoth Spanish-style hotel restored to some of its former grandeur. For authentic American and local specialties, such as home-made burgers and lemon pepper grouper, the *Sebring Diner*, 4040 US-

27 S (Ⓣ863/385-3434), comes through, in a snazzy replica of an old-fashioned Art Deco structure, all chrome and glass.

Well away from the sound of revving engines, the orange grove and cypress swamp trails inside **Highlands Hammock State Park**, six miles west of Sebring on Route 634 (daily 8am–sunset; cars $3.25, pedestrians and cyclists $1), add up to a well-spent afternoon. Keep an eye out for the white-tailed deer, and time your visit to coincide with the informative ranger-guided **tram tour** ($3; for times, call Ⓣ863/386-6094).

Twelve miles north of Sebring lies **Avon Park** (Ⓣ863/453-3350, Ⓦwww.apfla.com), which acquired its name from an early English settler born in Stratford-upon-Avon. Information on her and the community's general history is available at the **Avon Park Museum**, 3 N Museum Ave (Mon–Fri 10am–2pm, free; Ⓣ863/453-3525), housed in a restored pink stucco train depot. Once **downtown**, several miles away, spin by the quaint row of flea markets and antique shops on East Main Street, and have breakfast or lunch at the typical small-town eatery, the *Sandwich Depot*, 21 W Main St (Ⓣ863/453-5600). If you feel inclined **to stay** the night, the restored *Hotel Jacaranda*, 19 E Main St (Ⓣ863/453-2211; ❸), evokes the town in its glory days, and its *Palm Room* and *Citrus Room* (closed Sat) are elegantly appointed for dining, with Southern cooking buffets a specialty.

Travel details

Trains (Amtrak)

Hollywood to: Boca Raton (39min); Delray Beach (51min); Fort Lauderdale (15min); West Palm Beach (1hr 16min).

Tri-Rail

Mon–Fri 14 per day, Sat 7 per day, Sun 6 per day Ⓣ1-800/874-7245, Ⓦwww.trirail.com.

Buses

Clewiston to: Belle Glade (1 daily; 25min); West Palm Beach (1 daily; 1hr 30min).

Fort Lauderdale to: Daytona Beach (4 daily; 6hr 20min–7hr 25min); Delray Beach (2 daily; 55min); Fort Pierce (12 daily; 2hr–2hr 50min); Miami (19 daily; 40min–1hr); Orlando (9 daily; 4hr 30min–5hr 20min); Stuart (4 daily; 3hr 15min); Vero Beach (5 daily; 3hr 55min); West Palm Beach (16 daily; 1hr–1hr 45min).

Hollywood to: Daytona Beach (5 daily; 6hr 55min–10hr 30min); Fort Lauderdale (11 daily; 20min); Miami (6 daily; 40min); West Palm Beach (13 daily; 1hr 30min).

West Palm Beach to: Clewiston (1 daily; 1hr 30min); Daytona Beach (4 daily; 5hr 10min–6hr 25min); Fort Pierce (15 daily; 1hr); Miami (16 daily; 1hr 50min–2hr 45min); Tampa (6 daily; 6hr 30min–7hr 30min); Vero Beach (4 daily; 2hr 30min).

5

Sarasota and the Southwest

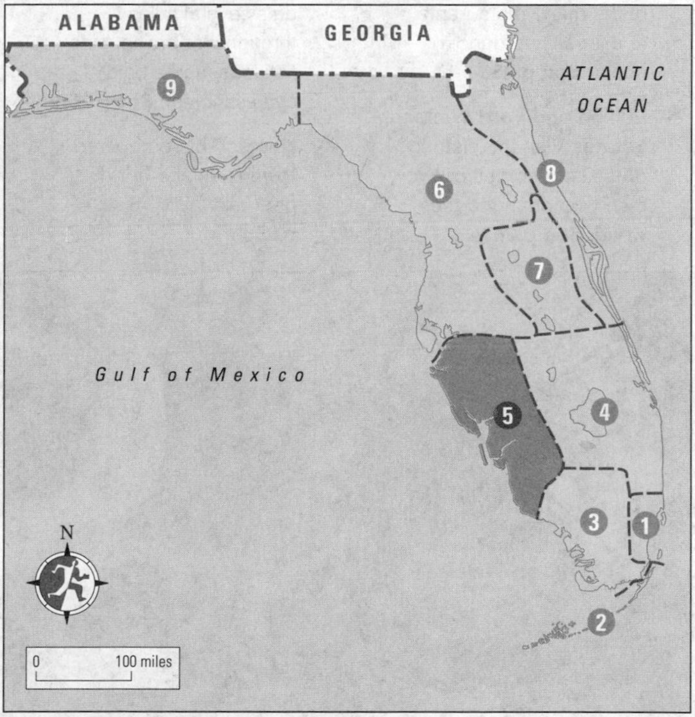

CHAPTER 5 # Highlights

* **Cà d'Zan and the Ringling Museums** A historic home, circus exhibition, and breathtaking art museum rolled into one. **See pp.232–233**
* **St Armands Circle** Spend an afternoon trolling the upscale shops, then dine in one of the many restaurants at this festive roundabout. **See p.236**
* **Edison and Ford Winter Estates** Visit the historic off-season homes of two men who changed the world. **See p.247**
* **Sanibel Island** The antithesis of the standard Florida beach spot, offering a wildlife refuge and miles of relatively unpopulated shore. **See p.251**
* **Corkscrew Swamp Sanctuary** Best seen from the impressive boardwalk, which meanders several miles through wet prairie, pine flatlands, and a bald cypress forest. **See p.256**
* **Naples** This pampered town is all about indulgent relaxation. **See p.256**

△ Edison House

5

Sarasota and the Southwest

A string of barrier-island beaches runs the length of the gulf in Florida's **SOUTHWEST**. And while it may be the beaches that draw the crowds, the mainland towns that provide access to them have a lot in their favor as well. The first of any consequential size is **Sarasota**, the custodian of an arts legacy passed down at the turn of the twentieth century by John Ringling, the circus entrepreneur. Further south, Thomas Edison was one of a number of scientific pioneers who took a fancy to palm-studded **Fort Myers**, which neighbors two atmospheric islands – **Sanibel** and **Captiva**. Several unique towns flavor the 150 miles of coast here, with origins dating back to the early days of Florida's incorporation into the US. Residents here lead more tranquil lives away from the bustle of the big city, and until the last few decades had an easy job preserving their seclusion. Nowadays, newer communities in the vicinity are beginning to expand at a colossal rate and large-scale tourism is prevalent. Accommodation prices double in high season – December to April – and can be hard to find on the weekends in more popular areas. However, for those prepared to venture off the tourist trail, there is more to Florida's southwest coast than sun, sand, and sea. A mixture of history, culture, and wildlife awaits discovery in this fine balance of mainland sights and beaches begging for exploration.

The southwest coast is easy to get around. **US-41** connects the main southwest coastal settlements and is often known as the **Tamiami Trail**, a nickname incorporating Tampa and Miami, from its time as the only road link crossing the Everglades (see p.169) between the two cities. These days, the bland **I-75** is a faster alternative to the trail. Greyhound services number five daily each way through the southwest coast and a few towns are also connected by Amtrak buses from Tampa (see p.265). The bigger centers have adequate **public transport**, though the barrier islands do not.

Sarasota and around

Rising on a gentle hillside beside the blue waters of Sarasota Bay, bright **SARASOTA** is both affluent and welcoming, an intriguing combination lack-

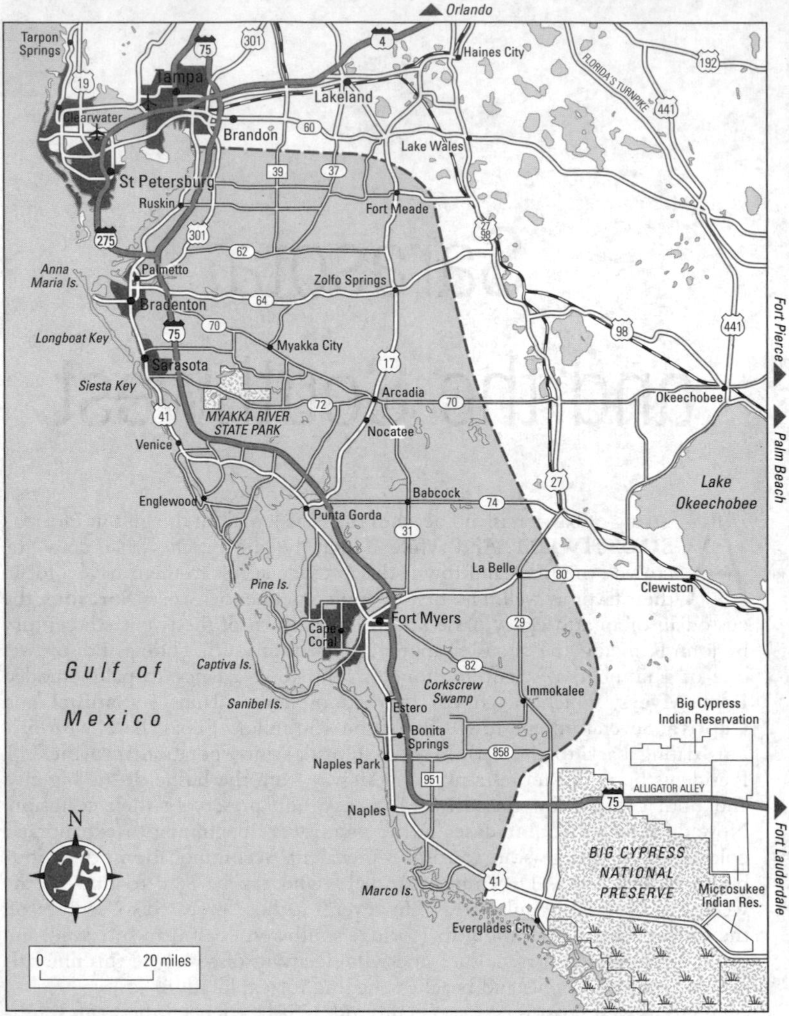

ing in other West Coast communities such as Naples (see p.256). This is the city where golf was first introduced to Florida from Scotland – the first course was laid in 1886. It remains a popular sport and there are more than thirty courses within minutes of the downtown area. Sarasota is also one of the state's leading cultural centers: home to numerous writers and artists, and the base of several respected performing arts companies. This is a place where opera and theater-goers in formal attire join hip students in coffee bars, and the tone of the town is intelligently upbeat. The community is far less stuffy than its wealth might suggest, and downtown Sarasota is fairly lively, with cafés, bars, and eateries complementing the excellent grouping of bookstores for which the place is known. A few miles north up the Tamiami Trail (US-41), the **Ringling Museum Complex** – home of the late art-loving circus magnate – is a fine diversion. And the barrier-island **beaches**, a couple of miles away across the bay, are the lounger's paradise.

Arrival, transport, and information

Whether you're arriving from north or south, **US-41** (always referred to here as the Tamiami Trail) zips through Sarasota, passing the main causeway to the islands just west of downtown and skirting the Ringling estate in the north. I-75 runs parallel to the Tamiami, and while it's not as enticing, it's a lot quicker. Downtown Sarasota is an easy grid of streets mostly named for fruits, while Main Street contains most of the city's restaurants and nightlife venues.

Local **bus** routes run by Sarasota County Area Transit (4.30am–8.30pm, except Sun; ⓣ941/861-1234) radiate out from the downtown Sarasota terminal on Lemon Avenue, between First and Second streets. **Useful routes** are #2 or #15 to the Ringling estate; #4 to Lido Key; #18 to Longboat Key; #11 to Siesta Key; and #17 (to #V) to Venice Beach. Fares are 50¢ per journey; there are no transfers and no Sunday service. The Amtrak bus from Tampa also pulls into the Lemon Avenue station, but all passengers arriving on Greyhound buses are dropped at 575 N Washington Blvd (ⓣ941/955-5735). The Sarasota Tampa Express provides a direct connection with Tampa airport and runs frequently throughout the day ($24 one way; ⓣ941/727-1344 or 1-800/326-2800). If you're around for a week or more, a good way to explore the town and the islands is by **renting a bike** for around $15 per day from Sarasota Bicycle Center, 4048 Bee Ridge Rd (ⓣ941/377-4505), or the Backyard Bike Shop, on Longboat Key at 5610 Gulf of Mexico Drive (ⓣ941/383-5184). In addition to bikes, Siesta Sports Rental, 6551 Midnight Pass Rd, Siesta Key (ⓣ941/346-1747, ⓦwww.siestasportsrentals.com), also rent out kayaks, motor scooters, and beach equipment. For a **taxi**, try Diplomat Taxi (ⓣ941/355-5155) or Yellow Cabs of Sarasota (ⓣ941/955-3341).

Information

For **information** in Sarasota, call at the **Convention and Visitors Bureau**, 655 N Tamiami Trail (Mon–Sat 9am 5pm, Sun 11am–3pm; ⓣ1-800/522-

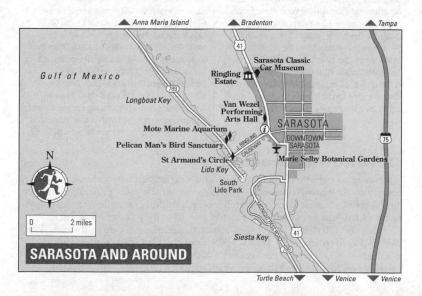

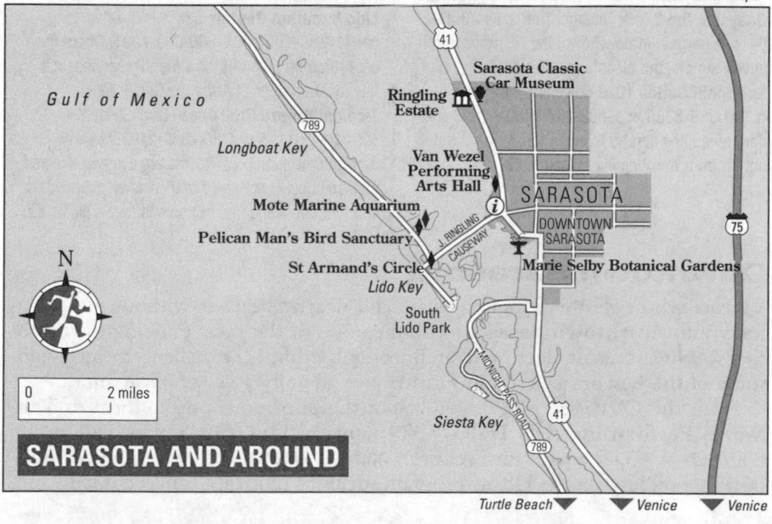

9799, Ⓦ www.sarasotafl.org), or the **Chamber of Commerce**, 1819 Main St (Mon–Fri 9am–5pm; Ⓣ 941/955-8187). On **Siesta Key**, you'll find a Chamber of Commerce at 5100 Ocean Blvd (Mon–Fri 9am–5pm; Ⓣ 941/349-3800). Besides the customary discount coupons and leaflets, look for the free magazines *Sarasota Visitors Guide, Sunny Day*, and *See*, and the Friday edition of the *Sarasota Herald Tribune*, whose pullout section, "Ticket," has entertainment listings.

Accommodation

On the **mainland**, you're most likely to end up in the corridor of chain hotels and motels that run the length of US-41 between the Ringling estate and south of downtown Sarasota. Prices are higher at the **beaches**, where many properties rent by the week.

Downtown

Best Western Golden Host Resort 4675 N Tamiami Trail 1 Ⓣ 941/355-5141 or 1-800/722-4895. A good bet for reasonable off-season rates, this chain features tropical gardens and a cocktail lounge, *Bahi Hut*, known for serving killer Mai Tais. ❸

The Cypress 621 Gulfstream Ave Ⓣ 941/955-4683. This comfortable inn, with sepia and yellow interiors, is within walking distance of Bayfront Park and Marie Selby Botanical Gardens. Generous breakfast also served. ❻

Hyatt Sarasota 1000 Blvd of the Arts Ⓣ 941/953-1234. Centrally located hotel near the Ringling Causeway, with tasteful rooms, business amenities like dataports and voicemail, and a tranquil view of Sarasota Bay. ❻

Holiday Inn Lakewood Ranch 6231 Lake Osprey Drive Ⓣ 941/782-4400 or 1-866/782-4401. New but somewhat dated-looking décor characterizes this standby, about 15min north of downtown. ❹

Quayside Inn 270 N Tamiami Trail Ⓣ 941/366-0414. A bargain in downtown, the *Quayside* is relatively simple, but clean and reliable. ❸

Springhill Suites 1020 University Parkway Ⓣ 941/358-3385 or 1-888/287-9400. All the standard amenities can be found in this Marriott hotel, not far from the Ringling Museum. ❹

The beaches

Aloha Kai 6020 Midnight Pass Rd, Siesta Key Ⓣ 941/349-5410. The secluded villas and studios here come with screened verandas, full kitchens, and attractive décor, and guests have access to a very large pool and recreation room. ❹

Beau Lido Suites 149 Tyler Drive, Lido Key Ⓣ 941/388-3227, Ⓦ www.beaulido.com. Studios and one- and two-bedroom apartments all are fairly basic but have kitchenettes with stove and refrigerator. ❷

Capri International 6782 Sara Sea Circle, Siesta Key Ⓣ 941/349-2626, Ⓦ www.capriinternational.com. Plain, though pleasant, motel of efficiencies located near Stickney Point Bridge in the middle of the island. ❹

Helmsley Sandcastle 1540 Ben Franklin Drive, Lido Key Ⓣ 941/388-2181 or 1-800/225-2181. Mid-priced option with decent-sized rooms, accented in yellows and floral prints, two pools, a restaurant, and a lovely stretch of beach. ❺

Lido Vacation Rentals 528 S Polk Drive, Lido Key Ⓣ 941/388-1004 or 1-800/890-7991. Offers the best rates on Lido Key, and friendly service, in a fine location near St Armands Circle. ❸

Tropical Breeze 5150 Ocean Blvd, Siesta Key Ⓣ 941/349-1125 or 1-800/300-2492, Ⓦ www.tropicalbreezeinn.com. Rooms are average size and a bit colorless, but there's free continental breakfast, and four pools and four hot tubs to take a dip in. ❹

Downtown Sarasota

Visitors who ogle the Ringling estate and nearby beaches without making a foray into **downtown Sarasota** will miss one of the most enticing towns on the southwest coast. Restored architectural oddities, excellent theater, and some of the best art galleries in Florida give the city a very upbeat aura.

From the CVB (see p.229), you'll spot the enormous purple form of **Van Wezel Performing Arts Hall**, 777 N Tamiami Trail (Ⓣ 941/953-3368 or 1-800/826-9303, Ⓦ www.vanwezel.org). Named one of the five hundred most notable buildings in the US, its program includes musicals, dance, comedy, and

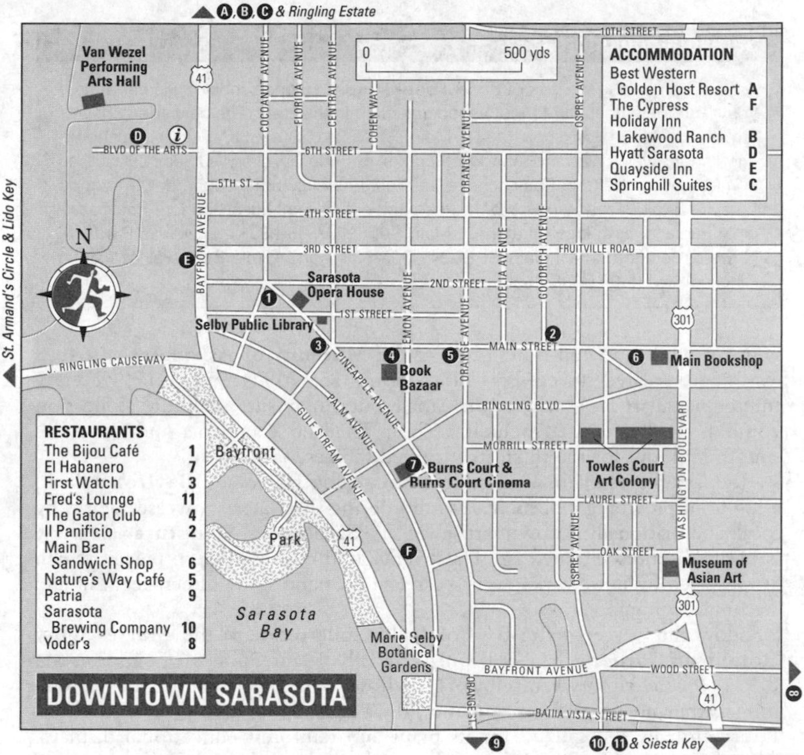

plays (see "Entertainment and nightlife," p.237). For those who wish to explore behind the scenes, backstage tours are on offer (call for times and ticket prices).

Heading into the heart of downtown, don't miss a visit to the **Selby Public Library**, 1331 First St (Mon–Thurs 9am–9pm, Fri & Sat 9am–5pm, Sun 1–5pm; ⓣ941/861-1100), which from the outside looks like it belongs in a grandiose Hollywood epic, while inside it's a clean, functioning library, complete with a fishtank and loads of computers with free **Internet** access. Opposite the library on the corner of First Street and Pineapple Avenue is the **Sarasota Opera House** (ⓣ941/953-7030, ⓦwww.sarasotaopera.org). Opened in 1926, this Mediterranean Revival building hosted the Ziegfeld Follies and a young Elvis Presley (see p.237).

South of Main Street, a few blocks past the pretty Methodist Church, is **Burns Court**, a hidden enclave of 1920s bungalows, each with Moorish details. Almost all the Spanish/Mediterranean buildings in town were built just before the Depression, when the style was most in vogue. At the end of this lane stands the startlingly pink **Burns Court Cinema**, a great alternative film house run by the Sarasota Film Society (see also listing on p.238). Walk a few blocks east to reach the **Towles Court Artist Colony**, a cluster of bungalows and cottages taking up a several-block stretch of Morrill Street and Adams Lane (between Osprey Avenue and US-301/Washington Boulevard; ⓣ941/330-9817). You can browse the galleries here, which are open to the public (Tues–Sat 11am–4pm), or take a two-hour tour and meet the artists (Nov–April 10am; $20, lunch included). Just south of here,

Sarasota bookstores

Anyone bemoaning the lack of decent **bookstores** in Florida should take heart: here you'll find the biggest and most varied selection in the state. The best-filled shelves are at the Main Bookshop, 1962 Main St (Ⓣ941/336-7653, Ⓦwww.mainbookshop.com), which has thousands of books on virtually every subject as well as comics, records, and old easy chairs that foster a relaxed atmosphere. Other good bets are Book Bazaar, which stocks used and out-of-print titles, and rare book dealer A. Parker's, both located at 1488 Main St (Ⓣ941/366-2898), as well as Sarasota News & Books at 1341 Main St (Ⓣ941/365-6332) and Circle Books at 478 John Ringling Blvd (Ⓣ941/388-2850).

you can while away an hour or so at the **Museum of Asian Art**, at 640 S Washington Blvd (Wed–Fri 11am–5pm; $5; Ⓣ941/954-7117, Ⓦwww.museumasianart.org), where the small but impressive sculpture collection comes from all over Asia, including China, Thailand, Cambodia, and Nepal. Be sure to look out for the intricately carved Chinese jade.

Back on the Tamiami Trail, just past Ringling Boulevard, **Bayfront Park**, aside from providing a pleasant lawn bordering the water, showcases works by local and nationally known artists in its **Season of Sculpture** (Ⓦwww.sarasotaseasonofsculpture.org). The twenty-odd mostly modern pieces, which are replaced by new works every year or two, stand some fifteen-feet tall and are quite striking.

Follow the curve of the bay for half a mile south to the **Marie Selby Botanical Gardens**, 811 S Palm Ave (daily 10am–5pm; $10, children $5; Ⓣ941/366-5731, Ⓦwww.selby.org), whose walled perimeter hides a startling gathering of growths – some 20,000 plants, including 6000 orchids. Internationally recognized for its plant and rainforest educational displays, the garden (complete with butterflies and a koi pond) can't fail to improve the mood of anyone who spends time meandering along the fragrant pathways.

The Ringling Museum Complex and around

Two miles north of downtown Sarasota is the **Ringling Museum Complex**, containing the house and art collections of John Ringling, a multi-millionaire who not only poured money into the fledgling community beginning in the 1910s, but also gave it a taste for fine arts that it has never lost. One of the owners of the fantastically successful Ringling Brothers Circus, which began touring the US during the 1890s, Ringling – an imposing figure over six feet tall and weighing nearly 280 pounds – plowed the circus's profits into railways, oil, and land. By the Twenties, he had acquired a fortune estimated at $200 million. Charmed by Sarasota and recognizing its investment potential, Ringling built the first causeway to the barrier islands and made the town his circus's winter base, saving a fortune in northern heating bills and generating tremendous publicity for the town in the process. His greatest gift to Sarasota, however, was a Venetian Gothic mansion – a combination of European elegance and American-millionaire extravagance – and an incredible collection of European Baroque paintings, displayed in a museum built for the purpose beside the house. Grief-stricken following the death of his wife in 1927 and losing much of his wealth through the Wall Street crash two years later, Ringling died in 1936, reportedly with just $300 to his name.

Ringling Museum practicalities

The **Ringling Museum Complex**, beside US-41 at 5401 Bay Shore Rd (daily 10am–5.30pm; $15, children under 12 free; ⓣ941/359-5700, recorded info at ⓣ941/351-1660, ⓦwww.ringling.org), ranges over 66 acres, and its buildings are linked by pathways, easy to walk between and clearly signposted, though there are trams connecting the areas too. To get there from downtown Sarasota via public transport, use **bus** #2 or #10.

The Ringling House: Cà d'Zan

Begin your exploration of the Ringling estate by walking through the gardens to the former Ringling residence, **Cà d'Zan** ("House of John," in Venetian dialect). A lavish though not tasteless piece of work serenely situated beside the bay, it was the inappropriate setting for the 1998 film adaptation of *Great Expectations*. The multitude of attractive trees was a gift from Thomas Edison, who nurtured the young seeds at his Fort Myers home (see p.247). The most dramatic, a Chinese banyan, shades the circular *Banyan Café* (ⓣ941/359-3183), where you can grab lunch for around $8. Completed in 1925, reputedly at a cost of $1.5 million, the house was planned around an airy, two-story living room marked on one side by a fireplace of carved Italian marble and on the other by a $50,000 organ – though neither Ringling nor his wife could play the thing. The other rooms are similarly filled with expensive items (largely gained from the estate sales of New York mansions, at a cost of $400,000), but unlike their mansion-erecting contemporaries elsewhere in Florida, John and Mable Ringling knew the value of restraint. Their spending power never exceeded their sense of style, and the house remains a triumph of taste and proportion – and an exceptionally pleasant place to walk around. Take the free **guided tour** departing regularly from the entrance, then roam on your own.

The Art Museum

The mix of inspiration and caution that underpinned Ringling's business deals also influenced his art purchases. On trips to Europe to scout for new circus talent, Ringling became obsessed with **Baroque art** – then wildly unfashionable – and over five years, led largely by his own sensibilities, he acquired more than five hundred Old Masters, a collection now regarded as one of the finest of its kind in the US. To display the paintings, many of them as epic in size as they were in content, Ringling selected a patch of Cà d'Zan's grounds and erected a spacious **museum** around a mock fifteenth-century Italian palazzo, decorated by his stockpile of high-quality replica Greek and Roman statuary. As with Cà d'Zan, the very concept initially seems absurdly pretentious but, like the house, the idea works: the architecture matches the art with great aplomb. Here also, you should take the free **guided tour** departing regularly from the entrance, before wandering around at your leisure. The paintings are exhibited in a beautiful series of rooms, the dark wood wainscoting, luxurious wallpaper, and deep, rich hue of the walls befitting the striking artwork. Five enormous paintings by **Rubens**, commissioned in 1625 by a Hapsburg archduchess, and the painter's subsequent *Portrait of Archduke Ferdinand*, are the undisputed highlights of the collection, though they shouldn't detract from the excellent canvases in succeeding rooms: a wealth of talent from Europe's leading schools of the mid-sixteenth to mid-eighteenth centuries. Watch out, in particular, for the finely composed and detailed *The Rest on the Flight to Egypt*, by Paolo Veronese, and the entertaining *Building of a Palace* from Piero de Cosimo.

The Circus Gallery

The Ringling fortune had its origins in the big top, and the **Circus Gallery** is worth a visit for a glimpse into the family business. One large room is ringed by tiger cages and wagons used to transport other animals and equipment, and standing at the center is an impressive scale model of the Big Top and the preparatory tents. The rest of the gallery consists of rotating exhibitions, which have in the past spotlighted Cecil B. DeMille's film, *The Greatest Show on Earth* (some of which was filmed in Sarasota), cuttings and memorabilia of famous dwarfs and performers, and a tribute to Gunther Gebel-Williams, the great animal trainer who never missed a day of work in over 12,000 performances before passing away in 2001.

The Asolo Theater and Asolo Center for the Performing Arts

Ringling transported an eighteenth-century, Italian-court playhouse from the castle of Asolo to the grounds of his estate. Its interior, although fascinating, is only open for special events and conferences, but plans are afoot to transform the building into a public performance venue over the next few years. The **Asolo Center for the Performing Arts**, not to be confused with the Asolo Theater, is right next door and usually offers a strong program of theatrical events throughout the year. The main stage was brought over from Dunfermline, Scotland, where it was built in 1903. While not as enticing as the off-limits Asolo Theater, the center has an elegant, gilded interior. Free back-stage tours are available (for performance details, see p.238).

Sarasota Classic Car Museum

Vintage car enthusiasts and devotees of old music boxes will love the **Sarasota Classic Car Museum**, across US-41 from the entrance to the Ringling Museum Complex (daily 9am–6pm; $8.50; ⓣ941/355-6228, ⓦwww.sarasotacarmuseum.org). Nearly 200 aged vehicles – including John Lennon's Mercedes and Stephen King's "Christine" – are gathered together with hurdy-gurdies, cylinder discs, an enormous Belgian pipe organ, and nickelodeons. There's also an antique game room filled with arcade games from the 1930s and 1940s. Real car buffs should take the detailed guided tours, while casual visitors would do best just to wander. Even if you don't pay to enter the museum, check out the gift shop for some unusual souvenirs and collectibles.

The Sarasota beaches

Increasingly the stomping ground of European package tourists spilling south from the St Petersburg beaches, the powdery white sands of the **Sarasota beaches** – fringing two barrier islands, which continue the chain beginning off Bradenton – haven't exactly been spared the attentions of property developers. For all that, the Sarasota beaches are worth a day of anybody's time – either to lie back and soak up the rays, or to seek out the few remaining isolated stretches. And the sunsets alone make them worth a visit. Both islands, **Lido Key** and **Siesta Key**, are accessible by car or bus from the mainland, though there's no link directly between them. If you are traveling by car, the beach roads are very busy in high season and the tailbacks to leave the beach toward the end of the day can ruin any relaxation you might have gained throughout the day.

Lido Key

Financed by and named for Sarasota's circus-owning sugar daddy, the Ringling Causeway crosses the yacht-filled Sarasota Bay from the foot of Main Street to

△ Horseshoe crabs, J.N. "Ding" Darling National Wildlife Refuge

Lido Key and flows into **St Armands Circle** (take bus #4 or #18). This roundabout ringed by upmarket shops and restaurants is dotted with some of Ringling's replica classical statuary – musclebound torsos emerging surrealistically from behind palm fronds. The shops aren't cheap, but there is plenty of parking and it's worth having a stroll around, especially as this is a handy transfer point between buses. After a look around head to the north end of Lido Key beach, which is relatively condo-free, and then trek south along Benjamin Franklin Drive. This route passes more accessible beaches, fine in and of themselves though overrun by the holiday-making set. After two miles, you'll find the more attractive **South Lido Park** (daily 8am–sunset; free), a belt of dazzlingly bright sand beyond a large grassy park, with walking trails shaded by Australian pines. Busy with barbecues and tanned bodies on Saturday and Sunday, the park is a delightfully subdued spot for weekday rambles.

Away from the beaches the only place of consequence on Lido Key, the **Mote Marine Aquarium**, 1600 Ken Thompson Parkway (daily 10am–5pm; $12, children $8; ⓣ941/388-4441, ⓦwww.mote.org) on Lido Key, is a mile north of St Armands Circle. The public off-shoot of a marine laboratory studying the ecological problems threatening Florida's sea life, such as the ride tide – a mysterious algae that blooms every few years, devastating sea life – the aquarium has an assortment of live creatures, from seahorses to loggerhead turtles. The centerpiece of the 22 aquariums is a massive outdoor shark tank, wherein you can view several species, but the tanks of ghostly jellyfish are a close second.

Adjacent to the Mote Aquarium you'll find **Pelican Man's Bird Sanctuary**, 1708 Ken Thompson Parkway (daily 10am–5pm; $6; ⓣ941/388-4444, ⓦwww.pelicanman.org), where injured and sick migratory birds (55 different species) from all over the world, together with native Floridian species, are cared for by over two hundred volunteers. You'll come away with facts about how our feathered friends are nursed back to health; some are released into the wild, others with irreparable injuries remain at the sanctuary.

Siesta Key

Far more refreshing and laidback than Lido or Longboat keys, **Siesta Key** (arrive via Siesta Drive off US-41 about five miles south of downtown Sarasota) attracts a younger crowd and has less-manicured surroundings than other spots on the coast. The affluent, however, have not ignored Siesta Key – this is, after all, where Paul Simon has a condo. Beach-lovers should hit **Siesta Key Beach**, beside Ocean Beach Boulevard, where the sand has an uncommon sugary texture due to its origins as quartz (not the more usual pulverized coral). It's a wide white strand that can – and often does – accommodate thousands of partying sun-worshippers. To escape the crowds, continue south past Crescent Beach, which meets a second road (Stickney Point Road) from the mainland, and follow Midnight Pass Road for six miles to **Turtle Beach**, a small, secluded stretch of sand.

Eating

Owing to the increase in nightlife venues and the resurgence of a youthful downtown scene, Sarasota's **restaurant** and **café culture** has taken off. Exquisite restaurants with prices to match are popping up everywhere, but you'll still find plenty of options catering to every taste and budget. Though a bit touristy, St Armands Circle in Lido Key is a lively option, with shops and a wide range of restaurants open until late. If you're staying on US-41, especially in a motel closer to the airport than downtown, good places to eat can be hard to find and what is available is usually closed by 9pm.

Downtown

The Bijou Café 1287 First St ⓣ941/366-8111. Expensive lunch and dinner menus of seafood, fowl, and meat served in surprisingly basic surroundings.

El Habanero 417 Burns Court ⓣ941/362-9562. Good Cuban food (and huge portions) served in what looks like a private home for just a few dollars.

First Watch 1395 Main St ⓣ941/954-1395. There isn't much character to the joint, but the excellent American-style breakfast and inexpensive lunch offerings assure there's always a line.

Il Panificio 1703 Main St ⓣ941/366-5570. Italian deli, bakery, and coffee shop with superb (and huge) home-made pizzas, sandwiches, and strong espressos.

Main Bar Sandwich Shop 1944 Main St ⓣ941/955-8733. Delicious and reasonably priced sandwiches have been served here since 1958. Closes 4pm.

Nature's Way Café 1572 Main St ⓣ941/954-3131. A good vegetarian option known for its sandwiches, fresh-fruit salads, and frozen yogurt. Closed Sun.

Patria 8383 S Tamiami Trail ⓣ941/927-8587. Superbly prepared seafood, steak, and chicken dishes, as well as more unusual ones like pheasant and elk, served in a sleek interior. Dinner entrees run $24–38, but you can always try it for lunch or brunch. Reservations suggested.

Yoder's 3434 Bahia Vista St ⓣ941/955-7771. There are thriving Mennonite and Amish communities in the Sarasota area and this local favorite has won awards for the home-made goodness of its old-fashioned Amish cuisine. Closed Sun.

St Armands Circle

Blue Dolphin Café 470 John Ringling Blvd ⓣ941/388-3566. The hearty breakfasts (and especially the French toast) are guaranteed to fill you up at this convivial blue diner.

Cha-Cha Coconuts 417 St Armands Circle ⓣ941/388-3300. A young crowd spills out of the very busy, very loud bar. The inexpensive menu claims to feature "Caribbean cuisine," but it's really just fish sandwiches and burgers, and there's also live music on some nights.

Crab & Fin 420 St Armands Circle ⓣ941/388-3964. Classy (but not too fancy) local favorite, with seafood entrees starting at $20, but there are some bargains too, plus an impressive wine list. Daily raw bar selections.

Hemingway's Retreat 325 Ringling Blvd ⓣ941/388-3948. Tasty steak and seafood standards served in tropical-flavored surroundings.

Hungry Fox Tree Top Bistro 419 Ringling Blvd ⓣ941/388-2222. A tropically themed bistro bursting with such American favorites as hamburgers and stuffed sandwiches.

Watson's Pump 328 Ringling Blvd ⓣ941/388-0155. British-style pub, with a menu featuring fish and chips and bangers and mash, plus the usual American favorites – and plenty of draft ale to wash it all down.

Siesta Key

The Broken Egg 210 Avenida Madera ⓣ941/346-2750. Popular with locals looking for a filling, inexpensive, all-American breakfast or lunch. Try the broken egg breakfast for $5.49 or the homemade banana nut bread French toast for $4.59.

Javier's 6621 Midnight Pass Rd ⓣ941/346-1199. For a taste of Peru and a menu including seafood, steaks, ribs, pasta, and decadent desserts, this is an excellent mid-priced option ($12–20).

Turtles 8875 Midnight Pass Rd, Turtle Beach ⓣ941/346-2207. Outstanding seafood dinners served at tables overlooking Little Sarasota Bay, at the very southern tip of Siesta Key.

Entertainment and nightlife

There's no shortage of arts in Sarasota (billed along with the surrounding area as "Florida's Cultural Coast"), and the Convention and Visitors Bureau (see p.229) has full details of events; also check out the Sarasota County Arts Council website (ⓦwww.sarasota-arts.org). Some of the state's top small theatrical groups are based in Sarasota. **Drama** devotees should scan local newspapers for play listings or phone the theaters directly. For **opera** buffs, the Sarasota Opera House has been staging grand performances since the 1920s, and, though not known for his arias, Elvis Presley also performed here in his younger days. For information and tickets call ⓣ941/366-8450; the box office is open daily, 10am–4pm. The daily *Sarasota Herald Tribune* is a good source of entertainment information.

On weekend evenings, the **nightlife** along Main Street in Sarasota attracts both students looking to chill and a more rough-and-ready, good-old-boys crowd. Another spot to head for are the main avenues on Siesta Key.

Theaters and cinemas

Asolo Center for the Performing Arts 5555 N Tamiami Trail ⓣ941/351-8000 or 1-800/361-3833, ⓦwww.asolo.org. The major repertory, the Asolo Theater Company, stages plays both classic (Shaw, Miller, Coward) and modern (tickets $30–45, gallery seats $13, students $6; $7 tickets are sometimes available on the day).
The Burns Court Cinema Burns Court ⓣ941/364-8662. The cinema that hosts Sarasota's film festival in January, showing over forty of the best international films of the year. To purchase tickets and hear a schedule for regular shows, call the box office between noon and 5pm at ⓣ941/955-3456.
Florida Studio Theater 1241 N Palm Ave ⓣ941/366-9000, ⓦwww.fst2000.org. Sarasota's most contemporary theater (Mon 9am–6pm, Tues–Sat 9am–9pm, Sun 10am–9pm; tickets $18–30).
Golden Apple Dinner Theater 25 N Pineapple Ave ⓣ941/366-5454. For theater with cocktails and candlelit dining.
Hollywood 20 1993 Main St ⓣ941/954-5768. All mainstream films are shown at this distinctive (and popular) pure Art Deco theater. Inside, a neon-lilac glow bathes the popcorn-devouring crowds.
The Van Wezel Performing Arts Hall 777 N Tamiami Trail ⓣ941/953-3368 or 1-800/826-9303, ⓦwww.vanwezel.org. Sometimes referred to as "the Purple Cow" by locals (first dismissively, now affectionately), the hall was built in 1968 and has a varied program of musicals and dance performances.

Bars and nightclubs

Beach Club 5151 Ocean Blvd, Siesta Key ⓣ941/349-6311. Find driving rock-n-roll here, both local and some smaller national acts.
Daiquiri Deck 5250 Ocean Blvd, Siesta Key ⓣ941/349-8697. This place specializes in frozen daiquiris and is hugely popular as an after-beach venue.
Fred's Lounge 1917 Osprey Ave ⓣ941/364-5811. Dark bar, with a good buzz and a large assortment of mixed drinks and beers.
The Gator Club 1490 Main St ⓣ941/366-5969. The *Gator* continually wins the prize for loudest bar. Set in a huge warehouse, it has dance-type music performed live every night at 9.30pm.
Old Salty Dog 5023 Ocean Blvd, Siesta Key ⓣ941/349-0158. This is one of the more popular bars on Siesta Key; English-theme, fish and chips optional.
Sarasota Brewing Company 15516607 Gateway Ave ⓣ941/925-2337. Sports bar and brew joint (with seven homebrews offered) for the easygoing.
Speakeasy 5254 Ocean Blvd, Siesta Key ⓣ941/346-1379. Cozy, laidback joint, the *Speakeasy* sponsors jazz or r&b every night, with wine, a pool table, and the island's largest selection of beers as accoutrements.

Gay and lesbian bars and clubs

For **gay nightlife**, there's *Triangles,* 1330 Dr Martin Luther King Way (ⓣ941/953-5945), with a mostly local crowd that enjoys billiards tournaments (Tues–Thurs) as well as weekend dancing and DJs. Outside the downtown area at 3218 Clark Rd, *Therapy Night Club* has gay nights on Thursday and Saturday. **Films** of gay interest are most likely to appear at the Burns Court Cinema. For information on local events visit ⓦwww.outinsarasota.org.

North of Sarasota: Bradenton and around

A major producer of tomato and orange juice, **BRADENTON**, across the broad Manatee River from Palmetto, is a hard-working town whose center comprises several unlovely miles of office buildings along the river's south bank. While mainland Bradenton is far from exciting, **Anna Maria Island** (the northernmost point of a chain of barrier islands running from here to Fort Myers) and the **Bradenton beaches** eight miles west of downtown make up for Bradenton proper's lack of charm. It's well worth traveling along Route 789, known along Lido Key as Gulf of Mexico Drive, for a more picturesque (if slightly longer) route to Sarasota than the inland options.

The town and around

In central Bradenton, the **South Florida History Museum, Bishop Planetarium, and Parker Manatee Aquarium**, 201 Tenth St (Mon–Sat 10am–5pm, Sun noon–5pm; $9.50 – extra fees for astronomy presentations; ⓣ941/746-4131, ⓦwww.sfmbp.org), are well worth time away from the beaches. The museum takes a wide-ranging look at the region's past. If you're around in April, check out the month-long **Florida Heritage Festival**, which culminates with a ceremonial crowning of a local as the new Hernando de Soto (see below). The most popular attraction here is not, however, the museum artifacts but the **aquarium**, home to manatees Snooty and Mo. Born in 1948, Snooty is the oldest manatee born in captivity, while the considerably younger Mo was rescued in 1994 from Crystal River after being orphaned. Ten minutes of watching them glide about is enough, but the aquarium is intelligently laid out to provide varying views of the creatures. Feeding times – 12.30pm, 2pm, and 3.30pm – are more lively and included in the entry price. The **Bishop Planetarium** is open throughout the day – weekday mornings, however, are reserved for school visits. Daily Starshows, which take you on an educational tour of the universe, are on offer at 1pm and 4pm, while at 2.30pm the laser light show is more spectacular than informative. On Fridays and Saturdays at 7pm live astronomy presentations are given, and at 9pm and 10.30pm, a remarkable rock and roll laser light show does dramatic things to the music of Pink Floyd, Jimi Hendrix, Pearl Jam, and Led Zeppelin. In addition, weather permitting, on Saturday mornings between 11.30am and 1pm, you can view the sun through a large telescope from the rooftop observatory.

More of the region's history is on display at the **Manatee Village Historical Park**, on the corner of Manatee Avenue East and Fifteenth Street East (Mon–Fri 9.30am–4.30pm; free; ⓣ941/749-7165), which has a courthouse, church, general store, and "cracker" cottage dating from Florida's rough-and-ready frontier days.

Five miles west of central Bradenton, Manatee Avenue (the main route to the beaches) crosses 75th Street West, at the northern end of which is the **De Soto National Memorial** (daily 9am–5pm; free; ⓣ941/792-0458, ⓦwww.nps.gov/deso). This is believed to mark the spot where Spanish conquistador

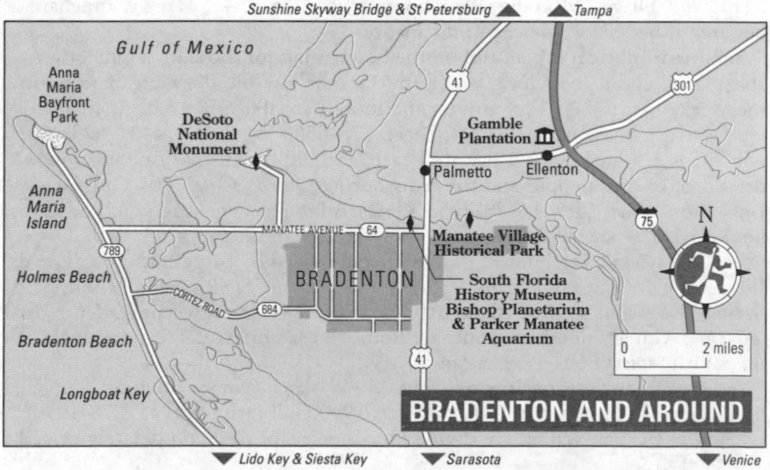

Hernando de Soto came ashore in 1539. The three-year de Soto expedition, hacking through Florida's dense subtropical terrain and wading through its swamps, led to the European discovery of the Mississippi River – and numerous pitched battles with Native Americans. The visitor center contains artifacts and exhibits explaining the expedition's effect on American Indians, and a film depicting the expedition is shown continuously. From December to April, park rangers dressed as sixteenth-century Spaniards offer informative tidbits on the lifestyles of Florida's first adventurers (five programs daily); for more about the de Soto expedition, see "History" in Contexts, p.462

Anna Maria Island and the Bradenton beaches

In contrast to central Bradenton's grayness, the ramshackle beach cottages, seaside snack stands, and beachside bars on **Anna Maria Island** ten miles away are bright and convivial. From the end of Manatee Avenue, turn left along Gulf Drive for **Coquina Beach**, where the swimming is excellent and the weekend social life is youthful and merry; if you have a quieter time in mind, take a right turn along Marina Drive for the calm **Anna Maria Bayfront Park**. For a break from the beach, the **Anna Maria Island Historical Museum**, 402 Pine Ave (Tues–Thurs & Sat 10am–noon; ⓣ941/778-1514), exhibits interesting old photos, islands artifacts, and videos of interviews with early residents. Further down the road, bikes can be hired from Neumann's Island Beach Store, 427 Pine Ave (ⓣ941/778-3316).

South of Anna Maria Island, **Longboat Key** is all about privacy: its pricey homes are shielded by rows of tall Australian pines and, while all the sands along this nineteen-mile-long island are public property, access points are few and far between, making the beach almost impossible to reach for non-residents. Not until you reach Lido Key, further south, are there more useable beaches (see "The Sarasota beaches," p.234).

Practicalities

In central Bradenton, the **Chamber of Commerce**, 222 Tenth St (Mon–Fri 9am–5pm; ⓣ941/748-3411, ⓦwww.manateechamber.com), has the usual tourist information. The **Anna Maria Island Chamber of Commerce**, 5313 Gulf Drive (Mon–Fri 9am–5pm; ⓣ941/778-1541, ⓦwww.amichamber.org), is better for its beach information.

Accommodation is plentiful on the beaches but for those on a budget suitable places tend to be a long way from the beach. While the rates increase on the weekend, the best bets among the motels are the *Silver Surf Motel*, 1301 Gulf Drive, Bradenton Beach (ⓣ941/778-6626 or 1-800/441-7873; ➎), which has a heated pool, a private beach, and big rooms that can accommodate three or four people; and the neighboring *Queen's Gate*, 1101 Gulf Drive, Bradenton Beach (ⓣ941/778-7153; ➎–➏). A little cozier – and you'll need to book ahead – are the *Duncan House* bed and breakfast, 1703 Gulf Drive (ⓣ941/778-6858; ➏), built in the 1880s and moved by barge from its original site up the Manatee River in 1946; or the pleasant *Siam Garden Resort*, 512 Spring Ave, Anna Maria Island (ⓣ941/778-2000, ⓦwww.siamgardenresort.gov; ➎), with antique bathrooms and some nice architectural features, including a Thai "spirit house" by the pool.

You should do your **eating** on Anna Maria Island. One of the most popular local places for breakfast is *Gulf Drive Café*, 900 Gulf Drive (ⓣ941/778-1919), where the Belgian waffles are divine. Top choices for fresh, moderately priced seafood lunches or dinners are *The Sandbar*, 100 Spring Ave (Ⓣ941/778-0444), which serves fried alligator and Cajun grouper on its decks on the beach; *Waterfront Restaurant* (Ⓣ941/778-1515), with a relaxing view of the pier and not much else but ocean; and *Top of the Island Grill & Pub* (Ⓣ941/778-3909), which also features live music on weekends. On Holmes Beach, try *Paradise Bagels*, 3210 E Bay Drive (Ⓣ941/779-1212), for a variety of bagels, spreads, and great coffee. *Mama Lo's*, 101 S Bay Blvd, Anna Maria Island (Ⓣ941/779-1288), a simple luncheonette, is just the place for a cool coffee drink or some thirty flavors of ice cream.

Palmetto and the Gamble Plantation

Frequently dismissed in favor of neighboring Bradenton (see p.238), the little town of **PALMETTO** makes for a pleasant foray and is untouched by the commercialism of the bigger towns and beaches beyond. Perched on the northern shore of the Manatee River, Palmetto's prettiest section is Riverside Drive, an avenue of grand old mansions. The 1889 **J.A. Lamb House** at no. 1100, a stunning villa carved from heart pine with fairytale-like features in its twenty rooms, is probably the most impressive – though it's a private residence and not open to the public.

Next door, *The Palmetto House*, at no. 1102 (Ⓣ941/723-1236 or 1-800/658-4167, Ⓦwww.thepalmettohouse.com), is a fine **place to stay** (rooms start at $100), and serves as a good base for visiting Bradenton and the beaches. Built in 1910, the house's interior has graceful arches and antique furniture, and breakfast and cocktails are served to guests on a sweeping veranda.

If you have time to spare, veer east from Palmetto along Tenth Street (US-301) to **ELLENTON**, a riverside settlement where the 1840s **Gamble Plantation**, 3708 Patten Ave (Ⓣ941/723-4536), is one of the oldest homes on Florida's West Coast and the only slave-era plantation this far south. Composed of thick, tabby walls (a mixture of crushed shell and molasses) and girded on three sides by sturdy columns, the house belonged to a Confederate major, Robert Gamble, a failed Tallahassee cotton planter who ran a sugar plantation here before financial uncertainty caused by the impending Civil War forced him to leave. In 1925, the mansion was designated the **Judah Benjamin Confederate Memorial** in remembrance of Confederate Secretary Benjamin, who took refuge here in 1865 after the fall of the Confederacy. With Union troops in hot pursuit, he hid here until friends found him a boat in which he sailed from Sarasota Bay to England, where he joined the English Bar and practiced law. A showcase of wealthy (and white) Old South living, the house – stuffed to the rafters with period fittings – is open Thursday to Monday 9am–5pm; however, admission is only by **guided tour** (six times daily) that costs $4. Besides describing the building, its contents, and owners, the tour offers a very Confederate view of the Civil War.

Inland from Sarasota: Myakka River State Park

Should your knowledge of Florida be limited to beaches and theme parks, broaden your horizons by traveling fourteen miles inland from Sarasota on Route 72. Here you'll find a great tract of rural Florida barely touched by humans, where the marshes, pinewoods, and prairies form **Myakka River**

State Park, 3715 Jaffa Drive (daily 8am–sunset; $2 for one person, $4 for two to eight people; ⓣ941/365-0100). On arrival, drop into the **interpretive center** for an insight into this fragile (and threatened) ecosystem. Begin exploring it by walking along the numerous paths or canoeing on the calm expanse of the Upper Myakka Lake. Myakka Wildlife Tours (ⓣ941/365-0100) offer narrated tram and airboat tours through the wildlife habitats, explaining the ecology of the area and providing views of the animals; both tours cost $8 and run at regular intervals throughout the day. If you're equipped for **hiking**, following the forty miles of trails through the park's **wilderness preserve** is a better way to get close to the cotton-tailed rabbits, deer, turkey, bobcats, and alligators that live in the park; before commencing, register at the entrance office and get maps and check weather conditions – be ready for wet conditions during the summer storms. Other than the five basic campgrounds on the hiking trails ($13–16), park **accommodation** (details and reservations: ⓣ941/361-6511) comprises two well-equipped **campgrounds** and a few four-berth **log cabins** ($55 a night); these are very popular so it's a good idea to book in advance.

South from Sarasota: Venice and around

In the Fifties, the Ringling Circus moved its winter base twenty miles south from Sarasota to **Venice**, a pleasant small town with Italianate architecture and surrounded by water, modeled on its European namesake. Parking at the beachfront is limited, but it's a lovely walk from downtown along a palm-lined avenue; the parking time is limited away from the beaches. The downtown area itself has a more relaxed, friendly feel than many other tourist destinations on this coastline, but most people come for the gorgeous **beaches**, which are used by a range of people, from watersports enthusiasts to pensioner sunbathers. Swimming is a pleasure in the ocean here, but beware of the jellyfish – if there's a blue flag flying on the beach it means that there are lots of them around. Even if this is the case and swimming is out of bounds, you can always entertain yourself by watching flocks of pelicans dive into the waves, or by searching for the sharks' teeth commonly washed ashore. Anyone with their own transport can also explore the little-visited coastline around **Englewood beaches**, south of Venice on Route 775, which are pockmarked by small islands and creeks.

Practicalities

If you're arriving in Venice by Greyhound bus, you'll be dropped at 225 S Tamiami Trail (ⓣ941/485-1001), from which your first port of call might be the **Chamber of Commerce**, 597 S Tamiami Trail (Mon–Fri 8.30am–5pm; Nov–March also Sat 9am–noon; ⓣ941/488-2236, ⓦwww.venicechamber.com), for local information. **Local buses** (SCAT; ⓣ94/316-1234) #13 and #16 (25¢ fare) link Venice with the beaches and surrounding areas.

Spending a night in this quiet community might seem an attractive proposition, though prices can be steep; of the motels, try the *Kon-Tiki*, 1487 Tamiami Trail (ⓣ941/485-9696; ❹), or the *Venice Beach Resort*, 501 W Venice Ave (ⓣ941/488-1580; ❸). The *Inn at the Beach Resort*, 725 W Venice Ave (ⓣ1-800/255-8471; ❸) aims for a resort-like feel, with more personalized service and a palm-fringed pool. The *Venice Campground* is at 4085 E Venice Ave (ⓣ941/488-0850, ⓦwww.campvenice.com; $28–32 per tent site), in an oak hammock by the river.

Among the **places to eat**, don't miss the *Soda Fountain,* 349 W Venice Ave (Ⓣ941/412-9860), for delicious milkshakes; *The Frosted Mug,* 1856 S Tamiami Trail (Ⓣ941/497-1611), which has been here since 1957 and serves the best root beer and burgers in the area; and *TJ Carney's Pub and Grill,* 231 W Venice Ave (Ⓣ941/480-9244), for evening entertainment as well as inexpensive to moderately priced food throughout the day.

Continuing south: Punta Gorda

Punta Gorda, about thirty miles from Venice, is easily dismissed as one of the retirement communities that populate the West Coast and, although there is not much here to detain you for long, it does warrant exploring. Don't expect to find impressive beaches here, but you will encounter large, Southern-style houses facing the sea and an unhurried pace of life that contrasts sharply with the frantic US-41 that runs through it. One of the surprises of Punta Gorda is its excellent public art; large murals adorn walls and a plethora of small statues appear at frequent intervals along its main street. Situated on the banks of the Peace River, the **Fishermen's Village**, a quaint collection of unusual shops and a working marina housed in the old city docks, was established by Cuban fishermen. A collection of boat-tour operators line the pier offering trips around the harbor and further afield to Cayo Costa Island and Cabbage Key (see p.255). **King Fisher Cruises** (Ⓣ941/639-0969, Ⓦwww.kingfisherfleet.com) run full- and half-day cruises and shorter sunset boat trips, starting at $7.50. The **Charlotte County Historical Center**, 22959 Bayshore Road (Mon–Fri 10am–5pm, Sat 10am–3pm; $2; Ⓣ941/629-7278), features exhibits of state and local history, as well as Florida's natural history, but won't keep you for more than an hour.

Telegraph Cypress Swamp

For anyone interested in untamed Florida, but lacking the desire to traipse through the wild for days, **Babcock Wilderness Adventures**, 8000 State Rd 31 at Punta Gorda (Ⓣ1 800/500-5583, Ⓦwww.babcockwilderness.com), is a must. Forty miles inland and northeast of Fort Myers (take exit 143 on I-75), this eco-tourism outfit offers you a choice of either a ninety-minute swamp-buggy tour or a three-hour off-road bike tour through the Babcock Ranch and **Telegraph Cypress Swamp** (Nov–April 9am–3pm, May–Oct 9am–noon, reservations essential; swamp-buggy tours $18, children $10; bike tours $35, $30 children). Excellent guides lead the tours through their vast ranch (it's three times the size of Washington DC), which was bought in 1914 by Edward Babcock and adapted as a wildlife refuge by his son Fred. From open fields with wild pigs and bison to swamp areas where alligators carpet the pathway, the tours will take you through a wild, ever-changing terrain. Among the highlights – and there are plenty – is the **bald cypress swamp**, a primeval scene of stunning trees and blood-red bromeliads reflected in still, tea-colored water. Another highlight is the gold Florida panthers, although they're not pure-bred. Only around fifty true Florida panthers are left, and inbreeding has caused most of the young to be stillborn. You'll also be offered the opportunity to stroke the surprisingly dry, smooth belly of a baby alligator, and learn about how trade in the reptile's meat and skin is carried out – an unexpected aspect to this essentially very caring establishment. There's also a museum where visitors can learn more about the history of the ranch and take a break from the wilderness by viewing all the Florida memorabilia.

Practicalities

If you are charmed enough by Punta Gorda to want to stay the night, ignore the motels on US-41 and try one of the waterfront **accommodation** options in the town itself. Villas are available for rent at the *Fishermen's Village*, 1200 W Retta Esplanade (Ⓣ941/639-8721 or 1-800/639-0020, Ⓦwww.fishville.com; ❹), whose amenities include a beach area, tennis courts, free use of bikes, and heated pool; you'll get all the same amenities with a bit more glamour at the *Best Western Waterfront*, 300 Retta Esplanade (Ⓣ941/639-1165, Ⓦwww.bestwestern.com/waterfront; ❺). The *Banana Bay Waterfront Motel,* 23285 Bayshore Rd (Ⓣ941/743-4411, Ⓦwww.bananabaymotel.com; ❸), is a more secluded option, tucked away beside the Fisherman's Village.

Good **eating** options include *Harpoon Harry's* (Ⓣ941/637-1177) at the end of the pier, a restaurant and bar renowned for its raw oysters, clams, and its special firehouse chili. There's also *Portabellos*, 5000 Burnt Shore Rd (Ⓣ941/639-3650), where cocktails are served in cozy surroundings and Sunday brunch is a specialty. The terrace dining area offers a brilliant view of Charlotte Harbor, excellent food, and entertainment on the weekend.

Fort Myers

Though lacking the sophistication of Sarasota (fifty miles north) and the exclusivity of Naples (twenty miles south), **FORT MYERS** is one of the up-and-coming communities of the southwest coast. The town took its name from Abraham Myers, who helped establish a fort here in 1860 after the Seminole War. During the war, the town was activated as a base where cattle were rounded up to supply beef to federal gunboats patrolling the gulf off Sanibel Island (see p.251). Fortunately, most of the town's late-twentieth-century growth occurred on the north side of the wide Caloosahatchee River, leaving the traditional center relatively unspoiled. The workplace of inventor Thomas Edison, who lived in Fort Myers for many years, provides the strongest interest in a town that otherwise relies on its scenery. Its riverside setting and regimental lines of palm trees along the main thoroughfares are arresting enough to delay your progress toward the local beaches, fifteen miles south, or the islands of **Sanibel** and **Captiva**, a similar distance west.

Arrival and information

Fort Myers, like many south Florida towns, sprawls farther than you initially imagine. East of I-75, **Southwest Florida International Airport** lies on Daniels Parkway. US-41 is known here as Cleveland Avenue. Hwy-80 runs through downtown Fort Myers and curves into McGregor Boulevard to the west, where you'll find the Edison home. Most tourist maps fail to refer to downtown and the wider city on the same map, and the fact that there's only a mile between Edison's house and downtown is not always clear. If you're arriving from US-41, the exit for McGregor Boulevard is clearly marked and, for those on mass transit, it's covered by the #20 **local bus** (Ⓣ239/275-8726, Ⓦwww.lee-county.com/leetran) and a trolley service. To get from downtown Fort Myers to the beaches, take the #140 south to Bell Tower and then change to the #50 to Fort Myers beach. Fares are $1 and there is only limited service to the beaches on Sundays. The Greyhound station is at 2275 Cleveland Ave (Ⓣ239/334-1011), just south of downtown Fort Myers. Stacks of **information** await you at the **Visitor and Convention Bureau**, 2180

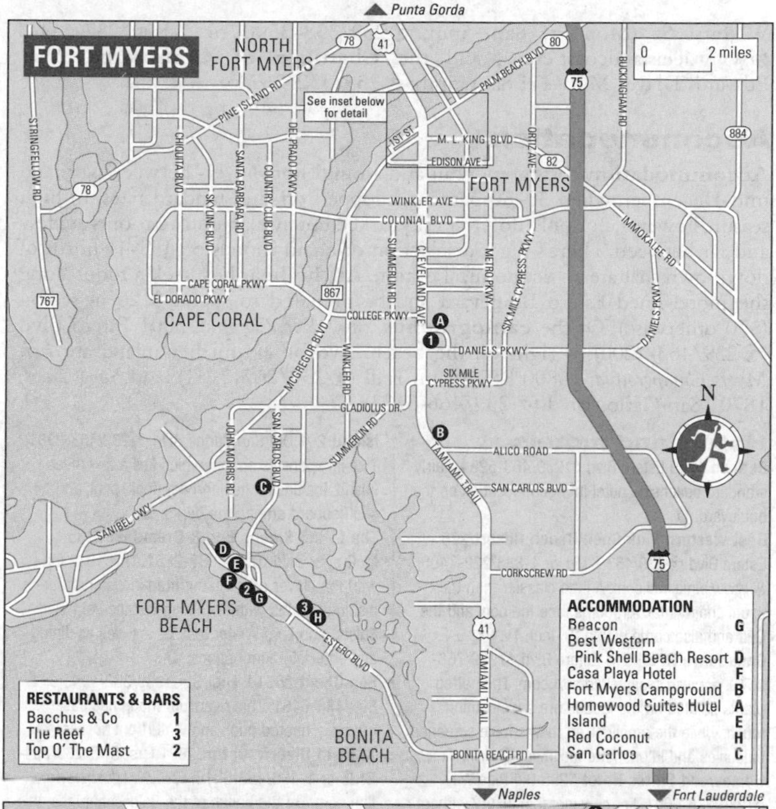
FORT MYERS
Punta Gorda
NORTH FORT MYERS
See inset below for detail
0 2 miles
PINE ISLAND RD
PALM BEACH BLVD
STRINGFELLOW RD
CHIQUITA BLVD
SANTA BARBARA RD
COUNTRY CLUB BLVD
DEL PRADO PKWY
SKYLINE BLVD
1ST ST
M. L. KING BLVD
EDISON AVE
ORTIZ AVE
BUCKINGHAM RD
FORT MYERS
WINKLER AVE
COLONIAL BLVD
IMMOKALEE RD
SUMMERLIN RD
CLEVELAND AVE
METRO PKWY
SIX MILE CYPRESS PKWY
DANIELS PKWY
CAPE CORAL PKWY
EL DORADO PKWY
CAPE CORAL
COLLEGE PKWY
MCGREGOR BLVD
WINKLER RD
SIX MILE CYPRESS PKWY
GLADIOLUS DR.
JOHN MORRIS RD
SAN CARLOS BLVD
SUMMERLIN RD
TAMIAMI TRAIL
ALICO ROAD
SAN CARLOS BLVD
SANIBEL CWY
CORKSCREW RD
FORT MYERS BEACH
ESTERO BLVD
BONITA BEACH
BONITA BEACH RD
N
RESTAURANTS & BARS
Bacchus & Co 1
The Reef 3
Top O' The Mast 2
ACCOMMODATION
Beacon G
Best Western Pink Shell Beach Resort D
Casa Playa Hotel F
Fort Myers Campground B
Homewood Suites Hotel A
Island E
Red Coconut H
San Carlos C
Naples
Fort Lauderdale

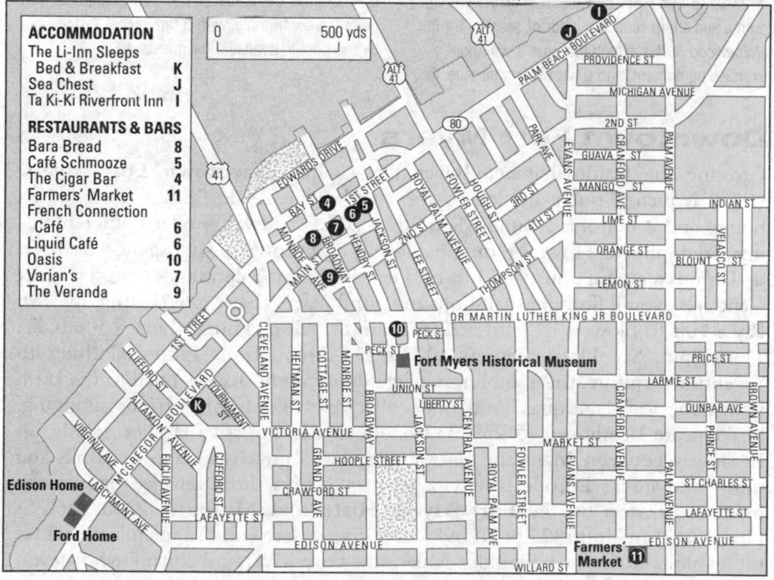
ACCOMMODATION
The Li-Inn Sleeps Bed & Breakfast K
Sea Chest J
Ta Ki-Ki Riverfront Inn I
RESTAURANTS & BARS
Bara Bread 8
Café Schmooze 5
The Cigar Bar 4
Farmers' Market 11
French Connection Café 6
Liquid Café 6
Oasis 10
Varian's 7
The Veranda 9
0 500 yds
PALM BEACH BOULEVARD
PROVIDENCE ST
MICHIGAN AVENUE
2ND ST
GUAVA ST
MANGO ST
LIME ST
ORANGE ST
LEMON ST
EDWARDS DRIVE
BAY ST
1ST STREET
ROYAL PALM AVENUE
FOWLER STREET
HOUGH ST
PARK AVE
EVANS AVENUE
CRANFORD AVE
PALM AVENUE
INDIAN ST
VELASCO ST
BLOUNT ST
3RD ST
4TH ST
THOMPSON ST
MONROE ST
MAIN ST
BROADWAY
HENDRY ST
JACKSON ST
2ND ST
LEE STREET
DR MARTIN LUTHER KING JR BOULEVARD
PECK ST
Fort Myers Historical Museum
UNION ST
LIBERTY ST
1ST STREET
CLIFFORD ST
BOULEVARD
TOURNAMENT ST
ALTAMONT AVENUE
MCGREGOR BLVD
VIRGINIA AVE
EUCLID AVENUE
CLIFFORD ST
CLEVELAND AVENUE
HEITMAN ST
COTTAGE ST
MONROE ST
BROADWAY
VICTORIA AVENUE
HOOPLE STREET
GRAND AVE
CRAWFORD ST
JACKSON ST
CENTRAL AVENUE
ROYAL PALM AVE
FOWLER STREET
EVANS AVENUE
MARKET ST
CRANFORD AVENUE
PALM AVENUE
PRICE ST
LARMIE ST
DUNBAR AVE
PRINCE ST
BROWN AVENUE
ST CHARLES ST
LAFAYETTE ST
EDISON AVENUE
LAFAYETTE ST
EDISON AVENUE
WILLARD ST
Farmers' Market
Edison Home
LARCHMONT AVE
Ford Home

W First St (Mon–Fri 8am–5pm; ⓣ239/338-3500 or 1-800/237-6444, ⓦwww.leeislandcoast.com), and the **Chamber of Commerce**, 2301 Edwards Drive (Mon–Fri 8am–5pm; ⓣ239/332-3624).

Accommodation

Accommodation costs are low in and around Fort Myers between May and mid-December, when 30–60 percent is lopped off the standard rates. In high season, however, not only do prices skyrocket, but available spare rooms are few and far between. There's a good selection of chain motels on US-41 north of downtown that are an economical option. **At the beaches**, seek a room along the motel-lined Estero Boulevard and be prepared to spend $120 in season ($70 otherwise). Of the **campgrounds**, only *Red Coconut*, 3001 Estero Blvd (ⓣ239/463-7200), is right on the beach. Two others further inland are *Fort Myers Campground,* 16800 S Tamiami Trail (ⓣ239/267-2141), and *San Carlos*, 18701 San Carlos Blvd (ⓣ239/466-3133).

Hotels and motels

Beacon 1240 Estero Blvd ⓣ239/463-5264. Fairly standard beachside hotel in a good location on the boulevard. ❸

Best Western Pink Shell Beach Resort 275 Estero Blvd ⓣ239/463-6181 or 1-888/222-7465, ⓦwww.pinkshell.com. A little classier than the usual chain hotel. All rooms face the pool and the Gulf and also come with a 27-inch TV. ❻

Casa Playa Hotel 510 Estero Blvd ⓣ239/765-0510, ⓦwww.casaplayaresort.com. The potted plants painted on the facade are a welcoming touch, while the amply sized rooms have screened balconies and kitchenette facilities. ❹

Homewood Suites Hotel 5255 Big Pine Way ⓣ239/275-6601. For considerable luxury without pomp, and sharp reductions out of season, try the *Homewood Suites*, which features a whirlpool, exercise equipment, and a babysitting service. ❼

Island 201 Old San Carlos Blvd ⓣ239/463-2381. This inexpensive option, which lies a few miles inland, includes a fishing/boat dock, pool, and shuffleboard among the perks. ❸

The Li-Inn Sleeps Bed & Breakfast 2135 McGregor Blvd ⓣ239/332-2651. This 1912 inn with the clever name is outfitted in Victorian furnishings and is within walking distance of the Edison and Ford Winter Estates, as well as dining and entertainment options. ❹

Sea Chest 2571 E First St ⓣ239/332-1545 or 1-800/438-6461. This riverfront motel has basic rooms, a heated pool, and waterfront access. ❷

Ta Ki-Ki Riverfront Inn 2631 First St ⓣ239/334-2135 or 1-866/453-0016, ⓦwww.takikiriverfrontinn.com. On the banks of the Caloosahatchee, this hotel is very friendly, with a family feel. Barbecue by the pool is available for guests. ❸

Downtown Fort Myers

Crossing the Caloosahatchee River, US-41 hits **downtown Fort Myers**, which is picturesquely nestled by the river's edge. Aside from a few restored homes and storefronts around Main Street and Broadway, modern office buildings predominate. However, time exploring downtown is well spent. The Patio de León is a quaint courtyard just off First Street – the central downtown street – and here you'll find unusual shops and good places to eat (see "Eating," p.248). Pay a visit to Flowers to Fifties, 2229 Main St (Mon–Thurs 11am–5.30pm, Fri 11am–8pm, Sat 11am–5.30pm; ⓣ239/334-2443): from Fifties' clothing to Seventies' furniture, this rambling vintage department store is filled to the brim with American "antiques" and odd collectibles. For more serious shopping, Shakespeare Beethoven (ⓣ239/332-8300) in the attractive Collier Arcade, on Broadway between Main and First streets, has a good selection of books and music and stocks European newspapers, too. For a thorough insight into the town's past, stop by the **Fort Myers Historical Museum**, 2300 Peck St (Tues–Sat 9am–4pm; $2.50; ⓣ239/332-5955), where exhibits include details on the exploits of Doctor Franklin Miles, the Fort Myers inhabitant who developed Alka Seltzer. The invention of the world's great hangover cure was overshadowed, however, by the deeds of Thomas Edison, comprehensively recalled a mile west of downtown Fort Myers on McGregor Boulevard – also the route to the Fort Myers beaches and the Sanibel Island causeway.

The Edison and Ford Winter Estates

In 1885, six years after inventing the light bulb, workaholic **Thomas Edison** collapsed from exhaustion and was instructed by his doctor to find a warm working environment or face an early death. While on holiday in Florida, the 37-year-old Edison noted a patch of bamboo sprouting from the banks of the Caloosahatchee River and bought and cleared fourteen acres of it. Henry Ford, a close friend of Edison's since 1896 (when the latter had been one of the few people to speak admiringly of his ambitious car ideas), bought the house next door in 1915, by which time he was established as the country's top automobile manufacturer. The combined **Edison and Ford Winter Estates** at 2350 McGregor Blvd (Mon–Sat 9am–5pm, Sun noon–5pm; guided tours every 30min; $14, children $7.50; Ⓣ239/334-3614, Ⓦwww.edison-ford-estate.com) provide some small insight into these men of innovation.

Edison's liking for bamboo was no idle fancy: he was a keen horticulturist and often used the chemicals produced by plants and trees in his experiments. The **gardens** of the house (in-depth botanical tours are given for $19) are sensational, and the over 100 varieties from Africa, South America, and Asia provided Edison with much raw material: a variety of tropical foliage, from the extraordinary African sausage tree to a profusion of wild orchids, intoxicatingly scented by frangipani, that the inventor nurtured. By contrast, Edison's **house**, where he spent each winter until his death in 1931, is an anticlimax: a palm-cloaked wooden structure with an ordinary collection of period furnishings glimpsed only through the windows. A reason for the plainness of the abode may be that Edison spent most of his waking hours inside the **laboratory**, attempting to turn the latex-rich sap of *solidago Edisoni* (a giant strain of goldenrod weed that he developed) into rubber. A mass of test tubes, files, and tripods are scattered over the benches, unchanged since Edison's last experiment, performed just before his death.

Not until the tour reaches the **museum** does the full impact of Edison's achievements become apparent. A design for an improved ticker-tape machine provided him with the funds for the experiments that led to the creation of the phonograph in 1877 and financed research into passing electricity through a vacuum, which resulted in the incandescent lightbulb two years later. Scores of cylinder and disc phonographs with gaily painted horn-speakers, bulky vintage lightbulbs, and innumerable spin-off gadgets, make up an engrossing collection. Here, too, you'll see some of the ungainly cinema projectors derived from Edison's Kinetoscope – bringing the inventor a million dollars a year in patent royalties from 1907.

Unlike the Edison home, you can go inside the Ford Winter Home, though the interior, restored to the style of Ford's time, lacks almost all of the original fittings and bears an unassuming appearance: despite becoming the world's first billionaire, Ford lived with his wife in modest surroundings.

Before leaving the old homes, pause to admire the sprawling **banyan tree** outside the ticket office: grown from a seedling given to Edison by tire-king Harvey Firestone in 1925, it's now the largest tree in the state.

The Fort Myers beaches

Still being discovered by the holidaying multitudes, the **Fort Myers beaches**, fifteen miles south of downtown Fort Myers, are appreciably different in character

Getting to Key West

If you're heading to Key West from Fort Myers, there are a handful of ferry operators who will whisk you there on their high-speed catamarans, a trip that takes about four hours each way. **Key West Shuttle** (ⓣ239/394-9700, ⓦwww.keywestshuttle.com) leaves from Salty Sam's Marina in Fort Myers Beach and costs $90 round-trip for return on the same day, $10 more for different day return. Departing from Fisherman's Wharf, **X-Press to Key West** (ⓣ239/765-0808, ⓦwww.keywestferry.com), which charges $70 one way, $120 return, also runs between Key West and the Marco River Marina on Marco Island (see p.258). Call for schedules.

from the West Coast's more commercialized beach strips, with a cheerful seaside mood that's worth getting acquainted with. Accommodation (see p.246) is plentiful on and around Estero Boulevard – reached by San Carlos Boulevard, off McGregor Boulevard – which runs the seven-mile length of **Estero Island**; the hubs of activity are the short fishing pier and the **Lynne Hall Memorial Park** at the island's northern end.

Estero Island becomes quieter and increasingly residential as you press south. Estero Boulevard eventually swings over a slender causeway onto the barely developed **San Carlos Island**. A few miles ahead, at **Lovers Key** (daily sunrise to sunset; cars $3.25, pedestrians and cyclists $1), a footpath picks a trail over a couple of mangrove-fringed islands and several mullet-filled creeks. Although this area has recently experienced some build-up, it remains one of the quietest and prettiest beaches in the region – the perfect base for stress-free beachcombing and sunbathing, although canoes and kayaks are available to rent if you want to be a bit more active. If you don't fancy the half-mile walk, a free trolleybus will transport you between the park entrance and the beach.

Eating

Dining options in Fort Myers are scattered over a wide area, but you'll find clusters of places to eat in the downtown area, as well as the northern section of Estero Boulevard in Fort Myers Beach.

Bacchus & Co 13499 S Cleveland Ave ⓣ239/415-9463. Ginger, saffron, or wasabi are likely to spice up your meal at this restaurant, which serves a wide range of international cuisines (entrees $18–28).

Bara Bread 1520 Broadway ⓣ239/334-8216. Try the deliciously fresh pastries at this inexpensive downtown bakery and bistro, the latter serving omelets, salads, and quiche at lunch.

Café Schmooze 1532 Jackson St ⓣ239/337-3400. This place has it all, from comfort foods, homemade soups, and desserts, to more substantial dinners (starting at $13) of pork or duckling.

Farmers' Market Restaurant 2736 Edison Ave ⓣ239/334-1687. Despite its grim appearance and 1950s signs, try the reasonably priced *Farmers'* for such good country cooking as smoked ham hocks and barbecued ribs.

The French Connection Café 2288 First St ⓣ239/332-4443. This convivial place for an evening bite serves inexpensive French onion soup, crepes, and excellent Reuben sandwiches.

Oasis Restaurant 2260 Dr Martin Luther King Blvd ⓣ239/334-1566. For cheap breakfast and large burger lunches, head for this super-friendly spot, wedged into the Edison Ford Square Shopping Center.

The Reef 2601 Estero Blvd ⓣ239/463-4181. If you have a massive appetite, you'll want to try this beachside restaurant for all-you-can-eat nightly specials, ranging from catfish to frogs' legs.

Top O' The Mast 1028 Estero Blvd ⓣ239/463-9424. This casual restaurant by the beach is a solid bet for seafood, with prices topping out at $15.

The Veranda 2122 Second St ⓣ239/332-2065. The casual elegance of the Old South lives on in this restaurant, which occupies two 1902 houses and has a lush courtyard of mango trees. The classic and regional specialties on offer are expensive at dinner but extremely reasonable at lunch. Reservations recommended.

Nightlife

Fort Myers' **nightlife** scene is small but constantly changing; a stroll through the downtown area can usually turn something up, or check Ⓦwww.downtownftmyers.com for more options.

The Downtown Cigar Bar 1502 Hendry St Ⓣ239/337-4662. Laidback yet stylish bar, filled with leather chesterfields, a grand piano, and the mounted heads of bison, oryx, and bears sporting cigars. Choose from a huge range of bourbons and single malts (and smokes). The attached cigar shop stocks everything from $1 cigarillos to pre-embargo Cuban cigars that cost $35 each.

The Liquid Cafe 2236 First St Ⓣ239/461-0444. The spot for a relaxing drink in a stylish setting, with a good casual food menu and live guitar music on Saturday nights. Open until 2am every night except Sunday (closes at midnight).

Varian's 33 Patio de Leon Ⓣ239/461-2727. An inside and outside bar (and restaurant) offers plenty of choices, among them Latin night Tuesdays and DJs and occasional theme parties on weekends.

Gay and lesbian bars and clubs

For **gay nightlife**, your best bet is *The Bottom Line*, 3090 Evans Ave (Ⓣ239/337-7292), a cavernous bar and club isolated in a desolate stretch of downtown; nightly themes range from drag shows (Mon) to DJs (weekends) to go-go boys (Wed). For a drink in a congenial if somewhat gloomy, unlit pub, try *The Office*, at 3704 Cleveland Ave (Ⓣ239/936-3212), in the Pizza Hut Plaza opposite the *Red Lobster* sign. More gregarious and inviting is *Tubby's*, at 4350 Fowler St (Ⓣ239/274-5001), a very friendly locals' bar with dancing and occasional karaoke.

Inland from Fort Myers: the Calusa Nature Center

Just as the beaches are kept in good condition, so is much of the eastern perimeter of the town, which is protected by a series of parks that make scenic spots for picnicking, canoeing, and walking. For a more informative look at the local landscape, spend a couple of hours at the **Calusa Nature Center and Planetarium**, 3450 Ortiz Ave, five miles west of I-75 off exit 136 (Mon–Sat 9am–5pm, Sun 11am–5pm; $7, children $4; Ⓣ239/275-3435, Ⓦwww.calusanature.com), and trek the boardwalk trails through cypress and pine woods. Cast an eye, too, around the aviary where injured birds regain their strength before returning to the wild, and the indoor **museum**. Here, alongside general geological and wildlife exhibits, you'll find a caged specimen of each of the state's four varieties of poisonous snakes; the facial expressions of the mice, fed to each snake once a day, are not a sight for the faint-hearted. The museum also features a re-creation of a Seminole Indian village as well as exhibitions on the history of southwest Florida.

Lee County Manatee Park

One creature you won't find at Babcock Ranch (p.243) is a manatee. Fortunately, just one stop further north on I-75, they're the center of attention at the **Lee County Manatee Park** (Nov–March 8am–5pm, April–Oct 8am–8pm; 75¢ per hour parking fee, $3 maximum; Ⓣ239/694-3537). Here, along the banks of the Orange River, large information boards explain how manatees are identified by their scar patterns, which are caused by collisions with boat propellers. Those most often sighted – and, therefore, the most scarred – are given names. Due to its proximity to the Interstate and the Fort Myers Power Company, the park isn't too aesthetically pleasing. Still, the manatees enjoy the warm water generated by the plant, especially in the winter, and if you wander to the first inlet, where they congregate in the calm, shallow waters, you are likely to see them. Although they are easiest to spot in the early morning, there's a good chance you'll see at least a couple at any time of day.

ECHO

For more eco-tourism pay a visit to **ECHO** (Educational Concerns for Hunger Organization), 17891 Durrance Rd (tours given Jan–March Tues–Sat 10am, April–Dec Tues, Fri & Sat 10am; donations suggested; ⓣ239/543-3246, ⓦwww.echonet.org), a 21-acre farm devoted to the development of Third World farming techniques. Greenhouses simulate different environments in which workers experiment with plants to find out which ones thrive in them, while gardens in such unlikely settings as old tires and rooftops prove that it is possible to create a garden anywhere.

Sanibel and Captiva islands

Hailed as paradise by many package-tour operators, Sanibel and Captiva islands, 25 miles southwest of Fort Myers, have more of a sense of paradise lost than the perfect holiday destination. The lack of public transport both to and on the islands makes day-trips virtually impossible without a car. When the Lee County authorities (who are responsible for the whole Fort Myers area) decided to link **Sanibel Island**, the most southerly of an island grouping around the mouth of the Caloosahatchee River, by road to the mainland in 1963, Sanibel's thousand or so occupants fought tooth and nail against the scheme, but eventually lost. A decade later, they got their revenge by seceding from the county, becoming a self-governing "city" and passing strict land-use laws to prevent their island sinking beneath holiday homes and hotels. To its credit, there are no high resorts to mar the view; however, much of the island is dominated by motels and restaurants, and visitors always outnumber the not-always-welcoming residents. Sizeable areas are set aside as nature preserves, so that when these are combined with all the resort-dominated territory, a day-trip can leave you with the sense that you've seen little of the island. North of Sanibel, a road continues to **Captiva Island**. Even less populated, its only concession to modern economics is an upmarket holiday resort at its northern tip, from where you can take boat trips to some of the otherwise inaccessible neighboring islands.

Arrival and information

To reach Sanibel and Captiva from mainland Fort Myers, take College Parkway west off of US-41, turning almost immediately onto Summerlin Road. Summerlin winds its way to Sanibel Causeway, which links to the island. There's a $3 vehicle **toll** to get onto Sanibel.

Your first stop on Sanibel should be the **Visitor Center**, 1159 Causeway Rd (Mon–Sat 9am–7pm, Sun 10am–5pm; ⓣ239/472-1080, ⓕ472-1070, ⓦwww.sanibel-captiva.org), which is packed with essential **information** and numerous free publications. There is no public transport on the island so without a car, you'll have to rent a **bike**: Finnimore's Cycle Shop, 2353 Periwinkle Way (ⓣ239/472-5577), and The Bike Rental Inc, 2330 Palm Ridge Rd (ⓣ239/472-2241), offer a good selection; bike rental is around $5 an hour. Billy's Rentals, 1470 Periwinkle Way (ⓣ239/472-5248), also provides a good cycle guide with rentals at the same prices. It's worth bearing in mind that no bikes are allowed on the beaches.

Accommodation

Accommodation on the islands is always expensive, more so than on the mainland, and per-day rates can be $100 higher in high season than the rest of the year between May and November. Sanibel does have a **campground**, *Periwinkle Trailer Park*, 1119 Periwinkle Way (ⓣ239/472-1433), where it costs $30–37 to pitch a tent.

Gulf Breeze Cottages 1801 Shell Basket Lane, Sanibel ⓣ239/472-1626, ⓦwww.gbreeze.com. Choose from four efficiencies in a Victorian house or one of the more expensive cottages; all are clean, well furnished, and have Gulf views. Efficiencies ❺, cottages ❻

Kona Kai 1539 Periwinkle Way, Sanibel ⓣ941/472-1001 or 1-800/820-2385. This inexpensive option three-quarters of a mile from the beach has a large pool but if your heart is set on the sands, the motel will provide bikes to get there. ❸

Seahorse 1223 Buttonwood Lane, Sanibel ⓣ239/472-4262. Comfortable and simply decorated cottages come equipped with oak furniture and both A/C and paddle fans, and there's a garden pool too. ❹

'Tween Waters Inn 15951 Captiva Rd, Captiva ⓣ239/472-5161 or 1-866/893-3646. Actually an old-fashioned resort, with everything you need on the premises: tennis courts, three restaurants, a marina, pool, and fitness center. ❼

Waterside Inn on the Beach 3033 W Gulf Drive, Sanibel ⓣ239/472-1345 or 1-800/741-6166, ⓦwww.watersideinn.net. Colorful and friendly place, right on the beach, with spacious accommodation in rooms and cottages. ❻

Sanibel Island

People visit **SANIBEL ISLAND** for its beaches and although there are a number of them, public access is limited and they are not always as spectacular as the glossy brochures would have you believe. Signs prohibit parking wherever you look and the parking lots at the main beaches are clogged with vacationers lining up for a precious, and sometimes expensive, space. The further west and north you travel the more likely you are to find space; however, by this time you can be fairly frazzled and wishing you'd opted for the free roadside beaches before the toll bridge, where the sea, sun, and views are pretty much the same.

The first sight you'll come across on the island is the undramatic gray **Sanibel Lighthouse** (erected in 1884), a relic most arrivals feel obliged to inspect (from the outside only) before spending a few hours on the presentable beach at its foot. After the beach, trace your way along Periwinkle Way and turn right into Dunlop Road, acknowledging the island's tiny city hall on the way to the **Sanibel Historical Village and Museum**

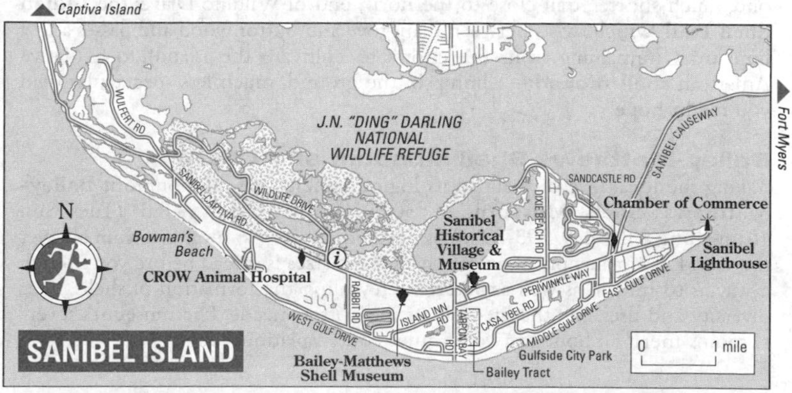

(June–Aug Wed–Sat 10am–4pm, Nov–May also Sun 1–4pm; $3; ⓣ239/472-4648). The museum is a century-old, pioneer settler's home with furnishings and photos of early Sanibel arrivals – those who weren't seafarers tried agriculture until the soils were ruined by saltwater blown up by hurricanes – and displays on the Caloosa Indians, including a thousand-year-old skeleton. Continue along Periwinkle Way to Tarpon Bay Road, which cuts north-south to the coasts; going north, you'll pass the rampant vegetation of the **Bailey Tract**, a jungle-like rectangle of land in the midst of a residential area; poorly marked trails – for the careful and courageous only – will take you deep among the alligators and the wildfowl. In either direction from the southern end of Tarpon Bay Road, resorts and tourists mark the beaches. Turning left along Casa Ybel Road and Algiers Lane leads to the more promising **Gulfside City Park**, a slender sandy strip shaded by Australian pines and bordered by a narrow canal, with a nicely secluded picnic area. Before you leave, follow the bike path off Algiers Road for a few yards to a tiny **cemetery**, where a few wooden markers remember those who perished in their attempts to forge an existence on the then inhospitable island some hundred years ago.

The J.N. "Ding" Darling National Wildlife Refuge

In contrast to the smooth beaches along the Gulf side of Sanibel Island, the opposite edge comprises shallow bays and creeks and a vibrant wildlife habitat under the protection of the **J.N. "Ding" Darling National Wildlife Refuge** (daily except Fri sunrise–sunset; cars $5, cyclists and pedestrians $1; ⓣ239/472-1100); you can also take the tram tour ($10, children $7; ⓣ239/472-1351) conducted by Tarpon Bay Explorers (ⓣ239/472-8900, ⓦwww.tarponbayexplorers.com). The main entrance and **information center** are just off Sanibel-Captiva Road. Alligators, brown pelicans, and ospreys are usually easy to spot, but much of what you'll see at the refuge is determined by when you come: during the fall, migrating songbirds are plentiful, thousands of wintering ducks show up in subsequent months, and in spring, graceful roseate spoonbills sweep by just before sunset. The five-mile **Wildlife Drive** requires slow speeds and plenty of stops if you're to see the well-camouflaged residents by car. If you're cycling, heed the wind direction before entering; you'll usually keep the wind at your back and not in your face by pedaling north to south. You'd do better, though, to plod the less-traveled four miles of the **Indigo Trail**, beginning just beyond the information center. There's a second, much shorter, trail close to the north end of Wildlife Drive; the **Indian Shell Trail**, which twists between mangrove and buttonwood and passes a few lime trees (remaining from the efforts to cultivate the island) to a Native American **shell mound** – a hump in the ground, much less spectacular than you might hope.

Bailey-Matthews Shell Museum and CROW

Taking the local love of shells to its logical conclusion, the nonprofit **Bailey-Matthews Shell Museum**, at 3075 Sanibel-Captiva Rd (Tues–Sun 10am–4pm; $5; ⓣ239/395-2233), is devoted entirely to mollusks from all over the world. A cornucopia of colors, shapes, and sizes is spread before you in such a way as to inform as well as entertain, revealing the formation of shells, their diversity and uses, and the lifecycle of the critters inside. The museum's several rooms merit an hour or two of quiet contemplation.

Shelling on Sanibel and Captiva islands

One thing that both Sanibel and Captiva share are **shells**. Literally tons of them are washed ashore with each tide, and the popularity of shell collecting has led to the bent-over condition known as "Sanibel Stoop." The potential ecological upset of too many shells being taken away has led to laws forbidding the removal of any live shells (ones with a creature still living inside) on pain of a $500 fine or a prison sentence. Novices and seasoned conchologists alike will find plenty to occupy them on the beaches; to identify your find, use one of the shell charts drawn in most of the giveaway tourist magazines – or check the exhibits at the Bailey-Matthews Shell Museum (opposite) or at the **Sanibel Shell Festival** in early March.

Still on Sanibel-Captiva Road, at no. 3883 near the entrance to the J.N. "Ding" Darling Wildlife Refuge (see opposite), you'll find a "hospital" for injured, orphaned, and sick native wildlife from all over southwest Florida. Several thousand patients are treated here each year (mostly due to interaction with humans), and **CROW** (Care and Rehabilitation of Wildlife Inc) puts some of its energy into educating the public about the threats we often unwittingly pose. This ten-acre sanctuary, established thirty years ago and largely staffed by volunteers, offers **guided tours** for small groups (Dec–April only, Mon–Fri at 11am, Sun at 1pm; $3; to book ahead, call ⓣ239/472-3644). A short but enlightening talk on the dangers posed by carelessly discarded fishing lines and other detritus is followed by a walk around the sanctuary's outdoor enclosures, which house a multitude of mammals, birds, amphibians, and reptiles until they are (hopefully) ready for release back into the wild. It all serves as a poignant reminder of man's impact on the environment, as well as the healing powers of nature.

Bowman's Beach

Sanibel's loveliest, and most popular, swathe of sand is **Bowman's Beach,** which lies to the west of the island; to reach it, watch for Bowman's Beach Road off Sanibel-Captiva Road just prior to Blind Pass. Attracting shell-hunters and suntan-seekers, it offers showers and a shady picnic spot, along with spectacular sunsets. **Naturists** seeking to perfect their all-over tans should beware: as the visitor center will remind you, nude sunbathing is forbidden by Florida state law.

Captiva Island

Immediately north of Bowman's Beach, Sanibel-Captiva Road crosses Blind Pass by bridge and reaches **CAPTIVA ISLAND**, markedly less developed than Sanibel and inhabited by only a few hundred people. If you're not going to call on one of them, the sole site of note is the tiny **Chapel-by-the-Sea**, at 11580 Chapin (down Wiles Drive). Mostly used for weddings, the chapel is unlikely to be open and you should walk instead around the unusual **cemetery**, just opposite, where many of the island's original settlers are buried. With crashing waves a shell's throw away and the graves protected from the sun by a roof of seagrape, it's a fitting final resting place for an islander. A few miles further, Captiva's northern tip is covered by the tennis courts, golf courses, and Polynesian-style villas of the ultra-posh *South Sea Plantation*, where the cheapest beds are $150 a night in season. There's no point in hanging around here, though, except for the **boat trips** to the neighboring islands (see box overleaf).

Boat trips from Captiva Island

Several organized **boat trips** leave from the docks at the *South Sea Plantation*. The trips on offer include dolphin-spotting cruises and shelling trips, but the best of them is the lunch cruise, departing at 10.30am and returning at 3.30pm, allowing two hours ashore at either Cabbage Key (see opposite) or at a gourmet restaurant on Useppa Island; cost is $27.50. The price does not include food while ashore – there's no obligation to eat once you land, but taking your own food on the boat isn't allowed. Another option is the six-hour cruise to Boca Grande or Pine Island (see p.174) for $35. Whenever you sail, you're likely to see **dolphins**: many of them live in the warm waters around the islands, sometimes leaping above the water to turn somersaults for your benefit. For further **details** and to make **reservations** for all sailings, contact Captiva Cruises (ⓣ239/472-5300, ⓦwww.captivacruises.com).

Eating and drinking

The islands' isolation makes for a quiet **eating** and **drinking** experience and more of an opportunity to bond with total strangers. Establishments can be found all over Sanibel, while Captiva's haunts are few and far between, except for a cluster of places toward the island's northern tip.

Restaurants

Amy's Over Easy Cafe 630 Tarpon Bay Rd, Sanibel ⓣ239/472-2625. Bright primary colors and bright, amiable staff populate this diner. Try the Egg Reuben sandwich on a bagel ($5) or the Gulf shrimp, tomato, and cheese omelet ($9).

Bubble Room 15001 Captiva Drive, Captiva ⓣ239/472-5558. "Bubble scouts," complete with uniforms, take your order at this campy restaurant. The portions are huge, with the menu leaning toward creations like Guava Gabor (sauteed scallops and peppers with guava barbecue sauce).

Lighthouse Café 362 Periwinkle Way, Sanibel ⓣ239/472-0303. Tuck into breakfast or lunch in a diner-like setting, where the red-sauce frittata and turkey Benedict are distinct highlights.

Matzaluna 1200 Periwinkle Way, Sanibel ⓣ239/472-1998. Fill up on pasta, pizza, or classics like *vitello saltimbocca* or chicken cacciatore.

Mucky Duck 11546 Andy Rosse Lane, Captiva ⓣ239/472-3434. The reasonably priced menu is heavy on seafood, but also includes steak and sausage pie and Captiva chicken (baked with oil, wine, onions, herbs, and capers). Lunch usually costs under $10 and is served until 2.30pm. Closed Sun.

Old Captiva House 15951 Captiva Rd at the *'Tween Waters Inn*, Captiva ⓣ239/472-5161, Fine dining spot offering plenty of alternatives besides the usual seafood, including chicken Wellington ($20) and duckling in pecan butter ($24).

Pippin's 1975 Periwinkle Way, Sanibel ⓣ239/395-2676. *Pippin's* has a wide selection of Caribbean-spiced steak, chicken, ribs, and fish.

Sanibel Steakhouse 1473 Periwinkle Way, Sanibel ⓣ239/472-5700. One of the few restaurants that caters to meat-eaters in an area known for its seafood. Quality isn't cheap (all dishes are over $20), but you do get your choice of home-made steak sauces.

Twilight Café 751 Tarpon Bay Rd, Sanibel ⓣ239/472-8818. The striking local artwork here is matched by stunning plates and inventive offerings such as grilled scallops with tangerine linguine and cowboy steak with roasted green-apple glaze ($20–25).

Bars

Bungalow corner of Sanibel-Captiva Road and Rabbit Road, Sanibel ⓣ239/395-3502. A low-key version of a sports bar, with the usual pool table, jukebox, dartboard, and many, many beers.

The Jac Bar 1223 Periwinkle Way, Sanibel ⓣ239/472-1771. The livelier side of the *Jacaranda* restaurant, this bar has live music every night (reggae on weekends), and an appealing open-air feel thanks to the adjacent patio and a multitude of tiny white lights strung on the trees and bushes.

McT's Tavern 1523 Periwinkle Way, Sanibel ⓣ239/472-3161. The place where locals come to lift a few lagers, this tavern is also an excellent restaurant in its own right, specializing in shrimp (available 14 different ways).

Beyond Captiva Island: Cabbage Key

Of a number of small islands just north of Captiva, **Cabbage Key** is the one to visit. Even if you arrive on the lunch cruise from Captiva (see the box opposite), skip the unexciting food in favor of prowling the footpaths and the small marina: there's a special beauty to the isolated setting and the views across Pine Island Sound. Take a peep into the **restaurant** of the *Cabbage Key Inn* to see an estimated $30,000 worth of dollar bills, each one signed by the person who left it pinned up in observance of a Cabbage Key tradition. The lunchtime menu is reasonable, but if you're planning to stay for dinner expect to pay about $100 for the works. In case you get the urge **to stay** longer, the inn has six simple rooms on offer at $89 a night and a few rustic two-bedroom cottages in the grounds at $145; reserve at least a month in advance (Ⓣ239/283-2278).

South of Fort Myers

While Sanibel and Captiva islands warrant a few days of exploration, there's less to keep you occupied on the mainland on the seventy-mile journey **south of Fort Myers** toward Everglades National Park. The towns you'll pass will hold less appeal than the nearby beaches or the vistas of Florida's interior. Set aside a few hours, however, to examine one of the stranger footnotes to Florida's history: the oddball religious community of the Koreshans.

The Koreshan State Historic Site

Around the turn of the twentieth century, some of the nation's radicals and idealists began viewing Florida as the last earthly wilderness – a subtropical Garden of Eden where the wrongs of modern society could be righted. Much to the amusement of hard-living Florida farmers, some of the idealists came south to experiment with utopian ways, though few braved the humidity and mosquitoes for long. One of the more significant arrivals was also the most bizarre: the **Koreshan Unity** community, which came from Chicago in 1894 to build the "New Jerusalem" on a site now preserved as the **Koreshan State Historic Site**, 22 miles from Fort Myers, just south of Estero beside US-41 (daily 8am–sunset; cars $3.25, pedestrians and cyclists $1; Ⓣ239/992-0311).

The flamboyant leader of the Koreshans, **Cyrus Teed**, was an army surgeon when he witnessed the "great illumination": an angel appearing and informing him that the Earth was concave, lining the inner edge of a hollow sphere, at the center of which was the rest of the universe. Subsequently, Teed changed his name to "Koresh," which is Hebrew for Cyrus, meaning "the anointed of God," and gained a following among Chicago intellectuals who, like him, were disillusioned with established religions and sought a communal, anti-materialistic way of life. Among the tenets of the Koreshan creed were celibacy outside marriage, shared ownership of goods, and gender equality. The aesthetes who came to this desolate outpost, accessible only by boat along the alligator-infested Estero River, quickly learned new skills in farming and house building and marked out thirty-foot-wide boulevards, which they believed would one day be the arteries of a city inhabited by ten million enlightened souls. In fact, at its peak in 1907, the community numbered just two hundred. After Teed's death in 1908, the Koreshans fizzled out, the last member – who arrived in 1940, fleeing Nazi Germany – dying in 1982. Ranger-led tours are available and there are over forty **campgrounds** available in the pine lands along the river at $21 a night.

The Koreshan library and museum

The Koreshan site will be a disappointment unless you first call at the **Koreshan library and museum**, 8661 Corkscrew Rd (tours Mon–Fri at 1pm, 2pm, 3pm, & 4pm; $1; four-person minimum; ⓣ239/992-2184), for some background on the Koreshans' beliefs, plus the chance to see numerous photos and portraits of Teed, some of his esoteric books, and copies of the Koreshan newspaper, *The American Eagle*. Along the broad thoroughfares at the neighboring **site**, several of the Koreshan buildings have been restored. Among them are Teed's home; the Planetary Court, meeting place of the seven women – each named for one of the seven known planets – who governed the community; and the Art Hall, where the community's cultural evenings were staged. Koreshan celebrations (such as the solar festival in October and the lunar festival in April) still occur here, and this is also where the rectilinator, a device that "proved" the Koreshan theory of the concave Earth, can be seen.

Bonita Springs and the Corkscrew Swamp Sanctuary

A fast-growing residential community, **Bonita Springs**, seven miles south of the Koreshan site, has negligible appeal aside from providing access to quiet **Bonita Beach**, along Bonita Beach Road, and the less impressive **Everglades Wonder Gardens**, on the corner of Terry Street and US-41 (daily 9am–5pm; $9), which keeps a multitude of the state's indigenous creatures in cramped confinement.

Make more of an effort and you'll get a better impression of natural Florida fifteen miles **inland** on Route 846 (branching from US-41 a few miles south of Bonita Springs) at the National Audubon Society's **Corkscrew Swamp Sanctuary,** 375 Sanctuary Rd, Naples (Oct–March daily 7am–5.30pm; April–Sept 7am–7.30pm; $8; ⓣ239/348-9151), an enormous gathering of Spanish-moss-draped cypress trees rising through a dark and moody swamp landscape. Tempering the initial impression is the knowledge that all of the much larger area – presently safeguarded by the Big Cypress National Preserve (see "The Everglades," p.177) – used to look like this; uncontrolled logging felled the 500-year-old trees, partly for war efforts, and severely reduced Florida's population of wood stork, which nest a hundred feet up in the tree tops. The remaining wood stork colony is still the largest in the country, but now faces the threat of falling water levels. The two-and-a-quarter-mile **self-guided boardwalk tour** is excellent; leaflets and binoculars ($8) are available from the visitor center.

A unique facet of this park, though, is found at the outset, on the way to the rest rooms. Here, a remarkably simple "living machine" aids water management in the park by recycling waste from the rest rooms through a purely natural environment to produce purified water. Within a visually pleasing plant-filled glasshouse construction, the cycle relies on sunlight, bacteria, algae, and snails to break down the waste, a process that is later continued by vegetation, small insects, and animals. The result is purified water. It's mildly amusing to think that if you avail yourself of the facilities in Corkscrew Swamp, a part of you will remain here for some time to come, helping to preserve it.

Naples

Twenty miles south of Corkscrew, **NAPLES** is cushioned in wealth. Hardly a soul walks and the most action in town is from the sprinklers that spray the obsessively manicured lawns. You'll get the hang of the place on Fifth Avenue, where

Getting to the Everglades from Naples

There's no public transport to the Everglades (p.167), so if you don't have a car a good option for visiting them is to take a day-trip from Naples or Marco Island (see p.258). **Everglades Excursions** (ⓣ239/262-1914 or 1-800/592-0848, ⓦwww.everglades-excursions.com), runs full- and half-day tours that include safari guided transportation, a jungle cruise through Everglades National Park, and a tour of Everglades City. Half-day tours cost $59, and full-day $89 – including lunch. It is possible to pick up discount coupons of up to $5 from the tourist booklets at the Chamber of Commerce (see below).

the boatyards have been turned into upscale clothes shops, art galleries, and restaurants. The eleven miles of public **beaches** and preserves, however, are lovely and make the pervading social snobbishness more than bearable. **Lowdermilk Park**, about two miles north of the pier, is the most gregarious of the local sands, especially on weekends.

A good way to explore Naples and learn of its history is to take a **Naples Trolley Tour**. Running daily 8.30am to 5.30pm (ⓣ239/262-7300), these entertaining and educational tours last nearly two hours, departing from the Old Naples General Store and Trolley Depot downtown. The tour passes such sights as **Palm Cottage**, at 137 Twelfth Ave, one of the few houses left in Florida built of tabby mortar (made by burning seashells), and the building that now houses **Fantozzi's Café** (see p.258), a cube built in 1922 that has been everything to Naples – from its first town hall, to a courthouse, drugstore, movie theater, Presbyterian church, Catholic church, tap-dance shop, and zoo. Fares are $17 for the trolley, including an all-day boarding pass.

To ogle the fruits of Naples' wealth, head north up US-41 to the *Ritz-Carlton Hotel* (ⓣ239/598-3300, ⓦwww.ritzcarlton.com) at the end of Vanderbilt Beach Road. While you'd need $3500 for a night in the presidential suite, sweeping through the grand entrance for a coffee at the bar is an inexpensive way to appreciate the hotel's towering splendor. The building looks like a 1930s vision of classical decadence, but it actually appeared in the late 1980s. More grandeur on a smaller scale can be found at the *Ritz-Carlton Golf Resort* (see p.258).

Information and accommodation

For **information**, try the **Chamber of Commerce**, 895 Fifth Ave S (daily 9am–5pm; ⓣ239/262-6141, ⓦwww.napleschamber.org). They're not always exceedingly friendly, but if you push hard enough, they'll supply you with local bus schedules. Greyhound **buses** stop in Naples at 2669 Davis Blvd S (ⓣ239/774-5660 or 1-800/231-2222 for schedules).

Accommodation, not surprisingly, is more expensive the closer you get to the beach – between high-season months of December and April, even expensive accommodation can be hard to find. It's worth making the Chamber of Commerce (see above) your first stop as they have a list of all available accommodation when it's in high demand. The nearest campground is the *KOA* site, 1700 Barefoot Williams Rd (ⓣ239/774-5455 or 1-800/562-7734, ⓔnaples@koa.net), where you can pitch a tent for $35 a night or rent a Kamping Kabin for $55. You can park your RV at *Rock Creek RV Resort*, at 3100 North Rd (ⓣ239/643-3100; $40 per day).

The Cove Inn on Naples Bay 900 Broad Ave S ⓣ239/262-7161. This reasonably priced inn is convenient for walking everywhere in Old Naples. ❸

Flamingo Apartment Motel 383 Sixth Ave S ⓣ239/261-7017, ⓦwwww.flamingonaplesfl.com. An old-style Fifties motel set in a cozy tropical courtyard and featuring a pool, shuffleboard, and picnic tables. ❸

The Inn on Fifth 699 Fifth Ave S ⓣ239/403-8777, ⓦwww.naplesinn.com. This Mediterranean-style boutique hotel on Naples' main drag fits right in with the subdued wealth and chic stores. The well-appointed rooms all have terraces. ❼

The Lemon Tree Inn 250 Ninth St S ⓣ239/262-1414, ⓦwww.lemontreeinn.com. There's free lemonade in the lobby and bike rental for guests at this homey inn. ❸

Lighthouse Inn 9140 Gulfshore Drive ⓣ239/597-3345. This small and friendly lodging has a riverside restaurant, boats and sun decks, and a large pool, though rooms lack character and phones. ❸

Ritz-Carlton Golf Resort 2600 Tiburon Drive ⓣ239/593-2000, ⓦwww.ritzcarlton.com. Similar to Naples' other *Ritz-Carlton*, except the grounds are lusher, the glitziness more low key, and the staff more cordial. All the amenities you could possibly think of (for a price). Check for off-season specials. ❼

Eating

There's a welcome lack of the usual fast-food chains in Naples. Even the food in casual restaurants is done well here, though not surprisingly it's more expensive than elsewhere in the state.

bha!bha! 847 Vanderbilt Beach Rd ⓣ239/594-5557. Classical and new Persian cuisine, with most dishes around $17 to $22. Try the delicious lamb *bademjune*, in a tomato and lemon sauce, with grilled vegetables, sautéed eggplant, and sour grapes.

Bistro 821 821 Fifth Ave S ⓣ239/261-5821. Local favorite that carries vaguely Asian entrees flavoured with miso and lemongrass, alongside updated comfort foods ($17–30).

Fantozzi's Café 1148 Third St S ⓣ239/262-4808. Convenient for the old town and the beach, this popular café serves frozen yogurts and gourmet sandwiches.

McCabe's Irish Pub and Grill 699 Fifth Ave S ⓣ239/403-7170. Traditional Irish fare (and some old pub standards), along with Irish ale and traditional Irish entertainment attract a young crowd.

Old Heidelberg 10711 N Tamiami Trail ⓣ239/592-7900. An Old World German-style restaurant, where you can expect to find *Hasenpfeffer* (rabbit stew) and plenty of pork on the menu.

Riverwalk at Tin City 1200 Fifth Ave S ⓣ239/263-2734. This excellent seafood restaurant by the water also offers a wide range of beers and exotic cocktails.

Spanky's Speakeasy 1550 N Airport Pulling Rd ⓣ239/643-1559. Worth seeking out for its unique atmosphere of old America, complete with a 1924 Model T truck and antiques in every nook and cranny. Try the fried catfish sandwich or the Louisiana barbecue shrimp.

Starplace 770 Fifth Ave S ⓣ239/435-7701. Pleasant gourmet Italian option, serving pizzas, antipasti, sandwiches, and desserts. An off-shoot of the **Vergina** down the street at no. 700, which offers a more formal setting with tablecloths and candles.

Zoe's 720 Fifth Ave S ⓣ239/261-1221. The eclectic menu features smoked Thai chicken, Gulf shrimp, and lots of noodle dishes, with main courses ranging from $12 to $27. *Zoe's* is open until 10pm as a restaurant, but the bar (with its extensive wine selection) and live music go on until late. Reservations recommended.

Marco Island

There's not all that much reason to visit **Marco Island** (directly south of Naples), where artificial bald eagle nests are among the techniques dreamed up by property developers to bring back the wildlife that their high-rise condos have driven away. However, the island is relatively unvisited and makes a pleasant detour if you need a break from the crowds found elsewhere. A good way to see the island is on a trolley tour, which runs daily 10am–5pm ($16; ⓣ239/394-1600); the complete narrated journey takes about ninety minutes, but you can hop on and off as many times as you like. At the northern end of the island, the old village of Marco has some charm, and **Tigertail Beach**

Park, at the end of a boardwalk from Hernando Drive, is a fine place to relax – though neither really makes the journey (seven miles along Route 951 off US-41) worthwhile. Also, a few fairly authentic **fish shacks** are located near the eastern edge of the island – worth a stop if you're hungry. Still, the Everglades, within easy striking distance, are a far superior target.

Seventeen miles south of Naples on US-41, the landscape becomes an unbroken swathe of forest. **Collier-Seminole State Park**, at 20200 E Tamiami Trail (8am–sunset; cars $3.25, cyclists or pedestrians $1; Ⓣ239/394-3397), is a tropical hammock filled with Florida royal palms and a six-and-a-half-mile walking trail; a guide to hiking trails is available at the park's main office. Boat tours run throughout the day taking passengers along the Black Water River, which runs through the park; fares are $10. If you want to camp here (and it's not a bad base from which to explore the Everglades), there are two sites: one for tents, the other for RVs (both around $10 a night; enquire at the office at the above number).

Heading inland from Marco Island you'll reach the national parks that form the **Everglades**, the largest subtropical wilderness in America (covered in "The Everglades," starting on p.167).

Travel details

Buses

Fort Myers to: Fort Lauderdale (6 daily; 3hr); Miami (6 daily; 4hr 30min); Naples (4 daily; 1hr); Orlando (5 daily; 5hr 30min); Sarasota (6 daily; 2hr 15min); Tampa (7 daily; 4hr).

Sarasota to: Fort Lauderdale (4 daily; 5hr 30min); Miami (4 daily; 6hr 30min); Ft Myers (4 daily; 2hr 30min); Orlando (4 daily; 4hr 30min); Tampa (6 daily; 1hr 45min).

6

Tampa Bay and the Northwest

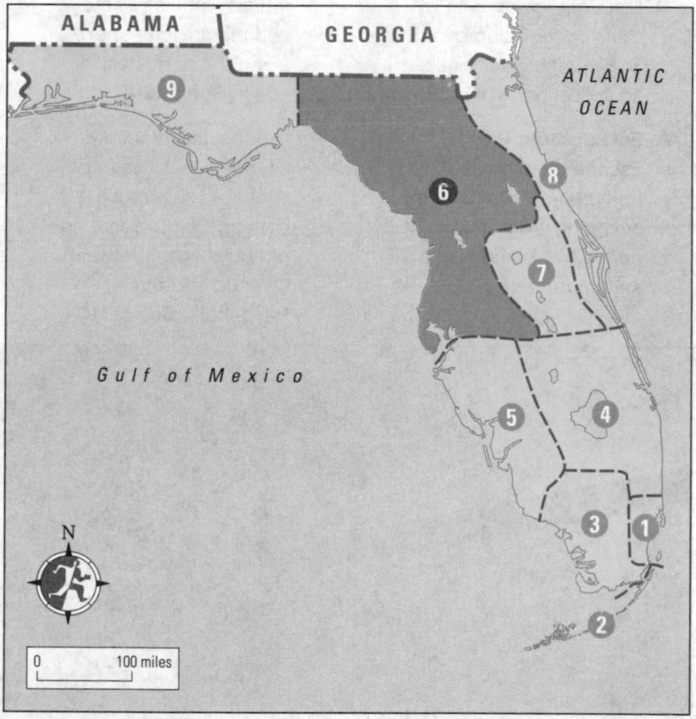

CHAPTER 6

Highlights

* **Ybor City** This neighborhood is ground zero for Tampa Bay's most exciting nightlife and dining; sample the Cuban music and flamenco dancing at the *Columbia*. See p.271
* **The Salvador Dalí Museum** View Dalí masterpieces such as the Discovery of America by Christopher Columbus at St Petersburg's unlikeliest art collection. See p.284
* **Fort de Soto Park** Escape the crowds at St Petersburg's beaches by spending a day or two on the five islands of this state park. See p.291
* **Swimming with manatees** Don't miss the chance to swim or scuba dive with these fascinating endangered creatures. See p.302
* **Cedar Key** Oyster harvesting and an intoxicatingly slow pace of life still hold sway over tourism at this remote and picturesque spot along the northwest coast. See p.304
* **Gainesville** This university town is an oasis of youthful exuberance – combined with some fine old buildings – between Orlando and the Panhandle. See p.313

△ Tampa Skyline Bridge

6

Tampa Bay and the Northwest

Served by an international airport and situated at the end of I-4 from central Florida, the diversely populated **TAMPA BAY** area, midway along Florida's three-hundred-mile west coast, is well placed to entice tourists away from nearby Orlando. Buzzing, youthful towns, a selection of good museums and galleries, a theme park to match those of Disney and Universal, and, crucially, miles of beaches with sunset views rivaled only by those of the Florida Keys have made Tampa Bay a firm, if somewhat unheralded, fixture on the Florida tourist circuit. Those wanting to get off the beaten track should head north along the coast of the largely beachless **NORTHWEST** or along I-75 toward the Panhandle and Georgia, where placid fishing hamlets, forests, horse ranches, and insular villages speak of a Florida largely ignored by the brochures – but one that's well worth exploring.

The largest city on Florida's west coast, 83 miles east of Orlando, **Tampa** itself probably won't detain you long, though it has more to offer than its power-dressers and corporate towers would suggest. Ybor City, for example, is Tampa's – and one of the state's – hippest and most culturally eclectic quarters.

Directly across the bay, **St Petersburg** once took pride in being the archetypal Florida retirement community. In the past ten years or so, it has been recast in a younger mold and is riding high on its acquisition of a major collection of works by the surrealist Salvador Dalí. For most visitors, though, the Tampa Bay area begins and ends with the **St Petersburg beaches** – miles of sea, sun, and sand fringed by uninspired vacation developments. The beaches are pure vacation territory but are also a good base for exploring the Greek-dominated community of **Tarpon Springs**, just to the north.

The coast **north of Tampa** (known as the **Big Bend** for the way it curves toward the Panhandle) is consumed by flat marshes, large chunks of which are wildlife refuges with little public access. No settlement here boasts a population of more than a few thousand, and the area receives little attention from visitors bolting through on their way to the beach territories further south. It is, however, one of Florida's hidden treasures. Scattered throughout is evidence of much busier and prosperous times, like the prehistoric sun-worshipping site at **Crystal River**. **Cedar Key**, which was a thriving port over a century ago, is now the perfect retreat. Locals here have preserved a laidback way of life and

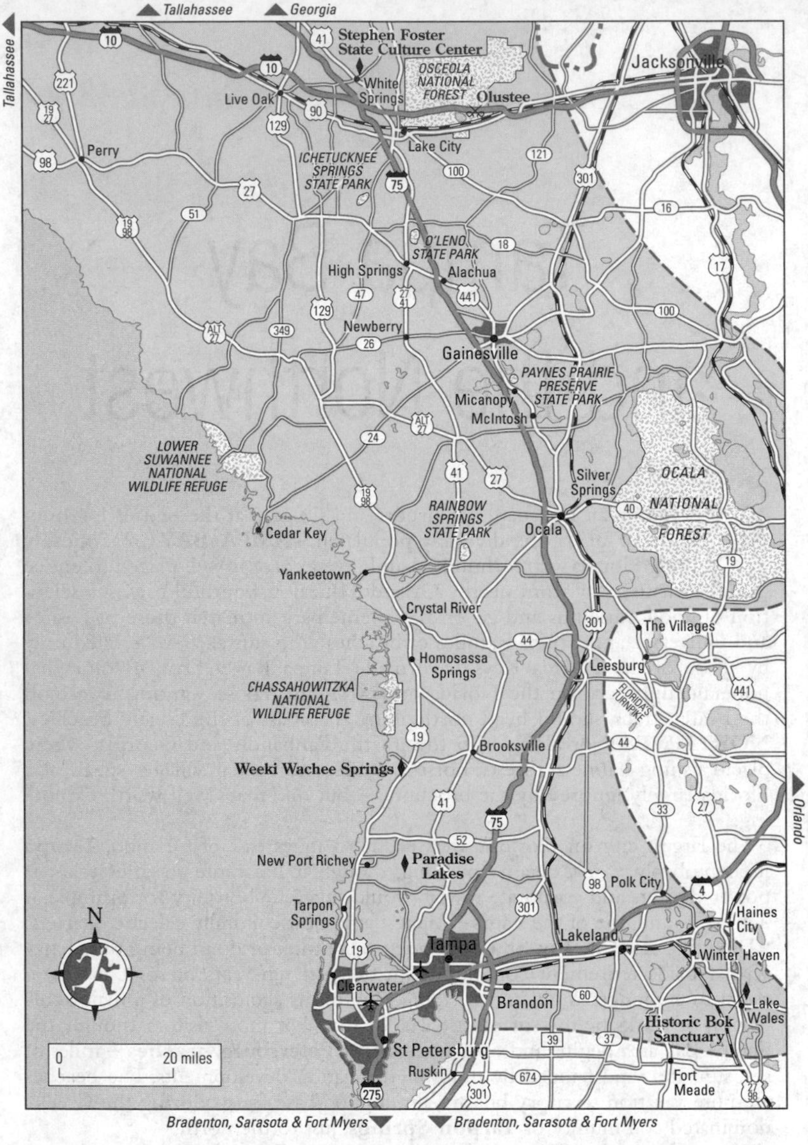

the community is a time-warped enclave of excellent restaurants and rewarding sights. The wildlife park at **Homossasa Springs**, fifteen miles south of Crystal River, offers the chance to view some of Florida's beautiful yet endangered animals. The alternative route north from Tampa is along I-75, passing through **north central Florida**, another area of unexpected discoveries, not least of which are the huge forest and numerous horse ranches around **Ocala** and the historic villages and natural springs near the lively university town of **Gainesville**.

Most people arrive in the Tampa Bay area via **I-4** from Orlando or **I-75**, which passes by Tampa on its way north from the southwest coast through north central Florida toward Georgia and beyond. From Tampa through the Big Bend, **US-19** is the only route, served by two Greyhound **buses** daily in each direction. Greyhound services between Tampa and Ocala and Gainesville are more regular (six to eight daily). The bigger centers have adequate **public transport**, though most towns in the Big Bend do not. Note that you will need your own transport to get to Cedar Key.

The Tampa Bay area

The geographic and economic nerve center of the region, the **Tampa Bay area**, consisting of Tampa and St Petersburg, has a population greater than Miami's. But people do live here for reasons other than work. The wide waters of the bay provide a scenic backdrop for Tampa itself, which is a stimulating city. And the barrier-island beaches along the coast let the locals swap metropolitan bustle for luscious sunsets and miles of glistening sands. With sun, sand, and sea, however, comes the inevitable assortment of chain restaurants and accommodations for the touring masses.

Tampa

TAMPA is a small city with an infectious, upbeat mood. You'll only need a day or two to explore it thoroughly, but you'll depart with a lasting impression of a city on the rise. Tampa has been one of the major beneficiaries of the flood of people and money into Florida, and the city's main vibe is that of a business hub. Yet despite cultural and artistic offerings envied by many larger communities and an international airport in its back yard, Tampa rarely gets more than a passing glance. Tourists speed through to Busch Gardens, a theme park on the city's outskirts, and the Gulf Coast beaches half an hour's drive west – missing out totally on one of Florida's most youthful and energetic urban communities.

Tampa began as a small settlement beside Fort Brooke (a US Army base built to keep an eye on local Seminole Indians during the 1820s), and remained tiny, isolated, and insignificant until the 1880s, when the railway arrived and the Hillsborough River – on which the city stands – was dredged to allow seagoing vessels to dock. It became a booming port and simultaneously acquired a major tobacco industry as thousands of Cubans moved north in 1886 from Key West to the new cigar factories of neighboring Ybor City. Although the Depression stalled the economic surge, the port remained one of the busiest in the country. And while the social problems that blight any decent-sized US city are evident, Tampa continues to emerge as a forward-thinking, financially secure community.

Despite the deals being struck in its towering office blocks, which are surprisingly thoughtfully designed, **downtown Tampa** is quiet and compact. An art museum, a sensational Spanish Revival film house, and the *Tampa Bay*

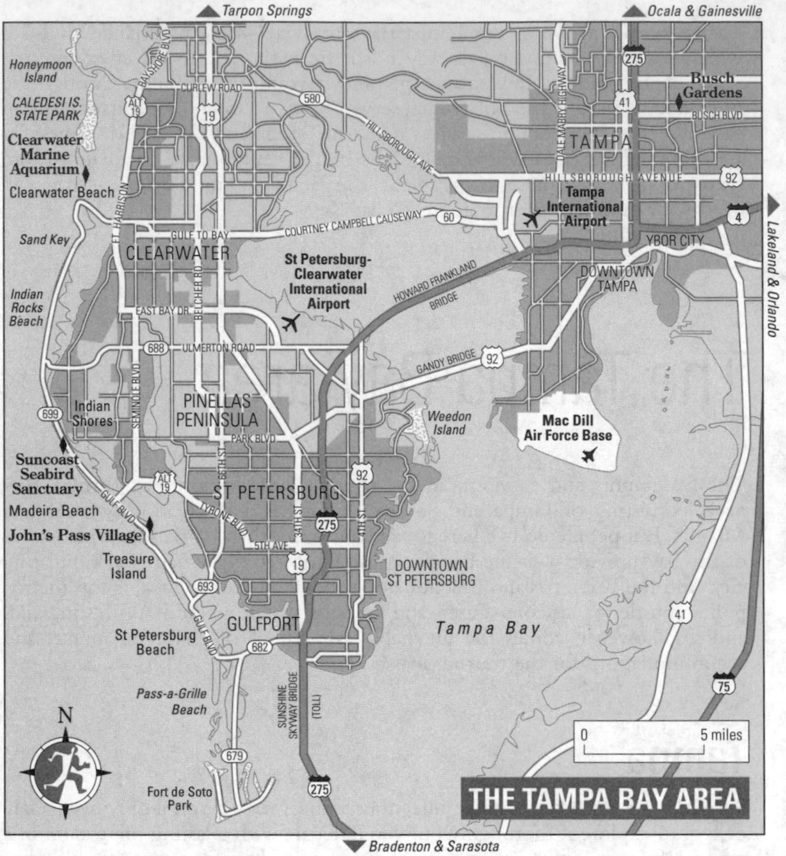

Hotel – one of the few reminders of earlier times – form the basis for a half-day ramble. What downtown may lack in atmosphere and history is made up for one mile northeast in the **Ybor City** quarter, whose Latin American character derives from migrant cigar workers. Ybor now boasts a plethora of historical markers to the heady days of the struggle for Cuban independence.

Venture a mile south of downtown into **Hyde Park**, and you will find the homes of Tampa's wealthiest early settlers. **Busch Gardens** and the **Museum of Science and Industry** are also worth a stop, or you could just amble into the wilds of the open country that appears remarkably quickly just north of the busy city.

Arrival, information, and getting around

The city's international **airport** (Ⓣ813/870-8700, Ⓦwww.tampaairport.com) is five miles northwest of downtown Tampa. Local bus #30 is the least costly connection ($1.25) to downtown Tampa. The **taxi** fare from the airport to downtown Tampa or a Busch Boulevard motel is $15–35; to St Petersburg or the St Petersburg beaches, $35–40. The main firms are United (Ⓣ813/253-

2424) and Yellow (Ⓣ813/253-0121). All the major **car rental** companies have desks at the airport.

If you arrive **by car** from St Petersburg, the main route into Tampa is I-275, which crosses Old Tampa Bay and ends up in the west of downtown. From east or central Florida, you'll come in on the I-4, which intersects with I-75. Be advised that from I-75, it's essential to exit at Hwy-60 (signposted Kennedy Blvd) for downtown Tampa. There are seven less convenient exits and if you miss this one and end up in north Tampa, the city's fiendish one-way system will keep you in your car for hours.

Long-distance public transport terminates in downtown Tampa: Greyhound **buses** at 610 E Polk St (Ⓣ813/229-2174 or 1-800/231-2222) and **trains** at 601 N Nebraska Ave (Ⓣ813/221-7600 or 1-800/872-7245).

Information

In downtown Tampa, collect vouchers, leaflets, and general information at the **Visitors Information Center**, 615 Channelside Drive, Suite 108A (Mon–Sat 9.30am–5.30pm, Sun 11am–5pm; Ⓣ813/226-0293 or 1-800/44-TAMPA, Ⓦwww.visittampabay.com). In Ybor City, visit the **Ybor City Visitor Information Center**, 1600 E Eighth Ave, Suite B104 (Mon–Sat 10am–6pm, Sun noon–6pm; Ⓣ813/241-8838, Ⓦwww.ybor.org). Opposite Busch Gardens, the **Tampa Bay Visitor Information Center**, 3601 E Busch Blvd (Mon–Sat 10am–5.30pm, Sun 10am–2pm; Ⓣ813/985-3601), has local and state-wide information.

Getting around

Although downtown Tampa and Ybor City are easily covered on foot, to travel between them – or to reach Busch Gardens or the Museum of Science and Industry – without a car, you'll need to use **local buses** (HARTline Ⓣ813/254-4278, Ⓦwww.hartline.org; one-way $1.25; day pass $3), whose routes fan out from Marion Street at the northern edge of downtown Tampa. **Useful bus numbers** are the #8 to Ybor City; #5 or #39 to Busch Gardens; #6 to the Museum of Science and Industry; and #30 to the airport. The free **Uptown/Downtown Connector** trolley service runs Monday to Friday 6am–6pm from the Marion Street terminal through downtown Tampa to Harbour Island and back again. Commuter (express) buses run **between Tampa and the coast**: #100X to St Petersburg (for schedule information for this bus only, call Ⓣ813/530-9911) and #200X to Clearwater. Alternatives are the numerous daily Greyhound buses or the twice- or thrice-daily Amtrak bus. Another way to travel between downtown Tampa and Ybor City is on the **TECO Line Streetcar System** (Ⓣ813/254-4278, Ⓦwww.tecolinestreetcar.org), a vintage replica streetcar that runs daily several times an hour, and until 2am on Fridays and Saturdays. The route takes you via Harbour Island and the Florida Aquarium (see p.269) and costs $1.25 one way.

Accommodation

Except for the area around Busch Gardens, Tampa is not generously supplied with low-cost **accommodation**. Within Tampa, the cheaper **motels** are all on East Busch Boulevard close to Busch Gardens. Other than the site at the Hillsborough River State Park (see "Around Tampa," p.274), the only local **campground** where tents are welcome is the *Camp Nebraska RV Park*, 10314 N Nebraska Ave/US-41 (Ⓣ813/971-3460 or 1-877/971-6990), which lies a mile and a half north of Busch Gardens.

Hotels, motels, and inns

Best Western All Suites 301 University Center Drive, behind Busch Gardens ⓣ813/971-8930. This resort serves as a reasonable base for seeing the city by car. It's so close to Busch Gardens that the parrots escape into their trees. Features a happy hour every afternoon and free breakfast each morning. ❹

Days Inn Busch Gardens Maingate 2901 E Busch Blvd ⓣ813/933-6471. The closest hotel to Busch Gardens, it has a 24-hour restaurant and is within walking distance of plenty of others. ❷

Don Vincente de Ybor Historic Inn 1915 Avenida Republica de Cuba ⓣ813/241-4545 or 1-866/206-4545, ⓦwww.donvincente.com. A luxurious B&B option in Ybor City featuring sixteen one-bedroom suites, a fine restaurant, and a cigar and martini bar that has live entertainment Thursday and Friday nights. ❺

Gram's Place 3109 North Ola Ave ⓣ813/221-0596, ⓦwww.grams-inn-tampa.com. Named for music legend Gram Parsons, this inn has a relaxed, laidback atmosphere and both private rooms, themed in different musical styles (complete with music to match the room), and youth-hostel-style accommodation in a simulated train carriage ($15–25 for a dorm bed). With a recording studio in the basement and the strains of jazz, blues, folk, country, and rock and roll everywhere, it's a music lovers' paradise. ❸

Hilton Garden 1700 E Ninth Ave ⓣ813/769-9267, ⓦwww.tampayborcity.gardeninn.com. Comfortable rooms, even if the decor is a little sterile for a place in the heart of Tampa's most historically rich neighborhood. ❺

Marriott Waterside 700 S Florida Ave ⓣ813/221-4900. Downtown Tampa's newest, largest, and most luxurious hotel, towering above the nearby Convention Center and Channelside entertainment complex. Top-notch facilities and stellar views of the bay. ❻

Radisson Riverwalk 200 N Ashley Drive ⓣ813/223-2222, ⓦwww.radisson.com/tampafl_riverwalk. In a very convenient downtown location and attractively situated on the banks of the Hillsborough River. Rooms are generously large, the waterfront ones having balconies overlooking the river. ❹

Downtown Tampa

Downtown Tampa's prosperity is most evident in its office towers, especially at **Lykes Gaslight Square**, where massive, mirrored structures jut into the sky. But aside from the riverside warehouses in various states of dilapidation around the northern end of pedestrian-friendly **Franklin Street** (once a pulsating main drag and still the best place to get your bearings), any hint of the city's past is left largely to text-bearing plaques that detail everything from the passage of sixteenth-century explorer Hernando De Soto to the site of Florida's first radio station. The single substantial relic of the past is the **Tampa Theatre**, 711 Franklin St (ⓣ813/274-8981, ⓦwww.tampatheatre.org), one of the few surviving "atmospheric theaters" erected by designer John Eberson during the Twenties. When silent movies enthralled the masses, Eberson's movie houses heightened the escapist mood: ceilings became star-filled skies, balconies were chiseled to resemble Moorish arches, gargoyles leered from stuccoed walls, and replica Greek and Roman statuary filled every nook and cranny. Having fallen on hard times with the arrival of TV, the Tampa Theatre is now enjoying a new lease on life as the home of the Tampa Theatre Film Society and boasts a full program of movies. Paying $8 for a ticket (see "Nightlife," p.278) is one way to gain access to the splendidly restored interior. Another is the "Balcony to Backstage" guided tours ($5), which are highly entertaining but are held only twice a month (call theater for dates and times). In addition to the theater's magnificent lighting system that cultivates the feel of an open auditorium at night, a Wurlitzer organ rises from the orchestra pit fifteen minutes before each screening to serenade the crowd.

Tampa Museum of Art

None of the contemporary buildings in downtown Tampa better reflects the city's striving for cultural recognition than the **Tampa Museum of Art**, on the banks of the Hillsborough River at 600 N Ashley Drive (Tues–Sat 10am–5pm, third Thurs of every month 10am–8pm, Sun 11am–5pm; $7; Ⓣ813/274-8130, Ⓦwww.tampamuseum.com). The highly regarded museum specializes in an incongruous mix of classical antiquities and twentieth-century American art. Selections from the permanent modern stock, which includes an outstanding collection of Greek pottery and paintings by Rockwell Kent and Abraham Walkowitz, are cleverly blended with loaned pieces from the cream of contemporary US painting, photography, and sculpture. A third gallery is devoted to major traveling exhibitions. The sculpture gallery, which houses a collection of not-so-thrilling contemporary pieces, affords lovely views of the *Tampa Bay Hotel* (see p.270) across the river.

Harbour Island and the Aquarium

Continuing south, you'll feel like an insignificant speck at the feet of the city's tallest structures. For a better view of them – and their surroundings – walk or take the free Uptown/Downtown Connector (see p.267) to **Harbour Island**, a posh residential district with some shops on a small island dredged from the Hillsborough Bay. If strapped for time, walk through the concrete walkway of the Nations Bank Plaza and take the elevator to the 31st floor – the view is an exquisite vista of the whole city.

The **Florida Aquarium**, 701 Channelside Drive (daily 9.30am–5pm; $15; parking $4; ⓣ813/273-4000, ⓦwww.flaquarium.org), houses lavish displays of Florida's fresh- and salt-water habitats, ranging from springs and swamps to beaches and coral reefs. The permanent residents include an impressive variety of exotic fish and native creatures such as otters, turtles, baby alligators, and countless species of bird. Certified scuba divers also have the opportunity to dive in the shark tank (reservations ⓣ813/367-4005).

Northeast from downtown Tampa

The only other attractions in downtown that might warrant a look are two churches. Built in 1898, **Sacred Heart Catholic Church**, 509 Florida Ave (ⓣ813/229-1595), has a gleaming facade of mottled marble and a rich interior illuminated by stained glass. **St Paul African Methodist Church**, just a few minutes' walk north at 1100 Marion St, cannot match Sacred Heart's grandeur, but its Victorian-style red-brick and vivid stained glass are worth a visit.

Far from the glamorous skyscrapers, the northeast section of the city has an unsafe reputation. If you're heading to Ybor City (see opposite) on foot, this rather desolate area is on the route, and though there isn't much reason to linger in this part of town, it's worth a detour to **Oaklawn Cemetery**, at the junction of Morgan and Harrison streets, just north of downtown, which was set aside to bury the town's dead ("whites and slaves alike") in 1850. Along with the bones of one Florida governor and two Supreme Court judges, the picturesque graveyard guards the remains of soldiers from the Second Seminole War, the Mexican War, the Billy Bowlegs Indian War, the Civil War, the Spanish American War, and both World Wars. Hidden away at the far end of the cemetery, in the shadow of the faceless Morgan Street Penitentiary, is the tomb of the **Ybor family** – whose name lives on in Tampa's most exotic quarter, Ybor City.

Across the river: the Tampa Bay Hotel

From the east bank of the Hillsborough River, you can't miss the silver minarets, cupolas, and domes of the main building of the University of Tampa – formerly the **Tampa Bay Hotel**. A fusion of Moorish, Turkish, and Spanish building styles and financed to the tune of $2 million by steamship and railway magnate **Henry B. Plant**, the structure is as bizarre a sight today as it was on its opening in 1891, when its 500 rooms looked out on a community of just 700 people. For a good look, walk across the river on Kennedy Boulevard and climb down the steps leading into the small patch of green that is Plant Park.

Plant had been buying up bankrupt railways since the Civil War and steadily inching his way into Florida to meet his steamships unloading at Tampa Harbor. Like Henry Flagler, whose tracks were forging a trail along Florida's east coast and whose upscale resorts in St Augustine (see "The Northeast," p.371) were the talk of US socialites, Plant was wealthy enough to realize his fantasy of creating the world's most luxurious hotel. While the hotel boosted the prestige of the town, Plant's intention of "turning this sandheap into the Champs Elysées, the Hillsborough into the Seine" was never accomplished, and the hotel stayed open for less than ten years. Neglect (the hotel was only used during the winter months and left to fester during the scorching summer), and Plant's death in 1899, hastened its transformation from the last word in comfort to a pile of musty, crumbling plaster. The city authorities bought the place in 1905 and halted the rot, before leasing the building to the fledgling University of Tampa 23 years later.

In a wing of the main building, the **Henry B. Plant Museum**, 401 W Kennedy Blvd (Tues–Sat 10am–4pm, Sun noon–4pm; $5; ⓣ813/254-1891, ⓦwww.plantmuseum.com), has several rooms, including an original suite containing what's left of the hotel's furnishings. This is a gorgeous clutter of Venetian mirrors, elaborate candelabras, ankle-deep rugs, Wedgwood crockery, and intricate teak cabinets – all the fruits of a half-million-dollar shopping expedition undertaken by Plant and his wife across Europe and Asia. Incredibly, when the hotel was closed up for five years, it was left unlocked and many of the antiques disappeared.

The hotel was Florida's first building to be installed with electricity, and low-wattage Edison carbon filters are used today to ensure the original, authentic gloom, which is perfect for taking in the richness of the Cuban mahogany doors. You can almost imagine guests calling room service for a grand piano (there were twelve). Note the reassembled *Rathskellar*, a gentleman's social room previously in the hotel basement (now a student snack bar), complete with a German wine cooler and billiard tables. The final room reveals Mrs Plant's affection for oversized ornamental swans.

A few strides from the museum, the former lobby is a popular rendezvous point for the university's three thousand students, who display their tans from the hotel's overstuffed leather chairs surrounded by antique French statuary. You can roam around much of the building at will and a self-guided tour brochure is available to help put the details of the building and its history into place. Make sure you see the evocative photographs of society life from the hotel's heyday in the long corridors. As for the furniture, though, there's precious little left – what human looters left behind, the termites finished off.

Hyde Park

If they don't ensconce themselves in bay-view condos, Tampa's yuppies snap up the old wooden homes of **Hyde Park**, a mile southwest of downtown Tampa just off Bayshore Boulevard. Attracted by the glamour of the *Tampa Bay Hotel*, well-heeled arrivals in the 1890s duplicated the architectural mold that defined the wealthier sections of the turn-of-the-century's American towns: a mish-mash of Mediterranean, Gothic, Tudor, and Colonial revival jobs, interspersed with Queen Anne cottages and prairie-style bungalows – rocking chairs on porches being the sole unifying feature. Such complete "blasts from the past" are rare in Tampa and, provided you're driving (they don't justify a slog around on foot), the old homes are easy to appreciate on a twenty-minute drive on and around Swann and Magnolia avenues and Hyde Park and South boulevards. Even Tampans who prefer modern living quarters descend on Hyde Park to lay waste to their wages in the fashionable stores of **Olde Hyde Park Village**, beside Snow Avenue, where several classy restaurants offer affordable refreshment (see "Eating," p.276). "Tow Away Zone" signs pepper Hyde Park, so if you want to browse or lunch here, go to the free parking garage right in the village at the corner of Bristol Avenue and South Rome Avenue.

Continuing south from Hyde Park, incidentally, brings you to the gates of **Mac Dill Air Force Base**. The nerve center of US operations during the 1991 Gulf War, this was where the Queen of England knighted General "Stormin' Norman" Schwarzkopf later the same year.

Ybor City

In 1886, as soon as Henry Plant's ships (see opposite) ensured a regular supply of Havana tobacco into Tampa, cigar magnate Don Vincente Martínez Ybor cleared a patch of scrubland three miles northeast of present-day downtown

Tampa and laid the foundations of **Ybor City**. Around 20,000 immigrants – mostly Cubans drawn from the strife-ridden Key West cigar industry, joined by a smattering of Spaniards and Italians – settled here, creating an enclave of Latin American life and producing the top-class hand-rolled cigars that made Tampa the "Cigar Capital of the World" for forty years. Mass-production, the popularity of cigarettes, and the Depression proved a fatal combination for skilled cigar makers. Ybor City lost its *joie de vivre* and, while the rest of Tampa expanded, its twenty tight-knit blocks of cobbled streets and red-brick buildings were engulfed by drab and dangerous low-rent neighborhoods.

Today, Ybor City is in the midst of a revival; it buzzes with tourists and at night the atmosphere reaches carnival proportions, especially at weekends. It is trendy, culturally diverse, and a terrific place to wander at will. Yet commercialism is taking hold fast. Shops still sell hand-rolled cigars, but, owing to rising rents, the little hole-in-the-wall cafés that once doled out freshly baked Cuban bread and fresh-brewed coffee have all but disappeared, replaced by a new breed of stylish but essentially generic café-bars and restaurants. There are still some sensational, authentic places to savor Cuban cooking, but they are being forced further and further off the main drag.

Ybor City Museum

Ybor City's Cuban roots are immediately apparent and explanatory background texts adorn many buildings. Soak up the atmosphere during the day, but don't expect the place to really get going until the evening. The **Ybor City Museum** (which is officially designated a state park), 1818 Ninth Ave (daily 9am–5pm; $2; ⓣ813/247-6323, ⓦwww.ybormuseum.org), offers just enough to help you grasp the main points of Ybor City's creation and its multi-ethnic make-up. Enormous wall photographs show cigar rollers at work: thousands sat in long rows at bench-tables making 25¢ per cigar and cheering or heckling the *lector* (or reader), who recited the news from Spanish-language newspapers. On the grounds is a cigar worker's cottage, which you can enter to get a taste of the simple domestic arrangements – more interesting than riveting. The museum also offers cigar-rolling demonstrations (Fri–Sun 10am–1pm) and historic walking tours (Sat 10.30am).

Ybor Square and the local brewery

The old Stemmenzy-Zago building, where cigar rolling actually took place, at 1901 Thirteenth St on the corner of Eighth Avenue, is now called **Ybor Square**. This cavernous structure – three stories supported by sturdy oak pillars – had been converted into a collection of tourist-aimed shops and restaurants, a depressingly commercialized market of fairy lights draped over T-shirt shops, and cafés without a local in sight. Perhaps such an enterprise was doomed to failure, and the current role of Ybor Square is as an office block essentially closed to the public.

Standing on the cigar factory's iron steps in 1893, the famed Cuban poet and independence fighter José Martí spoke to thousands of Ybor City's Cubans, calling for pledges of money, machetes, and manpower for the country's anti-Spanish, pro-independence struggles. It's estimated that expatriate Cuban cigar workers contributed ten percent of their earnings, most of which was spent on the illicit purchase and shipment of arms to rebels in Cuba. A stone marker at the foot of the steps records the event and, across the street, the **José Martí Park** remembers Martí with a statue.

Ybor City even has its own brewery whose beers – the most famous of which is Ybor Gold – can be found all over Florida. The **Ybor City Brewing**

△ Cigar exhibit, Yorba City State Museum

Company, 2205 N Twentieth St (Ⓣ813/242-9222), housed in what used to be a storage warehouse for the Hava–Tampa Cigar Company, runs guided tours (Mon–Fri 1pm; $3), where you can learn how the beer is brewed and give it an all-important taste test.

Ybor's social clubs

From the earliest days, each of Ybor City's ethnic communities ran its own **social clubs**, published newspapers, and even organized a medical insurance scheme that led to the building of two hospitals. The hospitals still function today, as do several of the social centers. Stepping inside one of the centers (opening hours vary wildly) reveals patriotic paraphernalia and sometimes, in the basement, men-only dens of dominoes and drinking (although visiting this part of the club might not be as easy as taking a peek at the decor upstairs). If you can, visit *Centro Español* (now the *Big City Tavern* restaurant – see "Eating," p.277) at 1600 E Eighth Ave; *The Cuban Club*, 2010 Avenida Republica de Cuba N; or *Centro Asturiano*, 1913 N Nebraska Ave, for a look at Ybor City life that most visitors miss. One Ybor City institution out-of-towners invariably do find is the *Columbia* restaurant, 2117 E Seventh Ave (see "Eating," p.277). Now filling a whole block, the *Columbia* opened in 1905 as a humble coffee stop for tobacco workers; inside, newspaper cuttings plaster the walls and recount the restaurant's lustrous past.

Around Tampa

The collar of suburbia around downtown Tampa offers few reasons to stop, though the city's least expensive motels cluster around the **Busch Gardens** theme park, which ranks among the state's top tourist attractions. While it's as enjoyable as any of its ilk, you might be inclined to skip the park and divide your attentions between the **Lowry Park Zoo,** the **Museum of Science and Industry,** and (provided you're driving, for it's unreachable by public transport) the 3000 pristine acres of the **Hillsborough River State Park**. On the way, don't be tempted by the Seminole Indian Village (5221 N Orient Rd), part of a Seminole reservation where a token collection of Native American arts and crafts is on sale to tourists, and high-stakes bingo is played.

Busch Gardens

Incredible as it may seem, most people are drawn to Tampa by a theme-park re-creation of colonial Africa in the grounds of a brewery, at 3000 E Busch Blvd (two miles east of I-275 or two miles west of I-75, exit 54, signposted Fowler Ave). In glossing over a period of imperial exploitation in the name of entertainment, **Busch Gardens** (daily 9.30am–6pm; longer hours in high season; $56, children $46; parking $7 a day; Ⓣ1-888/800-5447, Ⓦwww.buschgardenstampabay.com), which opened in 1959 as a brewery and was developed into a theme park six years later, brazenly reshapes world history just as much as its arch-rival, Walt Disney World.

Traversable on foot or by pseudo-steam train, the 300-acre park divides into several areas. You'll first enter **Morocco**, where Moroccan crafts are sold at un-Moroccan prices, snake-charmers and belly dancers weave through the crowds, and the Mystick Sheiks Marching Band blast their trumpets into the ears of passersby. Then comes the **Myombe Reserve**, where a collection of chimps and gorillas are kept in a tropical environment complete with waterfall. Follow the signs to **Nairobi** and you'll find small gatherings of elephants, giant tortoises, alligators, crocodiles, and monkeys in varying states of liveliness. Directly ahead in **Timbuktu**, animals are less in evidence than amusement rides: a small roller coaster and a children's fairground ride called "Sandstorm," neither of which comes near to matching the park's larger coasters. If the Ubanga-Banga bumper cars in the **Congo** don't hold lasting appeal, gird your loins for the swirling and very wet raft trip around the Congo River Rapids – which may induce you to cross Stanleyville Falls on a roller coaster, the best feature of neighboring **Stanleyville**. Whatever you do, don't miss the park's excellent **thrill rides**: Congo's devastating "Kumba," which, along with "Gwazi" (near the entrance) and "Montu" (tucked away in the park's eastern corner), are among the largest and fastest roller coasters in the southeastern US, with all the high-speed drops, twists, and turns to satisfy the most serious of adrenaline junkies.

The biggest single section of the gardens, the eighty-acre **Serengeti Plain**, roamed by giraffes, buffaloes, zebras, antelopes, black rhino, and elephants, is the closest the place gets to showing anything genuinely African, even if the exhibits are really no better than those at a good zoo; look down on the beasts from the Skyride cable car or get a closer view from the train. After all this, retire to the Hospitality House of the Anheuser-Busch Brewery, purveyors of Budweiser and owners of the park, where the beer is free but limited to two drinks (in a paper cup) per person.

Park practicalities

Despite the exotic names given to each section of the park, on the whole, the landscaping and design of Busch Gardens lack the imagination and attention to detail of the Orlando theme parks, and the overall impression is less enchanting. Predictably, **waiting times** can be long and, in the absence of an express line system akin to those at Disney and Universal, unavoidable. Ask a member of staff for actual waiting times, which are often considerably shorter than the gloomy predictions of the clocks at the entrance (at times up to 90min). Bear in mind that you'll have to store your bags in a **locker** (50¢) while riding the roller coasters – a situation made more annoying by the fact that the most convenient lockers (at the entrance) cost $1.

The Lowry Park Zoo

Five and a half miles north of downtown Tampa, two miles southwest of Busch Gardens and just west of I-275, the **Lowry Park Zoo**, 1101 W Sligh Ave (daily 9.30am–5pm; $9.50; ⓣ813/935-8552, ⓦwww.lowryparkzoo.com), established in the late 1930s, was Tampa's first zoo. Today it is home to about 1500 animals, kept on some forty acres of natural habitats; many of them are rare and endangered. There are five major exhibits: the Florida Manatee and Aquatic Center, Native Florida Wildlife Center, Asian Domain, Primate World, and Wallaroo Station (the latter an Australian-themed kids' zoo), with an eleven-acre African exhibit to be added in 2004. All are supported by regular educational events – including courses given at the "Zoo School" – and shows held in outdoor amphitheaters, which makes this a good place to learn about Florida's wildlife, especially if most of your trip centers on the beaches and theme parks.

The Museum of Science and Industry

Two miles northeast of Busch Gardens, at 4801 E Fowler Ave, the **Museum of Science and Industry** (daily 9am, closing times seasonal; $14.95; ⓣ813/987-6100, ⓦwww.mosi.org) will entertain adults as much as it does kids. Intended to reveal the mysteries of the scientific world, the hands-on displays and machines will easily fill half a day. To get the most from your visit, study the program schedule carefully upon arrival: the main – and most interesting – features run at fixed times throughout the day. Plan your time around the Challenger Learning Center, an engrossing simulated spacecraft and mission control. The Gulf Coast Hurricane is a convincing demonstration that allows begoggled participants to feel the force of the strongest winds known. High Wire Bicycle gives you the somewhat daunting opportunity to peddle a bike 98 feet along a one-inch steel cable suspended thirty feet above the ground. After this excitement, relax in the Saunders Planetarium and gaze at the stars or catch a movie in Florida's first IMAX (or "maximum image") film theater in a dome, which shows films of outstanding visual and audio quality. The entrance fee includes admission to a single IMAX screening.

Hillsborough River State Park

Twelve miles north of Tampa on US-301, shaded by live oaks, magnolias, and sable palms, the **Hillsborough River State Park** (daily 8am–sunset; cars $3.25, pedestrians and cyclists $1; ⓣ813/987-6771) holds one of the state's rare instances of rapids – outside of a theme park. Here, the Hillsborough River tumbles over limestone outcrops before pursuing a more typical meandering course. Rambling the sizeable park's walking trails and canoeing the gentler sections of the river could fill a day nicely (and the park makes an enjoyable place for **camping**; $13 without electricity), but on weekends you should devote part of the afternoon to the **Fort Foster Historic Site**, a reconstructed 1836 Seminole War fort that can only be seen on one of the **guided tours** (Sat 2pm & Sun 11am). Stemming from the US attempts to drive Florida's Seminole Indians out to reservations in the Midwest and make the state fit for the white man, the Seminole Wars raged throughout the nineteenth century and didn't officially end until 1937 (see Contexts, p.465–466). Once a month period-attired enthusiasts occupy the fort and recount historical details, including the fact that more soldiers died from tropical diseases than in battle. Not surprisingly, the Seminoles give a somewhat different account of the conflict, and both sides make for interesting listening. For an extra $2 you can also swim in the pool (summer Mon–Fri 10am–5pm, Sat & Sun 9am–6pm).

Eating

Eating in Tampa means good quality and lots of choice – except in **downtown**, where street stands dispensing snacks to lunching office workers are the culinary norm. Some of the best and most interesting meals are served in Ybor City, whose Latin heritage and hip reputation have made it a restaurant haven. Another good place to go is Hyde Park, where a diverse range of restaurants can be found on South Howard Avenue (also known as SoHo). Bear in mind that the majority of Tampa's downtown restaurants are only open for lunch.

Canoeing on the Hillsborough River

To spend two hours or a whole day gliding past the alligators, turtles, wading birds, and other creatures that call the Hillsborough River home, contact **Canoe Escape**, 9335 E Fowler Ave (ⓣ813/986-2067, ⓦwww.canoeescape.com), who have devised a series of novice-friendly routes along the tea-colored river. Prices range from $18 to $38 depending on length of trip and the type of kayak, and you should make a reservation at least 24 hours in advance.

Downtown

C'Est La Vie 200 E Madison St ⓣ813/221-4748. Serving coffee and croissants in the morning and quiche and baguette sandwiches at lunch, this good French bakery is, unusually for a downtown eatery, open Sundays.

La Teresita Cafeteria 3246 W Columbus Drive, north of downtown near the Raymond James Stadium ⓣ813/879-4909. Cuban sandwiches go for under $3, and dishes such as *patas de cerdo* (pigs' feet) and *rabo encendido* (oxtail) are served with superb Cuban coffee. Locals chat and often break into fits of singing and guitar playing at the bar.

Manhattan Bagel Bar 602 Franklin St ⓣ813/307-0555. Bagels with various tasty fillings provide an alternative to the sandwich- and salad-dominated delis in the downtown business district.

Ole Style Deli 110 E Madison St ⓣ813/223-4282. A worthy address where office workers devour $4 sandwiches. Service can be very slow, but breakfasts and salads are good.

Hyde Park

Bella's Italian Café 1413 S Howard Ave ⓣ813/254-3355. Reliable pasta dishes preceded by tasty starters such as lobster bisque and polished off with a slice of rich molten chocolate cake at this long-standing SoHo restaurant.

Bern's Steak House 1208 S Howard Ave ⓣ813/251-2421. The most memorable charcoal-broiled steaks you'll ever have, starting from around $20. The restaurant also boasts the largest working wine cellar in the world.

Blackhawk Coffee Café 1628 W Snow Circle ⓣ813/258-1600. A favorite haunt of locals, this café offers great coffee and is open late every night (Sun–Thurs until 11pm, Fri & Sat until midnight).

Café DeSoto 504 E Kennedy Blvd ⓣ813/229-2566. The Cuban lunch specials, like roast chicken, black beans, rice, and Cuban bread – all for $4.25 – are a steal.

Ybor City

Bernini 1702 Seventh Ave ⓣ813/248-0099. An Italian joint serving up wood-fired pizza and pasta in the lovely old Bank of Ybor City (note the giant-insect door handles).

Big City Tavern 1600 E Eighth Ave ⓣ813/247-3000. Housed in the former *Centro Español* social club (see p.274), this atmospheric restaurant caters to Tampa's chic set, serving American cuisine spiced with plenty of ginger and other Asian influences amid bare brick walls and a tin ceiling.

Cephas 1701 E Fourth Ave ⓣ813/247-9022. A funky Jamaican restaurant run from the political-poster-decorated front room of Cephas Gilbert, who arrived in Ybor via Birmingham, England, and serves jerk chicken, curry goat chicken, and fish while regaling guests with his vivid life story.

Columbia 2117 E Seventh Ave ⓣ813/248-4961. Serving refined yet moderately priced Spanish and Cuban food, this Tampa institution – the city's oldest restaurant – has become a fixture on the tourist circuit. Its eleven rooms hold nearly 2000 people, who are entertained six nights a week by flamenco dancers. Reservations recommended.

Green Iguana 1708 E Seventh Ave ⓣ813/248-9555. Perhaps better known for its nightlife (see p.278), the *Green Iguana* is a good spot for a filling lunch or a pre-party dinner of burgers, sandwiches, and particularly tasty wraps (all served with excellent fries).

Joffrey's Coffee House 1616 Seventh Ave ⓣ813/248-5282. The delectable aromas of fruit, coffee, and chocolate are always thick in the air at this reasonably priced coffee house.

Nightlife

Tampa's **nightlife scene** may have the reputation of being strong on drinking and live rock music, but there are alternatives for those seeking more from a night out. For details on upcoming arts and cultural events, phone the Artsline at ⓣ813/229-ARTS; to purchase tickets, call Ticketmaster at ⓣ813/287-8844. For a list of all things nightlife-related, pick up a copy of the free *Weekly Planet* (every Thurs), or try their website ⓦwww.weeklyplanet.com, or the Thursday edition of the *Tampa Tribune*. Although **Ybor City** has long been the focus of **Tampa's** nightlife possibilities, the opening of two entertainment complexes – **Channelside**, in the downtown area next to the Florida Aquarium (ⓣ813/223-4250), and the **International Plaza and Bay Street**, near the airport at the junction of West Shore and Boy Scout boulevards (ⓣ813/342-3790, ⓦwww.shopinternationalplaza.com) – has proved popular with locals, and the clientele is generally slightly older than the crowds of teenagers that flock to Ybor City.

Performing arts and film

Tampa's cultural profile is improved by regular high-quality shows at the **Tampa Bay Performing Arts Center**, 1010 N W.C. MacInnes Place (box office open Mon–Sat 8am–6pm, Sun noon–6pm and 90min prior to performances; ⓣ813/229-7827, ⓦwww.tbpac.org), a state-of-the-art performance venue that features top US and international names. The **Gorilla Theatre**, 4419 N Hubert Ave (tickets $15–25; ⓣ813/879-2914, ⓦwww.gorilla-theatre.com), is a more intimate, but just as professional, theater with a program including contemporary comedies and dramas, as well as the classics. For a full list of **films** playing around the city, check the Thursday edition of the *Tampa Tribune*. Foreign-language, classic, or cult films crop up only at the **Tampa Theatre**, 711 Franklin St (see "Downtown Tampa," p.268); pick up a schedule from the building itself or call ⓣ813/274-8981; tickets are $8. The multi-screen cinema at Channelside shows mainstream movies and IMAX films.

Drinking, live music, and nightclubs

Ybor City is brimming with clubs and music bars and many of the area's restaurants also offer entertainment, such as the famous *Columbia* (see "Eating," p.277), which has live music at weekends in its *Cigar Bar*, plus live Spanish flamenco dance performances in the main restaurant. One of the busiest places for a **drink** or five is the *Green Iguana*, 1708 E Seventh Ave (ⓣ813/248-9555), which also has rock bands playing daily and DJs to keep the young crowd very much in the party mood. Another good drinking spot in Ybor is the *Irish Pub*, 1721 E Seventh Ave (ⓣ813/248-2099). Outside of Ybor, one of the best-looking crowds congregates at the *Blue Martini* at the International Plaza and Bay Street (ⓣ813/873-2583). Tampa's most dependable **live music** club is the blues- and reggae-dominated *Skipper's Smokehouse*, 910 Skipper Rd (ⓣ813/971-0666). For dancing, it's best to head back to Ybor City for the best selection of **nightclubs**, including the techno-orientated *Amphitheater*, 1609 E Seventh Ave (ⓣ813/248-2331, ⓦwww.amphitheaterybor.com); the Gothic-inspired *Castle*, 2004 Sixteenth St, at Ninth Ave (ⓣ813/247-7547, ⓦwww.castle-ybor.com); or, just to the west of Ybor City, *Rain Lounge*, 302 S Nebraska Ave (ⓣ813/229-7246, ⓦwww.rainlounge.com), which has a sushi and sake bar and an outdoor patio.

Comedy clubs

Tampa has two notable **comedy clubs**. *Side Splitters*, 12938 N Dale Mabry Hwy (ⓣ813/960-1197, ⓦwww.sidesplitterscomedy.com), is one of the best in the area and has a line-up featuring national and regional comedians. The other, also with well-known performers, is the *Improv Comedy Theater*, 1600 E Eighth Ave (ⓣ813/864-4000, ⓦwww.tampaimprov.com), right in the heart of Ybor City. Cover charges range from $8 to $16 at both venues.

Gay and lesbian Tampa

With the constant addition of more bars, clubs, and resource centers, **gay and lesbian** life in Tampa is improving all the time, and it's a very gay-friendly city. For plenty of information on Tampa's gay life, visit ⓦwww.gaytampa.com; a good bookstore to try is Tomes & Treasures, just west of Hyde Park at 408 S Howard Ave (ⓣ813/251-9368). Every October, Tampa hosts the International Gay and Lesbian Film Festival; check ⓦwww.pridefilmfest.com for up-to-date information.

The clothing-optional option

Somewhat unsurprisingly given its plentiful sunshine and agreeable year-round temperatures, the Tampa Bay area has gained a reputation as the site of clothing-optional resorts. **Paradise Lakes**, 17 miles north of Tampa in the town of Land O' Lakes (ⓣ813/949-9327 or 1-866/SWIM-NUDE, ⓦwww.paradiselakes.com), is the largest nudist resort in North America, and definitely worth a visit – even for just a day – for those interested in shedding their clothes. Once inside the confines of the 81-acre resort, where accommodation ranges from poolside hotel rooms to two-bedroom condos ($75–175 per night), you're free to be naked anywhere and at any time. Nudity is virtually uniform around the two pools; less common in the evenings at the restaurant and disco. Special events such as murder mystery weekends, nude fashion shows, and a massive Halloween party are organized by the dynamic staff, when, in most cases, the clothes go on. Holiday weekends at *Paradise Lakes* are extremely busy, so book well in advance. A day pass entitling you to use all of the resort's facilities costs $27.

Gay and lesbian bars and clubs

The clean, dimly lit *Baxters*, 1519 S Dale Mabry Hwy (ⓣ813/258-8830), is currently enjoying its third reincarnation, and has pool tables and dancers on Friday nights. Other pulsating gay clubs include *2606*, 2606 N Armenia Ave (ⓣ813/875-6993, ⓦwww.2606.com), a very leather club; *Metropolis*, 3447 W Kennedy Blvd (ⓣ813/871-2410, ⓦwww.metrotampa.com), open seven days a week (with strippers on four of them) and no cover charge; and *The Cherokee Club*, 1320 E Ninth Ave (ⓣ813/247-9966), which is geared primarily to lesbians.

Listings

Amtrak ⓣ813/221-7600 or 1-800/872-7245.
Car rental Avis, at Tampa Airport ⓣ813/396-3500; Budget ⓣ1-800/527-0700; Dollar ⓣ1-800/800-4000.
Dentists For referral: ⓣ1-800/428-8771.
Directory enquiries (local only) ⓣ411.
Doctor For referral: ⓣ1-800/822-3627.
Hospital Tampa General on Davis Island ⓣ813/844-7000. Emergency room ⓣ813/844-7100.
Left luggage At the Greyhound station, 610 Polk St; the train station, 601 Nebraska Ave. There is no left luggage at the airport.
Pharmacy Eckerd Drugs, 611 S Howard Ave (ⓣ813/259-9911), is open 24hr.
Police Emergencies ⓣ911.
Post Office 5201 W Spruce St (airport) or 925 N Florida Ave (downtown). In Ybor City, at 1900 E Twelfth Ave.
Sports The city's professional football team and winners of the 2003 Superbowl, the Tampa Bay Buccaneers (ⓦwww.buccaneers.com), play at Raymond James Stadium, 4201 N Dale Mabry Hwy (box office and information ⓣ813/870-2700). The local baseball team, the Tampa Bay Devil Rays (ⓦwww.devilrays.com), actually play in St Petersburg; see p.282. Tampa's hockey team, the Tampa Bay Lightning (ⓣ813/229-8800, ⓦwww.tampabaylightning.com), play at the St Pete Forum.
Travelers Aid ⓣ813/264-9949.
Weather information ⓣ813/645-2323.

St Petersburg

Situated on the eastern edge of the Pinellas Peninsula, **ST PETERSBURG** (named by a homesick Russian) may be physically close to Tampa, but location is about the only thing the cities share. St Petersburg holds the world record for the number of consecutive days of sunshine – 768 in total, set in 1967–69 – and enjoys on average 361 days of sunshine a year. It should come as no sur-

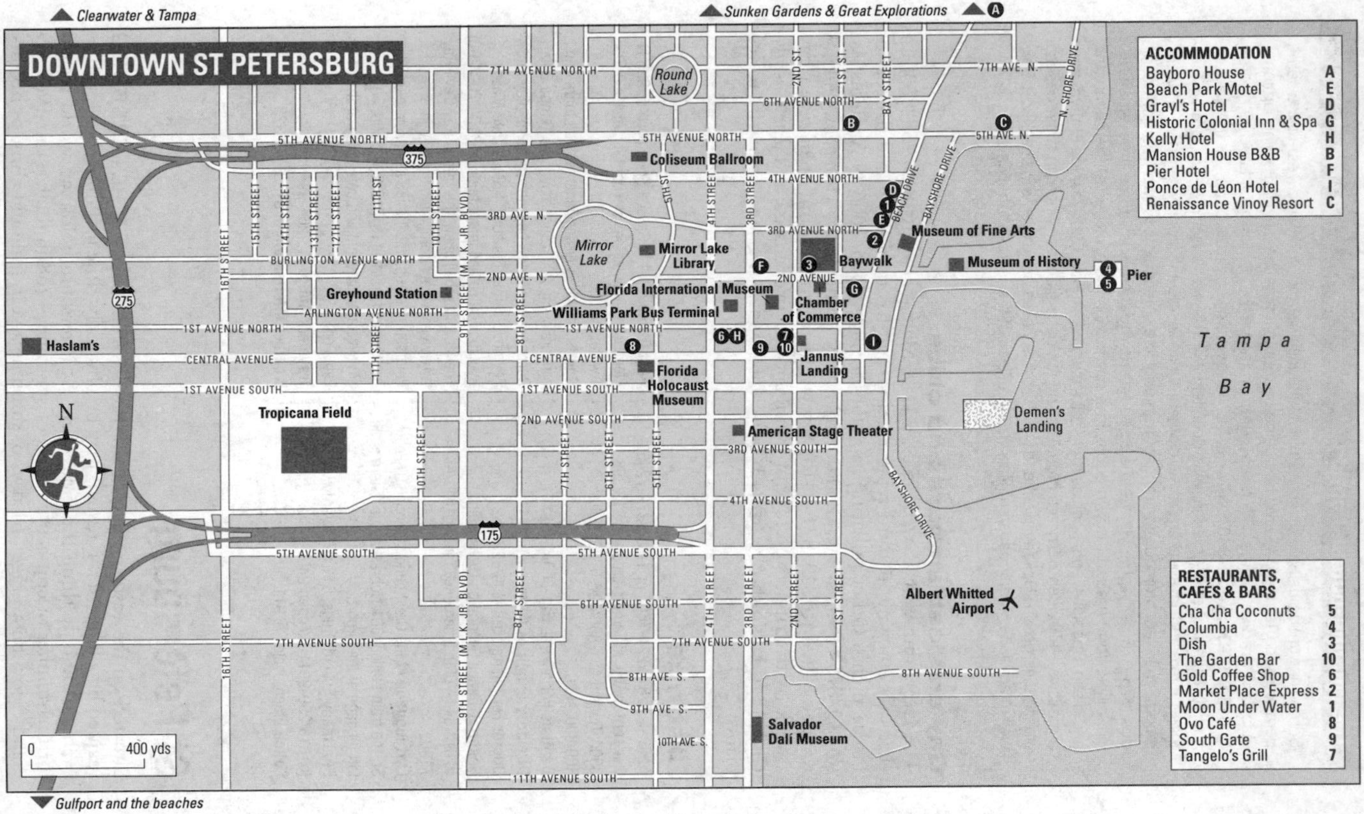
Clearwater & Tampa
Sunken Gardens & Great Explorations
A
DOWNTOWN ST PETERSBURG
ACCOMMODATION
Bayboro House A
Beach Park Motel E
Grayl's Hotel D
Historic Colonial Inn & Spa G
Kelly Hotel H
Mansion House B&B B
Pier Hotel F
Ponce de Léon Hotel I
Renaissance Vinoy Resort C
RESTAURANTS, CAFÉS & BARS
Cha Cha Coconuts 5
Columbia 4
Dish 3
The Garden Bar 10
Gold Coffee Shop 6
Market Place Express 2
Moon Under Water 1
Ovo Café 8
South Gate 9
Tangelo's Grill 7
Coliseum Ballroom
Round Lake
Mirror Lake
Mirror Lake Library
Florida International Museum
Williams Park Bus Terminal
Greyhound Station
Haslam's
Tropicana Field
Florida Holocaust Museum
American Stage Theater
Baywalk
Chamber of Commerce
Jannus Landing
Museum of Fine Arts
Museum of History
Pier
Demen's Landing
Albert Whitted Airport
Salvador Dalí Museum
Tampa Bay
7TH AVENUE NORTH
7TH AVE. N.
6TH AVENUE NORTH
5TH AVENUE NORTH
5TH AVE. N.
4TH AVENUE NORTH
3RD AVE. N.
3RD AVENUE NORTH
BURLINGTON AVENUE NORTH
2ND AVE. N.
2ND AVENUE
ARLINGTON AVENUE NORTH
1ST AVENUE NORTH
CENTRAL AVENUE
1ST AVENUE SOUTH
2ND AVENUE SOUTH
3RD AVENUE SOUTH
4TH AVENUE SOUTH
5TH AVENUE SOUTH
6TH AVENUE SOUTH
7TH AVENUE SOUTH
8TH AVE. S.
8TH AVENUE SOUTH
9TH AVE. S.
10TH AVE. S.
11TH AVENUE SOUTH
16TH STREET
15TH STREET
14TH STREET
13TH STREET
12TH STREET
11TH ST.
11TH STREET
10TH STREET
9TH STREET (M.L.K. JR. BLVD)
8TH STREET
7TH STREET
6TH STREET
5TH STREET
5TH ST
4TH STREET
3RD STREET
2ND ST.
2ND STREET
1ST ST.
1ST STREET
BAY STREET
BEACH DRIVE
BAYSHORE DRIVE
N. SHORE DRIVE
375
275
175
N
0
400 yds
Gulfport and the beaches

prise that this city wasted no time in attracting the recuperating and the retired to its climate. At one point, the city put 5000 green benches on its streets to take the weight off elderly backsides, and by the early 1980s, few people under 50 lived in the town. Although it remains a haven for the retired, St Petersburg has worked hard to attract young blood. In addition to the rejuvenated pier, which now offers something for every age, its diverse selection of museums and plethora of art galleries have contributed to its emergence as one of Florida's richest cultural cities. The mixture of old and new architecture and the landscaped parks around the seafront make this city a good option if you are looking for a break from the beaches nine miles west on the Gulf Coast (see "The St Petersburg beaches," p.288).

Arrival, information, and getting around

St Petersburg-Clearwater International Airport (ⓣ727/453-7800, ⓦwww.fly2pie.com) is served by several major carriers as well as charters. If you are arriving at Tampa airport (see p.266) and need to get to St Petersburg or the beaches, Super Shuttle (ⓣ727/572-1111 or 1-800/282-6817, ⓦwww.supershuttle.com) can get you there for $17 per person, or $34 for a round-trip ticket. The main route **by car** into St Petersburg is I-275 – and don't get off before the "Downtown St Petersburg" exit or you'll face a barrage of traffic lights. The Greyhound **bus** station is centrally located at 180 Ninth St N (ⓣ727/898-1496 or 1-800/231-2222). A day-trip to Tampa is difficult without a car; there are no trains between Tampa and St Petersburg, just a twice- or thrice-daily Amtrak bus link (ⓣ727/221-7600 or 1-800/872-7245), which drops you at the Pinellas Square Mall at 7200 US-19 N. The only **bus** service to Tampa is the 100X commuter service that runs between the out-of-town Gateway Mall, on Ninth Street and 77th Avenue, and downtown Tampa and is both inconvenient to reach and infrequent during the day. Most bus services arrive at and depart from the Williams Park terminal, at the junction of First Avenue N and Third Street N, where an information booth (Mon–Sat 7am–5.45pm, Sun 8–11.30am & 12.30–4pm) gives route details. Most bus journeys cost $1.25 (except the 100X, which is $1.50). The best option if you're planning to take several buses in one day is to purchase a **Go Card pass**, which allows unlimited travel for a day. It costs $3 and can be purchased on board. You can reach the St Petersburg beaches on PSTA local buses (ⓣ727/530-9911, ⓦwww.psta.net), though these are not always direct. There is also a **trolley** (#3) to Treasure Island beach that is probably your best option (for more on transportation, see the "Buses between St Petersburg and the beaches" box on p.289). The **Looper** is a pink trolley bus that runs every 30 minutes (Mon–Fri 10am–5pm, Sat & Sun 11am–5pm), connecting all the museums and attractions. It costs $1 a ride and there are pink Looper stops all around the downtown area. The driver gives a guided tour to boot.

Gather the usual tourist **information** and discount coupons from the **Chamber of Commerce**, 100 Second Ave N (Mon–Fri 8am–5pm, Sat 10am–4pm, Sun noon–4pm; ⓣ727/821-4715, ⓦwww.stpete.com), and look out for the "Weekend" section of the *St Petersburg Times* for entertainment and nightlife listings, also available on their website (ⓦwww.stpetetimes.com). The first floor of the pier (see p.283) also has a well-stocked tourist counter.

Accommodation

Sleeping in St Petersburg can be less costly than at the beaches. **Motels** are plentiful and can be easy on the pocket – between $40 and $80 year-round depending on location. The *Kelly Hotel* in the historic *Bay Park Arms* building at 326 First Ave N (ⓣ727/822-4141) has dormitory-style accommodation ($20 for a place in a four-bed dorm), as well as private rooms ($25).

Bayboro House 1719 Beach Drive ⓣ727/823-4955, ⓦwww.bayborohousebandb.com. Victorian mansion just south of town on the shores of Tampa Bay, with plenty of verandas from which to enjoy the views, plus a small beach, pool, and hot tub. ❺

Beach Park Motel 300 Beach Drive NE ⓣ727/898-6325 or 1-800/657-7687. A good budget option, especially in low season when room specials are available, with an attractive waterfront location to boot. ❸

Grayl's Hotel 340 Beach Drive NE ⓣ727/896-1080 or 1-888/508-4448, ⓦwww.graylshotel.com. Check out the excellent views of St Petersburg and the coast from the rooftop deck at this eighteen-room boutique hotel in a distinctive white Spanish mission-style building. ❹

Historic Colonial Inn & Spa 126 Second Ave NE ⓣ727/896-6400, ⓦwww.colonialinnandspa.com. Vintage chic rooms with high ceilings in a very centrally located 1925 building. Hotel guests receive a discount on massages, facials, manicures, and such offered at the first-floor spa. ❹

Mansion House 105 Fifth Ave ⓣ727/821-9391 or 1-800/274-7520, ⓦwww.mansionbandb.com. Antique and traditional furnishings, pine floors, and four-poster beds, all in a charming house just north of the pier. ❺

Pier Hotel 253 Second Ave N ⓣ727/822-7500, ⓦwww.thepierhotel.com. Pricey yet bright and tastefully decorated rooms at an upscale hotel that offers free evening cocktails to the strains of live piano music. ❻

Ponce de León Hotel 95 Central Ave ⓣ727/550-9300, ⓦwww.poncedeleonhotel.com. The hotel's restaurant and piano bar have more class than the ordinary rooms – one of which was once occupied by the late President Nixon. Discounts available if you book online. ❸

Renaissance Vinoy Resort 501 Fifth Ave NE ⓣ727/894-1000 or 1-800/468-3571, ⓦwww.renaissancehotels.com/tpasr. If you want to stay over in style, you have to experience this pink hotel opened in 1925 as a haven for the rich and famous. Now beautifully restored, it offers two swimming pools, twelve tennis courts, a golf course, an excellent gym and health spa, grandiose ballrooms, and gourmet restaurants. Check out the special packages combining rooms with golf, tennis, and spa treatments. ❼

The Town

However you reach downtown St Petersburg, the first thing you'll see is **Tropicana Field** on the western edge of town at 1 Stadium Drive. Formerly the Thunderdome, this huge building, shaped like a half-collapsed soufflé, opened in the spring of 1998 as home to the local major league baseball team, the **Tampa Bay Devil Rays** (ⓦwww.devilrays.com). To reserve tickets for a game (the season lasts from April to October) call ⓣ727/898-RAYS or 813/282-RAYS.

Once in downtown, be sure to walk along **Fourth Avenue**, passing the grandstands of the **Shuffleboard Club**, no. 536 N, the original home of this popular game. Directly across Fourth Avenue N is the Mediterranean Revival facade of the **Coliseum Ballroom**, built in 1924 and still throbbing to big-band sounds (see "Nightlife," p.286). If art galleries are more your style, try *Take a Walk on the Art Side* on the second Saturday of every month, a walk created by the St Petersburg Downtown Arts Association that incorporates 24 art galleries in the downtown area. Pick up a free leaflet at any of the downtown galleries, many of them on Central Avenue, and set aside a day for the entire tour.

St Petersburg museum pass

A good option for those intending to visit all of St Petersburg's main museums is to purchase an **Arts Pass** for $30, which gets you in to The Salvador Dalí Museum, the Museum of Fine Arts, the Florida International Museum, the Museum of History, the Florida Holocaust Museum, and Great Explorations. Buy the pass at any of the participating museums.

If you want a swim, try the excellent **North Shore Pool**, 901 N Shore Drive NE (Mon–Fri 9am–4pm, Sat 10am–4pm, and Sun 1–4pm; $2; ⓣ727/893-7727); in addition to the large pool, there is a sun terrace near the waterfront where you can soak up St Petersburg's abundant sunshine. Though a considerable trek west along Central Avenue, **Haslam's**, 2025 Central Ave (Mon–Sat 10am–6.30pm; ⓣ727/822-8616, ⓦwww.haslams.com), Florida's largest bookstore, will keep browsers occupied for hours. Opened in the Depression to provide avid readers with used magazines and books at bargain prices, the store stocks over 300,000 new and used books on all topics. If it's virtual information you need, your best option for Internet access is the **Mirror Lake Library**, 280 Fifth St N (Mon–Fri 9am–6pm, Sat 9am–5pm; ⓣ727/893-7268, ⓦwww.st-petersburg-library.org), which offers free use of online computers.

The pier and around

The focal point of downtown St Petersburg is its quarter-mile-long **pier** (open Mon–Thurs 10am–9pm, Fri & Sat 10am–10pm, and Sun 11am–7pm, ⓦwww.stpete-pier.com), which juts from the end of Second Avenue N. There is a shuttle tram that runs between the parking lots and the end of the pier. Arts and crafts exhibitions often line the pier and you'll find stacks of tourist information at the **Chamber of Commerce** desk (Mon–Sat 10am–8pm, Sun noon–6pm; ⓣ727/821-6164), which is near the entrance. The five-story, inverted-pyramid-like building is packed with restaurants, shops, fast-food counters, and an aquarium. Outside at the bait house, you can buy fish to feed the many pelicans that congregate at the end of the pier.

Opposite the entrance to the pier is the **Museum of History**, 335 Second Ave NE (Mon–Sat 10am–5pm, Sun 1–5pm; $5; ⓣ727/894-1052, ⓦwww.museumofhistoryonline.org). Modest displays recount St Petersburg's early twentieth-century heyday as a winter resort (which lasted until the wider and sandier Gulf Coast beaches became accessible), and the inaugural flight of the world's first commercial airline, which took off from St Petersburg in 1914. There's documentation, too, on **Weedon Island**, five miles north of the town and once the base of a small film industry. Significant pottery finds were unearthed from Native American burial mounds here, but they were ransacked by looters in the 1960s. Now a state-protected wildlife refuge, the island is mostly used for fishing.

One block west of the pier, a group of Mediterranean Revival buildings houses the **Museum of Fine Arts** at 255 Beach Drive NE (Tues–Sat 10am–5pm, Sun 1–5pm; $8 including free guided tour on Sun; ⓣ727/896-2667, ⓦwww.fine-arts.org). This elegant Mediterranean-villa-style building, set in a landscaped park with sculptures and banyan trees, is a work of art in itself. Opened in 1965, its twenty galleries hold more than 400 objects from antiquity to the present day. Inside, the works of seventeenth-century art are competent but not imposing; more inspiring is the section on modern European art, featuring drawings by Kandinsky, Monet's *Houses of Parliament*, and Daumier's amusing *Connoisseur of Prints*. Also on display are pre-Columbian pieces, plus ceramics, glasswork, and antiquities from Europe and Asia. The American contemporary room displays include Georgia O'Keeffe's vibrant *Poppy* and George Luks' *The Musician*.

A short walk south of the Museum of Fine Arts is the massive **Florida International Museum**, 100 Second St N (during exhibition periods only, Mon–Sat 10am–5pm, Sun noon–5pm, last entry 4pm; $12, students $6; ⓣ727/822-3693, ⓦwww.floridamuseum.org), which encompasses an entire block. The museum opened in 1995 with the first of its exhibitions, "Treasures of the Czars," which contained works from the Moscow Kremlin Museum. Grand in scale, with subject matter ranging from ancient Egypt to John F. Kennedy, the exhibitions each last for about a year and are usually very good.

Florida Holocaust Museum

Dedicated to encouraging public awareness, education, and understanding of the Holocaust, the emotionally wrenching **Florida Holocaust Museum**, at 55 Fifth St, on the western edge of the central part of downtown (Mon–Fri 10am–5pm, Sat & Sun noon–5pm, last entry 4pm; $8; ⓣ727/820-0100 or 1-800/960-7448, ⓦwww.flholocaustmuseum.org), chronicles the genocide of Europe's Jewish population with sensitivity and intelligence, and puts the history of anti-Semitism, from the first anti-Jewish legislation in Europe in 1215 AD, into context. The museum has both permanent and temporary exhibits, including an expansive second-floor gallery focusing on Holocaust art, and eleven eternal flames – symbolizing the eleven million victims of the Nazis – form part of the building's facade.

The brainchild of local businessman and World War II veteran Walter Loebenberg, who escaped Germany in 1939, the center includes among its exhibits a massive, original boxcar – #1130695-5 – that carried thousands of starving victims to their deaths and is the only one of its kind in the US. There are also some stunning sculptures on Jewish and secular themes, though for the best of these, you'll need to be here during the last week of January for the superb annual art festival at Temple Beth El, 400 Pasadena Ave S (ⓣ727/347-6136, ⓦwww.templebeth-el.com).

The Salvador Dalí Museum

Few places make a less likely depository for the biggest collection of works by maverick artist Salvador Dalí than St Petersburg. However, the **Salvador Dalí Museum**, 1000 S Third St (Mon–Sat 9.30am–5.30pm, Thurs 9.30am–8pm, Sun noon–5.30pm; $13, $5 Thurs after 5pm; ⓣ727/823-3767, ⓦwww.salvadordalimuseum.org), a mile and a half south of the pier, stores more than a thousand Dalí works from the collection of a Cleveland industrialist who struck up a friendship with the artist in the Forties, bought stacks of his works, and ran out of space to show them – until this specially built gallery opened in 1982.

Hook up with the hour-long **free tours** that run continuously throughout the day. They trace a fact-filled path around the chronologically arranged paintings (some shown on rotation), from early experiments with Impressionism and Cubism to the ectoplasmic watches of the seminal surrealist canvas *The Disintegration of the Persistence of Memory*, and on to works from Dalí's "Classic" period in the Forties, which play upon the fundamentals of religion, science, and history. Some canvases – such as the overwhelming *The Discovery of America by Christopher Columbus*, and *The Hallucinogenic Toreador*, with its multiple double-images – are so big they have been hung in a specially deepened section of the gallery.

The Sunken Gardens and Great Explorations

If you've had your fill of museums, head for the **Sunken Gardens**, 1825 Fourth St N (Wed–Sun 10am–4pm; tours Tues, Fri, & Sun 11am, Sat 1pm; $7; ⓣ727/551-3100), a mile north of the pier. In 1935, a water-filled sinkhole was drained and planted with thousands of tropical plants and trees, forming what is now four acres of shady and sweet-scented gardens. Fifteen feet below street level, lush tropical gardens are combined with flowing ponds and waterfalls. For a crash-course in exotic botany, scrutinize the texts along the pathway that descends gently through bougainvillea, hibiscus, and staghead ferns.

Next to the Sunken Gardens at 1925 Fourth St N, **Great Explorations** (Mon–Sat 10am–4.30pm, Sun noon–4.30pm; $8; ⓣ727/821-8992, ⓦwww.greatexplorations.org) is a hands-on science museum, which, like Tampa's much larger Museum of Science and Industry (see p.275), strives to make the rudiments of science accessible with inventive games, such as shooting tennis balls high in the air using compression techniques and playing synthesized music on a harp with diode lasers instead of strings. Although aimed more at children than adults, this museum can be both fun and educational for all ages and new exhibits are added regularly.

Eating

As the atmosphere in St Petersburg grows increasingly hipper, so does the choice of places to **eat.** Good places for a meal are the BayWalk complex (see below), where you can often dine to live music, as well as the pier and Central Avenue.

Cha Cha Coconuts 800 Second Ave N, 5th floor ⓣ727/822-6655. Inexpensive Caribbean dishes, such as blue mountain voodoo ribs, tropical tuna salad, and Caribbean steak, accompanied by tall, frosty island drinks and live entertainment.

The Chattaway 358 22nd Ave ⓣ727/823-1594. A one-time grocery store, gas station, and trolley stop, *The Chattaway* is now a great and inexpensive American diner, famous for its Chattaburger, with all the trimmings.

Columbia 800 Second St, 4th floor ⓣ727/822-8000, ⓦwww.columbiarestaurant.com. High-quality Cuban and Spanish dishes for $10–15, some drawing on traditional family recipes. One of several *Columbia* restaurants, the most famous of which is in Ybor City (see p.277).

Dish 197 Second Ave N, in the BayWalk complex ⓣ727/894-5700. Choose your ingredients – from plenty of meats, vegetables, and sauces – and the style in which they should be cooked on the huge grill that forms the restaurant's centerpiece.

Gold Coffee Shop 336 First Ave N ⓣ727/822-4922. Inexpensive and simple, this spot is a good bet for an all-American breakfast. Lone diners will blend in easily thanks to the seating at communal tables. Closes at 2pm.

Marchand's Bar & Grill at the *Renaissance Vinoy Resort* ⓣ727/894-1000, ext 2136. Well presented and moderately expensive Mediterranean grill food at this, the best restaurant in St Petersburg's best hotel. The lovely large dining room frequently reverberates with piano music and sometimes live jazz.

Market Place Express 284 Beach Drive ⓣ727/894-3330. Open at 7am weekdays, this delightful deli with outside terrace is a great place for breakfast. It also sells good-quality, though quite expensive, deli-style food and wine.

Moon Under Water 332 Beach Drive NE ⓣ727/896-6160. Overlooking the waterfront, this inexpensive British Colonial tavern is well known for its cocktails, curries, and baked salmon. Try the killer Key Lime pie for dessert.

Ovo Café 515 Central Ave ⓣ727/895-5515. A blast of pure chic, but if you keep to salads and drinks, you can enjoy the minimalist, classic decor without smashing your budget. Closed Sun.

South Gate Restaurant 29 Third St N ⓣ727/823-7071. Family-style fare at reasonable prices. Try the blueberry waffles for breakfast or the lamb and beef gyros at lunchtime.

Tangelo's Grill 226 First Ave N ⓣ727/894-1695. Excellent Cuban café offering hearty economical meals, such as fantastic black beans and rice, sweet potato fries, and Cuban sandwiches, plus great music.

Ted Peters' Famous Smoked Fish 1350 Pasadena Ave ⓣ727/381-7931. Indulge in hot smoked-fish dinners with all the trimmings. Order a menu item such as smoked mullet or catch your own fish and have it cooked in the restaurant's red oak smoker. Expensive but worth it.

Nightlife

It's been said that if you fire a cannon down Central Avenue after 9pm on any night, you won't hit a soul, but enough bars and cafés have now opened to make this more of a risk. The arrival of the **BayWalk** entertainment complex (Ⓣ27/384-6000) has been a boon for night owls, as several of the restaurants here double as bars, with live music and a fair amount of activity at weekends. At one of the more popular venues, *Marino's Martini Bar* (Ⓣ727/895-8558), you can watch the weekend **jazz** bands quite well from the sidewalk without forking over the $5–10 cover charge to enter the bar itself. If you're at the pier, go up to the roof level to hear the free band playing at *Cha Cha Coconut's* (Ⓣ727/822-6655) – the cool ocean breeze and St Petersburg skyline make the lightweight rock sounds palatable. Another restaurant offering live jazz at the weekends is *The Garden*, 217 Central Ave (Ⓣ727/896-3800), a Mediterranean bistro with an outdoor martini lounge beneath an ancient banyan tree; it's open every night until 2am. **Country music** enthusiasts should head for *The Bull Pen Lounge*, 3510 34th St N (Ⓣ727/526-3366), where pool tables, video games, and karaoke share the spotlight with the live music at the weekends. Elsewhere, a steady procession of bands playing rock, reggae, folk, and the like appear at *Jannus Landing*, 19 Second St N (Ⓣ727/896-1244, Ⓦwww.januslanding.net), the oldest (and one of the largest) outdoor concert venues in Florida. Turn up with your own booze (there's no bar) at the *Coliseum Ballroom*, 535 Fourth Ave (Ⓣ727/892-5202, Ⓦwww.stpete.org/coliseum), a **big band** venue for decades that boasts one of the biggest dance-floors in the US; weekend cover is around $15 depending on the event, less during the week, and $5 (including instruction 11.30am–12.30pm) for the Wednesday tea dances (1–3.30pm). The **American Stage,** 211 Third St (Ⓣ727/823-7529, Ⓦwww.americanstage.org), is the oldest **theater** in the Tampa Bay area. A nonprofit organization with a mission to "entertain, educate, and enlighten," it presents American classics and Broadway shows. Each spring the theater stages a Shakespeare in the Park Festival at **Demen's Landing**, a waterfront park facing the pier. Ticket prices range from $9 to $22.

Gay and lesbian bars and clubs

There are a few friendly, dependable **gay bars** in town. To the south of St Petersburg, just north of the Skyway Bridge, the lively *Sharp A's Lounge,* 4918 Gulfport Blvd S (Ⓣ727/327-4897), is an entertainment complex offering shows, dancing, karaoke, and pool tables to its predominantly male clientele, while *Georgie's Alibi*, 3100 Third Ave at 31st St (Ⓣ727/321-2112, Ⓦwww.georgiesalibi.com), has an extended happy hour, a dance floor with live DJs, and bar food. The *Suncoast Resort*, 3000 34th St (Ⓣ727/867-1111, Ⓦwww.suncoastresort.com), is the world's largest all-gay holiday resort, and its clubs and bars are worth checking out. For more information options in and around St Petersburg, visit Ⓦwww.gaytampa.com.

Gulfport

Absent from most tourist brochures and unseen by the thousands of visitors who hustle between downtown and the St Petersburg beaches, **GULFPORT** is a charming enclave of peaceful eateries, interesting art galleries, and unusual shops. There's little glamour to this former fishing community and not a high-rise hotel in sight, making this one of the best places to stay in the area if you want to get off the tourist trail.

From downtown St Petersburg, travel a few miles south on I-275 to exit 6, then turn right at the bottom of the exit onto Gulfport Boulevard (22nd Avenue S), which, after about two miles, serves as the central axis for the town. If you are traveling by bus, catch #23 from the Williams Park terminal to Shore

Boulevard. Much of Gulfport is an unpretentious and rather bland mix of weather-beaten houses, coin laundries, and little grocery stores. Turn off Gulfport Boulevard onto Beach Boulevard, however, and you'll discover a stretch of antique shops and restaurants shaded by oak trees dripping with Spanish moss. At the end of the road is the **Gulfport Casino**, 5500 Shore Blvd (Ⓣ727/893-1070), where **ballroom dancing** with a live orchestra has the locals strutting their stuff on Sundays and Tuesdays, while fans of swing have it their way on Wednesdays.

Practicalities

The *Sea Breeze Manor*, 5701 Shore Blvd (Ⓣ727/343-4445 or 1-888/343-4445, Ⓦwww.seabreezemanor.com; ❺), is a gloriously restored, seaside house with sumptuous beds, antique furnishings, and home-baked breakfasts that makes a great alternative to staying in St Petersburg proper. Another comfortable place to lay your head is the *Peninsula Inn & Spa*, 2937 Beach Blvd (Ⓣ727/346-9800 or 1-888/900-0466, Ⓦwww.innspa.net; ❺), with its British Colonial–style decor, Indonesian hand-crafted furniture, and full-service spa. Renowned as one of the best Cuban restaurants in the Tampa Bay area, *Habana Café*, 5402 Gulfport Blvd (Ⓣ727/321-8855), serves shrimp of all sorts (Guantanamo Bay, Creole butterfly, *ajillo*), all for around $10 for a main course. Try *H.T. Kanes*, 5501 Shore Blvd (Ⓣ727/347-6299), which faces the casino at the junction of Shore and Beach boulevards, for inexpensive grouper, clam, ribs, and catfish; or *La Côte Basque*, 3104 Beach Blvd (Ⓣ727/321-6888), which has moderately priced flounder, veal, liver, and lamb dishes. Upscale dining is available at *Six Tables*, the restaurant at the *Peninsula Inn & Spa* (dinner only; closed Mon; Ⓣ727/346-9806), where a fixed-price dinner of *canard à l'orange*, roasted venison or poached salmon will set you back $65 excluding wine. For **nightlife**, *O'Maddy's*, 5403 Shore Blvd (Ⓣ727/323-8643), has a good view of the sea and a happy hour between 4pm and 8pm. Otherwise, there's always the casino (see above).

South from Tampa Bay

Taking I-275 south from St Petersburg (a preferable route to the lackluster I-75 or US-41 from Tampa), you'll soar over Tampa Bay on the **Sunshine Skyway Bridge**, high enough to allow ocean-going ships to pass beneath and for the outlines of land and sea to become blurred in the heat haze. The original Sunshine Skyway was rammed by a phosphate tanker during a storm in May 1980, causing the central span of the southbound section to collapse. With visibility reduced to a few feet, drivers on the bridge failed to spot the gap, and 35 people, including the occupants of a Greyhound bus, plunged 250 feet to their deaths; this tragedy was the worst of several fatal accidents on the Sunshine Skyway. The southern and northern sections of the remains have now been turned into the longest fishing piers in the world (access costs $3 per vehicle), while the central section, submerged in the waters at the mouth of Tampa Bay, creates an artificial reef. The Sunshine Skyway Bridge, which cost $215 million to build, is rife with tales of phantom hitchhikers who thumb rides across only to vanish into thin air before reaching the other side. For the dollar toll, it rivals anything at Walt Disney World.

Beyond the Sunshine Skyline Bridge you enter Florida's southwest coast, which is covered in "Sarasota and the Southwest," starting on p.225.

The St Petersburg beaches

Framing the Gulf side of the Pinellas Peninsula – a bulky thumb of land poking out between Tampa Bay and the Gulf of Mexico – is 35 miles of barrier islands that form the **St Petersburg beaches**, a convenient name for one of Florida's busiest coastal strips. Although each beach area has a name of its own, collectively they are often referred to as "the Holiday Isles," or the "Pinellas County Suncoast," and in reality merge together in one long, built-up strip of tourism at its tackiest. When the famed resorts of Miami Beach lost their allure during the Seventies, the St Petersburg beaches grew in popularity with Americans and later evolved into an established destination for package-holidaying Europeans. There's no denying that the beaches themselves are beautiful, the sea warm, and the sunsets fabulous, yet in no way is this Florida at its best. That said, staying here can be very cost-effective (especially during the summer) and if you're prepared to travel beyond the major built-up areas, you will find that some of the islands deserve exploration. It's quite feasible to combine lazing on the beach with day-trips to the more interesting inland areas. A word of warning – alcohol is prohibited on all municipal beaches in Florida, and glass containers are also illegal. Police in this area are particularly vigilant in chucking the drunk and disorderly in jail.

Information

Several beach areas have **Chambers of Commerce** readily dispensing handy information: St Petersburg Beach, 6990 Gulf Blvd (Mon–Fri 9am–5pm; ⓣ727/360-6957, ⓦwww.tampabaybeaches.com); Treasure Island, 152 107th Ave (Mon–Fri 9am–5pm; ⓣ727/363-6181); Madeira Beach, 501 150th Ave (Mon–Fri 9am–5pm; ⓣ727/391-7373). In Clearwater Beach, visit the booth at Pier 60, 1 Causeway Blvd (daily 10am–7pm; ⓣ727/442-3604), or the Clearwater Welcome Center, 3350 Gulf-to-Bay Blvd (daily 9am–5pm; ⓣ727/726-1547), which is convenient if you are arriving from St Petersburg-Clearwater International Airport.

Accommodation

The accommodation options along St Petersburg's beaches are limited to **hotels** – including resorts with facilities and activities galore for families – and less expensive **motels** that line mile after mile of Gulf Boulevard and the

The Pinellas Trail

If you're looking for an intriguing alternative to the usual beach-hopping paths of tourists up and down the coast, take the **Pinellas Trail,** a 34-mile hiking/cycling track that runs between St Petersburg and Tarpon Springs. You can pick up a free, informative, and highly portable guide to the trail at any of the Chambers of Commerce or visitor centers between these two destinations. The guide describes the route and picks out points of interest, providing easy-to-manage maps and mileage charts. Numerous exit and entry points encourage a leisurely approach, so allow yourself time to meander off the well-marked confines of the trail and, if you don't feel inclined to tackle its entirety, you can take a bus or drive to selected areas for day excursions. Despite some uglier sections through urban centers (tricky on a bike), the trail offers enjoyable scenery along its rural portions and a chance for contemplation away from tanning and watersports. Keep in mind that Florida law requires everyone under 16 to wear a helmet when they ride a bike – no matter where they ride.

Buses between St Petersburg and the beaches

The best way to access the beaches by bus is the **Suncoast Trolley** service. A beach trolley (PSTA service #3) operates daily from the Williams Park terminal in St Petersburg to **Treasure Island Beach** (daily every hour 5.50am–9.05pm, Fri & Sat until 11.50pm). Change here for the Suncoast Trolley that travels along Gulf Boulevard and connects all the beaches from **Sand Key** to **Pass-a-Grille** (daily every half-hour 5.45am–9.25pm; Fri & Sat until 12.40am). Alternatively, there's a direct connection from Williams Park **to Indian Rocks Beach** with #59, **St Pete Beach** with #35, and to **Clearwater** with #18 and #52, where #80 continues **to Clearwater Beach**. PSTA bus fares are $1.25 one way. If you are making a number of journeys in one day, a daily Go Card can be purchased on board for $3 and provides unlimited trips on any PSTA vehicle for one day, while $12 buys a seven-day unlimited pass – a real bargain if you're planning to explore the beaches over a number of days. Bicycles can be taken on buses. For further transport details, see "Buses around Clearwater Beach," p.292.

neighboring streets. The latter typically cost $50–75 in winter, $15–20 less during the summer, though if you're staying long enough, many offer discounted weekly rates. Some motels also have **self-catering** amenities (such as a fridge and stove) for $5–10 above the basic room rate. Remember that a room on the beach side of Gulf Boulevard costs $5–10 more than an identical room across the street. Note that the lack of competition causes prices in **Pass-a-Grille** to be around $10 higher than you might pay a few miles north, but the district is much less built up than other areas and makes an excellent base. Otherwise, there's not much difference between staying at the southern or the northern sections of the St Petersburg beaches, save for a bit more small town atmosphere in Clearwater Beach than you'll find along Gulf Boulevard.

In **Clearwater Beach**, you'll find the West Coast's only IYHA **youth hostel**, the *Clearwater Beach Hostel*, 606 Bay Esplanade (Ⓣ727/443-1211, Ⓦwww.clearwaterbeachhostel.com), which has a pool, shuffleboard, free use of canoes, and bike rental ($5 a day). Dorm beds cost $13 and private rooms are available from $36 a night. Reservations are advisable during December–April and at all times for private rooms.

There are no **campgrounds** along the main beach strip, though the nearest and nicest spot, at Fort de Soto Park (see p.291; Ⓣ727/582-2267; tent site $27.75), is adjacent to sand and sea; all reservations must be made in person (not by telephone) at this site. An inland alternative is *St Petersburg KOA*, 5400 95th St N (Ⓣ727/392-2233 or 1-800/562-7714). Situated five miles east of Madeira Beach and tucked away on a mangrove bayou, this campground rents "kamping kabins" from $59 a night or tent sites for $30. Bike rental is also available. *Clearwater/Tarpon Springs KOA*, 37061 US-19 N (Ⓣ727/937-8412 or 1-800/562-8743), six miles north of Clearwater, is handier for Clearwater Beach and charges $23 to pitch a tent.

The southern beaches

Don Cesar 3400 Gulf Blvd, St Petersburg Beach Ⓣ727/360-1881 or 1-800/282-1116, Ⓦwww.doncesar.com. The venerable hotel (see p.290) now features 277 newly renovated rooms and even "etiquette classes" in an attempt to regain its past glory. The high price tag is what sets the place apart from most other hotels by the beach. ❼

Island's End Resort 1 Pass-a-Grille, Pass-a-Grille Ⓣ727/360-5023, Ⓦwww.islandsend.com. Five one-bedroom cottages and a three-bedroom cottage with its own private pool, all occupying a tranquil spot at the southernmost tip of Pass-a-Grille. ❺

Lamara Motel & Apartments 520 73rd Ave, St Petersburg Beach Ⓣ727/360-7521 or 1-800/211-5108, Ⓦwww.lamara.com. The landscaped, flower-filled gardens give this motel a quiet and secluded feel despite the location in the heart of St Pete Beach. ❷

Pass-a-Grille Beach Motel Co-op 709 Gulf Way, Pass-a-Grille ⓣ727/367-4726, ⓦwww.geocities.com/pagbeachmotel. Individually owned studios and apartments rented out to lucky – or unlucky, depending on the owner's taste in decor – visitors. Deposit required for stays of two days or more. ❸

Sea Chest Motel 11780 Gulf Blvd, Treasure Island ⓣ727/360-5501 or 1-888/525-0043, ⓦwww.seachestmotel.com. A good-value and comfortable motel option just a few steps from the sands of Treasure Island Beach. ❷

Shoreline Island Resort 14200 Gulf Blvd, Madeira Beach ⓣ727/397-6641 or 1-800/635-8373, ⓦwww.shorelineislandresort.com. A motel featuring many resort-style facilities and activities, but minus the onsite restaurants and hundreds of screaming kids (all guests here must be 21 or older). ❹

The northern beaches

Belleview Biltmore 25 Belleview Blvd, Clearwater ⓣ727/373-3000 or 1-800/237-8947, ⓦwww.belleviewbiltmore.com. At the southern edge of Clearwater, high on a bluff overlooking the water, this beautiful 1897 wooden structure was originally owned by the railroad magnate Henry B. Plant, who entertained shippers and celebrities here. All 244 rooms have been immaculately preserved. ❹

Clearwater Beach Hotel 500 Mandalay Ave, Clearwater Beach ⓣ727/441-2425 or 1-800/292-2295, ⓦwww.clearwaterbeachhotel.com. Once the only hotel on Clearwater Beach, this elegant, family-run establishment has been caught up by the competition in terms of comfort and facilities, but remains a charming place to stay with attentive service. ❺

Gulf Beach Motel 419 Coronado Drive, Clearwater Beach ⓣ727/447-3236 or 1-800/486-5432, ⓦwww.gulfbeachmotel.com. Reasonable accommodation within easy walking distance of the beach and on the local bus route, making this a convenient option for travelers without cars. ❷

Sheraton Sand Key 1160 Gulf Blvd, Sand Key ⓣ727/595-1611 or 1-800/325-3535, ⓦwww.sheratonsandkey.com. One of the best and most popular hotels (especially for conferences) on the St Petersburg beaches. Benefits from its location on an uncrowded strip of sand, and boasts an attractive poolside area with pleasant gardens, a great restaurant, and the best-equipped gym hereabouts (where you can also treat yourself to a superb massage). ❻

Traveler Motel 408 E Shore Drive, Clearwater Beach ⓣ727/442-3217 or 1-800/813-1163, ⓦwww.travelermotel.com. Right in the thick of the action, this British-owned motel, one of the cheapest around, nevertheless manages to maintain a certain tranquility, not least around the pool, which is situated in a tropical garden. ❶

The southern beaches

In twenty or so miles of heavily touristed coast, just one section has the feel of a genuine community with a history attached to it. The slender finger of **Pass-a-Grille**, at the very southern tip of the barrier island chain, was discovered in the early 1500s by Spanish explorers and became one of the first beach communities on the west coast. Settled by fishermen in 1911, it is now recognized in the National Historic Registry. Named by French fishermen – "la passe aux grilleurs" because they grilled their catch at this pass – modern Pass-a-Grille comprises two miles of tidy houses, well-kept lawns, small shops, and a cluster of bars and restaurants. On weekends, locals come to Pass-a-Grille's beach to enjoy one of the area's liveliest stretches of sand and the unobstructed views of the tiny islands that dot the entrance to Tampa Bay. **The Gulf Beaches Historical Museum**, 115 Tenth Ave (Thurs & Sat 10am–4pm, Sun 1–4pm; free; ⓣ727/552-1610), is situated here in what was the first church built on the barrier islands. The museum adequately traces the history of the islands, from the 1500s to the present day, through photographs, news clippings, and artifacts. The **Suncoast Beach Trolley** serves Pass-a-Grille (see "Buses between St Petersburg and the beaches," p.289).

The Don Cesar Hotel and around

A mile and a half north of Pass-a-Grille, at St Petersburg Beach, you won't need a signpost to locate the **Don Cesar Hotel**, 3400 Gulf Blvd (ⓣ727/360-1881 or 1-800/282-1116, ⓦwww.doncesar.com). Contrasting sharply with the turquoise sea, this grandiose pink castle with white-trimmed arched windows and vaguely Moorish turrets, and filling seven beachside acres, was conceived by a Twenties property speculator, Thomas J. Rowe. The *Don Cesar* opened in 1928, but its glamour was shortlived. The Depression forced Rowe to use part of the hotel as a warehouse and later drove him to allow the New York Yankees baseball team to make it their spring training base. After decades as a military hospital and then as federal offices, the building received a $1-million facelift during the Seventies and regained its hotel function (see p.289 for details) – a vacation base for anyone with upwards of $200 a night to spare. The present interior bears little resemblance to its original appearance, but you should stride past the marble columns and crystal chandeliers of the lobby into the lounge, where you can soak up the understated elegance from the depths of a sofa or, just outside, from the poolside. The hotel offers live music every night, both indoors and outdoors, and of course great sunsets.

Just beyond the *Don Cesar*, Pinellas County Bayway cuts inland and makes a good route to take to Fort de Soto Park (see below). Keeping to Gulf Boulevard brings you into the main section of **St Petersburg Beach** (or St Pete Beach), a series of uninspiring rows of hotels, motels, and eating places grouped along Gulf Boulevard and continuing for several miles. A very short break in the monotony is provided by a batch of pseudo-English shops around Corey Avenue. Further north, **Treasure Island** is even less varied, but does offer abundant watersports for those bored with lying in the sun. An arching drawbridge crosses over to **Madeira Beach** and the wood-walled, tin-roofed shops, restaurants, and bars of **John's Pass Village**, 12901 Gulf Blvd. Linked by a creaking boardwalk, the shops and the local fishing and pleasure-cruising fleet moored close by are mildly entertaining if you're at a (very) loose end. Madeira Beach itself is another sleepy spot and if you can't make it to Pass-a-Grille, the local beach justifies a weekend fling. **Hubbard's Marina** (Ⓣ727/393-1947 or 1-800/755-0677, Ⓦwww.hubbardsmarina.com) offers deep-sea fishing, and the adjacent *Friendly Fisherman Seafood Restaurant* (daily 7am–10pm; Ⓣ727/391-6025) will cook the fish caught from their boats for you.

Suncoast Seabird Sanctuary

Four miles north of Madeira Beach, at **Indian Shores**, the **Suncoast Seabird Sanctuary**, 18328 Gulf Blvd (daily 9am–sunset; donations suggested; Ⓣ727/391-6211, Ⓦwww.seabirdsanctuary.org), offers a break from bronzing. The sanctuary is the largest wild-bird hospital in North America, treating between 400 and 600 convalescing birds, including pelicans, herons, and cormorants at any one time, in state-of-the art facilities. These birds, commonly injured by fishing lines or environmental pollution, are released back into their natural habitat once well.

Fort de Soto Park

If you have a car, you can soak up some of the history surrounding the St Petersburg beaches by heading across the Pinellas County Bayway (85¢ toll on bridges), immediately north of the *Don Cesar*, then turning south along Route 679 to spend a day on the five islands comprising **Fort de Soto Park** (sunrise–sunset; free; Ⓣ727/866-2662, Ⓦwww.fortdesoto.com). The Spaniard credited with discovering Florida, Juan Ponce de León, is thought to have anchored here in 1513 and again in 1521 when the islands' indigenous inhabitants inflicted on him what proved to be a fatal wound. Centuries later, the islands became a strategically important Union base during the Civil War, and in 1898 a fort was constructed to forestall attacks on Tampa during the Spanish-American War. The remains of the fort – which was never completed

– can be explored on one of several **walking trails**, which wind through an impressively untamed, thickly vegetated landscape featuring Australian pines and oaks, with plenty of palm-shaded picnic tables along the way. Pick up a leaflet for the self-guided walking tour of the fort, or join a guided walking tour offered on Saturdays at 10am. Free nature tours through the park are also available at weekends departing from various locations.

Three miles of swimmer-friendly **beaches** line the park, which possesses an intoxicating air of isolation during the week – a far cry from the busy beach strips. The best way to savor the area is by **camping**; see "Accommodation," p.288.

The northern beaches

Much of the **northern section** of **Sand Key**, the longest barrier island in the St Petersburg chain, is lined by stylish condos and time-share apartments – this is one of the wealthier stretches of the coast. It ends with the pretty **Sand Key Park**, where tall palm trees frame a scintillating strip of sand. The classic beach vista is a good spot to watch dolphins, though the view is marred by the nearby high-rises.

The 65 acres of Sand Key Park occupy one bank of Clearwater Pass, across which a belt of sparkling white sands characterize **Clearwater Beach**, another community devoted to the holiday industry. Motels fill its side streets, while more expensive accommodation overlooks the Gulf. The endearing small-town ambience makes this a pleasant place to spend a couple of days, certainly preferable to Clearwater's dull downtown. A crucial plus for nondrivers is the regular bus links between Clearwater Beach and the mainland town of **Clearwater** – reached by a two-mile causeway – where you'll find connections to St Petersburg and Tarpon Springs, and a Greyhound station (see box below). Clearwater has its own **information point** separate from that of Clearwater Beach at 1130 Cleveland St (Mon–Fri 8.30am–5pm; ⓣ727/461-0011, ⓦwww.clearwaterflorida.org).

The Clearwater Marine Aquarium, 249 Windward Passage (Mon–Fri 9am–5pm, Sat 9am–4pm, Sun 11am–4pm; $8.75; ⓣ727/441-1790 or 1-888/239-9414, ⓦwww.cmaquarium.org), is well worth a break from the beach. At this nonprofit working aquarium, where injured marine mammals, sea turtles, and dolphins are rescued and rehabilitated, visitors can learn ways to help protect these animals and check out exhibits on Florida's coastal ecology and tanks of stingrays and sharks. Beyond its sands and two long piers, there's not much else to do in Clearwater Beach: if the brine beckons, board a mock pirate vessel for a two-hour *Captain Memo's* "pirate cruise" (daily 10am & 2pm,

Buses around Clearwater Beach

Clearwater Beach is good news for travelers without cars. **Around the beach strip**, the Jolly Trolley (ⓣ727/445-1200) runs daily (10am–10pm) between Sand Key (from the *Sheraton Sand Key Resort*) and Clearwater Beach (along Gulfview Boulevard, Mandalay Avenue, and Acacia Street); fares are $1. **To the mainland**, another Jolly Trolley runs between the beach and downtown Clearwater for 50¢. Alternatively, catch bus #80, which operates between Clearwater Beach and Clearwater's Park Street terminal (info: ⓣ727/530-9911). **Useful routes** from the terminal are #18 and #52 to St Petersburg; #66 to Tarpon Springs; and #200X (weekdays and rush hours only) to Tampa. A much less frequent mainland link is provided [illegible] two (and sometimes three) daily Amtrak buses, running from Tampa in lieu [illegible]ns; they stop in Clearwater at 657 Court St, and at Clearwater Beach's Civic C[illegible] The Greyhound station in Clearwater is at 2811 Gulf-to-Bay Blvd (ⓣ727/796-[illegible]

$28; evening Champagne Cruises at varying times through the year, $30; ⓣ727/446-2587, ⓦwww.pirateflorida.com) from the marina just south of the causeway; or, more adventurously, make a day-trip to the Caladesi or Honeymoon islands, a few miles north.

Honeymoon and Caladesi islands

These islands were created in 1921 when a hurricane tore the aptly named Hurricane Pass out of what was a single, five-mile island. These islands are now protected state parks (each $4 per car; $1 pedestrians and cyclists) that offer a chance to see the jungle-like terrain that covered the whole west coast before the bulldozers arrived. Of the two, only **Honeymoon Island** can be reached by road; take Route 586 off US-19 just north of Dunedin. The island earned its name when Paramount newsreels and *Life* magazine gave away all-expenses-paid honeymoons on the island as a grand prize in a 1940s contest. Today the condos that sprout from Honeymoon Island dent its natural impact, but a wild pocket at the end of the road is well worth exploring by way of the walking trail that runs around the edge of the entire island.

For a glimpse of what these islands must have looked like before the onset of mass tourism, make for **Caladesi Island**, just to the south. From a signposted landing stage beside Route 586 on Honeymoon Island, the **Caledesi Connections** ferry ($7 round-trip; ⓣ727/734-1501) crosses between the islands daily on the hour every hour on weekdays and (if busy) every half-hour at weekends, between 10am and 5pm. Once ashore at Caladesi's mangrove-fringed marina, you'll find boardwalks leading to a beach of unsurpassed tranquillity: perfect for swimming, sunbathing, and shell collecting. While here, though, summon up the strength to tackle the three-mile **nature trail**, which cuts inland through saw palmetto and slash pines to an observation tower. Be certain to bring food and drink to the island, as the poorly stocked snack bar at the marina is the sole source of sustenance.

Eating

The restaurants of the St Petersburg beaches are a jumble of diners, fast-food joints, and casual and fine-dining establishments. As you'd expect at any beach resort, **buffets** are popular, and you'll find the pinnacle of buffet-style dining at the *Don Cesar*, 3400 Gulf Blvd, St Petersburg Beach (ⓣ727/360-1881), where from 10.30am to 2.30pm you can tuck into as many made-to-order crêpes and as much smoked salmon as you can eat for $31.95 per person. Cheaper and more mundane buffet breakfasts, lunches, and dinners are available at *Shephard's*, 601 S Gulfview Blvd, Clearwater Beach (ⓣ727/441-6875).

The southern beaches

Fetishes 6690 Gulf Blvd, St Petersburg Beach ⓣ727/363-3700. An intimate restaurant with expensive American cuisine and only eight tables (so reservations are a must). Good wine selection.

Guppy's on the Beach 1701 Gulf Blvd, Indian Rocks Beach ⓣ727/593-2032. Tasty meals, including sashimi tuna, upper potato crust salmon, and filet mignon, served in a beachfront setting that's ideal for sunset watching.

Hurricane 807 Gulf Way, Pass-a-Grille ⓣ727/360-9558. Dine from a well-priced seafood menu on the terrace overlooking Tampa Bay, to the tunes of some of the area's top jazz musicians.

The Wharf 2001 Pass-a-Grille Way, Pass-a-Grille ⓣ727/367-9469. Forming part of the marina and a popular place with locals – an enormous bowl of mouthwatering clam chowder will only set you back around $3.

The northern beaches

Frenchy's Café 41 Baymont St, Clearwater Beach ⓣ727/446-3607. Opened in 1981 as the original *Frenchy's* (see below). The small menu features favorites such as seafood gumbo, smoked fish spread, and some of the best grouper sandwiches on the beach.

Frenchy's Rockaway Grill 7 Rockaway St, Clearwater Beach ⓣ727/446-4844. A beachside grill with great atmosphere and decent-enough grilled grouper, mahi mahi, and chicken, along with a daily schedule of beach games, music, and much cocktail drinking.

Rusty's Bistro at the *Sheraton Sand Key*, Sand Key ⓣ727/595-1611. That rare restaurant where seafood dishes are as good as the meat offerings, including a choice selection of steaks. All dishes are under $20, making this place fairly good value.

Tio Pepe 2930 Gulf-to-Bay Blvd, Clearwater ⓣ727/799-3082. One of the area's longstanding restaurants, serving good Spanish, Mediterranean, and Latin American cuisine, plus an extensive wine list. Closed Mon.

Nightlife and entertainment

As you'd expect, most of the **nightlife** is aimed at tourists, though there are exceptions. Many hotel and restaurant bars have lengthy **happy hours** and lounges designed for watching the sunset while sipping a cocktail – look for the signs and ads in the free tourist magazines. Otherwise, check out the "Weekend" section of the *St Petersburg Times* or the free *Weekly Planet* for entertainment and nightlife listings. In downtown Clearwater, the Royalty Theatre, 405 Cleveland St (ⓣ727/441-8868, ⓦwww.royaltytheatre.org), offers country music, jazz, and the like, and all proceeds from ticket sales are used to further renovate this beautiful historic building. *Sunsets at Pier 60* (two hours before and two hours after sunset; ⓣ727/449-1036, ⓦwww.sunsetsatpier60.com) is a free daily street festival that celebrates the sunsets hereabouts, with street entertainers and live music of all kinds on offer around Pier 60 in the heart of Clearwater Beach. A couple of **beach bars**, *Frenchy's Rockaway Grill*, 7 Rockaway St, Clearwater Beach (ⓣ727/446-4844; see "Eating" above), and *Sloppy Joe's on the Beach*, 10650 Gulf Blvd, at the *Bilmar Beach Resort*, Treasure Island (ⓣ727/367-1600), are ideal places to enjoy a sundowner and **live music** day and night in an informal setting. Another popular bar on the beach, again with live music – spoiled somewhat by the stench of dead fish – is the *Backyard Tiki Bar*, 616 S Gulfview Blvd, Clearwater Beach (ⓣ727/442-5107), part of *Shephard's Beach Resort*. Also at *Shephard's*, *Catch the Wave* is one of the more popular of the beaches' **nightclubs**, a state-of-the-art venue attracting a youngish crowd, while *Liquid Blue*, 22 N Fort Harrison, Clearwater (ⓣ727/446-4000), in an old theater, has the leopard-print carpeting and mirrored walls to satisfy anyone seeking Seventies- and Eighties-style kitsch. Both of these nightclubs play dance music and the like.

Inland from Tampa Bay: Lakeland and around

LAKELAND, thirty miles east of Tampa, plays the suburban big brother to its more rural neighbors and provides sleeping quarters for Orlando and Tampa commuters, who emerge on weekends to stroll the edges of the town's numerous lakes.

Aided by its busy railway terminal, Lakeland's fortunes rose in the Twenties, and a number of its more important buildings have been maintained as the **Munn Park Historic District** on and close to Main Street. Pay attention to the 1927 **Polk Theater**, 124 S Florida Ave, and the restored balustrades, lampposts, and gazebo-style bandstand on the promenade around Lake Mirror, at the east end of Main Street. A few minutes' walk from the town center, the generous size of the **Polk Museum of Art**, 800 E Palmetto St (Tues–Sat

10am–5pm, Sun 1–5pm; $3; ⓣ863/688-7743), suggests Lakeland is striving to raise its cultural profile: the spacious temporary galleries air the latest innovative pieces by up-and-coming Florida-based artists.

A stronger draw, and something of a surprise in such a tucked-away community, is the largest single grouping of buildings by **Frank Lloyd Wright**, who redefined American architecture in the Twenties and Thirties. Maybe it was the rare chance to design an entire communal area that appealed to Wright – the fee he got for converting an eighty-acre orange grove into **Florida Southern College**, a mile southwest of Lakeland's center, certainly didn't; the financially strapped college paid on credit and got its students to provide the labor.

Much of the integrity of Wright's initial concept has been lost: buildings have been crudely adapted and used for purposes other than those for which they were intended, and newer structures have distorted the college's overall harmony. Even so, the campus is an inventive statement and easily negotiated using the free **maps** provided in boxes along its covered walkways. Interestingly, Wright's contempt for air-conditioning caused him to erect thick masonry structures to shield the students from the Florida sun, and his desire to merge his work with the natural environment allowed the creeping vegetation of the orange grove (which has now given way to lawns) to wrap around the buildings and provide further insulation. To sign up for the regular guided **tours** (Thurs at 11am; $5) of the Wright buildings, call ⓣ863/680-4110; otherwise, you can walk amongst them at your leisure (Mon–Fri 10am–4pm, limited hours and access on the weekend).

Practicalities

Get a descriptive **walking tour map** of the Munn Park Historic District from the **Chamber of Commerce**, 35 Lake Morton Drive (Mon–Fri 8.30am–5pm; ⓣ863/688-8551). For **eating**, the *Reececliff*, 940 S Florida Ave (ⓣ863/686-6661), a spartan diner in business since 1934, has ridiculously cheap breakfasts and lunches; *Harry's Seafood Bar & Grille*, 101 N Kentucky Ave (ⓣ863/686-2228), provides a large menu of Cajun and Creole-inspired food in a fern-bar atmosphere; and the *Silver Ring Café*, 106 Tennessee Ave (ⓣ863/687-3283), features sizeable Cuban sandwiches. But if you're in the mood for a posh meal, *The Terrace Grill*, in the newly restored, vintage 1924 *Terrace Hotel*, 329 E Main St (ⓣ863/688-0800), offers superb dishes, such as the salmon with fresh *mozzarella di buffala* salad, in a chic Mediterranean Revival setting.

For further **accommodation** options, the atmospheric *Lake Morton Bed & Breakfast*, 817 South Blvd (ⓣ863/688-6788; ❸), is an oak-decorated period boarding house near the campus and the main lake. There are inexpensive motels, such as the *Royalty Inn*, 3425 US-98 N (ⓣ863/868-4481; ❷), a walk around the lake from the historic center, or the *Scottish Inn*, 244 N Florida Ave (ⓣ863/687-2530; ❷), a more basic choice, but near enough to everything of interest. Lakeland nightlife centers around *Mojo's*, 215 E Main St (ⓣ863/616-9966), which features an eclectic mix of live music (everything from rock to soul to techno) Thursdays to Mondays, and a variety of other musical events the rest of the week.

Polk City: Fantasy of Flight

Ten miles northeast of Lakeland, near Polk City, **Fantasy of Flight**, 1400 Broadway Blvd SE (daily 9am–5pm; ⓣ863/984-3500, ⓦwww.fantasyofflight.com; $25, children $14), draws both tourists and aviation enthusiasts. Part themed attraction and part private aircraft collection, Fantasy of Flight allows visitors to climb aboard a World War II B-17 Flying Fortress and pretend to drop bombs amid the sounds of anti-aircraft fire. You can be closed into "flight simulators" to get a somewhat realistic flavor of mid-air combat, or you can fly 500 feet into the air in an "Ultralight" airplane. Perhaps most interesting is the owner's collection of thirty-plus vintage planes, including the Lockheed Vega, which was the first plane ever flown around the globe.

Lake Wales and around

Southeast of Lakeland (25 miles south of I-4 on US-27), **Lake Wales** (Ⓦwww.cityoflakewales.com) is a lackadaisical town with more of note on its fringes than in its center, though the pink stucco **Lake Wales Depot Museum**, 325 S Scenic Highway (Mon–Fri 9am–5pm, Sat 10am–4pm; free; Ⓣ863/678-4209), contains an entertaining collection of train parts, remnants of the turpentine industry on which the town was founded in the late 1800s, and a Warhol-like collection of crate labels from the citrus companies that prospered during the early 1900s. They also have an ongoing program of special exhibitions, such as a huge collection of fine vintage quilts, and a recently restored caboose to check out.

At the museum, confirm directions to **Spook Hill**, an optical illusion that's been turned into a transparently bogus "legend" (which you can read about on a plaque), worth seeing as a unique example of local Florida kitsch (conveniently, it's on the way to Historic Bok Sanctuary; see below). By car, cross Central Avenue from the museum and turn right onto North Avenue, and then take a left at the T-intersection, following the one-way system. Just before meeting Hwy-17A, a sign indicates the spot to brake and put your vehicle into neutral. As you do so, the car appears to slide uphill. Looking back reveals the difference in road gradients that creates the effect.

Historic Bok Sanctuary

"A more striking example of the power of beauty could hardly be found, better proof that beauty exists could not be asked for," rejoiced landscape gardener William Lyman Phillips in 1956 upon visiting **Historic Bok Sanctuary**, a rolling garden of greenery two miles north of Lake Wales on Hwy-17A (daily 8am–6pm, last admission 5pm; $8, children 5–12 $3; Ⓣ863/676-1408). As sentimental as it may sound, Phillips' comment was, and is, accurate. Whether it's the effusive entanglements of ferns, oaks, and palms; the bright patches of magnolias, azaleas, and gardenias; or just the sheer novelty of a hill (this being the highest point in peninsular Florida), Bok Tower Gardens is one of the state's most lush and lovely places.

Not content with winning the Pulitzer Prize for his autobiography in 1920, Dutch-born office-boy turned author and publisher **Edward Bok** resolved to transform the pine-covered Iron Mountain (as this red-soiled hump is named) into a "sanctuary for humans and birds," in gratitude to his adopted country for making his glittering career possible. President Coolidge, one of Bok's many famous friends, showed up to declare it open in 1929.

Marvelous though they are, these 128 acres would be just a glorified botanical garden were it not for the **Singing Tower** and the **mansion**. The tower, two hundred feet of marble and coquina, rises steeply above the foliage, poetically mirrored in a swan- and duck-filled lily pond. Originally intended to conceal the garden's water tanks, the tower features finely sculpted impressions of Florida wildlife on its exterior and fills its interior with a 53-bell carillon: richly timbred chimes resound through the garden at regular intervals. Only

Chalet Suzanne

In 1931, gourmet cook and world traveler Bertha Hinshaw, recently widowed and made penniless by the Depression, moved to an isolated site two miles north of Lake Wales, beside US-17, to open a restaurant called **Chalet Suzanne.** Armed with her own recipes and tremendous powers of culinary invention – adding chicken livers to grilled grapefruit, for instance – Bertha created what's now among the most highly rated meal stops in the country, and one that's still run by her family.

Aside from the food (a multi-course lunch costs upward of $50, dinner upward of $80; call for reservations ⓣ800/433-6011), the quirky architecture grabs the eye: part Arabic, part Renaissance, whimsical, Hobbit-like buildings painted in confectionery pinks, greens, and yellows, topped by twisting towers and exotic turrets. Even if you're not dining or staying in one of the boudoir-like guest rooms (ⓦwww.chaletsuzanne.com; ❼), you're free to wander through the public rooms – whose furnishings are as loopy as the architecture, with decorative pieces picked up from Bertha's seven around-the-world trips.

The one conventional structure is the **soup cannery**, where "Romaine" soup – another of Bertha's creations – begins its journey to the nation's gourmet food stores. While here, don't be frightened by low-flying aircraft: a small runway beside the cannery is where corporate execs and freeloading food critics breeze in by private plane for a slap-up meal.

the 3pm recital is "live" (all the others are recordings), but you can discover more about its workings in the **visitor center**, which provides every detail imaginable about the garden and tower. Near the garden's entrance is an old "cracker" cottage. ("Cracker" was the nickname given to the state's early cattle farmers, perhaps because of the sound of the whips they handled with such precision.) The twenty room Mediterranean-style estate, named Pinewood, opened in 1995, its rooms decorated with 1920s furnishings. Guided tours last for one hour and cost $5.

A portion of the grounds has been left in its raw state, allowing wildlife to roam and be surreptitiously viewed through the glass front of a wooden hut. Hardier visitors can hack their way for twenty minutes along the **Pine Ridge Trail**, through the pine trees, saw-edged grasses, and wild flowers that once covered the entire hill.

Lake Kissimmee State Park

Nineteenth-century Floridian farming techniques may not seem the most inspiring subject in the world, but the 1876 Cow Camp section of **Lake Kissimmee State Park** (daily 7am–sunset; cars $3.25, pedestrians and cyclists $1; ⓣ863/696-1112), nine miles east of Lake Wales off Route 60, is an enjoyable and instructive re-creation of a pioneer-era cattle farm, complete with park rangers tending genuine cows and horses.

In the park picnic area, an observation platform above Lake Kissimmee can be utilized for bird- and alligator-spotting.

Tarpon Springs

Greek sponge-divers driven out of Key West by xenophobic locals during the early 1900s resettled in **TARPON SPRINGS**, ten miles north of Clearwater off US-19 (use Alt 19 – called Pinellas Avenue here – to arrive in the center, and have a map on hand). These early migrants began what has become a sizeable Greek community in a town previously the preserve of wealthy wintering northerners. Demand for sponges was unprecedented during World War II (among other attributes, sponges are excellent for mopping up blood), but the industry was later devastated by a marine blight and the development of synthetic sponges. The Greek presence in Tarpon Springs remains strong, however, and is most evident every January 6 when around 30,000 participate in the country's largest Greek Orthodox Epiphany celebration. Each year, an even greater number of visitors traipse around the souvenir shops lining the old sponge docks, largely neglecting the rest of the small town which – from restored buildings to weeping icons – has much more to offer.

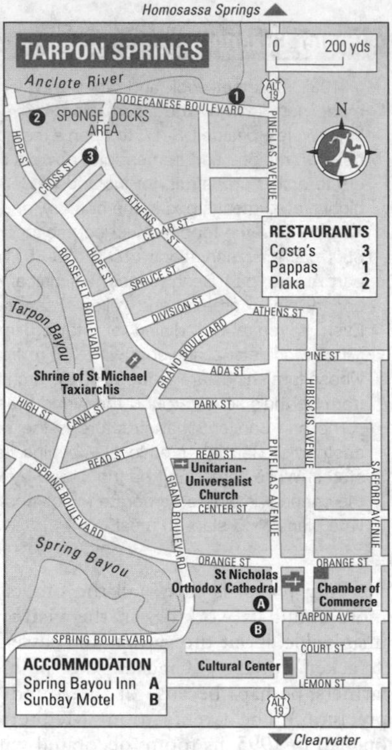

The Town

Greek names appear on virtually every shop front throughout Tarpon Springs, and although most of the shops lining busy Pinellas Avenue bill themselves as antique dealers, their displays gleam with newness. Don't stop here, but follow the "docks" signs. On the right you'll see the strongest symbol in this Greek community: the resplendent Byzantine-Revival **St Nicholas Orthodox Cathedral**, 36 N Pinellas Ave, at Orange Street (Mon–Fri 9am–4pm; free; ⓣ727/937-3540), partly funded by a half-percent levy on local sponge sales and finished in 1943. The full significance of the cathedral's ornate interior will inevitably be lost on those not of the faith, though the icons and slow-burning incense create an intensely spiritual atmosphere.

After leaving the cathedral, drop into the nearby **Tarpon Springs Cultural Center**, 101 S Pinellas Ave (Mon–Fri 9am–4pm; free except for special events; ⓣ727/942-5605), which regularly stages imaginative exhibitions about Tarpon Springs' past and present, as well as art exhibitions. For $2, you can also pick up a forty-page pamphlet detailing a self-guided walking tour of historic Tarpon Springs, which has to be one of the best ways to absorb the history and architecture of this area. The Neoclassical building that houses the Cultural Center has served as the city hall since 1915, when Tarpon Avenue, a street away, was a bustling commercial strip where butchers, bakers, and grocers once plied their trades from stumpy masonry structures, many of which still stand. Several have now been converted into curio-filled antique shops, which make for a good half-hour's walk.

The Unitarian-Universalist Church and George Innes Junior Collection

Walking west along Tarpon Avenue takes you downhill to **Spring Bayou**, a crescent-shaped lake ringed by the opulent homes of Tarpon Springs' pre-sponge-era residents, who were primarily a mix of tycoons and artists.

The **Unitarian-Universalist Church**, 230 Grand Blvd, at Read Street (Oct–May Tues–Sun 2–5pm; donations suggested; ⓣ727/937-4682), is known for its collection of whimsical paintings by the early-twentieth century landscapist George Innes Junior. To mark what would have been the 100th birthday of his late father (George Innes Senior, also a renowned artist), Innes painted a delicate rendition of the Spring Bayou, now the centerpiece of the church's collection. Innes spent much of his career mired in depression and mediocrity, but this singular work seemed to ignite a creative spark and prompted the series of hauntingly beautiful paintings that dominate the church's walls today. The paintings once hung in the Louvre, but after George Junior's death, his widow paid for their safe return. Helpful locals guide you through the collection; of particular note are the murals Innes painted to stop up the church's windows, which were blown out by a hurricane in 1918.

Keeping to a religious theme and just a few minutes' walk from the Unitarian-Universalist Church, the simple wooden **Shrine of St Michael Taxiarchis**, at 113 Hope St (always open), was erected by a local woman in gratitude for the unexplained recovery of her "terminally ill" son in 1939. Numerous instances of the blind regaining their sight and the crippled throwing away their walking sticks after visiting the shrine have been reported, all detailed in a free pamphlet.

The sponge docks

Along Dodecanese Boulevard, on the banks of the Anclote River, the **sponge docks** are a disappointing conglomeration of one-time supply stores turned into restaurants and gift shops touting cassettes of Greek "belly-dancing music" and, of course, sponges. A boat departs regularly throughout the day on a half-hour **sponge-diving trip** from the St Nicholas Boat Line, 693 Dodecanese Blvd ($7; ⓣ727/942-6425). The trip includes a cruise through the sponge docks, a talk on the history of sponge-diving, and a demonstration of harvesting performed in a traditional brass-helmeted diving suit. These days, though, only a few sponge boats still operate commercially.

You'll pay less, and learn more about the local community and sponge-diving, in a group of shops at 510 Dodecanese Blvd, whose **Sponge Factory** (Mon–Sat 10.30am–6pm, Sun 11.30am–6pm; free; ⓣ727/938-5366) includes the Museum of Sponge Diving and a half-hour film detailing where sponges grow and how they are harvested. It also traces the history of Tarpon Springs' Greek settlers and shows the primitive techniques still used in the industry. Some of the museum exhibits are showing signs of age, and sponging terminology sounds much more raunchy than it really is – "nude sponging" and "thrusting hookers" are two themes explored in the displays. One shop even sells alligator heads with their mouths held open, but the only real reason to hang around is the free **sponge-diving shows**, which run roughly half-hourly in the theater.

Once you've had your fill of sponges and tourist shops, the **Konger Tarpon Spring Aquarium**, 850 Dodecanese Blvd (Mon–Sat 10am–5pm, Sun noon–5pm; $5; ⓣ727/938-5378), is a small aquarium with a simulated coral reef, complete with native plants and tropical fish, and a tidal pool that offers a closer look at such creatures as starfish and hermit crabs. For a really lazy and very pleasurable half day, you can take a **boat tour** to nearby **Anclote Key**, four miles of sandy beach with a lighthouse at its southern end. Contact Island Wind Tours, 600 Dodecanese Blvd ($7 for a 75-minute cruise; ⓣ727/934-0606, ⓦwww.islandwindtours.com).

Practicalities

Pick up general **information** and a map guide to historical sites and points of interest in downtown from the **Chamber of Commerce**, 11 E Orange St, opposite the cathedral (Mon–Fri 9am–5pm; ⓣ727/937-6109, ⓦwww.tarpon-springs.com). On weekends, when the chamber is closed, head for the **visitor center** at the City Marina (daily 10.30am–4.30pm; ⓣ727/937-9165).

Tarpon Springs makes a sensible **overnight stop** if you're continuing north. A number of motels dot the junctions with US-19, but the most central is the *Sunbay Motel*, 57 W Tarpon Ave (ⓣ727/934-1001; ❷); or, for bed and breakfast, try the *Spring Bayou Inn*, across the road from the *Sunbay* at 32 W Tarpon Ave (ⓣ727/938-9333).

Among the **eating** options, check out *Pappas Restaurant*, 10 W Dodecanese Blvd (ⓣ727/937-5101), whose large parking garage is a blessing in itself (there aren't many places to leave your car in the center of town), and the large if rather pricey portions of Greek-inspired seafood and other dishes are very satisfying. For more Greek food, sample the inexpensive offerings at *Costa's*, 510 Athens St (ⓣ727/938-6890), or *Plaka*, 769 Dodecanese Blvd (ⓣ727/934-4752), which specializes in seafood, salads, and souvlaki. If excellent syrupy pastries are more your thing, or to stock up on homemade Greek breads, head to *Apollo Bakery* at the docks, and don't forget to sample their chocolate baklava. Cheap breakfasts, hot sandwiches, hummus, baklava, and the like can be found at the *Bread and Butter Deli*, 1880 Pinellas Ave (ⓣ727/934-9003).

The Big Bend

Popularly known as the **BIG BEND** for the way it curves toward the Panhandle, Florida's **northwest coast** is one of its best-kept secrets. Far from the tourist beaches and theme parks, this sparsely populated coastline offers thousands of mangrove islands and marshlands, wide spring-fed rivers, and quiet roads leading to small communities. Here you will find some of the best wildlife Florida has to offer and – in one instance – an outstanding Native American ceremonial site. Sand-crazy visitors miss it all by barreling toward the Tampa Bay beaches on US-19, the region's only major road, ignoring the Big Bend. For the more inquisitive visitor, this area offers a rewarding taste of the real Florida.

Homosassa Springs and around

The main highway out of Tampa Bay, US-19, is a roadside clutter of filling stations and used-car lots and something of a parking lot, until you reach **New Port Richey** – an uninteresting series of condos and time-share properties. A quicker route out of the area is to take I-275, which becomes I-75 after it leaves

Tampa, then head west on US-98 at junction 61. By the time you reach US-19, after approximately twenty miles, it has become a more soothing, if often monotonous, landscape of hardwood and pine forests along with expanses of swamp. Those taking this quicker way to the Big Bend who are planning a visit to Weeki Wachee Springs should join Hwy-50 at Brooksville, while those on US-19 will remain on it until the junction with Hwy-50, about thirty miles north of Clearwater. **Weeki Wachee Springs** (daily 10am–4pm; $18.95, children 3–10 $15; ⓣ352/596-2062, ⓦwww.weekiwachee.com) opened in 1947 and has attracted numerous celebrities – including Elvis – to its thoroughly kitsch underwater shows performed by "mermaids" in one of the Big Bend's many natural springs. The park also offers a Wilderness River Cruise, a petting zoo, and bird shows and is now part of its own city. There are plenty of places to stay, although it can be visited as a day-trip from Clearwater. During the summer months it is possible to buy a combination ticket that allows access to the adjacent **Buccaneer Bay Water Park** (daily 10am–6pm in summer; ⓣ352/596-2062), where you can swim and play on the water slides to your heart's content.

The desire to see animals and (real) sea life is better satisfied twenty miles north at **HOMOSASSA SPRINGS**, the first community of any size on US-19, and one of the best places anywhere in the world to catch tarpon (May and June are the prime fishing months for the fish). The **Homosassa Springs Wildlife State Park** (daily 9am–5.30pm; $7.95; ⓣ352/628-2311 or 628/5354, ⓦwww.homosassasprings.org) is a showcase of Florida's native wildlife, offering a chance to see animals, birds, and plants in their natural setting. Walking trails lead to a gushing spring and an underwater observatory where you can see numerous fish and manatees up close, while daily educational programs offer the opportunity of learning more about the wildlife on show. The park also serves as a rehabilitation center and refuge for endangered West Indian manatees that have been orphaned or injured in the wild.

To get a feel for the town, go a couple of miles west along the oak-lined Route 490, passing the crumbling walls and rusting machinery of the **Yulee Sugar Mill**, originally owned by David Yulee, Florida's first congressman and the financier of the 1860s Cedar Key to Fernandina Beach rail line (see "Cedar Key," p.304), which he extended to Homosassa Springs. With the railway long gone this tranquil town's old wooden houses are finding favor with young artists: drop into the Riverworks Gallery, 10844 W Yulee Drive (ⓣ352/628-0822), to see some of the better works, or the Old Mill House Printing Museum, 10466 W Yulee Drive (ⓣ352/628-1081), which, in addition to an art gallery, has antique printing presses on display.

Practicalities

Homosassa Springs is a good option if you're seeking a place **to stay** off the beaten track. Avoid the usual chain motels on US-19 and spend a night at *MacRae's*, 5300 S Cherokee Way (ⓣ352/628-2602; ❸), the place of choice for fishermen for kicking back in a rocking chair and barbecuing the day's catch, or the *Homosassa Riverside Resort*, 5297 S Cherokee Way (ⓣ352/628-2474 or 1-800/442-2040, ⓦwww.homosassariverside.com; ❷). **Boat rental** is available at both establishments. **Campers** should head for the centrally located *Nature Resort Campground and Marina*, 10359 W Halls River Rd (ⓣ352/628-9544 or 1-800/301-7880), which charges $21 per night to pitch a tent. The obvious place to **eat** is *Charlie Brown's Crab House* at the marina next to the *Homosassa Riverside Resort* (ⓣ352/621-5080), where the best spot to consume your blue crabs, grouper sandwiches, and fried shrimp is at a table overlooking the river and small island inhabited by monkeys.

Crystal River and around

Seven miles further north along US-19, **CRYSTAL RIVER** is among the region's larger communities – its population is a whopping four thousand. Many residents are retirees, fearful of the crime in Florida's urban areas and unable to afford the more southerly sections of the coast. You'd never guess it from the drab US-19, but quite a few arrivals are also drawn here by the sedate beauty of the clear river from which the town takes its name. **Manatees** take a shine to it as well: they can be seen all year round, but during the winter greater numbers are found at the **Chassahowitzka National Wildlife Refuge** (Mon–Fri 7.30am–4pm; ⓣ352/563-2088), accessible by turning west on US-19 at Paradise Point Road in Crystal River. Here you can also swim, snorkel, and scuba dive and there are also plenty of boat trips in the area. The American Pro Diving Center, 821 SE US-19 (ⓣ352/563-0041 or 1-800/291-3483, ⓦwww.americanprodiving.com), offers all kinds of guided dives from $30 to $50 and rents convenient waterfront villas from $80 a night, so you can step right out into a boat in the morning.

Crystal River's present dwellers are by no means the first to have lived by the waterway – it provided a source of food for Native Americans from at least 200 BC. To gain some insight into Indian culture, take State Park Road off US-19 just north of the town to the **Crystal River State Archaeological Site**, 3400 N Museum Point (daily 8am–sunset; cars $2, pedestrians and cyclists $1; ⓣ352/795-3817), where the temple, burial, and shell midden mounds are still visible. Inside the **visitor center** (daily 9am–5pm) there is an enlightening assessment of finds from the 450 graves discovered here, indicating trade links with tribes far to the north. More fascinating, however, are the connections with the south. The site contains two *stele*, or ceremonial stones, much more commonly found in Mexico, and the engravings – thought to be faces of sun deities – suggest that large-scale solar ceremonies were conducted here. The

Manatees

Manatees are one of Florida's most beloved creatures, but sadly also one of its most endangered. More closely related to elephants and aardvarks than to other sea life, it's hard to believe that these large animals – they can grow up to thirteen feet tall and weigh up to 3500 pounds – are the source of the mermaid myth. Manatees are harmless and love to graze on seagrasses in shallow water, surfacing every three to four minutes to breathe. They have been on the endangered species list since 1973, and there are only a few thousand left in Florida waters. With no natural predators, a third of manatee deaths have human-related causes, such as accidents with boats, pollution, and flood control gates that automatically close. Although scientists believe that manatees can live to 60 or longer, their slow development to sexual maturity and low birth rate do little to compensate for their disproportionately high death rate. Manatees may be endangered, but Florida law prohibits breeding them; resources, they say, are better spent on the care and rehabilitation of wild manatees that have suffered the blows of ship's propellers or river poisoning. You should never approach, feed, or touch manatees in the wild and if you see an injured or dead one, a calf with no adult around, or see anyone harassing one, call the Florida Marine Patrol on ⓣ352/447-1633. To learn more about manatees and their conservation, read *Manatees: An Educator's Guide* produced by the Save the Manatee Club, 500 N Maitland Ave, Maitland, FL 32751 (ⓣ1-800/432-5646, ⓦwww.savethemanatee.org). Most of the dive shops in Crystal River offer snorkeling and diving trips geared to swimming with the manatees (starting from $30).

sense of the past and the serenity of the setting make the site a highly evocative educational experience. Don't pass it by.

Practicalities

Other than diving and visiting the archaeological site, Crystal River doesn't have much to justify a long stop, though if you're traveling by Greyhound (the station is at 200 N US-19; ⓣ352/795-4445), it's useful for an overnight rest. The best **accommodation** is at the *Plantation Inn*, within walking distance of the bus station at 9301 W Fort Island Trail or Route 44 (ⓣ352/795-1601 or 1-800/524-7733, ⓦwww.plantationinn.com; ❹), surrounded by attractive bayfront lawns, with an onsite dive shop and a golf course nearby. If you're planning on swimming with the manatees or playing golf, the manatee and golf packages (which include accommodation at the inn) are more cost effective. The *Best Western*, 614 NW US-19 (ⓣ352/795-3171; ❹), also has a dive shop, while the *Days Inn*, just north of the town on US-19 (ⓣ352/795-2111; ❷), has the cheapest rooms in town.

The closest **campground** is *Rock Crusher Canyon*, 275 Rock Crusher Rd (ⓣ352/795-3870, ⓦwww.rockcrushercanyon.com), where it costs $35 a night to pitch a tent. The site, which was an old phosphate mine, is also home to Florida's largest natural amphitheater, where a wide variety of live music is regularly performed (closed during summer). For **food**, try *Cravings on the Water*, 614 NW US-19, next to the *Best Western* (ⓣ352/795-2027), a great place for authentic Cuban sandwiches and bread, as well as delicious home-made flan and Key lime pie. Alternatives include the seafood-based *Charlie's Fish House*, 224 NW US-19 (ⓣ352/795-3949), with river views and an adjoining fish market, and the basic but dependable *Crystal Paradise Restaurant*, 508 Citrus Ave (ⓣ352/563-2620).

The **Chamber of Commerce**, 28 NW US-19 (Mon–Fri 9am–4pm, Sat 10am–2pm; ⓣ352/795-3149, ⓦwww.citruscountychamber.com), can supply general information on Crystal River and around.

Yankeetown and around

Ten miles north of Crystal River, US-19 spans the **Florida Barge Canal**. Conceived in the 1820s to provide a cargo link between the Gulf and Atlantic coasts, work on the canal only started in the 1930s and – thanks largely to the efforts of conservationists – was abandoned in the 1970s with just six miles completed. The bridge offers a view of the Crystal River nuclear power station, the area's major employer and the reason why local telephone books carry instructions on how to survive a nuclear catastrophe.

Further on, taking any left turn off US-19 will invariably lead to some tiny, eerily quiet community where fishing on the local river is the only sign of life. One such place is **YANKEETOWN**, five miles west of Inglis on Route 40, reputedly named for some Yankee soldiers who moved here following the Civil War. Yankeetown's claim to fame is that in 1961 Elvis filmed *Follow That Dream* in several locations around the area: the bridge over Bird Creek was the main set, and Route 40 is also known as Follow That Dream Parkway. Those who follow it to the very end will be rewarded with a large stretch of serene, isolated water, populated only by herons and the ubiquitous fishermen.

The area around Yankeetown contains many parks and preserves, most with something to recommend them. Two of the largest are **Withlacoochee State**

Forest (south of Route 44) and **Chassahowitzka National Wildlife Refuge** (west of US-19, see p.302). Further north, the protected wildlife habitats of the **Wacassassa State Preserve** cover the salt marshes and tidal creeks on the coastal side of US-19 as you travel on from Yankeetown. A breeding ground for deer and turkey, and sometimes visited by black bear and Florida panthers, these swampy lands are intended to allow the state's indigenous creatures to replenish their numbers. Humans are not allowed free rein, though there are periodic ranger-guided **canoe trips** through the area; call ⓣ352/543-5567 for details. More information can be found at the **Chamber of Commerce**, 167 Hwy-4 W (Thurs–Sat 9am–1pm, hours may vary; ⓣ352/447-3383). For motel **accommodation** try the *Withlacoochee Motel*, 66 US-19 S (ⓣ352/447-2211; ❷), or you can **camp** on the banks of the Withlacoochee River at *B's Marina*, 6621 Riverside Drive (ⓣ352/447-5888, ⓦwww.bmarinacampground.net; $15). After a devastating fire, the local landmark *Izaak Walton Lodge*, Riverside Drive at 63rd Street (ⓣ352/447-2311; ❺), rents two cabins by the river, but is better known for being Yankeetown's best **restaurant**, where seafood, steak, prime rib, and wild game dishes start around $20 (closed Mon).

Cedar Key

Whatever you do on your way north, don't deny yourself a day or two at the splendidly isolated and charmingly scenic community of **CEDAR KEY**. To find it, turn west off US-19 onto Route 24 at the hamlet of Otter Creek and drive for 24 miles until the road ends. In the 1860s, the railroad from Fernandina Beach (see "The Northeast," p.371) ended its journey here, turning the community – which occupies one of several small islands – into a thriving port. When ships got bigger and moved on to deeper harbors, Cedar Key began cutting down its cypress, pine, and cedar trees to fuel a pencil-producing industry. Inevitably, the trees were soon gone, and by 1900 Cedar Key was all but a ghost town. The few who stayed eked out a living from fishing and harvesting oysters, as many of the thousand-strong population still do. Cedar Key has, however, undergone a revival. Many decaying, timber-framed warehouses have been turned into restaurants and shops, and more holiday homes are appearing. Given the town's remoteness, however (there's no public transport from other communities in the area), it's unlikely that Cedar Key will ever be deluged with visitors – the only remotely busy periods are during the Seafood Festival sponsored by the Cedar Key Lions Club (ⓣ352/543-5600) in October and the arts and crafts show during April – and the place remains a fascinating example of the Old South. The **Chamber of Commerce**, next door to the former city hall on Second Street (Mon, Tues, Wed, & Fri 9am–1pm, Sun 10am–2pm; ⓣ352/543-5600, ⓦwww.cedarkey.org), has a cozy visitor's center with all the usual neighborhood information. When this is closed, try the Cedar Key State Museum (see opposite) or Cedar Key Bookstore on Second Street for information.

Accommodation

As befits the town's picture-postcard setting, the accommodation options tend to be atmospheric and pretty, most with fine waterfront views. Prices are higher in the center of town, while reasonable rates can be found if you're prepared to stay on the islands closer to the mainland. You can pitch a **tent** at *Sunset Isle RV Park*, one mile from the center on Route 24 (ⓣ352/543-5375; $16).

Cedar Key Bed & Breakfast 810 Third St ⓣ352/543-9000 or 1-877/543-5051, ⓦwww.cedarkeybandb.com. Relax in this beautiful wooden house with a garden dominated by a 400-year-old live oak tree. Choose from six comfortable rooms or a more private "Honeymoon Cottage." ❹

Dockside Motel 491 Dock St ⓣ352/543-5432 or 1-800/541-5432, ⓦwww.dockside-cedarkey.com. You won't find anything cheaper or as centrally located as this motel, which is situated on the dock a few steps away from the fishing-friendly pier. Ten well-furnished suites, one with a full kitchen, are also available. ❷

Island Hotel 373 Second St, at B Street ⓣ352/543-5111 or 1-800/432-4640, ⓦwww.islandhotel-cedarkey.com. An undeniably atmospheric place with sloping wooden floors, overhanging verandas, sepia murals dating from 1915 – and supposedly a ghost – marred somewhat by indifferent service. ❹

The Island Place First Street, at C Street ⓣ352/543-5307 or 1-800/780-6522, ⓦwww.islandplace-ck.com. One- and two-bedroom suites with fully equipped kitchens and balconies overlooking the pool and the waters of the Gulf. ❹

Pirates' Cove Route 24 ⓣ352/543-5141, ⓦwww.piratescovecottages.com. The location about half a mile from the center between the second and third bridges results in cheaper rates and views of the bayou, with its diverse birdlife. Accommodation is in six refurbished cottages, and fishing gear is provided should you wish to try your hand from the fishing deck. ❷

The island and around

With its rustic, ramshackle galleries, old wooden houses on Second Street, and the glittering reflections off the waters of Cedar Key's unspoiled bay, the island is perfect for exploring. The **Cedar Key State Museum**, 12231 SW 166 Court (Thurs–Mon 9am–5pm; $1; ⓣ352/543-5350), exhibits household items from the past and boasts an enormous collection of exotic shells from around the region. The **Historical Society Museum**, on the corner of D and Second streets (Sun–Fri 1–4pm, Sat 11am–5pm; $1; ⓣ352/543-5549), reveals the fact that this, in fact, is not the original site of Cedar Key. The uninhabited island cloaked in foliage across the water bore the town's name until the end of the nineteenth century, when a hurricane tore every building to pieces. The devastated ruins of a bed-and-breakfast still sulk near the dock and now serve as the adopted home of a troupe of pelicans, whose presence has helped make this Cedar Key's most popular postcard scene. The museum also supplies various leaflets, and sells maps of Cedar Key and a **historic walking tour** guide for $4.50.

If you're staying for several days, take a boat trip out to the twelve islands within a five-mile radius of Cedar Key – set aside in 1929 by President Hoover as the **Cedar Keys National Wildlife Refuge**. *Island Hopper*, at the City Marina on Dock Street (ⓣ352/543-5904, ⓦwww.cedarkeyislandhopper.com), operates daily cruises to **Seahorse Key** for $12 and also rents out boats. Seahorse Key boasts a pretty lighthouse built in 1851. At 52 feet, it stands on the highest point of land on the Gulf Coast. Landing is prohibited on the key between March and June when the island becomes a sanctuary for nesting birds; during this time the *Island Hopper* lands at another key. For a more personalized tour of the area, consider the **kayak tours** run by Wild Florida Adventures (ⓣ352/528-3984 or 1-877/945-3928, ⓦwww.wild-florida.com), which explore much of the Big Bend as well as the lower Suwannee River. Their half-day tours cover the **Lower Suwannee National Wildlife Refuge**, which fronts 26 miles of the Gulf of Mexico and is an ideal place to see the nesting grounds of a multitude of birds, including white ibis, egret, blue herons, ospreys, and brown pelicans. *Island Hopper* also offers a sunset/moonrise tour during which you can watch the moon rise over the water and maybe even spot a dolphin in the moonlight. Both tours cost $50.

Bikes, cars, and Cedar Key's slow pace

Cedar Key is made for walking, but renting a **bike** from Fishbonz on Third Street near the dock (closed Mon; ⓣ352/543-9922) is also an enjoyable option. If you're driving, the one thing you're sure to notice is the absurdly slow speed limits – sometimes down to fifteen miles per hour despite the absence of traffic. Don't be lulled into thinking the traffic police don't bother. They do.

Eating

While there aren't a lot of **places to eat** in Cedar Key, it is nevertheless the best place in the Big Bend for dining out, offering the largest selection of restaurants and cafés between Tampa Bay and the Panhandle. Sampling freshly caught seafood is an enjoyable way to spend a few hours in Cedar Key: oysters, smoked mullet, and fried trout are among the local, rather expensive specialties.

Annie's Café Route 24, at Sixth Street ⓣ352/543-6141. A quiet place, away from the main drag of the dock, to enjoy home-style breakfasts and lunches.
Blue Desert Café 12815 Route 240 ⓣ352/543-9111. The food – all of it cooked from scratch, so be patient – includes fine pizzas, bruscetta, and a salsa dip to die for. A friendly ambience and thirty different types of beer add to the appeal. Closed Sun & Mon.
Captain's Table 222 Dock Street ⓣ352/543-5441. One of a string of restaurants on Dock Street with the usual seafood offerings, plus live music and dancing – as much a reason for coming here as the food.
Cook's Café Second Street ⓣ352/543-5548. A good bet for breakfast as well as for the fresh grouper mullet, and shrimp served at reasonable prices during the day.
The Island Room 192 Second St ⓣ352/543-6520. Cedar Key's most elegant restaurant, boasting a justly famous crab bisque and dishes made with homegrown ingredients.
Pat's Red Luck Café 390 Dock St ⓣ352/543-6840. Regarded by locals as one of the town's best eateries, this café has enough on the menu to satisfy vegetarians – which is not always the case elsewhere.

North toward the Panhandle

Back on US-19, there's a featureless ninety-mile slog to the next noticeable town, **PERRY**. The lumber industry for which the place is famous is celebrated in the **Forest Capitol State Museum**, one mile south of the town, at 204 Forest Park Drive (Thurs–Mon 9am–noon & 1–5pm; $1; ⓣ850/584-3227); exhibits include an 1860 furnished "cracker" home (see p.297) of limited interest. The only reason to stay in Perry is if you're too tired to travel any further, and there are a number of motels on US-19 set up for just this contingency, one of the best deals being the *Southern Inn*, 2238 S US-19 or Byron Butler Parkway (ⓣ850/584-4221; ❶). Otherwise, nothing breaks the journey **north toward the Panhandle**, fifty miles distant. Gas stations are less frequent and more expensive on this stretch of road, so if you're driving, fill up in advance. To reach Tallahassee, stick to US-19 (from here also known as US-27), or, for the Panhandle coast, branch west with US-98. The Panhandle is fully detailed in Chapter 9.

North central Florida

The alternative and quicker option to taking US-19 from the Tampa Bay area to the Panhandle would be to follow I-75 up through the center of the state, then, instead of continuing north into Georgia, turn west onto I-10 to Tallahassee. As unrelentingly ordinary as I-75 is, just a few miles to the east of the interstate are the villages and small towns that typified Florida before the arrival of made-to-measure vacations and mass tourism. The region has just two appreciably sized towns, one of which, **Gainesville**, holds a major university and a terrain that varies from rough scrub to resplendent grassy acres lubricated by dozens of natural springs. The other, **Ocala**, is the access point to a sprawling national forest. This part of Florida is definitely worth a few days of your time, as much for its charming atmosphere compared with points further south as for things to see or do. Costs here can be relatively low, too.

Ocala and around

Known throughout the US for the champion runners bred and trained at the thoroughbred horse farms occupying its green and softly undulating surrounds (the 1978 Triple Crown winner, *Affirmed*, was bred here), **OCALA** itself is a town without much to shout about – though it makes an agreeable base for seeing more of the immediate area, which is noted for its pristine natural springs. The **visitor center**, 110 E Silver Springs Blvd (daily 10am–4pm; Ⓣ352/629-8051), can supply local facts, issue walking maps of the town's mildly interesting historic districts, and tell you which of the **horse farms** are open for free self-guided tours.

The Don Garlits and Appleton museums

Ten miles south of Ocala, exit 67 off I-75, the **Don Garlits Museum of Drag Racing** (daily 9am–5pm; $8 for the drag racing exhibit, or $12 if adding on the antique car exhibit; Ⓣ352/245-8661, Ⓦwww.garlits.com) parades

"The Villages" in central Florida

The nondescript town of **Leesburg**, thirty miles south of Ocala on US-27, is dotted with communities, sometimes described as "country clubs," where seniors can live out their remaining years in peace, and sometimes considerable luxury. One such community, **The Villages**, 1100 Main St (Ⓣ352/753-2270 or 1-800/346-4556, Ⓦwww.thevillages.com), sprawling on either side of US-27, nine miles north of Leesburg, is among the fastest growing in the US. Indeed, in these parts The Villages is considered to be a town in its own right. Thanks to five eighteen-hole golf courses and a multitude of shops, restaurants, and services, including a fully equipped hospital, residents rarely have the need – or inclination – to venture beyond the gates. Should you wish to sample Floridian retirement living on its grandest scale, you can do so surprisingly cheaply. Four-, five-, six- and seven-night stays at a fully furnished guest villa cost from $400 to $700; and for each night you stay you'll receive 75 "Village dollars," which can be spent on most goods and services in The Villages.

dozens of low-slung drag-racing vehicles, including the "Swamp Rat" machines that propelled local legend Don Garlits to 270mph over the drag tracks during the mid-Fifties. Yellowing press cuttings and grainy films chart the rise of the sport, and a subsidiary display of Chevys, Buicks, and Fords – and the classic hits pumped out by a Wurlitzer jukebox – evoke an *American Graffiti* atmosphere.

An outstanding assembly of art and artifacts is found about seven miles east of I-75, inside the **Appleton Museum of Art**, 4333 NE Silver Springs Blvd (daily 10am–6pm; $6, under-18s free; ⓣ352/236-7100, ⓦwww.appletonmuseum.org). Spanning the globe and five thousand years, the exhibits, collected by a wealthy Chicago industrialist, go together with remarkable cohesion, and there's barely a dull moment over two well-filled floors. Early Rembrandt etchings, a Rodin *Thinker* cast from the original mold, and paintings by Jules Breton amid an exquisite stock of nineteenth-century French canvases are admirable enough, but the handicrafts are really special: look for the Turkish prayer rugs, the brightly colored Naxco ceramics, the wooden Tibetan saddle, and the massed ranks of "Toggles" – Japanese *netsuke* figures carved from ivory.

Silver Springs

Approximately one mile east of Ocala at 5656 SR-40/Silver Springs Blvd, **Silver Springs** (daily 10am–5pm; $33, children 3–10 $24; ⓣ352/236-2121, ⓦwww.silversprings.com) has been winning admirers since the late 1800s when Florida's first tourists came by steamboat to stare into the spring's deep, clear waters.

During the 1930s and 1940s, six of the original *Tarzan* films, starring Johnny Weissmuller, were shot here. Today, the park operates as a highly commercial enterprise: a menagerie of imported animals, such as monkeys, giraffes, and llamas, plus the inevitable petting zoo mar an otherwise attractive spot where you can happily wile away the day. The admission fee, however, is high, especially considering the proliferation of springs all across central and northern Florida, some of them just a few miles east in the Ocala National Forest (see p.310) or north of Gainesville (see p.317). From a conservationist point of view, Wakulla Springs near Tallahassee (see p.428) is a far better bet. However, if you do decide to visit Silver Springs, you'll get the most from the **Glass-Bottomed Boat Tour** (the best of several boat rides available; and given a certain historical resonance by the fact that the glass-bottomed boat was invented here in 1878), the **Jungle Cruise**, and the **Jeep Safari**, all of which run regularly through the day. The **Big Gator Lagoon** attraction is fun during feeding time, when you get to throw tasty morsels at the alligators and watch them jump for the food. **World of Bears** offers a glimpse of the creatures as well as an educational program about their lives at Silver Springs. Other attractions include **Panther Prowl**, an up-close look at the lives of these endangered felines, and the **Lost River Voyage**, which takes you around the Silver River and back into primeval Florida. Silver Springs also now offers a full schedule of popular music concerts, including big names from country to rock and roll. If you feel like cooling off, or have kids in tow, buy a combo ticket, which allows entry to the adjacent **Wild Waters** (late March to mid-Sept, daily 10am–5pm; 10am–7pm during summer; ⓦwww.wildwaterspark.com), a typical water park with slides, wave pools, amusement arcades, and so on.

If you decide you want to spend a couple of days visiting Silver Springs and Wild Waters, the best choice for **lodging** is the *Holiday Inn*, right across from the entrance at no. 5751 (ⓣ352/236-2575, ⓦwww.holiday-inn.com/silversprings; ❸), an attractive establishment with two pools (one for the kids) and an attached *Denny's* 24-hour restaurant.

Rainbow Springs State Park

A more natural setting for a walk and a swim is **Rainbow Springs State Park**, located about twenty miles west of Ocala and three miles north of Dunnellon, off US-41 (daily 8am–sunset; walk-in only, $1 per person; ⓣ352/489-8503, camping ⓣ352/489-5201; $14 per night). From 1890 until the 1960s, this park rivaled Silver Springs as a commercial venture, but has thankfully been allowed to return to its natural state. A popular haunt for locals, it's busy on weekends, with families picnicking on the grass and splashing around in the springs. At other times you can enjoy exploring woodland **trails** in peace and quiet, keeping an eye out for bobcats, raccoons, wild pigs, otters, and a great variety of birdlife, then have a swim in the cool, crystal-clear waters. Phone ahead to take advantage of the **ranger-led walks** (winter only) and **snorkeling** tours (summer). Day-trippers to the park can take advantage of canoe and kayak rentals for $5 per hour. If you're camping, inner-tube rentals are also available for a leisurely drift down the Blue Run River.

Accommodation: Ocala and around

Motels line Silver Springs Boulevard between Ocala and Silver Springs. One of the cheapest is the *Southland Motel*, no. 1260 E (ⓣ352/351-0113; ❶), while the *Days Inn–Ocala East*, no. 5001 E (ⓣ352/236-2891; ❷), costs slightly more for satisfactory rooms and the standard facilities. The *Ritz Historic Inn*, 1205 E Silver Springs Blvd (ⓣ352/671-9300 or 1-888/382-9390, ⓦwww.ritzhistoricinn.com; ❹), with its attractive mosaic tile swimming pool, fountains, and gardens, has considerably more charm and historic appeal. For real luxury, try the *Seven Sisters Inn Bed & Breakfast*, in Ocala's historic district at 820 SE Fort King St (ⓣ352/867-1170 or 1-800/250-3496, ⓦwww.7sistersinn.com; ❺), where you can stay in rooms decorated to recall such far-flung places as Argentina, Egypt, and India. For other upscale lodgings around Ocala – convenient if you're visiting a horse ranch – see box below. The only local

Horseback riding

A visit to the Ocala area isn't really complete without seeing one of its numerous **horse ranches**, but you'll need a car to reach them. If you actually want to go horseback riding, rather than simply view the ranches from the road, try **Young's Paso Fino Ranch**, four miles along SR-326, off I-75, at no. 8075 NW (ⓣ352/867-5305, ⓦwww.youngspasofino.com; book ahead). One of the country's top ranches for breeding and training Paso Fino horses (the name means "fine gait" in Spanish), Young's offers instruction before taking you out on a trail ($30 for 1hr 30min, including instruction). The horses' easy disposition and exceptionally smooth gait make them an ideal choice for beginners as well as more advanced riders.

An ideal place to rest your saddle-sore butt after a hard day's horseback riding is the **Heritage Country Inn**, set in ranch country at 14343 W Hwy-40, off I-75 (ⓣ352/489-0023 or 1-888/240-2233, ⓦwww.heritagecountryinn.com; ❺). There are six unique bedrooms, ranging from The Plantation Room to The Thoroughbred Room, and a favorite among guests is the home-baked cinnamon bread.

West of Ocala, handy for Silver Springs, is another great option that combines horseback riding with a commodious B&B: **Rosslor Manor**, 3230 NE 55th Ave, just north of Wild Waters (ⓣ352/236-4219 or 1-800/404-2362, ⓦwww.rosslor.com; ❼). The friendly, urbane owners offer an extended continental breakfast, instruction for all levels, and pure luxury. You can bring your own horses or rent one from the Rosslor stables.

campground (aside from camping in the Ocala National Forest) to allow tents is the *KOA*, five miles southwest of Ocala off Route 200 at 3200 SW 38th Ave (☎352/237-2138). You can pitch a tent here for $32 or rent a cabin for $52.

Eating and drinking: Ocala and around

You'll seldom need to spend more than $5 for a filling **meal** in town, what with a wide selection of eateries along East Silver Springs Boulevard. For lunch or dinner, *Piccadilly Cafeteria*, no. 1602 (☎352/622-7447), has home-style foods served cafeteria-style, including four vegetables and bread for under $5 and meals with meat for a dollar or so more. At the other end of the scale, *Carmichael's*, no. 3105, about eight miles east of Ocala (☎352/622-3636), is one of the area's most elegant choices and features a large, eclectic menu for breakfast, lunch, and dinner. *Richard's Place*, also on East Silver Springs Boulevard, though right in town at no. 316 (☎352/351-2233), is the place locals go for a full, American-style breakfast, while *Harry's*, 24 SE First Ave (☎352/840-0900), with outdoor seating directly on the central square, specializes in New Orleans cooking and has great seafood – and a fun-loving atmosphere. Ocala **nightlife**, such as it is, is limited to the few nondescript bars and bistros grouped around the town square.

Ocala National Forest

Translucent lakes, bubbling springs, and a splendid 65-mile hiking trail bring weekend adventurers to the 400,000-acre **OCALA NATIONAL FOREST** (free), five miles east of Silver Springs on Route 40. Steer clear of the busy bits, and you'll find plenty to savor in seclusion. Alternatively, if you only have time for a quick look, take a spin along Route 19 (meeting Route 40, 22 miles into the forest) running north–south in the shade of overhanging hardwoods near the forest's eastern edge.

Juniper, Alexander, and Salt springs

For swimming, canoeing (rent on the spot; $26 per one-way outing), gentle hiking, and lots of other people, especially on weekends and holidays, the forest has three warm-water springs that fit the bill; and each of them has a campground. The easiest to reach from Silver Springs is **Juniper Springs** (☎352/625-3147; $3 per person; $13 per campsite), fifteen miles ahead on Route 40, particularly suited to hassle-free canoeing with a seven-mile marked course. **Alexander Springs** (☎352/669-3522; $3 per person; $13 per campsite),

Ocala National Forest information

The Ocala **Chamber of Commerce**, 110 E Silver Springs Blvd (visitor center: daily 10am–4pm; ☎352/629-8051), has maps and general information, and visitor centers are located at three park entrances (daily 9am–5pm; ☎352/236-0288, 685-3070 or 669-7495), offering details on every campground. The latest camping updates are available by phoning the camping areas at Juniper, Alexander, and Salt springs (see above). For specialist hiking tips, call one of the district ranger offices – the northern and southern halves of the forest are administered respectively by the Lake George Ranger District, 17147 E Hwy-40, Silver Springs (☎352/625-2520), and the Seminole Ranger District, 40929 Route 19, Umatilla (☎352/669-3153).

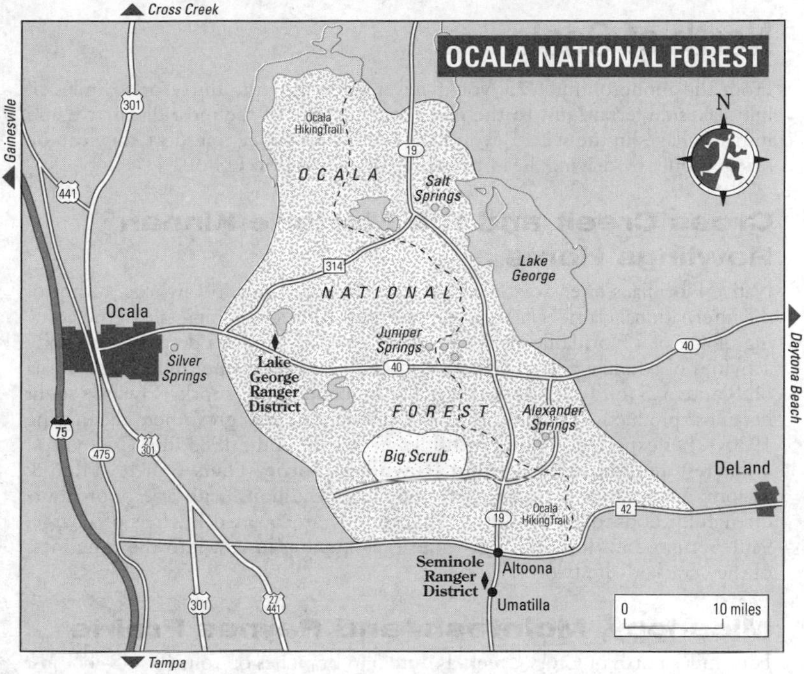

on Route 445 off SR-19 about ten miles southeast of Juniper Springs, has good canoeing, too, and its see-through waters are perfect for snorkeling.

To the north of the forest, reachable on Route 314 or Route 19, the most developed site – it even has a gas station and laundromat – is **Salt Springs** (☎352/685-2048; $3 per person; $13 per campsite). Despite the name, the springs here flow with 52 million gallons of fresh water a day, and the steady 72°F temperature stimulates a semi-tropical landscape of vividly colored plants and palm trees. Swimming and canoeing are as good here as at the other two springs, but people come mainly for the **fishing**, casting off in anticipation of catfish, large-mouthed bass, and speckled perch.

The Ocala Hiking Trail

The 67-mile **Ocala Hiking Trail** runs right through the forest, traversing many remote, swampy areas, and passing the three springs mentioned above. Very **basic campgrounds** (free) appear at regular intervals (be warned that these are closed during the mid-November to early January hunting season). At the district rangers' offices (see the box opposite), pick up the excellent leaflet describing the trail, which is part of the Florida State Scenic Trail.

However keen you might be, you're unlikely to have the time or stamina to tackle the entire trail, though one exceptional area that merits the slog required to get to it is **Big Scrub**, an imposingly severe landscape with sand dunes – and sometimes wild deer – moving across its semi-arid acres. The biggest problem at Big Scrub is lack of shade from the scorching sun, and the fact that the nearest facilities of any kind are miles away – don't come unprepared. Big Scrub is in the southern part of the forest, seven miles along Forest Road 573, off Route 19, twelve miles north of Altoona.

North of Ocala

From the monotonous I-75, you'd never guess that the thirty or so miles of hilly, lakeside terrain just to the east contain some of the most distinctive and insular villages in the state. Beyond the bounds of public transport, they can be reached only by driving; head **north from Ocala** on US-301.

Cross Creek and the Marjorie Kinnan Rawlings Home

Native Floridians often wax lyrical about Marjorie Kinnan Rawlings, author of the international classic *The Yearling*, the Pulitzer Prize–winning tale of the coming of age of a Florida farmer's son, and *Cross Creek*, which describes the daily activities of country folk in **CROSS CREEK**, about twenty miles from Ocala on Route 325 (off US-301). Leaving her husband in New York, Rawlings spent her most productive years writing and tending a citrus grove here during the 1930s – her experience being faithfully re-created in the 1983 film *Cross Creek*.

The restored **Marjorie Kinnan Rawlings Home** (Thurs–Sun 10–11am & 1–4pm; guided tours of up to ten people on the hour, with afternoon tours often fully booked; $3, children $2; grounds are open daily, free of charge, 9am–5pm; ⓣ352/466-3672) gives an eye-opening insight into the toughness of the "cracker" lifestyle.

Micanopy, McIntosh, and Paynes Prairie

Four miles north of Cross Creek, Route 346 branches off to meet US-441 just outside **MICANOPY**. A voguish vacation destination during the late 1800s, Micanopy, named after a Seminole chief, has made an effort to win back visitors by restoring many of its century-old brick buildings and turning some

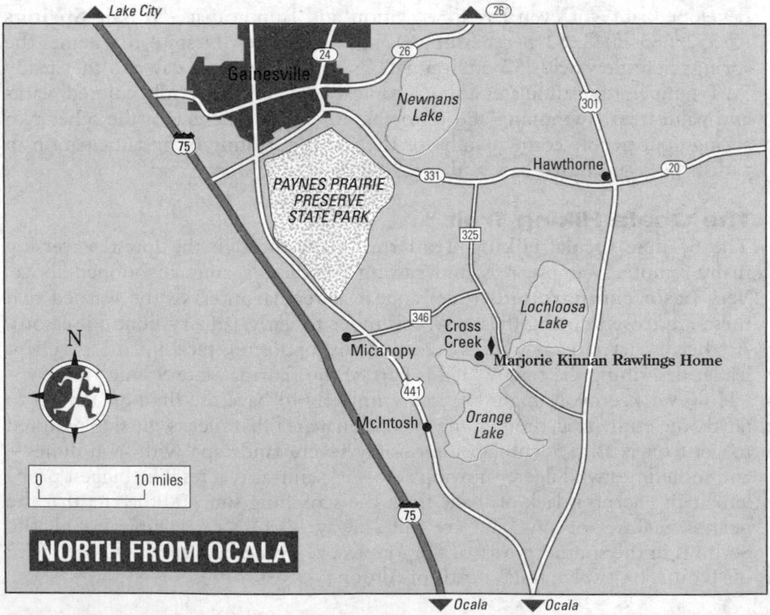

into antique and craft shops. The atmosphere is most evocative of the slowed-down pace of the Old South, with its enormous live-oak trees and the Spanish moss trailing down to the ground, and you may even be drawn to **stay**. Top choice would certainly be the glorious Greek-revival *Herlong Mansion*, 402 NE Cholokka Blvd (ⓣ352/466-3322, ⓦwww.herlong.com; ❹), whose facade of Corinthian columns will make you feel you've just come home to Tara. For great home cookin', try **lunch** on the veranda of the *Old Florida Café*, right downtown (ⓣ352/466-3663).

If you have time, you might want to travel a few miles south along US-441 to another village, **MCINTOSH**, whose 400-strong population dresses up every October in Victorian costumes for the **1890 festival** to escort visitors around the restored homes. There you'll find several antique stores and on the way, just four miles south of Micanopy and two miles north of McIntosh, you can stop to check out the Historic Harvest Village shops and its *Sisters 3 Café* (ⓣ352/591-1191), with its full range of international choices and great array of homemade desserts.

In contrast to the conviviality found in these quaint towns of the Old South, the marshy landscapes of the **Paynes Prairie Preserve State Park** (daily 8am–sunset; cars $3.25, cyclists and pedestrians $1), filling a broad sweep of land (18,000 acres) between Micanopy and Gainesville, can't help but strike a note of foreboding. It's an eerie place in many ways, though one well stocked with wildlife: cranes, hawks, waterfowl, otters, turtles, and various wading birds all make homes here, as do many alligators. During weekends from November to April, **ranger-led hikes** (free; reservations ⓣ352/466-4100) uncover the fascinating natural history of the area – and some of the social history: habitations have been traced back to 10,000 BC. Without a guide, you can bone up on the background at the **visitor center** (daily 9am–4pm), about a mile from Micanopy off US-441, and peer into the moody wilderness from the nearby **observation tower**.

Gainesville and around

Without the University of Florida, **GAINESVILLE**, 35 miles north of Ocala, would be just another slow-paced rural community nodding off in the Florida heartland. As it is, the daintily sized place, once called Hogtown, is given a boost by its 40,000 students, who bring a lively, liberal spirit and account for the only decent **nightlife** in central Florida outside Orlando. This, combined with a few low-key targets in and around the town and some attractive and reasonable accommodation, makes Gainesville a deserving base for a day or two.

Arrival, information, and getting around

Gainesville's Greyhound **bus** station is centrally located at 516 SW Fourth Ave (ⓣ352/376-5252), with services going either north to Tallahassee or south to Orlando and Miami. The old buildings are easily tracked down with the *Historic Gainesville* brochure issued by the **Visitors and Convention Bureau**, 30 E University Ave (Mon–Fri 8.30am–5pm; ⓣ352/374-5231 or 1-866/778-5002, ⓦwww.visitgainesville.net). From the town center, it's an easy fifteen-minute walk along University Avenue to the university; though if you're feeling very lazy, take a **bus** (any number from #1 to #10) from beside the Clock Tower.

Accommodation

Although Gainesville has rows of low-cost **motels**, inconveniently located a couple of miles out of the center along Southwest Thirteenth Street, be warned that these fill quickly when the University of Florida Gators are playing at home. Gainesville also has some of the most pleasant **B&Bs** in the state. The closest tent-friendly **campground** is ten miles south at the Paynes Prairie Preserve State Park (Ⓣ352/466-3397; $10 without electricity) – see p.313.

Bambi 2119 SW Thirteenth St Ⓣ352/376-2622 or 1-800/342-2624. Slightly nearer to downtown than most of the inexpensive motels, this is a rudimentary establishment that will appeal to penniless students. ❶

Gainesville Lodge 413 W University Ave Ⓣ352/376-1224. Within easy walking distance of downtown and the campus, so the most convenient location of all the motels. Basic rooms, friendly service. ❶

Hilton 1714 SW 34th St Ⓣ352/371-3600. The most luxurious hotel in Gainesville is strategically located right next to the UF campus (but about three miles from downtown), presumably for the benefit of visiting parents and professors. ❺

Laurel Oak Inn 221 SE Seventh St Ⓣ352/373-4535, Ⓦwww.laureloakinn.com. Relatively small, five-room B&B in a quiet part of town littered with historic homes. This 1885 Queen Anne Victorian stands out as one of the more beautiful. ❸

Magnolia Plantation B&B 309 SE Seventh St Ⓣ352/375-6653 or 1-800/201-2379, Ⓦwww.magnoliabnb.com. A romantic and dreamy historic mansion, with elegant yet cozy rooms decorated in a plush Victorian style, surrounded by lush gardens and waterfalls. Enjoy the company of the owners' dogs, cats, and ducks, or bring your own pets to this pet-friendly establishment. ❹

Sweetwater Branch Inn B&B 625 E University Ave Ⓣ352/373-6760 or 1-800/451-7111, Ⓦwww.sweetwaterinn.com. Spacious, beautifully laid out, and convenient to everything the town has to offer, housed in two gracefully restored period homes. ❹

The town and university

Impressive sights are few in Gainesville's quiet center, where most of the people you'll see are office workers going to or from work or nipping out to lunch. At the junction of University Avenue and Northeast First Street you'll spot the **Clock Tower**, an undramatic relic culled from Gainesville's nineteenth-century courthouse. Inside are the clock workings and some photos from the old days. If these whet your historical appetite, explore northwards along Third Street, which reveals many of the showcase homes of turn-of-the-nineteenth-century Gainesville – Queen Anne, Colonial, and various Revival styles dominate – and the palm-fronted **Thomas Center**, 302 NE Sixth Ave (Mon–Fri 9am–5pm, Sat & Sun 1–4pm; free; Ⓣ352/334-5064), once a plush hotel and restaurant, which now hosts small-scale art and historical exhibitions.

The University of Florida

Most of Gainesville's through traffic passes half a mile west of the town center along Thirteenth Street (part of US-441), from which the **University of Florida (UF)** campus stretches three miles west from its main entrance by the junction with University Avenue. Visit the **information booth**, facing Southwest Second Street, for a free map, without which it's easy to get lost in the extensive grounds.

After the university opened in 1906, the early alumni gave Florida's economy a leg-up by pioneering the state's fantastically successful citrus farms. These days, the curriculum is no longer devoted solely to agriculture and the university's modern buildings dominate the campus, though the first you'll see are the red-brick "Collegiate Gothic" structures favored by US turn-of-the-nineteenth-century academic institutions. In the center of the campus, the 1953 **Century Tower** serves as a navigational aid and a time-keeping device – its electric bells issue a nerve-shattering carillon every hour.

University sports venues

Beyond the tower, the 83,000-seat **Florida Field/Ben Hill Griffin Stadium**, nicknamed "The Swamp" – home of the Gators football team and a monument to the popularity of college sports in Florida – can hardly be missed, and neither can the adjacent **O'Connel Center** (ⓣ352/392-5500), an indoor sports venue, entering which is akin to walking into a giant balloon. Aside from staging evening volleyball and basketball games, and entertaining design buffs, the building offers only a cool, refreshing breather.

University museums, gardens, and cultural venues

For a quick respite from the sun, take in the temporary shows in the **University Gallery**, inside the Fine Arts Building (Tues 10am–8pm, Wed–Fri 10am–5pm, Sat 1–5pm; free), which capture the best student art. Head back outdoors and walk about two miles west along Museum Road to the tidy **University Garden**, where a concealed footpath leads to **Lake Alice**, overlooked by a wooden observation platform gradually losing its battle against the surrounding vegetation. You could come here for a picnic, but the roar of insects, the constant scampering of lizards, and the plentiful alligators mean keeping your guard up as you gaze over the sizeable lake.

At the corner of Southwest 34th Street and Hull Road is the **University of Florida Cultural Complex**, where the **Florida Museum of Natural History** (Mon–Sat 10am–5pm, Sun 1–5pm; free; ⓣ352/846-2000, ⓦwww.flmnh.ufl.edu) focuses on Florida's prehistory and wildlife. The **Harn Museum of Art** (Tues–Fri 11am–5pm, Sat 10am–5pm, Sun 1–5pm; free) has an intriguing permanent collection with an emphasis on ethnic works and hosts about twelve temporary exhibitions per year. The nearby **Center for the Performing Arts**, 315 Hull Rd (ⓣ352/392-2787 or 1-800/905-2787 for ticket information, ⓦwww.performingarts.ufl.edu), brings in traveling Broadway plays, symphonies, popular music, family entertainment, and educational programs.

Eating

Gainesville is not a difficult place in which to find a good **meal**, with plenty of restaurants around the town center and the university. As a general rule, head to the town center for a more refined dining experience; the places around the UF campus offer filling meals at rock-bottom prices.

Burrito Brothers Taco Co 16 NW Thirteenth St ⓣ352/378-5948. This UF institution has been lining students' stomachs with tasty and very cheap burritos for over 25 years.

Cameo Tea Room 230 NW Second Ave ⓣ352/379-5889, ⓦwww.cameotearoom.com. Experience the gentility and good eatin' of the Old South in these appealingly decorated rooms, where a lunch of home-made quiche, tea, and scones will cost around $10. Lunch only; closed Sun & Mon.

Harry's Seafood Bar and Grill 110 SE First St ⓣ352/372-1555. A sidewalk café serving New Orleans–style seafood, pasta, chicken, burgers, and salads.

Leonardo's 706 706 W University Ave ⓣ352/378-2001. California pizzas and lots of seafood offerings. Don't miss the made-to-order mid-priced Sunday brunch whose unusual items include French toast made from home-made challah bread, and filet mignon with eggs and hollandaise sauce.

Mark's US Prime 201 SE Second Ave ⓣ352/336-0077. Upscale steak restaurant with some of the tenderest alligator tail in town. Most main dishes cost over $20. Closed Sun.

Paramount Grill 12 SW First Ave t352/378-3398. The elegant (and pricey) nouvelle cuisine and stylish dining room would be enough to make this place trendy if it didn't shut at 9.30pm (10.30 at weekends).

The Top 30 N Main St ⓣ352/337-1188. Young, arty, and hip – a good choice if all you want is a pleasant spot to refuel on salads or sandwiches for about $5.

The Wine and Cheese Gallery 113 N Main St ☎352/372-8446. An amazing selection of international wines and cheeses, and all the fresh breads, hors d'oeuvres, crudités, and pastries to go with them, in a warm, inviting setting. Prices range from $5 to $15.

Drinking, entertainment, and nightlife

The town's students keep a bright **nightlife** in motion, live rock music being especially easy to find. Check the "Scene" section of Friday's *Gainesville Sun*, or the free *Insite* newspaper, found in most bars and restaurants, for details. You could quite easily pass a couple of sedate hours in one of the town's **coffee shops** in the company of studious students and their laptop computers, or you may also find some of the restaurants listed above suitable for a drink or two. From April to October in the Downtown Plaza, opposite the Clock Tower, you can catch special events such as jazz concerts and open-air film screenings on Friday evenings.

Fat Tuesdays 116 SE First St ☎352/375-3466. Bar specializing in the sweet, crushed-ice drinks that go down all too easily on warm evenings, laced with considerable amounts of alcohol.

Hippodrome State Theatre 25 SE Second Place ☎352/375-4477. This grandiose building dominating the town center hosts contemporary plays, films, and exhibits by local artists.

Lillian's Music Store 112 SE First St ☎352/372-1010. A Gainesville institution, featuring live bands that play grunge, indie, Southern, and acoustic rock. More of a local spot than a student hangout.

Market Street Pub and Brewery 120 SW First Ave ☎352/377-2927. Brews its own beer and provides jazz, blues, and rock Thurs–Sat to help it down.

Maude's 101 SE Second St ☎352/336-9646. A smaller, more intimate place to enjoy a coffee and a slice of cake than the *Starbucks* opposite.

The University Club 18 E University Ave ☎352/378-6814, ⓦwww.ucclub.com. Downtown's no. 1 gay venue, with three levels (a bar, club, and disco). Always crowded and lively, with a deck out back.

Vibe 6 E University Ave ☎352/381-9044. Miami-style club with a hip, well-dressed clientele. House, acid, techno, and classic disco grooves Thurs–Sun. Friday night is gay night.

Kanapaha Botanical Gardens

Flower fanciers shouldn't miss the 62-acre **Kanapaha Botanical Gardens** (Mon, Tues, & Fri 9am–5pm, Wed, Sat, & Sun 9am–sunset; $5, children 6–13 $3, ☎352/372-4981, ⓦwww.kanapaha.org), five miles southwest of central Gainesville on Route 24 (also known as Archer Road), reachable on bus #1. More than most, the summer months are a riot of color and fragrances, although the design of the gardens means there's always something in bloom. Besides vines and bamboos, and special sections planted to attract butterflies and hummingbirds, the highlight is the herb garden, whose aromatic bed is raised to nose-level to encourage sniffing.

Dudley Farm

Between Gainesville and Newberry, seven miles west of I-75 off Route 26, a worthwhile excursion is a trip to the **Dudley Farm Historic State Park**, 18730 W Newberry Rd (tours of the farm Wed–Sun 9am–4pm; cars $4, pedestrians and cyclists $1; ☎352/472-1142), a working farm in the sense that park staff, dressed in clothes that the Dudley family would have worn when the farm was at its peak in the late 1800s, perform daily chores and allow visitors to feed the chickens and try their hand at harvesting and other rural activities. The farm's buildings have been, or are in the process of being restored to their original condition, and there's also a rotating exhibit at the visitor center chronicling the history of the Dudley family.

The Devil's Millhopper

Of thousands of sinkholes in Florida, few are bigger or more spectacular than the **Devil's Millhopper**, set in a state geological site (Wed–Sun 9am–5pm; cars $2, pedestrians and cyclists $1; free guided tour Sat 10am; ⓣ352/955-2008), seven miles northwest of Gainesville at 4732 NW 53rd Ave. Formed by the gradual erosion of limestone deposits and the collapse of the resultant cavern's ceiling, the lower reaches of this 120-foot-deep bowl-shaped dent have a temperature significantly cooler than the surface, allowing species of alpine plant and animal life to thrive. A winding boardwalk delivers you into the thickly vegetated depths, where dozens of tiny waterfalls trickle all around you.

North of Gainesville

Traveling **north of Gainesville** puts you in easy striking distance of the Panhandle to the west, and Jacksonville, the major city of the northeast coast, but it's best not to be in a hurry. Choose to stop a night or two here and you'll find yourself smack in the heart of some of the most pristine natural springs in the state – as well as some of the most charming, out-of-the-way towns of the Florida of yesteryear.

Alachua, High Springs, and the Parks

Continuing about twelve miles north of Gainesville on US-441, the town of **ALACHUA** is worth a stop for **lunch** and a bit of window-shopping. The restored old part of downtown has a broad selection of browsable shops, and *Govinda's*, 14603 Main St (ⓣ386/462-4500, ⓦwww.govindas.net; closed for remodeling at the time of writing), is a superb restaurant in a finely restored, enormous old home, run by the local Hare Krishna group, who do amazing things with vegetables.

Sticking to US-441 for another six miles puts you in **HIGH SPRINGS** (Chamber of Commerce ⓣ386/454-3120), voted by the readers of *Florida Living* magazine Florida's friendliest small town. If you decide to experience it for yourself, top choice for a few nights' **stay** is the *Grady House*, 420 NW First Ave (ⓣ386/454-2206, ⓦwww.gradyhouse.com; ❹), where the owners have poured their hearts into creating one of the most attractive gazebo gardens of any B&B anywhere to go with the comfortable rooms (some have antique iron beds). For less expensive accommodation, there's *The High Springs Country Inn*, along US-441, 520 NW Santa Fe Blvd (ⓣ386/454-1565, ⓦwww.highsprings.com/cinns; ❷), whose scrubbed oak and cherry wood furniture give the motel-style rooms a homely feel. Scrumptious **food** can be found downtown at the *Great Outdoors Trading Company & Café*, 65 N Main St (ⓣ386/454-2900), where the hot artichoke dip with raw veggies and chips is sensational.

The High Springs area is replete with crystal-clear sources: **Poe Springs** (9am–7.30pm; $4, children 6–13, $3; ⓣ386/454-1992), **Blue Springs** (9am–7pm; $10, children 5–12, $3; camping $15, children 5–12, $6; ⓣ386/454-1369), and **Ginnie Springs**, just to the west along County Road 340 (Mon–Thurs 8am–7pm, Fri & Sat 8am–10pm, Sun 8am–8pm; closes one hour earlier in winter; $10, children 7–14, $3; camping $16, children 7–14, $6; cottage $150 per night for up to four adults; ⓣ386/454-7188, ⓦwww.ginniespringsoutdoors.com). There's also **O'Leno State Park** (8am–sunset; cars $3.25, pedestrians and cyclists $1; ⓣ386/454-1853) and **Ichetucknee Springs State Park** (daily 8am–sunset; cars $3.25, pedestrians and cyclists $1,

☎386/497-2511) to the north and northwest, off US-441. All of these parks, both state and private, are endowed with springs, streams, and rivers – waters that lend themselves to leisurely kayaking, canoeing, or inner-tube rafting. **Canoes** can be rented in most of the parks for $15–25 a day. Weekdays, when beavers, otters, and turtles sometimes share the river, are the best time to come to the area; weekend crowds scare much of the wildlife away. Ginnie and Ichetucknee springs both also offer the possibility of cave diving, using scuba equipment to explore the mysterious, labyrinthine domain of the underground rivers; at Ginnie Springs the cost is $27 a day for certified divers, plus the cost of renting whatever equipment you may need.

There's no point in stopping in unremarkable **Lake City**, thirteen miles north of the springs, nor in the **Osceola National Forest**, to the east of Lake City. This, the smallest of the state's three federally protected forests, is mostly visited by hardened fishermen bound for its Ocean Pond, and you should aim instead for a couple of more fulfilling attractions in the near vicinity (see below).

The Stephen Foster State Culture Center

Twelve miles north of Lake City, off US-41, the **Stephen Foster State Culture Center** (daily 8am–sunset; cars $3.25, pedestrians and cyclists $1; ☎386/397-2733, Ⓦwww.stephenfostercenter.com) offers a tribute to the man who composed Florida's state song, *The Old Folks At Home*, immortalizing the waterway ("Way down upon the S'wanee river. . .") that flows by here on its 250-mile meander from Georgia's Okefenokee Swamp to the Gulf of Mexico. As it happens, Foster never actually saw the river but simply used "S'wanee" as a convenient Deep South–sounding allusion. Besides exploring Florida's musical roots, the center has a sentimental display about Foster, who penned a hatful of classic American songs including *Camptown Races*, *My Old Kentucky Home*, and *Oh! Susanna* – instantly familiar melodies, which ring out through the oak-filled park from a bell tower. Foster died in New York in 1863, at the age of 37.

The Olustee Battlefield Site

The **Olustee Battlefield Site**, thirteen miles west of Lake City beside US-90 (daily 8am–sunset; free; ☎386/758-0400), is a sure sign you're approaching the Panhandle, and was a Confederate power base during the Civil War. The only major battle of the conflict in Florida took place here in February 1864, when 5000 Union troops pressing west from Jacksonville squared up to a similar-sized Confederate force. The five-hour battle, which left three hundred dead, nearly two thousand wounded, and both sides claiming victory, is marked by a monument and a small interpretive center at the entrance (daily 9am–5pm), and by a trail around the respective troop positions. It's hard to imagine the carnage that took place in what is now – as it was then – a peaceful pine forest.

Travel details

Trains (Amtrak)

Ocala to: Jacksonville (1 daily; 2hr); Miami (1 daily; 7hr); Tampa (1 daily; 2hr 30min).
St Petersburg to: Orlando (2 daily; 2hr 55min).
Tampa to: Jacksonville (1 daily; 4hr 10min); Miami (1 daily; 5hr 20min); Orlando (2 daily; 2hr 20min).

Buses

Clearwater to: Crystal River (3 daily; 1hr 50min); St Petersburg (4 daily; 30min); Tallahassee (3 daily; 5hr 30min); Tampa (6 daily; 30min).
Crystal River to: Clearwater (2 daily; 2hr 5min); Tallahassee (3 daily; 2hr 35min); Tampa (2 daily; 2hr 30min).

Gainesville to: Miami (5 daily; 9hr 5min); Ocala (10 daily; 45min); Orlando (6 daily; 2hr 25min); Tallahassee (4 daily; 2hr 35min); Tampa (4 daily; 3hr 40min).

Lakeland to: Avon Park (1 daily; 2hr 15min); Lake Wales (1 daily; 1hr 5min); Sebring (1 daily; 2hr 35min); West Palm Beach (5 daily; 6hr 15min–7hr 55min).

Ocala to: Gainesville (10 daily; 45min); Miami (8 daily; 7hr 50min); Orlando (8 daily; 1hr 25min); Tallahassee (5 daily; 3hr 30min); Tampa (6 daily; 2hr).

St Petersburg to: Clearwater (3 daily; 30min); Tampa (8 daily; 30min).

Tampa to: Clearwater (9 daily; 30min); Crystal River (3 daily; 2hr 20min); Fort Myers (6 daily; 2hr 40min); Gainesville (5 daily; 3hr 5min); Jacksonville (7 daily; 4hr 40min); Miami (5 daily; 8hr 20min); Ocala (6 daily; 1hr 35min); Orlando (6 daily; 1hr 40min); Sarasota (5 daily; 1hr 45min); St Petersburg (8 daily; 35min); Tallahassee (4 daily; 5hr 50min).

7

Orlando and Disney World

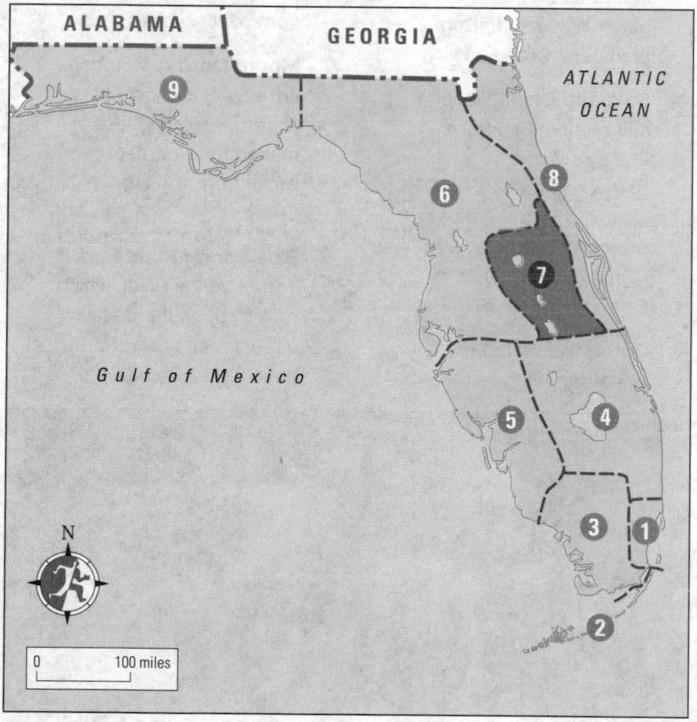

CHAPTER 7

Highlights

✱ **Blizzard Beach** Demonstrating that it can work its magic in all domains, Disney has created this excellent water park to provide a break from trudging around the theme parks. **See p.350**

✱ **Islands of Adventure** The rides don't get any better or more thrilling than here. **See p.356**

✱ **Splendid China** Despite stiff competition from Disney's World Showcase at the EPCOT Center, this is the most extensive tribute to a foreign culture on offer in Orlando. **See p.361**

✱ **Gatorland** Watch the alligators being fed – or wrestled – at this less heralded theme park between Orlando and Kissimmee. **See p.362**

✱ **Celebration** An easy day-trip from Orlando, this essay in urban planning, if not incredibly compelling in itself, has provoked a storm of controversy. **See p.363**

✱ **Mount Dora** A Victorian-era town just north of Orlando, Mount Dora makes for a genteel break from the crowds. **See p.365**

✱ **Blue Spring State Park** The St Johns River, which runs through the park, is a great place to watch manatees. **See p.367**

△ Walt Disney World

7

Orlando and Disney World

It's highly ironic that **Orlando**, an insubstantial, quiet farming town in the heart of peninsular Florida a little over thirty years ago, now has more people passing through its environs than any other place in the state. Reminders of the old Florida are still easy to find in and immediately north of Orlando. Most people, however, get no closer to Orlando's heart than a string of cheap motels along US-192, fifteen miles south of town, or **International Drive**, five miles southwest of Orlando: a long boulevard of posher motels, convention hotels, shopping malls, and schmaltzy restaurants.

The cause of the area's transformation is, of course, **Walt Disney World**, a group of state-of-the-art theme parks southwest of Orlando that lures millions of people a year to a 43-square-mile plot of previously featureless scrubland. It's possible to pass through the Orlando area and not visit Walt Disney World, but there's no way to escape its impact – even the road system was reshaped to accommodate the place, and, whichever way you look, billboards tout more ways to spend your money there. Amid a plethora of fly-by-night, would-be tourist targets, only **Universal Studios** and **SeaWorld Orlando** offer serious competition to the most finely realized concept in escapist entertainment anywhere on earth.

Orlando's tentacles have wrapped themselves firmly around much of what lies **south of Orlando**, the seemingly perfect, Disney-like town of **Celebration** being a case in point. Venture a few miles **north of Orlando**, however, and the "real world" starts to reassert itself, albeit it very gently, in the form of a quaint Victorian-era town called **Mount Dora** and the hidden village of **Cassadaga**, populated almost entirely by spiritualists.

Arrival and information

The region's primary **airport**, **Orlando International** (Ⓣ407/825-2001, Ⓦwww.orlando-mco.com), is nine miles south of downtown Orlando. Shuttle buses, such as those operated by Mears Transportation Group (Ⓣ407/423-5566), will carry you from the airport to any hotel or motel in the Orlando area. The flat rate from the airport to a hotel on International Drive is $14. If

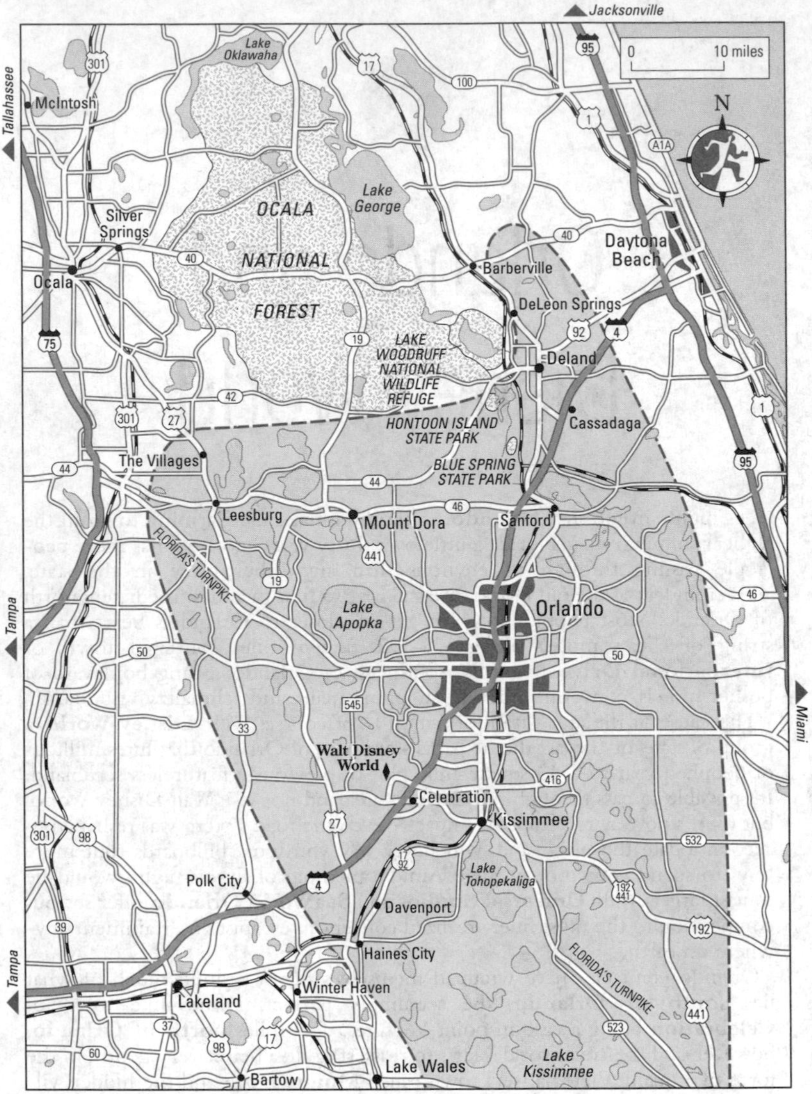

you're headed for downtown Orlando, use local bus #11 (a forty-minute journey), or #42 for International Drive (both buses depart from the airport's "A Side" concourse every thirty minutes between 5.30am and 11.30pm for #11 and 6am to 10.30pm for #42). A taxi (see p.326) to downtown Orlando, International Drive, or the motels on US-192 will cost from $30 to $45.

A second airport, **Orlando Sanford International** (Ⓣ407/585-4000, Ⓦwww.orlandosanfordairport.com), is a small but growing facility twenty miles north of downtown Orlando that receives a lot of charter flights from Great Britain. A taxi from Sanford to downtown Orlando costs about $55.

Orlando area orientation: the major roads

The major cross-Florida **roads** form a web-like mass of intersections in or around Orlando and Walt Disney World: **I-4** passes southwest–northeast through Walt Disney World and continues in elevated form through downtown Orlando; **US-192** (the **Irlo Bronson Memorial Highway**) crosses I-4 in Walt Disney World and charts an east–west course fifteen miles south of Orlando; **Hwy-528** (the **Beeline Expressway**) stems from International Drive and heads for the east coast; and **Florida's Turnpike** (for which there is a toll) cuts northwest–southeast, avoiding Walt Disney World and downtown Orlando altogether.

Arriving by **bus** or **train**, you'll wind up in downtown Orlando at the Greyhound terminal, 555 N John Young Parkway (Ⓣ407/292-3422), or the train station, 1400 Slight Blvd (Ⓣ407/843-7611). Other train stops in the area lie in Winter Park, 150 W Morse Blvd (Ⓣ407/645-5055), and Kissimmee, 111 E Dakin Ave (Ⓣ407/933-1170).

Free magazines, strewn virtually wherever you look, are packed with handy facts, but a better source of reliable **information** is the **Official Visitor Center**, 8723 International Drive, Suite 101 (daily 8am–7pm; Ⓣ407/363-5872, Ⓦwww.orlandoinfo.com), where you should pick up the free *Orlando Official Visitors Guide* and browse among the hundreds of leaflets and discount coupons. You can also purchase discounted park tickets here. The **Winter Park Chamber of Commerce**, 150 New York Ave (Mon–Fri 9am–5pm; Ⓣ407/644-8281 or 1-877/972-4262, Ⓦwww.winterparkcc.org), has good local information and brochures not found at the Official Visitor Center. If you're using the motels along US-192, drop by the equally well-stocked **Kissimmee–St Cloud Convention & Visitors Bureau**, 1925 E US-192 in Kissimmee (Mon–Fri 8am–5pm; Ⓣ407/847-5000 or 1-800/333-KISS, Ⓦwww.floridakiss.com). The best entertainment guide to the area is the Friday "Calendar" section of the *Orlando Sentinel* newspaper.

Getting around

With most routes operating from 6.30am to 8pm on weekdays, 7.30am to 6pm on Saturdays, and 8am to 6pm on Sundays, **local bus lines** (Ⓣ407/841-2279 or 1-800/344-LYNX, Ⓦwww.golynx.com) converge at the downtown Orlando terminal between Central and Pine streets. The system is known as the "Lynx," and bus-stop signs are cleverly marked with paw prints. You'll need **exact change** ($1.25 one-way; $3 day pass) if you pay on board; a weekly pass for $10 is available from the terminal's information booth. The single fare includes a free transfer to another Lynx service, valid for travel within one and a half hours of the initial ticket purchase. Given the expanse of the network and the considerable journey times, you'll often be hard-pressed to catch your second bus before the ticket expires. The "Lynx" system makes about 4000 stops in three counties, and the **most useful bus routes** (from downtown Orlando) are #1 to Loch Haven and Winter Park; #11 to the airport; #8 to International Drive – where you can connect with #42 to **Orlando International Airport** (an hour-long journey) – and #50 to Disney's The Magic Kingdom. Along International Drive, between SeaWorld Orlando and Universal Studios, the **I-Ride** trolley service (Ⓣ407/248-9590 or 1-866/243-7483, Ⓦwww.iridetrolley.com) operates every fifteen minutes daily from 8am

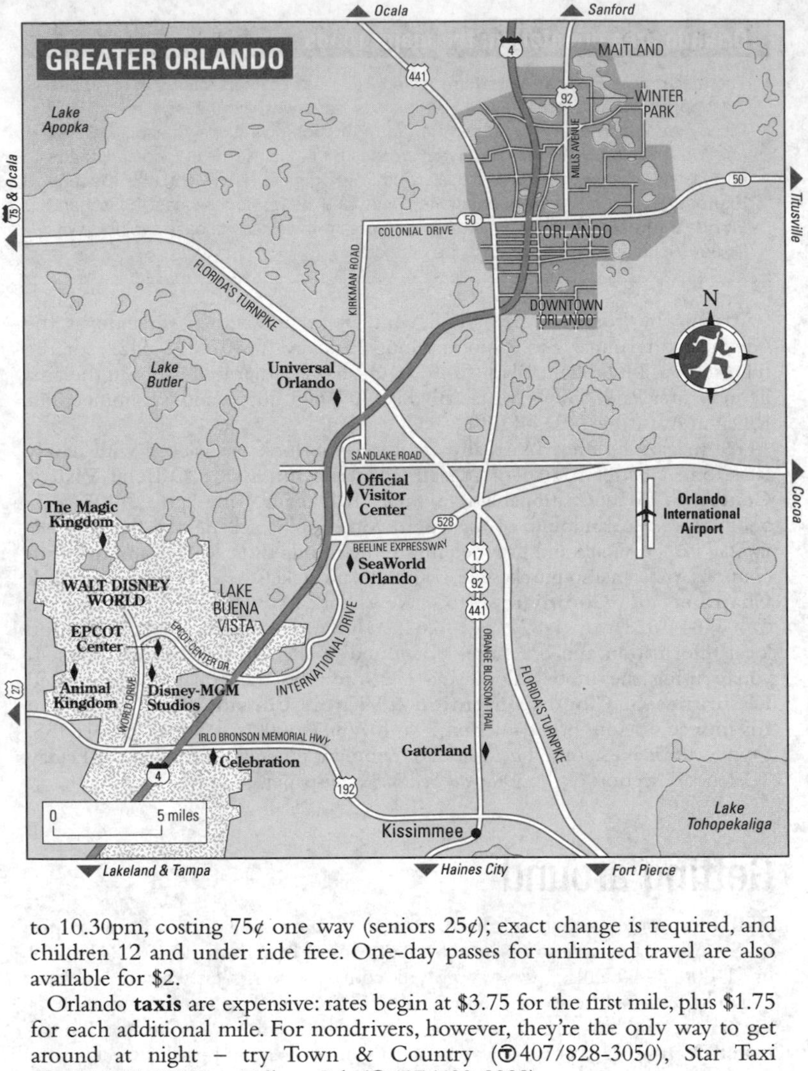

to 10.30pm, costing 75¢ one way (seniors 25¢); exact change is required, and children 12 and under ride free. One-day passes for unlimited travel are also available for $2.

Orlando **taxis** are expensive: rates begin at $3.75 for the first mile, plus $1.75 for each additional mile. For nondrivers, however, they're the only way to get around at night – try Town & Country (☎407/828-3050), Star Taxi (☎407/857-9999), or Yellow Cab (☎407/699-9999).

Cheaper than taxis, but more expensive and quicker than the I-Ride, are the **shuttle buses**, minivans, or coaches run by private companies connecting the main accommodation areas, such as International Drive and US-192, with Walt Disney World, SeaWorld Orlando, Universal Studios, and the airports. You should phone at least a day ahead to be picked up, and confirm a time for your return. Mears Transportation Group (☎407/423-5566) charges $11–13 for a round-trip ride from International Drive or US-192 to all the major attractions, and $14 one way to Orlando International Airport.

All the main **car rental** firms have offices at or close to Orlando International Airport. Demand is strong despite the high rates, so call in advance during busy seasons (for phone numbers, see "Getting around" in Basics).

Orlando

Despite the enormous expansion of the Nineties, **ORLANDO** itself remains impressively free of the commercialism that surrounds it. Bearing north from Orlando's compact **downtown** and its small but growing crop of high-rise office buildings, you'll get a taste of Florida living without the mouse-ear hats. For this is an area of smart residential neighborhoods such as **Loch Haven Park** and **Winter Park**, adorned by parks and lakes and offering the moderately high-brow museums and art galleries which, for all their varying degrees of quality, will be a refreshing change for those with theme-park fatigue. This said, most visitors haven't come to Orlando to sample more than an afternoon or two of its unheralded cultural refinement, and will inevitably gravitate southwest of the downtown area before too long to join the fun and frolics at the parks. Here, along the strip of hotels, restaurants, shopping malls, and multitude of other tourist traps that is **International Drive**, the Orlando you had always expected rears its mouse-eared head, to the great relief of kids and kids-at-heart.

Accommodation

Unless you're staying on Disney or Universal property and planning a Disney- or Universal-only vacation, you'll need to be mobile wherever you stay in the far-flung Orlando area. Price, therefore, should be more of a concern than location when looking for **accommodation**. If you're dependent on public transport, however, downtown Orlando and International Drive, both areas with good local bus connections (see p.325), are the best places to stay.

Genuinely budget-priced accommodation is offered only by the scores of cheap motels lined up **along US-192** between Walt Disney World and Kissimmee; many offer special rates that are yours simply by picking up a discount coupon at one of the information offices mentioned above. **International Drive** is dominated by expensive chain hotels and is where you're likely to end up if you come on a package trip – but bargains can be found during the slower winter periods. Accommodation, though expensive, is also available within Disney World itself and just outside Disney property in the Lake Buena Vista area (see p.339), as well as at Universal (see p.354). **Campgrounds** are plentiful on and around US-192 close to Kissimmee (see p.363). The *Kissimmee/Orlando KOA*, 2644 Happy Camper Place (ⓣ407/396-6851 or 1-800/562-7791; $20), is suited to tents and offers a large heated pool as well as a playground and game room for the kids. For a more peaceful setting, pitch your tent at *Richardson's Fish Camp*, 1550 Scotty's Rd (ⓣ407/846-6540; $17), a few miles south of Kissimmee beside West Lake Tohopekaliga, where the pace is leisurely and more fuss is made about fishing than visiting Mickey Mouse.

If you have a car, an excellent option is to **rent a villa** from Sunsplash Travel, 3710 CR 54, Davenport, FL 33837 (ⓣ863/424-6193 or 1-800/505-1359, ⓦwww.sunsplash.com; from $110 a night). The three-, four-, and five-bedroom houses come with their own pools, garages, kitchens, washing machines, and so on, and are located in an upscale residential area thirty minutes from Orlando International Airport, fifteen minutes from Disney World, and fifteen minutes from Haines City, the nearest town. The staff can provide discount tickets to Disney World and other attractions in the Orlando area, and will even furnish a prospective itinerary for your stay. Be sure to book as far ahead as possible.

Downtown Orlando

The Courtyard at Lake Lucerne 211 N Lucerne Circle E ⓣ407/648-5188 or 1-800/444-5289, ⓦwww.orlandohistoricinn.com. A lush flower garden and four separate antique inns, one of which is the oldest house in Orlando, comprise this peaceful oasis of grace and hospitality nestled right in the busy downtown area. ❹

Embassy Suites Hotel 191 E Pine St ⓣ407/841-1000, ⓦwww.embassysuites.com. Stylish luxury high-rise in the heart of downtown where all 167 suites open onto a busy atrium. Cooked-to-order and all-you-can-eat breakfast and evening reception are included in the price. ❹

Eo Inn 227 N Eola Drive ⓣ407/481-8485 or 1-888/481-8488, ⓦwww.eoinn.com. A very chic establishment right on Lake Eola, with modern furnishings and plenty of rooms with lake views. An onsite spa offers a full range of massages, facials, and the like. ❻

Four Points Sheraton 151 E Washington St ⓣ407/841-3220, ⓦwww.fourpoints.com. The first hotel built overlooking Lake Eola in the Thirties, now completely modernized and including all the comforts you'd expect at a Sheraton hotel. Better rates if you book online. ❹

Travelodge 409 N Magnolia Ave ⓣ407/ 423-1671. Good-value motel-style accommodation within walking distance of everything. Private pool and non-smoking rooms, plus free HBO cable TV, newspaper, and local calls. ❷

Veranda Bed & Breakfast Inn 115 N Summerlin Ave ⓣ407/849-0321 or 1-800/420-6822, ⓦwww.theverandabandb.com. Charming and friendly twelve-room bed and breakfast located in five period buildings nestled around a courtyard garden, in Orlando's Thornton Park district, one block from Lake Eola. ❺

Winter Park

Fortnightly Inn 377 E Fairbanks Ave ⓣ407/ 645-4440. A night or two at this personable five-room bed and breakfast makes for a relaxing break from the rampant commercialism of the Orlando area. Rooms come with fresh flowers and cream sherry, and there is free use of bicycles. ❹

Park Plaza 307 Park Ave S ⓣ407/ 647-1072 or 1-800/228-7220, ⓦwww.parkplazahotel.com. Reminiscent of New Orleans' French Quarter, this Twenties hotel is stuffed with wonderful wicker furniture and brass fittings. Be sure to book early. Continental breakfast is included. ❹

International Drive and around

Clarion Universal 7299 Universal Blvd ⓣ407/351-5009 or 1-800/445-7299, ⓦwww.clarionuniversal.com. A mid-sized easygoing hotel with nicely furnished rooms. Handiest location for Universal Studios and Wet 'n' Wild. Substantial off-season discounts if you book online. ❸

Days Inn Lakeside 7335 Sand Lake Rd ⓣ407/ 351-1900 or 1-800/777-3297. An enormous branch of the nationwide chain in a lakeside location a quarter of a mile from the action on International Drive and one mile to Universal. Facilities include a small beach and three pools. ❷

DoubleTree Castle Hotel 8629 International Drive ⓣ407/345-1511 or 1-800/952-2785, ⓦwww.doubletreecastle.com. This elaborate theme-hotel, complete with Renaissance music and medieval decor, such as armor, offers all the luxuries – plus complimentary chocolate chip cookies. ❹

Howard Johnson 7050 S Kirkman Rd ⓣ407/351-2000 or 1-800/327-3808, ⓦwww.howardjohnsonhotelorlando.com. Good-sized rooms, three pools, and free shuttle buses to the major theme parks make this a good base for nondrivers concentrating on the big attractions. Very reasonable rates. ❷

Peabody Orlando 9801 International Drive ⓣ407/352-4000 or 1-800/PEABODY, ⓦwww.peabodyorlando.com. Twenty-seven stories of opulent rooms primarily aimed at delegates using the massive Orange County Convention Center across the street. If money's no object and you like in-room luxuries, access to a fitness center, and floodlit tennis courts, this one's for you. Ducks parade through the lobby twice a day. ❻

Radisson Barcelo Hotel 8444 International Drive ⓣ407/345-0505 or 1-800/333-3333. While speed-swimming records have been set at the adjacent YMCA's Olympic-sized pool (to which hotel guests have free access), those looking for relaxation will find the spacious rooms and the location, directly opposite the restaurants of the Mercado Mediterranean Shopping Village (see "Eating," p.336), a winning combination. ❹

Renaissance Orlando Resort 6677 Sea Harbor Drive ⓣ401/351-5555 or 1-800/327-6677. Ten-story hotel with an attractive atrium, large rooms, conference facilities, and an unbeatable location for SeaWorld visitors – directly opposite the park's entrance. ❻

Ritz-Carlton Orlando 4012 Central Florida Parkway ⓣ407/206-2400, ⓦwww.grandelakes.com. One of the newest luxury hotels in Orlando, this elegantly imposing building with its Italian decor shares the 500-acre *Grande Lakes Resort* estate with another hotel and a golf course.

Hiking and picnicking

Just north of Universal Orlando, next to Florida's Turnpike, lies **Turkey Lake Park**, 3401 Hiawassee Rd (daily 8am–7pm; cars $4, pedestrians and cyclists free; ⓣ407/299-5581), a quiet place to have lunch by a lake, take a short hike, or let the kids run around a terrific playground. Five miles west of downtown Orlando off Hwy-50 is the **West Orange Trail** (ⓣ407/654-5144), nineteen miles of scenic, paved walkways that run from historic Winter Garden to the hills of Lake County. West Orange Trail Bikes and Blades Co. (ⓣ407/877-0600) rent bikes ($5 per hour) and skates ($6 per hour).

Features immaculate facilities, several restaurants, and a full-service spa. ❼

Wellesley Inn and Suites 8687 Commodity Circle ⓣ407/248-8010. Very comfortable rooms with kitchens in an out-of-the-way spot, close enough (three miles) but not too close to the hub-bub on International Drive. The Lynx bus stop next to the hotel makes this a viable option for travelers without a car. ❸

Along West US-192 (Irlo Bronson Memorial Highway)

Many of the following accommodations are officially located in the town of **Kissimmee** (see p.363).

Best Western Eastgate 5565 W US-192 ⓣ407/396-0707 or 1-800/223-5361. Basic, comfortable, and extremely convenient to Disney World, with its own pool and sheltered from the noise of the highway by a small lake. ❷

Comfort Inn Maingate West 9330 W US-192 ⓣ407/424-8420 or 1-800/440-4473. This hotel's yellow exterior is a foretaste of the bright, cheerful rooms inside. A pleasant, economical place to stay, six minutes west of Disney. ❷

Comfort Suites Maingate Resort 7888 W US-192 ⓣ407/390-9888 or 1-888/390-9888. All suites here have every convenience, amid beautifully laid-out parklands with two pools. ❸

DoubleTree Resort–Villas at Maingate 4787 W US-192 ⓣ407/397-0555 or 1-800/222-TREE, ⓦwww.doubletree.com. Bi-level Mediterranean-style villas, with two or three bedrooms, situated in fifteen acres of attractive gardens. ❹

Holiday Inn Nikki Bird Resort 7300 W US-192 ⓣ407/396-7300 or 1-800/20-OASIS. A good hotel for children, with specially designed "Kidsuites" featuring bunks, playrooms, and video games. Just one mile from Disney. ❸

Howard Johnson Express & Parkside 4311 W US-192 ⓣ407/396-7100 or 1-800/388-7698. The recently refurbished rooms are spacious, clean, and cheap. Also has two pools (one Olympic-sized) and free shuttles to Disney, Universal, and SeaWorld. ❷

Howard Johnson Maingate Resort West 8660 W US-192 ⓣ407/396-4500 or 1-800/638-7829, ⓦwww.orlandohojomaingate.com. An elaborate HoJo with no less than three pools, two restaurants, tennis, volleyball, shuffleboard, and a panoply of other services, including free transportation to the Disney parks. Good value. ❷

Motel 6 5731 W US-192 ⓣ407/396-6333 or 1-800/4-MOTEL-6. Not all that close to the theme parks, but if you have your own transportation, you might consider staying at this, one of the cheapest options around. ❶

Quality Suites Maingate East 5876 W US-192 ⓣ407/396-8040 or 1-800/268-6048, ⓦwww.qualitysuitesmaingate.com. Apartment-style accommodation, built around a tropically landscaped garden with a large, heated pool. Free continental breakfast and shuttles to Disney included. ❸

Sevilla Inn 4640 W US-192 ⓣ1407/396-4135 or 1-800/367-1363, ⓦwww.sevillainn.com. A refreshing change from the chain hotels, this unpretentious motel has simple, cheap, but perfectly satisfactory rooms and a humble pool. ❶

Super 8 Motel 1815 W US-192 ⓣ407/847-6121 or 1-800/325-4348, ⓦwww.abcsuites.com. Choose from standard rooms or apartment-style suites in an attractive garden setting; the latter come complete with full kitchen, living and dining areas, and two bedrooms. Free continental breakfast. ❶

Downtown Orlando

Except to sample its nightlife (see p.337), few visitors make their way into **downtown Orlando**, which, despite the half-dozen corporate towers in its midst, is still redolent, in size and mood, of the tobacco-chewing cow town that it used to be. Everything of consequence in the tiny downtown can be visited on foot within an hour.

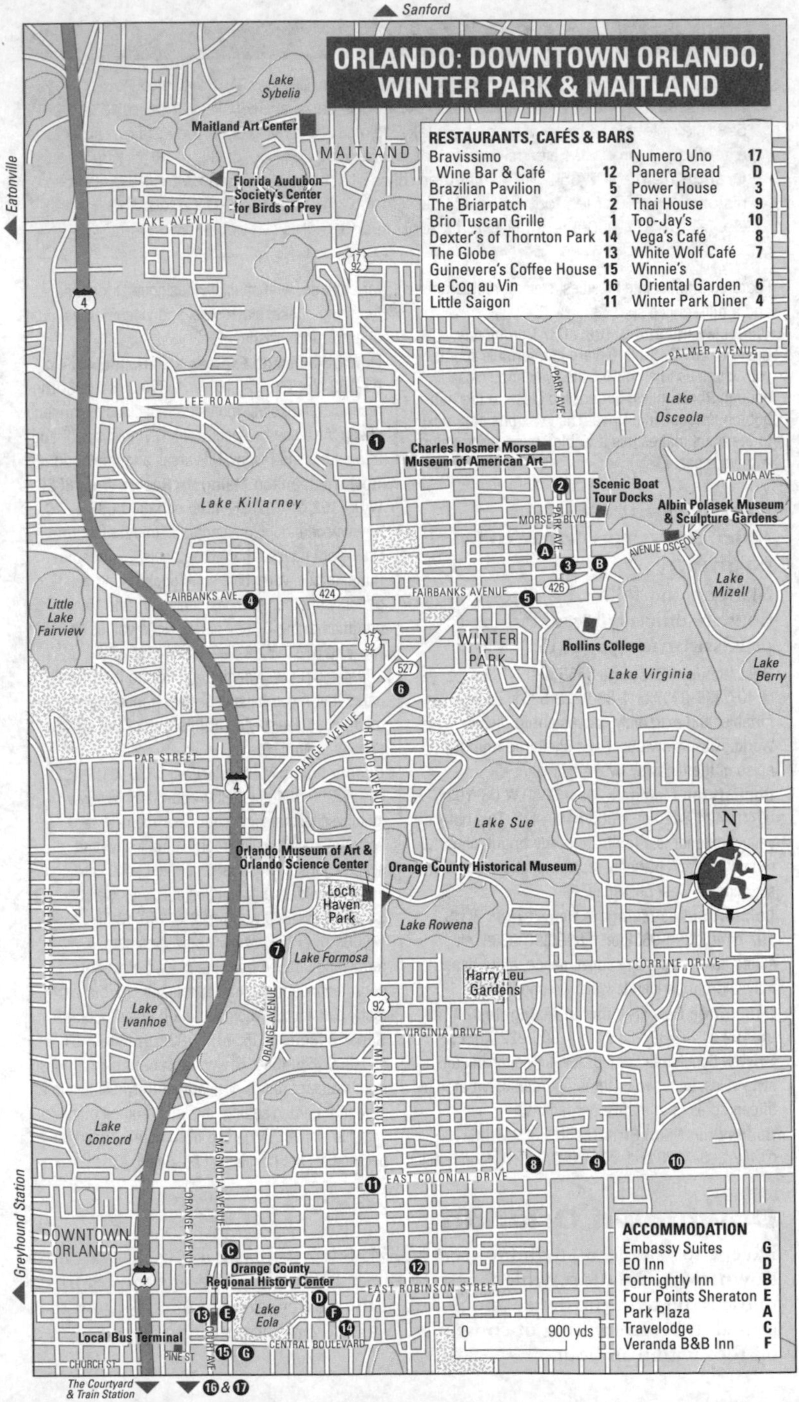
ORLANDO: DOWNTOWN ORLANDO, WINTER PARK & MAITLAND
RESTAURANTS, CAFÉS & BARS
Bravissimo Wine Bar & Café 12
Brazilian Pavilion 5
The Briarpatch 2
Brio Tuscan Grille 1
Dexter's of Thornton Park 14
The Globe 13
Guinevere's Coffee House 15
Le Coq au Vin 16
Little Saigon 11
Numero Uno 17
Panera Bread D
Power House 3
Thai House 9
Too-Jay's 10
Vega's Café 8
White Wolf Café 7
Winnie's Oriental Garden 6
Winter Park Diner 4
ACCOMMODATION
Embassy Suites G
EO Inn D
Fortnightly Inn B
Four Points Sheraton E
Park Plaza A
Travelodge C
Veranda B&B Inn F
Sanford
Eatonville
Greyhound Station
The Courtyard & Train Station
16 & 17
Lake Sybelia
Maitland Art Center
MAITLAND
Florida Audubon Society's Center for Birds of Prey
LAKE AVENUE
PALMER AVENUE
PARK AVE.
Lake Osceola
LEE ROAD
Charles Hosmer Morse Museum of American Art
ALOMA AVE.
Scenic Boat Tour Docks
Albin Polasek Museum & Sculpture Gardens
Lake Killarney
MORSE BLVD
AVENUE OSCEOLA
Lake Mizell
FAIRBANKS AVE.
FAIRBANKS AVENUE
Little Lake Fairview
WINTER PARK
Rollins College
Lake Virginia
Lake Berry
ORANGE AVENUE
ORLANDO AVENUE
PAR STREET
Lake Sue
Orlando Museum of Art & Orlando Science Center
Orange County Historical Museum
Loch Haven Park
Lake Rowena
EDGEWATER DRIVE
Lake Formosa
CORRINE DRIVE
Harry Leu Gardens
Lake Ivanhoe
VIRGINIA DRIVE
MILLS AVENUE
Lake Concord
MAGNOLIA AVENUE
EAST COLONIAL DRIVE
DOWNTOWN ORLANDO
Orange County Regional History Center
EAST ROBINSON STREET
Lake Eola
Local Bus Terminal
COURT AVE.
CENTRAL BOULEVARD
PINE ST
CHURCH ST
0 900 yds
N

Begin by dawdling along **Orange Avenue**, which is mostly trawled by lunch-seeking office workers. Pass the late-Twenties **First National Bank** building (now a college) on the corner of Church Street, and continue a few blocks north to the easily identifiable **McCrory's Five and Dime** building, which has been closed for some years but is nevertheless a good example of early Art Deco. One block east of Orange Avenue, on Heritage Square, you'll find the state-of-the-art **Orange County Regional History Center**, now housed in the restored Orange County Courthouse at 65 E Central Blvd (Mon–Sat 10am–5pm, Sun noon–5pm; $7; ⓣ407/836-8500 or 1-800/965-2030, ⓦwww.thehistorycenter.org). The exhibitions trace the history of the area from 10,000 BC to the present day, and many of the most effective displays and artifacts, from old photos to recreated hotel lobbies and grocers' stores, do an admirable job of reviving a time when, far from being a global tourist destination, Orlando epitomized the American frontier town.

Some of the wooden homes built by Orlando's first white settlers in the mid-1800s stand around scenic **Lake Eola**, a ten-minute walk east of Orange Avenue. Many are undergoing expensive restoration as their owners strive to become bed-and-breakfast moguls. There's a good view of the houses from the oak-filled park that rings the placid lake. From here you can contemplate the city's first hundred years – not to mention the freeway and the fact that Orlando's early black inhabitants didn't live in these leafy environs but in a much less picturesque district west of the railway line, parallel to Orange Avenue, which is still today very much the wrong side of the tracks.

Loch Haven Park

A large lawn wedged between two small lakes, **Loch Haven Park**, three miles north of downtown Orlando, contains several buildings of varying degrees of interest. The **Orlando Museum of Art**, 2416 N Mills Ave (Tues–Fri 10am–4pm, Sat & Sun noon–4pm; $6; ⓣ407/896-4231, ⓦwww.omart.org), is likely to take up at least an hour: permanent collections of recent and ancient American art and African artifacts back up the usually excellent temporary exhibitions of modern paintings, sculptures, and the like culled from some of the finest collections in the world.

Children will enjoy roaming around the nearby **Orlando Science Center**, 777 E Princeton St (Mon–Thurs 9am–5pm, Fri–Sat 9am–9pm, Sun noon–5pm; $10–16, depending on whether you watch a film; ⓣ407/514-2000 or 1-888/672-4386, ⓦwww.osc.org), a stunning, state-of-the-art, $44-million complex where hundreds of interactive exhibits explain the fundamentals of physics, biology, agriculture, astronomy, and more to formative minds. The center's CineDome is the world's largest Iwerks domed theater and Digistar II planetarium.

Harry P. Leu Gardens

A mile east of Loch Haven Park, the fifty-acre **Harry P. Leu Gardens**, 1920 N Forest Ave (daily 9am–5pm; $4, including a tour of Leu House; ⓣ407/246-2620, ⓦwww.leugardens.org), was purchased by a green-thumbed Orlando businessman in 1936 to show off plants collected from around the world. After seeing and sniffing the orchids, roses, azaleas, and the largest camellia collection in the southern US, take a trip around **Leu House** (guided tours only; daily 10am–3.30pm), a late-nineteenth-century farmhouse bought and lived in by Leu and his wife, now maintained in the simple but elegant style of their time and laced with family mementos.

Winter Park

A couple of miles northeast of Loch Haven Park, **Winter Park** has been socially a cut above the rest of the city since it was launched in 1887 as "a beautiful winter retreat for well-to-do people." For all its obvious money – a mix of new yuppie dollars and old wealth – Winter Park is a very likeable place, with a pervasive sense of community and a touch of California-style, New Age affluence.

On Fairbanks Avenue, which brings traffic from Loch Haven Park into Winter Park, stand the Mediterranean Revival buildings of **Rollins College**, the oldest college in the state and a tiny but respected liberal arts college. Other than its neat landscaping, the campus has just one thing in its favor: the **Cornell Fine Arts Center** (Tues–Fri 10am–5pm, Sat & Sun 1–5pm; free; ⓣ407/646-2526, ⓦwww.rollins.edu/cfam), which offers a staid bundle of modest nineteenth-century European and American paintings, rather more interesting temporary shows, and an eccentric collection of old watch keys.

You'll find a more personal art collection a mile east of the college on Osceola Avenue, at the **Albin Polasek Museum and Sculpture Gardens**, no. 633 (Sept–June Tues–Sat 10am–4pm, Sun 1–4pm; $4; ⓣ407/647-6294, ⓦwww.polasek.org): the former home of Czech-born sculptor Albin Polasek, who arrived penniless in the US in 1901 and spent most of his time over the next fifty years winning big-money commissions. The profits were eventually channeled into the creation of this house, studio, and three-acre garden, which contain more than 200 of his technically accomplished, realist works.

Park Avenue: the Morse Museum and boat tours

The showpiece of Winter Park's upmarket status is **Park Avenue**, a row of top-of-the-line outfitters, jewelers, and spick-and-span restaurants, which meets Fairbanks Avenue close to Rollins. Worth a special stop are the Scott Laurent Galleries, 348 N Park Ave (Mon–Sat 10am–6pm, Sun noon–5pm; ⓣ407/629-1488), a shop with an impressive collection of art, glass, ceramics, and jewelry.

Should window-shopping not appeal, drop into the **Charles Hosmer Morse Museum of American Art**, 445 Park Ave N (Tues–Sat 9.30am–4pm, Sept–May Fri 9.30am–8pm, Sun 1–4pm; $3; ⓣ407/645-5311, ⓦwww.morse-museum.org), which houses the collections of its namesake, one of Winter Park's founding fathers. The major exhibits are drawn from the output of Louis Comfort Tiffany, a legend for his innovative Art Nouveau lamps and windows that furnished high-society homes around the turn of the last century. Great creativity and craftsmanship went into Tiffany's work: he molded glass while it was still soft, imbuing it with colored images of water lilies, leaves, and even strutting peacocks. Tiffany's work is so stunning that the rest of the museum's possessions, including paintings by Norman Rockwell, pale in comparison.

To discover why those who can afford to live anywhere choose Winter Park, take the **scenic boat tour** from the dock at 312 E Morse Blvd (departures every hour daily 10am–4pm; $8; ⓣ407/644-4056, ⓦwww.scenicboattours.com). The one-hour, narrated voyage provides a picture-postcard view, usually reserved exclusively for the owners of the big-buck waterside homes.

Eatonville

Just to the east of Winter Park is the small town of **Eatonville**, the first incorporated African-American municipality in the United States. The town was founded by three black men in 1875 so that, according to an 1889 notice published in the local newspaper, black Americans could "solve the great race problem by securing a home...in a Negro city governed by Negroes," and land was

△ SeaWorld Orlando

sold for $5–10 an acre to encourage relocation. Renowned author Zora Neale Hurston, an Eatonville native, used the town as the setting for novels such as *Their Eyes Were Watching God*. The town is worth a stop to see the **Zora Neale Hurston National Museum of Fine Arts**, 227 E Kennedy Blvd (Mon–Fri 9am–4pm; free; ⓣ407/647-3307), which rotates exhibits of artists of African descent, and also has a complete collection of Zora Neale Hurston's books.

Maitland

The luscious sunsets over Lake Sybelia in **Maitland**, directly north of Winter Park, inspired a young artist named André Smith to buy six acres on its banks during the Thirties. With the financial assistance of Mary Bok (wealthy widow of Edward Bok; see p.296), Smith established what is now the **Maitland Art Center**, 231 W Packwood Ave (Mon–Thurs 9am–5.30pm, Sat & Sun noon–4.30pm; free; ⓣ407/539-2181, ⓦwww.maitartctr.org), a collection of stuccoed studios, offices, and apartments decorated with Aztec- and Mayan-style murals and grouped around garden courtyards. Smith invited other American artists to spend working winters here, but his abrasive personality scared many potential guests away. The colony continued in various forms until Smith's death in 1959, never becoming the aesthetes' commune he'd hoped for. There are temporary exhibitions and a permanent collection, but it's the unique design of the place that demands a visit. While here, spare a thought for Smith's ghost, which, according to a number of local painters and sculptors who claim to have felt its presence, dispenses artistic guidance.

A few steps from the Maitland Art Center are the **Maitland Historical Museum** and the **Telephone Museum**, 221 W Packwood Ave (Thurs–Sun noon–4pm; $2; ⓣ407/644-2451). The front rooms of the combined museums host rotating exhibits with some bearing on Maitland life, but the back room is filled with wonderful vintage telephones, commemorating the day in 1910 when a Maitland grocer installed telephones in the homes of his customers, enabling them to order groceries from the comfort of their armchairs. The only other thing to make you dally in Maitland is the **Florida Audubon Society's Center for Birds of Prey**, 1101 Audubon Way (Tues–Sun 10am–4pm; $5, children $4; ⓣ407/644-0190), the headquarters of the Florida Audubon Society, the state's oldest and largest conservation organization. The house is primarily an educational center and gift shop, but the adjacent viewable rehabilitation facility is the largest in the Southeast, treating injured and orphaned birds, such as ospreys, owls, hawks, eagles, falcons, and the odd vulture.

International Drive

Devoid of any of the traditional charm one might find in downtown Orlando and adjacent communities, **International Drive**, five miles southwest of Orlando and smack between Disney World, Universal Studios, and SeaWorld Orlando, is still worth a short visit for those interested in gawking at big-budget tourism at its most obscenely creative. The strip boasts an **F.A.O. Schwartz** toy store at Pointe Orlando, no. 9101 (ⓣ407/248-2838), whose location is marked by a 380-foot-high Raggedy Ann. Other wonders include a **Ripley's Believe It or Not Museum**, at no. 8201, housed in a dramatically lopsided building, **WonderWorks**, at no. 9067, in an upside-down house, and the **Skull Kingdom**, a haunted mansion built to look like a castle with a skull face emerging from the front wall (for more on these attractions, see p.361). A Belz outlet shopping complex (ⓣ407/352-9611) on International Drive's north end is good for heavily discounted Disney merchandise, Levi's, and other name brands.

Eating

Given the level of competition among restaurants hoping to attract hungry tourists, **eating** in Orlando is never difficult and – if you escape the clutches of the theme parks – need not be expensive. In **downtown Orlando**, choices are quite good, and the need to satisfy a regular clientele of lunch-breaking office workers keeps prices low. With a car, you might also investigate the local favorites scattered in the outlying areas away from downtown. Affluent **Winter Park** promises more variety, generally with higher standards and prices, though it does have a few serviceable low-cost diners.

Tourist-dominated **International Drive** offers a greater range, if less intimacy. The culinary hot spots are the gourmet ethnic restaurants, but strict-budget travelers will relish the opportunity to eat massive amounts at one of several buffet restaurants – all for less than they might spend on a tip elsewhere. Buffet eating reaches its ultimate expression along **US-192**, where virtually every buffet restaurant chain has at least one outlet, leaving the discerning glutton spoiled for choice.

Discount coupons in tourist magazines bring sizeable reductions at many restaurants, including "Show Restaurants," where $40 per head not only buys a multi-course meal and (usually) limitless beer, wine, and soft drinks but also entertainment ranging from intriguing whodunits to medieval knights jousting on horseback.

Orlando

Bravissimo Wine Bar & Cafe 337 N Shine Ave ⓣ407/898-7333. Authentic Italian cuisine, outdoor garden seating, and aria-singing waiters in an out-of-the-way neighborhood about ten blocks from downtown. Main dishes for around $10.

Bubbalou's Bodacious Bar-B-Q 5818 Conroy Rd ⓣ407/295-1212. One of a fun local chain, featuring smoked meat sandwiches and platters at down-home prices, just north of Universal Studios. Daily specials for a little over $5.

Dexters of Thornton Park 808 E Washington St ⓣ407/648-2777. Trendy foods priced right ($10 and up for entrees), plus an extensive beer menu, attract a young, urban clientele.

The Globe 25 Wall St Plaza ⓣ407/849-9904. Always packed with young artsy types, this is the perfect place for inexpensive Nouveau American snacks and light meals. Eat sushi next door at the *Tuk Tuk Room* or dance the night away another door down at *Slingapores* nightclub – all three establishments are under the same ownership.

Guinevere's Coffee House 37-39 S Magnolia Ave, at E Pine ⓣ407/992-1200. A relaxing place for a coffee before or after a visit to the adjoining art gallery, one of the city's hippest. Closed Mon.

India Palace 8530 Palm Parkway, Vista Center ⓣ407/238-2322. Traditional Indian, offering tandoori and great seafood dishes for under $20, all in a quiet, appealing setting. Lunch buffet Tues–Sun, $6.95.

Le Coq au Vin 4800 S Orange Ave ⓣ407/851-6980. French restaurant with surprisingly low prices for top-notch dishes such as bronzed grouper and oven-roasted salmon. Closed Mon.

Little Saigon 1106 E Colonial Drive ⓣ407/423-8539. Tempting Vietnamese treats – don't miss the summer rolls with peanut sauce.

Numero Uno 2499 S Orange Ave ⓣ407/841-3840. A small, good-value Cuban restaurant, reputed to be the best Cuban food in town. Try the black beans and rice with grouper or the paella Valenciana for two at $39.95. Closed Sun.

Panera Bread 227 N Eola Drive ⓣ407/481-1060. One of a great local chain, with a wonderful array of baked goods, soups, salads, and sandwiches.

Thai House 2117 E Colonial Drive ⓣ407/898-0820. Tasty Thai food priced under $10 (slightly more for the seafood); wash the spicy dishes down with the Thai iced tea. Weekends, dinner only.

Too-Jay's 2624 E Colonial Drive ⓣ407/894-1718. This casual New York–style deli is part of an attractive local chain with a big menu that includes beef kebabs.

Vega's Café 1835 E Colonial Drive ⓣ407/898-5196. Cuban diner with great-value lunches provided you can make do with Cuban sandwiches and Spanish soups – which is all they do.

Winter Park

Brazilian Pavilion 140 W Fairbanks Ave ⓣ407/740-7440. Sumptuous Brazilian creations; try the *peixe a Brasileira* (filet of snapper with tomatoes, scallions, and coconut milk).

The Briarpatch 252 Park Ave N ⓣ407/628-8651. Well-prepared eclectic lunches and dinners with salads that are especially huge – and pricey (around $10). Eat inside or on the terrace.

Brio Tuscan Grille 480 N Orlando Ave ⓣ407/622-5611. A bright and bustling Italian restaurant that belies its location in a shopping mall. Wonderful *bruschetta* topped with shrimp and mozzarella.

Power House 109-111 E Lyman Ave ⓣ407/645-3616. Raise your energy level with a vitamin-packed fruit juice, sample one of the tasty soups, or try the Middle Eastern specialties.

White Wolf Café 1829 N Orange Ave ⓣ407/895-5590. Down-to-earth café/antique store known for creative sandwiches and generous salads on a menu that ranges from lasagna to pork chops to quiche. Closed Sun.

Winnie's Oriental Garden 1346 Orange Ave ⓣ407/629-2111. Applauded by locals as the best Chinese restaurant in town with entrees ranging from $15 to $22. Its specialties include crispy sea bass and moo shoo vegetables, or, for an appetizer, soft-shell crab.

Winter Park Diner 1700 W Fairbanks Ave ⓣ407/644-2343. In business longer than most people can remember, and still serving generous portions of classic diner food at prices sure to please.

International Drive and around

Bahama Breeze 8849 International Drive ⓣ407/248-2499. Decent Caribbean food in an upbeat atmosphere. Dinner only; open late (until 1am most nights).

Bergamo's Mercado Mediterranean Shopping Village, 8445 International Drive ⓣ407/352-3805. Good-quality and slightly expensive pasta and seafood dishes, served by singing waiters who perform Broadway hits, opera, and Neopolitan folk songs as you eat. Dinner only.

Boston Lobster Feast 8731 International Drive ⓣ407/438-0607. Just what the name implies – all-you-can-eat lobster from $25 to $30. The buffet also includes some simple sushi items.

Café Tu Tu Tango 8625 International Drive ⓣ407/248-2222. Fill up on creative appetizers and pizza at this lively hot spot. The walls are decorated with artworks for sale, and some of the artists use the place as an atelier.

China Garden Mercado Mediterranean Shopping Village, 8445 International Drive ⓣ407/226-9933. This spacious restaurant offers an all-you-can-eat "super buffet" of authentic Chinese cuisine at great prices.

Christini's Ristorante Italiano 7600 Dr Phillips Blvd ⓣ407/345-8770. One of the truly excellent tables in southwest Orlando. The menu, which includes linguini in white clam sauce and veal marsala, and service are so superb it's worth the high prices (most entrees $18–30), though it's a bit of a drive to get there.

The Crab House 8291 International Drive ⓣ407/352-6140 and 8496 Palm Parkway, in the Vista Center ⓣ407/239-1888. Lively and packed seafood house specializing in many kinds of crab. Its all-you-can-eat seafood and salad bar for $20.99 is very popular, so expect to wait for a table.

Cricketers Arms Mercado Mediterranean Shopping Village, 8445 International Drive ⓣ407/354-0686. Fish and chips, pies, and pasties complement a range of imported ales and lagers at this inexpensive nook. It has a cozy, authentic feel, the latest soccer scores – and sometimes the matches themselves on giant TV screens.

Don Pablo 8717 International Drive ⓣ407/354-1345. The decor will make you swear you're in a Tijuana cantina, and you'll find such Mexican favorites as enchiladas, fajitas, and tostados, complemented by Mexican beer.

Ming Court 9188 International Drive ⓣ407/351-9988. Chinese cuisine of an exceptionally high standard makes this a good choice; less costly than you might expect when you see the fabulously flash decor. Dim sum is available, and sushi, too.

Passage to India 5532 International Drive ⓣ407/351-3456. The full menu includes the curry and other Indian dishes you'd expect but emphasizes the "rich but not fatty" and "spicy but not hot" nature of the food.

Punjab 7451 International Drive ⓣ407/352-7887 and 3404 US-192 ⓣ407/931-2449. Everything's spiced to your personal taste. There's a wide range of curries, including a good vegetarian selection.

Race Rock 8986 International Drive ⓣ407/248-9876. A motorsports-themed restaurant with auto memorabilia on walls, serving such eclectic American choices as burgers, milkshakes, and malts at super-reasonable prices.

Roy's 7760 W Sand Lake Rd ⓣ407/352-4844. One of a chain founded in Hawaii and offering an innovative Hawaiian fusion cuisine. Try the fixed-price, three-course menu ($30) for a good sampling of what's on offer.

Timpano 7488 W Sand Lake Rd ⓣ407/248-0429. Italian eatery reminiscent of the classic restaurants and clubs of Chicago and New York, where you can tuck into steaks, chops, and the usual pasta dishes, as well as choose from a good wine list.

Along US-192

Cracker Barrel Old Country Store 5400 W US-192 ⓣ407/396-6521. Wholesome country cookin' in an Americana atmosphere, complete with country store.

Key W Kool's 7225 W US-192 ⓣ407/239-7166. For a break from buffets, sample the seafood and steaks – cooked in an open-pit oak grill – and served for lunch and dinner in this tropically themed restaurant.

Perkins 7451 W US-192 ⓣ407/896-3725. The place to go for pot roast, all-day breakfasts or freshly baked goods from the onsite bakery.

Show restaurants

Arabian Nights 6225 W US-192 ⓣ407/239-9223 or 1-800/553-6116. Considered by Orlando locals to be one of the best dinner theaters around. Sixty-plus live horses help tell a comic version of the classic story.

Disney's Spirit of Aloha Dinner Show Disney's *Polynesian Resort* ⓣ407/939-3463. All the colorful and highly entertaining native dance performances of the South Pacific that you would expect, plus a fairly good outdoor barbecue.

Hoop-Dee-Doo Musical Revue Disney's *Fort Wilderness Campground* ⓣ407/939-3463. Vaudeville-style entertainment provided by hokey cowboys as you dine on corn, baked beans, and fried chicken.

Makahiki Luau Sea Fire Grill, SeaWorld Orlando ⓣ407/363-2559 or 1-800/327-2424. So-so Hawaiian and Pacific island food, but the captivating, nonstop show features rhythmic music, dance, and authentic costumes.

Medieval Times Dinner & Tournament 4510 US-192 ⓣ407/396-1518 or 1-888/WE-JOUST. Knights joust on horseback as you feast inside this replica of an eleventh-century castle. Choose from a meat-laden menu.

Murderwatch Mystery Theatre *Grosvenor Resort*, 1850 Hotel Plaza Blvd ⓣ407/827-6534, ⓦwww.murderwatch.com. The cast interacts with the audience in this whodunit, which is played out in the dining room in between trips to the excellent prime rib buffet. One of the best of the show restaurants for the food quality.

Pirate's Dinner Adventure 6400 Carrier Drive ⓣ407/248-0590 or 1-800/866-2469. Shivering timbers, peg-leg buccaneers, scalawags, cannons, sword fights, and a host of stunts will divert your attention from the ordinary food.

Sleuth's Mystery Dinner Show 7508 Universal Blvd ⓣ407/363-1985 or 1-800/393-1985. If you know red herring isn't a seafood dish, you're well on the way to solving the murder mystery as you eat in this Agatha Christie–style set.

Nightlife

Nightlife in downtown Orlando used to revolve around the complex of bars and restaurants called Church Street Station, until the owner went bankrupt and all but a few of the nightspots closed. There is constant talk of reopening the complex, but for the time being most of the after-dark action is focused along Orange Avenue, where the atmosphere still evokes the raunchy honky-tonk feel of a bygone era. Otherwise, area entertainment, like everything else, has been swallowed whole by **Downtown Disney** (see p.353) and **Universal CityWalk** (see p.357), and, as always with theme parks, the fun can seem somewhat artificial and predigested.

Downtown Orlando

Howl at the Moon Saloon 55 W Church St ⓣ407/841-9118. It's hard to concentrate on your drink as dueling pianists whizz through a sing-along selection of rock and roll classics and show tunes.

Sky 60 64 N Orange Ave ⓣ407/246-1599. South Beach in style, this club is where beautiful people come to mingle with their kin, either on the dance floor or on the mellow rooftop terrace with its private cabanas.

The Social 54 N Orange Ave ⓣ407/246-1599. Southern, grunge and alternative rock, local bands, you name it. Check the website for a full list of coming attractions.

Southern Nights 375 S Bumby Ave ⓣ407/898-0424. Orlando's main gay venue. Monday is Latin House Night and weekends feature lots of zany drag acts, with the emphasis on the ladies at Saturday's Lesbo A-Go-Go.

Tabu 46 N Orange Ave ⓣ407/648-8363. An upscale nightclub (with reasonable cover charges) featuring a wide range of musical styles, as well as fashion shows and special evenings, such as Thursday's College Night when you can drink as much as you want for $10.

Wall Street Cantina 19 N Orange Ave ⓣ407/420-1515. Primarily a Tex-Mex restaurant, but with a great street terrace for people watching and refreshing cocktails. A popular place for after-work drinks and socializing.

Walt Disney World

As significant as air-conditioning in making the state what it is today, **WALT DISNEY WORLD** turned a wedge of Florida grazing land into one of the world's most lucrative vacation venues within a decade of its opening in 1971. Bringing growth and money to Central Florida for the first time since the citrus boom a century earlier, the immense and astutely planned empire (and Walt Disney World really *is* an empire) also pushed the state's profile through the roof: from being a down-at-heel and slightly seedy mixture of cheap motels, retirement homes, and clapped-out alligator zoos, Florida suddenly became a showcase of modern international tourism and in doing so, some would claim, sold its soul for a fast buck.

Whatever your attitude toward theme parks, there's no denying that Disney World is the pacesetter: it goes way beyond Walt Disney's original "theme park" – Disneyland, which opened in Los Angeles in 1955 – delivering escapism at its most technologically advanced and psychologically brilliant in a multitude of ingenious guises across an area twice the size of Manhattan. In a crime-free environment where wholesome all-American values hold sway and the concept of good clean fun finds its ultimate expression, Disney World often makes the real world – and all its problems – seem like a distant memory.

Here, litter is picked up within seconds of being dropped (by any of the "cast members," as all employees are called, who happen to spy it), subtle mind-games soften the pain of standing in line, the special effects are the best money can buy, and Disney minions grin merrily as snotty-nosed kids puke down their legs. It's not cheap, forward planning is essential, and there are times when you'll feel like a cog in a vast machine – but Walt Disney World unfailingly, and with ruthless efficiency, delivers what it promises.

Costs may come as a shock, especially to families (children under 3 are admitted free of charge, though note that little is designed specifically for their entertainment), but the basic admission fee allows unlimited access to all the shows and rides in a particular park – and you'll need *at least* a day per park to go on everything in each of the **four main parks**. Remember that Disney World comprises over 46 square miles in all and is not easy to take in, even if spread over a week. Restaurants and snack bars – each as clinically themed as the parks – are plentiful but pricey. No alcohol is served in the Magic Kingdom.

Disney information: ⓣ407/824-4321

Getting around

With its multiple attractions and similarly named resort hotels (see p.341), Disney property will seem complicated to get around until you pick up the *Transportation Guide/Map* from Guest Relations at any of the parks or at the resorts themselves. This leaflet will tell you exactly how to get from one park to another, lending some sense of order to the chaotic comings and goings of Disney's fleet of **buses**. As a general rule, buses to all destinations depart at roughly twenty-minute intervals from all of the resorts. Intra-park travel, meanwhile, will sometimes involve changing buses at The Transportation and Ticket Center (near the Magic Kingdom) or another park. For example, to get to Disney's Wide World of Sports, you will have to catch a bus from Disney-MGM Studios. Transportation between the Transportation and Ticket Center,

A brief history of Disney

When brilliant illustrator and animator Walt Disney devised the world's first theme park, California's **Disneyland** – which brought to life his cartoon characters Mickey Mouse, Donald Duck, Goofy, and the rest – he had no control over the hotels and restaurants that quickly engulfed it, preventing growth and raking in profits that Disney felt were rightfully his. Determined that this wouldn't happen again, the Disney Corporation secretly began to buy up 27,500 acres of Central Florida farmland, and by the late Sixties had acquired – for a comparatively paltry $6 million – a site a hundred times bigger than Disneyland. With the promise of a jobs bonanza for Florida, the state legislature gave the corporation – thinly disguised as the Reedy Creek Improvement District – the rights of any major municipality: empowering it to lay roads, enact building codes, and enforce the law with its own security force.

Walt Disney World's first park, the Magic Kingdom (see p.344), opened in 1971; based, predictably, on Disneyland, it was an equally predictable success. The far more ambitious **EPCOT Center** (see p.346), unveiled in 1982, represented the first major break from cartoon-based escapism. Millions visited, but the rose-tinted look at the future received a mixed response. Partly because of this reaction, and some cockeyed management decisions, the Disney empire (Disney himself died in 1966) faced bankruptcy by the mid-Eighties.

Since then, clever marketing has brought the corporation back from the abyss, and it now steers a tight and competitive business ship, always looking to increase Walt Disney World's daily attendance figures of 100,000 visitors and stay ahead of its rivals. **Disney-MGM Studios**, for example, puts a sizeable dent in Universal Studios' trade (see p.355), while **Downtown Disney** is always finding new ways to wow you in order to keep ahead of Universal CityWalk (see p.357). It may trade in fantasy, but where money matters, the Disney Corporation's nose is firmly in the real world.

the Magic Kingdom, and EPCOT Center is via the **monorail**. Although in theory it's possible to **walk** from one park to another, distances are deceptively long and there are few pedestrian walkways.

Accommodation

If you want to escape the all-pervasive influence and high prices of Walt Disney World for the night, refer to the accommodation listings under "Orlando," p.327, or opt to stay at one of the hotels situated in the vicinity of nearby **Lake Buena Vista** (see p.352), from where it only takes a few minutes' drive to get to any of the parks. If you can't bring yourself to leave, you'll be relieved to find a large number of **hotels** on Disney property, most of which are, in fact, fully equipped resorts. Predictably, each follows a particular theme to the nth degree, and prices are much higher – sometimes more than $300 per night – than you'll pay elsewhere. *All-Star Resorts*, however, is specifically intended for the less affluent visitor, costing $77 to $124 a night, and staying on the property is, after all, the most convenient way of doing Disney World – if that is your primary goal in coming to the Orlando area.

Each resort occupies its own landscaped plot, usually encompassing several swimming pools and a beach beside an artificial lake, and has several restaurants and bars. The Disney resorts are located in several areas, and transport, be it by boat, bus, or monorail, between them and the main theme parks is free (see "Getting around," opposite). Disney guests can also use resort **parking** lots for free. Theme park admission tickets are available at each resort, saving you valuable time otherwise spent lining up at park ticket booths. The standard of serv-

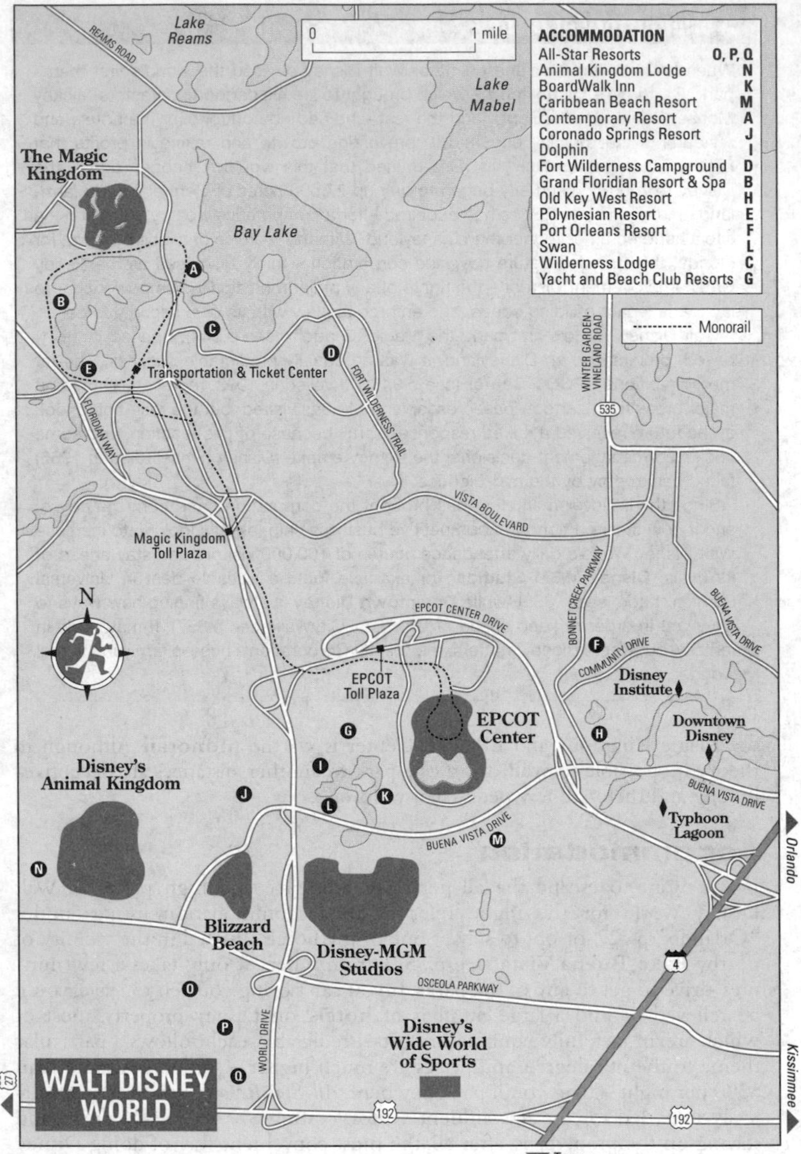

ice should be excellent; if it isn't, make a stiff complaint and you'll probably be treated like royalty throughout the remainder of your stay. Another advantage of staying at a Disney resort comes in the shape of the **Extra Magic Hour**, when each day one of the four parks is opened an hour early exclusively for resort guests, giving them the opportunity of some quality time with Mickey and relatively unimpeded access to the wildest rides – although if you're not a morning person, the idea of a stomach-churning roller coaster could be more daunting than the afternoon crowds.

At quiet times, rooms may be available at short notice, but with Disney resorts pitching themselves to convention-goers as much as vacationers, you may turn up to find that there is no space at all, even in 1000-room properties, such as the *Contemporary Resort*. To be assured of a room, book as far ahead as possible – nine months is not unreasonable. **Reservations** can be made by phone or on the Internet (Ⓣ407/939-7429, Ⓦwww.disneyworld.com).

Disney's Animal Kingdom Resort Area

All-Star Resorts The most affordable and garish of Disney's resorts, divided into the *All-Star Music Resort,* which is decorated with giant-sized, brightly colored cowboy boots, guitar-shaped swimming pools, and the like; the *All-Star Sports Resort*, complete with huge Coca-Cola cups, American football helmets, and so on; and the *All-Star Movies Resort*, featuring humongous reminders of Disney movies looming over you. Each complex has its own pools and over 1500 rooms. The much larger, 5000-plus room *Pop Century Resort* at Disney's Wide World of Sports will be unveiled in December 2003, devoted to mammoth pop icons from each decade of the twentieth century. ❹

Animal Kingdom Lodge Disney World's newest luxury accommodation and its most spectacular, a place where you can wake up to see African wildlife grazing outside your window. ❼

Coronado Springs Resort Moderately priced resort paying homage to the cultures of Mexico and the American Southwest, with its nearly 2000 rooms built around a faux-Mayan pyramid. The food court is good for family meals. ❻

Downtown Disney Resort Area

Old Key West Resort Caribbean-style painted wooden homes and shaded verandas make for a tropical ambience based on a turn-of-the-nineteenth-century Key West resort. ❽

Port Orleans Resort Combining two Southern themes: the row houses and cobbled streets of New Orleans at the *French Quarter*, and the grandiose manors overlooking the Mississippi River at the *Riverside*. ❻

EPCOT-MGM Resort Area

BoardWalk Inn Styled after a mid-Atlantic seaside resort in the Thirties, this place goes to show that no theme is too humble for the Disney treatment. Accommodation in hotel rooms or residential-style villas. ❽

Caribbean Beach Resort Disney's first attempt at a budget-priced hotel still works rather well. Typical rooms at this plushly landscaped property are located in one of six "island villages," each with its own beach. ❻

Dolphin Topped by the giant sculpture of a dolphin and decorated in dizzying pastel shades and reproduction artwork from the likes of Matisse and Warhol. Although this property and its partner, the *Swan*, are on Disney property, they are the only hotels not owned by Disney. ❽

Swan Intended as a partner to the *Dolphin* (see above), from which it's separated by an artificial lake and beach, and likewise whimsically decorated and equipped with every conceivable luxury. ❽

Yacht and Beach Club Resorts Turn-of-the-nineteenth-century New England is the cue for these twin hotels, complete with clapboard facades and a miniature lighthouse. Amusements include a mini water park reminiscent of a Nantucket beach. ❽

Magic Kingdom Resort Area

Contemporary Resort The Disney monorail runs right through the center of this hotel, which takes its exterior design from the futuristic fantasies of The Magic Kingdom's Tomorrowland, but is disappointingly characterless inside. ❼

Fort Wilderness Campground A 700-acre site where you can pitch your tent or hook up your RV ($35–82) or rent a six-berth cabin (from $229) – a good deal for larger groups. Entertainment includes nightly, open-air screenings of classic Disney movies, marshmallow roasts, and campfire sing-alongs.

Grand Floridian Resort & Spa Gabled roofs, verandas, and crystal chandeliers are among the frivolous variations on early Florida resort architecture at this elegant and relaxing base. ❽

Polynesian Resort An effective, if tacky, imitation of a Polynesian beach hotel; the concept is most effective if you spend your time on the lakeside beach under the shade of coconut palms. ❽

Wilderness Lodge This magnificent, oversized replica of a frontier log cabin is furnished with massive totem poles, a wood-burning fire in the lobby, and Southern-style wooden rocking chairs. ❼

Lake Buena Vista

Embassy Suites 8100 Lake Ave ⓣ407/239-1144 or 1-800/EMBASSY, ⓦwww.embassysuitesorlando.com. Luxuriously appointed two-room suites including free cooked-to-order breakfast and in-room refrigerators and microwaves. Includes excellent indoor and outdoor pools. ❺
Holiday Inn Family Suites 14500 Continental Gateway ⓣ407/387-5437 or 1-877/387-5437, ⓦwww.hifamilysuites.com. The leader in kid-friendly resorts, with bunk bed– and video game–equipped "Kidsuites," free kids' meals, and even a spa for the little ones. Grown-ups will also enjoy the "Cinema Suites," with their sixty-inch TVs, and the "Sweetheart Suites," which feature heart-shaped hot tubs. ❺
Perri House Acres Estate B&B Inn 10417 Vista Oaks Court ⓣ407/876-4830 or 1-800/780-4830, ⓦwww.perrihouse.com. An eight-room bed and breakfast hidden on four wooded acres – also a bird sanctuary – just a stone's throw from the opulent resorts of Disney, making this the perfect antidote to all the theme-park frenzy. The rooms are clean and bright; the atmosphere friendly. Pool and hot tub are also available. ❺
Westgate Lakes Resort & Spa 10000 Turkey Lake Rd ⓣ407/345-0000 or 1-800/801-9954, ⓦwww.westgateresorts.com. Choose from studios, two-, three-, or four-bedroom apartments, all with full kitchen facilities, at this resort spread across a 90-acre lakeside site. Rent a paddleboat to cross the lake to Paradise Island. ❻

The main parks: an overview

Walt Disney World's four main theme parks are quite separate entities. The Magic Kingdom is the Disney park everyone imagines, the signature castle towering over it all, where Mickey Mouse mingles with the crowds and the emphasis is on fantasy and fun – very much the park for kids. Recognizable for its giant, golfball-like geosphere, **EPCOT Center** is Disney's attempted celebration of science and technology, coupled with a very Disneyfied trip around various countries and cultures: dull for young kids, it's a sprawling area that involves a lot of walking. **Disney-MGM Studios** suits almost everyone; its special effects are enjoyable even if you've never seen the movies they're derived from, and the Backlot Tour, despite moments of tedium, at least visits *real* studios – reality being a rare commodity in Walt Disney World. Disney's newest addition, the more relaxed **Disney's Animal Kingdom**, is part new-age zoo, part theme park, remarkable in bringing an African and Asian feel to the swamplands of southwest Orlando.

Doing any kind of justice to all four parks will take at least five days – one should be set aside for rest – and you shouldn't tackle more than one on any single day. If you only have a day to spare, pick the park that appeals most and stick to it: day tickets are only valid for one location anyway. For visiting several parks over a few days, the **Park Hopper** ticket is the economical solution (see p.344 for details on this and other ticket options).

When to visit

While EPCOT Center in particular absorbs crowds easily, it's best to avoid the **busiest periods**: during summertime, and over Thanksgiving (fourth Thurs in Nov), Christmas, and Easter. The quietest months of the year are January, May, and September. The busiest days vary from park to park (though, on average, Sunday is the least-crowded day), so plan your itinerary once you've arrived or contact Disney information (see box, p.338) for help.

Provided you **arrive early** at the park (just before opening time is best), you'll get through the most popular rides before the mid-afternoon crush, when lines can become monstrously long. If you're staying at a Disney World resort, you may be offered early entrance to the parks (before opening time) to help beat the crowds (for more tips on minimizing waiting times, see opposite). If you can't arrive early, don't show up until 5pm or 6pm, which in some seasons still leaves

Disney's FastPass

In an effort to keep outrageous waiting times from wiping the smiles off visitors' faces, Disney set up a system (also employed at Universal Orlando) to give people the chance to avoid the long lines – if they are prepared to return to the attraction later in the day. Once you have your park ticket, you can reserve VIP treatment by simply inserting your ticket in a special turnstile at the entrance to the attraction. The system then prints out a FastPass for you, indicating the time you should return. In effect, you book a time to enter the FastPass line, which bypasses the regular line and gets you into the attraction in just a few minutes. You can save lots of time booking ahead all day long, but keep in mind that you can only hold one FastPass for one attraction at any one time.

FastPasses are free and currently available at the following attractions: **Magic Kingdom** (Big Thunder Mountain Railroad, Buzz Lightyear's Space Ranger Spin, The Haunted Mansion, Jungle Cruise, The Many Adventures of Winnie the Pooh, Peter Pan's Flight, Space Mountain, Splash Mountain); **EPCOT Center** (Honey, I Shrunk the Audience, Living with the Land, Maelstrom, Test Track); **Disney-MGM Studios** (Indiana Jones Epic Stunt Spectacular, Rock 'n' Roller Coaster, Star Tours, The Twilight Zone Tower of Terror, Voyage of the Little Mermaid, Who Wants to be a Millionaire – Play it!); and **Disney's Animal Kingdom** (DINOSAUR, It's Tough to be a Bug, Kali River Rapids, Kilimanjaro Safaris, Primeval Whirl).

time to do plenty before the place shuts. Each park has regularly updated notice boards showing the latest **waiting times** for each show and ride – at peak times often about an hour and a half for the most popular rides and up to forty minutes for others.

Beating the crowds

As wonderful and unique as each of the Disney parks is, the sheer number of people in them and the often horrendous waiting times for the attractions risk turning your visit into a war of attrition against the crowds. The single most effective way to increase your chances of going on all of the rides and seeing everything in the shortest time possible is to plan your visit during the quietest months (see opposite). You could also avoid the park on days when it opens early for guests of the Disney resorts – when it's sure to be more crowded than usual.

Once there, your best option is to use the FastPass system (see box above). It also pays to avoid standing in line at attractions where FastPasses are available if you don't want your waiting position constantly usurped by FastPass holders waltzing to the front of the line. Savvy Disney visitors use different time-saving tactics depending on the park they are in. At the **Magic Kingdom** most people turn right (counterlockwise) upon entering; therefore, consider starting your tour in a clockwise direction, starting at Adventureland and working your way toward Tomorrowland. At **EPCOT Center**, new arrivals tend to make straight for the geosphere, beside the entrance, to wait in line for Spaceship Earth, which makes heading to the World Showcase and returning to Future World later in the day a sensible plan. By far the most popular attraction at **Disney's Animal Kingdom** is Kilimanjaro Safaris, so visit this one at off-peak times or use a FastPass for it.

Opening times and tickets

Opening times vary greatly depending on what park you are visiting and at what time of year. The parks are generally **open** daily from 9am to around 9pm or 10pm during holidays and in the summer, and from 9am to 6pm or later the rest of the year, with extended hours on holidays. Disney's Animal Kingdom closes at

5pm. During peak seasons the *Orlando Sentinel* lists each park's hours on the front page. A one-day, one-park ticket costs $53.25 (children 3–9 $42.60; under-3s get in free), is available from any park entrance, and allows entry to one park only.

For seeing multiple parks, spread your visits over four or five days using a **Park Hopper** pass that permits entry to all four major parks and free use of the shuttle buses around the complex. A four-day pass costs $211.94 (children 3–9 $169.34), five-day $243.89 (children 3–9 $195.96). The **Park Hopper PLUS** pass adds on other Disney area attractions to the four major theme parks, including the water parks, Pleasure Island, and Disney's Wide World of Sports: a five-day pass costs $275.86 (children 3–9 $221.53); six-day $307.81 (children 3–9 $247.10); and seven-day $339.75 (children 3–9 $272.65). Note that admission prices given for the park include tax. There's also a $369 year-long pass ($314 for children), strictly for fanatics. If you're staying at a Disney World resort, you are eligible for reductions on all these prices and can purchase an **Ultimate Park Hopper** ticket – a more elaborate version of the Park Hopper PLUS, giving access to additional Disney attractions. You can also save around $20 off the front gate price by purchasing passes online at Ⓦ www.disney.com.

As obvious as it may sound, if you arrive by car be sure to follow the signs to the park you want to visit and use its **parking lot** ($7 a day, which covers you for all the Disney World parking lots; free if you're staying at a Disney World resort). These lots are enormous, so make a note of exactly where you're parked. Parking lots and hotels are linked to the main attractions by a comprehensive **transport system** made up of buses and a monorail (free to guests of Disney World resorts), further details of which are on p.338.

The Magic Kingdom

Anyone who's been to Disneyland in LA will recognize much of the Magic Kingdom. Like the original Disney theme park, it's divided into several themed sections, each with its own identity. Building facades, rides, gift shops, even the particular characters giving hugs contribute to the distinct feel of each section. The areas are called **Adventureland**, **Tomorrowland**, **Fantasyland**, **Frontierland**, **Liberty Square**, and **Mickey's Toontown Fair**. Some of the rides are identical to their Californian forebears, some are greatly expanded and improved – and a few are much worse. Like its older sibling, the place is best experienced with enthusiasm: jump in with both feet and go on every ride you can.

A warning: don't promise the kids (or yourself) too much beforehand. Unless you cleverly use your FastPass option (see p.343), lines are sometimes so long that it may be better to pass up some attractions. Although waiting times are usually posted, lines can be deceiving: Disney masterfully disguises their true length and keeps you cool with shade, fans, and air-conditioning wherever possible.

The park

From the main gates, you'll step into Main Street USA, a bustling assortment of souvenir shops selling the ubiquitous mouse-ear hats and other Disney paraphernalia in old-fashioned, town-square stores. Don't spend too much time here, as you can buy most of the same items throughout the park and in Disney hotels.

At the end of Main Street you'll see **Cinderella's Castle**, a stunning pseudo-Rhineland palace that looks like it should be the most elaborate ride in the park. In fact, it's merely a shell that conceals all the electronics and machinery that drive the whole extravaganza. You simply walk through a tunnel in its center, and use it as a reference point if you lose your bearings.

If you arrive early, beat the lines by heading immediately for the popular thrills-and-spills rides, which tend to draw the biggest crowds. The most nerve-jangling of these is **Space Mountain**, in essence an ordinary roller coaster, yet one whose total darkness makes every jump and jolt unexpected. The ride may last less than three minutes, but many breathe a sigh of relief once it's over. **Splash Mountain** employs water to great effect, culminating in a stunning 52-foot death-drop down a waterfall. Like most rides, you must be of adequate height to board Splash Mountain, so if you have a tot who's too tiny, there's a playground placed discreetly to the right of the ride. **Big Thunder Mountain Railroad** puts you on board a runaway train, which hurtles through Gold Rush California in about three minutes. There's also the kid-oriented **The Barnstormer**, a milder attraction perfect for thrillseekers-in-training.

You don't have to be a roller coaster junkie to enjoy the Magic Kingdom. Many of the best rides in the park rely on "AudioAnimatronic" characters – impressive vocal robots of Disney invention – for their appeal. The most up to date are seen in **The ExtraTERRORestrial Alien Encounter**, which will appeal especially to those who are fans of the *Alien* films, though the sensation of being brushed by unseen things in the dark may be too close an encounter for others. A wonderful visual treat is **The Timekeeper**, where you're taken on a trip through time by a zany robot (whose voice is provided by Robin Williams). A whole slew of realistic robots inhabit **Pirates of the Caribbean**, the classic boat ride through a pirate-infested Caribbean island complete with drunken debauchery and general mayhem.

Elsewhere, the **Haunted Mansion** is worth the wait, as much for the duration of the ride – one of the longest in the park – as for the clever special effects that include holograms: there's a sliding ceiling in the entrance room and macabre goings-on as your "doom buggy" passes through a spook-filled cemetery. The leisurely **Jungle Cruise** is narrated by a pun-loving guide, who takes you through waterfalls and cannibal camps in Africa's most "dangerous" territory. **Buzz Lightyear's Space Ranger Spin** is much like being inside a video game, as you try to help Buzz zap the enemy that threatens from every side. With no prior explanation of the rules, however, most visitors will derive their pleasure from using the joysticks to spin their buggies in various directions.

Fantasyland is the one place where the Magic Kingdom shows its age (the park opened in 1971), but it also caters to the imaginations of its youngest visitors, making it one of the most visited corners of the park. **It's a Small World** is a slow, pleasant boat ride past multi-ethnic childlike robots who sing the theme song over and over and over again. **Peter Pan's Flight** and **Snow White's Scary Adventures** are creaky, low-tech amusements, still very popular with young kids, but which wouldn't be out of place in a fairground. **The Many Adventures of Winnie the Pooh** ride has replaced **Mr Toad's Wild Ride**, to the chagrin of many nostalgic Disney buffs, but it is suitable for small children. **The Enchanted Tiki Room (Under New Management)** in Adventureland has dozens of AudioAnimatronic tropical birds and Tiki-god statues that sing and whistle their way through a program of updated Broadway-show-style numbers – unfortunately, the infectious original melody that once sent visitors away humming is no more.

Apart from thrill rides, the park offers a few low-key attractions. While in Fantasyland, head to the **Fantasyland Character Festival** area, set up between the **Mad Tea Party** and **Dumbo the Flying Elephant**, where you can meet and greet Disney's myriad characters. Otherwise, visit **Mickey's Toontown Fair**, where you're guaranteed to see several, or stay for the character-saturated **parade**. Check for the parade times, as they change depending on the day and season. The best vantage point is from a bench in Frontierland. Hint: stake one out around an hour before the event.

EPCOT Center

Even before the new Magic Kingdom opened, Walt Disney was developing plans for the **EPCOT** (Experimental Prototype Community of Tomorrow) **CENTER**. It was conceived in 1966 as a real community that would experiment and work with the new ideas and materials of a technologically advancing US. The idea failed to take shape as Disney had envisaged: EPCOT didn't open its gates until 1982, when global recession and ecological concerns had put a damper on the belief in the infallibility of science. One drawback of this park is simply its immense size: twice as big as the Magic Kingdom and, ironically, given its futuristic themes, very sapping on mankind's oldest mode of transport – the feet.

The park

EPCOT's 180-foot-high **geosphere** (unlike a semi-circular geodesic *dome*, the geo*sphere* is completely round) houses information desks and souvenir shops and sits in the heart of the **Future World** section of the park, which keeps close to EPCOT's original concept of exploring the history and researching the future of agriculture, transport, energy, and communication. Inside the geosphere is **Spaceship Earth**, a fifteen-minute ride that looks at communication, beginning with a pre-Cro-Magnon time tunnel and ending with a blast into the future to explore cutting-edge technologies. The highlight of the ride is the ascent into the star-filled core of the geosphere.

Future World is divided into eight pavilions (including Spaceship Earth), each corporate-sponsored, and having its own rides, films, interactive computer exhibits, and games. **Innoventions** highlights the newest trends in technological gadgetry, such as virtual-reality viewing helmets and computerized dwellings, with Innoventions **East** appealing to young and old, and Innoventions **West** to the kids.

The **Wonders of Life** pavilion has a diverse selection of attractions, including **Body Wars**, an exciting, if rather wrenching and somewhat dated, flight-simulator trip through a human body. While here, be sure to catch the entertaining **Cranium Command**, in which an AudioAnimatronic character is detailed to control the brain of a 12-year-old all-American boy – a good mix of Disney imagination and humor – and **The Making of Me**, certainly one of the most sensitive and affecting treatments for younger visitors of conception and childbirth ever put together, including actual footage of a developing fetus.

Concentrate on beating the lines that often stretch outside the **Universe of Energy**, a celebration of the harnessing of the earth's energy. Its centerpiece is **Ellen's Energy Adventure**, starring actress Ellen DeGeneres, the highlight of which is a ride through the primeval forests where dinosaurs roamed and today's fossil fuels originated. Although ultimately educational and with some impressive effects, its rather disjointed story line and the overplayed dinosaur theme make this attraction only just worth the wait.

In the **Imagination!** pavilion, a 3-D cinematic thrill called **Honey I Shrunk the Audience** keeps you on the edge of your seat with the excellent "feelies," which add sensations of touch and smell to the state-of-the-art 3-D visuals and surround-sound effects (as imagined in Aldous Huxley's *Brave New World*).

The Living Seas, the world's largest artificial saltwater environment, occupied by a multitude of fish, sharks, turtles, and other sea creatures, also has a great deal to offer those who enjoy gawking at marine life – not to mention the chance to climb inside a diving suit.

One of EPCOT's most successful attractions, no doubt because it's the only full-fledged thrill ride in the park, is **Test Track**, where you can experience firsthand what it might be like to be a test driver for a high-performance car. Reaching sixty miles per hour and lasting eight minutes, it's among the fastest and longest rides Disney World has to offer.

The Land offers the very rich and informative **Living with the Land**, a tour of the world's various biomes and alternative means of food production, marred somewhat by commentary touting the availability of certain species of fish at the park's restaurants. **The Circle of Life** is another worthwhile stop, with its powerful message about keeping the earth a viable habitat for all of its creatures, not just humans. Consider having a bite to **eat** in the food court, where the choice of eateries is more varied than the burgers-and-fries fare found elsewhere in Future World.

For the newest pavilion, **Mission: SPACE**, which opened in August 2003, Disney worked with NASA advisors, astronauts, and scientists to recreate as realistically as possible the sensations of being launched in a rocket to Mars.

Arranged around a forty-acre lagoon, the **World Showcase** section of EPCOT attempts to mirror the history, architecture, and culture of the eleven nations that responded to Disney's worldwide appeal when the original idea of creating a futuristic ideal community using the latest technology was being developed in the Seventies. Each section features an instantly recognizable landmark – Mexico has a Mayan pyramid, France an Eiffel Tower – or a stereotypical scene, such as a British pub or a Moroccan bazaar. The elaborate reconstructions show careful attention to detail; highlights include the Viking longboat ride through Norway, Japan's gardens and cultural museum, and the *Wonders of China* film. Each country also offers its own cuisine in often excellent restaurants where the decor can be as impressive as the food – notably Mexico's recreation of a balmy night in a picturesque Mexican village – and the staff are almost all natives. The most crowded place is usually **The American Adventure** inside a replica of Philadelphia's Liberty Hall, where AudioAnimatronic versions of Mark Twain and Benjamin Franklin give a somewhat sanitized account of two centuries of US history in under half an hour. It's worth staying on till late evening to see performances by many of the countries whose natives perform a variety of singing and dancing acts for passing crowds. At night, the lagoon also transforms into the spectacular sound-and-light show, **IllumiNations: Reflections of Earth**, which starts half an hour before closing. During the rest of the day, a boat crosses the lagoon at regular intervals, linking the entrance to Future World, Morocco, and Germany.

Disney-MGM Studios

When the Disney Corporation began making films and TV shows for adults – most notably *Who Framed Roger Rabbit?* – it also began plotting the creation of a theme park geared as much toward adults as kids. Buying the rights to the gem-filled Metro-Goldwyn-Mayer (MGM) collection of films and TV shows, Disney acquired a vast array of instantly familiar images to mold into shows and rides. Opening in 1990, **DISNEY-MGM STUDIOS** overshadowed the opening of Florida's Universal Studios (see p.355) and at the same time found an extra use for the real film studios based here – the people you'll see laboring over storyboards on the Backlot Tour aren't there for show: they are genuinely making films. Most of the things to do at MGM take the form of rides or shows, and there are fewer exhibit-style attractions compared to the other Disney parks. This means that you could do MGM in less time than it would take to explore, say, the EPCOT Center or Disney's Animal Kingdom.

The park

The first of several highly bowdlerized imitations of Hollywood's famous streets and buildings – which cause much amusement to anyone familiar with the seedy state of the originals – **Hollywood Boulevard** leads into the park, its length brightened with re-enactments of famous movie scenes, strolling film-star lookalikes and the odd Muppet.

Avoid a long wait in the sun by arriving early and going straight to the half-hour **Studios Backlot Tour**. A narrated tram-ride tour takes you behind the scenes, whisking you past the windows of animation studios and production offices (where you might see costumes and props being created) to the climax: the exploding **Catastrophe Canyon**, an ingenious set that demonstrates special effects at disturbingly close range. The tour's interest level rises and falls, depending on the movies in production at the time, but you won't feel as though you've had your money's worth if you miss it. The same applies to **The Magic of Disney Animation**, a 35-minute self-guided tour with a hilarious ten-minute instructional film featuring Robin Williams. Also not to be missed, **The Indiana Jones Epic Stunt Spectacular** recreates and explains many of the action-packed set pieces from the Steven Spielberg films.

Sharp turns and collisions with asteroids make **Star Tours**, a flight-simulator trip to the Moon of Endor piloted by *Star Wars* characters R2D2 and C-3PO, one of the more physical rides in the park – passengers' seatbelts are carefully checked before lift-off, but as simulator rides go, it's not one of the best. **Rock 'n' Roller Coaster** takes the prize for extreme edginess: a heavy-metal soundtrack, a breakneck-speed launch, and any number of full inversion loop-the-loops – all in the pitch dark – make it a pure claustrophobic panic-attack at its finest. Another really scary ride is **The Twilight Zone Tower of Terror**, a thirteen-story free-fall that's enough to put you off elevators for life. The series of drops that make up the ride changes from one ride to the next, adding to the fear factor.

For a rundown on Walt Disney – the man, the movies, the theme parks – pop into **Walt Disney: One Man's Dream**, where museum-style exhibits and a fourteen-minute film with some old footage help to put the Disney phenomenon into context. Just like the TV show it attempts, with admirable accuracy, to recreate, **Who Wants to be a Millionaire – Play it!** is a very popular attraction. It is held in a TV studio with working cameras and an appropriately cheesy host, and the members of the audience (you) earn the right to advance to the "hot seat" by answering questions with the aid of a keypad. A computer ranks everyone according to the speed and quality of their answers, and once in the spotlight, you'll be playing for a top prize of a three-day Disney Line cruise (see p.351) to the Bahamas (for full details of the rules and regulations of this game, go to Guest Relations at the park entrance). Good laughs courtesy of Kermit, Miss Piggy, and the gang can be had at **Jim Henson's MuppetVision 3D**, a three-dimensional film whose special effects put you right inside the *Muppet Show*, using more of the "feelies" technology.

Adding a welcome dimension to the park are two theater productions: **Beauty and the Beast** and **Voyage of the Little Mermaid**. Both are live performances of shortened versions of the Disney movies. The costumes, sets, and talents make them worth a visit.

Inside a replica of Mann's Chinese Theater in Hollywood is **The Great Movie Ride** (closed for refurbishment at time of writing), which repays the (usually) long wait with a ride that allows visitors to enter scenes from classic movies such as *The Wizard of Oz* and *Casablanca*. This enjoyable, 22-minute voyage employs more than sixty AudioAnimatronic figures, which are surprisingly lifelike. Afterwards, consider **refreshments** at either the *50's Prime Time Café,* decorated with Fifties formica kitchen tables and other period pieces, or the *Sci-Fi Dine-In Theater*, where patrons are served in Fifties-style cars while watching science-fiction trailers and cartoons in a drive-in theater.

Disney's Animal Kingdom

DISNEY'S ANIMAL KINGDOM was opened in April 1998 as an animal-conservation park with Disney's patented over-the-top twist. The result is a 500-acre theme park, Disney World's largest by far, divided into six major "lands": **Africa**, **Camp Minnie-Mickey**, **DinoLand USA**, **Discovery Island, Rafiki's Planet Watch**, and **Asia**. The Animal Kingdom is a true tribute not only to wildlife but also to the versatility of concrete, which is colored, imprinted upon, and formed into an endless variety of shapes to help create authentic-looking settings for each land.

The park

Upon entering the park, visitors find **The Oasis**, where they are greeted by flamingos and other exotic birds, reptiles, and mammals. Just beyond is **Discovery Island**, the center of which is **The Tree of Life**, a 145-foot-high concrete imitation tree. Depictions of animals are cleverly and intriguingly woven into the trunk and branches, and there's an amusing 3-D "feelie" **It's Tough to be a Bug!** shown inside – children with a fear of "things that creep and crawl in the dark" are advised not to enter.

The park's main thrill ride is in **DinoLand USA**, where **DINOSAUR**, a roller coaster–style vehicle, makes small drops and short stops in the dark as the beasts pop out of nowhere and roar all the while.

Disney's Animal Kingdom has four live shows, three for all ages, and one particularly for younger visitors. Head to DinoLand USA for *Tarzan Rocks!*, in which amazing gymnast-actors swing to the high energy rock music. Across the park at **Camp Minnie-Mickey** is the *Festival of the Lion King*, a participatory production of upbeat music with some nifty acrobatics, loosely based on its namesake film. Also in Camp Minnie-Mickey, for the kiddies, there's *Pocahontas and Her Forest Friends*, featuring the legendary Native American maid and a host of live animals. The *Flights of Wonder* bird show, on Asia's **Caravan Stage**, showcases falcons, vultures, owls, and other wonderful birds that interact with the audience.

In **Africa**, you'll find one of the most involving and best-realized attractions: the **Kilimanjaro Safaris**. Climb into a good facsimile of a jeep transport and be swept into what feels very much like a real safari through African wildlands (local oak trees have been trimmed to look like African acacias). You not only view the many animals – giraffes, zebras, elephants, lions, gazelles, and rhinos – but also take part in anti-poacher maneuvers. **Asia** offers the **Kali River Rapids Run** for thrills and wet chills, which compare favorably with those offered by Splash Mountain in the Magic Kingdom (see p.345). However, as with all flume rides at Disney, the saturation far outweighs the excitement – except for the kids, where the saturation *is* the excitement.

The remainder of the park requires no more than casual strolling, but all of its corners warrant exploration. **Rafiki's Planet Watch**, accessible by the

Wildlife Express Train, features the **Conservation Station**, the most educational part of the park. Here you can observe as veterinarians treat animals, and this is where you'll find **Song of the Rainforest**, a simple yet extremely effective attraction where the sounds of the rainforest – from screeching birds to buzzing chainsaws – come alive as you sit with earphones in a small booth. Rafiki's is also the site of the **Affection Section**, a particularly well-run petting zoo. To see more of the park's impressive collection of animals from around the globe, head back to Africa and take a stroll along the **Pangani Forest Exploration Trail**, home to a troop of lowland gorillas, hippos (view them underwater at the aquarium), and innumerable exotic creatures; or experience Asia's **Maharajah Jungle Trek**, which gives you an astoundingly up-close look at the healthiest-looking tigers in captivity frolicking amidst ruins, as well as a host of other creatures from that continent. Wander the **Discovery Island Trails** to catch sight of lemurs, kangaroos, and other eye-catching creatures; and, once you have bored of wildlife, make for the **Character Greeting Trails** in Camp Minnie-Mickey, where you can track down classic Disney characters and get them to sign their autographs.

The water parks

If you're planning to visit the four main Disney parks, consider splitting your itinerary with a day at either **Blizzard Beach** or **Typhoon Lagoon**. Both water parks follow the fantastic themes typical of Disney, and their straightforward and often quite thrilling rides, along with artificial white sand beaches and thousands of deckchairs, should appeal to kids and worn-out parents alike.

Blizzard Beach

Near Disney-MGM Studios and *All-Star Resorts* (see "Accommodation," p.341). Daily 10am–6pm in low season, 9am–6pm or later in high season; ☎407/560-5408; $33.02, children 3–9 $26.63.

An inviting and immensely popular water park, **Blizzard Beach** is a combination of sand and fake snow surrounding Melt Away Bay, which lies at the foot of a snow-covered "mountain," complete with a ski lift and water slides. The quickest way down is via **Summit Plummet**, designed to look like a ski jump but in fact an incredibly steep water slide 120 feet high. This ride offers possibly the most exhilarating ten seconds in Disney World, as well as commanding views of well-known landmarks such as the geosphere at the EPCOT Center and The Twilight Zone Tower of Terror at Disney-MGM Studios as you wait in line. The chairlift that transports you to the starting point of this and most of the park's other rides is really an attraction in itself (complete with waiting lines); walking up the stairs is a far quicker option. Alternatively, you can lounge around in deckchairs on the sand and soak up some rays, then cool off in one of the pools rippled by wave machines. Arrive early in summer to beat the inevitable crowds. If the entrance charge wasn't steep enough, you have to fork out an additional $7 for a locker and $1 for towel rental.

Typhoon Lagoon

Just south of Pleasure Island (see "Nightlife: Downtown Disney," p.353). Daily 10am–5pm in low season, 9am–6pm or later in high season; ☎407/560-6296; $33.02, children 3–9 $26.63.

Typhoon Lagoon, busiest in the summer and on weekends (often reaching full capacity), consists of an imaginatively constructed "tropical island" around a two-and-a-half-acre lagoon, rippled at regular intervals by four-foot waves. The rides are generally less daunting than what's on offer at Blizzard Beach (see above), but exciting enough to justify the price of entrance. **Humunga Kowabunga**, three speed-slides fifty feet up the "mountain" beside the lagoon, is the most exhilarating ride, followed by several smaller slides and a saltwater **Shark Reef** where snorkelers fearful of the open seas can explore a coral reef and be sniffed by real (but not dangerous) nurse and bonnethead sharks. When you're exhausted, take an inner tube (provided at the park's start point) and float around **Castaway Creek**, a half-hour meander through grottoes and caves, only interrupted by a sudden drenching from a tropical storm.

Unlike the major parks, you can bring **food** to Typhoon Lagoon, but no alcohol or glass containers.

The rest of Walt Disney World

Several other **Disney-devised amusements** exist to keep people on Disney property as long as possible and to offer therapeutic recreation and relaxation to those suffering theme-park burn-out.

Disney Institute

Buena Vista Drive, north of Downtown Disney; ⓣ407/939-8687, ⓦwww.disneyinstitute.com.

The **Disney Institute**, modeled on a university campus done in Florida-style architecture, offers various business-related courses. The interest for visitors, however, are the **tours** run by the Institute giving a behind-the-scenes look at many aspects of Walt Disney World. The best – and most expensive at $199 (including lunch) – is the "Backstage Magic" tour, which takes you along the tunnel system beneath the Magic Kingdom and offers a look at some of the backstage technology at the EPCOT Center and Disney-MGM Studios. If you're on this tour, there is no admission charge to the three parks.

Disney's Wide World of Sports

Two miles east of Disney's Animal Kingdom on Osceola Parkway. Hours depend on daily events; $10, children $7.50; ⓣ407/828-3267, ⓦwww.disneyworldsports.com.

Professional and amateur sporting events are frequently held at the Mediterranean-style **Disney's Wide World of Sports** complex, a collection of stadiums. Among them are the 9500-seat baseball field in which the Atlanta Braves hold their spring training; and the 30,000-square-foot, 5000-seat Milk House, used for everything from basketball to wrestling. Other features include a series of interactive games called the Multi Sport Experience, where amateurs can test various sporting skills using professional equipment; and a themed *All-Star Café* restaurant with baseball mitt-shaped booths and large-screen TVs. Stop at the retail shop for stuffed Disney characters in athletic uniforms.

Disney cruise line

Disney is also solidly in the cruise ship business. On the *Disney Wonder* and *Disney Magic*, you can book three- and four-day voyages combined with land-based vacations. The elegant ships – the luxurious decor includes inlaid Italian woodwork – depart from Port Canaveral, an hour from the theme park (parking $30, $40, and $70 for the three-, four-, and seven-day cruises respectively), and sail to Nassau and then Disney's own Bahamian island, **Castaway Cay**. Live shows are different every night, and separate entertainment areas are provided for children, adults, and families. Cabins in high season average about $1225 per person for seven nights, including three nights at a Disney resort and four nights on board. In general, rates run from $829 to $4999 per person, depending on accommodation choices and season. For roughly the same price, not including airfare, you could also choose a seven-night cruise to various destinations in the Caribbean. For more information: ⓣ407/566-7000 or 1-800/939-2784, ⓦwww.disneycruiseline.com.

Richard Petty Driving Experience

Walt Disney World Speedway (at the south end of the Magic Kingdom Parking Lot); ⓣ1-800/237-3889, ⓦwww.1800bepetty.com. Daily 9am–5pm, sporadic closures during Oct, Nov, and Dec.

The **Richard Petty Driving Experience** offers race-car fanatics and wannabes four ways to fulfill their fantasies: they can take a sixteen-lap stock-car ride around a one-mile tri-oval track driven by an expert for $94.34; for $369.94, an intensive three-hour "Rookie Experience" course, at the end of which participants drive eight laps themselves; or the "King's Experience" ($740.94) and the "Experience of a Lifetime" ($1270.94), longer variations whereby participants get to drive eighteen and thirty laps respectively. In all cases, a valid driver's license must be presented.

Eating

Besides the generally mundane and overpriced fare available at the theme parks, there are plenty of **places to eat** on Disney property. Some upscale dining opportunities are to be found at the resorts, Downtown Disney is a safe bet for dinner, and the World Showcase at EPCOT Center, with its multi-ethnic cuisines, offers the best food among the theme parks.

Bongo's Cuban Café Downtown Disney West Side, 1498 E Buena Vista Drive ⓣ407/828-0999. Gloria and Emilio Estefan's fair-but-fun Cuban cuisine. The decor is wildly fabulous and there are shows Fri and Sat.

California Grill on the 15th floor of the *Contemporary Resort* ⓣ407/939-3463. Disney's culinary showpiece, with a menu from sushi to stews prepared in an open kitchen and served in a bustling dining room. A great selection of Californian wines is also available, along with impressive views over the Magic Kingdom.

Chefs de France the French Pavilion at EPCOT Center's World Showcase ⓣ407/939-3463. Definitely the best, most authentic French cuisine around, served in perfect style. Fresh produce is flown in daily from France. Wonderful wines, too.

Flying Fish Café at the *BoardWalk Inn* ⓣ407/939-3463. Excellent but pricey seafood as well as meat, game, and vegetable dishes, prepared New American–style and served in an energetic dining room. Considered Disney World's best by many locals.

The Hollywood Brown Derby Disney-MGM Studios ⓣ407/939-3463. A faithful recreation of the mythic Hollywood landmark, with the famous original recipes to match. Try their famous Cobb Salad, invented by the Brown Derby's original chefs. One of Disney World's very best.

House of Blues Downtown Disney West Side, 1490 E Buena Vista Drive ⓣ407/934-2583. Decent Creole- and Cajun-inspired food. Consider going during Sunday's popular all-you-can-eat Gospel brunch ($30).

Jiko – The Cooking Place at the *Animal Kingdom Lodge* ⓣ407/939-3463. An upscale and cosmopolitan addition to Disney World's restaurants, offering delicacies from around the world, including banana leaf–steamed Chilean sea bass and oven-baked garlic chicken *tagine*.

Planet Hollywood Downtown Disney Pleasure Island, 1506 E Buena Vista Drive ⓣ407/827-7836. One of the world's top-grossing restaurants, serving burgers inside a giant globe. Its popularity stems from the brand name rather than the mediocre quality of the food.

Rainforest Café Downtown Disney West Side (ⓣ407/827-8500) and at Disney's Animal Kingdom (ⓣ407/938-9100). These safari-themed restaurants, with faux animals poking out through the trees, are worth a walk through for their creative decor, but you'll find better-value meals elsewhere.

Victoria & Albert at the *Grand Floridian Resort & Spa* ⓣ407/939-3463. Venison, fine wines, and harp music in the background set the tone at what is possibly the best place for gourmet dining at Disney World. Reserve far in advance to sit at the Chef's Table in the kitchen, where you'll be attended to by the chef himself.

Wolfgang Puck Downtown Disney West Side, 1482 E Buena Vista Drive ⓣ407/938-9653. Four restaurants in one multi-level location: *The Dining Room* upstairs for upscale dining; *The Café* for casual; *The Express* for self-service; and *B's Lounge & Sushi Bar* for sushi. Meals are moderately priced (except in *The Dining Room*) and creatively prepared. Pizzas, rotisserie chickens, and good sandwiches are available at *The Express*, which has another location in Downtown Disney Marketplace ⓣ407/828-0107.

Nightlife: Downtown Disney

Around a half-hour before closing, most of the Walt Disney World parks hold some kind of bash, usually involving fireworks and fountains. For more solid night-time entertainment for adults, the corporation devised the six-acre **Pleasure Island**, exit 26B off I-4, part of **Downtown Disney** (for information, Ⓣ407/939-2648), which also includes **West Side** and **Marketplace**, the two areas where restaurants (see "Eating" opposite) and shops predominate. On this remake of an abandoned island, pseudo-warehouses are the setting for a mixture of theme shops, bars, and nightclubs. Admission to Pleasure Island is free from 10am to 7pm; after 7pm there's a charge of $21.25 – unless you have an Ultimate Park Hopper or Park Hopper Plus ticket that includes Pleasure Island (see p.344) – which allows you limitless entry into the bars and clubs. Anyone under 18 must be accompanied by a parent, and alcohol will only be served to those who are 21 or over. Take your ID and be prepared to pay high prices for food and drink.

Five shows a night keep things lively at the *Comedy Warehouse*, where a handful of comedians do an improvisational act and are not afraid to send up Mickey Mouse. The *House of Blues* (in West Side), built by the Blues Brothers themselves, now headlines top artists from the world of soul, blues, and rock and roll. The *Pleasure Island Jazz Company* offers live combos and groups, with taped music between shows, plus a limited menu and a wine list. For dancing, *Mannequins Dance Palace* is a swish, and rather risqué by Disney standards, disco that favors techno music and doesn't get cracking until midnight; the less ostentatious *8Trax* spins exclusively Seventies and Eighties pop hits; the *Rock 'n' Roll Beach Club* jams to the all-time greatest hits, with both DJs and live bands; and the *BET SoundStage Club*, owned by Black Entertainment Television, caters to the throngs that love rhythm and blues, soul, and hip-hop music.

The most original – and most enjoyable – place on Pleasure Island is the **Adventurers Club**, loosely based on a 1930s gentlemen's club and furnished with a motley collection of face masks (some of which unexpectedly start speaking), deer heads, and assorted flea-market furniture. Between scheduled shows, actors and actresses move surreptitiously (despite their period attire) among the crowd and strike up loud and eccentric conversations with unsuspecting audience members.

Back on the mainland, next to Pleasure Island and glowing with neon lights, sits *Planet Hollywood*. Housed in a sphere, it seats 400 people and is the biggest branch in the restaurant chain to date. As well as some interesting dining alternatives, **Downtown Disney West Side** has DisneyQuest ($33.02, children $26.63), a five-story, hi-tech arcade – a bastion of virtual-reality games, including a canoe course where you paddle through a digital river, getting splashed with very real water. The Cirque du Soleil (Ⓣ407/939-1298, Ⓦwww.cirquedusoleil.com) has made Downtown Disney its permanent home, and they perform ten times a week in a 1600-seat theater – the shows are fascinat-

Orlando FlexTicket

In the hopes of prying tourists from Disney's clutches, competitors have teamed up to offer special multi-park passes. The **Orlando FlexTicket** offers unlimited admission for fourteen days to Universal Studios, SeaWorld Orlando, and Wet 'n' Wild (a water park) for $187.39 (adults), $152.25 (children 3–9). For $223.77 (adults) or $187.56 (children), you can throw Busch Gardens Tampa Bay (two hours away) into the deal, with a free shuttle from Orlando to Busch Gardens included. For details on Busch Gardens, see p.274.

ing, but tickets are exorbitantly priced: $77 or $87 depending on where you sit. On the other side of Pleasure Island is **Marketplace**, a shopping emporium crammed with the world's largest Disney store, a Christmas shop, and a Lego store where kids can ogle massive Lego creations of, among others, a dragon and a spaceship, and also play with every type of Lego known.

Universal Orlando

For some years, it seemed that US TV and film production would be shifting away from expensive California to Florida, which, with its lower taxes and cheaper labor, was more amenable, and the opening of Universal Studios in June 1990 appeared to confirm that trend. So far, for various reasons, Florida has not proved to be a fully realistic alternative, but that hasn't stopped the Universal enclave here, now known as **UNIVERSAL ORLANDO**, from expanding enormously and becoming even more successful.

The sequel to the long-established and immensely popular Universal Studios tour in Los Angeles, Florida's original Universal, like its rival Disney-MGM, is a working studio, filling over 400 acres with the latest in TV- and film-production technology. However, as the result of a multi-billion-dollar cash infusion, it is now much more than a glorified backlot and is competing with Disney World on more than one front. **Universal Studios** has added **Islands of Adventure**, which definitely has far zingier roller-coaster rides and zowier hi-tech special effects than Disney, and **CityWalk**, an earthier, more realistic lure for nightlife dollars that would otherwise go to Downtown Disney.

Universal has proved to be extremely popular, becoming one of the most visited theme parks in the US. Overall, the mood is more hip and the rides are more spectacular than at Disney, but service can be snippy and the parks can feel less welcoming – as though almost everything is aimed primarily at hyper-energetic adolescent boys who want things louder, faster, and with more attitude. For the overwhelming majority of visitors, two days will be sufficient.

Accommodation

A sign of Universal Orlando's popularity has been the relatively recent opening of three resort hotels on Universal property, all of them luxurious, expensive,

Visiting Universal Orlando

Universal Orlando (ⓣ407/363-8000, ⓦwww.uescape.com) is located half a mile north of exits 29B or 30A off I-4. The park is open daily from 9am, with closing times varying by season. A one-day studio pass costs $55.33 for adults, $45.75 for children 3–9; a two-day **Escape Pass** $103.26 for adults, $89.41 for children; three-day, $119.23 for adults, $103.26 for children. Note that the admission prices given for the park include tax.

Universal has also devised **Universal Express** – a system similar to Disney's FastPass (see p.343) – to help get visitors around long waits in line. Unlike at Disney, more than half of the park's attractions are covered under this scheme. Another good way to **beat the crowds** at Universal is to join the much quicker single rider lines – whereby you fill up the odd seat not taken by groups wishing to experience the attraction together – that you'll find at some rides, notably the roller coasters. All guests at the Universal resorts can join the Express lines simply by presenting their room key card.

and incredibly convenient for visiting Universal Studios, Islands of Adventure, and CityWalk (regular complimentary water taxis run between the three resorts and a dock at CityWalk). To make reservations at any of the Universal resorts, call ⓣ1-888/322-5541.

Hard Rock Hotel Stuffed with rock memorabilia, stylish rooms equipped with high-quality CD players, and familiar tunes blaring out at poolside, make this the least tranquil of the park's resorts – and the most popular with the younger generation. ❼

Portofino Bay Hotel A lavish recreation of the Italian seaside village of Portofino, complete with vintage Alfa Romeos and Fiats parked in the piazza. Enjoy every possible luxury at one of the top-rated hotels in Florida. ❽

Royal Pacific Resort Nothing very original about the South Pacific island theme, although the kids will enjoy the lagoon-style pool, and the rooms, decked in bamboo and other tropical accents are the height of comfort. The most economical of the park's resorts. ❼

Universal Studios

The first thing you'll encounter upon entering are street sets replicating New York, Hollywood, San Francisco, and Amity – the New England town where *Jaws* took place and where the detail goes right down to the chewing gum painted onto the pavements. The park itself, arranged around a large lagoon, is nominally divided into several areas: the Front Lot, World Expo, Woody Woodpecker's KidZone, the aforementioned cities, and Production Central. But they are by no means that distinct, so there's no real need to follow a particular order in your explorations.

For sheer excitement, nothing in the park compares to **Back to the Future The Ride**, a bone-shaking flight-simulator time-trip ranging from 2015 to the Ice Age, which, along with The Amazing Adventures of Spider-Man at Islands of Adventure (see p.356), is the most rewarding and successfully realized simulator ride of all the Orlando theme parks. The park's other ride using simulator technology is **Jimmy Neutron's Nicktoon Blast**, most memorable for its impressive animated graphics. After Back to the Future, the next best attraction in the park is **Earthquake–The Big One**, which gives you an intensely claustrophobic two minutes of terror as you experience what it's like to be caught on a subway train when an 8.3 Richter-scale quake hits. Along the same lines, **Twister...Ride It Out** is a suffocating but gripping experience in which you stand beside an imitation tornado, complete with simulated lightning, flying objects, and rain (cover all camera equipment). **Jaws** owes its success to anticipation of horror and classy special effects, but the ride is over all too quickly. **Terminator 2 3-D Battle Across Time** offers second-to-none special effects – like the "plasma blasts" that let the audience feel the heat and shock of its explosions – and is definitely worth the wait. The **Men in Black Alien Attack** ride puts you smack inside a video game, where you rack up points zapping aliens – or get zapped – and return a hero, or a loser. For something a little more sedate, you could check out **Lucy: A Tribute** – snippets, clips, props, costumes, bits, and bobs in memory of the zany, irrepressible redhead.

Moving on, **E.T. Adventure** is a rather dull ride on pretend bicycles to ET's home planet, although ET speaking your name (recorded earlier by a computer) as you leave is a pleasing touch. This and another tame ride, **Woody Woodpecker's Nuthouse Coaster**, are ideal for younger kids – and for adults who aren't into all the hyperactive jerks, spins, and zooms. Nearby, **Curious George Goes to Town** provides an interactive aqua-playground, with special emphasis on splashing, squirting, and getting drenched. Another playground option for tots or tots-at-heart is **Fievel's Playland**, where every piece of equipment is oversized and fun to climb on. The kiddies might also go for **Nickelodeon Studios**, a peek behind the scenes at where most of the cable network's programming is put together.

You'll also find a number of live stage shows on offer throughout the park: *The Wild, Wild, Wild West Stunt Show*, with dysfunctional cowboys and rather tame stunts (which you are nevertheless warned not to try at home); the *Universal Horror Make-Up Show*, where movie makeup secrets are revealed amidst comic repartee; *Animal Planet Live*, featuring amusing cameos and tricks performed by household animals and more exotic creatures; and *Beetlejuice's Graveyard Revue*, which, as the title suggests, is just plain wacky.

Islands of Adventure

Billed as one of two Universal parks, **ISLANDS OF ADVENTURE** is really five superb miniparks, each with its own unique spin: **Seuss Landing**, fun for the little ones and those who grew up with the good Dr S's whimsical creations; **The Lost Continent**, where ancient myth meets edgy technology; **Jurassic Park**, in which thunder lizards once again rule the earth; **Toon Lagoon**, whose classic cartoons come to giddy life; and **Marvel Super Hero Island**, which takes you into the supercharged comic-book world of your youth. The park has a truly remarkable number of amazing thrill rides and it must be said that it outshines anything Disney World has to offer in that department – even though no one has yet equaled Disney for the sheer seamless perfection of its imagined environments made real. There is also a live show, an area in which Disney still holds the edge, and a number of great hands-on play areas spread throughout.

The very best of the rides is also one of the newest: **The Amazing Adventures of Spider-Man**, which uses every trick imaginable – 3-D, sensory stimuli, motion simulation, and more – to spirit you into another dimension that's not to be missed. **Dueling Dragons** may be the next most exciting ride: twin roller coasters ("Fire" and "Ice" – separate waiting lines for each) engineered to provide harrowing near misses that will literally have your hair standing on end at several points. Here, more than on other roller coasters, the front seats provide the greatest thrills; the seats themselves keep your feet dangling in mid-air, adding to the sense of danger. Another exciting ride is the **Incredible Hulk Coaster**, with its catapult start, seven full inversions, and two precipitous plunges.

Heading the second tier of thrill rides is **Jurassic Park River Adventure**, a generally tame river-raft trip where the only thing to shout about is an 85-foot drop. If the lines are long, you might consider bypassing the twin towers of **Doctor Doom's Fearfall**, which look frightening enough, but the very short ride – a controlled drop during which you experience a few seconds of weightlessness – is an anti-climax. The views from the top of the towers are good, though. **Storm Force Accelatron** is a ride for all ages, placing visitors in tub-like cars that spin and whirl in a domed space enveloped by a noisy light show. **Poseidon's Fury** offers some impressive effects using water and fire as you play your part in an Indiana Jones–style tour of the ancient ruins of Poseidon's temple, even if the storyline is only mildly engaging.

In somewhat less adrenaline-pumping mode, you could go for **Dudley Do-Right's Ripsaw Falls**, a flume ride with its share of drops and lots of surprises; **Popeye & Bluto's Bilge-Rat Barges**, a river ride that's all about getting soaked; and **The Flying Unicorn**, a fanciful flight through an enchanted forest. Seuss Landing has even tamer, but enchanting, offerings for kiddies, including **Caro-Seus-el**, a merry-go-round adorned with Seussian characters; the interactive **One Fish, Two Fish, Red Fish, Blue Fish** and **If I Ran the Zoo**; and **The Cat in the Hat**, another endearing Seuss–inspired ride. Unless you have tons of time to kill, most of it waiting in line, give the **Pteranodon Flyers** gondola ride a miss.

Hands-on playgrounds and other attractions include **Triceratops Discovery Trail** and the **Jurassic Park Discovery Center**, the former a petting zoo with a docile ten-foot-tall, 24-foot-long interactive robot, the latter a learning center where the focus is on, of course, more dinosaurs; **Me Ship, *The Olive***, in which kids of all ages can climb, crawl, and scramble around to their heart's content; and the best, **Camp Jurassic**, an extensive, elaborate play area full of hidden treasures such as bones and fossils.

There's one live performance offered throughout the day: *The Eighth Voyage of Sinbad* stunt show, a nonstop extravaganza of swashbuckling adventure and pyrotechnics, where the set, stunts, and effects are as good as the jokes are bad.

Eating

Besides being Orlando's premier nightlife venue (see below), CityWalk has a good selection of restaurants – at least better than those on offer inside neighboring Universal Studios and Islands of Adventure. Add to these some noteworthy eateries at the resorts, and Universal visitors won't have to look hard for a decent bite to eat.

Delfino Riviera at the *Portofino Bay Hotel* ⓣ407/503-3463. An elegant Italian restaurant serving up authentic Ligurian specialties in a romantic setting overlooking the hotel's large piazza and "Portofino Bay."

Emeril's CityWalk, 6000 Universal Blvd ⓣ407/224-2424. CityWalk's most upscale dining option, where the largely New Orleans cuisine is overseen by TV chef Emeril Lagasse.

Hard Rock Cafe CityWalk, 6050 Universal Blvd ⓣ407/351-7625. Orlando boasts the world's largest *Hard Rock Café*, known as much for its T-shirts and music memorabilia as its All-American, hamburger-rich menu.

Jimmy Buffett's Margaritaville CityWalk, 6000 Universal Studios Plaza ⓣ407/224-2230, ⓦwww.margaritaville.com/orlando. Caribbean-style food served in an appropriately tropical setting, complete with a volcano exploding with margarita mix. Busy and reasonably priced.

Latin Quarter CityWalk, 6000 Universal Blvd ⓣ1-888/745-2846, ⓦwww.thelatinquarter.com. Traditional dishes of Latin America are given a contemporary touch on the "Nuevo Latino" menu, which includes paella among the decent selection.

Nightlife: CityWalk

CITYWALK (ⓣ407/363-8000, ⓦwww.citywalkorlando.com) has actually surpassed both Downtown Disney and downtown Orlando as a nightlife venue. Since it doesn't have the hyper-wholesome Disney image to live down, it's a much hipper place than Disney World could ever manage; and Orlando's after-dark area simply doesn't seem to have the imagination, or the budget, to match it. Add to that the fact that one very reasonable price includes all-night access to every club: the $8.95 **Party Pass** (add $3 if you want to take in a movie). Free parking after 6pm makes Downtown Disney seem like the most abject tourist gouger.

CityWalk features a friendly mix of restaurants (see "Eating" above), live music, dance clubs, theaters, bars, eateries, and shops. If you want to dance, try the drop-dead-hip **The Groove**, a huge, intense, multi-faceted space filled with deafening decibels and pulsing photons, or the **Latin Quarter**, for devotees of every type of Latin beat. Live music abounds at **Bob Marley – A Tribute to Freedom**, which celebrates the "King of Reggae"; **CityJazz**, which offers a cooler, more sophisticated ambience and showcases all types of jazz, funk, R&B, soul, and rock; **Hard Rock Live**, a concert hall in-the-round featuring live performers, occasionally famous ones, almost every evening; and **Jimmy Buffett's Margaritaville**, whose live island-style music captures the famous laidback Florida mood perfectly. A couple of other restaurant/bars complement the festive, musical atmosphere: at **Motown Café** the clientele creates its own music, singing and bopping along to the endless stream of great hits, and **Pat O'Brien's** perfectly recreates the feel of Old New Orleans, with its dueling pianos and wrought-iron balconies. Check out the daily **happy hours**, which vary from bar to bar.

SeaWorld Orlando

It may have as many souvenir shops as fish, but **SEAWORLD ORLANDO** is the cream of Florida's sizeable crop of marine parks and as such shouldn't be missed. Like Busch Gardens in Tampa (see p.274), SeaWorld Orlando is owned by Anheuser-Busch (which explains the incongruous homage to the brewery's Clydesdale horses, the company symbol, at SeaWorld's **Clydesdale Hamlet**). To see it all and get the best value for your money, you'll need to allocate a whole day and be certain to pick up the free map and show schedule at the entrance. To **beat the crowds**, try going on the park's thrill rides during one of the immensely popular live animal shows, when the number of people milling about the park can be significantly reduced.

The big event is the *Shamu Adventure Show* – thirty minutes of tricks performed by a playful killer whale; the night show, *Shamu Rocks America,* is also terrific. Bear in mind that at both shows the first fourteen rows will get drenched during the performance. Nearby **Shamu's Happy Harbor** is a paradise for children, offering inner tubes, slides, remote-control boats, and even an area where they can catapult water balloons at each other. The **Wild Arctic** complex (complete with artificial snow and ice) brings you close to beluga whales, walruses, and polar bears, while a simulated ride takes you on a stomach-churning helicopter flight through an arctic blizzard.

The charming and funky **Key West** area invites visitors to pet slimy stingrays at **Stingray Lagoon**, or feed them smelt at $4 a tray; and the **Key West Dolphin Stadium** wows 'em with leaping dolphin and whale-riding shows. SeaWorld's first thrill ride, **Journey to Atlantis**, is part water slide, part roller coaster, and has a sixty-foot drop. While it's less visually impressive than similar rides at Disney, you will get drenched. Inside the adjacent gift shop are two aquariums: a 25,000-gallon, underfoot aquarium filled with stingrays, and another one overhead (6000 gallons) with hammerhead sharks; odd-looking illuminated jellyfish are in tanks built into a nearby wall. On **Kraken**, SeaWorld Orlando's exhilarating roller-coaster ride, you'll be flung around at speeds of up to 65mph, free-flying and looping-the-loop.

Visiting SeaWorld Orlando

SeaWorld Orlando (Ⓣ407/351-3600 or 1-800/4-ADVENTURE, Ⓦwww.seaworld.com) is located on Sea Harbor Drive, at the intersection of I-4 and the Central Florida Expressway, or I-4 and the Bee Line Expressway; exit 27A if you're coming from the west on I-4, exit 28 if you're coming from the east on I-4. The park is open daily 9am–7pm in low season, longer hours in peak season. Tickets are $55.33, children 3–9 $45.74. Note that the admission prices given for the park include tax.

With substantially less razzmatazz, plenty of smaller tanks and displays around the park offer a wealth of information about the undersea world. Among the highlights, the **Penguin Encounter** recreates Antarctica with scores of the waddling birds scampering over a make-believe iceberg and swimming underwater; the young occupants of the **Dolphin Nursery** assert their advanced intellect by flapping their fins and drenching passersby; and **Shark Encounter** includes a walk through a glass-sided and roofed tunnel, offering the closest eyecontact you're ever likely to have with sharks and other scary predators.

The **Nautilus Theater** offers live entertainment that changes periodically; be delighted and amazed at the current *Cirque de la Mer*, a fantastic blend of dance, gymnastics, mime, music, and special effects. At the **SeaWorld Theater** you'll be charmed by *Pets Ahoy!*, in which animals rescued by the local humane society do their best to win you over. Perhaps the best show takes place at the **Sea Lion and Otter Stadium**, where the stalwart mammals put on a grand entertainment entitled *Clyde and Seamore Take Pirate Island*. Be sure not to miss the mime artist on hand fifteen minutes or so before the show starts to make fun of spectators as they file into the stadium – very amusing and, in the context of Orlando theme parks, risqué entertainment. Just behind the Sea Lion and Otter Stadium, at **Pacific Point Preserve**, check out more barking sea lions in a stunning replica of their natural Pacific Coast habitat.

If you've never been lucky enough to see a manatee in the wild, don't leave SeaWorld Orlando without taking in **Manatees: The Last Generation?**, a huge tank in which you can see a few of the endangered creatures and learn about the threat faced by their species (for more on Florida's manatees, see p.302). For wildlife buffs, the small **Turtle Point** exhibit offers a behind-the-scenes look at how SeaWorld Orlando rescues and rehabilitates manatees, sea turtles, and other marine life. One of the most successfully realized exhibits is **Tropical Reef**, a series of aquariums offering dazzling, multi-hued recreations of undersea worlds that are filled with marvelous and exotic sea creatures, the highlight being the sea dragons from Southern Australia.

Discovery Cove

Seaworld's latest attraction, **DISCOVERY COVE**, is slightly different from anything else you'll find in Orlando: a theme park without a theme; a water park without the slides; an aquarium without the glass tanks. Discovery Cove is billed as a multi-environment tropical paradise where the star turn is swimming – or, more accurately, standing waist-deep in water – with actual dolphins in the chilly salt waters of the **Dolphin Lagoon**. On entry to the park you'll be given a time for your dolphin encounter, which lasts for about half an hour and involves stroking, playing, and riding on the dorsal fin of the docile creatures. Other attractions in the park include an **Aviary** that you have to swim under a waterfall to get to; a **Coral Reef** well stocked with colorful fish to snorkel through; the **Ray Lagoon**, where you can wade with hundreds of the fascinating creatures (all with their stingers safely removed); and a **Tropical River** and beaches to

Visiting Discovery Cove

Discovery Cove (ⓣ407/370-1280 or 1-877/4-DISCOVERY, ⓦwww.discoverycove.com) is located next to SeaWorld Orlando on Central Florida Parkway. The park is open daily 8am–5.30pm. Tickets cost $137.38 without dolphin swim, $243.88 with dolphin swim, and both prices include tax and seven-day access to SeaWorld Orlando.

explore however you like. Access to Discovery Cove is limited to about a thousand visitors a day, so it's advisable to reserve well in advance. The high cost of admission does include use of equipment (wet suits, snorkeling gear, towels, lockers, animal-friendly sunscreen) and a meal with soft drinks, although once you've done your business with the dolphins and been on a few snorkeling expeditions, there's not much else to do than lounge around on the beach.

Other attractions in and around Orlando

The Orlando area's small-time entrepreneurs are nothing if not inventive. No end of tacky, short-lived, would-be attractions spring up each year and a large number of them swiftly sink without trace. The list below represents the best – or just the longest-surviving – of the thousand-and-one little places to visit in and around Orlando. Several other highly worthwhile attractions in the Orlando area, including Gatorland, are detailed starting on p.362.

Air Florida Helicopters

8990 International Drive. Daily 10am, last flight varies with the season; $20–395/person, depending on the flight plan; minimum two people. Ⓣ407/354-1400, Ⓦwww.airfloridahelicopters.com.

Take in the Orlando area from your own private piloted helicopter. Nine different flight plans whisk you over the major attractions, even all the way out to the east coast of Florida, if you like.

Airboat Rentals

Guide Marker 15, US-192, Kissimmee. Daily 9am–5pm; 2-person canoes $5/hr; 6-person electric boats $22/hr; 4-person airboats $27/hr. Ⓣ407/847-3672, Ⓦwww.airboatrentals.com.

Here's a chance to explore a pristine Florida cypress swamp on your own terms. All the boats are silent so as not to disturb any of the local fauna; you'll see alligators, otters, turtles, blue herons, and countless other birds as you meander through their natural habitat.

Flying Tigers Warbird Air Museum

231 N Hoagland Blvd, next to Kissimmee airport. Daily 9am–5pm; $9, children 7–12 $8. Ⓣ407/933-1942, Ⓦwww.warbirdmuseum.com.

The main hangar contains battle-weary Tiger Moths, Mustangs, and assorted bombers and biplanes in various states of repair – all being commercially restored.

Hard Rock Vault

8437 International Drive, in the Mercado. Daily 9am–midnight; $14.95, children 5–12 $8.95. Ⓣ407/599-7625, Ⓦwww.hardrock.com/vault.

One of Orlando's most recent attractions will appeal especially to music buffs, but casual fans too will enjoy listening to the enthusiastic and knowledgeable guides explain the often convoluted histories of the music memorabilia on display, which range from Elvis's costumes to a hand-written list of twelve things the Sex Pistols' Sid Vicious liked about his girlfriend, Nancy.

Old Town

5770 W US-192, Kissimmee. Daily 10am–11pm, rides noon–11pm; free, rides $2 to $25. Ⓣ407/396-4888, Ⓦwww.old-town.com.

Old-fashioned amusement rides and 75 interesting, if slightly tacky, shops. The go-kart track and Ferris wheel are a hoot, as are the bumper cars and laser-tag game.

Pirate's Cove Adventure Golf

Two locations: in the Mercado, 8501 International Drive (ⓣ407/352-7378) and Exit 27 off I-4 at Crosswoods, Lake Buena Vista (ⓣ407/827-1242, ⓦwww.piratescove.net). Daily 9am–11.30pm; $8.95–12.45, children $7.95–11.45, depending on which course you choose.

This is miniature golf at its inventive best: choose from several challenging, fanciful courses, and putt your way through caves, over footbridges, and under waterfalls, with pirates scrutinizing your every stroke.

Reptile World Serpentarium

5705 US-192, just over four miles east of St Cloud. Tues–Sun 9am–5.30pm; $5.50, children 6–17 $4.50, children 3–5 $3.50. ⓣ407/892-6905.

A research center for the production of snake venoms, which are sold for research to produce anti-venoms. Visitors are introduced to a caged collection of poisonous and nonpoisonous snakes from around the world, and are shown demonstrations of venom extraction at noon and 3pm.

Ripley's Believe It or Not!

8201 International Drive. Daily 8–1am; $15.95, children 4–12 $10.95. ⓣ407/345-0501, ⓦwww.ripleysorlando.com.

A model of the world's tallest man, a chunk of the Berlin Wall, and a Rolls-Royce built from a million matchsticks are among the innumerable oddities packed into these noninteractive displays in a building that was designed to appear as if it's half-sunk into the earth.

Skull Kingdom

5933 American Way at International Drive, across from Wet 'n' Wild. Mon–Fri 6–11pm, Sat & Sun noon–midnight; $14.95. ⓣ407/354-1564, ⓦwww.skullkingdom.com.

A standard haunted house packaged in a nifty skull-faced castle. The scariest part is having costumed employees such as the "Vampire Vixens" and "Mr Dragon" terrorizing your every move. Realistic-looking animatronic characters being tortured add a particularly morbid touch. Too scary for ages 7 and under.

SkyCoaster

2850 Florida Plaza, on US-192, next to Old Town. Daily noon–midnight; $37–81, depending on the number flying together ⓣ407/397-2509, ⓦwww.skyfun.com.

Bungee-jumping for one to three people at a time, soaring between two joined poles; rather like skydiving and hang-gliding at once.

SkyVenture

6805 Visitors Circle, off International Drive, across from Wet 'n' Wild. Mon–Fri 2pm–midnight, Sat & Sun noon–midnight; $38.50, children 12 and under $33.50. ⓣ407/903-1150, ⓦwww.skyventureorlando.com.

Fly on a column of air without a parachute in this virtual-reality freefall skydiving simulator. The whole process takes about an hour, although the actual diving only lasts for a couple of minutes or so.

Splendid China

3000 Splendid China Blvd, two miles west of Disney World, off US-192. Daily 9.30am–8pm; no shows Mon; $28.88, children 5–12 $18.18. ⓣ407/396-7111 or 1-800/244-6226, ⓦwww.floridasplendidchina.com.

The best of the smaller Orlando attractions, this park features over sixty authentic replicas celebrating 5000 years of Chinese architecture and history. Painstakingly reconstructed miniatures (including the Great Wall, the Forbidden City, the Leshan Buddha, and the Terracotta Warriors), plus museum exhibits, a variety of shows, and fascinating displays, make this an intriguing place to spend the day. A highlight is *The Mysterious Kingdom of the Orient* with its incredible dancers, acrobats, and martial artists (Tues–Sun 6pm). The best time to visit is toward evening when the park is beautifully illuminated. A dining and shopping area called Chinatown charges no admission fee and is a nice stop for dinner.

Titanic: Ship of Dreams

The Mercado, 8445 International Drive. Daily 10am–8pm; $16.95, children 6–12 $11.95. ⓣ407/248-1166 or 1-877/410-1912, ⓦwww.titanicshipofdreams.com.

Full-scale replicas of the famous ship's Grand Staircase, authentic artifacts from the wreckage, and the stories of many of the ship's passengers and crew all await you at this well-researched attraction.

Wet 'n' Wild

6200 International Drive. Daily 10am–5pm, longer hours in summer; $31.95, children 3–9 $25.95. After 2pm, you get $10 off regular prices. ⓣ407/351-9453 or 1-800/992-9453, ⓦwww.wetnwildorlando.com.

Water slides, chutes, rapids, wave machines, bungee cords, and more – the perfect thing for a day when the thermometer soars. Since the water's well heated in winter, it's open all year round.

WonderWorks

9067 International Drive at Pointe Orlando. Daily 9am–midnight; $16.95, children 4–12 $12.95. ⓣ407/351-8800, ⓦwww.wonderworksonline.com.

A collection of more than one hundred hi-tech interactive gizmos housed cleverly inside an upside-down creaking house. Check out "Old Sparky," Florida's electric chair, which smokes just as the original did when it accidentally set a victim on fire. Also of interest are contraptions in which you experience simulated earthquakes and hurricanes. Perfect for 13-year-old boys.

A World of Orchids

2501 N Old Lake Wilson Rd, 1 mile south of US-192, Kissimmee. Tues–Sun 9.30am–4.30pm. Free. ⓣ407/396-1881, ⓦwww.a-world-of-orchids.com.

An enthralling, air-conditioned tropical rainforest garden that showcases thousands of rare, exotic, and beautiful flowering orchids from around the world. Blooms all year round.

South of Orlando

Not much fills the rough acres directly **south of Orlando**, though Gatorland, one of the area's oldest and, in its way, most amusing destinations, sits on what's called the **Orange Blossom Trail** (known variously as US-92, US-17, and US-441), which runs the sixteen miles between Orlando and Kissimmee.

Gatorland

An oversized alligator mouth serves as the entrance for **Gatorland**, 14501 S Orange Blossom Trail (daily 9am–sunset; $19.95, children 3–12 $9.95; ⓣ407/855-5496 or 1-800/393-JAWS, ⓦwww.gatorland.com), which has been giving visitors an up-close look at the state's most feared and least understood animals since the 1950s. Surprisingly lazy beasts, the residents of the park (actually a working farm, licensed to breed alligators for their hides and meat) only show signs of life at the organized feeding – the Gator Jumparoo show – when hunks of chicken are suspended from a wire and the largest alligators, using their powerful tail muscles, propel themselves out of the water to grab their dinner: a bizarre spectacle of heaving animals and ferociously snapping jaws. When you arrive, pick up a schedule for the four main shows: Gator Jumparoo, Gator Wrestlin', Jungle Crocs of the World, and Up Close Animal Encounters. This last performance features some of Florida's most deadly snakes – coral snakes, pygmy rattlesnakes, cottonmouth moccasins, and diamond-back rattlesnakes – none of which you'd enjoy meeting in the wild, but the show serves as a handy recognition exercise just in case you ever do.

Kissimmee

A country-bumpkin counterpoint to the modern vacation developments that ring it, **KISSIMMEE**, at the end of Orange Blossom Trail, has most of its fun during the Wednesday lunchtime cattle auctions at the **Livestock Market**, 805 E Donegan Ave. The **motels** close to the town on US-192 (see "Accommodation," p.329) make Kissimmee a cheap place to stay, and even without a car getting to the theme parks and elsewhere in the region is relatively simple: **trains** stop at 111 E Dakin St, Greyhound **buses** at 103 E Dakin St (Ⓣ407/847-3911), and there are frequent **shuttle bus** links to the major Orlando area attractions (see "Getting around," p.325). For visitor information, drop by the **Kissimmee–St Cloud Convention & Visitors Bureau**, 1925 E US-192 (Mon–Fri 8am–5pm; Ⓣ407/847-5000 or 1-800/333-KISS, Ⓦwww.floridakiss.com).

In shabby downtown Kissimmee, take a walk around the fifty-foot obelisk called **Kissimmee Monument of States**, on Monument Avenue. Comprising garishly painted concrete blocks adorned with pieces of stone and fossil representing all of the American states and twenty foreign countries, this funky monument was erected in 1943 to honor the former president of the local All-States Tourist Club.

A peaceful, rural back street is the setting for **Green Meadows Petting Farm**, 1368 S Poinciana Blvd (daily 9.30am–4pm; $17; Ⓣ407/846-0770, Ⓦwww.greenmeadowsfarm.com), a refreshing change of pace from the major parks. Take a leisurely (sometimes painfully slow) two-hour tour of this old-fashioned petting zoo, where kids can milk a cow and ride a pony.

Finding anything decent to **eat** in the town center can be a bit of a challenge at dinnertime, but for good home cooking at breakfast, lunch, or (early) dinner, there's *Mrs. Mack's Restaurant*, 215 Broadway (Ⓣ407/847-5771; closed Sat lunch and all day Sun).

Celebration

If you just can't get enough of the squeaky-clean Disney concept, you might consider buying a home in **CELEBRATION** (Ⓦwww.celebrationfl.com), a 4900-acre town nestled between Kissimmee and Disney's theme parks (off US-192) that was created by Disney and officially opened in 1996. The Disney people did massive sociological research before settling on the design they believed would capture the American ideal of community: old-fashioned exteriors, homes close to the road so neighbors are more likely to interact, and a congenial old-fashioned downtown area. World-famous architects were brought in to design major buildings: Phillip Johnson, Ritchie & Fiore designed the Town Hall; Michael Graves the post office; Cesar Pelli the movie house; and Robert A.M. Stern the health center. The first 350 home sites sold out before a single model was even complete. Enthusiasts applaud Celebration's friendly small-town feeling, where new neighbors are greeted with home-baked brownies, each home is fully hooked up to all the others by an elaborate intercom system, town events are well attended, and children can walk carefree to school, all without being a gated community, as spokespersons are quick to point out. Detractors use words such as "contrived" and "sterile," and point to stringent rules, such as the insistence that all window treatments facing the outside must be white. The town, though, is growing rapidly and is worth a short visit – and not only for the architecture and some of the best restaurants in the region. Stop by to determine for yourself whether this homogeneous blandness is an evolutionary stage of the American Dream, a touch of elitist Big Brother, or some sort of smug cult.

Practicalities

The luxurious, neo-old-fashioned *Celebration Hotel*, 700 Bloom St (Ⓣ407/566-6000 or 1-888/499-3800, Ⓦwww.celebrationhotel.com; ❻), makes a pleasant base for exploring the area, and each of Celebration's restaurants, facing the town's small lake, can be recommended for its own reasons. The *Market Street Café*, 701 Front St (Ⓣ407/566-1144), is a classic inexpensive diner, featuring home-made potato chips and fried-chicken salad; *Café d'Antonio*, 691 Front St (Ⓣ407/566-2233), offers fine, fairly pricey Italian wood-fired specialties made with chicken, steak, salmon, and, for vegetarians, eggplant; and the *Columbia Restaurant*, 649 Front St (Ⓣ407/566-1505), looks like an Iberian villa and serves superb, moderately priced Spanish cuisine, featuring red snapper Alicante and paella Valenciana.

North of Orlando

Back-to-back residential areas dissolve into fields of fruit and vegetables **north of Orlando**'s city limits. Around here, in slow-motion towns harking back to Florida's frontier days, farming still has the upper hand over tourism. Although it's easy to skim through on I-4, the older local roads connecting the major settlements have far more atmosphere.

Sanford and around

Its position on the south shore of Lake Monroe, fifteen miles north of Maitland on US-92 (also known as US-17 along this section), allows **SANFORD** to take advantage of riverboat cruises for a fair share of its tourist dollars. Three-hour lunch cruises (Ⓣ1-800/423-7401; from $35) embark from the marina on North Palmetto Avenue. For insight into the modestly sized town – and Shelton Sanford, the turn-of-the-nineteenth-century lawyer and diplomat who created it – pop into the **Sanford Museum**, 520 E First St (Tues–Fri 11am–4pm, Sat 1–4pm; free; Ⓣ407/302-1000). Once called "Celery City" on account of its major agricultural crop, Sanford hasn't had a lot going for it since the boom years of the early twentieth century, a period fondly chronicled in the museum. For more relics of the halcyon days, collect a self-guided tour map from the **Chamber of Commerce**, 400 E First St (Mon–Fri 9am–noon & 1–5pm; Ⓣ407/322-2212), and venture around 22 buildings of divergent classical architecture in the adjacent old downtown district, most of which are now doing business as drugstores and insurance offices.

On the way back to US-92 at Sanford's southwest corner, the **Seminole County Historical Museum**, 300 Bush Blvd (Tues–Fri 9am–noon & 1–4pm, Sat 1–4pm; free; Ⓣ407/321-2489), carries a multitude of objects from all over the county, including an intriguing selection of medicine bottles. You can also rummage around **Flea World** (Fri, Sat, & Sun 8am–5pm; free), near the Historical Museum on US-17/92 – a large-scale attempt to sell items that nobody in their right mind would ever buy.

If Sanford's historic buildings, antique shops, and quiet charm appeal, consider **staying overnight** at *The Higgins House*, a Queen Anne Victorian B&B just a few blocks from downtown, at 420 S Oak Ave (Ⓣ407/324-9238 or 1-800/584-0014, Ⓦwww.higginshouse.com; ❺); it has three rooms and huge, healthy breakfasts. If this is full, a good, lakeside alternative is the *Best Western Marina Hotel*, next to the marina at 530 N Palmetto Ave (Ⓣ407/323-1910; ❸). A special place to **eat** lunch or dinner is *Morgan's Gourmet Café*, 112 E First St (Ⓣ407/688-4745), for its fine mid-priced (entrees $12–16) international menu. Closed Sunday.

Mount Dora

To see an authentic Victorian-era Florida village on a pristine lake, take Route 46 west of Sanford for 21 miles and feast your eyes on the picket fences, wrought-iron balconies, and fancy wood-trimmed buildings that make up **MOUNT DORA**. The **Chamber of Commerce**, 341 Alexander St (Mon–Fri 9am–5pm, Sat 10am–4pm; Ⓣ352/383-2165, Ⓦwww.mountdora.com), has a free guide to the old houses and the excellent antique shops that now occupy many of them. Of the stores that dot the hilly streets, visit Double Creek Pottery, 430 N Donnelly St (Ⓣ352/735-5579), for fine handmade creations. To get the most out of Lake Dora, you can rent a boat from Fun Boats at the dock in front of the *Lakeside Inn* (from $10/hr; bikes $8/hr; Ⓣ352/735-2669). One of the area's original railways is still operating here, too; take the 1920s-era *Dora Doodlebug* on a one-hour scenic spin along the lake (Mon–Fri; $12, children $8) or the *Mount Dora Cannonball*, dating from 1913, which does the 74-mile round-trip between Orlando and Mount Dora (daily: departs Orlando 9am, departs Mount Dora 2pm; $40, children 3–9 $32). The Mount Dora Trolley also offers narrated historic and scenic tours of the town's parks, monuments and significant buildings, lasting about an hour and leaving from next to the *Lakeside Inn* (daily, times vary; $8, children $5.50; Ⓣ352/357-9123).

A **stay** at Mount Dora's genteel *Lakeside Inn*, 100 N Alexander St (Ⓣ352/383-4101 or 1-800/556-5016, Ⓦwww.lakeside-inn.com; ❺), might just transport you back to Old Florida; the long front porch is excellent for sunset-watching, too. Bed-and-breakfasts fit in perfectly with Mount Dora's quaintness, and they are not in short supply. A good, central option is *Simpson's Bed & Breakfast*, 441 N Donnelly St (Ⓣ352/383-2087, Ⓦwww.simpsonsbnb.com; ❹), which has six suites of either two or three rooms.

One of the most popular places to **eat** is *The Goblin Market*, hidden down a quiet side street at 330 Dora Drawdy Lane (Ⓣ352/735-0059), with its intimate dining room, outside patio, and gourmet meals such as stuffed pork loin and mushroom chicken ragout (reservations recommended). Another safe bet, this time easier to find opposite the park, is *The Park Bench Restaurant*, 116 E Fifth Ave (Ⓣ352/383-7004), where Alaskan halibut and chicken Chardonnay meals are served in a bright, airy dining room. It would be sacrilegious to come to Mount Dora and not take tea and scones at one of the many English-inspired teahouses dotted around town, a good example of which is *The Windsor Rose Tea Room*, 144 Fourth Ave (Ⓣ352/735-2551), where tea and scones will cost $20, and other hearty English delicacies such as Cornish pasties and Scotch eggs are also available. *La Cremerie*, 424 N Donnelly St (Ⓣ352/735-4663), has good ice creams and cheap coffee.

Cassadaga

A village in the deep forest populated by spiritualists may conjure up images of beaded curtains and thumping tabletops in forbidding houses, but the few hundred residents of **CASSADAGA**, just east of I-4, fifteen miles north of Sanford, are disarmingly conventional citizens in normal homes, offering to reach out and touch the spirit world for a very down-to-earth fee ($50 for a thirty-minute session). A group of northern spirit mediums bought this 35-acre site in 1875 and quickly caught the imagination of Florida's early settlers – for whom contacting the Other Side was a lot easier than communicating with the rest of the US.

Throughout the year, seminars and lectures cover topics ranging from UFO cover-ups to out-of-body traveling. For more details, visit the official **Cassadaga Camp Bookstore** in the Andrew Jackson Davis Building, on the corner of Route 4139 (Cassadaga Road) and Stevens Street (Mon–Sat 10am–5.30pm, Sun noon–5.30pm; ⓣ386/228-2880, ⓦwww.cassadaga.org), which doubles as an **information center** and psychic bookshop. Rival enclaves include The Universal Centre of Cassadaga, across the street at 460 Cassadaga Rd ($35 for 15 min, $50 for 30 min; ⓣ386/228-3190, ⓦwww.universalcentre.net), which claims to be home to the finest psychics anywhere; and *The Cassadaga Hotel*, across the street at 355 Cassadaga Rd ($50 for 30 min, $100 for an hour; ⓣ386/228-2323, ⓦwww.cassadagahotel.com; ❸), which offers its own stable of seers – some with names like Philomena and Birdie. Yet another possibility is the Purple Rose, 1079 Stevens St ($30 for 15 min, $50 for 30 min; ⓣ386/228-3315, ⓦwww.cassadaga-purplerose.com).

Just outside Cassadaga, on the way to nearby Lake Helen, *Clauser's Bed and Breakfast*, 201 E Kicklighter Rd (ⓣ386/228-0310 or 1-800/220-0310, ⓦwww.clauserinn.com; ❺), makes a wonderful, woodsy getaway. The atmosphere is very friendly, and you'll find every comfort has been seen to in advance.

DeLand and around

Intended as the "Athens of Florida" when founded in 1876, **DELAND**, four miles north of Cassadaga, west off I-4, is really just an old-fashioned central Florida town featuring a domed courthouse, an old theater, and a welcoming atmosphere. It boasts the state's oldest private educational center, **Stetson University**, on Woodland Boulevard (ⓣ386/822-8920, ⓦwww.stetson.edu), whose red-brick facades have stood since the 1880s. The school is named for hat manufacturer John B. Stetson, a generous donor to the university and one of its founding trustees. Pick up a free tour map from the easily found DeLand Hall for a walk around the vintage buildings. Also on the campus, on the corner of Michigan and Amelia avenues, the **Gillespie Museum of Minerals** (closed for renovation at the time of writing; ⓣ386/822-7330) displays Florida quartz, calcite, and limestone, plus gemstones gathered from all over the world.

Around the corner from the town's Chamber of Commerce (see below) is the **Henry A. DeLand House Museum**, 137 W Michigan Ave (Tues–Sat noon–4pm; free), built in 1886 and refurbished in period style. Of particular note are a wood carving of The Lord's Prayer, antique kitchen appliances, and an exhibit devoted to "Citrus Wizard" Lue Gim Gong, a Chinese botanist who lived in DeLand from 1888 until 1925.

Practicalities

For general information, visit DeLand's super-friendly **Chamber of Commerce**, 336 N Woodland Blvd (Mon–Fri 8.30am–5pm; ⓣ386/734-4331 or 1-800/749-4350, ⓦwww.delandchamber.org), which provides detailed pamphlets of walking and driving tours in the area. Anyone **spending the night** in DeLand should stay at the pleasant *DeLand Artisan Inn*, 215 S Woodland Blvd (Ⓣ386/736-3484, Ⓦwww.delandartisaninn.com; ❹), where each room has a different theme, such as Literary, Mediterranean, or Tropical; the hotel also has a lively restaurant. For dining in a lush garden setting, *Holiday House*, 704 N US-17/92, right across from Stetson University (Ⓣ386/734-6319), has great buffet **meals** with salads and a carvery.

DeLeon Springs, Lake Woodruff National Wildlife Refuge, and Barberville

DeLeon Springs State Recreation Area (daily 8am–sunset; cars $4, pedestrians and cyclists $1; Ⓣ386/985-4212), ten miles north of DeLand on US-17, is one of the better-known sites in the area where thousands of gallons of pure water bubble continuously up from artesian springs. Fascination with the labyrinths of underground water that permeate north central Florida is not limited only to tourists, however, for **DeLeon Springs** is a very popular place for locals, too. There's swimming, canoeing, and picnicking in and beside the spring, and you can even make your own pancakes in the *Old Spanish Sugar Mill & Griddle House* (Mon–Fri 9am–4pm, Sat & Sun 8am–4pm; Ⓣ386/985-5644), which is set in a historic sugar mill on the park grounds.

Following US-17 a few miles west to Grand Avenue, you will find the stunning **Lake Woodruff National Wildlife Refuge** (open sunrise to sunset; free), a 22,000-acre section of untouched wetlands that is home to over 200 species of birds, including the endangered Southern bald eagle, many types of fish, and other creatures. **Boat tours** of the refuge are run by Safari River Tours, 222 Lucerne Drive, DeBary (Ⓣ386/668-1002, Ⓦwww.safaririvertours.com; $16, children 6–10 $10), and leave from the sugar mill. A good bet for dinner in the town of DeLeon Springs is *Karling's Inn*, 4640 N US-17 (Tues–Sat 5–9pm; Ⓣ386/985-5535), a continental restaurant featuring such entrees as crisp-roasted duck Montmorency and rainbow trout in lemon sauce.

Seven miles further north on US-17, the tiny crossroads community of **Barberville** celebrates rural Florida with its **Pioneer Settlement for the Creative Arts** (Mon–Fri 9am–4pm, Sat 9am–2pm; $3; Ⓣ386/749-2959), a small collection of turn-of-the-nineteenth-century buildings, including a train station, a log cabin, a turpentine still, a bridgehouse, and a general store. Here, an assembly of pottery wheels, looms, and other tools are put to use during the informative guided tour, which should take between one-and-a-half and two hours.

Blue Spring and Hontoon Island

The year-round 72°F (22°C) waters at **Blue Spring State Park** (daily 8am–sunset; cars $4, pedestrians and cyclists $1), seven miles south of DeLand (off US-17/92, on West French Ave) in Orange City, attract **manatees** between mid-November and mid-March. Affectionately known as "sea cows," these best-loved of Florida's endangered animals swim here from the cooler waters of the St Johns River, and the colder it is there the more manatees you'll see here. Aside from staking out the manatees from several observation platforms (and watching a twenty-minute slide show describing their habits), there's also the chance to see **Thursby House**, a large frame dwelling built by pioneer settlers in 1872. **Accommodation** in the park includes an $18.86-a-night campground and cabins for $111.52 for two nights (minimum) that sleep up to four people (Ⓣ386/775-3663).

Not far from Blue Spring is **Hontoon Island State Park**, a striking dollop of wooded land set within very flat and swampy terrain. Without a private boat,

Hontoon Island is reachable only by the free **ferry** that runs daily from 8am to about one hour before sunset from a landing stage off Route 44 (the continuation of DeLand's New York Avenue). Unbelievably, the island once held a boatyard and cattle ranch, but today it's inhabited only by the hardy souls who decide to stay over in one of its six rustic **cabins** (⊕386/736-5309, or for reservations ⊕1-800/326-3521; $20 for four people, $25 for six people), or at one of its very basic **campgrounds**.

Travel details

Trains (Amtrak)

Orlando to: DeLand (2–3 daily; 1hr); Jacksonville (2–3 daily; 3hr 15min); Kissimmee (2 daily; 20min); Miami (2 daily; 5hr 35min); Sanford (2–3 daily; 45min); Tallahassee (1 daily; 7hr 15min); Tampa (2–3 daily; 2hr); Winter Park (2–3 daily; 18min).

Buses

Orlando to: Daytona Beach (6 daily; 1hr 5min); DeLand (4 daily; 50min); Fort Lauderdale (12 daily; 4hr 15min); Fort Pierce (5 daily; 2hr 20min); Gainesville (5 daily; 2hr 10min); Jacksonville (7 daily; 2hr 30min); Lakeland (6 daily; 1hr); Kissimmee (8 daily; 40min); Miami (10 daily; 5hr 30min); Ocala (6 daily; 1hr 20min); Sanford (3 daily; 30min); Tallahassee (4 daily; 5hr 10min); Tampa (6 daily; 2hr); West Palm Beach (8 daily; 3hr 10min); Winter Haven (6 daily; 55min).

8

The Northeast

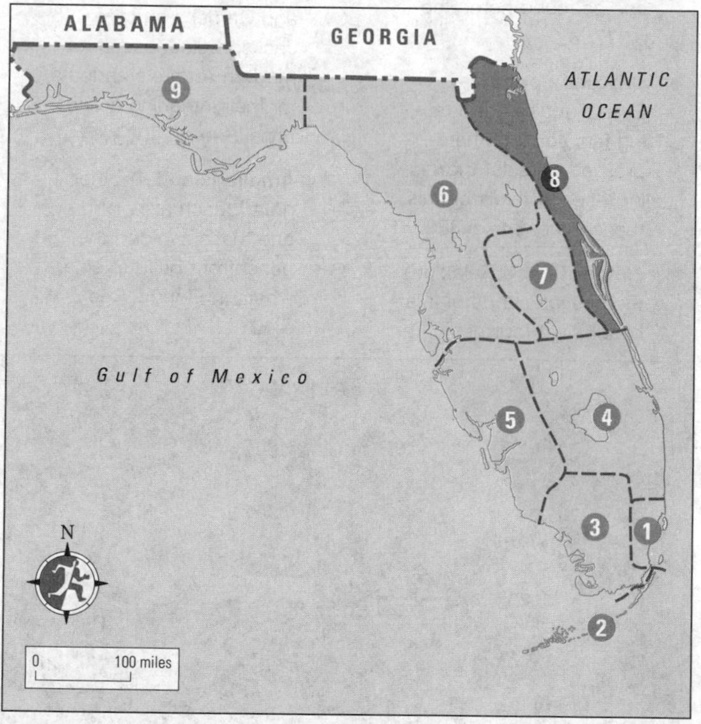

CHAPTER 8

Highlights

✱ **Kennedy Space Center** Watch awe-inspiring nighttime launches against the clear sky. See p.373

✱ **Merritt Island National Wildlife Refuge** An incredible array of wildlife, birds especially, can be found here. See p.377

✱ **Daytona Speedway** Even if you're not a racing fan, you'll be hard-pressed to resist the high-speed thrills on this racecourse. See p.388

✱ **Flagler Beach** Relax on the pristine sands of this beach, just fourteen miles from more crowded Daytona. See p.390

✱ **St Augustine** America's oldest city, with European charm, narrow streets, and an eventful history. See p.391

✱ **Jacksonville museums** The Cummer Museum and Gardens and the Jacksonville Museum of Modern Art are standouts for their intriguing collections. See pp.403–404

✱ **Amelia Island** Another great beach area, and one that's avoided the beachfront buildup elsewhere in Florida. See p.407

△ Jacksonville Landing

8

The Northeast

Substantially free of commercial exploitation, with washed-up sharks' teeth sometimes more evident on its beaches than people, the 190 miles of coastline dominating Florida's **NORTHEAST** are tailor-made for leisurely exploration. You'll often feel like doing nothing more strenuous than settling down beside the ocean, but throughout the region signs of the forces that have shaped Florida – from ancient Native American settlements to the launch site of the space shuttle – are easy to find and worth exploring. When planning your trip, remember that, owing to the less tropical climate, the northeast coast's tourist **seasons** are the reverse of those of the southeast coast: the crowded time here is the summer, when accommodation is more expensive and harder to come by than during the winter months.

Besides sharing a shoreline, the towns of the northeast coast have surprisingly little in common. Those making up the **Space Coast**, the southernmost area, primarily serve the hordes passing through to visit the impressively efficient **Kennedy Space Center**, birthplace and still the launching pad of the nation's space exploits. Its public image is unrelentingly positive, but the Space Center is definitely worth a visit, as is the wildlife refuge that surrounds it. Seventy miles north of the Space Coast lies **Daytona Beach**, a small town with a big strand, where the legendary excesses of Spring Break gained international notoriety in the Eighties until local authorities began to discourage all sorts of teenage carousing. The result is that things are downbeat, and a bit squalid, in Daytona now.

Along the northerly section of the coast, the plentiful evidence of Florida's early European landings is best displayed in the comprehensively restored town of **St Augustine**, where sixteenth-century Spaniards established North America's earliest foreign settlement. In addition to the attractions of the town itself, there's the surrounding coast, part of a divine strand extending to the **Jacksonville Beaches**, twenty miles north, where lying in the sun and tuning into the sprightly local nightlife will fill a few decadent days. Just inland, the city of **Jacksonville**, struggling to shrug off its gray industrial image, merits more than a cursory glance, as you strike out toward the state's northeastern extremity. Here, overlooking the coast of Georgia, slender **Amelia Island** is fringed by gorgeous silver sands and features a quirky, posh Victorian-era main town.

The **road network** is very much a continuation of the southeast coast's system: **Hwy-A1A** hugs the coastline, with occasional breaks, while **US-1** charts a less appealing course on the mainland and is a lot slower than **I-95**, which divides the coastal area from the eastern edge of central Florida. Greyhound **buses** are frequent along US-1 between the main towns, but, as with the rest of Florida, the best way to get around is by car. Forget the **train** – only Jacksonville has a station.

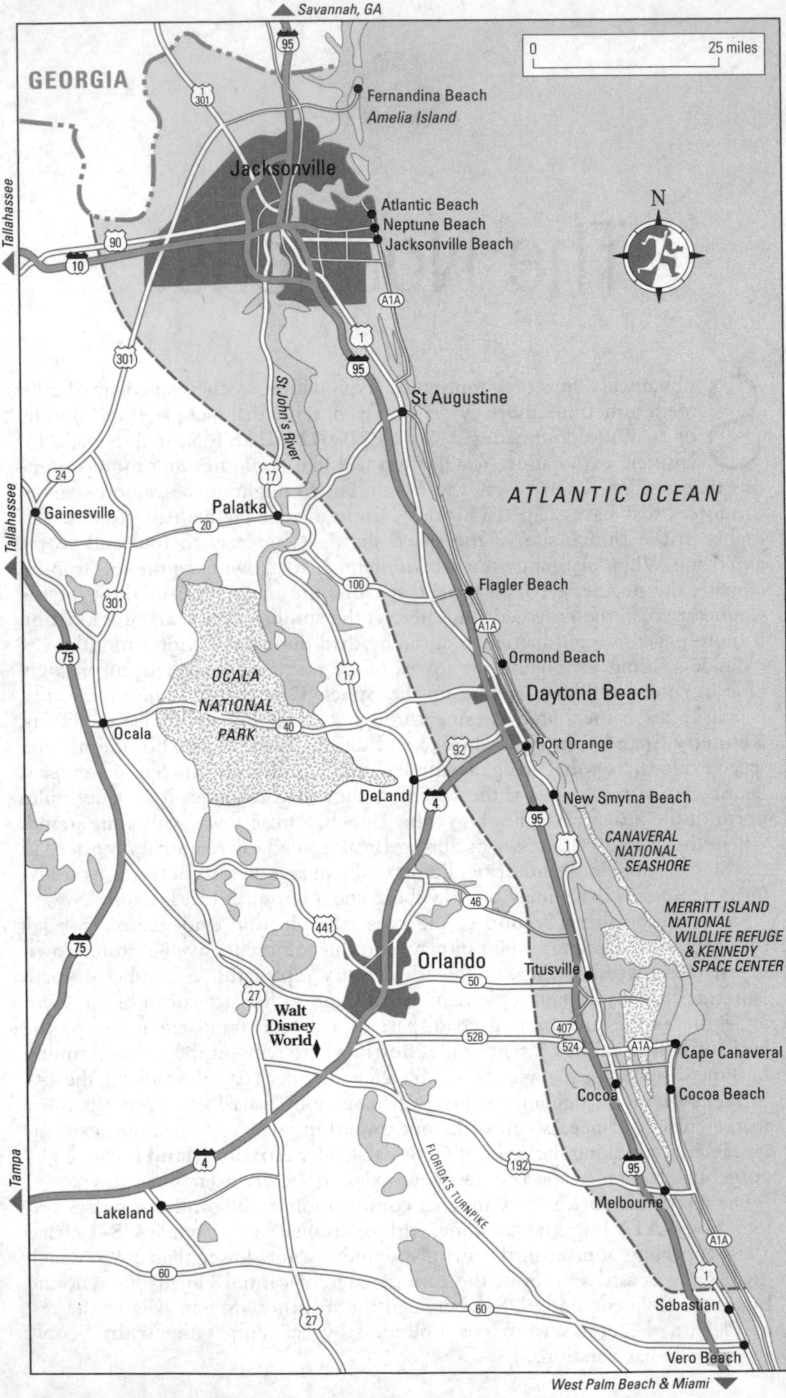
Savannah, GA
GEORGIA
0
25 miles
N
Fernandina Beach
Amelia Island
Jacksonville
Atlantic Beach
Neptune Beach
Jacksonville Beach
Tallahassee
St Augustine
St John's River
ATLANTIC OCEAN
Gainesville
Palatka
Tallahassee
Flagler Beach
Ormond Beach
Daytona Beach
OCALA
NATIONAL
PARK
Ocala
Port Orange
DeLand
New Smyrna Beach
CANAVERAL
NATIONAL
SEASHORE
MERRITT ISLAND
NATIONAL
WILDLIFE REFUGE
& KENNEDY
SPACE CENTER
Orlando
Titusville
Walt
Disney
World
Cape Canaveral
Cocoa
Cocoa Beach
FLORIDA'S TURNPIKE
Tampa
Melbourne
Lakeland
Sebastian
Vero Beach
West Palm Beach & Miami
95
301
90
10
A1A
1
301
17
24
20
100
301
75
17
40
92
4
95
1
46
441
75
50
27
407
528
524
A1A
192
95
4
A1A
1
60
60
27

The Space Coast

The barrier islands that occupy much of the Treasure Coast (see "The Southeast," p.183) continue north into what's known as the **SPACE COAST**, the base of the country's space industry and site of the Kennedy Space Center, which occupies a flat, marshy island bulging into the Atlantic just fifty miles east of Orlando. Many of the visitors who flock here are surprised to find that the land from which the space shuttle leaves earth is also a sizeable wildlife refuge framed by several miles of rough coastline. Except for the beach-oriented communities on the ocean, the towns of the Space Coast are of little interest other than for low-cost overnight stops on the way to St Augustine or points north, or for meal breaks. General information about the area is available on the 24-hour Space Coast hotline (Ⓣ1-800/93-OCEAN).

The Kennedy Space Center

Justifiably the biggest attraction in the area, the **Kennedy Space Center** (KSC) is the nucleus of the US space program: it's here that space vehicles are developed, tested, and blasted into orbit. The first launches actually took place across the water at the US Air Force base on Cape Canaveral (renamed Cape Kennedy in 1963 and changed back to the original in 1973), from which rockets still lift off. After the space program was expanded in 1964 and the Saturn V rockets proved too large to launch from there, the focus of activity was moved to Merritt Island, positioned between Cape Canaveral and the mainland, and directly north of Cocoa Beach.

The Space Center is well worth a visit for its solid documentation of US achievements, revealing how closely success in space is tied to the nation's sense of well-being.

The Kennedy Space Center: practical info and tips

The only **public entry roads** to the Kennedy Space Center are Hwy-405 from Titusville and Route 3 off Hwy-A1A between Cocoa Beach and Cocoa: on either approach, follow signs for the Kennedy Space Center **Visitor Complex** (daily 9am–6pm), which underwent a massive revamping in late 2000 and contains a museum, a life-size Space Shuttle Explorer replica, the Universe Theater, exhibit halls, the Astronaut Memorial, the Rocket Garden, and an IMAX film theater.

It makes sense to **arrive early** to be able to devote the better part of a day here; unfortunately, **crowds** of patrons do the same, so plan accordingly. The complex is most full during the summer and during school vacations. To take the bus tour or to see one of the two IMAX films, you should **buy tickets** from the ticket pavilion as soon as you arrive. The **Maximum Access Badge** ($34, children $24; after the last bus tour has left, the sales plaza offers a reduced-price ticket) covers the entire Visitor Complex and includes a bus tour and an IMAX show. **Add-on** tours like "Cape Canaveral: Then and Now" and "UpClose" take in other attractions. You can also buy virtually all tickets online at Ⓦwww.KennedySpaceCenter.com.

To **see a launch** from the Space Center, phone Ⓣ321/449-4444 or 1-800/KSC-INFO for recorded schedule information, **launch dates**, and times; you can purchase a pass for access to a special restricted viewing area six miles away. Note, however, that the sheer magnitude of the blast delivers an extraordinary, unforgettable experience from anywhere within a forty-mile radius of the launch pad, especially at night when launches are the most spectacular.

The Kennedy Space Center Visitor Complex

Everything at the **KSC Visitor Complex** is within easy walking distance of the parking lot, as is the departure point for the bus tour (see below). The complex will keep anyone with the faintest interest in space exploration entertained for at least an hour or two. Everything you might expect to see is here: actual mission capsules, space suits, lunar modules, a granite memorial to those who gave their lives in the quest to explore space, a full-sized, walk-through mock-up of the space shuttle, and an interactive exhibit on the 1997 Pathfinder mission to Mars, where scientists may have discovered signs of possible extraterrestrial bacterial life embedded in rocks. The rockets standing outside the museum in the **Rocket Garden** are deceptively simple in appearance and far daintier than the gigantic Saturn V (only seen on the bus tour) that launched the Apollo missions.

In the center of the complex, the IMAX **theater** shows two films, using 70mm film projected onto a five-story screen. The better of the two, *The Dream Is Alive* (40min), is very rah-rah but effective, and features dramatic shots from an orbiting Space Shuttle. It captures the sensations of space flight as well as the daily business of living in space. Elsewhere, the **Robot Scouts** exhibit is also very entertaining, as computer-generated versions of unmanned probes – Viking (Mars exploration), Voyager (Jupiter and beyond), and Cassini (the Saturn system) – explain how new technology aids in the collection of mission data. Other offerings include the **Astronaut Encounter**, a daily chance to meet a real live astronaut, and **Exploration in the New Millennium**, a futuristic exhibit tracing the history of human civilisation's urge to go where no one has gone before, an educational journey that includes the chance to touch an actual piece of the planet Mars.

As far as **eating** goes, there are four canteens and various snack bars scattered around the Visitor Complex that provide standard pizza-and-hot dog fare at just short of stratospheric prices. Though convenient for snacks and drinks (you can eat futuristic ice cream in solid-pellet form called "space dots"), you might be better off packing your meal (no coolers allowed, though) and eating in the aptly named "Lunch Pad."

The Kennedy Space Center Tour

The **bus tour** (daily; tours leave from 10am to 2.15pm; included with Maximum Access Badge – see box on p.373) around the rest of the Merritt Island complex provides a dramatic insight into the colossal grandeur of the space program. After zooming through the main gate and passing countless alligators on the side of the road, you'll see the **Vehicle Assembly Building** (where space shuttles, like Apollo and Skylab before them, are put together and fitted with payloads) looming ahead. At 52 stories, it's the largest scientific building in the world. Unfortunately, access is prohibited, but if a door is open you'll catch a glimpse inside one of the world's largest structures. Equivalent in volume to three and a half Empire State Buildings, the VAB is the second largest in the world and the first stop for the "crawlerway" – the huge tracks along which Space Shuttles are wheeled to the launch pad.

With luck, a Space Shuttle will be in place for take-off when the bus takes a loop around the **launch pad** – no different in reality from what you've seen on TV, and no more interesting than any other large pile of scaffolding if a Shuttle isn't present (obviously, when a countdown is under way there are no bus tours; see the box on p.373 for launch-watching tips).

Besides a nose-to-nozzle inspection of a Saturn V rocket, which took the first Apollo mission into space and produced enough power upon blastoff to light

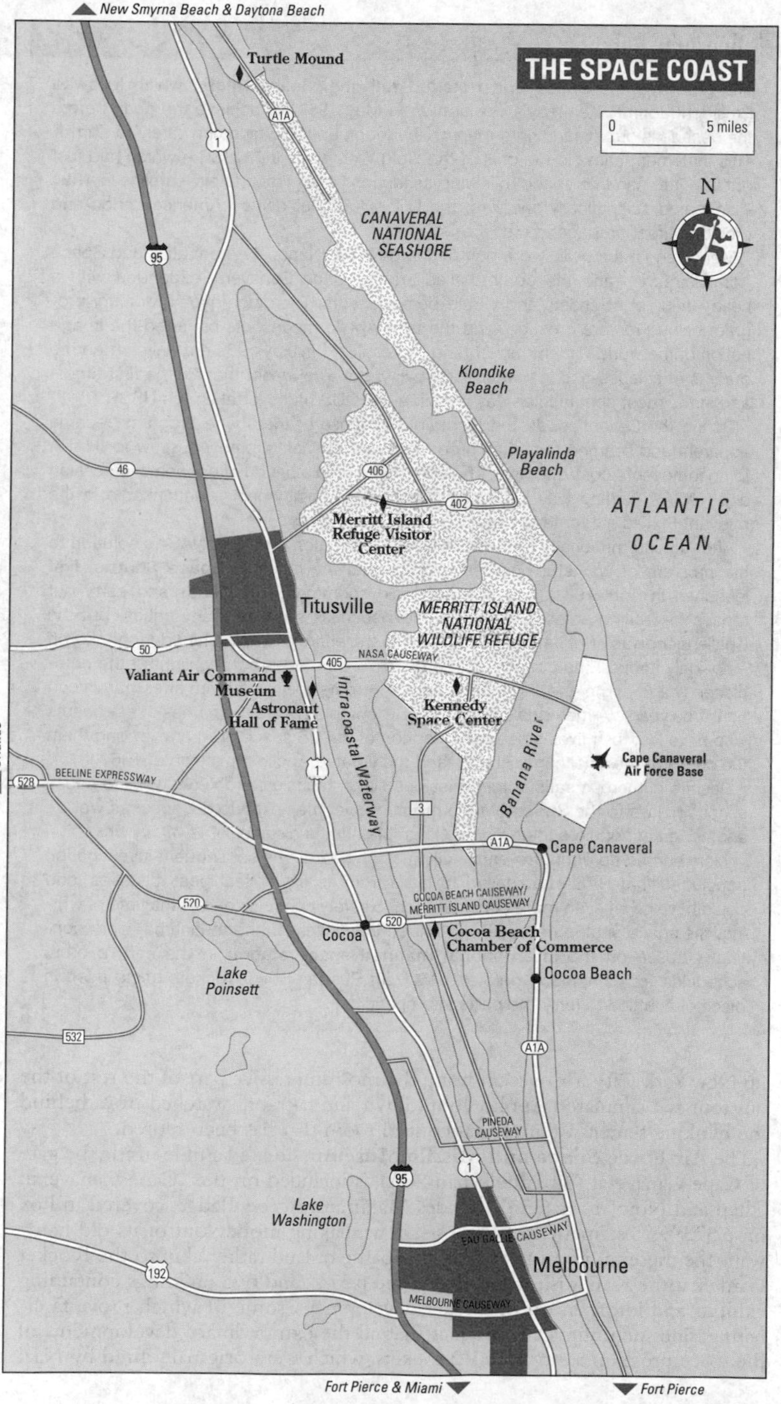
THE SPACE COAST
0 5 miles
N
New Smyrna Beach & Daytona Beach
Turtle Mound
A1A
1
95
CANAVERAL NATIONAL SEASHORE
Klondike Beach
Playalinda Beach
46
406
402
Merritt Island Refuge Visitor Center
ATLANTIC OCEAN
Titusville
MERRITT ISLAND NATIONAL WILDLIFE REFUGE
50
405
NASA CAUSEWAY
Valiant Air Command Museum
Astronaut Hall of Fame
Intracoastal Waterway
Kennedy Space Center
Banana River
Cape Canaveral Air Force Base
Orlando
528
BEELINE EXPRESSWAY
3
A1A
Cape Canaveral
COCOA BEACH CAUSEWAY/ MERRITT ISLAND CAUSEWAY
520
520
Cocoa
Cocoa Beach Chamber of Commerce
Cocoa Beach
Lake Poinsett
St. Cloud
532
A1A
PINEDA CAUSEWAY
1
95
Lake Washington
EAU GALLIE CAUSEWAY
192
Melbourne
MELBOURNE CAUSEWAY
Fort Pierce & Miami
Fort Pierce

Americans in space

The growth of the Space Coast started with the "**Space Race**," which followed President John F. Kennedy's declaration in May 1961 to "achieve the goal, before the decade is out, of landing a man on the moon and returning him safely to Earth." This statement came in the chill of the Cold War, when the USSR – which had just put the first man into space following its launch of the first artificial satellite in 1957 – appeared scientifically ahead of the US, a fact that dented American pride and provided great propaganda for the Soviets.

Money and manpower were pumped into **NASA** (National Aeronautics and Space Administration), and the communities around Cape Canaveral expanded with a heady influx of scientists and would-be astronauts. The much-hyped Mercury program helped restore prestige, and the later Apollo moonshots captured the imagination of the world. The moon landing by Apollo 11 in July 1969 not only turned the dreams of science-fiction writers into reality, but also meant that for the first time – and in the most spectacular way possible – the US had overtaken the USSR.

During the Seventies, as the incredible expense of the space program became apparent and seemed out of all proportion to its benefits, pressure grew for NASA to become more cost-effective. The country entered a period of economic recession and NASA's funding was drastically slashed; unemployment – unthinkable in the buoyant Sixties – threatened many on the Space Coast.

After the internationally funded Skylab space station program, NASA's solution to the problem of wasteful one-use rockets was the reusable **Space Shuttle**, first launched in April 1981, and able to deploy commercial payloads and carry out repairs to orbiting satellites. The Shuttle's success silenced many critics, but the Challenger disaster of January 1986 – when the entire crew perished during take-off – not only imbued the country with a deep sense of loss but highlighted the complacency and corner-cutting that had crept into the space program after many accident-free years. (A memorial inside the KSC complex bears the names of astronauts who have lost their lives since the inception of the US space program, among them the crews of the Challenger shuttle and the ill-fated Apollo 1 mission of 1967.)

Despite numerous satisfactory missions since, technical problems were to cause serious delays to the Space Shuttle program over the next two decades, as well as another catastrophic accident: the Columbia shuttle disaster of 2003, in which the vehicle burned up during re-entry, killing all on board. The subsequent investigation concluded that NASA had failed to learn from its earlier technical mistakes (and could have given even more consideration to safety controls), and at the time of writing, the space shuttle had been grounded indefinitely. In the meantime, work continues apace on the **international manned space station** in the earth's orbit, scheduled for completion before 2010, with Russian Soyuz rockets being used in place of shuttles to ferry the parts into space.

up New York City for over an hour, the most impressive part of the rest of the bus tour is a simulated Apollo countdown and take-off, watched from behind the blinking screens of an actual control room that has been retired.

The **Air Force Space and Missile Museum**, situated a mile inside the gate of Cape Canaveral (on launch pad 26A), is included on the "Cape Canaveral: Then and Now" tour ($53, includes Maximum Access Badge, covered in box on p.373). A testament to NASA's skill at making money out of its old hardware, the museum consists of a large expanse of land rather akin to the Rocket Garden at the KSC Visitor Complex (see p.374), and two buildings containing exhibits and information on rocket development, some of which prove fascinating: one such nugget is the fact that all the extraordinary developments of the space program stem from V2 rockets, which were originally fired by Nazi

Germany against Britain in the closing years of World War II – and were subsequently launched into orbit by America in 1950. A tour of the Mercury, Gemini, and Apollo launch pads are also included, as well as a visit to the dramatic black-and-white striped Cape Canaveral lighthouse.

For yet another angle on space travel, visit the **Astronaut Hall of Fame** (see Titusville, p.381; admission is included with Maximum Access Badge), just down the road from the Kennedy Space Center.

Merritt Island National Wildlife Refuge

NASA shares its land with the **Merritt Island National Wildlife Refuge** (daily sunrise–sunset; free), entered via Route 402 from Titusville. Here you'll find alligators, armadillos, raccoons, bobcats, and one of Florida's greatest concentrations of birdlife living alongside some of the world's most advanced technology.

Even if you're only coming for a day at the Space Center, it would be a shame to pass up such a spectacular place – though it has to be said that Merritt Island, on first glance, looks anything but spectacular, comprising acres of estuaries and brackish marshes interspersed with occasional hammocks of oak and palm, and pine flatwoods where a few bald eagles construct nests ten feet in circumference. Winter is the **best time to visit**, when the island's skies are alive with thousands of migratory birds from the frozen north, and when mosquitoes are absent. At any other period, and especially in summer, the island's Mosquito Lagoon is worthy of its name; bring ample insect repellent.

Seeing the refuge

Seven miles east of Titusville on Route 406, the seven-mile **Black Point Wildlife Drive** gives a solid introduction to the basics of the island's ecosystem. At the entrance you can pick up a highly informative free leaflet that describes specific stops along the route. From one you'll spot a couple of bald eagle nests, while another by the mudflats affords a good vantage point for watching a wide variety of wading and shore birds angling for their dinner.

Be sure to do some walking within the refuge, too. Off the wildlife drive, the five-mile **Cruickshank Trail** weaves around the edge of the Indian River. If the whole length is too strenuous for you, there's an observation tower just a few minutes' walk from the parking lot. For a more varied landscape, drive a few miles further east along Route 402 – branching from Route 406 just south of the wildlife drive – passing the **visitor center** (Mon–Fri 8am–4.30pm, Sat & Sun 9am–5pm; closed Sun April–Sept; ⓣ321/861-0667), and tackle the half-mile **Oak Hammock Trail** or the two-mile **Palm Hammock Trail**, both accessible from the parking lot.

The Canaveral National Seashore

A slender, 25-mile-long beach dividing Merritt Island's Mosquito Lagoon from the Atlantic Ocean, the **Canaveral National Seashore** (winter 6am–6pm, summer 6am–8pm; $5; ⓣ321/267-1110) begins at **Playalinda Beach** on Route 402, seven miles east of the refuge's visitor center. The National Seashore's entire length is top-notch beachcombing and surfing territory and also suitable for swimming. Except when rough seas and high tides submerge it completely, you should take a wind-bitten ramble along the palmetto-lined path to wild **Klondike Beach**, north of Playalinda Beach, its sands often coated with intriguing shells and marked from May through September by the tracks left by sea turtles crawling ashore at night to lay eggs. The Space Coast is the second largest **turtle nesting** area in the world and, not surprisingly, turtle-watching is a popular local pastime. For more information, call ⓣ1-800/93-OCEAN.

At the northern tip of the National Seashore, on **Apollo Beach** (accessible only by road from New Smyrna Beach, eight miles north of Apollo; see "Heading north: New Smyrna Beach," p.381), is **Turtle Mound**. Known as a "midden," the mound is a 35-foot heap of oyster shells and other refuse left by the Timucua Indians over several generations of living here. The site became prominent enough over time to be marked on maps by Florida's first Spanish explorers, being visible several miles out to sea. Take a few minutes to walk along the boardwalks, through the dense, fragrant vegetation to the top of the mound – aside from its historical significance, the greenery provides some welcome shade in an otherwise desert-like environment.

Cocoa Beach

A few miles south of the Kennedy Space Center, **Cocoa Beach** comprises just a ten-mile strip of shore and a few residential streets off Atlantic Avenue (Hwy-A1A). As well as being unquestionably the best base from which to see the Space Coast, it's also a favored haunt of surfers, who are attracted here by some of the most "radical" waves in Florida. Major (and minor) surfing contests are held here during spring and summer, and throughout the year the place has a perky, youthful feel. There's also a big beach volleyball contingent here, setting and spiking on four permanent courts, as well as free music around the pier and beachside parks often on weekends. To get an idea of the community's prime concerns you need only take a walk around the original **Ron Jon Surf Shop**, 4151 N Atlantic Ave (ⓣ321/799-8820 or 1-888/RJ-SURFS), a virtual surfing theme park with its colorful, high-energy vibes, and its WaterSports rental shop just a stone's throw away. Both are open 24 hours a day and packed with surfboards (rental per day is $30 for a fiberglass board), bicycles ($10 for two hours or $50 per week), and wetsuits (same prices as for bikes), kites, and extrovert beach attire. Enthusiasts will want to stop by the tiny **surf museum** inside the Natural Art Surf Shop, 2370 S Atlantic Ave (ⓣ321/783-0764), for its eclectic collection of old photos, magazines, memorabilia, and surfboards dating from the Sixties and Seventies. If you feel like taking the surfing vibes home with you, drop by **Beach Culture**, 158 N Atlantic Ave (ⓣ321/784-0720), which carries surf-inspired artwork.

Arrival, information, and getting around

The nearest Greyhound station is on the mainland in Cocoa at 302 Main St (ⓣ321/636-6531). The Cocoa Beach Shuttle (ⓣ321/784-3831) runs to and from Orlando International Airport for about $20 one way; call to be collected from any hotel on Hwy-A1A.

Tourist information is available seven days a week at 3670 N Atlantic Avenue (9am–6pm; ⓣ321/784-3223) or from the Cocoa Beach **Chamber of Commerce**, located on Merritt Island at 400 Fortenberry Rd (Mon–Fri 9am–5pm; ⓣ321/459-2200).

A local **bus** service (Space Coast Area Transit; ⓣ321/633-1878) runs daily (Mon–Sat 7am–9pm, Sun 8am–5pm) to and from Cape Canaveral through Cocoa Beach (#9: Beach Trolley), and #6 runs from downtown Cocoa to Cocoa Beach; a ride costs $1 each way. To get around the beach area, rent a **bike** from the Ron Jon Surf Shop (see above).

Accommodation

Accommodation bargains are rare in Cocoa Beach. You can expect prices to be highest during February, March, July, and August – and during space shuttle launches. The most tent-friendly **campground** is *Jetty Park*, 400 Jetty Drive (Ⓣ321/783-7111; $17), five miles north at Cape Canaveral.

Days Inn 5500 N Atlantic Ave Ⓣ321/784-2550 or 1-888/799-1631. Located next door to the Cocoa Beach pier, with balconies outside all rooms. Some rooms also come with a microwave or recliner. ❸

Fawlty Towers 100 E Cocoa Beach Causeway Ⓣ321/784-3870. Nothing like the television show, this friendly, roomy, pink-towered motel on the beachfront is centrally located, with a pool and cable TV. ❸

Luna Sea 3185 N Atlantic Ave Ⓣ321/783-0500 or 1-800/586-2732. This bed and breakfast/motel lays on a continental breakfast of muffins, bagels, and cheeses each morning. Rooms are clean and neat, and some include kitchens. ❸

Sea Esta Villas 686 S Atlantic Ave Ⓣ321/783-1739 or 1-800/872-9444. Apartments in this little oasis are cheaper if rented by the week. Choose from one- or two-bedroom units that come with full kitchen, spacious bath, and access to the pool and gardens. ❻

Surf Studio Beach Resort 1801 S Atlantic Ave Ⓣ321/783-7100. Clean, comfortable, and convenient to the island's more southerly beaches. ❹

Eating and nightlife

Many restaurants here strive to undercut each other, resulting in some good **eating** deals if you have your own transportation; see "Inland," below, for other suggestions, and scan free magazines (found in motels and at the Chamber of Commerce) such as *Restaurant Dining Out*, *The Dining Out Guide*, and *Space Coast* for money-saving coupons.

For great oysters and an excellent water view, head for *Sunset Café Riverfront*, 500 E Cocoa Beach Causeway (Ⓣ321/783-8485) – but go early as it's frequently mobbed. A great dinner option is *The Pier Restaurant*, on the pier (Ⓣ321/783-7549), which has a quality (and somewhat expensive) menu especially strong on seafood and features a Sunday champagne brunch. Or you can opt for the tasty Italian dinners at *Alma's*, 306 N Orlando Ave (Ⓣ321/783-1981). A lovely spot for coffee and pastries is the tiny *Il Sogno*, 24 N Orlando Ave (closed Mon; Ⓣ321/783-0219), where you can sit surrounded by local artwork under a ceiling painted sky blue.

Nightlife is most enjoyable if you start early at one of the beachside **happy hours**: try *Marlins' Good Time Grill*, also part of the pier complex (Ⓣ321/783-7549). As the evening draws on, the *Pig and Whistle*, 801 N Atlantic Ave (Ⓣ321/799-0724), offers TV soccer and English bitter, while the party-hearty *Coconuts*, 2 Minuteman Causeway (Ⓣ321/784-1422), has drinking and **live music** on the beach (with no cover).

Inland: Melbourne, Cocoa, and Titusville

The chief attractions of the Space Coast's sleepy **inland towns**, strung along US-1, are cheaper accommodation and food than at the beaches, plus areas of historical interest that provide a welcome change from the usual tourist drag.

Melbourne

Just twenty miles south of Cocoa Beach lies the pretty yet dull town of **Melbourne**. You can take in the **Brevard Zoo**, 8225 N Wickham Rd (daily 10am–5pm; $9, children $6; Ⓣ321/254-WILD), with its Latin American, Australian, and native Floridian fauna, or the collections at the **Brevard Museum of Art and Science**, 1463 Highland Ave (Tues–Sat 10am–5pm, Sun 1–5pm; $5; Ⓣ321/242-0737, Ⓦwww.artandscience.org). Melbourne's **restaurants** aren't bad: *Conchy Joe's*, 1477 Pineapple Ave (Ⓣ321/253-3131), has seafood, live reggae in the evenings, and great views of the Indian River, while the friendly, busy *New England Eatery*, 5670 Hwy-A1A (Ⓣ321/723-6080), offers fresh seafood at terrific prices.

After eating, stroll along **Crane Creek**, a stretch of water between the US-1 road bridge and the railway bridge, which is a **manatee-watching** area, though the viewing opportunities further north are better. A shoreline boardwalk, lined with oak trees and sabal palms, provides an attractive spot from which to glimpse these shy, endangered creatures. Each June and July, the Sea Turtle Preservation Society organizes popular nighttime **turtle walks** (reservations required, $7 donation; Ⓣ321/676-1701) on the beach. Following an informative talk and video, you can walk on the beach to witness the huge, reticent loggerhead turtles crawling onto the sands to lay their eggs – the only time in their lives they venture out of the water.

If you're **staying** overnight, try the comfortable *Ramada Inn*, 420 S Harbor City Blvd (Ⓣ321/723-5320; ❸), which has a pool and exercise room (a breakfast at nearby *Denny's* is included).

Cocoa

In **Cocoa**, thirty miles north of Melbourne and eight miles inland from Cocoa Beach, the brick-paved sidewalks and turn-of-the-nineteenth-century buildings of **Cocoa Village** fill several small blocks south of King Street (Hwy-520) and make for a relaxing stroll. Among the rather quaint antique shops and boutiques, seek out the Porcher House, 434 Delannoy Ave (Mon–Fri 9am–5pm; free; Ⓣ321/639-3500), a grand Neoclassical abode built in 1916.

For a greater insight into the town's origins, head a few miles west to the **Brevard Museum of History and Natural Science**, 2201 Michigan Ave (Mon–Sat 10am–4pm, Sun noon-4pm; $5.50; Ⓣ321/632-1830), whose displays recount Cocoa's birth as a trading post when the first settlers arrived in the 1840s by steamboat and mule. There's also a respectable exhibit of Florida wildlife and some informative leaflets that are particularly useful if you're planning to visit the Merritt Island National Wildlife Refuge (see p.377) further north.

The **Astronaut Memorial Planetarium and Observatory**, 1519 Clearlake Rd (Wed 1.30–4.30pm, Fri & Sat 6.30–10.30pm; $14; Ⓣ321/634-3732, Ⓦwww.brevardcc.edu/planet), which offers planetarium shows, large-screen movies and laser shows, is a halfhearted attempt to attract tourist dollars from the overflow of the nearby Kennedy Space Center and will interest only the most devoted of space enthusiasts.

If you're **staying** in Cocoa, there are some small and uninviting motels lining Cocoa Boulevard. The best of these is the *Econo Lodge Space Center* at no. 3220 N (Ⓣ321/632-4561 or 1-888/721-9423; ❷), which has a pool. For **eating**, try *Lone Cabbage Fish Camp*, 8199 W Hwy-520 (Ⓣ321/632-4199), good for catfish, frog legs, and alligator tail (and airboat rides as well). Alternatively, *Café Margaux*, 220 Brevard Ave (closed Tues; Ⓣ321/639-8343), is a stylish spot for a pasta lunch.

Titusville

If you don't visit the Kennedy Space Center, you'll at least get a great view of the towering Vehicle Assembly Building from **Titusville**, twenty miles north of Cocoa. If you find you have time on your hands here, visit the **Valiant Air Command Museum**, 6600 Tico Rd (daily 10am–6pm; $9; Ⓣ321/268-1941), a celebration of slightly more pedestrian flying machines than those at the Kennedy Space Center. Originally formed to commemorate the US Air Force's involvement in preventing Japan's invasion of mainland China in 1941, the museum today exhibits lovingly restored planes, with examples from all wars since that date. The best way to see them is in March, when the VAC holds an air show and most of these war veterans take to the skies.

Apart from this, all that's commendable about Titusville is its ease of access to the Kennedy Space Center (via Hwy-405) and the Merritt Island National Wildlife Refuge (via Hwy-402). On the way to either place, visit the **Astronaut Hall of Fame** (daily 10am–6pm; $14, children $10 admission included with Maximum Access Badge; ⓣ321/449-4444, ⓦwww.astronauthalloffame.com), one of Florida's most entertaining interactive museums. Simulation rides allow visitors to experience stomach-churning G-forces, weightlessness, and 360-degree spins. There's also a mock space shuttle and tours of **SpaceCamp USA**, where young aspiring astronauts spend several weeks spinning in contraptions designed to simulate the extreme G-forces of space travel

Inexpensive **hotels and motels** are plentiful along Washington Avenue (US-1): *Holiday Inn KSC*, no. 4951 S (ⓣ321/269-2121; ❸), and *Siesta*, no. 2006 S (ⓣ321/267-1455; ❷), are just two. Otherwise, try the *Best Western Space Shuttle Inn*, 3455 Cheney Highway (ⓣ321/269-9100; ❹), which also offers eco-tourism packages for exploring the unique flora and fauna of the area, such as sawgrass, loggerhead turtles, and indigo snakes.

For **food**, search out the seafood at locally famous *Dixie Crossroads*, 1475 Garden St (ⓣ321/268-5000), or the Asian specialties at *Dragon & Phoenix*, 3520 S Washington Ave (ⓣ321/269-7393).

When it's time to move on, there's a Greyhound **bus** station at 1220 S Washington Ave (ⓣ321/267-8760).

Heading north: New Smyrna Beach

After the virgin vistas of the Canaveral National Seashore, the tall beachside hotels of **New Smyrna Beach**, thirty miles north of Titusville on US-1, create the impression of a likeable low-key beach community, where the sea – protected from dangerous currents by offshore rock ledges – is perfect for **swimming** and **surfing**, especially at Smyrna Dunes State Park, located on the south side of Ponce Inlet, to the north. To reach the beach (or the northern section of the Canaveral National Seashore, see p.377), you have to pass through the inland section of the town, before swinging east on Hwy-A1A.

New Smyrna Beach started life as a Mediterranean colony founded by wealthy Scottish physician **Andrew Turnbull**, who bought land here in the mid-1700s and set about recruiting Greeks, Italians, and Minorcans to work for seven years on his plantation in return for fifty acres of land per person. The colony didn't last: bad treatment, language barriers, culture clashes, disease, and financial disasters hastened its demise, and many of the settlers moved north to St Augustine (see p.391).

The immigrants worked hard, however (by most accounts, they had little choice), laying irrigation canals, building a sugar mill, and commencing work on what was to be a palatial abode for Turnbull. Close to US-1, the **ruins** of the mill (at the junction of Canal Street and Mission Road) and his unfinished house (at Riverside Drive and Julia Street) are substantial enough to merit a look. The nearby **visitor center**, 2242 State Rd 44, just off I-95 (Mon–Fri 9am–5.30pm, Sat 9am–5pm, Sun 10am–2pm; ⓣ386/428-1600 or 1-866/397-6976, ⓦwww.nsbfla.com), has a handy historical brochure, as well as the usual local information. You can also stop by the Southeast Volusia County **Chamber of Commerce** downtown, closer to the remains of the mill, at 115 Canal St (ⓣ386/428-2249). For surfing tips, visit Inlet Charlie's (ⓣ386/423-2317) and Quiet Flight (ⓣ386/427-1917), surf shops right next door to each other at nos. 508 and 510 Flagler Blvd.

△ Daytona International Speedway

Practicalities

From Orlando International Airport, Greyhound **buses** will drop you in New Smyrna Beach at Majestic Gas Station, 600 W Canal St (Ⓣ386/428-8211) – and then you can use the local Votran buses (Ⓣ386/424-6800) to get around.

If you want to stay over, there are cheap and basic **motels** on US-1 (locally called the Dixie Freeway), like the *Smyrna Motel*, no. 1050 N (Ⓣ386/428-2495; ❷), which has an eagle's nest on its property. If you're in the mood for a truly luxurious and super-welcoming bed and breakfast, don't bypass the *Night Swan Intracoastal B&B*, within walking distance of downtown at 512 S Riverside Drive (Ⓣ386/423-4940 or 1-800/465-4261, Ⓦwww.nightswan.com; ❺), with its own dock, the perfect spot for viewing shuttle launches. Across the arching causeway bridge and out to the beach itself, the pink stucco *Sea Vista Ocean Front Resort*, 1701 S Atlantic Ave, Hwy A1A (Ⓣ386/428-2915 or 1-800/874-3917, Ⓦwww.seavistaresort.com; ❷), has a pool and a beachside tiki bar serving cocktails, snacks, as well as a full menu. The grouper sandwich is a coastal favorite.

For the area's finest upscale **dining**, there's *Norwood's*, on the beach side of the causeway at 400 Second Ave (Ⓣ386/428-4621); stop by on a Friday (5–7pm), when they have one of their popular wine-tastings to complement the mouth-watering seafood. Otherwise, there's the *New Smyrna Steakhouse*, 723 E Third Ave (Ⓣ386/424-9696), for wood-grilled steaks and ribs, or *Heavenly Sandwiches & Smoothies*, 115 Flagler Ave (Ⓣ386/427-7475), which runs toward healthy drinks and wraps (not counting their home-made ice cream).

Continuing north from New Smyrna Beach, Hwy-A1A joins with US-1 for ten miles before splitting off oceanward near Ponce Inlet, five miles south of mainland Daytona Beach.

Daytona Beach

The consummate Florida beach town, with rows of airbrushed-T-shirt shops, amusement arcades, and wall-to-wall motels, **DAYTONA BEACH** owes its existence to twenty miles of light brown sand where the only pressure is to relax and enjoy yourself.

For decades, Daytona Beach was invaded by half a million college kids going through the Spring Break ritual of underage drinking and libido liberation. In the mid-Nineties, the town ended its love affair with the nation's students and tried to emulate Fort Lauderdale (see "The Southeast," p.183) by cultivating a more refined image – an attempt that has been only partially successful, to say the least, since now it seems to cater mainly to bikers and race-car fanatics. In fact, Daytona Beach presents a decidedly seedy air these days. It's as if the rowdy kids have moved on and no one at all has come to replace them – except for the rowdy adults.

The resort is the center of three major annual events: the world-famous **Daytona 500** stock-car meeting, held at the Daytona International Speedway; **Bike Week** (also known as Biketoberfest), when thousands of leather-clad motorcyclists converge for races at the Speedway; and the relatively new **Fall Cycle Scene**, which is much the same idea (see box on p.388 for more info on all three events).

Even before the students and bikers, the beach was a favorite with pioneering auto enthusiasts such as Louis Chevrolet, Ransom Olds, and Henry Ford, who came here during the early 1900s to race their prototype vehicles beside the ocean. The land speed record was regularly smashed, five times by million-

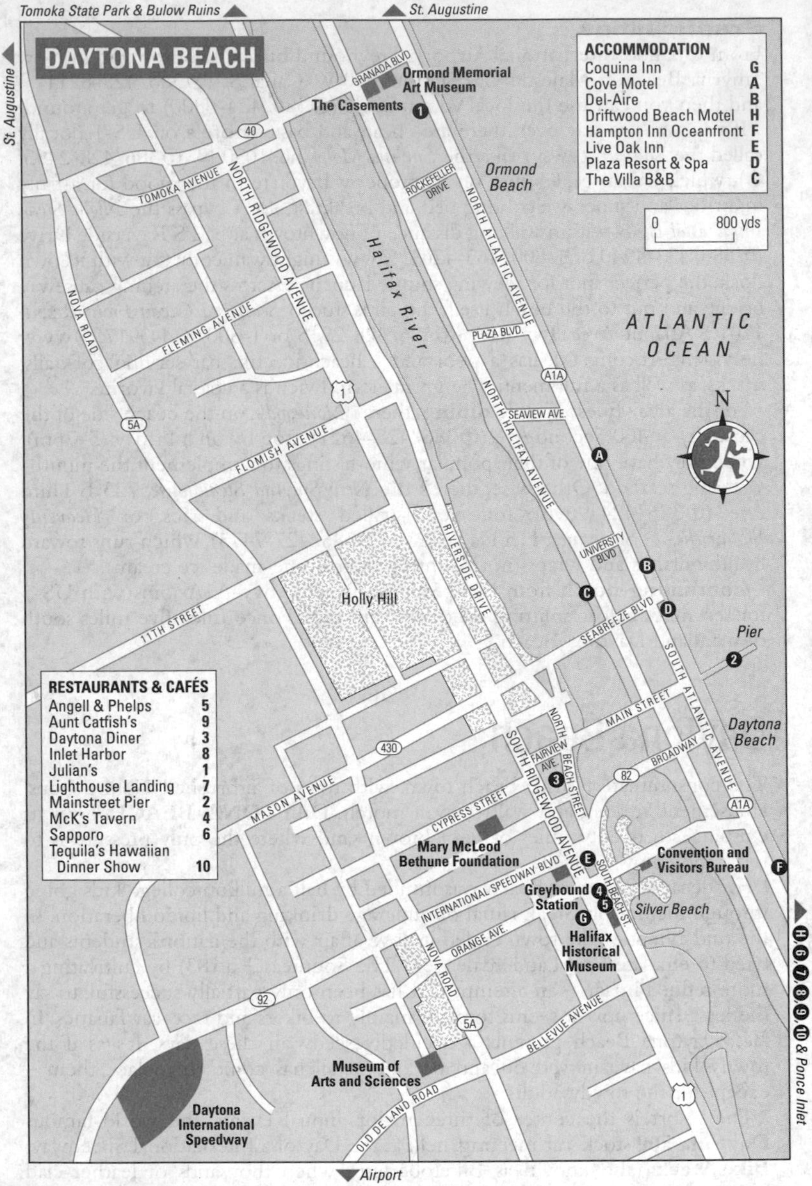

aire British speedster Malcolm Campbell who, in 1935, roared along at 276mph. As a legacy of these times, Daytona Beach is one of the few Florida towns where the dubious thrill of **driving on the beach** is permitted: pay $5 at any beach entrance, stick to the marked track, observe the 10mph speed limit, park at right-angles to the ocean – and beware of high tide.

Arrival, information, and getting around

As Ridgewood Avenue, **US-1** steams through **mainland Daytona Beach**, passing the Greyhound station, at no. 138 S (ⓣ386/255-7076 or 1-800/231-2222). By car, you should keep to **Hwy-A1A** (known as Atlantic Avenue), which enters the beachside area – filling a narrow sliver of land between the ocean and the Halifax River (part of the Intracoastal Waterway) a mile from the mainland.

The **Convention and Visitors Bureau**, located in the Chamber of Commerce building at 126 E Orange Ave (Mon–Fri 9am–5pm; ⓣ1-800/854-1234, ⓦwww.daytonabeach.com), is on the way to the beach and has a wealth of free information.

Local buses (Votran ⓣ386/761-7700, ⓦwww.votran.org) connect the beaches with the mainland and the Greater Daytona Beach area, though night and Sunday services are limited. The bus terminal is at the junction of US-1 and Bethune Boulevard in mainland Daytona Beach. At the beach, **trolleys** ($1) run until midnight along the central part of Atlantic Avenue. A **taxi** between the airport and the beach will cost around $10; try AAA Metro Taxi (ⓣ386/253-2522) or Yellow Cab (ⓣ386/255-5555).

Accommodation

From mid-May to November, scores of small **motels** on Atlantic Avenue slash their rates to $40–55 for a double. These rates go up by $10–20 from December to January, and soar to $80-plus during February through April (coinciding with racing season). Pick up the free *Superior Small Lodging Guide* from the Convention and Visitors Bureau for helpful hints on where to stay.

Hotels, motels, and bed and breakfasts

Coquina Inn 544 S Palmetto Ave ⓣ386/254-4969 or 1-800/805-7533. This homespun bed and breakfast is located a little inland. ❹

Cove 1306 N Atlantic Ave ⓣ386/252-3678 or 1-800/828-3251. This family-friendly motel has some rooms with kitchenettes and private balconies. ❷

Del-Aire 744 N Atlantic Ave ⓣ386/252-2562 or 1-/800-253-4920. Friendly, centrally located beachfront motel, with spacious rooms, cable TV, free local calls, and a pool. ❷

The Driftwood Beach Motel 657 S Atlantic Ave, Ormond Beach ⓣ386/677-1331 or 1-800/490-8935. This beachfront motel a couple miles north of the action accommodates limited budgets. ❷

Hampton Inn Oceanfront 3135 S Atlantic Ave ⓣ386/767-8533 or 1-800/822-8008, ⓦwww.hamptoninndaytonabeach.com. One of the more luxurious options, offering private balconies, a large pool, and a Jacuzzi. Located a bit south of Atlantic Avenue's busiest section. ❹

Live Oak Inn 444-448 S Beach St ⓣ386/252-4667 or 1-800/881-4667. This Colonial-style bed and breakfast (listed in the National Register of Historic Places) is both charming and reasonable. Dinner available Tues–Sat. ❺

Plaza Resort & Spa 600 N Atlantic Ave ⓣ386/255-4471 or 1-800/874-7420, ⓦwww.plazaresortandspa.com. Though the rooms (with fridge and microwave) are plain, the onsite spa gives this large hotel an upscale feel compared to much of Atlantic Ave, and there's a lively bar as well (review of *600 North* on p.390). ❺

The Villa 801 N Peninsula Drive ⓣ386/248-2020, ⓦwww.thevillabb.com. Situated in a Spanish-style mansion on the Intercoastal Waterway, this pleasant B&B includes a pool, spa, and gardens. ❻

Camping

Daytona Beach Campground 4601 S Clyde Morris Blvd ⓣ386/761-2663. Tent sites from $24, with pool access and a small store on the grounds.

Nova Family Campground 1190 Herbert St, Port Orange ⓣ386/767-0095. Ten miles south of mainland Daytona Beach (accessible by buses #17A, #17B, or #7), with a pool and laundromat. Tent sites $16 (more during Daytona speed weeks – see box on p.388).

Tomoka State Park seven miles north of mainland Daytona, in Ormond Beach ⓣ386/676-4050. Though tent sites are cheap ($10–15; cabins and RV sites also available), the real attraction is the leafy park itself. Bus #1B stops a mile down the road.

Buses between Daytona Beach and Orlando International Airport

If you're enjoying yourself at the beach but have to fly home from Orlando, you can take advantage of the **Daytona-Orlando Transit Service** (DOTS; ⓣ1-800/231-1965), whose shuttle buses run every ninety minutes (4am–9.30pm) from the corner of Nova Road and Eleventh Street to Orlando International Airport. On request, the buses also make stops in DeLand and Sanford. The one-way fare is $27 ($49 round-trip). Call ahead for details and reservations.

The beach and around

Without a doubt, the best thing about Daytona Beach *is* the **beach**: a seemingly limitless affair – 500 feet wide at low tide and, lengthways, fading dreamily into the heat haze. There's little to do other than develop your tan, take the occasional ocean dip, or observe one of the many pro volleyball tournaments that set up camp during the summer. Even the **pier**, at the end of Main Street, isn't a source of action: you can loiter in one of two characterless bars; enjoy panoramic views of the town from the Space Needle ($3); take the Sky Ride, a run-down cable-car-like conveyance that ferries you slowly from one end of the pier to the other over the heads of patient anglers; or try the Sky Coaster Ride, a 60mph amusement ride to curl your hair.

Nearby, Main Street (the center of motorcycle culture here) and Seabreeze Boulevard have better bars and cafés (see "Eating," p.389, and "Drinking and nightlife," p.390), but for more diverse pursuits – such as rambling around sand dunes, climbing an old lighthouse, or discovering Daytona Beach's history – you need to head twelve miles south to Ponce Inlet, three miles north to Ormond Beach or cross the Halifax River to the mainland.

South to Ponce Inlet

As you travel south along Atlantic Avenue, small motels and fast-food dives give way to the towering beachside condos of affluent Daytona Beach shores. As you approach **Ponce Inlet**, four miles ahead, the outlook changes again, this time to single-story beach homes and large sand dunes.

Here, at the end of Peninsula Drive – parallel to Atlantic Avenue – the 176-foot-high **Ponce Inlet Lighthouse** (Sept–May 10am–4pm, June–Aug 10am–9pm; $5; ⓣ386/761-1821) illuminated the treacherous coast from the late 1800s until 1970, giving seaborne access to New Smyrna Beach (see p.381). Stupendous views make climbing the structure (the tallest in Florida) worthwhile, and the outbuildings hold engaging artifacts from its early days, as well as mildly interesting displays on US lighthouses in general. Several **nature trails** scratch a path through the surrounding scrub-covered dunes to a (usually) deserted **beach**; pick up a map from the **ranger station** at the end of Riverside Drive. Once you've trekked up an appetite, drop into the eccentric *Lighthouse Landing* (see "Eating," p.389), beside the lighthouse, whose cheap seafood is brought ashore at the adjoining marina.

North to Ormond Beach

In 1890, as part of his plan to bring his East Coast railway south from St Augustine, oil baron Henry Flagler bought the local hotel, built a beachside golf course, and helped give **Ormond Beach**, three miles north of Main Street, the refined tone that it retains to this day. Millionaires like John D. Rockefeller wintered here, and the car-happy fraternity of Ford, Olds, and

Chevrolet used Flagler's garage to fine-tune their autos before powering them along the beach. Note, however, that beach driving is now prohibited in Ormond Beach, from North Granada Boulevard.

Facing the Halifax River at the end of Granada Boulevard, Flagler's **Ormond Hotel** stood until 1993, when it was demolished to much public mourning. However, the **Casements**, a three-story villa on the other side of Granada Boulevard that Rockefeller bought in 1918, is in fine shape (all the original furniture, though, was sold, and what remains was donated by neighbors). **Guided tours** of the house (25 Riverside Drive; Mon–Fri 10am–2.30pm, Sat 10–11.30am; free; ⓣ386/676-3216) – which, oddly enough, now holds displays of Hungarian folklore and Boy Scouts of America bric-a-brac – run every thirty minutes and tell you more than you'll ever need to know about Rockefeller and his time here, which was mostly spent playing golf and pressing dimes into the hands of passers-by.

At 78 E Granada Blvd, the Polynesian-style **Ormond Memorial Art Museum and Gardens** (Mon–Fri 10am–4pm, Sat & Sun noon–4pm; suggested donation $2; ⓣ386/676-3347) puts on decent temporary art shows – if they don't appeal, the gallery's jungle-like **gardens**, with shady pathways winding past fishponds to a gazebo, just might.

For **information** on Ormond Beach, drop by the Chamber of Commerce, 165 W Granada Blvd (ⓣ386/677-3454, ⓦwww.ormondchamber.com), which is located west of the museum, across Halifax River.

The mainland

When you're tired of the sands or nursing your sunburn, cross the river to **mainland Daytona Beach**, where several waterside parks and walkways contribute to a relaxing change of scene, and four museums will keep you out of the sun for a few hours.

Near the best of the parks, on Beach Street, a few turn-of-the-nineteenth century dwellings have been tidied up and turned into office space. At no. 252 South is the **Halifax Historical Museum** (Tues–Fri 10am–4pm, Sat 10am–noon; $4, free on Sat; ⓣ386/255-6976), which captures, with an absorbing stock of objects, models, and photos, the frenzied growth of Daytona Beach and Halifax County. Amid the fine stash of prehistoric archaeological artifacts and historic memorabilia, don't overlook the immense wall paintings of long-gone local landscapes.

One former Daytona Beach resident mentioned in the museum is better remembered by the **Mary McLeod Bethune Foundation**, a couple of miles north at 640 McLeod Bethune Blvd. Born in 1875 to freed slave parents, Mary McLeod Bethune was a lifelong campaigner for racial and sexual equality, founding the National Council of Negro Women and serving as a presidential advisor to Calvin Coolidge and Franklin Roosevelt on racial issues, especially the education of African-American women. In 1904, against the odds, she founded the state's first black girls' school here – with savings of $1.50 and five pupils. The white-framed **house** (Mon–Fri 9am–4pm; free; ⓣ386/481-2122), where Bethune lived from 1914 until her death in 1955, contains scores of awards and citations alongside furnishings and personal effects, and sits within the campus of Bethune-Cookman College, which has grown up around the original school.

If you're keen on paleontology and prehistory, stop off at the **Museum of the Arts and Sciences**, 1040 Museum Blvd (Tues–Fri 9am–4pm, Sat & Sun noon–5pm; $8; ⓣ386/255-0285, ⓦwww.moas.org), a mile south of

International Speedway Boulevard, to scrutinize bones and fossils dug up from the numerous archaeological sites in the area. These include the ferocious-looking reassembled remains of a million-year-old giant ground sloth, measuring thirteen feet long. There is also a **Planetarium** ($3, children $2) that is only worth it if you desire a long nap under a virtual star-scape. The other sections of the constantly expanding museum are intriguingly diverse: a stash of American paintings, furnishings, and decorative arts from the seventeenth-century onward illuminates early Anglo-American tastes. A major African collection displays domestic and ceremonial objects from thirty of the continent's cultures, including pieces donated – strangely enough – by some bygone television stars. Finally, Cuban paintings spanning two centuries (donated by Cuba's former dictator, Fulgencio Batista, who spent many years of exile in a comfortable Daytona Beach house) provide a glimpse of the island nation's important artistic movements.

Daytona International Speedway

About three miles west along International Speedway Boulevard, at no. 1801 West (Ⓣ386/254-2700), accessible by bus #9A and #9B, stands an ungainly configuration of concrete and steel that has done much to promote Daytona Beach's name around the world: the **Daytona International Speedway**, home of the Daytona 500 stock-car meeting and a few other less famous races. When high speeds made racing on Daytona's sands unsafe, the solution was this 150,000-capacity temple to high-performance thrills and spills, which opened in 1959.

Though it doesn't quite capture the excitement of a race, the guided **trolley tour** (daily 9.30am–4pm, except on race days; every 30min) gives visitors a chance to see the sheer size of the place and the remarkable gradient of the curves, which help make this the fastest racetrack in the world – 200mph is not uncommon.

Inside, the interactive exhibits put you in the driver's seat: see how fast you can jack a race car off the ground during a sixteen-second pit stop; feel the engines revving in your chest as you watch the "thunder-round sound" Daytona 500 wide-screen movie; or call a race as it happens at the interactive commentator booth. Other exhibits showcase the history of NASCAR (National Association of Stock Car Auto Racing) and the evolution of the race car.

Daytona speed weeks and more

The Daytona Speedway hosts several major race meetings each year, starting in early February with the **Rolex 24**: a 24-hour race for GT prototype sports cars. A week or so later begin the qualifying races leading up to the biggest event of the year, the **Daytona 500** stock-car race in mid-February. Tickets (see below) for this are as common as Florida snow, but many of the same drivers compete in the **Pepsi 400**, for which tickets are much easier to get, held on the first Saturday in July. The track is also used for motorcycle races: **Bike Week**, in early March, sees a variety of high-powered clashes, highlighted by **American Motorcycle Association** championship racing; and the **Fall Cycle Scene**, held the third week in October, features the **Championship Cup Series races.**

Tickets for the bigger events sell out well in advance, and it's advisable to book accommodation at least six months ahead (the cheapest are $50 for car-racing, $95 for the Daytona 500, $25 for motorcycle races). For **information** and ticket details call Ⓣ386/253-RACE or check Ⓦwww.daytonainternationalspeedway.com.

If you can't catch a race, **Daytona USA** (daily 9am–7pm; $16 to enter, $7 for speedway tours, $20 for a combo ticket/$14 for children; ⓣ386/947-6800, ⓦwww.daytonausa.com), located next to the speedway, is the next best thing. You can also get behind the wheel of a stock car yourself – for a price – at the **Richard Petty Driving Experience** in Orlando; for details, see "Walt Disney World," p.352.

North to Tomoka State Park and the Bulow Ruins

At the meeting point of the Halifax and Tomoka rivers, just off US-1 six miles north of International Speedway Boulevard (bus #1B, then a mile's walk), the attractive **Tomoka State Park** (daily 8am–sunset; cars $3.25, cyclists and pedestrians $1; ⓣ386/676-4050) comprises several hundred acres of marshes and tidal creeks, bordered by magnolias and moss-draped oaks. It's ripe for exploration by canoe ($3 per hour or $15 per day) or on foot along its many paths.

A 1972 addition to the park, the tiny **Fred Dana Marsh Museum** (9.30am–4.30pm; admission included in park entrance fee) details the life and work of the man who, in the 1910s, was the first American artist to create large-scale murals depicting "the drama and significance of men at work." In the 1920s, Marsh also designed a then (and in some ways still) futuristic home for himself and his wife in Ormond Beach. The house is located just north of Granada Boulevard on Hwy-A1A, though unfortunately it's not open to the public. Within the park itself, Marsh's immense sculpture *The Legend of Tomokie* is worth a look.

Take full advantage of the park by camping overnight (see "Accommodation," p.385), which leaves time to visit the **Bulow Plantation Ruins** (daily 9am–5pm; $2; ⓣ386/517-2084) – scant and heavily vegetated remains of an eighteenth-century plantation destroyed by Seminole Indians (five miles north of the park off Route 201). Picnicking is encouraged and canoe rentals are available.

Eating

No one comes to Daytona Beach for the food, and while most tourists satisfy themselves with the casual and fast-food **restaurants** along Atlantic Avenue, there are a few worthwhile options scattered around as well.

Angell & Phelps Restaurant & Wine Bar 156 S Beach St ⓣ386/257-2677. Creative American-style gourmet fare served in an informal setting, with live local talent Thurs–Sat.

Aunt Catfish's on the River 4009 Halifax Drive, Port Orange ⓣ 386/767-4768. Mighty portions of ribs and seafood are prepared in traditional Southern style. Lunch from $6, dinner from $11.

Daytona Diner 290 1/2 N Beach Blvd ⓣ386/258-8488. A Harley-Davidson presence dominates this Fifties-style diner, with a menu featuring the usual staples.

Inlet Harbor 133 Inlet Harbor Rd, Ponce Inlet ⓣ386/767-5590. Dine on seafood right on the marina, as local bands play their hearts out.

Julian's 88 N Atlantic Ave ⓣ386/677-6767. A dimly lit mock-Tahitian-style lounge with a solid, varied menu (entrees $10–24) and the same chef for 35 years.

Lighthouse Landing beside the Ponce Inlet Lighthouse ⓣ386/761-9271. Offering the freshest seafood around in a quirky and festive setting.

Mainstreet Pier Restaurant at the Daytona Beach pier ⓣ386/253-1212. Try the clam chowder or the fried fish at this long-standing favorite, while gazing at the sunset.

McK's Tavern 218 S Beach St ⓣ386/238-3321. A relaxed spot for a filling meal, with juicy burgers and an extensive beer selection.

Sapporo 3340 S Atlantic Ave ⓣ386/756-0480. Choose from a menu of well-executed sushi and hibachi-seared steaks.

Tequila's Hawaiian Dinner Show 2301 S Atlantic Ave ⓣ386/255-5411. A regular dinner is transformed by the less-than-serious erupting volcano and fire dancers.

Drinking and nightlife

Even without the Spring Break invasion of party-crazed students, it seems likely that Daytona Beach will retain its reputation as one of the best spots on Florida's east coast for merrymaking when the sun goes down.

600 North 600 N Atlantic Ave ⓣ386/255-4471. The nucleus of beachside nightlife, with bars and discos, live rock and rave alternative, and ceaseless wet T-shirt competitions.

Boot Hill Saloon 310 Main St ⓣ386/258-9506. They say it's "better here than across the street," referring to the neighboring cemetery, but this slightly rowdy biker bar is at least several notches above that.

Oyster Pub 555 Seabreeze Blvd ⓣ386/255-6348. Dirt-cheap oysters and a loud jukebox enhance the atmosphere at this sports bar.

Razzles 611 Seabreeze Blvd ⓣ386/257-6236. The wildly popular *Razzles* (the line often stretches down the block) has headache-inducing light shows and throbbing music for dancers, plus four pool tables and 20 TVs for everyone else. Drink specials every night.

Rockin' Ranch 801 S Nova Rd ⓣ386/673-0904. If country and western is your thing, come here Wed, Fri, or Sat for live C&W, or early evening on Wed or Sun, when everyone is line dancing.

North of Daytona Beach

Assuming you don't want to cut twenty miles inland along I-4 or Hwy-92 to DeLand and the Orlando area (see "Orlando and Disney World," p.321), keep on Hwy-A1A **northward** along the coast toward St Augustine. The first community you'll encounter is **Flagler Beach**, fourteen miles from Daytona Beach, comprising a few houses and shops, a pier, and a very tempting beach. Nearby, at the **Flagler Beach State Recreation Area** (daily 8am–sunset; cars $3.25, cyclists and pedestrians $1), a good cross-section of coastal birdlife can be spotted, particularly at low tide when freshly exposed sands provide a feast for swift beaks. If the relative peace and solitude of Flagler Beach persuades you to stay, try the elegant, well-appointed *Topaz Motel/Hotel*, 1224 S Ocean Shore Blvd (ⓣ1-800/555-4735; ❸).

Further north, soon after passing the blazing blooms of **Washington Oaks State Gardens** (daily 8am–sunset; cars $3.25, pedestrians and cyclists $1), you can't miss the streamlined, yet crumbling, architecture of **Marineland** (daily 9.30am–4.30pm; $14, children $9; ⓣ904/460-1275), Florida's original sea-creature theme park. The state's biggest tourist draw when it opened in 1938, its status has been severely undermined by subsequent imitations, such as the far superior SeaWorld (see "Orlando and Disney World," p.358). Add to that the extensive damage done by a hurricane in 1999, and what you now see is a mere shadow of its former glory. Established as marine studios for underwater research and photography, the park's highlights are somewhat limited now; however, high points include sharks in a large viewing tank, performing porpoises, and, for additional fees, a chance to scuba or snorkel among manta rays, sea turtles, and fish of various sizes in a 450,000 gallon tank.

Hwy-A1A crosses a narrow inlet three miles beyond Marineland onto **Anastasia Island**, close to the Spanish-built eighteenth-century **Fort Matanzas** on Rattlesnake Island. Never conquered, partly due to the sixteen-foot-thick walls and the surrounding moat, the fort is accessible only by **ferry** (daily 9.30am–4.30pm on the half-hour; free; call ⓣ904/471-0116 to confirm schedule), but it's of minor appeal in comparison to history-packed St Augustine.

A better stop might be the **St Augustine Alligator Farm** (daily 9am–6pm; $15, children $9; ⓣ904/824-3337), a few miles further north along Hwy-A1A.

Visitors are greeted by shrieks from a vividly colored toucan and can take a walk through a wildlife-infested swamp. It's the only place in the world where you can meet all 23 members of the crocodillian family, and it's also home to thousands of visiting coastal birds in the Rookery from April through June (a great place for budding photographers to snap away). Time your visit to coincide with the alligator, reptile, or bird shows (three shows daily, call for exact times) or the alligator feeding demonstration – heart-stopping stuff, especially when you're listening to the crunch of capybara (a large South American rodent) bone between reptilian teeth.

Once past the Alligator Farm, you're well within reach of St Augustine, whose old center is just across Matanzas Bay, three miles ahead.

St Augustine

With the size and even some of the looks of a small Mediterranean town, there are few places in Florida as immediately engaging as **ST AUGUSTINE**, the oldest permanent settlement in the US and one with much from its early days still intact. St Augustine's eminently strollable narrow streets are lined by carefully renovated buildings whose architecture carries evidence of Florida's broad European heritage and the power struggles that led up to its statehood. There's plenty here to fill a day or two, and for variation you can visit two alluring lengths of beach located just across the small bay on which the town stands.

Ponce de León, the Spaniard who gave Florida its name, touched ground here on *Pascua Florida* (Easter Sunday) in 1513, but it wasn't until Pedro Menéndez de Aviles put ashore on St Augustine's Day in 1565 that settlement began with the intention of subduing the Huguenots based to the north at Fort Caroline (see "The Jacksonville beaches," p.400). Repeated battles with the British began when Sir Francis Drake's ships razed St Augustine in 1586, but Spanish control was only relinquished when Florida was ceded to Britain in 1763, by which time the town was established as an important social and administrative center – soon to become the capital of East Florida. Spain regained possession twenty years later, and kept it until 1821, when Florida joined the US. Subsequently, Tallahassee became the capital of unified Florida, and St Augustine's fortunes waned. A railway and a posh hotel stimulated a tourist boom at the turn of the twentieth century, but otherwise expansion bypassed St Augustine – which inadvertently made possible the restoration program that started in the Thirties. The current residential community is unsurprisingly proud of having flourished under five flags in its long history.

Arrival and information

From Anastasia Island, **Hwy-A1A** crosses over Mantanzas Bay into the heart of St Augustine; **US-1** passes a mile west along Ponce de León Boulevard. The Greyhound **bus** will drop you at 100 Malaga St (☎904/829-6401), a fifteen-minute walk from the center.

St Augustine has no public transport system, but this poses no problem in the town, which is best seen **on foot**. There are two **sightseeing trains**, distinguishable only by their colors: the red-and-blue St Augustine Sightseeing Train (3 Cordova St; $14; ☎1-800/226-6545) and the green-and-orange Old Town Trolley Tours (167 San Marco Ave; $15; ☎904/829-3800). Both operate daily 8.30am–5pm, and make approximately twenty stops during an hour-long narrated circuit of the main landmarks; you can hop on and off whenever you like.

In addition to the aforementioned addresses, **tickets** can be purchased from virtually any bed-and-breakfast or motel, and tickets entitle you to three days of travel.

After a few hours of hard exploration, **harbor cruises**, leaving eight to ten times a day from the Municipal Marina near the foot of King Street, make a relaxing break; Scenic Cruise offers four to six (depending on the season) daily 75-minute guided paddlewheeler trips around the bay for $10 – paying to ride one of the sightseeing trains will earn you a discount on the cruise. There is also the nightly sail on the fully equipped 72-foot *Freedom* ($28; ⓣ904/810-1010).

After delving into the town's trove of historical treasures, getting to the beaches means a two-mile hike, calling a **taxi** (ⓣ904/824-8161), or waiting for the Beach Bus ($5, children $2, free for Old Town Trolley customers; ⓣ904/829-3800).

The main **Visitor Center**, 10 Castillo Drive (daily 8am–5pm; ⓣ1-800/653-2489, ⓦwww.visitoldcity.com), offers the usual tourist brochures and discount coupons (it costs $5 to park there, but is convenient if you're strolling the streets). It also has a free film on the town's history, recommendations for a variety of historical guided tours, including those of Tour Saint Augustine (ⓣ1-800/797-3778, ⓦwww.staugustinetours.com), who offer well-organized and informative walking tours, tailored itineraries, and information on the numerous local festivals (including torch-lit processions and a Menorcan Fiesta). Also consider indulging in "A Ghostly Experience," a more historical than scary guided walking tour that reveals local legends, tall tales, and haunted and spook-filled sites; tours start at 8pm in front of the *Milltop Tavern* (for tickets call ⓣ904/461-1009 or 1-888/461-1009; $6).

But truth to tell, the atmosphere always seems festive here, especially on weekends, when it's usually full up with relaxed pleasure-seekers and the air seems filled with live music spilling from every bistro and café.

Accommodation

St Augustine attracts plenty of visitors, and its Old Town has many excellent restored inns offering **bed and breakfast.** Note that prices usually go up $25–40 on weekends for the bayfront **motels**. The best place to **camp** is the Anastasia State Recreation Area (ⓣ904/461-2033), four miles south, off Hwy-A1A (see "The Beaches," p.398), where you can pitch a tent for $17.

Hotels, motels, and bed & breakfasts

Anastasia Inn 218 Anastasia Blvd ⓣ904/825-2879 or 1-888/226-6181, ⓦwww.anastasiainn.com. Across the bay from the Old Town, on Anastasia Island, well within striking distance of all the sights and the beach, the *Anastasia Inn* has clean, simple rooms. ❸

Best Western Spanish Quarter Inn 6 Castillo Drive ⓣ904/824-4457 or 1-800/528-1234. About half a mile north of the town center, this gracious Spanish-style villa, with a whirlpool for night-time stargazing, is right beside the main Visitor Center (see above).

Carriage Way 70 Cuna St ⓣ904/829-2467 or 1-800/908-9832, ⓦwww.carriageway.com. Canopy and four-poster beds, clawfoot tubs, and antiques add to the period feel of this 1880s house. ❹

Casa de Suenos 20 Cordova St ⓣ904/824-0887 or 1-800/824-0804, ⓦwww.casadesuenos.com. This sumptuous bed and breakfast with five Spanish-themed rooms offers all amenities (even cream sherry in your room). ❺

Casa Monica 95 Cordova St ⓣ904/827-1888 or 1-800/648-1888, ⓦwww.casamonica.com. By far the most elegant, and costly, choice in the heart of Old Town. The magnificently restored, Spanish-style *Casa Monica* has 138 uniquely furnished rooms and an air of royalty – in fact, the tower suite has hosted the King and Queen of Spain. Book well in advance. ❻

Kenwood Inn 38 Marine St ⓣ904/824-2116 or 1-800/824-8151, ⓦwww.oldcity.com/kenwood. This charming, immaculate, and inviting inn features its own pool, and the friendly owners throw a wine cocktail hour every day. ❹

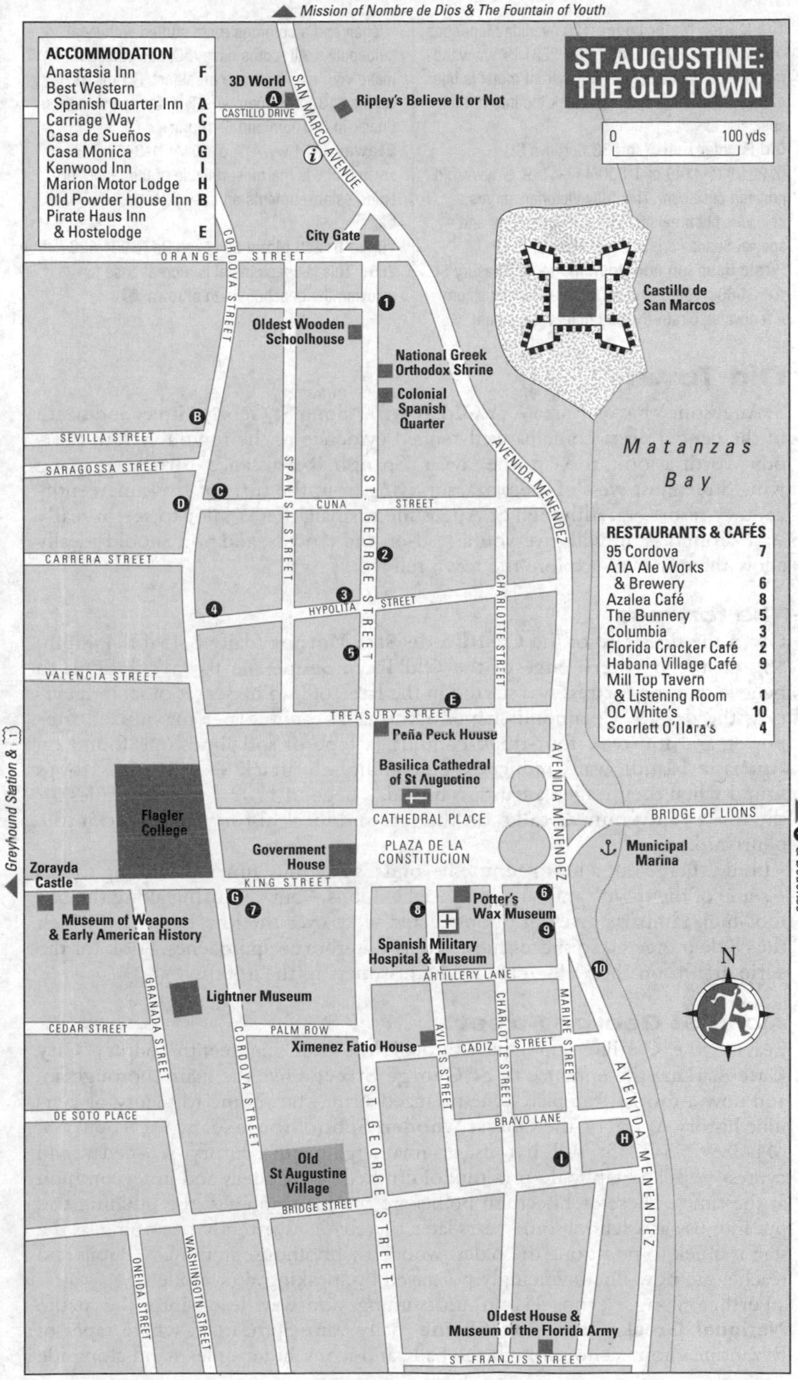
ST AUGUSTINE: THE OLD TOWN
Mission of Nombre de Dios & The Fountain of Youth
ACCOMMODATION
Anastasia Inn F
Best Western Spanish Quarter Inn A
Carriage Way C
Casa de Sueños D
Casa Monica G
Kenwood Inn I
Marion Motor Lodge H
Old Powder House Inn B
Pirate Haus Inn & Hostelodge E
RESTAURANTS & CAFÉS
95 Cordova 7
A1A Ale Works & Brewery 6
Azalea Café 8
The Bunnery 5
Columbia 3
Florida Cracker Café 2
Habana Village Café 9
Mill Top Tavern & Listening Room 1
OC White's 10
Scarlett O'Hara's 4
0
100 yds
3D World
Ripley's Believe It or Not
CASTILLO DRIVE
SAN MARCO AVENUE
City Gate
ORANGE STREET
CORDOVA STREET
Castillo de San Marcos
Oldest Wooden Schoolhouse
National Greek Orthodox Shrine
Colonial Spanish Quarter
AVENIDA MENENDEZ
Matanzas Bay
SEVILLA STREET
SARAGOSSA STREET
SPANISH STREET
ST. GEORGE STREET
CUNA STREET
CARRERA STREET
HYPOLITA STREET
CHARLOTTE STREET
VALENCIA STREET
TREASURY STREET
Peña Peck House
Basilica Cathedral of St Augustine
CATHEDRAL PLACE
PLAZA DE LA CONSTITUCION
BRIDGE OF LIONS
Flagler College
Government House
Municipal Marina
Greyhound Station & I-1
Zorayda Castle
KING STREET
Museum of Weapons & Early American History
Potter's Wax Museum
Spanish Military Hospital & Museum
F & Beaches
ARTILLERY LANE
N
Lightner Museum
GRANADA STREET
CEDAR STREET
PALM ROW
Ximenez Fatio House
AVILES STREET
CADIZ STREET
MARINE STREET
DE SOTO PLACE
BRAVO LANE
Old St Augustine Village
BRIDGE STREET
WASHINGOTN STREET
ONEIDA STREET
Oldest House & Museum of the Florida Army
ST FRANCIS STREET

The Marion Motor Lodge 120 Avenida Menéndez ⓣ904/829-2261 or 1-800/258-2261, ⓦwww.themarionmotorlodge.com. This bayfront motel is one of the better-value options; check the Internet for specials. ❸

Old Powder House Inn 38 Cordova St ⓣ904/824-4149 or 1-800/447-4149, ⓦwww.oldpowderhouse.com. This frilly Victorian serves a delicious hot breakfast in the dining room, and special Sunday brunches. No smoking. ❺

Pirate Haus Inn and Hostelodge 32 Treasury St ⓣ904/808-1999, ⓦwww.internationalhaus.com. A renovated pirate-themed hotel with a giant kitchen and a common room stuffed with local guidebooks. All rooms have A/C, and you can make your own pancake breakfast. Rooms ❷. Dorms $13 for HI members, $16 for nonmembers. Check-in 8–10am and 5–10pm.

Seaway 481 Hwy-A1A ⓣ904/471-3466. This small motel is the most reliable of the family-oriented establishments on busy St Augustine Beach. ❸

Vilano Beach Motel 50 Vilano Rd ⓣ904/829-2651. This laidback motel is a great base for enjoying the beaches north of town. ❸

Old Town

St Augustine's historic area – or **Old Town** – along St George Street and south of the central plaza contains well-tended evidence of the town's various periods. Worth a look, too, are the lavish "Spanish Renaissance" structures along King Street, just west of the plaza, surviving from the turn-of-the-nineteenth-century resort era. Although St Augustine is small, there's a lot to see: an early start, around 9am, will give you a lead on the crowds, and you should ideally allow three days to explore the town fully.

The fortress

Given the fine state of the **Castillo de San Marcos** (daily 8.45am–4.45pm; $5), on the northern edge of the Old Town beside the bay, it's difficult to believe that the fortress was started in the late 1600s. The secret of its longevity is the design: a diamond-shaped rampart at each corner maximized firepower, and fourteen-foot-thick coquina (a type of soft limestone found on Anastasia Island) walls reduced vulnerability to attack – as British troops found when they waged a fruitless fifty-day siege in 1702. Time schedules for the free twenty-minute **talks** on the fort and local history are posted in the courtyard.

Inside, there's not a lot to admire beyond a small museum and echoing rooms – some of them with military and social exhibits – but venturing along the 35-foot-high ramparts gives an unobstructed view over the low-lying city, which the castle protected so successfully, and its waterborne approaches. Look for the eerie graffiti on the walls, scrawled by prisoners in the 1600s.

Along St George Street

Leaving the Castillo, you'll pass through the little eighteenth-century **City Gate** marking the entrance to **St George Street**, once the main thoroughfare and now a tourist-trampled pedestrianized strip – but home to plenty of genuine history. At no. 14, the **Oldest Wooden Schoolhouse** (daily 9am–5pm; $3; ⓣ1-888/653-7245) still has its original eighteenth-century red-cedar and cypress walls and tabby floor (a mix of crushed oyster shells and lime, common at the time). These architectural points are the main interest: the building was put into use as a school some years later, thereby inadvertently becoming, as the staff is quick to point out, the oldest wooden schoolhouse in the US. Pupils and teacher are now unconvincingly portrayed by speaking wax models.

Further along, at no. 41, an unassuming doorway leads into the petite **National Greek Orthodox Shrine** (daily 9am–5pm; free), where tapes of Byzantine choirs echo through the halls, and icons and candles stand alongside hard-hitting accounts of the experiences of Greek immigrants to the US – some of whom settled in St Augustine from New Smyrna Beach (see p.381) in 1777.

More directly relevant to the town, and taking up a fair-sized plot at the corner of St George and Cuna streets, the **Colonial Spanish Quarter** (daily 9am–5.30pm; $6.50; ⓣ904/825-5033) includes nine reconstructed homes and workshops. Volunteers disguised as Spanish settlers go about their daily tasks at spinning wheels, anvils, and foot-driven wood lathes. The museum should be visited either early in the day or during an off-peak period; lines of camera-wielding tourists and rowdy school groups substantially lessen the effect. The main entrance is through the Triay House, on North St George Street.

For a more intimate look at local life during a slightly later period, head for the **Peña Peck House**, at no. 143 (Mon–Sat 12.30–3.30pm, Sun 10.30am–3.30pm; $4.50 suggested donation; ⓣ904/829-5064). Thought to have originally been the Spanish treasury, by the time the British took over in 1763 this was the home of a physician and his gregarious spouse, who turned the place into a high society rendezvous. The Pecks' furnishings and paintings, plus the enthusiastic spiel of the guide, make for an enjoyable tour.

Old St Augustine Village, 250 St George St (entrance on Bridge St; daily 9am–5pm; $7; ⓣ904/823-9722), presents a group of nine period buildings that have been beautifully restored. They're from every period and cultural stripe, not just Spanish, and the detailed tours offered by the guides will easily hold your attention. Particularly fascinating is the **Prince Murat House** (1790), briefly home to Napoleon's nephew (for whom it was named). Ravishing French Empire furniture graces its main room, and a glass case displays a letter penned by the emperor himself, along with one by the Revolutionary figure Lafayette, and one by Murat himself.

The plaza

In the sixteenth century, the Spanish king decreed that all colonial towns had to be built around a central plaza, and St Augustine was no exception: St George Street runs into **Plaza de la Constitucion**, a marketplace dating from 1598 that nowadays attracts shade seekers and the occasional wino. On the north side of the plaza, the **Basilica Cathedral of St Augustine** (daily 7am–5pm; donation requested) adds a touch of grandeur, though it's largely a Sixties remodeling of the late eighteenth-century original, with murals by Hugo Ohlms depicting life in St Augustine. Periodic **guided tours** (times are sometimes pinned to the door) revel in the painstaking details of the rebuilding and the undistinguished stained-glass windows. Slightly more worthwhile, the ground floor of **Government House** (daily 9am–5pm; $2.50; ⓣ904/825-5033), on the west side of the plaza, contains small displays of objects from the city's various renovation projects and archaeological digs. In contrast, on the south side of the square, seeking shelter from a thunderstorm might be the sole justification for entering **Potter's Wax Museum** (daily: summer 9am–9pm, winter 9am–5pm; $8; ⓣ904/829-9056 or 1-800/584-4781), populated by effigies of people you may have heard of but probably won't recognize.

South of the plaza

Tourist numbers lessen as you cross south of the plaza into a web of quiet, narrow streets with as much antiquity as St George Street.

Close by, at 20 Aviles St, the **Ximenez Fatio House** (Mon–Sat 11am–4pm; free; ⓣ904/829-3575) was built in 1789 for a Spanish merchant and proved popular with travelers during the late eighteenth century, drawn by the airy balconies added to the original structure. Although the upper floor is a bit rickety, a walk around is safe and quick in the company of a guide who points out illuminating details. At 3 Aviles St you can spend an interesting fifteen minutes in the small **Spanish Military Hospital & Museum** (Mon–Sat 10am–4pm, Sun noon–4pm; $3.50; ⓣ904/827-0807), built in 1791 and recreating the spartan care wounded soldiers could expect.

More substantial history is unfurled a ten-minute walk away at the **Oldest House**, 14 St Francis St (daily 9am–5pm; last admission 4.30pm; $6; ⓣ904/824-2872), occupied from the early 1700s (and, indeed, the oldest house in the town) by the family of an artillery hand at the castle. The second floor was grafted on during the British period, a fact evinced by the bone china crockery belonging to a former occupant, one Mary Peavitt. Her disastrous marriage to a hopeless gambler provided the basis for a popular historical novel, *Maria*, by Eugenia Price (the gift shop has copies). A smaller room shows the pine-stripped "sidecar" style made popular by the arrival of Flagler's railway, copying as it does the decor of a train carriage.

Entered through the back garden of the house, the less-than-riveting **Museum of the Florida Army** (entry included with admission to the Oldest House; same hours) gives an inkling, with its display of old uniforms, of the numerous conflicts that have divided Florida over the years. Anybody you might see striding by in modern military garb probably belongs to the Florida National Guard, whose headquarters are across the street.

West of the plaza: along King Street

A walk west from the plaza along **King Street** bridges the gap between early St Augustine and its turn-of-the-twentieth-century tourist boom. You'll soon notice, at the junction with Cordova Street, the flowing spires, arches, and red-tiled roof of **Flagler College**. Now used by liberal arts students, a hundred years ago it was – as the *Ponce de León Hotel* – an exclusive winter retreat of the nation's rich and mighty. The hotel was an early attempt by entrepreneur Henry Flagler to exploit Florida's climate and coast, but as he developed properties further south and extended his railway, the *Ponce de León* fell from favor – not helped by a couple of freezing winters. There are free guided tours in the summer. You can walk around the **campus** and the first floor of the **main building** (daily 10am–3pm) to admire the Tiffany stained glass and the painstakingly restored painted ceiling in the dining room.

In competition with Flagler, the eccentric Bostonian architect Franklin W. Smith – seemingly obsessed with poured concrete and Moorish design (see the Zorayda Castle, below) – built a rival hotel of matching extravagance directly opposite the *Ponce de León*. Named the *Casa Monica*, it was eventually sold to Flagler, who named it the *Cordova*. Fronted by a courtyard of palm trees and fountains, the building now holds the **Lightner Museum** (daily 9am–5pm; last admission 4.30pm; $6; ⓣ904/824-2874, ⓦwww.lightnermuseum.org), where you can easily pass an hour poring over the Victorian cut glass, Tiffany lamps, antique music boxes, and more. There's even a Russian malachite and ormolu urn from the Winter Palace of imperial St Petersburg. Much of the booty was acquired by publishing ace Otto C. Lightner from once-wealthy estates hard hit by the Depression.

A rather incongruous sight in St Augustine is Franklin W. Smith's recreation of the famed Alhambra. The architect was so impressed by the Moorish architecture he'd seen in Spain that he built a copy of one wing of the thirteenth-century palace here, in the late nineteenth century, at a tenth of the original size. Called the **Zorayda Castle**, 83 King St, it is now a private residence and not open to the public.

Just across the Zorayda's parking lot, a shack contains the **Museum of Weapons and Early American History** (daily 9.30am–5pm; $4; ⓣ904/829-3727). Reading the small collection of Civil War diaries gives an interesting personal view of the struggle, but this one-room cache will mainly appeal to survivalist types, with plenty of tools to shoot, stab, and batter foes to death.

North of Old Town: San Marco Avenue and around

Leading away from the tightly grouped streets of the Old Town, the traffic-bearing **San Marco Avenue**, beginning on the other side of the City Gate from St George Street, passes the sites of the first Spanish landings and settlements as well as some remains of the Timucua Indians who greeted them. A couple of other potential stops are of much less relevance to the town but can be good for an entertaining hour or two.

The **Ripley's Believe It or Not**, at 19 San Marco Ave (daily 9am–7pm; $10.95; ⓣ904/824-1606, ⓦwww.staugustine-ripleys.com), isn't the best but it contains a riveting collection of oddities gathered by Robert Ripley as he traveled around the world in the Twenties and Thirties. Among the items on display are a grandfather clock made from clothes pegs, the Lord's Prayer printed on the head of a pin, and a rendering of Degas' *L'Absinthe* composed entirely of toasted white bread.

Directly across the street from Ripley's is **3-D World**, 28 San Marco Ave (daily 10am–6pm; $10; ⓣ904/824-1220), which shows three films ranging from the calming waters of "Blue Magic," where scores of colorful fish dart past your eyes, to the two action-adventure films whose frenetic motion simulator pitches you headfirst into the "Castle of Doom" and then on to the "Curse of King Tut" – unadvisable for those susceptible to motion sickness.

Don't be discouraged, half a mile further along San Marco Avenue, by the dull, modern church that now stands in the grounds of **Mission of Nombre de Dios** (daily: summer 7am–8pm, rest of the year 8am–6pm; donation requested). This sixteenth-century mission was one of many in the southeast US established by Spanish settlers to convert Native Americans to Christianity, simultaneously exploiting their labor and seeking their support in possible confrontations with rival colonial powers.

A pathway leads to a 208-foot-tall stainless steel cross, glinting in the sun beside the river on the spot where Menéndez landed in 1565. Soon after, Father Francisco Lopez de Mendoza Grajales celebrated the first Mass in North America, recording that "a large number of Indians watched the proceedings and imitated all they saw," which was a bit unfortunate since the arrival of the Spanish signaled the beginning of the end for the Indians. A side-path takes a mildly interesting course around the rest of the squirrel-patrolled lawns, passing a few relics of the mission, on the way to a small, ivy-covered re-creation of the original chapel.

In addition to the prospect of finding gold and silver, it's said that Ponce de León was drawn to Florida by the belief that the fabled life-preserving "fountain of youth" was located here. Rather tenuously, this fact is celebrated at a mineral spring touted as **The Fountain of Youth**, 11 Magnolia Ave (daily 9am–5pm; $6; ⓣ1-800/356-8222) in a park at the end of Williams Street (off San Marco Ave), very near the point where he landed in 1513, and about half a mile north of the old mission site. It's unlikely, however, you'll live forever after drinking the fresh water (with the smelly bouquet of sulfur) handed to you as you enter the springhouse. The expansive acres of the park have far more significance as an archaeological site. Besides remains of the Spanish settlement, many Timucua Indian relics have been unearthed here, and you'll also come across some of the wiry plants that were the base of the "Black Drink," a thick, highly potent concoction used by the Timucuans to help them achieve mystical states.

The Beaches

If you've reached St Augustine with Hwy-A1A you'll need no introduction to the fine **beaches** that lie just a couple of miles from the Old Town. Few other people need one either, especially on weekends when the bronzers, beachcombers, and watersports fanatics descend in droves. A fine view of St Augustine and up and down the beaches is afforded by the **Lighthouse and Museum**, 81 Lighthouse Ave (daily 9am–6pm; $7; Ⓣ904/829-0745, Ⓦwww.lighthousestaug.com), which tells the story of the keepers and the lights they tended.

Across the bay on Anastasia Island, **St Augustine Beach** is family terrain, but here you'll also find the **Anastasia State Recreation Area** (daily 8am–sunset; cars $3.25, cyclists and pedestrians $1), offering a thousand protected acres of dunes, marshes, scrub, and a wind-beaten group of live oaks, linked by nature walks – though most people come here to catch a fish dinner from the lagoon. In the other direction (take May Street, off San Marco Avenue), **Vilano Beach** pulls a younger crowd and marks the beginning of a dazzling strand of vegetation hemming the road on both sides that continues for twenty undeveloped miles all the way to Jacksonville Beach (see opposite).

Eating

The tourist throng on and around St George Street makes **eating** in the Old Town an often pricey affair, particularly for dinner.

95 Cordova 95 Cordova St, at the *Casa Monica Hotel* Ⓣ904/810-6810. Reservations are necessary to partake of the masterful nouvelle continental cuisine at this elegant bistro.

Azalea Café 4 Aviles St Ⓣ904/824-6465. Cute little breakfast and lunch restaurant, with omelets, salads, club sandwiches, and soups served 9am–4pm, from 10am on weekends.

The Bunnery 121 St George St Ⓣ904/829-6166. Good coffee and economical breakfasts (and tempting home-made sandwiches and soups as well) served in an old Spanish bakery with a courtyard.

Columbia 98 St George St Ⓣ904/824-3341. A traditional Spanish/Cuban menu is appropriate for this eatery on the stone streets of Old Town, which is decorated by splashing fountains, wood beams, candlelight, and painted tiles. Entrees around $20.

Florida Cracker Café 81 St George St Ⓣ904/829-0397. Especially good for lunch, with eclectic combo salads (blackened shrimp and spinach), conch fritters, and home-made desserts.

The Oasis 4000 Ocean Trace Rd (Hwy-AlA) Ⓣ904/471-3424. Excellent burgers, with a multitude of toppings, can be found at this fun shack at St Augustine Beach.

Nightlife

St Augustine's **nightlife scene** offers many establishments with live music, even in the afternoon and especially on weekends, and many are decent eating establishments in their own right.

A1A Ale Works & Brewery 1 King St Ⓣ904/829-2977. A fun place to while away some time raising home brews (at least six kinds), but the food is nothing special.

Dunes Cracker House 641 Beach Blvd Ⓣ904/461-5725. The place to come after a lazy afternoon on the beach; the happy hour lasts from 3pm to 7pm daily. Weekend entertainment includes DJ music, and there's jazz on Mondays.

Habana Village Café 1 King Street ⓣ904/827-1700. You'll find live Latin music to dance to Thurs–Sat, potent home-made sangria, and yummy Cuban snacks at this upbeat hideaway. Also open for lunch and dinner.

Milltop Tavern and Listening Room 19 1/2 St George St ⓣ904/829-2329. Lots of local folk hang out at the top of the millwheel, where there's a terrific, funky atmosphere, live music in the afternoons and evenings, and an open-air view of the Castillo and harbor.

O.C. White's 118 Avenida Menéndez ⓣ904/824-0808. A lively crowd pervades this bayfront bar/restaurant, which has nightly entertainment, and grouper and crab cakes to absorb the beer.

Scarlett O'Hara's 70 Hypolita St ⓣ904/824-6535. You can get full meals here (barbecue is the specialty) and hear a variety of live music.

The Jacksonville beaches

However good the beaches around St Augustine may be, they're just the start of an unblemished coastal strip running northwards for twenty miles alongside Hwy-A1A, with nothing but the ocean on one side, and the swamps and marshes of the Talamato River (the local section of the Intracoastal Waterway) on the other. The scene begins to change when you near the sculptured golf courses and half-million-dollar homes of **Ponte Vedra Beach** – one of the most exclusive communities in northeast Florida. The crowd-free sands are prime beachcombing terrain – retreating tides often leave sharks' teeth among the more common ocean debris.

Four miles on, the much less snooty **Jacksonville Beach** (info on ⓣ904/249-3868; visitor center at 403 Beach Blvd ⓣ904/242-0024, ⓦwww.jaxcvb.com) is an affable beachside community whose residents relax here and commute to work in the city of Jacksonville, twelve miles inland. Though much cleaner than Daytona, the place is inexplicably neglected by tourists outside of the summer months. The **pier** is the center of activity, and a fried-fish sandwich from its snack bar is the right accompaniment to observing novice surfers grappling with modest-sized breakers. If you start itching for some action of your own, you could do worse than visit **Adventure Landing**, 1944 Beach Blvd (Sun–Thurs 10am–11pm, Fri & Sat 10am–1am; ⓣ904/246-4386). Getting in is free, but you pay for the attractions that most strike your fancy: highlights include a go-kart race track ($6), a game of laser-tag with pirates in the dark ($6), and baseball batting cages ($2). If you get tired of the ocean, you can splash about in the water park ($22); the "Nightflash" evening reduced-rate ticket lets you in for $15 between 4pm and 7pm (Mon to Fri).

Once you cross Seagate Avenue, less than two miles north of the pier, Jacksonville Beach merges with the more commercialized **Neptune Beach**, which in turn blurs (at Atlantic Boulevard) with the identical-looking **Atlantic Beach**. These last two places are more family-oriented than Jacksonville Beach, but all are great to visit for eating and socializing. Just north of Atlantic Beach, downbeat **Mayport** is dominated by its naval station, berth to some of the biggest aircraft carriers in the US Navy. It's best seen through a car window on the way to the Mayport ferry, which crosses the St Johns River, and the barrier islands beyond (see "Toward Amelia Island," p.406).

In contrast to the naval station is the **Kathryn Abbey Hanna Park**, 500 Wonderwood Drive ($1; ⓣ904/249-4700), just south of Mayport. Besides its mile and a half of unblemished beachfront, the park boasts 450 acres of woodland surrounding a large lake, around which wind ten miles of enjoyable biking and hiking trails. There's also a campground here (see "Accommodation," p.400).

Around the beaches

A few miles inland on Girvin Road (off Atlantic Boulevard), the **Fort Caroline National Memorial** (daily 9am–5pm; free; Ⓣ904/641-7155, Ⓦwww.nps.gov/foca) offers a historical interlude: a small museum details the significance of the restored Huguenot fort here, which provoked the first Spanish settlement in Florida (see "St Augustine," p.391). Another reason to visit is the great view from the fort across the mile-wide St Johns River and its ocean-going freighters.

Accommodation

Along the coast there will be plenty of bargains in winter, but during the summer be ready to spend upwards of $80 for a basic **motel** room, and book ahead. Kathryn Abbey Hanna Park (Ⓣ904/249-4700) is ideal for woodsy isolation while **camping**; tent sites cost $13, and sleeping cabins with electricity (but no furniture) are also available for $30 per night.

Best Western Oceanfront 305 N 1st St, Jacksonville Beach Ⓣ904/249-4949 or 1-800/897-8131, Ⓦwww.jaxbestwestern.com. A reliable standby where the comfortable rooms come with fridge and microwave. ❺

Comfort Inn Mayport 2401 Mayport Rd (Hwy-A1A), Atlantic Beach Ⓣ904/249-0313 or 1-800/968-5513. Not far from the Mayport ferry, this standard chain hotel includes a fitness room and even a popcorn machine. ❹

Pelican Path Bed & Breakfast 11 N 19th Ave, Jacksonville Beach Ⓣ904/249-1177 or 1-888/749-1177, Ⓦwww.pelicanpath.com. Rooms with bay windows look onto the sands at this cozy inn, and bicycles are available for guests' use. No smoking. ❺

Sea Horse Oceanfront Inn 120 Atlantic Blvd, Neptune Beach Ⓣ904/246-2175 or 1-800/881-2330, Ⓦwww.seahorseresort.com. This two-story pink stucco hotel has fairly ordinary rooms in a beachside location, which might account for the price. ❺

Sea Turtle Inn 1 Ocean Blvd, Atlantic Beach Ⓣ904/249-7402 or 1-800/874-6000, Ⓦwww.seaturtle.com. A romantic boutique hotel with its own beach and pastel-colored Mediterranean decor. ❺

Surfside 1236 N 1st St, Jacksonville Beach Ⓣ904/246-1583. This pleasant motel features renovated rooms, a pool, and continental breakfast. ❸

Eating, drinking, and nightlife

The **eating** and **nightlife** options are fairly good at the beaches, especially at Jacksonville Beach (on 3rd St), which tends to be a little louder and younger than the other beach communities. Check out restaurants like *Ragtime Tap Room* (Thurs–Sun) and *Sun Dog Diner* (Mon–Sun) for live music as well.

Restaurants

Harry's Seafood Bar & Grille 1018 N 3rd St, Jacksonville Beach Ⓣ904/247-8855. A lively New Orleans-style restaurant serving flavorful Cajun-influenced seafood dishes.

Ragtime Tap Room 207 Atlantic Blvd, Atlantic Beach Ⓣ904/241-7877. Boasting an extensive seafood menu, this restaurant is a favorite among locals and visitors alike.

Sliders Oyster Bar 218 1st St, Neptune Beach Ⓣ904/246-0881. The fresh seafood is superb; a platter of a dozen local oysters is only $6.

Sun Dog Diner 207 Atlantic Blvd, Neptune Beach Ⓣ904/241-8221. Better than your usual diner fare, with unusual specials like pan-seared red snapper with avocado and mango salsa.

Bars and clubs

The Fly's Tie 177 E Sailfish Drive, Atlantic Beach Ⓣ904/246-4293. An authentic Irish pub, the *Tie* usually features traditional Irish music on weekends.

Freebird Café 200 N 1st St, Jacksonville Beach Ⓣ904/246-2473. Named for Lynyrd Skynyrd's best-known song, the café has a slightly rough atmosphere that's softened by the spirited music, from funk to rock to jazz to bluegrass. Cover varies depending on the night, closed Mon and Tues.

Monkey's Uncle 1850 S 3rd St, Jacksonville Beach Ⓣ904/246-1070. Fun bar that offers a mix of karaoke, DJs, dance music, and trivia games (Tues 8pm).

Ocean Club 401 N 1st St, Jacksonville Beach ⓣ904/242-8884. This club has the loudest music on the beaches, with DJs spinning every night (Thurs is Reggae and Latin night).

Jacksonville

JACKSONVILLE's reputation has lagged somewhat behind its recent renewal. Most outsiders know it only as an industrial city, with a dusty seaport that remains a major transit point for cargo on the deep St Johns River, and a deeply conservative population. Residents, however, have witnessed the changes of the Nineties, when the city's insurance, technology, and service industries flourished and helped generate enough buzz to attract retail stores, construction projects, and new homebuyers into the area. At the same time, efforts to enhance Jacksonville's appeal have repaired roads and created parks and riverside boardwalks, though the sheer size of the city – at 841 square miles, the largest in the US – dilutes its character and makes it difficult to walk around and get a real feel for the city. For all that, Jacksonville is not an unwelcoming place and is gearing up for tourism. Thanks to increased funding for its museums, the city's cultural attractions are now among the best in the state.

Arrival, information, and getting around

The Greyhound **bus** station is at 10 N Pearl St (ⓣ904/356-9976). The **train** station is an awkward six miles northwest of downtown at 3570 Clifford Lane, from which a **taxi** (Taxi Terry ⓣ904/535-TAXI or Gator City Taxi ⓣ904/355-TAXI) downtown will cost around $8.

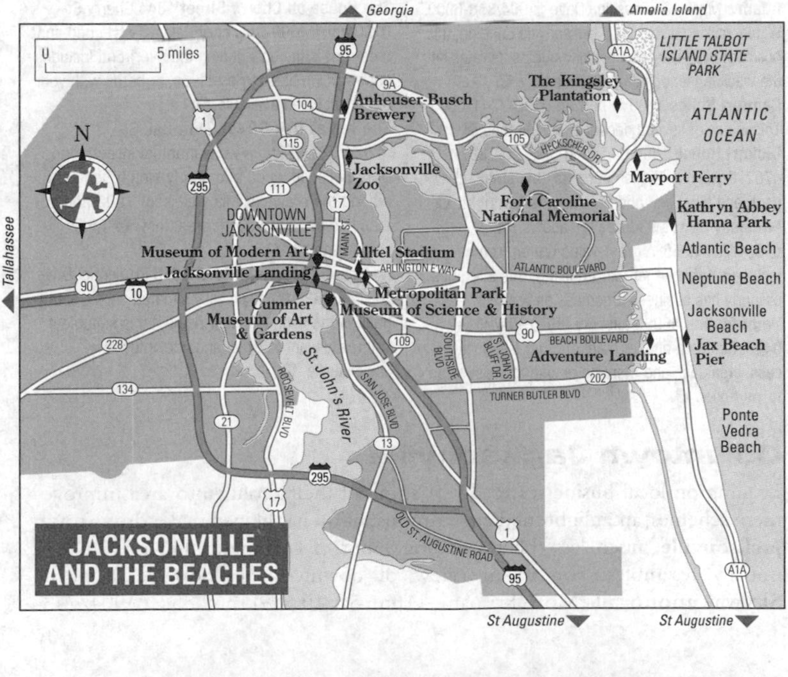

In downtown Jacksonville, the **Convention and Visitors Bureau**, 550 Water St, Suite 1000 (Mon–Fri 8am–5pm; ⓣ904/798-9111 or 1-800/733-2668, ⓦwww.jaxcvb.com), is an easy walk from the bus station and has plenty of tourist leaflets and discount vouchers (there are also affiliated information booths at the airport and in the Jacksonville Landing Mall).

The **local bus** service, JTA (75¢ a ride, or $1.35 to the beaches, exact change only; ⓣ904/630-3100, ⓦwww.ridejta.net), is comprehensive but confusing, so be sure to pick up a system map on JTA buses or at the CVB. In addition, free **trolleys** run on three routes through the north bank, with an additional one that meanders through the south bank and the San Marco neighborhood (call ⓣ904/743-3582).

Though maddening in spots, the city does offer ample opportunities for **cycling**, which are well laid-out in the pamphlet *Bike Ways of Northeast Florida*, available from the CVB or the Northeast Florida Regional Planning Council (ⓣ904/279-0880, ⓦwww.nefrpc.org). You can rent a bike from Open Road, 3544 St Johns Ave (ⓣ904/388-9066), for $25 per day, $100 for a week. Outside of downtown, be sure to check out the Jacksonville–Baldwin Rail Trail, where a bike path wends its way through fifteen miles of parkland along the track bed of a defunct railroad. The trail starts about ten miles outside of downtown's north bank and stretches west to Baldwin; call (ⓣ904/630-5401) for further information.

Accommodation

The city's far-flung layout means that you'll find **accommodation** concentrated in several neighborhoods, such as downtown's bustling Riverwalk and the suburban Riverside-Avondale area – a good base for exploring the nearby residences and the Cummer Museum (see p.404). Most budget chain hotels are located near the airport, nine miles north of downtown Jacksonville.

Adam's Mark 225 Coastline Drive ⓣ904/358-6800. Within walking distance of Jacksonville Landing, this business hotel is worth checking out, as its rates on the weekend tend to drop considerably. ⑤

Comfort Suites 1180 Airport Rd ⓣ904/741-0505. This is one of several decent airport hotels. ③

Dickert House 1804 Copeland St ⓣ904/387-4762. If you like English gardens, this small, elegant, and quiet bed and breakfast is just right. ⑥

Embassy Suites 9300 Baymeadows Rd ⓣ904/731-3555. A great-value option (rooms include a sofa bed for extra guests), this all-suites property has business amenities as well. ⑤

Hampton Inn 4690 Salisbury Rd ⓣ904/281-0443. Standard budget hotel offering free local calls, breakfast, and morning newspaper delivered to your door. ④

The House on Cherry Street 1844 Cherry St ⓣ904/384-1999. This cozy Colonial-style bed and breakfast is the only one on the riverfront. Includes home-grown blueberries, citrus, or herbs with your breakfast when available. ④

The Inn at Oak Street 2114 Oak St ⓣ904/379-5525, ⓦwww.innatoakstreet.com. Dark polished wood and comfy sleigh beds are among the draws at this well-kept 1902 house. Also serves an excellent breakfast. ⑥ (one smaller room ④)

Radisson Riverwalk Hotel 1515 Prudential Drive ⓣ904/396-5100. Scenically situated on the south bank of the river, this high-rise hotel is suitable if you really want to experience downtown Jacksonville. ④

Downtown Jacksonville

Leaning on local businesses to divert some of their profits into area improvement schemes, an enlightened city administration has helped make **downtown Jacksonville** much less the forbidding forest of corporate high-rises than it initially resembles. For an overview of downtown Jacksonville, take the **Skyway monorail** (Mon–Fri 6am–11pm, Sat 10am–11pm; 35¢; ⓣ904/743-

3582) from the Convention Center to Hemming Park, a ten-minute journey at eye-level with the high-rise offices. Otherwise, wander along the banks of the St Johns River, which snakes through the city center, dividing downtown Jacksonville in two.

The north bank

Within four blocks of Bay Street on the **north bank** of the river, you'll find the few structures that survived a major fire in 1901 – which claimed much of early Jacksonville – as well as some of the more distinctive buildings from subsequent decades. These are best examined with the aid of the free *Downtown Walking* leaflet from the Convention and Visitors Bureau (see "Arrival, information, and getting around," p.401). One noteworthy building is the **Florida Theater**, 128 E Forsyth St, which opened in 1927 and became a center of controversy thirty years later when Elvis Presley's pelvic thrusts shocked the city's burghers. Though rather nondescript from the outside, its interior has been restored with a dazzling gold proscenium arch, and the theater is now used for a variety of performances. The **Morocco Temple**, 219 N Newman St, currently occupied by an insurance company, was built by Henry John Kluthco, a classically minded architect who arrived to rebuild Jacksonville after the 1901 fire but later converted to Frank Lloyd Wright–inspired Modernism and erected this sphinx-decorated curiosity in 1912.

In this city of commerce and industry, you might not expect much from the **Jacksonville Museum of Modern Art** (Tues–Fri 11am–5pm, Sat & Sun noon–4pm; $6, free Wed 5–9pm; Ⓣ904/366-6911, Ⓦwww.jmoma.org), which you'll find at 333 N Laura St, in downtown Jacksonville. However, the scope and depth of its offerings in photography, painting, and sculpture pleasantly surprise, including the large Ed Paschke and James Rosenquist canvases on permanent display. Beyond maintaining its collection and hosting traveling exhibits, the museum provides support and studios for local artists, and the workspaces are often open to the public; further details are available at the reception desk.

The south bank

To cross to the **south bank** of the river, take the River Taxi ($3 one way, $5 round-trip) from the dock beside the gleaming **Jacksonville Landing** shopping mall, between Water Street and the river. You'll be dropped next to a mile-long pathway called the **Riverwalk**, a downtown boardwalk from where you can view the city's colorful bridges and its skyline. Three blocks on, you'll come to the oversized **Friendship Fountain**, best seen at night when colored lights illuminate its gushing jets. Finally, the **Museum of Science and History**, 1025 Museum Circle (Mon–Fri 10am–5pm, Sat 10am–6pm, Sun 1–6pm; $7, children $5; Ⓣ904/396-7062, Ⓦwww.themosh.org) has educational hands-on exhibits primarily aimed at kids, like the NFL Jacksonville Jaguars Hall of Fame and a planetarium offering hi-tech trips around the cosmos. Meanwhile, parents might be diverted by "Currents of Time," an engaging exhibit tracing the history of northern Florida over several hundred years.

Beyond the museum, traveling south along the western edge of the peninsula will bring you to the **San Marco** neighborhood. Worth a stroll of an hour or two, it's filled with sleepy shops and restaurants that give something of a small-town feel to sprawling Jacksonville.

Beyond downtown

Scattered about Jacksonville's sprawl are a few diverting points of interest, including a couple of reasonable art collections; if you've got a car – and the

Outdoor adventures

If you're interested in exploring out-of-the-way areas in this region, **Outdoor Adventures**, 1625 Emerson St, Jacksonville (Ⓣ904/393-9030, Ⓦwww.outdooradventuresfla.com) runs a series of reasonably priced canoeing, kayaking, cycling, and walking trips throughout an extensive area, ranging from as far afield as the Okefenokee Swamp and Suwanee River down to the Talbot Islands and the rivers and parks around Jacksonville.

time – aim to visit at least the Cummer Museum, the green fields of Metropolitan Park, and the Jacksonville Zoological Gardens.

The Cummer Museum and around

Just south of the Fuller Warren Bridge (I-95) lies the **Cummer Museum of Art and Gardens**, 829 Riverside Ave (Tues & Thurs 10am–9pm, Wed, Fri, & Sat 10am–5pm, Sun noon–5pm; $6, free Tues after 4pm; Ⓣ904/356-6857, Ⓦwww.cummer.org), on the former estate of the wealthy Cummer family. The spacious rooms and sculpture-lined corridors contain works by prominent European masters from the twelfth to nineteenth centuries, but American art is the strongest feature: Edmund Greacen's smoky cityscape *Brooklyn Bridge East River* and Martin Heade's *St Johns River* are particularly moving. The museum's signature piece is Thomas Moran's *Ponce de Leon in Florida*, a striking painting of the explorer's meeting with local Native Americans (though this event never occurred). Also worth lingering over is an extensive collection of eighteenth-century Meissen porcelain. Afterward, take a stroll through the flower-packed formal English and Italianate **gardens**, which roll down to the river's edge, providing an apt view of Jacksonville's sleek office towers.

If you have time to spare, consider taking a short walking tour of the surrounding **Riverside-Avondale district**, home to an eclectic assortment of residential architecture. Georgian Revival, Tudor, Mediterranean, and Prairie School are all represented, amid a number of Gothic Revival churches. All are marked in the walking tour brochure produced by Riverside-Avondale Preservation, 2623 Herschel St (Ⓣ904/389-2449, Ⓦwww.riverside-avondale.com), which can also provide heaps of information on the buildings themselves.

Metropolitan Park and Alltel Stadium

The plot of riverside greenery known as **Metropolitan Park** provides a venue for enjoyable free events most weekends plus some big free rock concerts during spring and fall. In midweek it's often deserted and makes a fine spot for a quiet riverside picnic. The "Northside Connector" NS-20 **bus** stops close by, and the water taxi stops here ($4) on event days. Next door, the 73,000-seat **Alltel Stadium** is home to the NFL's Jacksonville Jaguars (game tickets $20–220; Ⓣ1-877/4-JAGS-TIX, Ⓦwww.jaguars.com) and also the scene of the Florida-Georgia college football clash each November (an excuse for 48 hours of citywide drinking and partying) for which tickets for the actual match are notoriously hard to get.

Jacksonville Zoological Gardens

The **Jacksonville Zoological Gardens**, on Hecksher Drive, just off I-95 north of downtown Jacksonville (daily 9am–5pm; $9.50, children $5; Ⓣ904/757-4463), is hoping to develop into one of the better zoos around and affords its inmates plenty of space to prowl, pose, and strut. A justifiable source of pride are the white rhinos, seldom bred in captivity, which live in the eleven-acre "African veldt." A major new jaguar exhibit is scheduled to open in 2004.

Anheuser-Busch Brewery

After trekking about the US's largest city, you'll inevitably have worked up a thirst, and the **Anheuser-Busch Brewery**, 111 Busch Drive (Mon–Sat 10am–4pm; free; ⓣ904/751-8116), purveyor of Budweiser, would like to quench it for you. After taking the free tour, which follows the Germanic and Czech roots of America's most popular beer, including informative exhibits like a mural on the evolution of beer-can openers, visitors can indulge in the main attraction: free beer.

Eating

Dining selections are scattered all over the city. Try downtown's Jacksonville Landing Mall or the San Marco district for a concentration of choices.

Biscotti's Espresso Café 3556 St Johns Ave ⓣ904/387-2060. Part-coffeehouse, part-restaurant, with Mediterranean specials, large portions, and a superb Sunday brunch.

Bistro Aix 1440 San Marco Blvd ⓣ904/398-1949. Dine on the Mediterranean-style terrace from a range of well-prepared entrees (salads, pizzas, grilled fish, steaks). At lunchtime, $10–15 will buy you anything on the menu; dinner's slightly more costly.

Cool Moose Coffee Company 2708 Park St ⓣ904/381-4242. Sandwiches, wraps, and gourmet coffees served in rustic New England-style surroundings.

Juliette's at the Omni 1615245 W Water St ⓣ904/355-6664. Classy place offering a buffet for breakfast and made-to-order pasta dishes at lunch. Dinner is a combination of expensive American-style entrees and daily specials.

The Loop 4000 St Johns Ave ⓣ904/384-7301. Known for its Chicago- and California-style pizzas (a large pie, with toppings, from $16), *the Loop* serves plenty of other American food.

Matthew's 2107 Hendricks Ave ⓣ904/396-9922. Probably the finest restaurant in the city, four-star *Matthew's* features Australian lamb and Maine lobster among the highlights. Reservations recommended. Expensive.

Mossfire Grill 1537 Margaret St ⓣ904/355-4434. Highly recommended fresh Southwestern fare: try the barbecue shrimp tostada or chicken tortilla soup. This casual and reasonably priced place also has a selection of vegetarian dishes.

Panera Bread Company 1615 Hendricks Ave ⓣ904/306-9600. Gourmet bakery with panini sandwiches, coffee drinks, salads, and of course, dessert.

River City Brewing Company 835 Museum Circle ⓣ904/398-2299. Top-notch home-brews, seafood, and steaks ($15–25), served in an airy space near the Riverwalk.

Southend Brewery and Smokehouse 2 Independent Drive, at Jacksonville Landing ⓣ904/353-1188. This is heaven for those who love the smell of smoke (or the idea of it): meats are smoked or grilled over hickory wood, and pizzas are baked in a wood-burning oven. You can even smoke cigars here.

Wine Cellar 1314 Prudential Drive ⓣ904/398-8989. The ambience is French country at this local favorite, and the classic cuisine (with a few global touches) is best enjoyed in the attractive garden. Over 200 wines available.

Nightlife

Nightlife in Jacksonville is a pale shadow of the rave-ups at the beach (see "The Jacksonville beaches," p.399). You can move directly to interactive and electronic games from dinner elsewhere within *Dave & Busters,* 7025 Salisbury Rd (ⓣ904/296-1525). *Havana-Jax,* 2578 Atlantic Blvd (ⓣ904/399-0609), has live rock groups and the occasional Latin band to spice up its Cuban-American cuisine. There's also the *Art Bar,* 1261 King St (ⓣ904/381-0686), for indie rock and dance, trip-hop, and electronica; and *Jack Rabbits,* 1520 Hendricks Ave (ⓣ904/399-0609), a favorite among rock fanatics for live alternative bands.

Toward Amelia Island

Around thirty miles from Jacksonville lie the barrier islands, of which **Amelia Island** is particularly appealing, that mark Florida's northeast corner. To reach the islands, Hwy-105 will take you from Jacksonville along the north side of the St Johns River, but a much more enjoyable route is Hwy-A1A from the Jacksonville beaches, which crosses the river on the tiny **Mayport ferry** (6.20am–10pm; roughly every 30min; cars $2.75, cyclists and pedestrians $1). During this short voyage, pelicans can be seen swooping overhead to pluck morsels off the nearby shrimp boats.

The Kingsley Plantation

Near the ferry's landing point, Hwy-A1A combines with Hwy-105. Continuing north, you'll soon cross onto Fort George Island and, before long, encounter the entrance to the seemingly endless, tree-lined driveway of the **Kingsley Plantation** (daily 9am–5pm; free), the centerpiece of which is the elegant riverside house bought in 1817 by Scotsman Zephaniah Kingsley – though it's currently closed due to structural instability. The house and its 3000 acres were acquired with the proceeds from slavery, of which Kingsley was an advocate and dealer, amassing a fortune through the import and export of Africans. A pragmatic man, he wrote a treatise on the virtues of a patriarchal slave system more in keeping with the Spanish approach than the extremely brutal methods of the United States; he simply believed that well-fed, happier, and freer (though not free) slaves made better workers. Nonetheless, the restored plantation grounds and some original tabby slave quarters reveal much about the plight of the forced arrivals. Kingsley's remarkable wife, a Senegalese woman, ran the plantation and lived in extravagant style – perhaps compensating for her years as his servant. After returning to Hwy-A1A, keep an eye out for the **Huguenot Memorial Park** (daily 6am–sunset; 50¢ per person) on the east side of the road, another nesting area for Florida's shorebirds, and one of the few parks up north where you can drive on the beach. There's a **campground** here (☎904/251-3335) where you can pitch a tent for $6–8 per night, depending on whether you choose the interior or the riverfront sites.

The Talbot Islands

One mile further on from the park, Hwy-A1A runs through **Little Talbot Island State Park** (daily 8am–sunset; cars $3.25, cyclists and pedestrians $1; ☎904/251-2321), which takes up almost the whole of a thickly forested 3000-acre barrier island inhabited by 194 species of birdlife. The park has two tree-shaded, ocean-facing picnic areas and a superb four-mile **hiking trail**, which winds through a pristine landscape of oak and magnolia trees, wind-beaten sand dunes, and a chunk of the park's five-mile-long beach. **Canoes** can be hired for $4 an hour ($15 a day) and **bikes** for $2 an hour ($10 a day). If you're smitten by the natural charms and want to save the bother of finding accommodation on Amelia Island (see p.409), use the **campground** (☎1-800/326-3521; $16) on the western side of the park beside Myrtle Creek.

Alternatively, carry on across the creek, onto tiny Long Island and over onto **Big Talbot Island**, which has three points of interest. First, **Bluffs Scenic Shoreline** (signposted off the road), where the bluffs have eroded, depositing entire trees on the beach, some of them still standing upright with all their roots intact. Second, the **Black Rock Trail**, a one-and-a-half-mile hike through woods onto the Atlantic coast, to rocks once made from peat. Finally, there's **BEAKS,** the Bird Emergency Aid and Kare Sanctuary, 12084 Houston Ave (Tues–Sun, noon–4pm; Ⓣ904/251-2473, Ⓦwww.beaks.org), which also provides emergency care for other wildlife, 365 days a year. Back on Hwy-A1A, the road continues for a few miles toward Amelia Island.

Amelia Island

Most first-time visitors to Florida would be hard-pressed to locate **AMELIA ISLAND**, at the state's northeastern extremity, which perhaps explains why this finger of land, thirteen miles long and never more than two across, is so peaceful and only modestly commercialized despite the unbroken silver swathe of Atlantic beach gracing its eastern edge. Matching the sands for appeal, **Fernandina Beach**, the island's sole town, was a haunt of pirates before transforming itself into an outpost of Victorian-era high society – a fact proven by its immaculately restored old center.

Some parts of the island are being swallowed by upmarket resorts – much of the southern half is taken up by the *Amelia Island Plantation* (Ⓣ904/261-6161 or 1-888/261-6161, Ⓦwww.aipfl.com), a golf and tennis resort with private walking and biking trails, expensive restaurants, and pricey rooms – but it's still worth coming here. In Fernandina, at least, they still concern themselves more with the size of the shrimp catch than with pandering to tourists.

Fernandina Beach

Hwy-A1A runs more or less right into the effortlessly walkable town of **Fernandina Beach**, whose Victorian heyday is apparent in the restored painted wooden mansions with manicured lawns that line the short main drag, Centre Street. The English spelling of the street name reflects bygone political tug-of-wars (the Spanish named the town but the British named the streets), but an old-fashioned charm and Southern gentility are still very much in evidence. Beside the marina, at the western end of Centre Street and adjacent to a vintage train carriage, you'll spot the useful **visitor center** (Tues–Fri 9am–5pm, Sat 10am–2pm, Mon 10am–5pm; Ⓣ904/261-3248), where you can pick up the booklet *Walking/Driving Tour of Centre St*, produced by the local Chamber of Commerce (Ⓣ1-800/2AMELIA, Ⓦwww.ameliaisland.org), which highlights the forty historical buildings in the neighborhood.

Amelia Island history: the eight flags

Amelia Island is the only place in the US to have been under the rule of **eight flags**. Following settlement by Huguenots in 1562, the Spanish arrived and founded a mission here. This was destroyed in 1702 by the British, who returned forty years later to govern the island (naming it in honor of King George II's daughter). The ensuing Spanish administration was interrupted by the US-backed "Patriots of Amelia Island," who ruled for a day during 1812; the Green Cross of the Florida Republic flew briefly in 1817; and, oddest of all, the Mexican rebel flag appeared over Amelia Island the same year. US rule has been disturbed only by Confederate occupancy during 1861.

These shifts reflect the ebb and flow of allegiances between the great sea-trading powers over many years, as well as the island's geographically desirable location: Amelia Island offered a harbor to ocean-going vessels outside US control but within spitting distance of the American border.

Remarkably, given the present calm, President James Monroe described Fernandina as a "festering fleshpot" after the 1807 US embargo on foreign shipping caused the Spanish-owned town to become a hotbed of smuggling and other illicit activities to circumvent the ban. The acquisition of Florida by the US in 1821 did not diminish Fernandina's importance – this time as a key rail terminal for freight moving between the Atlantic and the Gulf of Mexico. More recently, however, its charm has been impaired by the unfortunate proximity of two smelly paper mills across the Intracoastal Waterway – if the winds are blowing the wrong way, the air carries an earthy sulfurous aroma. The locals, though, shrug it off as the "smell of money."

The Museum of History and around Centre Street

The obvious place to gain insights into the town is the **Museum of History**, 233 S Third St (Mon–Sat 10am–4pm; $5; ☎904/261-7378) – once the county jail – whose scattering of memorabilia is backed up by photographs and maps. The 45-minute **guided tours** (Mon–Sat at 11am & 2pm) of the museum are excellent, informatively covering 4000 years of the island's varied history with humor. Also recommended are the longer **historical walks** (Fri at 3pm, Sat at 10am from the visitor center; suspended June–Aug; $10) and ghost tours ($12), which feature many of the old buildings on and around Centre Street. The longer North and South Fernandina walking tours ($15 each) are conducted by appointment during the summer. Horse-drawn carriage tours are also on offer ($15, children $7.50; ☎904/277-1555), covering downtown, Fort Clinch, and Old Town, the original, funky settlement just to the north.

Even if you miss the tours, **walking around** on your own is far from dull. Centre Street and the immediate area are alive with Victorian-era turrets, twirls, and towers, plus many notable later buildings. Among them, **St Peter's Episcopal Church**, on the corner with Eighth Street, was completed in 1884 by New York architect Robert S. Schuyler, whose name is linked to many local structures and who never used the same style twice. The Gothic used for the church is a long way from the painted folly of the Italianate **Fairbanks House**, also by Schuyler, situated at the corner of Seventh and Cedar streets. This building, designed to look like a Florentine palace with a square tower rising above the center, was commissioned by a newspaper editor as a surprise for his wife, who hated it and refused to step over the threshold – at least according to local legend. Today it has been transformed into a sumptuous bed and breakfast (see "Accommodation," opposite).

The beach

Well suited to swimming and busy with beach sports, the most active of the island's **beaches** is at the eastern end of Fernandina's Atlantic Avenue, a mile from the town center. If you don't mind a long hike with sand between your toes, you can walk along the beach to Fort Clinch State Park, three miles north (see below). In the fall, you might be lucky enough to spot **whales** in the waters off Amelia Island. The right whale, an endangered species, moves into inland waterways to calve.

North to Fort Clinch State Park

After Florida came under US control in 1819, a fort was built on Amelia's northern tip, three miles from Fernandina, to protect seaborne access to Georgia. The fort now forms part of **Fort Clinch State Park** (daily 8am–sunset; cars $3.25, pedestrians and cyclists $1) and provides a home for a gang of

Civil War enthusiasts who pretend they're Union soldiers of 1864, the only time the fort saw action. Entrance to the fort itself costs $2, and the most atmospheric way to see it is with the soldier-guided **candle-lit tour** (most Fridays and Saturdays; $3; reservations essential: ⓣ904/277-7274). With the pseudo–Civil War garrison moaning about their work and meager rations, the tour may sound like a ham job, but in fact it is a convincing, informative – and quite spooky – hour's affair.

The rest of the park can hardly be overlooked: by road, you have to go through three miles of it before reaching the fort, passing an animal reserve (from which overgrown alligators often emerge, so if you do fancy a spot of hiking, stick to the marked 30- and 45-minute **nature trails**) and a turn-off for the stunning 2.5-mile long **beach**, where legions of crab catchers cast their baskets off a long fishing jetty. From both jetty and fort there's an immaculate view of Cumberland Island (only accessible by ferry from St Mary's, on the Georgia mainland, or by canoe or kayak on organized trips run by Outdoor Adventures, ⓣ904/393-9030, see box on p.404), a Georgian nature reserve famed for its wild horses – if you're lucky, a few will be galloping over the island's sands. You might also catch a glimpse of a nuclear-powered submarine gliding toward Cumberland Sound and the massive Kings Bay naval base. **Camping** in the park is available for $18.

Accommodation

While the best way to savor Fernandina's unique historic atmosphere is by staying in one of the town's antique-filled **bed-and-breakfasts**, more ordinary **accommodation** choices are the motels on the way to or on Fletcher Avenue (Hwy-A1A).

1735 House 584 S Fletcher Ave ⓣ904/261-4148 or 1-800/872-8531, ⓦwww.1735house-bb.com. To the east of the Old Town, right on Hwy-A1A and the sugary beach, lies this bed and breakfast, which offers a knotty-pine, nautical-theme ocean pad. ❻

Bailey House 28 S Seventh St ⓣ904/261-5390 or 1-800/251-5390, ⓦwww.bailey-house.com. One of the town's fabulous painted Victorian ladies with turrets and bay windows, this bed and breakfast has ten spacious and well-appointed rooms. ❻

Fairbanks House 227 S Seventh St ⓣ904/277-0500 or 1-800/261-4838, ⓦwww.fairbankshouse.com. This is one of the most historic bed-and-breakfast inns (see opposite). Ask for the top-floor honeymoon suite, with private turret. ❻

Florida House Inn 20 S Third St ⓣ904/261-3300 or 1-800/258-3301, ⓦwww.floridahouseinn.com. At the state's oldest hotel, you can sleep where Ulysses S. Grant and the Carnegies stayed. Children and pets are welcome, and there's also a cozy restaurant and pub onsite (see p.410 for review). ❹

Hampton Inn & Suites 19 S Second St ⓣ904/491-4911 or 1-800/426-7866, ⓦwww.hamptoninn.com. Fernandina's latest grand hotel, directly on the harbor, is harmoniously designed so as not to clash with the surrounding architecture. ❹

The Inn at Fernandina Beach 2707 Sadler Rd ⓣ904/277-2300. This is one of the better budget inns, a little bit out from the center of town. ❹

The Lighthouse 748 Fletcher Ave ⓣ904/261-5878. Book far in advance to secure a room in this small lighthouse, which has four rooms right on the sea. The top floor features a porch that wraps around the building. ❼

Eating and drinking

For its size, the island has an exceptionally good number of **places to eat**, the bulk of them on and around Fernandina's Centre Street. Besides the selections listed overleaf, you'll also find a limited menu of plain and simple dishes at the *Palace Saloon*, 117 Centre St (ⓣ904/261-6320), which claims to have the oldest bar in Florida, forty feet of hand-carved mahogany, built in 1878. You might prefer to save your visit for a night-time **drink**, not least because few other places warrant an after-dark investigation and the *Palace* has live music on weekends. This was the last tavern in the country to close after Prohibition began, taking two years to deplete its supply of spirits.

Beech Street Grill 801 Beech St ⓣ904/277-3662. A good, though expensive option for a fine dining experience. The inventive menu features items such as venison with blackcurrant sauce and local grouper with macadamia crust and curry citrus cream, and the wine list is extensive.

Brett's Waterway Café end of Centre St at the Fernandina Harbor Marina ⓣ904/261-2660. Generous portions of American food accompanied by great views.

Café Karibo 27 N Third St ⓣ904/261-2660. Moderately priced ($5–20) salads, sandwiches, and main dishes are served in a New Orleans-style atmosphere (try the spicy Cajun gumbo). Lunch and dinner served.

Crab Trap 31 N Second St ⓣ904/261-4749. Once past the unappealing poured concrete facade, you'll find tempting dishes such as alligator tail appetizer ($9) and the Crabber's Delight (fish, oysters, shrimp, deviled crab, and scallops; $20).

Down Under Intracoastal Waterway, at A1A, under the Thomas Shave Bridge ⓣ904/261-1001. Locals flock here to savor the fresh local seafood on the outdoor deck. There's usually evening entertainment as well.

Florida House Inn 20 S Third St ⓣ904/261-3300. Rich Southern-style meals served with plenty of hospitality; the biscuits, cornbread, fried chicken, and greens are seldom better. Brunch is a highlight ($10).

The Marina 101 Centre St ⓣ904/261-5130. One of the island's oldest restaurants, with a convivial atmosphere. Choose from cheese grits, eggs, and fried fish at breakfast, or the seafood-based menu at lunch and dinner.

O'Kane's Irish Pub and Eatery 318 Centre St ⓣ904/261-1000. Simple pub fare, best washed down with a cold tap brew.

Travel details

Trains

Jacksonville to: Miami (3 daily; 9-10hr); Orlando (2 or 3 daily; 3hr 30min–4hr 30min); Pensacola (1 on Tues, Thurs, & Sun; 8hr); Tallahassee (1 on Tues, Thurs, & Sun; 3hr 30min); Tampa (1 daily; 5hr).

Buses

Cocoa to: Daytona Beach (4 daily; 1hr 45min); Jacksonville (4 daily; 3hr 45min); Melbourne (6 daily; 35min); Titusville (4 daily; 30min).

Daytona Beach to: Jacksonville (10 daily; 1hr 40min–2hr); Orlando (6 daily; 1hr 30min); St Augustine (7 daily; 1hr).

Jacksonville to: Miami (11 daily; 8–13hr); Orlando (11 daily; 2hr 30min–5hr); St Petersburg (7 daily; 6hr 30min–8hr); Tallahassee (5 daily; 2hr 40min–3hr 40min); Tampa (10 daily; 5hr–6hr 30min).

St Augustine to: Jacksonville (6 daily; 50min).

9

The Panhandle

CHAPTER 9 Highlights

* **The Old City Cemetery** A good starting point for learning about African-American history in Tallahassee. See p.421

* **Havana** It may not be the one in Cuba, but this former tobacco plantation town has its own charms, including some worthy antique shops. See p.426

* **Apalachicola National Forest** The great outdoors reasserts itself in these woods, a world away from the Panhandle's busy tourist beaches – rent a canoe or hike some trails to explore. See p.429

* **Wakulla Springs** The best way to take the waters of this, one of the biggest and deepest natural springs in the world, is on a glass-bottomed boat tour. See p.428

* **Florida Caverns State Park** The deep caverns here, used by Seminole Indians to hide from Andrew Jackson's army, hold magnificent calcite formations. See p.432

* **Seaside** The dollhouse architecture and incredibly manicured streets and lawns of this resort should be seen to be believed. See p.444

* **National Heritage Coastline** The stretch of highway between Pensacola and Navarre beaches holds scenic reef dunes and other visual delights. See p.457

△ Dunes

9

The Panhandle

Butting up against the southernmost borders of both Alabama and Georgia, the long, narrow **Panhandle** has much more in common with the Deep South than it does with the rest of the state. Cosmopolitan sophisticates in Miami and Tampa tell countless jokes lampooning the folksy lifestyles of the people here – undeniably more rural and down-to-earth than their counterparts around the rest of the state – but the Panhandle has more to offer than many give it credit for. You certainly won't get a true picture of Florida without seeing at least some of it.

A century ago, the Panhandle actually *was* Florida. When Miami was still a swamp, **Pensacola**, at the Panhandle's western edge, was a busy port. Fertile soils lured wealthy plantation owners south and helped establish **Tallahassee** as a high-society gathering place and administrative center – a role that, as the state capital, it retains. The great Panhandle forests fueled a timber boom that brought new towns and an unrivaled prosperity, but the decline of cotton, the felling of too many trees, and the building of the East Coast Railroad eventually left the Panhandle high and dry.

Today, the region divides neatly in two. Much of the **inland Panhandle** consists of small farming towns that see few visitors, despite their friendly rhythm, fine examples of Old South architecture, and proximity to springs, sinkholes, and the **Apalachicola National Forest** – perhaps the best place in Florida to disappear into the wilderness. The **coastal Panhandle**, on the other hand, is inundated with tourists who flock in from the southern states and wreak havoc during the riotous student Spring Breaks. Indeed, **Panama City Beach**, while not being the best that the coastal Panhandle has to offer, has arguably become the most popular Spring Break destination in Florida, if not the entire country. Much of the coastline is marked by rows of hotels and condos, but there are also protected areas that are home to some of the finest stretches of unspoiled sand anywhere in the state. The blinding white sands are almost pure quartz, washed down over millions of years from the Appalachian mountains, and they squeak when you walk on them. Not to be outshone, the Gulf of Mexico's waters here are two-tone: emerald green close to the shore and deep blue further out.

Provided you're driving, **getting around** presents few problems. Across the inland Panhandle, **I-10** carries the through traffic, and **US-90** links the little places and many of the natural sights between Tallahassee and Pensacola. It's easy, too, to turn south off I-10 or Hwy-90 and get to the coast in under an hour. The main route along the coast is **US-98**, with a number of smaller, scenic roads leading off it. Several daily Greyhound **buses** connect the bigger centers, but rural and coastal services are fewer, and some parts see no bus servic-

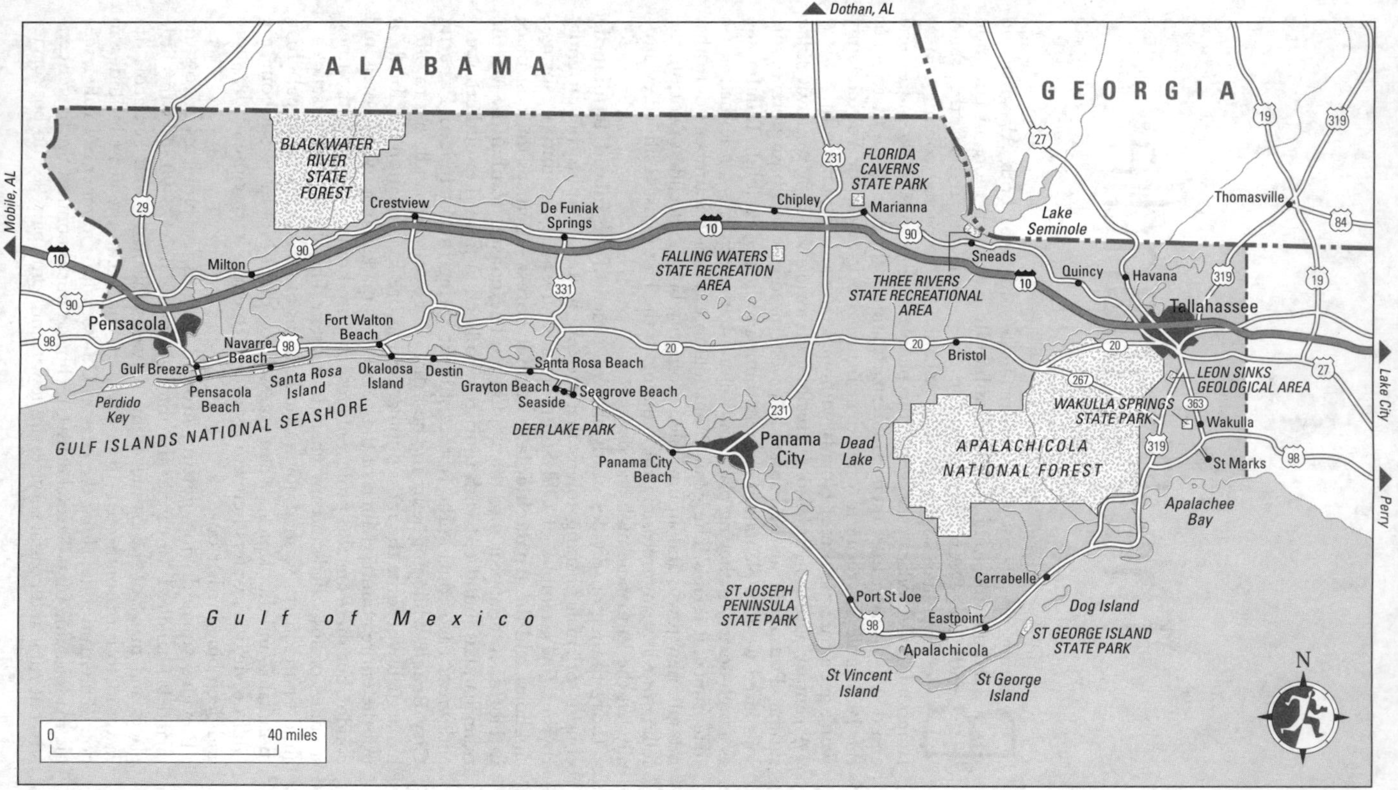
Dothan, AL
Mobile, AL
Lake City
Perry
ALABAMA
GEORGIA
BLACKWATER RIVER STATE FOREST
FLORIDA CAVERNS STATE PARK
FALLING WATERS STATE RECREATION AREA
THREE RIVERS STATE RECREATIONAL AREA
LEON SINKS GEOLOGICAL AREA
WAKULLA SPRINGS STATE PARK
APALACHICOLA NATIONAL FOREST
DEER LAKE PARK
GULF ISLANDS NATIONAL SEASHORE
ST JOSEPH PENINSULA STATE PARK
ST GEORGE ISLAND STATE PARK
Lake Seminole
Thomasville
Tallahassee
Havana
Quincy
Sneads
Marianna
Chipley
Bristol
De Funiak Springs
Crestview
Milton
Pensacola
Gulf Breeze
Pensacola Beach
Navarre Beach
Santa Rosa Island
Fort Walton Beach
Okaloosa Island
Destin
Santa Rosa Beach
Grayton Beach
Seaside
Seagrove Beach
Panama City Beach
Panama City
Dead Lake
Port St Joe
Apalachicola
Eastpoint
Carrabelle
Dog Island
St George Island
St Vincent Island
Perdido Key
Wakulla
St Marks
Apalachee Bay
Gulf of Mexico
10
90
98
29
331
20
231
267
363
319
19
27
84
0
40 miles
N

es at all. The Los Angeles–Jacksonville Amtrak **train** service *Sunset Limited* crosses the Panhandle, stopping at Tallahassee and Pensacola three times a week.

The inland Panhandle

Vast tracts of oak and pine trees, dozens of winding rivers, and a handful of moderately sized agricultural bases make much of the **inland Panhandle** powerfully evocative of Florida in the days before mass tourism took hold – and this distinct character is the main reason for making the effort to visit this part of the state. Despite the presence of the sociable state capital, **Tallahassee**, it's the insular rural communities strung along US-90 – between Tallahassee and the busy coastal city of **Pensacola** – that set the tone of the region. These small towns, including **Marianna**, **Chipley**, and **De Funiak Springs**, all grew rich from the timber industry at the turn of the twentieth century and now pull their earnings by working some of the richest soil in Florida. Thanks to some architectural gems, they warrant a look as you pass through to the area's compelling natural features, which include the state's only explorable caverns and two massive forests.

Tallahassee and around

State capital it may be, but **TALLAHASSEE** is a provincial city of oak trees and soft hills that won't take more than two days to explore in full. Around its small grid of central streets – where you'll find plenty of reminders of Florida's formative years – briefcase-clutching bureaucrats mingle with some of Florida State University's 25,000 students, who brighten the mood considerably and keep the city awake late into the night.

Though built on the site of an important prehistoric meeting place and taking its name from Apalachee Indian (*talwa* meaning "town," and *ahassee* meaning "old"), Tallahassee's **history** really begins with Florida's incorporation into the US and the search for an administrative base between the former regional capitals, Pensacola and St Augustine. Once this site was chosen, the local Native Americans – the Tamali tribe – were unceremoniously dispatched to make room for a trio of log cabins in which the first Florida government sat in 1823.

The scene of every major wrangle in Florida politics – including the controversial "dimpled ballot" recount of the 2000 presidential election – and the home of an ever-expanding white-collar workforce handling the paperwork of one of the country's fastest-growing states, Tallahassee's own fortunes have been hindered by the lightning-paced development of south Florida. Oddly distanced from most of the people it governs, the city has a slow tempo and a strong sense of the past.

Arrival, information, and getting around

I-10 cuts across Tallahassee's northern perimeter; turning off along Monroe Street takes you into downtown Tallahassee. **US-90** (known as Tennessee St)

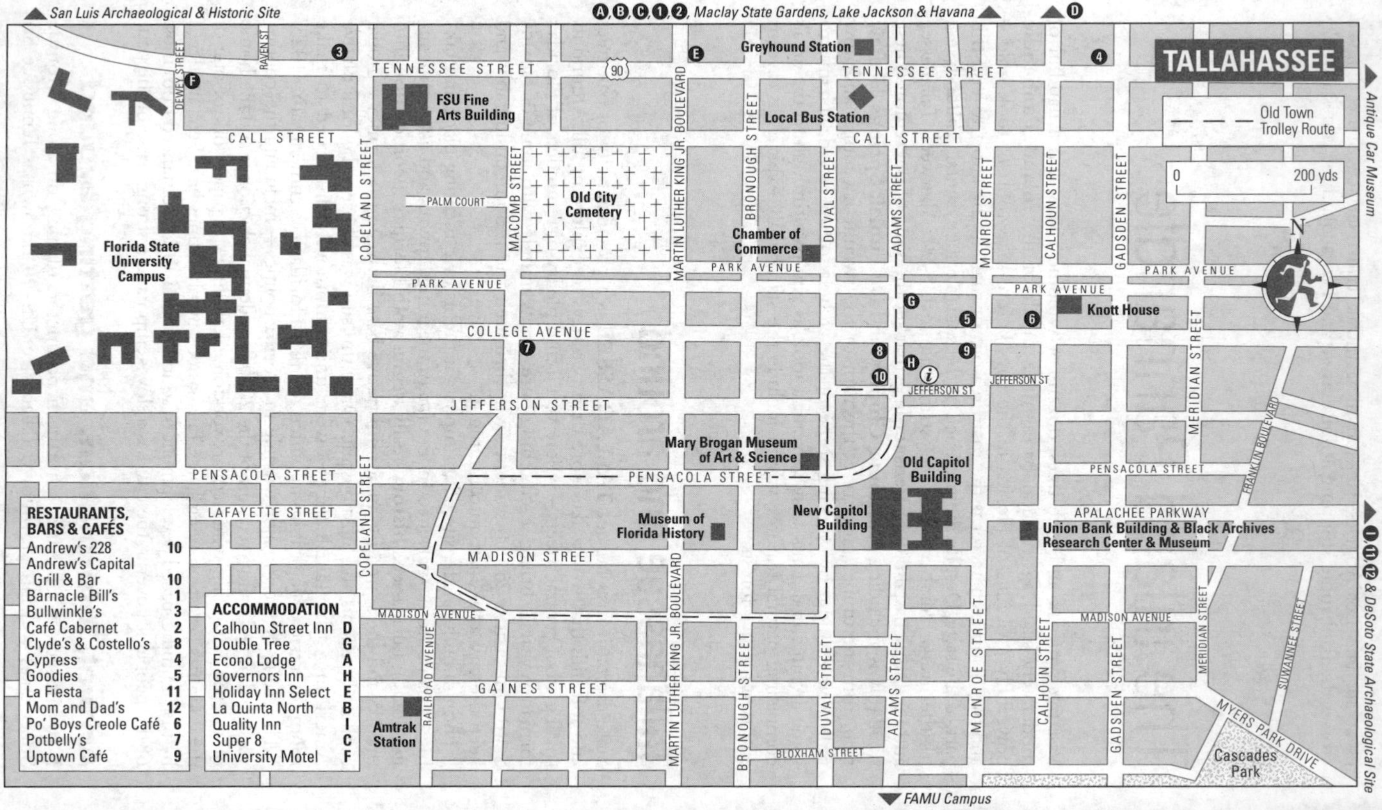
TALLAHASSEE
Old Town Trolley Route
0 200 yds
N
San Luis Archaeological & Historic Site
A, B, C, 1, 2, Maclay State Gardens, Lake Jackson & Havana
D
Antique Car Museum
I, 11, 12 & DeSoto State Archaeological Site
FAMU Campus
TENNESSEE STREET
CALL STREET
PARK AVENUE
COLLEGE AVENUE
JEFFERSON STREET
JEFFERSON ST
PENSACOLA STREET
LAFAYETTE STREET
MADISON STREET
MADISON AVENUE
GAINES STREET
BLOXHAM STREET
APALACHEE PARKWAY
FRANKLIN BOULEVARD
SUWANNEE STREET
MYERS PARK DRIVE
DEWEY STREET
RAVEN ST
COPELAND STREET
MACOMB STREET
PALM COURT
MARTIN LUTHER KING JR. BOULEVARD
BRONOUGH STREET
DUVAL STREET
ADAMS STREET
MONROE STREET
CALHOUN STREET
GADSDEN STREET
MERIDIAN STREET
RAILROAD AVENUE
90
Greyhound Station
Local Bus Station
FSU Fine Arts Building
Old City Cemetery
Florida State University Campus
Chamber of Commerce
Knott House
Mary Brogan Museum of Art & Science
Old Capitol Building
New Capitol Building
Museum of Florida History
Union Bank Building & Black Archives Research Center & Museum
Amtrak Station
Cascades Park
RESTAURANTS, BARS & CAFÉS
Andrew's 228 10
Andrew's Capital Grill & Bar 10
Barnacle Bill's 1
Bullwinkle's 3
Café Cabernet 2
Clyde's & Costello's 8
Cypress 4
Goodies 5
La Fiesta 11
Mom and Dad's 12
Po' Boys Creole Café 6
Potbelly's 7
Uptown Café 9
ACCOMMODATION
Calhoun Street Inn D
Double Tree G
Econo Lodge A
Governors Inn H
Holiday Inn Select E
La Quinta North B
Quality Inn I
Super 8 C
University Motel F

and **US-27** (Apalachee Parkway) are more central – arriving in or close to downtown. Coming by **bus** presents few problems. The Greyhound terminal is at 112 W Tennessee St (Ⓣ850/222-4249 or 1-800/231-2222), within walking distance of downtown and opposite the local bus station. The **train** station is housed in an 1855 building at the intersection of Gaines Street and Railroad Avenue (Ⓣ850/224-2779 or 1-800/872-7245), one block from Railroad Square in downtown Tallahassee. Tallahassee's **airport** is twelve miles southwest of Tallahassee (Ⓣ850/891-7800); frustratingly, no public transport services link it to the city. A **taxi** from the airport to the center will cost around $14 (try City Taxi Ⓣ850/562-4222, or Yellow Cab Ⓣ850/580-8080); some motels offer a free pick-up service.

Information

The **Chamber of Commerce**, 100 N Duval St (Mon–Fri 8am–5pm; Ⓣ850/224-8116), has a limited number of leaflets relating to the city and the surrounding area. A better option is the **Tallahassee Area Visitor Information Center**, 106 E Jefferson St (Mon–Fri 8am–5pm, Sat 9am–2pm; Ⓣ850/413-9200 or 1-800/628-2866, Ⓦwww.seetallahassee.com), which stocks large numbers of leaflets and guides for the city and also has a courtesy phone for making local calls. While there, be sure to pick up the engaging *Walking Guide to Historic Downtown Tallahassee* booklet, a free, comprehensive guide to the buildings and history of the area. For material covering the rest of the Panhandle – and much of the rest of the state – use the **FlaUSA Visitor Information Center** (Mon–Fri 8am–5pm) on the first floor of the New Capitol Building (see "Downtown Tallahassee," p.418).

Getting around

Downtown Tallahassee can easily be seen **on foot. Local buses** (TalTran Ⓣ850/891-5200, Ⓦwww.talgov.com) need only be used to reach outlying destinations, and rides cost $1 per journey. Collect a route map and timetable from the bus station (officially known as Transfer Plaza) at the corner of Tennessee and Duval streets. You can get a **free ride** into downtown Tallahassee from the bus station with the **Old Town Trolley**, which runs to the Civic Center (near the New Capitol Building) and back at ten-minute intervals on weekdays between 7am and 6pm; hop on at any of the "Trolley Stop" signs. The *Old Town Trolley Tour Guide* leaflet also gives a brief history of each of the eighteen stops and their surrounds. Despite the area's hills, there is plenty of good **cycling** terrain. Rent a bike from Tec's Bicycle Sport, 672 Gaines St (Ⓣ850/681-6979).

Accommodation

Finding **accommodation** in Tallahassee is only a problem during two periods: the sixty-day sitting of the state legislature beginning with the first Tuesday in March – if you're arriving then, try to turn up on a Friday or Saturday when the power-brokers have gone home – and on fall weekends when the Seminoles (Florida State University's immensely well-supported football team) are playing at home. If you can't avoid these periods, book well ahead. The Tallahassee Area Visitor Information Center has a hotel hotline (Ⓣ850/488-BEDS) that gives updated hourly information on room availability during peak periods. The cheapest **hotels** and **motels** are on North Monroe Street about three miles north of downtown.

There are no **campgrounds** within the city. The nearest place you can pitch a tent is the *Tallahassee RV Park*, 6504 Mahan Drive, which is also US-90

(Ⓣ850/878-7641; $25). Alternatively, try the *Tallahassee East KOA* in Monticello (Ⓣ850/997-3890), where you can either pitch a tent for $15 or rent a Kamping Kabin for $32.

Calhoun Street Inn 525 N Calhoun St Ⓣ850/425-5095, Ⓦwww.bbonline.com/fl/calhounstreet. Set in a Colonial Revival–style house on a tree-lined, historic street, this bed and breakfast is only a short walk from downtown. Each room features antique furniture, pine floors, and original fireplaces. ❸

Double Tree 101 S Adams St Ⓣ850/224-5000. Large, business-oriented hotel smack in the middle of downtown. Nondrivers will appreciate the complimentary airport shuttle; drivers the free parking in the hotel garage. ❹

Econo Lodge 2681 N Monroe St Ⓣ850/385-6155 or 1-800/553-2666. This basic chain motel offers complimentary continental breakfasts. All rooms have a microwave and a refrigerator, and there's a shopping mall within walking distance for stocking up on groceries and other supplies. ❷

Governors Inn 209 S Adams St Ⓣ850/681-6855 or 1-800/342-7717. A good alternative to the chain hotels, this luxurious downtown inn is well worth splurging for. The rooms are decorated with antique furniture, reflecting the period of the governor each is named for. Free cocktails and newspapers are also included. Book in advance. ❻

Holiday Inn Select 316 W Tennessee St Ⓣ850/222-9555 or 1-800/648-6135. Good facilities (pool, gym, quality restaurant, free local calls, and the like) and an excellent location (within easy walking distance of both downtown and the FSU campus) make this a good choice for visiting parents, business people, and tourists. ❺

La Quinta North 2905 N Monroe St Ⓣ850/385-7172 or 1-800/687-6667. This motel has much bigger and better rooms than the exterior suggests. If you'd prefer to stay in south Tallahassee, there's *La Quinta South* at 2850 Apalachee Parkway (US-27) Ⓣ850/878-5099. ❸

Quality Inn 2020 Apalachee Parkway (US-27) Ⓣ850/877-4437. Bright, modern rooms, free evening cocktails, and complimentary use of the facilities at the nearby YMCA are reasons for choosing this slightly upscale chain hotel. ❹

Super 8 2702 N Monroe St Ⓣ850/386-8818 or 1-800/800-8000. A reasonable option for the budget traveler, this motel offers simple rooms with basic amenities. ❷

University Motel 691 W Tennessee St Ⓣ850/224-8161, Ⓦwww.universitymotel.com. Looking a bit like another student dorm from the outside, this motel offers reasonably comfortable rooms on the perimeter of the FSU campus. ❷

Downtown Tallahassee

The soul of Tallahassee is the mile-square downtown area, where the main targets – the two Capitol Buildings, the Museum of Florida History, and the two universities – are within walking distance of the peaceful main drag: Adams Street, whose restored Twenties storefronts more often than not conceal attorneys' offices. A unique and charming feature of downtown Tallahassee is the **canopy roads**, thoroughfares lined with oak trees, whose branches, heavy with Spanish moss, arch across the road. Next to the allure of these splendid tree corridors – the best examples being Miccosukee, Centerville, Old St Augustine, Meridian, and Old Bainbridge roads – the **New Capitol Building**, at the junction of Apalachee Parkway and Monroe Street (Mon–Fri 8am–5pm; free), is an eyesore. Vertical vents make the seat of Florida's legal system resemble a gigantic air-conditioning unit. The only way to escape the sight of the structure, unveiled to much outrage in 1977, is to go inside, where the 22nd-floor observation level provides an unobstructed view over Tallahassee and its environs; on a clear day you can even see the Gulf of Mexico. If you're visiting from mid-February to April, stop off at the fifth floor for a glance at the state house of representatives or the senate in action.

Florida's growing army of bureaucrats made the New Capitol Building necessary. Previously, they'd been crammed into the **Old Capitol Building** (Mon–Fri 9am–4.30pm, Sat 10am–4.30pm, Sun noon–4.30pm; free; main entrance facing Apalachee Parkway), an 1845 Greek Revival building that stands in the shadow of its replacement. Designed on a more human scale than its modern counterpart, with playful red and white awnings over its windows, it's hard to imagine that the Old Capitol's walls once echoed with the decisions that shaped modern Florida. Proof is provided, however, by the recently opened political history **museum**, where the various exhibits lift the lid on the state's juiciest scandals and controversies. On display in a glass case is a ballot used for the contested 2000 Presidential election – with all of its chads successfully punched out – while elsewhere you can test your skills as a news reporter on camera or browse a small art gallery if you need a bit of creative relief from all the politics.

Along Apalachee Parkway from the Old Capitol's entrance is the nineteenth-century **Union Bank Building**. The bank's past has been unsteady: going bust in the 1850s after giving farmers too much credit, reopening to administer the financial needs of emancipated slaves after the Civil War, and later serving variously as a shoe factory, a bakery, and a cosmetics shop.

Black Archives Research Center and Museum at the Union Bank

Today, the Union Bank Building serves as an extension of the Florida Agricultural and Mechanical University's **Black Archives Research Center and Museum** (Mon–Fri 9am–4pm; free; ⓣ850/561-2603), and chronicles the history and persecution of Florida's black community. The first black Floridians arrived with Spanish explorers in the sixteenth century, and many more came as runaways in the early nineteenth century, taking refuge among the Creek and Seminole Indians. The museum explores their stories and the many facets of black culture through documents and displays. Among the most intriguing is a collection of black piggy banks depicting derogatory images of African-Americans, which were popular in some white households until the 1960s. Another exhibit charts the rise of Madame C.J. Walker, the first black female millionaire, whose line of beauty products, among other things, helped African-American women straighten their hair. In addition to tributes to such black American entertainers as Josephine Baker, the museum has some chilling Ku Klux Klan memorabilia, including an original Klan sword and a fairly recent application for membership, which proves the Klan is far from being ancient history; in 1997, the Klan won permission to march through town, but was turned back by protesting students on Monroe Street.

The Mary Brogan Museum of Art and Science

Situated one block behind the Capitol buildings is the **Mary Brogan Museum of Art and Science**, 350 S Duval St (Mon–Sat 10am–5pm, Sun 1–5pm; $6; ⓣ850/513-0700, ⓦwww.thebrogan.org), a unique institution offering a hands-on science center combined with rotating exhibitions of national art. There aren't many places where you can explore freshwater and marine fish in an Eco Lab one minute and view an exhibition of Impressionist art the next. In addition, the museum receives touring science shows and has a very active educational program providing lots of opportunities to learn more about the displays. There's also an interesting gift shop where you can buy a 5¢ eraser or a $7000 work of art made from beautiful colored glass.

The Museum of Florida History

For a well-rounded history – easily the fullest account of Florida's past anywhere in the state – visit the **Museum of Florida History**, 500 S Bronough St (Mon–Fri 9am–4.30pm, Sat 10am–4.30pm, Sun noon–4.30pm; free;

☎850/488-1484, Ⓦdhr.dos.state.fl.us/museum). Detailed accounts of Paleo-Indian settlements and the significance of their burial and temple mounds – some of which have been found on the edge of Tallahassee (see "Around Tallahassee," p.425) – provide valuable insights into Florida's prehistory. The colonialist crusades of the Spanish, both in Florida and across South and Central America, are also outlined by means of copious finds. However, other than portraits of hard-faced Seminole chiefs, whose Native American tribes were driven south into Florida backcountry, there's disappointingly little on the nineteenth-century Seminole Wars – one of the sadder and bloodier skeletons in Florida's closet. There's plenty, though, on the railroads that made Florida a winter resort for wealthy northerners around the turn of the century, and on the subsequent arrival of the "tin can tourists," whose nickname refers to the rickety Ford camper vans (forerunners of the modern Recreational Vehicles) they drove to what had by then been named the "Sunshine State."

Florida State University

West from Adams Street, graffiti-coated fraternity and sorority houses along College Avenue line the approach to **Florida State University (FSU)**. The institution has long enjoyed a strong reputation for its humanities courses, taught from the late 1800s in the Collegiate Gothic classrooms you'll see as you enter the wrought-iron gates, but has recently switched its emphasis to science and business, and the newer buildings on the far side of the campus have far less character. Shady oaks and palm trees make the grounds a pleasant place for a stroll, but there's little cause to linger. The student art of the **University Museum of Fine Arts** (Mon–Fri 9am–4pm; free; ☎850/644-6836), in the Fine Arts Building, might consume a few minutes, but you'd be better occupied rummaging around inside Bill's Bookstore, just across Call Street at 111 S Copeland St (☎850/224-3178), where the large stock includes many student cast-offs at reduced prices.

Despite being poorer, the more interesting of Tallahassee's universities is the Florida Agricultural and Mechanical University (Ⓦwww.famu.edu), about a mile south of the Capitol Buildings on Wahnish Avenue and Gamble Street. Founded in 1887 as the State Normal College for Colored Students, the university remains a major black educational center. Housed in the historic Carnegie Library on campus is the **Black Archives Research Center and Museum** (see p.419).

The Knott House

Another important landmark in Florida's black history, and one of the city's best-restored Victorian homes, is the **Knott House Museum**, 301 E Park Ave (Wed–Fri 1–3pm, Sat 10am–3pm; free; ☎850/922-2459), which was built by a free black in 1843 and later became home to Florida's first black physician. Florida's slaves were officially emancipated in May 1865 by a proclamation read from the steps of this very house. The house takes its name, however, from the Knotts, a white couple who bought it in 1928. William Knott, the state treasurer during a period of economic calamity (Florida had been devastated by two hurricanes just as the country entered the Depression), became one of Florida's most respected and influential politicians until his retirement in 1941. His wife, Luella, meanwhile, devoted her energies to the temperance movement (partly through her efforts, alcohol was banned in Tallahassee for a fifty-year period) and to writing moralistic poems, many of which you'll see attached to the antiques and furnishings that fill this intriguing relic and which give it the nickname of "the house that rhymes." The absence of intrusive ropes

Panhandle plantations

The largest concentration of plantations in the US lies between Tallahassee and the Georgia town of Thomasville, 28 miles to the northeast. In this relatively small section of the Panhandle, some seventy plantations – most of them cotton-growing – occupy an area totaling 300,000 acres, a reminder that Tallahassee's pre–Civil War days were notable less for their political events than for the wealthy people that the town managed to attract. Plantation owners included descendants of the first three US presidents and a nephew of Napoleon Bonaparte, and their houses were the epitome of fine Southern living. Several of the more notable addresses have been preserved for public viewing, of which **Goodwood**, about two miles east of downtown Tallahassee at 1600 Miccosukee Road (tours Tues–Fri 10am–4pm, Sat 10am–2pm; $5; ⓣ850/877-4202), is one of the more elaborate examples, situated in attractive grounds with plenty of trees. All of the antiques on display were actually in use at one point or another during the 130-year period when the house was occupied, and they range from stately mirrors to a bath painted with flowers, reflecting the diverse tastes of the various owners. Five miles south of Thomasville (and still in Georgia), **Pebble Hill** provides another good opportunity to see how the well-off of the time spent their money (see p.426), while **Bellevue**, a more modest 1840s plantation house that is part of the Tallahassee Museum of History and Natural Science (see p.425), was once home to George Washington's great-grandniece.

cordoning off the exhibits allows for an unusually intimate visit of the house and its history. Guided tours are available on the hour.

Old City Cemetery

A somewhat different perspective on Tallahassee's past is provided by walking around the **Old City Cemetery**, between Macomb Street and Martin Luther King Jr Boulevard (daily sunrise–sunset; free), which was established outside the city's original boundaries in 1829 and restored in 1991. Its layout, consisting of four quadrants, is a striking testament to segregation, even in death. Graves of Union soldiers lie in the southwest quarter, while those of Confederates are kept at a distance in the southeast portion; slaves and free blacks were consigned to the western half of the ground, while whites occupied the eastern part. Among the names marked on gravestones, you'll find many of Tallahassee's former leading figures: their stories are told in an informative leaflet, *Walking Tour of Old City Cemetery*, available at the Tallahassee Area Visitor Information Center (see p.417).

Eating

Tallahassee's **eating** options reflect the abiding presence of time-pressed bureaucrats and cash-strapped students. The downtown area is full of places to grab a sandwich or salad at lunchtimes, while restaurants serving reasonably priced, stomach-lining fare are most plentiful around the town's two college campuses. There is often live music at these establishments, which tend to become more bar than restaurant as the evening progresses, and while upscale dining can be found, such places remain the exception rather than the rule.

Andrew's 228 228 S Adams St. Fancier and more expensive than its near-namesake (the *Capital Grill & Bar*, see opposite), this elegant restaurant includes items such as tempura fried oysters and succulent roast lamb.

Andrew's Capital Grill & Bar (same address as *Andrew's 228*) ⓣ850/222-3444. A great lunch option with plenty of seating indoors and out. Choose from burgers and various chicken and pasta dishes, as well as a weekday brunch buffet.

Barnacle Bill's 1830 N Monroe St ⓣ850/385-8734. Low-cost seafood restaurant with a riotous atmosphere and constant music, much of it from the Fifties.

Café Cabernet 1019 N Monroe St ⓣ850/224-0322. A good choice for light, inexpensive California-style cuisine, this café also has one of the biggest wine selections in town. Live jazz can be heard here in the evening.

Capital Steak House in the *Holiday Inn Select*, 316 W Tennessee St ⓣ850/222-9555. Even confirmed white meat-eaters are bound to give this steak house rave reviews for its high-quality Angus beef. Count on spending $20 and up for a steak dinner. Some seafood is also available.

Cypress 320 E Tennessee St ⓣ850/513-1100. This small, rather chic and trendy option offers a Southern take on upscale dining, with seafood grits and the like replacing the more conventional side items.

Goodies 116 E College Ave ⓣ850/681-3888. One of the few places serving all-day breakfasts in downtown. The lunchtime sandwiches are tasty, if a little small and expensive.

Kool Beanz Café 921 Thomasville Rd ⓣ850/224-2466. Original and pricey starters, such as smoked rabbit and andouille gumbo, are followed by entrees like pecan-crusted mahimahi and crawfish tacos. Service is variable and be warned – the spice levels are set on hot. Closed Sun.

La Fiesta 2329 Apalachee Parkway ⓣ850/656-3392. Try this eatery for the very best Mexican food in the city. The number of cars outside at lunchtime gives away how good the food is.

Mom and Dad's 4175 Apalachee Parkway ⓣ850/877-4518. Delicious and affordable home-made Italian food served in a family atmosphere just outside downtown. Closed Sun–Mon.

Paradise Grill 1406 N Meridian Rd ⓣ850/224-2742. This cheap to moderately priced eatery is a fun place to go for seafood, gumbo, and British beer. Also has live music (see p.423).

Po' Boys Creole Café 224 E College Ave ⓣ850/224-5400, ⓦwww.poboys.com. A range of Creole delights such as jammin' jambalaya and Carmen's red beans and rice, plus a good selection of seafood is available here, generally for under $10. This restaurant is also one of Tallahassee's most popular live music venues (see below).

Uptown Café 111 E College Ave ⓣ850/222-3253. This homey café, complete with checkered tablecloths, has reasonably priced sandwiches and salads at lunchtime and various breakfast items.

Nightlife

Bolstered by its students, Tallahassee has a strong **nightlife** scene, with a leaning toward social drinking and live rock music (see below). There's also **comedy** at the Comedy Zone, *Ramada Inn*, 2900 N Monroe St (ⓣ850/386-1027), and a fair amount of **theater**, headed by the student productions at the University Theater on the FSU campus (box office Mon–Fri 11am–5.30pm; ⓣ850/644-6500), and the Tallahassee Little Theater, 1861 Thomasville Rd (ⓣ850/224-8474). Literary events are regularly held at Borders bookstore, 1302 Apalachee Parkway, which is also a great place to shop for books and music until 11pm. Find out **what's on** from the "Limelights" section of the Friday *Tallahassee Democrat* newspaper; the *Florida Flambeau*, the FSU student paper, publishes listings and recommendations; or, for live music details, listen to radio station WFSU at 89.7 FM.

Bars

Calico Jack's 2745 Capitol Circle NE ⓣ850/385-6653. Beer, oysters, and stomping Southern rock and roll records are featured here.

Clyde's & Costello's 210 S Adams St ⓣ850/224-2173. Pulls a smart and very cliquey crowd, which grows a bit rowdy during the early-evening happy hours. Friday nights are popular with students, no doubt on account of the free draft beer.

Halligan's 1700 Halstead Blvd, in Keiser Common ⓣ850/668-7665. This joint, north of downtown, is popular for its pool tables and chilled mugs of beer.

Po' Boys Creole Café 224 E College Ave ⓣ850/224-5400. Creole and acoustic music sets nicely complement the drink specials in this collegiate bar.

Potbelly's 455 W College Ave ⓣ850/224-2233. On the frat house–filled approach to the FSU campus, this rather grubby bar – with a stage for live music – is a major student watering hole.

Live music and clubs

American Legion Hall 229 Lake Ella Drive ⓣ850/222-3382. For a taste of the past, try this venue, which hosts a big-band dance night every Tuesday. The accent is on Latin music on Mondays and old-fashioned country the rest of the week.

Beta Bar 809 Railroad Ave St ⓣ850/425-2697. Showcases known and unknown indie rock acts, with covers ranging from $5 to $10.

Bullwinkle's 620 W Tennessee St ⓣ850/224-0651. Rock and blues dominate in this log-cabin-like setting, which also features DJs mixing the favorite dance music of the moment.

Late Night Library 809 Gay St ⓣ850/224-2429. At the apex of the nightclub scene, this cool dance-music club caters to a college crowd. Other musical genres, such as jazz, make for a mellower mood on some evenings. Dress-code and strict ID-checking are enforced.

Leon County Civic Center at the corner of Pensacola Street and Martin Luther King Jr Blvd ⓣ850/222-0400, ⓦwww.tlcc.org. Major touring acts play here – as does the FSU basketball team.

The Moon 1020 E Lafayette St ⓣ850/222-6666, ⓦwww.moonevents.com. Come for the big-name bands or Friday night's "Stetsons on the Moon" – a country music extravaganza with line dancing and much thigh slapping.

Paradise Grill 1406 Meridian Rd ⓣ850/224-2742. Popular with the 25-plus age group, with karaoke on Wed and live bands on Fri & Sat.

Gay clubs and bars

Brothers 926 W Tharpe St ⓣ850/386-2399, ⓦwww.brothersnightclub.com/brothers. Touted as a "pan-sexual playground," this design-conscious venue draws a friendly crowd and is almost exclusively gay on Sun, Thurs, Fri, and especially Sat when there is a drag show, The rest of the week pulls in a mixed clientele.

Club Jade 2122 W Pensacola St ⓣ850/574-1105. More of a lounge than a club, again with live drag shows on Saturdays. A good place to meet lesbians.

Listings

Art galleries Tallahassee has a credible arts scene centered around Railroad Square, close to the junction of Springhill Road and Gaines Street near the FSU campus. You'll find some innovative galleries here, and several local artists have open studios. Other contemporary art showcases include Nomads, 508 W Gaines St (ⓣ850/681-3222); The 621 Gallery, 621 Industrial Drive (ⓣ850/224-6163); and LeMoyne Art Foundation, 125 Gadsden St (ⓣ850/222-8800), which has an art museum and sculpture garden (Tues–Sat 10am–5pm, Sun 1–5pm; $1).

Car rental Most companies have branches at the airport (see p.417), and at the following locations: Avis, 3300 Capitol Circle (ⓣ850/576-4133); Budget, 628 N Monroe St (ⓣ850/915-0600); Lucky's, 2539 W Tennessee St (ⓣ850/575-0632); and Thrifty Car Rental, 1385 Blountstown Hwy (ⓣ850/576-7368).

Hospital Nonemergencies: Tallahassee Regional Medical Center, 1300 Miccosukee Rd ⓣ850/431-1155.

Pharmacy Walgreens, in the Tallahassee Mall, 2415 N Monroe St (ⓣ850/385-7145), open Mon–Sat 10am–9pm, Sun 12.30–5.30pm.

Sports Tickets for FSU baseball (March–May) and football (Sept–Nov) matches are on sale at the stadiums two hours before the games begin: ⓣ850/644-1073 and ⓣ850/644-1830 respectively. For info on FAMU sports teams, all known as the Rattlers, call ⓣ850/599-3200. Check the local telephone book for more details.

Western Union The most convenient location is at the Greyhound bus station (see p.417). Call ⓣ1-800/325-6000 for other locations.

Around Tallahassee

Scattered around the fringes of Tallahassee are half a dozen diverse spots that deserve brief visits, among them a remarkable antique car museum, prehistoric mounds, archaeological sites, and lakeside gardens. All are easily accessible by car, though most are much harder to reach by bus.

The Tallahassee Antique Car Museum

The **Tallahassee Antique Car Museum**, 3550 Mahan Drive (Mon–Sat 10am–5pm, Sun noon–5pm; $7.50, children $4; ⓣ850/942-0137, ⓦwww.tacm.com), is well worth the three-mile drive east along Tennessee Street, which turns into Mahan Drive. The museum's owner, DeVeo Moore, began his career modestly by shoeing horses. But through quiet determination, which inspires admiration or distaste depending on whom you ask in Tallahassee, he is now one of the

△ The Panhandle

region's richest men: selling just one of his businesses in early 1998 netted $37.5 million. The biggest crowd-puller in the collection is the gleaming 21-foot-long Batmobile from the Tim Burton *Batman* movie, bought for $500,000 and complete with Batman's suits and gloves and a flame-thrower attachment. While the most valuable car in the collection is a $1.2 million 1931 Duesenberg Model J, the most intriguing specimen is an 1860-built horse-drawn hearse believed to have carried Abraham Lincoln to his final resting place. The consummate collector, Moore didn't limit his collecting to automobiles. Among the eclectic exhibits are "anti-colic" baby bottles and whole rooms full of scooters and cash registers.

The San Luis and de Soto archaeological sites

Slowly being unearthed at the **San Luis Archaeological and Historic Site**, 2020 W Mission Rd, about three miles west of downtown Tallahassee (bus #21), the village of San Luis de Talimali was a hub of the seventeenth-century Spanish mission system, second only to St Augustine. At its zenith in 1675, its population numbered 1400. Stop by the **Visitor Center** (Tues–Sun 10am–4.30pm; free; ⓣ850/487-3655) for a general explanation and to see some of the finds. On some weekends, period-attired individuals re-enact village life – it sounds tacky but can be fun.

The **de Soto State Archaeological Site**, two miles east of downtown Tallahassee at the corner of Goodbody Lane and Lafayette Street (ⓣ850/922-6007), is where Spanish explorer Hernando de Soto is thought to have set up camp in 1539 and held the first Christmas celebration in North American history. The historical associations are more dramatic here than at the San Luis site, but there's much less tangible evidence of the past and the site is in fact closed to the public except for special events such as January's "De Soto's Winter Encampment," when exhibits, crafts, and various demonstrations bring to life what De Soto's sojourn must have been like. All there is to actually see is a few holes in the ground and it's not at all an essential stop even when it's open. For more information on the de Soto expedition, which was the first European team to cross the Mississippi River, see Contexts, p.461.

Tallahassee Museum of History and Natural Science

Three miles southwest of the city, the **Tallahassee Museum of History and Natural Science**, off Lake Bradford Road (bus #15) at 3945 Museum Drive (Mon–Sat 9am–5pm, Sun 12.30–5pm; $7; ⓣ850/576-1636, ⓦwww.tallahasseemuseum.org), is aimed primarily at kids, though it could fill an hour even if you don't have young minds to stimulate. The centerpiece is a working nineteenth-century-style farm, complete with cows and wandering roosters. Elsewhere, there's a short nature walk, a few cases of snakes, and a couple of old buildings of moderate note: a 1937 Baptist church, a vintage schoolhouse, and a plantation house (see box, p.421).

Maclay State Gardens

For a lazy half-day, head four miles northeast of downtown Tallahassee to **Maclay State Gardens**, set in a lakeside park at 3540 Thomasville Rd, north of I-10, exit 30 (park: daily 8am–sunset, cars $3.25, pedestrians and cyclists $1; garden: daily 9am–5pm, Jan–April $3, rest of year free; ⓣ850/487-9910). New York financier and amateur gardener Alfred B. Maclay bought this large piece of land in the Twenties and planted flowers and shrubs in order to create a blooming season from January to April. It worked: for four months each year the gardens are alive with the fragrances and fantastic colors of azaleas, camellias, pansies, and other flowers, framed by dogwood and redbud trees and towered over by huge oaks and pines. Guided tours of the gardens are conducted on weekends around mid-March (for details and times, call ⓣ850/487-4556), but they're worth visiting at any time, if only to retire to the lakeside pavilion for a snooze as lizards and squirrels scurry around your feet. The admission fee to the gardens also gets you into the **Maclay House** (open Jan–April only), which is filled with the Maclays' furniture and countless books on horticulture. While you're here, take your time to explore the rest of the park and Lake Hall. A picnic area gives great views of the lake, as does the short **Lake Overstreet Trail**, which meanders through the wooded hillside overlooking it. There is also a swimming area close to the parking area nearest the park's entrance.

Lake Jackson and the Indian Mounds

Most boat-owning locals moor their vessels beside the sizeable **Lake Jackson**, five miles north of downtown Tallahassee. On an inlet known as Meginnis Arm is the **Lake Jackson Mounds State Archaeological Site**, off US-27 at Crowder Road (daily 8am–sunset; free), where rich finds, such as copper breastplates and ritual figures, suggest that this eighty-acre site was once an important Native American ceremonial center. Other than large humps of soil and a sense of history, all that's here now are a few picnic tables and an undemanding nature trail over a small ravine. By car, follow the signs off Monroe Street; on foot, the site's a three-mile trek from the #1 bus stop.

North of Tallahassee

There's a wide range of roads that snake **north from Tallahassee** and a surprising number of them offer low-key but enjoyable forays. The Georgia border is only twenty miles away, and the most direct route is the Thomasville Road (Route 319) to, unsurprisingly, **THOMASVILLE**, a sleepy little town just across the Georgia border that was a winter haven for wealthy northerners who built magnificent plantations on the Florida side of the border. Five miles south of Thomasville (and still in Georgia), the **Pebble Hill Plantation** (Tues–Sat 10am–5pm, Sun 1–5pm, closed Sept; hour-long guided tour of house, with the last tour leaving at 4pm; $10, grounds only $3; ⓣ229/226-2344, ⓦwww.pebblehill.com) remains from the time of cotton picking and slavery and shows how comfortable things were for the wealthy whites who ran the show. Much of the original Pebble Hill burned down in the Thirties and what you see now is a fairly faithful rebuilding of the sumptuous main house, complete with the extensive fine art, antique, crystal, and porcelain collections that belonged to the house's final owner, Elisabeth Ireland Poe, and which were rescued from the fire. Note that babies and children aged 6 or under are not allowed in the house. Each April, the house comes back to life as people throng to a spring plantation ball.

If you're feeling carnivorous, take Centerville Road north from Tallahassee (Route 151), which, after twelve miles, leads to **Bradley's 1927 Country Store** (Mon–Fri 9am–6pm, Sat 9am–5pm; ⓣ850/893-1647). For over seventy years, Bradley's has been peddling Southern-style food, specializing in smoked sausages and unusual delicacies like country-milled grits, hogshead cheese, and liver pudding.

Havana

Twelve miles northwest of Tallahassee along Monroe Street (Route 27), tiny **HAVANA** (pronounced "Hey-vannah") is definitely worth time off the beaten track to explore. Providing an authentic taste of Americana, this historic little town takes a pride in its history and, although it has a number of shops catering to the tourist trade, tourism has done nothing to damage the community's sense of identity. The town even has a railroad running through it, and when a train passes, blowing its horn, for a moment those pioneering days of the past seem closer than the history books would have us believe. The town's name came from its tobacco plantations, which once supplied cigar-making factories in Cuba. Following the embargo against Cuba in 1958, the town could no longer sell tobacco leaves to Havana and went into decline, only to be rejuvenated again in 1984 when the first antique center opened and the community discovered that history can mean business.

The main body of shops and cafés huddle around Second Street; however, don't miss a detour to the **Havana Cannery** on East Eighth Avenue. Once a burgeoning fruit-canning business, packing seven million pounds of fruit during World War II, the company lost out to larger rivals and shifted to honey-packing until shutting down in 1994. Temporarily given a new lease of life as home to a maze of antique and curio stores – where you could buy anything from fried green tomato mix to antique furniture – the cannery is, once again, deserted and up for sale to the next entrepreneur with big plans for Havana's most famous landmark. Despite the demise of the cannery, the nearby Historical Bookshelf, 101 W Seventh Ave (☎850/539-5040), is still alive and well. This shop used to be the old town bank, and when the new owner dug into the floor to install an access ramp, the old brick road from Havana to Bainbridge, Georgia, was unearthed.

The **McLauchlin House**, at the corner of Seventh Avenue and Second Street (Wed–Sat 10am–6pm, Sun noon–5pm; ☎850/539-0901), is the home of six antique shops. This 150-year-old farmhouse is a gem with its wrap-around porch, sloping floors, and uneven doors. There's not much else to see in Havana, but if you hit town in April, look for the **MusicFest**, a three-day jazz and blues event (for information, call ☎850/539-7422).

Eating in Havana is never a problem. You're sure to come across *Bella's*, 211 NW First St (☎850/539-0014), situated amongst a plethora of antique shops; this fine Italian restaurant has a beautiful outdoor courtyard for eating al fresco when the weather allows. For a better deal and more fun, try *Slack Key Café*, 206 NW First St (☎850/539-6716). The owners are from Key West and serve Cuban sandwiches, luscious desserts (try a wicked chocolate-cheese cannoli), and great coffee. At *Confetti's Ice Cream Shoppe*, 102 E Seventh Ave (☎850/539-3178), you can eat ice cream in big, wide-booth seats straight from the Fifties.

Unfortunately, there is no accommodation in Havana. The nearest places to stay are the motels along North Monroe Street in Tallahassee (see p.418) and the bed and breakfasts in Quincy twelve miles west (see p.431).

South of Tallahassee

On weekends, many Tallahassee residents head south to the Panhandle's beaches (see "The coastal Panhandle," p.436). If you're not eager to join them, make a slower trek **south** along routes 363 or 61, tracking down a few isolated pockets of historical or geological significance; or take US-319 and lose yourself in the biggest and best of Florida's forests.

One of the most enjoyable ways to explore is by **cycling or rollerblading** the sixteen-mile Tallahassee–St Marks Historic Railroad Trail, a flat and straight course through placid woodlands following the route of a long-abandoned railroad. Bikes and blades can be rented from Tec's Pro Bicycle Sport, 672 Gaines St (ⓣ850/681-6979), in Tallahassee.

Leon Sinks Geological Area

Seven miles south of Tallahassee on Route 319 is the **Leon Sinks Geological Area** (8am–8pm; free), a fascinating karst (terrain that has been altered by rain and ground water dissolving underlying limestone bedrock). The area contains several prominent sinkholes, numerous depressions, a natural bridge, and a disappearing stream, all of which give a unique glimpse of the surrounding area before human interference. There are three manageable trails of between half a mile and three miles, described in a guide available from the ranger station at the entrance.

The Natural Bridge Battlefield State Historic Site and St Marks

Ten miles southeast of Tallahassee, a turn off Route 363 at Woodville leads after six miles to the **Natural Bridge Battlefield State Historic Site** (daily 8am–sunset; free; ⓣ850/922-6007), where, on March 4, 1865, a motley band of Confederate soldiers saw off a much larger group of Union troops, preventing Tallahassee from falling into Yankee hands. Not that it made much difference – the war ended a couple of months later – but the victory is celebrated by a monument and an annual re-enactment on or close to the anniversary involving several hours of shouting, loud bangs, and smoke.

Twelve miles south of Woodville, Route 363 expires at the hamlet of **St Marks**, where the **San Marcos de Apalache Historic State Park** (Thurs–Mon 9am–5pm; free, museum $1; ⓣ850/925-6216) offers decent pickings for students of Florida history – this sixteenth-century Spanish-built fort was visited by early explorers such as Pánfilo de Narváez and Hernando de Soto, and two hundred years later became Andrew Jackson's headquarters when he waged war on the Seminole Indians. Round off a visit at one of the nearby fishcamp eating places, such as *Posey's* (no phone), on Old Fort Drive.

If you prefer wildlife to history, backtrack slightly along Route 363 and turn east along US-98. Three miles on you'll find the main entrance to **St Marks National Wildlife Refuge** (daily sunrise–sunset; cars $4, pedestrians and cyclists $1), which spreads out over the boggy outflow of the St Marks River. Bald eagles and a few black bears reside in the refuge, though from the various roadside lookout points and observation towers you're more likely to spot otters, white-tailed deer, raccoons, and a wealth of birdlife. Apart from the natural attractions, a drive to the end of the road will bring you to the picturesque St Marks Lighthouse, completed in 1831. Just inside the entrance, a **visitor center** doles out useful information (Mon–Fri 8.15am–4.15pm, Sat & Sun 10am–5pm; ⓣ850/925-6121, ⓦsaintmarks.fws.gov).

Wakulla Springs

Fifteen miles south of Tallahassee, off Route 61 on Route 267, **Wakulla Springs State Park** (daily 8am–sunset; cars $3.25, pedestrians and cyclists $1; ⓣ850/224-5950) contains what is believed to be one of the biggest and deepest natural springs in the world, pumping up half a million gallons of crystal-clear pure water from the bowels of the earth every day – difficult to guess from the calm surface. The principal reason for visiting Wakulla Springs is to enjoy the barely touched scenery and to appreciate a part of Florida that is intact after hundreds of years.

It's refreshing to **swim** in the cool waters, but somewhat disconcerting to note that the marked areas are just inches from those where swimming is prohibited due to alligators. To learn more about the spring, you should take the twenty-five-minute narrated **glass-bottomed boat tour** ($4.50; only operates when the water is clear enough) and peer down to the shoals of fish hovering around the 180-foot-deep cavern through which the water comes. Join the 45-minute **river cruise** ($4.50) for glimpses of some of the park's other inhabitants: deer, turkeys, turtles, herons, and egrets – and the inevitable alligators. If déjà vu strikes, it may be because a number of films have been shot here, including several of the early *Tarzan* movies and parts of *The Creature from the Black Lagoon*. To see the alligators and snakes at their most active, take the **moonlight cruise** at twilight ($6; dinner cruise once a month, $25).

You shouldn't leave without strolling through the **Wakulla Lodge**, 550 Wakulla Park Drive (ⓣ850/224-5950; ❹), a hotel built beside the spring in 1937, which retains many of its original features: Moorish archways, stone fireplaces, and fabulous hand-painted Toltec and Aztec designs on the lobby's wooden ceiling. Take the opportunity, also, to pay your respects to the stuffed carcass of "Old Joe," one of the oldest and largest alligators ever known, who died in the Fifties, measuring eleven feet long and supposedly aged 200; he's in a glass case by the reception desk. The lodge and its surrounds have a relaxing ambience that can prove quite addictive. An added bonus is that once the day-trippers have departed, you'll have the springs and wildlife all to yourself.

Further south: the Apalachicola National Forest

With swamps, savannas, and springs dotted liberally about its half-million acres, the **Apalachicola National Forest** is the inland Panhandle at its natural best. Several roads enable you to drive through a good-sized chunk and several spots provide opportunities for a rest and a snack. But to see more of the forest than its picnic tables and litter bins, you'll have to make an effort. Leave the periphery and delve into the pristine interior and explore at a leisurely pace, following hiking trails, taking a canoe on one of the rivers, or simply spending a night under the stars at one of the basic campgrounds.

Practicalities

The northeast corner of the forest almost touches Tallahassee's airport, fanning out from there to the edge of the Apalachicola River, about 35 miles west. Most of the northern edge is bordered by Hwy-20, the eastern side by US-319 and US-98, while to the south lies the gruesome no-man's-land of Tate's Hell Swamp (see p.431).

Apalachicola National Forest information

Always equip yourself with maps, a weather forecast, and advice from a ranger's office before setting off on a hike or canoe trip through the forest (for more on how to travel in the backcountry safely, see "Basics," p.42). The Ochlockonee River divides the forest into two administrative districts and the following offices are responsible for the west and east sides of the forest respectively:

Apalachicola Ranger District Hwy-20, near Bristol ⓣ850/643-2282

Wakulla Ranger District Route 6, near Crawfordville ⓣ850/926-3561

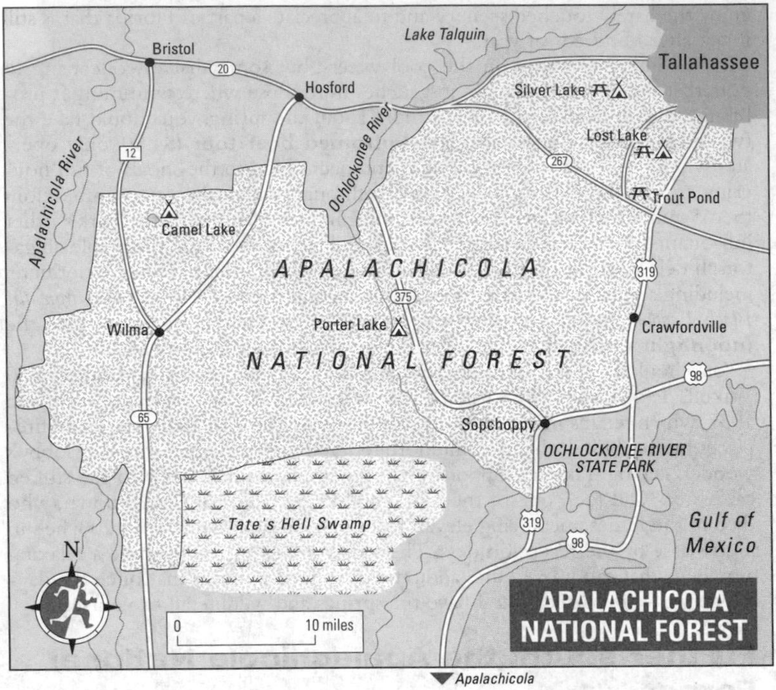

The main **entrances** are off Hwy-20 and US-319, and three minor roads – Routes 267, 375, and 65 – form cross-forest links between the two highways. **Accommodation** is limited to camping, and, with the exception of Silver Lake and Lost Lake (see below), all the sites are free and have basic facilities – usually just toilets and drinking water. For more information, call ⓣ850/643-2282. The only place to **rent a canoe** near the forest is TNT Hideaway (ⓣ850/925-6412), on US-98 two miles west of St Marks on the Wakulla River.

One section of the forest, Trout Pond (April–Oct only; cars $2), on Route 373 near Tallahassee airport, is intended for **disabled visitors** and their guests, with a wheelchair-accessible lakeside nature trail and picnic area.

The edge of the forest: Lost Lake and Silver Lake

For a brief taste of what the forest can offer, make for **Lost Lake**, seven miles from Tallahassee along Route 373, where there's little except a few picnic tables beside a small lake. The area's well suited to a nibble and a waterside laze, and is less busy than the campervan-infested **Silver Lake**, nine miles east of the city, off Hwy-20. You can swim in the lake and if you choose to stay, camping will cost $8; anticipate the company of too many other people, though.

Deeper into the forest: hiking and canoeing

Several short, clearly marked **nature walks** lie within the forest, but the major **hiking trail**, strictly for ardent and well-equipped backpackers, is the thirty-mile **Apalachicola Trail**, which begins close to Crawfordville, on US-319. This passes through the heart of the forest and includes a memorable (and sometimes difficult, depending on the weather conditions and water level) leg across an isolated swamp, the Bradwell Bay Wilderness. After this, the campground at Porter Lake, just to the west of the wilderness area, with its toilets and drinking water, seems the epitome of civilization.

The trail leads on to **Camel Lake**, whose campground has drinking water and toilets, and the less demanding nine-and-a-half-mile **Camel Lake Loop Trail**. By vehicle, you can get directly to Camel Lake by turning off Hwy-20 at Bristol and continuing south for twelve miles, watching for the signposted turn-off on the left.

Although there are numerous places to put in along its four rivers, **canoeists** can paddle right into the forest from the western end of Lake Talquin (close to Hwy-20), and continue for a sixty-mile glide along the Ochlockonee River – the forest's major waterway – to the Ochlockonee River State Park, close to US-319. Obviously, the length of trip means that to do it all you'll have to use the riverside **campgrounds** (info from the Supervisor's Office, National Forests Florida, 325 John Knox Rd, Suite F-100, Tallahassee; ⓣ850/523-8500). Those with drinking water are at Porter Lake, Whitehead Lake, and Mack Landing; be warned that these are often concealed by dense foliage, so study your map carefully.

South of the forest: Tate's Hell Swamp

Driving through the forest on Route 65 or Route 67, or around it on US-319 (which merges with US-98 as it nears the coast), you'll eventually pass the large and forbidding area called **Tate's Hell Swamp**. According to legend, Tate was a farmer who pursued a panther into the swamp and was never seen again. It's a breeding ground for the deadly water moccasin snake, and gung-ho locals sometimes venture into the swamp hoping to catch a few snakes to sell to less reputable zoos; you're well advised to stay clear.

West of Tallahassee

To discover the social character of the inland Panhandle, take US-90 **west from Tallahassee**: 180 miles of largely tedious rural landscapes and time-locked farming towns that have been down on their luck since the demise of the timber industry fifty or so years ago. If the scenery gets a little tiring, you can easily switch to the speedier I-10, or cut south to the coast. But the compensations are the endless supply of rustic eating places, low-cost accommodation, several appealing natural areas – and a chance to see a part of Florida that the travel brochures rarely reveal.

Quincy

Twenty miles west of Tallahassee on US-90 is **Quincy**, one of the first towns to strike it rich because of Coca-Cola. The Atlanta-based pharmacist who patented the fizzy drink sold company stock to friends in Quincy, who made a mint and built grandiose villas throughout the town at the beginning of the twentieth century. From the square on **Madison Street**, observe the immaculate **Court House**, surrounded by topiaries, and a grand marble memorial to slain Confederate soldiers. Just opposite, on East Jefferson Street, the wall of Padgett's jewelry store is covered with the original Coke ad. Painted here in 1905, it espouses coke as "delicious and refreshing, five cents at fountains and bottles." Most of the central square is unremarkable, looking like a dowdy film set from a B-grade cowboy movie. Take time to explore the **Gadsden Arts Center**, 13 N Madison St (Tues–Sat 10am–5pm, Sun 1–5pm; ⓣ850/875-4866, ⓦwww.gadsdenarts.com). One of the finest art galleries in the area, it hosts major traveling exhibitions as well as the work of local and regional artists.

Wealthy Quincy, with its bungalow homes of delicate trellises and sweeping verandas, begins on East Washington Street. The most exquisite mansions, though, are between Love and King streets. The finest of all also happens to be the **bed and breakfast** *McFarlin House*, 305 E King St (ⓣ850/875-2526, ⓦwww.mcfarlinhouse.com; ❹), an exquisite, turreted mansion whose sumptuous interior and 42-pillar porch were created for John McFarlin, Quincy's richest tobacco planter, in 1895. If this is out of your price range try the *Allison House Inn*, 215 N Madison St (ⓣ850/875-2511, ⓦwww.allisonhouseinn.com; ❸), an English-style bed and breakfast in another of the oldest houses in town. For a café-style **meal** try the *Gucchidadi Deli & Bakery*, 7 N Madison St (ⓣ850/627-6660); it has a great hometown, old-fashioned feel and a good selection of sandwiches, salads, and cakes.

Greyhound **buses** (three a day from Tallahassee) arrive opposite the big old Southern-style house that holds the **Chamber of Commerce**, 221 N Madison St (ⓣ850/627-9231), where you should pick up the excellent leaflet detailing a walking tour of the town's historic district.

Lake Seminole and the Three Rivers State Recreational Area

Fifty miles west of Tallahassee, close to the Georgia border, US-90 reaches **SNEADS**, a small town dominated by the large **Lake Seminole**, created by a Fifties hydroelectric project and popular for its massive and abundant catfish, bream, and bass. On the lake's Florida side (the other bank is in Georgia), spend an enjoyable few hours in the **Three Rivers State Recreational Area** (daily 8am–sunset; cars $3, pedestrians and cyclists $1), two miles from Sneads on Route 271. A mile-long **nature walk** from the park's **camping area** (ⓣ850/482-9006, reservations 1-800/326-3521; $8) leads to a wooded, hilly section where squirrels and alligators are two-a-penny and white-tailed deer and gray foxes lurk in the shrubbery. To spend a night by the lake without camping, use the ten-room *Seminole Lodge* (ⓣ850/593-6886; ❶), just outside Sneads at the end of Legion Road.

Marianna and the Florida Caverns State Park

Twenty-five miles west along US-90, **Marianna** is one of the larger inland Panhandle settlements, despite only having a four-figure population for whom the twice-monthly horse sale is the only source of excitement. There isn't much to recommend the place, except that it tries to sell itself (rather unsuccessfully) as "The Belle of the Panhandle" and that it has been the seat of Jackson County since 1829. Ask at the **Chamber of Commerce**, 4318 Lafayette St (Mon–Fri 9am–5pm; ⓣ850/482-8061), for a walking-tour map of the town.

There's a collection of motels on US-90 after exit 21 off the I-10 in case you want to **stay** in town. The delightful, if strange, *Hinson House* bed and breakfast, 4338 Lafayette St (ⓣ850/526-1500, ⓦwww.phonl.com/hinson_house; ❸), is a beautifully restored villa with authentic furnishings and

Crossing the time zone

Crossing the Apalachicola River, which flows north–south across the inland Panhandle, roughly 45 miles west of Tallahassee, takes you into the **Central Time Zone**, an hour behind Eastern Time and the rest of Florida. In the coastal Panhandle, the time shift occurs about ten miles west of Port St Joe, on the boundary between Gulf and Bay counties.

breakfasts served in a formal dining room. The owner has created a permanent sense of Christmas, with not only a year-round lit-up tree in the hallway, but twinkling lights on the stairs, windows patterned with fake frost, and golden reindeer all over the fireplace.

For **eating**, your best bet is the *Red Canyon Grill*, 3297 Caverns Rd (Ⓣ850/482-4256), which features such dishes as fajitas, wood-grilled shrimp, and a hearty corn soup at moderate prices. *Captain D's Seafood Restaurant*, 4253 Lafayette St (Ⓣ850/482-6230), serves inexpensive chicken and seafood dishes, while a popular eatery is the traditional and moderately priced *Old Mexican Restaurant*, 4434 Lafayette St (Ⓣ850/482-5552).

Florida Caverns State Park

The best thing about Marianna is its proximity to **Florida Caverns State Park** (daily 8am–sunset; cars $3.25, pedestrians and cyclists $1), three miles north on Route 167, where hourly **guided tours** (9am–4.30pm; $5) venture through 65-foot-deep caverns filled with strangely shaped calcite formations. Far from being new discoveries, the caves were mentioned in colonial Spanish accounts of the area and used by Seminole Indians to hide from Andrew Jackson's army in the early 1800s. Back in the sun, the park has a few other features to fill a day comfortably. From the **visitor center** (Ⓣ850/482-1228) by the caverns' entrance, a **nature trail** leads around the flood plain of the Chipola River, remarkable for the fact that it dips underground for several hundred feet as it flows through the park. At the **Blue Hole Spring**, at the end of the park road, you can canoe (rental is $10.75 for four hours, $16.13 for eight hours), swim, snorkel, or scubadive – and sleep at its **campground** ($14 with electricity).

Chipley and Falling Waters State Recreation Area

Continuing west, the next community of any size is **CHIPLEY**, 26 miles from Marianna. The town takes its name from William D. Chipley, who put a railroad across the Panhandle in the mid-1800s to improve the timber trade, which in turn gave rise to little sawmill towns such as Chipley. The railroad is still here (restricted locally to freight), but the boom times are long gone. The town itself is, for the most part, unexciting and the Neoclassical bulk of the **Washington County Court House** on US-90 (also called Jackson Avenue) seems very out of place. The only other building of interest is the large and elegant **First United Methodist Church**, built in 1910 and set on hand-hewn log foundations. If you can find someone to let you in, the interior is most unexpected. Towering over the vast, curved golden-oak pews are a huge pipe organ and semi-opaque stained glass that is especially radiant on a sunny day.

Chipley's historic district is on South Third Street, down the western side of the Court House. The houses here date from 1900 to 1920 and are not worth more than a cursory glance. More interesting, if only as a well-preserved example of the inland Panhandle's ubiquitous Main Streets, is the area just north of US-90, a charming row of old brick-faced shops along the railroad tracks. **Antique shops** abound here, and Chipley's best are at the Historic Chipley Antique Mall, 1368 Railroad Ave N (Ⓣ850/638-2535).

The Falling Waters State Recreation Area

Leave town along Route 77 and head for **Falling Waters State Recreation Area** (daily 8am–sunset; cars $3.25, pedestrians and cyclists $1), three miles south and the home of Florida's only **waterfall**. The fall is in fact a 100-foot drop into a tube-like sinkhole topped by a viewing platform. A trail passes several other sinks (without waterfalls), and another leads to a decaying oil well – remaining from an unsuccessful attempt to strike black gold in 1919. The park has a **campground** (Ⓣ850/638-6130; $10.90), but for **accommodation** under a roof, head back to Chipley where there are a number of chain motels on US-90, including the dull but cheap *Budget Inn*, 1184 E Jackson Ave (Ⓣ850/638-1850; ❶), or *Chipley Motel*, 1330 E Jackson Ave (Ⓣ850/638-1322; ❶). For **food**, try the *China Garden Restaurant*, next to the *Chipley Motel* at 1320 US-90 (Ⓣ850/638-3080). Local farmers pack into *Granny's Country Kitchen*, 1284 W Jackson Ave, open daily until 2pm, for hearty breakfasts and lunch buffets.

De Funiak Springs

A real jewel of the inland Panhandle, **De Funiak Springs**, forty miles west of Chipley on US-90, was founded as a fashionable stop on the newly completed Louisville–Nashville railroad in 1882. Drawn to the large, naturally circular lake, nineteenth-century socialites built fairy-tale villas to fringe the waters here. Three years later the Florida Chautauqua Alliance, a benevolent religious society espousing free culture and education for all, made the town its southern base. The alliance was headquartered at the grandiose Hall of Brotherhood, which still stands on Circle Drive – an ideal cruising lane to view the splendid villas, painted in gingerbread-house style with white or wedding-cake blue trim. With the death of its founders and the coming of the Depression, the alliance faded away, and in 1975 their 4000-seat auditorium was demolished by Hurricane Eloise. There has been renewed interest in the Chautauqua ethos, however, and a **Chautauqua Assembly Revival** is now held here around the end of February or the beginning of March (call Ⓣ1-800/822-6877 for details). In addition to putting on workshops and craft activities, the town also opens up its historic houses so you can view the interiors. If you miss that, the only building open to the public is the smallest, the **Walton-De Funiak Library**, 3 Circle Drive (Mon & Wed–Fri 9am–5pm, Tues 9am–8pm, Sat 9am–3pm; free; Ⓣ850/892-3624), which has been lending books since 1886 and has acquired a small stash of medieval European weaponry on display.

Another unlikely find is the **Chautauqua Winery** (Ⓣ850/892-5887), at the junction of US-331 and I-10, whose diverse wines may not be the world's finest, but have picked up a few awards in their fourteen years of existence (free tours and tastings daily 9am–5pm; last tour at 4pm). The actual vineyards are about twelve miles from the winery.

Stopping over in De Funiak Springs is a sound move if you're aiming for the more expensive coastal strip 25 miles south along US-331. The *Days Inn*, 475 Hugh Adams Rd (Ⓣ850/892-6115; ❷), has good rates but is closer to I-10 than the town. To stay in step with the town's historical mood, opt instead for *Hotel* *de Funiak*, 400 E Nelson Ave (Ⓣ850/892-4383, Ⓦwww.hoteldefuniak.com; ❸), a charmingly restored hotel in the old business district that is still close to the lake. Alternatively, you can rent a log cabin at *Sunset King Lake Resort*, 366 Paradise Island Drive (Ⓣ850/892-7229 or 1-800/774-5454, Ⓦwww.sunsetking.com; ❸), where there's also an outdoor pool and boat rentals. While in town, make sure to **eat lunch** amid the antiques at the delightful *Busy Bee Café*, 2 S Seventh St (Ⓣ850/892-6700). For **dinner**, the restaurant at *Hotel de Funiak* serves Italian food in the cozy atmosphere of its Chautauqua dining room. For cheaper eats try the *McLains Family Steakhouse*, on US-331 (Ⓣ850/892-2402), for a good selection of steaks, seafood, and salads, or head back to I-10 for the usual array of quick-stop restaurants.

The Blackwater River State Forest

Between the sluggish towns of Crestview and Milton, thirty miles west of De Funiak Springs, the creeks and slow-flowing rivers of **Blackwater River State Forest** are jammed each weekend with waterborne families enjoying what's officially dubbed "the canoe capital of Florida." In spite of the crowds, the forest is by no means over-commercialized, being big enough to absorb the influx and still offer peace, isolation, and unruffled nature to anyone intrepid enough to hike through it. Alternatively, if you're not game for canoeing or hiking, but just want a few hours' break, the **Blackwater River State Park** (daily 8am–sunset; cars $3, pedestrians and cyclists $1), within the forest four miles north of Harold off US-90, has some easy walking trails.

From Milton, US-90 and I-10 both offer a mildly scenic fifteen-mile drive over Escambia Bay to the hotels and freeways on the northern fringes of Pensacola, the city marking Florida's western extremity (see p.449).

Accommodation in the forest

With the exception of the restored 1800s "cracker" **cabins** and an *Old School House Inn* rented through **Adventures Unlimited** at Tomahawk Landing (see below; ❹–❻, depending on the comfort level), forest accommodation is limited to **camping** ($15–20). There are fully equipped sites at the Krul Recreation Area (Ⓣ850/983-5363), near the junction of Forest Road 4 and Route 19, and at the Blackwater River State Park (see above; Ⓣ850/983-5363). Free basic sites intended for hikers are dotted along the main trails.

Hiking and canoeing

Hardened **hikers** carrying overnight gear can tackle the 21-mile **Jackson Trail**, named after Andrew Jackson, who led his invading army this way in 1818, seeking to wrest Florida from Spanish control. On the way, two very basic shelters have handpumps for water. The trail runs between Karick Lake, off Hwy-189, fourteen miles north of US-90, and the Krul Recreation Area. The shorter **Sweetwater Trail** is a good substitute if your feet aren't up to the longer hike. An enjoyable four-and-a-half-mile walk, it leaves the Krul Recreation Area and crosses a swingbridge and the Bear Lake Dam before joining the Jackson Trail.

Canoeing in the forest is offered by Adventures Unlimited, at **Tomahawk Landing** on Coldwater Creek (Ⓣ850/623-6197 or 1-800/239-6864, Ⓦwww.adventuresunlimited.com), twelve miles north of Milton on Hwy-87. Here you can rent tubes, canoes, and kayaks for around $12, $17, and $22 respectively per day. Two- and three-day trips, with overnight gear and food provided, can also be arranged for $80 and $120 per person respectively.

The coastal Panhandle

Lacking the glamour and international renown of Florida's other beach strips, the **coastal Panhandle** is nonetheless no secret to residents of the Southern states who descend upon the region by the thousands during the summer. Consequently, a few sections of the region's 180-mile-long coastline are nightmarishly overdeveloped: **Panama City Beach** revels in its "redneck Riviera" nickname, and smaller **Destin** and **Fort Walton Beach** are only marginally more refined. By contrast, little **Apalachicola** and the **South Walton beaches**, both easily reached by car (they're inaccessible by bus) but out of the main tourist corridor, have much to recommend them as they have beautiful unspoiled sands and off-shore islands where people are a rarer sight than wildlife.

Apalachicola and around

A few miles south of the Apalachicola National Forest (see p.429), and the first substantial part of the coast you'll hit on US-98 from central Florida, the **Apalachicola area** contains much of value. Mainland beaches may be few, but sand-seekers are compensated by the brilliant strands of three barrier islands, and the small fishing communities you'll pass through are untainted by the aggressive tourism that scars the coast fifty miles west in Panama City Beach.

Apalachicola

Now a tiny port with an income largely derived from harvesting oysters (ten per cent of the nation's oysters come from here), **Apalachicola** once rode high on the cotton industry, which kept its dock busy and its populace affluent during the early 1800s. A number of stately columned buildings attest to former wealth; one, at 99 Market St, is occupied by the **Chamber of Commerce** (Mon–Fri 9am–5pm; ⓣ850/653-9419, ⓦwww.apalachicolabay.org), where you can pick up a map to find the attractions along an enjoyable half-hour's stroll.

To reach Apalachicola take US-98, which crosses the four-mile Gorrie Memorial Bridge, named for a physician held in high regard by Floridians. Arriving in the town in 1833, John Gorrie was seeking a way to keep malaria patients cool when he devised a machine to make ice (previously transported in large blocks from the north). He died, however, before the idea took off and became the basis of modern refrigerators and air-conditioners. The **John Gorrie State Museum**, on the corner of Sixth Street and Avenue D (Thurs–Mon 9am–5pm; $1; ⓣ850/653-9347), remembers the man and his work, as well as the general history of Apalachicola, and includes a replica of the cumbersome ice-making device – the original is in the Smithsonian Institute in Washington DC.

Accommodation and eating

There isn't a lot to Apalachicola, but the town makes a good base for visiting the barrier islands (see opposite) and there's plenty of good **accommodation** to choose from. Good bed and breakfast is available at the *Apalachicola River Inn*, 123 Water St (ⓣ 850/653-8139, ⓦwww.apalachicolariverinn.com; ❺), all of whose rooms have river views; the lovely *Coombes House Inn*, 80 Sixth St (Ⓣ850/653-9199, Ⓦwww.coombeshouseinn.com; ❹), which is in a Victorian-style mansion filled with antiques and oriental carpets, and has bicycles available for guests' use; and the *Gibson Inn*, 57 Market St (Ⓣ850/653-2191, Ⓦwww.gibsoninn.com; ❺), which offers murder-mystery weekends and a full lunch and dinner menu in their own somewhat pricey restaurant (closed Mon–Tues). You'll find lower prices just outside town, one and a half miles west, at the *Rancho Inn*, 240 US-98 (Ⓣ850/653-9435; Ⓦwww.ranchoinn.com; ❸).

Good places to **eat** in town include the inexpensive *Apalachicola Seafood Grill and Steakhouse*, 100 Market St (Ⓣ850/653-9510), for a wide range of lunch and dinner specials; and the *Boss Oyster Bar*, 123 Water St (Ⓣ850/653-9364), where you can tuck into fresh Apalachicola oysters. The motto of this place is "shut up and shuck," and it prepares its oysters in thirty-plus different ways: try the boss oyster combo for $15.95. Adjacent to the *Rancho Inn* you'll find the *Red Top Café* (Ⓣ850/653-8612), which serves inexpensive Southern cooking for lunch and dinner; while also on US-98, *That Place on 98* at no. 500 (Ⓣ850/670-9898) serves fresh seafood, pasta, and home-made desserts on a dining deck overlooking the Apalachicola Bay.

The barrier islands: St George, Dog, and St Vincent

A few miles off the coast, framing the Apalachicola Bay and the broad, marshy outflow of the Apalachicola River, the three Apalachicola **barrier islands** are well endowed with beaches and creatures – including thousands of birds that use them as resting stops during migration – and two of them hold what must be among the most isolated communities in Florida. It's worth seeing one of the islands if you have the chance, but only the largest island, St George, is accessible by road – Route 1A, which leaves US-98 at Eastpoint. Once here you can visit the rest with Journeys of St George's Island, 240 E Third St (Ⓣ850/927-3259, Ⓦwww.sgislandjourneys.com), which provides a variety of instructional guided canoe trips and hikes.

Twenty-seven miles of powdery white sands and Gulf vistas are not the only reason to come to **St George Island**, where shady live-oak hammocks and an abundance of osprey-inhabited pine trees add color to a day's lazy sunning. Occupying the island's central section are a few restaurants, beach shops, as well as the eight-room *St George Inn*, 135 Franklin Blvd (Ⓣ850/927-2903, Ⓦwww.stgeorgeinn.com; ❸), a beautiful wooden beachfront motel with its own heated pool, and the *Buccaneer Inn*, 160 W Gorrie Drive (Ⓣ850/927-2585, Ⓦwww.buccinn.com; ❹), with basic rooms and proximity to the island's restaurants and shops. The eastern sector is dominated by the raccoon-infested **St George Island State Park** (daily 8am–sunset; cars $4, or $2 if only two passengers, pedestrians and cyclists $1), where a three-mile **hiking trail** leads to a very basic **campground** ($3; there's a better-equipped site at the start of the hike, $14.84; Ⓣ850/927-2111).

A couple of miles east of St George, **Dog Island**, accessible only by boat (signs advertising crossings are all over the marina in Carrabelle, on US-98), has a small permanent population living in little cottages nestled among Florida's tallest sand dunes. Several footpaths lead around the windswept isle, which won't take more than a few hours to cover. The only **accommodation** is the pricey bed and breakfast at the *Pelican Inn* (Ⓣ1-800/451-5294, Ⓦwww.thepelicaninn.com; ❻), with its eight self-catering rooms (no maid service) in a wooden house on the beach. Reservations are essential.

The freshwater lakes and saltwater swamps of **St Vincent Island**, almost within a shell's throw of St George's western end, form a protected refuge for loggerhead turtles, wild turkeys, and bald eagles, among many other creatures. Trips to the island are available year-round with St Vincent Island Shuttle Services (ⓣ850/229-1065, ⓦwww.stvincentisland.com) from $10; they also organize bike rental for those who want to cycle their way around the twelve-acre island.

St Joseph Peninsula State Park and Port St Joe

For a final taste of virgin Florida coast before hitting heavily commercial Panama City Beach, take Route 30 – eighteen miles from Apalachicola, off US-98 – to the **St Joseph Peninsula State Park** (daily 8am–sunset; cars $3.25, pedestrians and cyclists $1). A long finger of sand with a short **nature trail** at one end and a spectacular nine-mile **hiking route** at the other, the park has rough **camping** with no facilities ($3) at its northern tip and better-equipped sites ($18.56 with electricity) and **cabins** ($55–70; ⓣ850/227-1327) about halfway along near Eagle Harbor.

The peninsula wraps a protective arm around **Port St Joe** on the mainland, another dot-on-the-map fishing port that has seen better days. One such day came in 1838 when a constitution calling for statehood (which Florida didn't acquire until seven years later) and liberal reforms was drawn up here – only to be deemed too radical by the legislators of the time. At the **Constitution Convention State Museum** (Thurs–Mon 9am–noon & 1–5pm; $1; ⓣ850/229-8029), signposted from US-98 as you enter the town, you'll find battery-powered waxworks that re-enact the deed. There are also more credible mementos of the town's colorful past, including an explanation of how the town's reputation for pirate pursuits earned it the title "Wickedest City in the Southeast" during its early years.

Panama City Beach

An orgy of motels, go-kart tracks, mini-golf courses, and amusement parks, **PANAMA CITY BEACH** is entirely without pretensions, capitalizing as blatantly as possible on the appeal of its 27-mile-long beach. The place is entirely commercial, but with the shops, bars, and restaurants all trying to undercut one another, there are some great bargains to be found – from airbrushed T-shirts and cut-price sunglasses to cheap buffet food. With everybody out to have a good time, there's some fine carousing to be done, too; not least during the Spring Break months of March and April when thousands of students – predominantly from the Deep South – descend upon Panama City Beach to drink and dance themselves into oblivion. Party town it may be, but Panama City Beach has zero drug tolerance and there are big signs along the beach to constantly remind you of this fact. As vulgar and crass as it often is, Panama City Beach cries out to be seen. Come here once, if only as a voyeuristic day trip – you may well be tempted enough by its tacky charm to stay longer.

Seasons greatly affect the mood. Throughout the lively **summer** (the so-called "100 Magic Days"), accommodation costs are high and advance bookings essential. In **winter**, prices drop and visitors are fewer; most are Canadians and – increasingly – northern Europeans, who have no problems sunbathing and swimming in the relatively cool (typically around 65°F) temperatures.

What Panama City Beach doesn't have is any **history** worth mentioning. It began as an offshoot of **PANAMA CITY**, a dull place of docks and paper mills eight miles away over the Hathaway Bridge (which US-98 crosses). Today there's little love lost between the two communities; they have nothing in common besides a name.

Arrival, information, and getting around

Since Panama City Beach is essentially a very long beach, **getting your bearings** could hardly be simpler, even if there are only two real, if rather similar landmarks (City Pier to the west, County Pier to the east). Much of the two piers was destroyed during Hurricane Opal in 1996, but restoration plans have returned them more or less to their original state. **Front Beach Road** (part of US-98A, which starts at the foot of the Hathaway Bridge) is the main track, a two-lane highway often called "the Strip" that's very much the place to prowl on weekends. When judging distances, count on having to go about a mile to get from, say, number 15,000 to 16,000 Front Beach Road. The speedier, four-lane **Hutchison Boulevard** loops off Front Beach Road for a few blocks around County Pier from the junction with **Thomas Drive** (which links the eastern extremity of the beach). If you don't want to see gaudy Panama City Beach at all, **Panama City Beach Parkway** (US-98) will take you straight through its anonymous residential quarter.

Greyhound **buses** pick up and drop off at the Shell station, 17325 W Hwy-98, leaving a fifteen-minute walk to the nearest motels. Note that this is a flag stop, meaning that you will have to ask the driver specifically to set you down here as opposed to the station in Panama City (917 Harrison Ave; ⓣ850/785-7861). To travel between Panama City and Panama City Beach, you'll need to use one of the four daily Greyhound services linking them or catch the Bay Town Trolley (see below).

For information, magazines, and discount coupons, drop into the **Visitors Information Center**, 17001 Panama City Beach Parkway (daily 8am–5pm; ⓣ1-800/722-3224, ⓦwww.800pcbeach.com).

In terms of getting around, Panama City Beach is incredibly bad for **walking**; **public transport** is scarce and **taxis** are prohibitively expensive, even for a short journey. The Bay Town Trolley (ⓣ850/769-0557, ⓦwww.baytowntrolley.com)

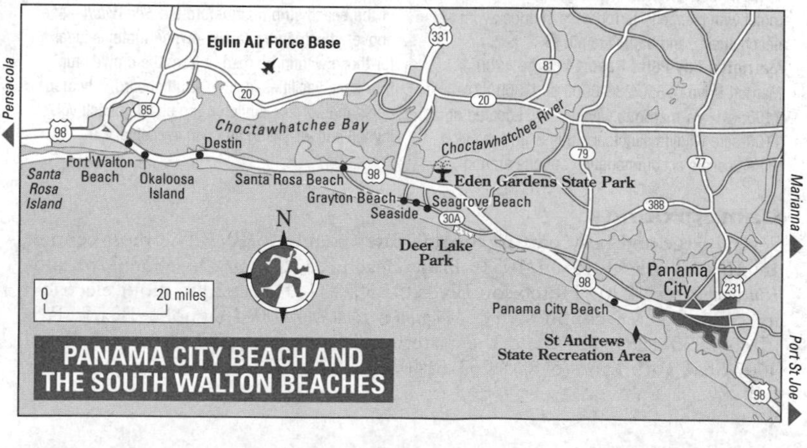

provides a limited service Monday through Friday (6am–6.30pm) around Panama City and along the beach. One-way fares are $1 and transfers 25¢. If you don't have a car, you can rent a **bicycle** (around $15 per day) or a **scooter** (around $45 per day; driver's license necessary) from any of the myriad beach shops.

Accommodation

Visitors to Panama City Beach outnumber residents, and though there are plenty of **places to stay**, these fill with amazing speed, especially on weekends. **Prices** are higher than you'll pay elsewhere in the Panhandle – $70–90 for a basic motel room in summer (March to Oct) – so if you're counting the bucks, stay inland and drive to the beach. In winter prices drop by 40–60 percent, with monthly rentals being even cheaper. **Campground** sites are rarely more expensive than their equivalents elsewhere, though only a couple are good for tents. As a very general rule, **motels** at the eastern end of the beach are smarter and slightly pricier than those in the center, and places at the western end are quiet and family-oriented. That said, you're unlikely to find much to complain about at any place that takes your fancy.

Blue Dolphin 19919 Front Beach Rd ⓣ850/234-5895 or 1-866/293-2583. A simple mid-range motel with a beachfront location away from the more built-up areas to the east. ❸

Flamingo Motel and Tower 15525 Front Beach Rd ⓣ850/234-2232 or 1-800/828-0400, ⓦwww.flamingomotel.com. This large motel is situated half a mile east of City Pier, featuring a tropical garden on the beach and kitchen-equipped rooms in the recently built tower. Cheaper rooms can be had on the nonbeach side of the road. ❷

Holiday Inn SunSpree 11127 Front Beach Rd ⓣ850/234-1111 or 1-800/633-0266. One of the most centrally located and comfortable hotels on the beach strip. All 340 rooms have balconies overlooking the palm-fringed pool – a useful aid to socializing for the young crowd that tends to congregate here. ❹

Impala 17751 Front Beach Rd ⓣ850/234-6462, ⓦwww.impalamotel.com. Cozy, basic beachfront motel with inexpensive rooms, a sundeck with beach chairs, and barbecue pit. ❷

Marriott's Bay Point Resort Village 4200 Marriott Drive ⓣ850/236-6000 or 1-800/874-7105, ⓦwww.marriottbaypoint.com. Located on a 1100-acre wildlife sanctuary, this is one of the more upscale accommodation options around. Every room has a view of either the sanctuary or the beach, and the resort offers four pools, whirlpools, an exercise room, as well as golf and tennis. ❻

Osprey 15801 Front Beach Rd ⓣ850/234-0303 or 1-800/338-2659, ⓦwww.ospreymotel.com. This relatively inexpensive, large beachfront motel offers heated pool, hot tub, and beach bar, and guests can also use the shuffleboard and volleyball facilities at the nearby *Driftwood Lodge*. All rooms have fully equipped kitchens. ❷

Sea Witch 21905 Front Beach Rd ⓣ850/234-5722 or 1-800/322-4571, ⓦwww.seawitchmotel.com. Situated in a secluded part of the beach known as Sunnyside, this family-oriented motel has a large Gulfside pool, jet-ski hire, gift shop, and a game room. ❷

Sugar Sands 20723 Front Beach Rd ⓣ850/234-8802 or 1-800/367-9221, ⓦwww.sugarsands.com. Located in a quiet spot on the western edge of the beach strip (just before the *Sea Witch* – see above), this friendly, family-owned motel is ideal for those wanting a respite from the crowds further east. Facilities include shuffleboard, a heated pool, and hot tub, while on the beach, beach volleyball and jet-skiing are also available. ❷

Campgrounds

Several large and busy **campgrounds** cater mainly to RVs. The most central are *Miracle Strip RV Resort*, 10510 Front Beach Rd (ⓣ850/234-3833; $25), and *Raccoon River*, 12209 Hutchison Blvd (ⓣ850/234-0181; $20 without electricity). For quieter confines, try *Magnolia Beach*, 4100 Magnolia Beach Rd (ⓣ850/235-1581; $25), and the waterfront *St Andrews State Recreation Area*, 4607 State Park Lane (ⓣ850/233-5140 or 1-800/326-3521; $8–17).

Scuba diving in Panama City Beach

While not as warm as the waters farther south, the Gulf of Mexico around Panama City Beach offers a greater variety of dive sites than is typically found elsewhere in Florida. Besides the natural reefs found a few miles off-shore at depths of between eighty and a hundred feet, the coastal waters include some fifty artificial reefs that were created by the Panama City Marine Institute as an aid to marine research. Known as the "Wreck Capital of the South," Panama City Beach also offers divers the opportunity of poking around a number of sunken ships, including a 441-foot World War II Liberty ship, a 160-foot coastal freighter, and, most famously, the 465-foot *Empire Mica*, a large freighter that was torpedoed and sunk in World War II.

The best time for diving in Panama City Beach is from April to September, when water temperatures are at their warmest. Of the several **dive shops** along the beach, try Panama City Dive Center, 4823 Thomas Drive (ⓣ850/235-3390, ⓦwww.pcdive-center.com) for dive packages, courses, and equipment rental.

Around the beach

Getting a tan, running yourself ragged at beach sports, and going wild at night are the main concerns in Panama City Beach – you'll get very strange looks indeed if you go around demanding history, art, and culture. Other than the beach-based activities, you can try your hand at a variety of waterborne pastimes such as jet-skiing, parasailing, fishing, snorkeling, and scuba diving (see box above), while go-kart rides and amusement parks are fodder for landlubbers. Panama City Beach's other main attractions are as follows:

Gulf World Marine Park

15412 Front Beach Rd. Daily 9am, closing times vary throughout the year; $19.42; ⓣ850/234-5271, ⓦwww.gulfworldmarinepark.com.

Allow about three hours to wander around the 20,000 square feet of this indoor tropical garden, where you can see dolphin, sea lion, and tropical bird shows, as well as view otters, alligators, penguins, and the like. Further attractions include the nightly "Splash Magic" laser show and the chance to become a dolphin trainer for the day.

Miracle Strip Park

12000 Front Beach Rd. Daily late May to early August, 6–11pm, Sat 2–11.15pm; $18; ⓣ850/234-5810, ⓦwww.miraclestrippark.com.

A throwback to the days when Florida amusement parks thrived on a wholesome recipe of cotton candy, popcorn, and rickety roller-coaster rides. The recent addition of "The O2 Tower," a 185-foot tower with an exhilarating three-second drop, has added some bite to this family-run park of forty years' standing, even if its charm and the absence of long waiting lines are the main reasons for a visit.

Museum of Man in the Sea

17314 W US-98. Daily 9am–5pm; $5; ⓣ850/235-4101.

All you ever needed to know about diving can be found in the museum's large collection, which includes enormous eighteenth-century underwater helmets, bulky air pumps, bodysuits, deep-sea cutting devices, and torpedo-like propulsion vehicles. A separate display documents *Sealab*, the US Navy's underwater research vessels, the first of which was fitted out in Panama City and now stands outside the museum. This entertaining stop makes an ideal prelude to a day's snorkeling.

Shell Island

Two three-hour cruises leave from Captain Anderson's Marina at the foot of Thomas Drive. Boat departures 9am and 1pm; return ticket $16. Alternatively, a five-minute voyage from St Andrews State Recreation Area departs every 30min 9am–5pm in summer and 10am–3pm in winter.

This seven-mile strip of sand is a haven for shell collectors and sun worshippers alike. As there's little shade on the undeveloped island, however, sunglasses are essential; the glare off the sands can be blinding. There are numerous boat trips from Captain Anderson Marina, most of which include a brief stop at Shell Island. Prices vary wildly among tour operators, so shop around.

Shipwreck Island Waterpark

12000 Front Beach Rd. Daily late May to early August, 10.30am–5.30pm; $24, locker rental $3; ⓣ850/234-0368, ⓦwww.shipwreckisland.com.

Gambling on the notion that people would pay for the privilege of being tossed and turned in water (when they could get it for free in the Gulf of Mexico over the road), this water park built its reputation around a wave pool that produces three foot waves roughly every ten minutes. So far at least, the venture appears to have paid off, and the wave pool, thrilling slides, and a play area for the kids make this a good break from a day on the beach.

St Andrews State Recreation Area

4607 State Park Lane. Daily 8am–sunset; cars $4, pedestrians and cyclists $1; ⓣ850/233-5140.

Get here early and you'll spot a variety of hopping, crawling, and slithering wildlife by following one of the nature trails around the pine forest and salt marshes within the park. By noon, however, the hordes will have arrived to swim, fish, and prepare picnics. If you're with kids, they'll enjoy splashing in the shallow lagoon sheltered by an artificial reef known as The Jetties. Clean enough that locals catch their dinner here, these crystal waters are ideal for swimming, snorkeling, diving, canoeing, and kayaking. Take advantage of the campground (see p.440) to enjoy the quietest times in this spot.

Zoo World

9008 Front Beach Rd. Daily 9am–7.30pm; $11.95; ⓣ850/230-4839.

If you're not opposed to animals being incarcerated, you'll enjoy this small collection of lions, tigers, orangutans, and other creatures, many of whom prefer to sleep through the midday heat, so try to time your visit for early morning or late afternoon.

Eating

As you would expect on such a touristy stretch of coast, places **to eat** are plentiful. Many of these are as down-at-heel as their surroundings, and you can fill up on mediocre food – much of it presented in buffet style – without changing out of your swimsuit. More refined dining can be found along Front Beach Road and Thomas Drive, with the more interesting choices concentrated at the eastern end of the beach strip. For more upmarket options try the marinas off Thomas Drive.

Panama City Beach is known for its **seafood** – most of it fresh when cooked – making seafood specialty dishes such as stuffed red snapper or grouper, seafood crêpes, or lobster thermidor good choices.

30° Blue 3900 Marriott Drive, at the Bay Point Marina ⓣ850/236-1115. The Cole Porter songs played in the background and impressive wine list make this place one of the more refined places to eat. Dinner only. Closed Sun.

Bishop's Family Buffet 12628 Front Beach Rd ⓣ850/234-6457. Features substantial buffet meals three times daily for $5–10, with a strong emphasis on seafood items such as snow crab legs and fried shrimp and oyster.

Capt. Anderson's 5551 N Lagoon Drive, in Captain Anderson's Marina ⓣ850/234-2225. Arguably the finest restaurant in town, with mainly seafood dishes – the grilled bay shrimp is highly touted – and a good enough selection of steaks to satisfy meat eaters. Dinner only. Closed Sun.

Hamilton's 5711 N Lagoon Drive ⓣ850/234-1255. Blackened alligator nuggets stand out among the more regular dishes. Opposite *Capt. Anderson's* (see above). Dinner only.

Mikato 7724 Front Beach Rd ⓣ850/234-1388. Watching the knife-throwing chefs is part of the show at this moderately priced sushi bar.

Mike's Diner 17554 Front Beach Rd ⓣ850/234-1942. This coffee shop opens early, closes late, and is great value throughout the day. Along with the staple diner-style dishes, it also has good home-made shakes and sundaes.

Ruthie T's 8503 Thomas Drive, two blocks east of Joan Avenue ⓣ850/234-2111. Moderately priced soul food with heart and a house special of blackened prime rib with attitude. The wine list is first rate.

Schooners 5121 Thomas Drive ⓣ850/235-3555. It may or may not be true to its billing as "last local beach club," but there is a good atmosphere at this restaurant on the beach where you can enjoy fresh seafood and listen to live music.

Shuckum's Oyster Pub & Seafood Grill 15614 Front Beach Rd ⓣ850/235-3214, ⓦwww.shuckums.com. Cheap oysters in many styles are available here, including fried in a sandwich.

Sweet Basil's 11208 Front Beach Rd ⓣ850/234-2855. Classy Italian food and the freshest seafood are offered at this moderately priced eatery.

The Treasure Ship 3605 Thomas Drive, in Treasure Island Marina ⓣ850/234-8881. A seafood restaurant built to resemble a wooden sailing ship, with pirates hopping around the tables.

Nightlife and entertainment

Even if you only stay a few minutes, you should visit one of the two beachside **nightlife** fleshpots, otherwise known as "superclubs": *Club La Vela*, 8813 Thomas Drive (ⓣ850/234-3866, ⓦwww.lavela.com), or *Spinnaker*, 8795 Thomas Drive (ⓣ850/234-7822, ⓦwww.spinnakerbeachclub.com) – both open 10am to 4am, with cover charges varying nightly (generally $5–15). Each has dozens of bars, several discos, live bands, and a predominantly under-25 clientele eagerly awaiting the bikini and wet T-shirt contests and "hunk shows." Because competition between the two clubs is so intense, there will often be free beer in the early evening. During the day, the action is by the clubs' open-air pools, where you're overdressed if covering anything more than your genitalia.

Everywhere else is tranquil by comparison. Although they may also have live music, a number of **bars** are worth a call simply for a drink. *Schooners* (see above) is a popular place to hang out at night, as is *Salty's by the Sea*, 11073 Front Beach Rd (ⓣ850/234-1913), another restaurant-cum-bar on the beach. You could also check out *Pineapple Willy's*, 9875 S Thomas Drive (ⓣ850/235-0928), with its sports bar atmosphere, or *Key West*, 6804 Thomas Drive (ⓣ850/230-9099), for your best chance of meeting the locals, be they long-haired bikers or shaven-headed types from the nearby military base. For more ideas tune in to **Beach TV**, a local television station with reports on various Panama City Beach bars.

Given the large number of visitors from the southern states of the US, **country music** is more popular here than it would be at almost any other beach resort in the world. The Ocean Opry Country Music Show, 8400 Front Beach Road (shows Mon–Sat during summer, three times a week, less at other times; ⓣ850/234-5464, ⓦwww.theoceanopryshow.com), features some good renditions of well-known country tracks, as well as comedy performances by cowboy boot- and dungaree-wearing comedians, and is one of the rare nightlife options in Panama City Beach suitable for the whole family.

West of Panama City Beach: the South Walton beaches

West of Panama City Beach, the motels eventually give way to the more rugged and less developed **beaches of South Walton County**: fifty miles of some of Florida's best-kept coastline. With a few exceptions, accommodation here is in resort complexes with sky-high rates, but it's a great area to spend a day. **Route 30A** (far superior to US-98, which takes an inland route) is an eighteen-mile scenic road linking the region's small beach communities. For **general information** on the South Walton beaches and surrounding area, phone the South Walton Tourist Development Council (daily 8am–4.30pm; ⓣ1-800/822-6877), or visit their offices at the junction of Route 331 and US-98, twenty miles west of Panama City Beach and ten miles east of San Destin.

Deer Lake Park and Seagrove Beach

Deer Lake Park, ten miles west of Panama City Beach on Route 30A, is a dramatic stretch of creamy-white sand dunes on a coastline studded with smooth driftwood. The best beach of the South Walton bunch, it somehow goes almost without mention in the area's tourist brochures. The road signposted "Deer Lake Park" ends at a parking lot, and a five-minute walk through scrubland leads to the beach, a favorite hideout for nude sunbathing – officially, it's forbidden, but the rules are enforced infrequently.

A few miles west, **Seagrove Beach** shares the same attractive shoreline as Deer Lake Park. If you wish to **stay**, the *Sugar Beach Inn Bed and Breakfast*, 3501 E Scenic 30A, at Seagrove Beach (ⓣ850/231-1577, ⓦwww.sugarbeachinn.com; ❻), is a luxurious Victorian-style inn with Gulf views within walking distance of the sea. For RV owners aged fifty and up (this place is only for seniors), there's the *Seagrove Beach RV Resort*, 4501 Hwy-30A (ⓣ850/231-3839 or 1-877/247-6878, ⓦwww.seagrovebeachrvresort.com; $33). Among the places to **eat**, *Cocoons*, Hwy-30A (ⓣ850/231-4544), is a great deli that offers take-out sandwiches, barbecued ribs, and roast chickens for picnicking on the beach. More upmarket and comfortable dining is available at the stylish *Café Thirty A*, Hwy-30A (ⓣ850/231-2166), a rotisserie and bar serving mainly fish and meat dishes. If you're keen to **cycle** or **paddle** around, Butterfly Bike & Kayak Rentals, 3657 Hwy-30A (ⓣ850/231-2826), is a good place to start.

Seaside and Grayton Beach

An exception to the casual, unplanned appearance of most South Walton beach towns, **SEASIDE** (ⓦwww.seasidefl.com), just west of Seagrove Beach, is an experiment in urban architecture begun in 1981 by a rich, idealistic developer named Robert Davies. The theory was that Seaside's pseudo-Victorian cottages, all gleaming white and incredibly well kept, would foster village-like neighborliness and instill a sense of community. In reality, they did nothing of the sort, and it's basically a wealthy and sterile resort these days. Still, as elitist and economically discriminating as this place is, there's no escaping the unique appeal of the streets; you won't see houses like this anywhere else, and though you'll never feel like you belong, it's well worth stopping to explore. The shops are interesting and unusual, offering high-quality arts and crafts, gourmet food, and expensive clothing, and the beach is fantastic. Everything is expensive, though, starting with the **accommodation** at *Josephine's*, 38 Seaside Ave (ⓣ850/231-1940 or 1-800/848-1840, ⓦwww.josephinesinn.com; ❼), the most elegant bed and (champagne) breakfast on the Gulf Coast. The owners can even arrange a massage followed by a glass on the veranda and more than likely a beautiful sunset for the final touch of perfection. Places to **eat** are equally pricey. *Bud and Alley's,* Route 30A (ⓣ850/231-5900), is widely renowned for its "carpet bag steak," a filet mignon stuffed with pan-fried oysters, while at lunchtime try *Café Spiazzia,* 183 Central Square (ⓣ850/231-1297), whose dishes use fresh ingredients, and the coffee is great. For luscious cakes and an earful of Seaside's local gossip, head for *Modica Market,* 109 Central Square (ⓣ850/231-1214), a fabulous gourmet grocery store.

The antidote to Seaside's sterility is just a few miles further along Route 30A at **GRAYTON**, whose secluded position (it's hemmed in by protected land) and ramshackle wooden dwellings have taken the fancy of a number of artists who now reside here. Check out some of their work at galleries such as Monet Monet, Hwy-30A (ⓣ850/231-5117), and The Studio Gallery, Logan Lane (ⓣ850/231-3331). For more information on the area visit the **Chamber of Commerce** at the junction of US-331 and US-98 (daily 8am–4.30pm; ⓣ850/267-3511). **Accommodation** is much cheaper here than at Seaside. One unusual option is the *Hibiscus Coffee and Guesthouse,* 85 De Funiak St (ⓣ850/231-2733, ⓦwww.hibiscusflorida.com; ❺), a coffee house serving basic snack food during the day. Nine simple yet comfortable rooms are available – four in the coffee house building and five in a renovated 1904 house. *Blue Luna Café,* 51 Upper Town, Grayton Circle (ⓣ850/231-0530), has a good dinner menu that won't break the bank, while for more formal dining, *Criolla's,* Hwy-30A (ⓣ850/267-1267), has excellent seafood served in Creole style.

Many who come to Grayton skip straight through to the **Grayton Beach State Recreation Area** (daily 8am–sunset; cars $3.25, pedestrians and cyclists $1), just east of the village. The recreation area is walled by sand dunes and touches the banks of a large brackish lake. A night at the park's **campground** (ⓣ850/231-4210; $15.40 without electricity; reservations recommended) leaves plenty of time for a slow exploration of the village and its natural surrounds. Continuing on to Destin (see p.446), route 30A rejoins US-98 seven miles west of Grayton.

Blue Mountain Beach and Santa Rosa Beach

Just west of Grayton the relatively undiscovered **Blue Mountain Beach** is a welcome escape from the Spring Break crowds that zip past without a second glance. Don't make the same mistake; the quiet beach is an expanse of creamy white sand bordered by unpretentious vacation homes. There's a gourmet grocery store at *Blue Mountain Plaza,* though for delicious, health-conscious lunches, wander across the street to *For the Health of It,* no. 2217 on Scenic Route 30A (ⓣ850/267-0558, ⓦwww.shopforthehealthofit.com), where lime-bean chowder and sesame pastas are served in the adjacent café and a huge selection of organic everything, as well as therapeutic massages, is available in the shop.

A mile further west is **Santa Rosa Beach**. Slightly more developed than Blue Mountain, Santa Rosa has one of the better places to **stay** in the region: *A Highlands House Bed & Breakfast,* 4193 W Scenic 30A (ⓣ850/267-0110, ⓦwww.ahighlandshousebbinn.com; ❺), an excellent, well-furnished lodging with panoramic views and a perfect beachside setting, all for considerably less than the selection of characterless new hotels that dot the area. A couple of good – though not cheap – places to **eat** here are *Goatfeathers Seafood Market & Restaurant,* 3865 W County Hwy-30A (ⓣ850/267-3342), which has excellent seafood, and *Café Tango* (ⓣ850/267-0054), down a tiny track called Vicki Street and serving Mediterranean and Deep South dishes in a pretty red and green cottage.

Hidden up Satinwood Road, just opposite *Goatfeathers*, is *The S. House* (Mon–Sat 10am–4pm; ⓣ850/267-2231), an **antique** shop dealing in a cache of vintage clothes, furniture, and collectable oddities from the region. If you ask, the friendly owner will show you his orchid house, which is dripping with color just outside.

Inland: Eden State Gardens

Away from the coast road, only **Eden Gardens State Park** (daily 8am–sunset; free), reached by Route 395 from Seagrove Beach a mile east of Seaside, is worth a visit. The gardens, now disturbed only by the buzz of dragonflies, were once the base of the Wesley Lumber Company, which helped decimate Florida's forests during the 1890s timber boom. Impressed with the setting, the company's boss pinched some of the wood to build himself a grandiose two-story plantation-style home, the **Wesley House** (guided tours on the hour Thurs–Mon 10am–3pm; $1.50; ⓣ850/231-4214). After the death of the last Wesley, the house stood empty for ten years until Lois Maxon, a journalist with an interest in antiques, bought it in 1963 as a showcase for her collections, which include a Chippendale cabinet and a Louis XVI mirror.

Destin and around

Heading west from Panama City, six miles before you encounter **DESTIN**, you will pass through San Destin, its newer, more resort-like cousin. San Destin is an exclusive and somewhat soulless collection of high-rise resorts and is best given a wide berth. The real Destin, once a small fishing village and a cult name among anglers for the fat marlin and tuna lurking in an undersea canyon a few miles offshore, is a less pristine version of San Destin. Towering condos emerge through the heat haze as you approach on US-98 and bear witness to more than two decades of unrestrained exploitation that have stripped away much of the town's character. Pick up tourist information at the **Visitors Center**, 1021 Hwy-98 (Mon–Fri 9am–5pm; ⓣ850/837-6241, ⓦwww.destin-fwb.com), signposted to your right as you arrive on US-98.

Accommodation

Most of the **accommodation** consists of rather monolithic hotels in central Destin, so head four miles east to the **motels** along Route 2378, also known as Old US-98 or Beach Road. *Surf High*, no. 3000 (ⓣ850/837-2366; ❹), is situated on the Gulf front and offers comfortable accommodation and a heated pool. A good alternative is the *Henderson Park Inn*, 2700 US-98 E (ⓣ850/654-0400 or 1-800/336-4853, ⓦwww.hendersonparkinn.com; ❹), an elegant beachside hotel that provides bed and breakfast in style and, for added romance, a restaurant offering candlelit dining. The free use of beach chairs for guests is also a thoughtful touch.

Of the **campgrounds**, only two accept tents: *Destin RV Resort*, 150 Regions Way (ⓣ850/837-6215, ⓦwww.destinrvresort.com; $24), and, in central Destin, *Destin Campground*, 209 Beach Drive (ⓣ850/837-6511; $15).

The town and beach

Evidence of Destin's sudden expansion can be found amid the fading photos of bygone days in the **Old Destin Post Office Museum** (Wed 1–5pm; free), opposite the library (Ⓣ850/837-8572) on Stahlman Avenue. The **Fishing Museum**, at 20009 Emerald Coast Parkway (Mon–Sat 11am–4pm; $2), with its mounted record-breaking catches and thousands of pictures of landed fish with their grinning captors, is proof of Destin's high esteem among hook-and-line enthusiasts.

An escape from the condo overkill is provided by enticing white sands situated just east of Destin. The **beach** here is family territory, but it offers relaxation, excellent sea swimming, and classic Gulf-coast sunsets. To reach it, take **Route 2378**, lined by unobtrusive motels and beach shops, which makes a coast-hugging loop off US-98, starting about four miles from Destin.

Eating and nightlife

On Old US-98, *The Back Porch*, at no. 1740 (Ⓣ850/837-2022), is Destin's oldest seafood and oyster house and one of the few places open late (until 11pm). Otherwise, the *Destin Diner*, 1083 US-98 (Ⓣ850/654-5843), dishes up hearty and economical breakfasts, burgers, and frothy milkshakes in surroundings of neon and chrome. Later in the day, there's a buffet at the *Flamingo Café*, 414 US-98 (Ⓣ850/837-0961), which is famous for its sea view and martinis. Along Route 2378, you can munch a fish sandwich or shrimp salad at *Captain Dave's*, no. 3796 (Ⓣ850/837-2627), while gazing over the ocean.

Destin's **nightlife** has little vigor: a few of the beachside bars and restaurants offer nightly drinks specials – look for the signs – and live music. Dance the night away at *Nightown*, 140 Palmetto Ave (Ⓣ850/837-6448; open until 4am), two blocks east of the Destin Bridge (see below), where you can choose to listen to live rock bands in one room or jig around to dance music in front of a video wall in another.

Okaloosa Island and Fort Walton Beach

US-98 leaves Destin by rising over the **Destin Bridge**, giving towering views of the two-tone ocean and intensely white sands, before hitting the crazy-golf courses and amusement parks of **OKALOOSA ISLAND**. The island's **beaches**, immediately west, are a better sight, kept in their unspoiled state by their owner – the US Air Force – and making a lively weekend playground for local youths and high-spirited beach bums.

A mile west, the neon motel signs that greet arrivals to **FORT WALTON BEACH** offer no indication that this was the site of a major religious and social center during the Paleo-Indian period – so important were the finds made here that the place came to be associated with a rigid form of tribal society, the so-called "Fort Walton Culture" (see Contexts, p.462, for more). These days it's military culture that dominates, as the town is home to Eglin, the country's biggest Air Force base. Aside from a few crewcuts and topless bars, however, you'll see little evidence of the base close to US-98, and much of Fort Walton Beach has a more downbeat and homely feel – and slightly lower prices – than Destin. Stop by the local **visitors center**, 1540 Miracle Strip Parkway (Mon–Fri 8am–5pm, Sat & Sun 10am–4pm Ⓣ850/651-7131 or 1-800/322-3319, Ⓦwww.destin-fwb.com), for information on eating and accommodation.

The main attraction here is the world's oldest marine show aquarium: the **Gulfarium**, 1010 Miracle Strip Parkway (daily: mid-May to early Sept 9am–8pm; early Sept to mid-May 9am–6pm; last admission two hours before closing time; $16.99; ⓣ850/244-5169, ⓦwww.gulfarium.com). Opened in 1958, it's now one of the best aquariums in the area, with all kinds of sea life on show. Sharks, moray eels, and sea turtles are displayed in their natural habitat and other exhibits include penguins and alligators. A program of dolphin and sea lion shows, each lasting about twenty minutes, is scheduled throughout the day and for an extra fee ($100) you can even get into the pool with the dolphins.

Accommodation

While it's not hard to find, **accommodation** in these parts varies little from the expensive, resort-style hotels and cheaper motels you'll find elsewhere in the coastal Panhandle. *Cayo Grande Suites Hotel*, 214 Racetrack Rd (ⓣ850/862-7540 or 1-800/827-9908, ⓦwww.cayogrande.com; ❹), is a luxury hotel with three pools, two saunas, tennis, a fitness center, and a putting green. Prices include breakfast and there is a good café on site. Most of the **motels** are along Miracle Strip Parkway (the local section of US-98). *Super 8,* no. 333 SW (ⓣ850/244-4999; ❸), is a very basic two-story motel with a small pool and some rooms with fridges and microwaves. *Greenwood*, 1340 US-98 (ⓣ850/244-1141; ❸), is good, economical accommodation with a heated pool.

The nearest **campground** is the RV-only *Playground RV Park*, four miles north on Hwy-189 (ⓣ850/862-3513); campers with **tents** should make for *Navarre Beach Campground* (ⓣ850/939-2188, ⓦwww.navbeach.com), just outside Navarre, where a site costs $26 and cabins start at $49.

The Indian Temple Mound and Air Force Armament museums

If you were inspired by the sizeable temple mound standing incongruously beside the busy highway into Fort Walton Beach, then you might wish to inspect the small **Indian Temple Mound Museum** (Mon–Fri 10am–4pm, Sat 9am–4pm; $2; ⓣ850/833-9595), at the junction of US-98 and Route 85, which is crammed with over four thousand elucidating relics.

For an insight into more contemporary culture, the **Air Force Armament Museum**, 100 Museum Drive, Eglin (daily 9.30am–4.30pm; free; ⓣ850/882-4062), six miles north of Fort Walton Beach on Route 85, has a large stock of what the local Air Force base is famous for – guns, missiles, and bombs, and the planes that carry them. The first guided missiles were put together here in the Forties, and work on developing and testing (non-nuclear) airborne weaponry has continued unabated ever since.

Eating and nightlife

The area's better **restaurants** are considerably easier to reach with your own transport. *Old Bay Steamer*, 1310 US-98 (ⓣ850/664-2795), serves good, fresh seafood and pasta dishes, while *Thai Saree*, 163 Eglin Parkway (ⓣ850/244-4600), has excellent Thai food for lunch and dinner at reasonable prices. But best of all are the high-quality steak and seafood dinners at the *Coach-N-Four*, 1313 Lewis Turner Blvd (ⓣ850/863-3443).

Fort Walton Beach **nightlife** amounts to little more than the usual **beachfront bars**, mostly on Okaloosa Island, with some good happy hours. The best are *Pandora's*, 1120 Santa Rosa Blvd (ⓣ850/244-8669), which draws tourists and locals to its nightly specials; and *Fudpucker's On the Island*, 108 Santa Rosa Blvd (ⓣ850/243-3833), which has live entertainment on "The Deck."

Pandora's attracts a mature clientele, while the crowd at *Fudpucker's On the Island* is much younger. A good **gay bar/club** (actually the only gay club between Panama City and Pensacola) is *Club Insatiable*, 217 Miracle Strip Parkway (Ⓣ850/664-2966, Ⓦwww.clubinsatiable.com), a friendly, lively place with drag shows and male strippers, as welcoming to lesbians as it is to gay men.

West from Fort Walton

If you're driving, travel **west from Fort Walton** along Hwy-98 and branch off on Route 399 for sixty scenic miles along **Santa Rosa Island** to the Gulf Islands National Seashore, near Pensacola Beach (see "Pensacola and around," below). The parallel route, the continuation of Hwy-98, is much duller but is the one the thrice-daily Greyhound **bus** takes from the station at 101 SE Perry Ave (Ⓣ850/243-1940).

Pensacola and around

Tucked away at the western end of the Panhandle, **PENSACOLA** is built on the northern bank of the broad Pensacola Bay, five miles inland from the nearest beaches. Although its primary features are a naval aviation school and some busy dockyards, Pensacola is also of considerable historic interest. In 1559, Spanish soldiers and colonists established a settlement at Pensacola that lasted two years before being destroyed by a hurricane. A permanent settlement was not established here until 1698, when Fort San Carlos was built. The fort repeatedly changed hands between the Spanish, French, and British before becoming the venue where Florida was officially ceded by Spain to the US in 1821. The city has retained enough evidence of its mercurial history to warrant a short visit, but it also makes a good base for exploring one of the prettiest and least-spoiled parts of the coastal Panhandle. Just cross the Bay Bridge to the coast, and you'll find Pensacola Beach neighboring the wild, protected beaches of the Gulf Islands National Seashore.

Arrival, information, and getting around

Pensacola Regional Airport, 2430 Airport Blvd (Ⓣ850/436-5005, Ⓦwww.flypensacola.com), is a fifteen-minute drive from downtown. Unless you're arriving from the inland Panhandle on I-10 or US-90, aim to take the scenic route to Pensacola, along Santa Rosa Island on **Route 399** (also known here as Via De Luna Drive). Doing this, you'll first strike Pensacola Beach, from which Pensacola Beach Road swings north, crossing the Santa Rosa peninsula and joining **US-98** before crossing the three-mile-long Pensacola Bay Bridge into the city. Unfortunately, the Greyhound **bus** station is far from central, being seven miles north of the city center at 505 W Burgess Rd (Ⓣ850/476-4800); bus #10A and #10B link it to Pensacola proper – see p.450 (#10B is the quicker of the two; note that there is no service on Sundays).

At the foot of the Bay Bridge, on the city side, is the **Visitor Information Center**, 401 E Gregory St (daily 8am–5pm; Ⓣ850/434-1234 or 1-800/874-1234, Ⓦwww.visitpensacola.com), packed with the usual worthwhile handouts. A more convenient source of information for those without a car is the downtown **Chamber of Commerce**, 117 W Garden St (Mon–Fri 8am–5pm; Ⓣ850/438-4081, Ⓦwww.pensacolachamber.com).

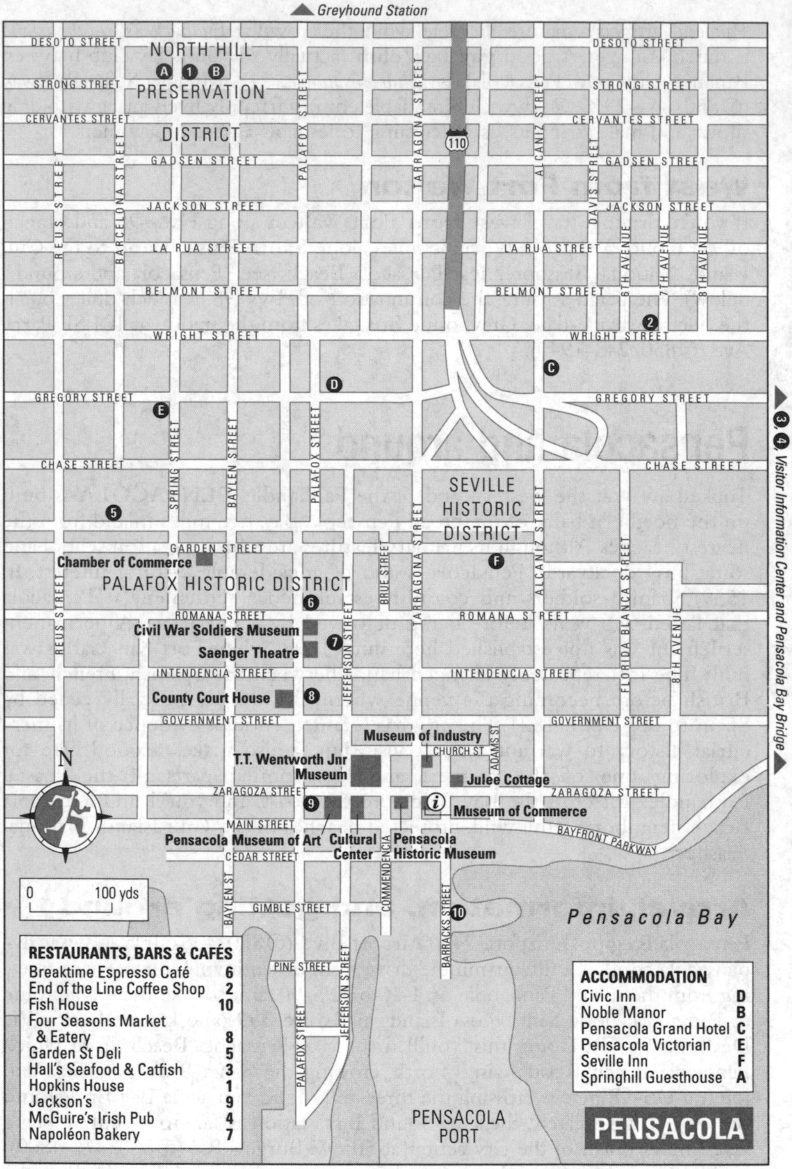

In the downtown area, you can easily get around on foot. Otherwise, **local buses** (for information call ⓣ850/595-3228, ext 30, ⓦwww.ecat.pensacola.com) serve the city, while route #21 goes to the beach three times daily; the main terminal is north of downtown at the junction of Fairfield Drive and L Street. There is also a beach trolley that only operates Friday to Sunday between May and September, which will take you up and down the beaches, but does not connect to downtown. Getting from the city to the beach by **taxi** will cost roughly $12–14; reliable cab companies include Cross Town Taxi (Ⓣ850/456-8294) or Yellow (Ⓣ850/433-3333). For **bike** hire on the beach try Tiki Island Golf & Games, 2 Vie De Luna Drive (Ⓣ850/932-1550).

Accommodation

The main approach roads from I-10 – North Davis Boulevard and Pensacola Boulevard – are both lined with unmissable billboards advertising **budget chain hotels** for $35–55 a night.

The closest **campground** is the *Fort Pickens Campground* ($20; reservation line Ⓣ1-800/365-2267), on the Gulf Islands National Seashore, a few miles west of Pensacola Beach (see p.457). Further out, options are *Big Lagoon*, ten miles southwest on Route 292A on Perdido Key (Ⓣ850/492-1595; $15.53), and *Navarre Beach Campground*, 9201 Navarre Parkway US-98 (Ⓣ850/939-2188 or 1-888/639-2188, Ⓔcampnbc@aol.com; $26), who also rent Kamping Kabins from $49 a night.

Downtown Pensacola

Civic Inn 200 N Palafox St Ⓣ850/432-3441. Cheap, if uninspiring, motel rooms in a convenient downtown location. Though there's a pool, it's located in the parking lot next to busy Palafox Street. ❷

Noble Manor 110 W Strong St Ⓣ850/434-9544, Ⓦwww.noblemanor.com. This bed and breakfast offers special packages and has a desirable location in the peaceful North Hill District. The rooms are cozy and comfortable; cookies, chocolates, and other tempting snacks are everywhere; breakfast is served in either the formal dining room or front porch, and, unusually for a B&B, there is a pool and two hot tubs. ❹

Pensacola Grand Hotel 200 E Gregory St Ⓣ850/433-3336 or 1-800/348-3336, Ⓦwww.pensacolagrandhotel.com. The most upscale lodgings in downtown, featuring a luxurious pool, gym, library, restaurant, and cocktail lounge. ❻

Pensacola Victorian 203 W Gregory St Ⓣ850/434-2818 or 1-800/370-8354, Ⓦwww.pensacolavictorian.com. Charming and comfortable, this bed and breakfast is in a Queen Anne-style home that was originally built for a captain who also founded the Pensacola Symphony Orchestra. ❸

Seville Inn 223 E Garden St Ⓣ850/433-8331 or 1-800/277-7275, Ⓦwww.sevilleinn.com. Standard, no-frills accommodation and as comfortable as the numerous chain motels around Pensacola, but in a much more central location. ❷

Springhill Guesthouse 903 N Spring St Ⓣ850/438-6887 or 1-800/475-1956, Ⓦwww.springhillguesthouse.com. The two suites here (one with a full kitchen; both with attractive fireplaces) have cheaper rates for weekly and monthly stays. Though it doesn't serve breakfast, it's directly opposite the popular *Hopkins House* restaurant (see p.454). ❺

Pensacola Beach

Hampton Inn 2 Via De Luna Drive Ⓣ850/932-6800 or 1-800/320-8108, Ⓦwww.hampton-beachresort.com. The comfortable rooms come with balconies and views of the Gulf, as well as the usual range of resort-style facilities. Expensive, but you generally get what you pay for. ❹

Hilton Garden Inn 12 Via De Luna Drive Ⓣ850/916-2999, Ⓦwww.pensacolabeach.gar-deninn.com. One of the beach's newer and most luxurious properties, geared to business guests as much as to vacationing families. Here you'll find Pensacola's largest convention space, the city's only indoor heated pool, and a "Kid's Club" with various activities to keep the youngsters entertained. ❹

Sandpiper Gulf Aire 21 Via De Luna Drive Ⓣ850/932-2319, Ⓦwwwparadisebeachhomes.com. Two separate motels, *Sandpiper* and *Gulf Aire*, have joined forces to make a good, cheap alternative to the large beachside resorts. A private beach compensates for the off-beach location, while a picnic area, BBQ, and pool are some of the other facilities. ❷

The City

While not as lively as it once was, Pensacola still warrants exploration due to a number of buildings of architectural merit and a relaxing atmosphere. The city is grouped in three distinct, adjoining **districts**: the south-central Palafox District, North Hill in the northern section of the city, and the Seville District in Pensacola's southeast quarter. The Palafox and Seville districts are the most interesting historically. The streets of Seville are flanked by house after house of interest. The only other attraction that might delay serious sunbathing at Pensacola Beach is a naval aviation museum.

The Palafox District

Pensacola was already a booming port at the turn of the nineteenth century, and the opening of the Panama Canal was expected to further boost the city's fortunes. Sadly, the surge in wealth never came, but the optimism of the era is apparent in the delicate ornamentation and detail in the buildings around the **Palafox District**. Take a look first at the **County Court House**, at the junction of Palafox and Government streets, which, besides its legal function, has also seen service as a customs house, a post office, and tax offices. Opposite, the slender form and vertically aligned windows of the **Seville Tower** exaggerate the height of what, in 1909, was the tallest building in Florida. A block further north, at 118 S Palafox Place, the Spanish Baroque **Saenger Theater** (see "Nightlife," p.455), is now the base of the Pensacola Symphony Orchestra. If the door is open, take the opportunity to have a peek at the interior – twice as opulent as the outside.

Also meriting a look is the **Civil War Soldiers Museum**, 108 S Palafox Place (Tues–Sat 10am–4.30pm; $5; ⓣ850/469-1900, ⓦwww.cwmuseum.org), which houses a collection of uniforms, weaponry, and many unsettling medical tools – all of which saw action in the Civil War – a graphic illustration of the conditions endured by soldiers during the conflict between the states. Ask at the entrance, which doubles as a well-stocked bookstore specializing in the Civil War, about the thirty-minute video that puts the exhibits into context.

North Hill

Between 1870 and 1930, Pensacola's professional classes took a shine to the **North Hill** area, just across Wright Street from the Palafox District, and commissioned elaborate homes in a plethora of fancy styles. Strewn across the tree-studded fifty-block area are pompous Neoclassical porches, cutesy Tudor Revival cottages, low-slung California-style bungalows, and rounded towers belonging to fine Queen Anne homes. These are private residences not open to the public, and the best way to see them is by walking or driving around Palafox, Spring, Strong, and Baylen streets.

The clamor to build houses in this fashionable neighborhood led to the dismantling of **Fort George**, which had once barracked two thousand British troops before falling to the Spanish at the Battle of Pensacola in 1781. Only an imitation cannon and a plaque at the corner of Palafox and La Rua streets commemorate the original location of the fort.

The Seville District: Historic Pensacola Village

As a commercial center, Pensacola kicked into gear in the late 1700s with a cosmopolitan mix of Native Americans, early settlers, and seafaring traders gathering here to swap, sell, and barter on the waterfront of the **Seville District**, just east of Palafox Street. Those who did well took up permanent residence, and many of their homes remain in fine states of repair, forming – together with several museums – the **Historic Pensacola Village** (Mon–Fri 10am–4pm; $6; ⓣ850/595-5985, ⓦwww.historicpensacola.org). Each ticket is valid for one week and allows access to all of the museums and former homes (and you should see them *all* – the effect of the whole is far greater than any of its parts) in an easily navigated four-block area. Start at the **Museum of Commerce**, next door to the **visitor center** (Mon–Fri 10am–4pm; ⓣ850/595-5985) on the corner of Zaragoza and Tarragona streets, an entertaining indoor recreation of Palafox Street in its heyday at the turn of the twentieth century, displaying many of the original storefronts and shop fittings. Much of the prosperity of Pensacola was based on the timber industry, a point celebrated by a noisy, working sawmill in the **Museum of Industry**, just across Zaragoza Street.

To catch up on earlier local history, cross Church Street to the sedate **Colonial Archaeology Trail**, where bits of pottery and weapons suggest the lifestyles of the city's first Spanish inhabitants and a marked path leads around the site of the Government House, an outpost of the British Empire which collapsed in the 1820s. Virtually next door (opposite the visitor center), the 1809 **Julee Cottage** belonged to Julee Panton, a "freewoman of color" who had her own land, business, and even her own slave. The building's exhibits record her life and deeds as well as the achievements of later black people with Pensacola associations.

Other **restored homes** in the vicinity signify the mishmash of architectural styles, from Creole to Greek Revival, favored by wealthier Pensacolians in the late 1800s. Filled with period furnishings, they make for an enjoyable browse – despite the somewhat corny period costumes of the attendants who sit in them during the summer season.

If you have neither the energy nor the inclination to visit all the museums and old homes of the Historic Village, head instead to the **Pensacola Historic Museum**, 115 Zaragoza St (Mon–Sat 10am–4.30pm; $2; ⓣ850/433-1559), operated by the Pensacola Historic Society and containing exhibits touching on pretty much every aspect of Pensacola's past.

The **T.T. Wentworth Jr Museum**, on Plaza Ferdinand (Mon–Sat 10am–4pm; $6, free admission with Historic Pensacola Village ticket), contains the random, garage-sale-like collections that once belonged to Mr Wentworth, who intended to create a museum of oddities. Thankfully, his ambitions were thwarted. The existing ephemera are briefly diverting, though it's the yellow-brick Renaissance building (constructed as the city hall in 1907) itself that is the real attraction. The upstairs has been converted to a museum of local history, which is comprehensive but not over-exciting. In the Plaza Ferdinand stands a statue to Andrew Jackson, the state's first governor, commemorating the fact that this is the spot where Florida was accepted into the US and, for the first time, an American flag was planted on US soil. If you want to learn more about the exhibits, join one of the tours that run regularly throughout the day.

Museum of Art

Cleverly incorporated into the old jailhouse, Pensacola's **Museum of Art**, opposite the Cultural Center at 407 S Jefferson St (Tues–Fri 10am–5pm, Sat & Sun noon–5pm; $2, free Tues; ⓣ850/432-6247, ⓦwww.pensacolamuseumofart.com), was built in 1906 on what was once the shoreline of Pensacola Bay (after ships started dumping their ballast stones, the shoreline was pushed out by half a mile). The art isn't of any particular distinction, but the building itself is worth exploring: old prison cells have been preserved as exhibition space, classrooms for children now occupy the former women's incarceration area, and temporary exhibits fill the upstairs all-male cell block.

The Museum of Naval Aviation and Fort Barrancas

You don't have to be a military fanatic to enjoy the **Museum of Naval Aviation** (daily 9am–5pm; free; ⓣ850/453-3604 or 1-800/327-5002,

ⓦwww.naval-air.org), inside the US naval base on Navy Boulevard, about eight miles southwest of downtown Pensacola and accessible by bus #14. Visitors can climb into many of the full-sized training cockpits and play with the controls. The main purpose of the museum, however, is to collect and display US naval aircraft, from the first flimsy seaplane acquired in 1911 to the Phantoms and Hornets of more recent times. Among them are a couple of oddities: a small Vietnamese plane, which carried a Vietnamese family onto a US carrier during the fall of Saigon, and the Command Module from the first Skylab mission in 1973, whose crew were naval pilots. It's all rather impressive and serves to underline Pensacola's role as the home base of US naval aviation. The base trains thousands of new pilots each year. Don't miss the seven-story-tall IMAX movie screen, on which a pilot's-eye view of flight makes for quite a visual sensation (tickets $6.50).

On the other side of the road lies the visitor center for **Fort Barrancas** (daily 8am–4.30pm; guided tours daily 2pm; free), part of the National Seashore area (see p.456). It's worth spending an hour or so at this well-preserved 1698 Spanish fort, whose design includes a fascinating system of connecting interior vaults.

Eating

The better **eating options** are to be found in and around the downtown area. Many of these establishments here cater to office workers and are only open during the day, but you'll always find restaurants that are open for dinner. Along the beach, the dining options are more homogeneous but the views – over the bay and Gulf coast – are far superior. The seafood is good, as it is along the whole stretch of the coastal Panhandle, and Pensacola's proximity to Alabama makes it one of the best places in Florida to sample authentic Southern cooking.

Pensacola

Breaktime Espresso Café 34 S Palafox St ⓣ850/438-7788. The best place for coffee that tastes of more than just flavored water. If you're hungry, consider ordering a filling wrap with your latte or cappuccino.

End of the Line Coffee Shop 610 E Wright St ⓣ850/429-0336. Munch on snacks and sandwiches in the Seventies-inspired interior, which is the frequent setting for poetry readings, an open-mike night (Thurs), and the like.

Fish House 600 S Barracks St ⓣ850/470-0003. A good local eatery featuring sushi and steaks with the seafood. The signature dish is "Grits a Ya-Ya" (smoked Gouda cheese grits covered with grilled mushrooms and shrimps).

Four Seasons Market & Eatery 212 S Palafox St ⓣ850/434-6771. Choose from enormous lunch plates of the meatloaf-and-mashed-potatoes variety or items from the self-serve salad bar.

Garden St Deli 236 W Garden St ⓣ850/470-0305. For cheap specialty sandwiches, try this deli, which serves excellent, inexpensive meals and a Sunday buffet brunch.

Hall's Seafood & Catfish 920 E Gregory St, at the foot of the Pensacola Bay Bridge ⓣ850/438-9019. Come here for fish-laden dinner buffets at reasonable prices and stellar views over the bay. Given its distance from downtown, you'll need your own transport.

Hopkins House 900 N Spring St ⓣ850/438-3979. Authentic and great-value Southern cooking eaten at communal tables in an old boarding house in the North Hill District. The hour-long waits for the fried chicken on Sundays is testament to the popularity of this local institution. Closed Sun dinner & Mon.

Jacksons 400 S Palafox St ⓣ850/469-9898. An elegant restaurant offering such delicacies as wood-fired salmon or filet mignon with fried oysters, and housed in a restored 1860 building overlooking the Plaza Ferdinand. Open for dinner only.

McGuire's Irish Pub 600 E Gregory St ⓣ850/433-6789. While the atmosphere at this popular tavern is very Irish (see opposite), the food menu is more mixed, ranging from down-to-earth corned beef and cabbage to excellent steaks.

Napoléon Bakery 101 S Jefferson St ⓣ850/434-9701. Good, if slightly pricey, European-style breads, cakes, and pastries, which you can enjoy with a cup of coffee and a newspaper in the adjoining dining room. Closed Sun.

Pensacola Beach

Bay on a Dolphin 400 Pensacola Beach Blvd, at the foot of Bob Sikes Bridge ⓣ850/932-7954. One of the more upscale options on the beach, slightly removed from the main drag, with seafood, steaks, pasta, good Greek salads, and views of the bay.
Flounder's Chowder & Ale House 800 Quietwater Beach Rd ⓣ850/932-2003. This pricey alehouse offers hearty seafood dinners such as shrimp salad, grouper, and, of course, flounder.
Jubilee 400 Quietwater Boardwalk ⓣ850/934-3108. Munch on burgers and fries in your swimsuit downstairs or dress up for Maine lobster and filet mignon dinners in the upscale restaurant upstairs, where your elevated position makes for some excellent views over the bay.
Peg Leg Pete's 1010 Fort Pickens Rd ⓣ850/932-4139, ⓦwww.peglegpetes.com. Known for its Cajun food and excellent raw bar, where you can slurp down oysters with various tasty accompaniments. The outdoor playground in the sand makes this a good place to bring the kids.

Nightlife

Pick up a copy of *The Weekender*, a supplement published every Friday with the *News Journal* daily newspaper, for information on the entertainment and nightlife possibilities in Pensacola. The city boasts two good **theaters** showing plays, musicals, and dance performances, as well as more lowbrow entertainment such as body building contests. The *Little Theatre*, 400 S Jefferson St (box office Mon–Fri 10am–5.30pm and one hour before curtain; tickets from $16; ⓣ850/432-2042, ⓦwww.pensacolalittletheatre.com), is housed in the Pensacola Cultural Center, and even if you don't see a production here, it's worth going inside just to look around. More architecturally impressive than the *Little*, the *Saenger Theater*, 118 S Palafox Place (box office Mon–Fri 10am–4pm and two hours before curtain; ⓣ850/444-7686, ⓦwww.pensacolasaenger.com), puts on plays, opera, and the like in a season that runs from October to April.

Pensacola

McGuire's Irish Pub 600 E Gregory St, Pensacola ⓣ850/433-6789. This lively pub brews its own ales and features nightly entertainment in each of its nine dining rooms. Beware: kissing the moosehead above the fireplace may be the price you pay for refusing to sing along to the Irish folk music. (See also review under "Eating," opposite.)
Seville Quarter 130 E Government St, Pensacola ⓣ850/434-6211. This tourist-oriented bar and disco decked out to reflect Pensacola's history is a bit more expensive than you might pay elsewhere, but it has atmosphere and can be fun.

Pensacola Beach

Bamboo Willie's 400 Quietwater Boardwalk, Pensacola Beach ⓣ850/916-9888. Overlooking the marina, with a long bar lined with machines churning lurid-colored frozen cocktails and enough space for a live band and the attendant dancing.
The Dock 4 Casino Beach Boardwalk, beside the pier, Pensacola Beach ⓣ850/934-3314, ⓦwww.thedock.pensacola.com. Packed every Friday and Saturday night when DJs set the mood, this club is also a venue for touring bands, local acts, and karaoke nights.
Flounder's Chowder & Ale House 800 Quietwater Beach Rd, Pensacola Beach ⓣ850/932-2003. Possibly the most hyped place to drink, this bar draws as many drinkers as diners and has live beach bands about once a week. (See also review under "Eating," above.)
Paddy O'Leary's Irish Pub 49 Via De Luna Drive, Pensacola Beach ⓣ850/916-9808. The place for a spot of traditional Irish music on the beach, plus Guinness stout served the way it was intended.
Sandshaker Lounge 731 Pensacola Beach Blvd, Pensacola Beach ⓣ850/932-2211. The self-professed home of the Bushwacker, an "adult milkshake" consisting of Kahlua, coconut, rum, and other ingredients – a popular tipple in these parts, and done very well at this bar.

Gay nightlife

For a city with a conservative reputation, Pensacola has a lively **gay scene** and a wild gay Memorial Day celebration that annually envelopes the city (see box,

The Memorial Day party

Every year between the Friday and Monday of the last week of May, Pensacola is consumed by a gay and lesbian party, which began when a 20-year-old local, Dickie Carr, threw a party at the *San Carlos Hotel* (recently demolished to build the courts of law). Dickie's father, who managed the hotel in the Seventies, said he would foot the bill for any of the five hundred rooms that weren't taken. They all were. The party took place on Memorial Day and has become an annual event involving most of the town and drawing large numbers of outsiders. Despite a brief and quickly squashed homophobic reaction from local businesses in 1985, the party gets bigger every year, pulling Americans from every state. The daytime festivities are mainly at the beach, while at night the partying shifts to the Pensacola nightclubs.

above). For a friendly local pub, head to *The Round Up*, 706 E Gregory St (ⓣ850/433-8482), which has a pleasant covered veranda but a strict ID policy – take official ID (like a passport) if you could be taken for under thirty. The biggest dance club for gays and lesbians in Pensacola is *Emerald City*, 406 E Wright St (ⓣ850/433-9491, ⓦwww.emeraldcitypensacola.com), which features drag shows, wet boxer contests, and plenty of thumping techno music (closed Tues). It's also a popular venue for the Memorial Day party.

Around Pensacola

On the other side of the bay from the city, the glistening quartz beaches of two **barrier islands** are ideal for sunbathing. Santa Rosa Island runs fifty miles from Fort Walton and contains Pensacola Beach, while Perdido Key sits to the west of Santa Rosa. The **Gulf Islands National Seashore**, a generic name for several parks, each with a specific point of interest (natural or historical), stretches 150 miles along the coast from here to Mississippi and includes the Naval Live Oaks Reservation, the western section of Santa Rosa Island, Fort Barrancas, and the eastern section of Perdido Key.

Gulf Breeze and the Naval Live Oaks Reservation

En route to Santa Rosa Island, via the three-mile-long Pensacola Bay Bridge, you'll pass through **Gulf Breeze**, a well-scrubbed, well-off community that's going all-out to attract homebuyers. Apart from a few supermarkets, the only reason to give it more than a passing thought is the **Naval Live Oaks Reservation** (daily 8am–sunset; free), about two miles east along US-98. In the 1820s, part of this live-oak forest was turned into a tree farm, intended to ensure a supply of shipbuilding material for years to come. Precise calculations were made as to how many trees would be needed for a particular ship, and the requisite number of acorns then planted – followed by a fifty-year wait. Problems were plentiful: the oak was too heavy for road transportation, wood rustlers cut down trees and sold them to foreign navies, and the final blow for the farm was the advent of iron-built ships.

The **visitor center** (daily 8am–5.30pm; ⓣ850/934-2600), near the entrance, has exhibits and explanatory texts on the intriguing forest, where fragments from Native American settlements from as far back as 1000 BC have been found. To escape the glare of the sun for an hour or so, take one of the short but shady **forest trails**, which include a two-mile section of what was, in the early 1800s, Florida's major roadway, linking Pensacola and St Augustine.

Pensacola Beach

From Gulf Breeze, another (shorter) bridge ($1 toll) leads across a narrow waterway to Santa Rosa Island and the epitome of a Gulf Coast strand, **Pensacola Beach**. Featuring mile after mile of fine white sands, rental outlets for beach and watersports equipment, a pier lined with fishermen, beachside bars, and snack stands, it's hard to beat for uncomplicated seaside recreation. With its sprinkling of motels and hotels (see p.451), Pensacola Beach also makes an alternative – if pricier – base to mainland Pensacola. The **Visitor Information Center** is opposite the pier at 735 Pensacola Beach Blvd (daily 9am–5pm; ⓣ850/932-1500 or 1-800/635-4803, ⓦwww.visitpensacolabeach.com).

Fort Pickens and Navarre Beach

From Pensacola Beach, it's just two and a half miles along the Fort Pickens Toll Road (7am–10pm; cars $8, pedestrians and cyclists $3) to the western end of Santa Rosa Island and the entrance to a part of the Gulf Islands National Seashore. Here, vibrant white sands are walled by a nine-mile stretch of high, rugged dunes, and the only reminder of civilization – other than the road – is a foliage-encircled campground. Hoofing over the dunes is strictly forbidden (as are bottles on the beach), but several tracks lead from the road to the beach. Once on the beach, you'll find plenty of space and seclusion – and sometimes even dolphins. To learn more about the dunes and the ecology of the island, join one of the frequent **ranger-led walks**; for details call ⓣ850/934-2600, or read the bulletin boards situated around the park.

At the western tip of the island are the substantial remains of **Fort Pickens**, which was built by slaves in the early 1800s to protect Pensacola from seaborne attack. There's plenty to be gleaned by walking around the fort's creepy passageways and rooms on your own: pick up the free tour leaflet at the **visitor center** (daily 8am–4.30pm; ⓣ850/934-2600). A small **museum** explains the origins of the structure, details the flora and fauna of the national seashore area, and records the travails of the seventeen Apache Indians who were imprisoned here in 1886. Among their number was a chief, Goyahkla, better known as **Geronimo**, who served his sentence roaming the sands. The Apaches, whose tribal lands covered much of the southwestern US, were one of the last Native American tribes to surrender to the advancing white settlers, signing a peace treaty with the sympathetic General Crook in 1886. Soon after, the higher-ranking General Sheridan reneged on the terms of the surrender and incarcerated Geronimo and his fellows, leading Crook to resign from the army in protest.

Beside the fort, some crumbling concrete walls remain from seacoast batteries erected in the Forties, which, together with the pillboxes and observation posts that litter the area, are a reminder that the fort's defensive function lasted until the end of World War II and only became obsolete with the advent of guided missiles.

If you head back east along Route 399, the stretch of sand between Pensacola Beach and Navarre Beach is clean and pristine. There are no developments (the area is part of the National Heritage Coastline) and inspirational vistas are plentiful. **Navarre Beach** itself (ⓦwww.navarrefl.com), unfortunately, is an explosion of unpleasant development, neither as pretty as Seaside nor as impersonally glamorous as San Destin. Yet just beyond where Route 399 curves north to cross the Pensacola Sound is one of the loveliest stretches of reef dunes and sand on the coast. In some places along this stretch there are no lifeguards, so swim in the sea at your own risk. Hurricane Opal did its best to raze the dunes to nothing in 1996, but impressive conservation work has restored much of the coast. For the best and most popular food on the beach, you have to pay a visit to the *Sailor's Grill*, 1451 Navarre Beach Causeway (⑦850/939-1092), where the breakfasts are scrumptious and the Key lime pie is legendary.

Perdido Key

Perdido Key, another barrier island to the west of Santa Rosa (Chamber of Commerce, 15500 Perdido Key Drive; ⑦850/492-4660 or 1-800/328-0107, Ⓦwww.perdidochamber.com), offers more pristine beaches. Its eastern section, protected as part of the Gulf Islands National Seashore, provides five miles of island untouched by roads. A one-and-a-quarter-mile nature trail allows you to explore the area, and if you're smitten with the seclusion, stick around to swim or pitch your tent at one of the primitive **campgrounds** (see p.451). The remainder of Perdido Key is much like Santa Rosa Island, a hotbed of sport, drinking, and suntanning rituals. One of the best **hotel** options is the *Best Western*, 13585 Perdido Key Drive (⑦850/492-2755; ❷), where prices rise dramatically at weekends.

Travel details

Trains

Pensacola to: Jacksonville (Mon, Wed, Sat; 10hr 10min); Tallahassee (Mon, Wed, Sat; 6hr).
Tallahassee to: Jacksonville (Mon, Wed, Sat; 4hr 10min); Pensacola (Tues, Thurs, Sun; 4hr 20min).

Buses

Panama City Beach to: Fort Walton Beach (2 daily; 1hr 5min); Panama City (2 daily; 30min); Pensacola (2 daily; 2hr 15min).
Pensacola to: Fort Walton Beach (3 daily; 1hr 5min); Mobile (6 daily; 1hr 5min); New Orleans (6 daily; 4hr 10min); Panama City Beach (3 daily; 1hr 55min); Tallahassee (6 daily; 3hr 15min).
Tallahassee to: Chipley (1 daily; 2hr 15 min); De Funiak Springs (1 daily; 3hr 5min); Gainesville (6 daily; 2hr 30min); Jacksonville (5 daily; 2hr 45min); Marianna (4 daily; 1hr 5min); Miami (7 daily; 11hr 40min); New Orleans (5 daily; 7hr 45min); Orlando (4 daily; 5hr 15min); Panama City Beach (3 daily; 2hr 20min); Pensacola (4 daily; 3hr 50min); Tampa (3 daily; 6hr); Thomasville (2 daily; 45min).

Contexts

Contexts

The historical framework

Contrary to popular belief, Florida's history goes back far beyond Walt Disney World and motel-lined beaches. For thousands of years, its aboriginal inhabitants lived in organized social groupings with contacts across a large section of the Americas. During the height of European colonization, it became a Spanish possession and, for a time, was under British control. Only in the nineteenth century did Florida become part of the US: the beginning of a period of unrestrained exploitation and expansion and the start of many of the problems with which the state continues to grapple today.

Origins of the land

Over billions of years, rivers flowing through what's now **northern Florida** carried debris from the Appalachian mountains to the coast, and their deposits of fine-powdered rock formed the beaches and barrier islands of the Panhandle. Further south, the highest section of a seabed plateau – the **Florida peninsula** – altered in shape according to the world's ice covering. The exposed land sometimes measured twice its present size; during other periods, the coastline was far inland of its current position, with wave action carving out still-visible bluffs in the oolitic limestone base. In the **present era**, beginning about 75 million years ago, rotting vegetation mixed with rainfall to form acid that burned holes in the limestone, and natural freshwater springs emerged; the underground water accumulated from heavy rains that preceded each Ice Age. Inland forests of live oak and pine became inhabited 20,000 years ago by mastodons, mammoths, and saber-toothed tigers, thought to have traveled – over many generations – across the ice-covered Bering Strait from Siberia.

First human habitation

Two theories exist regarding the origins of Florida's **first human inhabitants**. It's commonly believed that the earliest arrivals followed the same route as the animals from Siberia, crossing North America and arriving in northern Florida around 10,000 years ago. A minority of anthropologists takes the alternative view that the first Floridians were the result of migration by aboriginal peoples in South and Central America. Either way, the **Paleo** (or "Early") **Indians** in Florida lived hunter-gatherer existences – the spear tips they used are widely found across the central and northern parts of the state.

Around 5000 BC, social patterns changed: settlements became semi-permanent and diet switched from meat to shellfish, snails, and mollusks, which were abundant along the rivers. Traveling was done by dugout canoe and, periodically, a community would move to a new site, probably to allow food supplies to replenish themselves. Discarded shells and other rubbish were piled onto the **midden mounds** still commonly seen in the state.

Though pottery began to appear around 2000 BC, not until 1000 BC was there a big change in lifestyle, as indicated by the discovery of **irrigation** canals, patches of land cleared for **cultivation**, and cooking utensils used to prepare grown food. From the time of the Christian era, the erection of **burial mounds** – elaborate tombs of prominent tribes people, often with sacrificed kin and valuable objects also placed inside – became common. These suggest strong religious and trading links across an area stretching from Central America to the North American interior.

Spreading east from the Georgian coastal plain, the **Fort Walton Culture** became prevalent from around 200 AD, dividing society into a rigid caste system and forming villages planned around a central plaza. Throughout Florida at this time, approximately 100,000 inhabitants formed several distinct tribal groupings, most notably the **Timucua** across northern Florida, the **Caloosa** around the southwest and Lake Okeechobee, the **Apalachee** in the Panhandle, and the **Tequesta** along the southeast coast.

European settlement

After Christopher Columbus located the "New World" in 1492, Europe's great sea powers were increasingly active around the Caribbean. One of them, Spain, had discovered and plundered the treasures of ancient civilizations in Central America, and all were eager to locate other riches across these and neighboring lands. The **first European sighting** of Florida is believed to have been made by John and Sebastian Cabot in 1498, when they set eyes on what is now called Cape Florida, on Key Biscayne in Miami.

In 1513, the **first European landing** was made by **Juan Ponce de León**, a Spaniard previously employed as governor of Puerto Rico (a Spanish possession) and who was eager to carve out a niche for himself in the expanding empire. While searching for Bimini, Ponce de Leon sighted land during Pascua Florida, the Spanish Easter "Festival of the Flowers," and named what he saw **La Florida** – or "Land of Flowers." After landing somewhere between the mouth of the St Johns River and present-day St Augustine, Ponce de Leon sailed on around the Florida Keys, naming them Los Martires, for their supposed resemblance to the bones of martyred men, and Las Tortugas (now the Dry Tortugas), named for the turtles he saw around them.

Sent to deal with troublesome natives in the Lower Antilles, it was eight years before Ponce de Leon returned to Florida, this time with a mandate from the Spanish king to **conquer and colonize** the territory. Landing on the southwest coast, probably somewhere between Tampa Bay and Fort Myers, Ponce de Leon met a hostile reception from the Caloosa Indians and was forced to withdraw, eventually dying from an arrow wound received in the battle.

Rumors of gold hidden in Apalachee, in the north of the region, stimulated several Spanish incursions into Florida, all of which were driven back by the aggression of the indigenes and the ferocity of the terrain and climate. The most successful undertaking – even though it ended in death for its leader – was the **Hernando de Soto** expedition, a thousand-strong band of war-hardened knights and treasure seekers, which landed at Tampa Bay in May 1539. Recent excavations in Tallahassee have located the site of one of de Soto's camps, where the first Christmas celebration in North America is thought to have taken place, before the expedition continued north and eventually made the first European crossing of the Mississippi River – for a long time marking Florida's western boundary.

In time, news that Florida did not harbor stunning riches caused interest to wane. Treasure-laden Spanish ships sailing off the Florida coast between the Americas and Europe proved attractive to pirate ships, however, many of them British and French vessels hoisting the Jolly Roger. The Spanish failure to colonize Florida made the area a prime base for attacks on their vessels, and a small group of **French Huguenots** landed in 1562, building Fort Caroline on the St Johns River.

The French presence forced the Spanish to make a more determined effort at settlement. Already commissioned to explore the Atlantic coast of North America, **Pedro Menéndez de Aviles** was promised the lion's share of whatever profits could be made from Florida. Landing south of the French fort on August 28, 1562, the day of the Spanish Festival of San August'n, Menéndez named the site **St Augustine** – founding what was to become the longest continuous site of European habitation on the continent. The French were quickly defeated, their leader **Jean Ribault** and his crew massacred after being driven ashore by a hurricane; the site of the killing is still known as Matanzas, or "Place of Slaughter."

The first Spanish period (1585–1763)

Only the enthusiasm of Menéndez held Florida together during the early decades of Spanish rule. A few small and insecure settlements were established, usually around **missions** founded by Jesuits or Franciscans bent on Christianizing the Indians. It was a far from harmonious setup: homesick Spanish soldiers frequently mutinied and fought with the Indians, who responded by burning St Augustine to the ground. Menéndez replaced St Augustine's wooden buildings with "tabby" (a cement-like mixture of seashells and limestone) structures with palm-thatched roofs, a style typical of early European Florida. While easily the largest settlement, even St Augustine was a lifeless outpost unless a ship happened to be in port. Despite sinking all his personal finances into the colony, Menéndez never lived to see Florida thrive, and he left in 1571, ordered by the king to help plan the Spanish Armada's attack on Britain.

Fifteen years later, as war raged between the European powers, St Augustine was razed by a naval bombardment led by **Francis Drake**, a sign that the **British** were beginning to establish their colonies along the Atlantic coast north of Florida. Aware that the Indians would hold the balance of power in future colonial power struggles, the Spanish built a string of missions along the Panhandle from 1606; besides seeking to earn the loyalty of the natives, these were intended to provide a defensive shield against attacks from the north. By the 1700s the British were making forays into Florida, ostensibly to capture Indians to sell as slaves. One by one, the missions were destroyed, and only the timely arrival of Spanish reinforcements prevented the fall of St Augustine to the British in 1740.

With the French in Louisiana, the British in Georgia, and the Spanish clinging to Florida, the scene was set for a bloody confrontation for control of North America. Eventually, the **1763 Treaty of Paris**, concluding the Seven Years' War in Europe, settled the issue: the British had captured the crucial Spanish possession of Havana, and Spain willingly parted with Florida to get it back.

The British period (1763–83)

Despite their two centuries of occupation, the Spanish failed to make much impression on Florida. It was the British, already developing the colonies further north, who grafted a social infrastructure onto the region. They also divided Florida (then with only the northern section inhabited by whites) into separate colonies: **East Florida** governed from St Augustine, and **West Florida** governed from the growing Panhandle port of **Pensacola**.

By this time, aboriginal Floridians had largely died out through contact with European diseases, to which they had no immunity, and Florida's Indian population was becoming composed of disparate tribes arriving from the west, collectively known as the **Seminoles**. Like the Spanish, the British acknowledged the numerical importance of the Indians and sought good relations with them. In return for goods, the British took Indian land around ports and supply routes, but generally left the Seminoles undisturbed in the inland areas.

Despite attractive grants, few settlers arrived from Britain. Those with money to spare bought Florida land as an investment, never intending to develop or settle on it, and only large holdings – **plantations** growing corn, sugar, rice, and other crops – were profitable. Charleston, to the north, dominated sea trade in the area, though St Augustine was still a modestly important settlement and the gathering place of passing British aristocrats and intellectuals. West Florida, on the other hand, was driven by political factionalism and was also often the scene of skirmishes with the Seminoles, who received worse treatment than their counterparts in the east.

Being a new and sparsely populated region, Florida was barely affected by the discontent that fueled the **American War of Independence** in the 1770s, except for St Augustine, which served as a haven for British Royalists fleeing the war, many of whom moved on to the Bahamas or Jamaica. Pensacola, though, was attacked and briefly occupied in 1781 by the Spanish, who had been promised Florida in return for helping the American rebels defeat the British. As it turned out, diplomacy rather than gunfire signaled the end of British rule in Florida.

The second Spanish period (1783–1821)

The **1783 Treaty of Paris**, under which Britain recognized American independence, not only returned Florida to Spain but also gave it Louisiana and the prized port of New Orleans. Spanish holdings in North America were now larger than ever, but with Europe in turmoil and the Spanish colonies in Central America agitating for their own independence, the country was ill-equipped to capitalize on them. Moreover, the complexity of Florida's melting pot, comprising the British, smaller numbers of ethnically diverse European settlers, and the increasingly assertive Seminoles (now well established in fertile central Florida, and often joined by Africans escaping slavery further north), made it impossible for a declining colonial power to govern.

As fresh European migration slowed, Spain was forced to **sell land to US citizens**, who bought large tracts, confident that Florida would soon be under

Washington's control. Indeed, in gaining Louisiana from France in 1800 (to whom it had been ceded by Spain), and moving the Georgia border south, it was clear the US had Florida in its sights. Fearful of losing the commercial toehold it still retained in Florida, and aligned with Spain through the Napoleonic wars, Britain landed troops at Pensacola in 1814. In response, a US general, **Andrew Jackson**, used the excuse of an Indian uprising in Alabama to march south, killing hundreds of Indians and pursuing them – unlawfully and without official sanction from Washington – into Pensacola, declaring no quarrel with the Spanish but insisting that the British depart. The British duly left, and Jackson and his men withdrew to Mobile (a Floridian town that became part of Alabama as the Americans inched the border eastwards), soon to participate in the Battle of New Orleans, which further strengthened the US position on the Florida border.

The First Seminole War

Jackson's actions in 1814 had triggered the **First Seminole War**. As international tensions heightened, Seminole raids (often as a result of baiting on the US side) were commonly used as excuses for US incursions into Florida. In 1818, Jackson finally received what he took to be presidential approval (the "Rhea Letter," thought to have been authorized by President Monroe) to march again into Florida on the pretext of subduing the Seminoles but with the actual intention of taking outright control.

While US public officials were uneasy with the dubious legality of these events, the American public was firmly on Jackson's side. The US government issued an ultimatum to Spain, demanding that either it police Florida effectively or relinquish its ownership. With little alternative, Spain formally **ceded Florida to the US** in 1819, in return for the US assuming the $5 million owed by the Spanish government to American settlers in land grants (a sum that was never repaid). Nonetheless, it took the threat of an invasion of Cuba for the Spanish king to ratify the treaty in 1821; at the same time Andrew Jackson was sworn in as Florida's first American governor.

Territorial Florida

In territorial Florida it was soon evident that the East and West divisions were unworkable, and a site midway between St Augustine and Pensacola was selected as the new administrative center: **Tallahassee**. The Indians living on the fertile soils of the area were rudely dispatched toward the coast – an act of callousness that was to typify relations between the new settlers and the incumbent Native Americans for decades to come.

Under Spanish and British rule, the Seminoles, notwithstanding some feuding among themselves, lived peaceably on the productive lands of northern central Florida. These, however, were precisely the agriculturally rich areas that US settlers coveted. Under the **Treaty of Moultrie Creek** in 1823, most of the Seminole tribes signed a document agreeing to sell their present land and resettle in southwest Florida. Neither side was to honor this agreement: no time limit was imposed on the Seminole exodus, and those who did go found the new land to be unsuitable for farming. The US side, meanwhile, failed to provide promised resettlement funds.

Andrew Jackson spent only three months as territorial governor, though his influence on Florida continued from the White House when he became US president in 1829. In 1830 he approved the **Act of Indian Removal**, decreeing that all Native Americans in the eastern US should be transferred to reservations in the open areas of the Midwest. Two years later, James Gadsden, the newly appointed Indian commissioner, called a meeting of the Seminole tribes at Payne's Landing on the Oklawaha River, near Silver Springs, urging them to cede their land to the US and move west. Amid much acrimony, a few did sign the **Treaty of Payne's Landing**, which provided for their complete removal within three years.

The Second Seminole War (1821–42)

A small number took what monies were offered and resettled in the west, but most Seminoles were determined to stay, and the **Second Seminole War** ensued, with the Indians repeatedly ambushing the US militiamen who had arrived to enforce the law. The natives also ransacked the plantations of white settlers, many of whom fled and never returned. Trained for set-piece battles, the US troops were rarely able to deal effectively with the guerrilla tactics of the Seminoles. It was apparent that the Seminoles were unlikely to be defeated by conventional means and in October 1837 their leader, **Osceola**, was lured to St Augustine with the promise of a truce – only to be arrested and imprisoned, eventually to die in jail. This treachery failed to break the spirit of the Seminoles, though a few continued to give themselves up and leave for the west, while others were captured and sold into slavery.

It became the policy of the US to drive the Seminoles steadily south, away from the fertile lands of central Florida and **into the Everglades**. In the Everglades, the Seminoles linked up with the long-established Indians of south Florida, the "Spanish Indians," to raid the Cape Florida lighthouse and destroy the white colony on Indian Key in the Florida Keys. Even after bloodhounds were used to track the Indians, it was clear that total US victory would never be achieved. With the Seminoles confined to the Everglades, the US formally **ended the conflict** in 1842, when the Seminoles agreed to stay where they were – an area earlier described by an army surveyor as "fit only for Indian habitation."

The war crippled the Florida economy but stimulated the growth of a number of new towns around the army forts. Several of these, such as Fort Brooke (Tampa), Fort Lauderdale, Fort Myers, and Fort Pierce, have survived into modern times.

Statehood and secession (1842–61)

The Second Seminole War forestalled the possibility of Florida **attaining statehood** – which would have entitled it to full representation in Washington and to appoint its own administrators. Influence in Florida at this time was split between two camps. On one side were the wealthy slave-owning plantation farmers, concentrated in the "cotton counties" of the central section of the Panhandle, who enjoyed all the traditions of the upper rungs of Deep South society. They were eager to make sure that the balance of power in Washington did not shift toward the non-slave-owning "free" states, which would inevitably bring a call for the abolition of slavery. Opposing statehood were the smallholders scattered about the rest of the territory – many of whom were Northerners, already ideologically against slavery and fearing the imposition of federal taxes.

One compromise mooted was a return to a divided Florida, with the West becoming a state while the East remained a territory. Eventually, based on a narrowly agreed upon **constitution** drawn up in Port St Joseph on the Panhandle coast (on the site of present-day Port St Joe), Florida **became a state** on March 3, 1845. The arrival of statehood coincided with a period of material prosperity: the first railroads began spidering across the Panhandle and central Florida; an organized school system became established; and Florida's 60,000 population doubled within twenty years.

Nationally, things were less bright. The issue of slavery was to be the catalyst that led the US into civil war, though it was only a part of a great cultural divide between the rural Southern states – to which Florida was linked more through geography than history – and the modern industrial states of the North. As federal pressure intensified for the abolition of slavery, Florida formally **seceded from the Union** on January 10, 1861, aligning itself with the breakaway Confederate States in the run-up to the Civil War.

The Civil War (1861–65)

Inevitably, the **Civil War** had a great effect on Florida, although most Floridians conscripted into the Confederate army fought far away from home, and rarely were there more than minor confrontations within the state. The relatively small number of Union sympathizers generally kept a low profile, concentrating on protecting their families. At the start of the war, most of Florida's **coastal forts** were occupied by Union troops as part of the blockade on Confederate shipping. Lacking the strength to mount effective attacks on the forts, those Confederate soldiers who remained in Florida based themselves in the interior and watched for Union troop movements, swiftly destroying whatever bridge, road, or railroad lay in the invaders' path – in effect creating a stalemate, which endured throughout the conflict.

Away from the coast, Florida's primary contribution to the war effort was the **provision of food** – chiefly beef and pork reared on the central Florida farms – and the transportation of it across the Panhandle toward Confederate strongholds further west. Union attempts to cut the supply route gave rise to the only major battle fought in the state, the **Battle of Olustee**, just outside Live Oak, in February 1864: 10,000 participated in an engagement that left nearly 3000 dead or injured and both sides claiming victory.

The most celebrated battle from a Floridian viewpoint, however, happened in March 1865 at **Natural Bridge,** when a youthful group of Confederates defeated the technically superior Union troops, preventing the fall of Tallahassee. As events transpired, it was a hollow victory: following the Confederate surrender, the war ended a few months later.

Reconstruction

Following the cessation of hostilities, Florida was caught in an uneasy hiatus. In the years after the war, the defeated states were subject to **Reconstruction**, a rearrangement of their internal affairs determined by, at first, the president, and later by a much harder-line Congress intent on ensuring the Southern states would never return to their old ways.

The Northern ideal of free-labor capitalism was an alien concept in the South, and there were enormous problems. Of paramount concern was the future of the **freed slaves**. With restrictions on their movements lifted, many emancipated slaves wandered the countryside, often unwittingly putting fear into all-white communities that had never before had a black face in their midst. Rubbing salt into the wounds, as far as the Southern whites were concerned, was the occupation of many towns by black Union troops. As a backlash, the white-supremacist **Ku Klux Klan** became active in Tennessee during 1866, and its race-hate, segregationist doctrine soon spread into Florida.

Against this background of uncertainty, Florida's **domestic politics** entered a period of unparalleled chicanery. Suddenly, not only were black men allowed to vote, but there were more black voters than white. The gullibility of the uneducated blacks and the power of their votes proved an irresistible combination to the unscrupulous and power-hungry. Double-dealing and vote-rigging were practiced by diverse factions united only in their desire to restore Florida's statehood and acquire even more power. Following a constitution written and approved in controversial circumstances, Florida was **readmitted to the Union** on July 21, 1868.

Eventually, in Florida as in the other Southern states, an all-white, **conservative Democrat government** emerged. Despite emancipation and the hopes for integration outlined by the Civil Rights Act passed by Congress in 1875, blacks in Florida were still denied many of the rights reasonably regarded as basic. In fact, all that distanced the new administration from the one that led Florida into secession was awareness of the power of the federal government and the need to at least appear to take outside views into account. It was also true that many of the former slave-owners were now the employers of freed blacks, who remained very much under their white masters' control.

A new Florida (1876–1914)

Florida's bonds with its neighboring states became increasingly tenuous in the years following Reconstruction. A fast-growing population began spreading south – part of a gradual diminishing of the importance of the Panhandle, where ties to the Deep South were strongest. Florida's identity was forged by a new **frontier spirit**. Besides smallholding farmers, loggers came to work the abundant forests, and a new breed of wealthy settler started putting down roots, among them Henry DeLand and Henry S. Sanford, who each bought large chunks of central Florida and founded the towns that still bear their names.

As northern speculators invested in Florida, they sought to publicize the region, and a host of articles extolling the virtues of the state's climate as a cure for all ills began to appear in the country's newspapers. These early efforts to promote **Florida as a tourist destination** brought the wintering rich along the new railroads to enjoy the sparkling rivers and springs, along with naturalists keen to explore the unique flora and fauna.

With a fortune made through his partnership in Standard Oil, **Henry Flagler** opened luxury resorts on Florida's northeast coast for his socialite friends, and gradually extended his Florida East Coast Railroad south, giving birth to communities such as **Palm Beach** and making the remote trading post of **Miami** an accessible, expanding town. Flagler's friendly rival, **Henry Plant**, connected his railroad to **Tampa**, turning a desolate hamlet into a thriving port city and a major base for cigar manufacturing. The **citrus**

industry also revved into top gear: Florida's climate enabled oranges, grapefruits, lemons, and other citrus fruits to be grown during the winter and sold to an eager market in the cooler north. The **cattle farms** went from small to strong, with Florida becoming a major supplier of beef to the rest of the US: cows were rounded up with a special wooden whip that made a gunshot-like sound when used – hence the nickname "**cracker**" that was applied to rural settlers.

One group that didn't benefit from the boom years was the blacks. Many were imprisoned for no reason, and found themselves on chain gangs building the new roads and railroads; punishments for refusing to work included severe floggings and hanging by the thumbs. Few whites paid any attention, and those who were in a position to stop the abuses were usually too busy getting rich. There was, however, the founding of **Eatonville**, just north of Orlando, which was the first town in Florida – and possibly the US – to be founded, governed, and lived in by black people.

The Spanish-American War

By the 1890s, the US was a large and unified nation itching for a bigger role in the world, and as the drive in **Cuba** for independence from Spain gathered momentum, an opportunity to participate in international affairs presented itself. Florida already had long links with Cuba – the capital, Havana, was just ninety miles from Key West, and several thousand Cuban migrants were employed in the Tampa cigar factories. During 1898, tens of thousands of US troops, known as the Cuban Expeditionary Force, arrived in the state, and the **Spanish-American War** was declared on April 25. As it turned out, the fighting was comparatively minor. Spain withdrew, and on January 1, 1899, Cuba attained independence (and the US a big say in its future). But the war was also the first of several major conflicts that were to prove beneficial to Florida. Many of the soldiers would return as settlers or tourists, and improved railroads and strengthened harbors at the commercially significant ports of Key West, Tampa, and Pensacola did much to boost the economy.

The Broward era

The early years of the 1900s were dominated by the progressive policies of **Napoleon Bonaparte Broward**, who was elected state governor in 1905. In a nutshell, Broward championed the little man against corporate interests, particularly the giant land-owning railroad companies. Among Broward's aims were an improved education system, a state-run commission to oversee new railroad construction, a tax on cars to finance road building, better salaries for teachers and the judiciary, a state-run life insurance scheme, and a ban on newspapers – few of which were well disposed toward Broward – knowingly publishing untruths. Broward also enacted the first **conservation laws**, protecting fish, oysters, game, and forests; but at the same time, in an attempt to create new land to rival the holdings of the rail barons, he conceived the drainage program that would cause untold damage to the Everglades.

By no means did all of Broward's policies become law, and he departed Tallahassee for a US Senate seat in 1910. Nonetheless, the forward-thinking plans of what became known as the **Broward era** were continued through subsequent administrations – a process that went some way toward bringing a rough-and-ready frontier land into the twentieth century.

World War I and after

World War I continued the tradition of the Spanish-American War by giving Florida an economic shot in the arm, as the military arrived to police the coastline and develop sea-warfare projects. Despite the influx of money and the reforms of the Broward years, there was little happening to improve the lot of Florida's blacks. The Ku Klux Klan was revived in Tallahassee in 1915, and the public outcry that followed the beating to death of a young black on a chain gang was answered only by the introduction of the sweatbox as punishment for prisoners considered unruly.

Typically, most visitors to Florida at this time were more concerned with getting drunk than social justice. The coast so vigilantly protected from advancing Germans during the war was left wide open when **Prohibition** was introduced in 1919; the many secluded inlets became secure landing sites for shipments of spirits from the Caribbean. The illicit booze improved the atmosphere in the new resorts of **Miami Beach**, a picture-postcard piece of beach landscaping replacing what had been a barely habitable mangrove island just a few years before. Drink was not the only illegal pleasure pursued in the nightclubs: gambling and prostitution were also rife, and were soon to attract the attention of big-time **gangsters** such as Al Capone, initiating a climate of corruption that was to scar Florida politics for years.

The lightning-paced creation of Miami Beach was no isolated incident. Throughout Florida, and especially in the Southeast, new communities appeared almost overnight. Self-proclaimed architectural genius **Addison Mizner** erected the "million dollar cottages" of Palm Beach and began fashioning **Boca Raton** with the same mock-Mediterranean excesses, on the premise "get the big snob and the little snob will follow." Meanwhile, visionary **George Merrick** plotted the superlative **Coral Gables** – now absorbed by Miami – which became the nation's first preplanned city and one of the few schemes of the time to age with dignity.

In the rush of prosperity that followed the war, it seemed everyone in America wanted a piece of Florida, and chartered trains brought in thousands of eager buyers. The spending frenzy soon meant that for every genuine offer there were a hundred bogus ones: many people unknowingly bought acres of empty swampland. The period was satirized by the Marx Brothers in their first film, *The Cocoanuts*.

Although millions of dollars technically changed hands each week during the peak year of 1925, little hard cash actually moved. Most deals were paper transactions with buyers paying a small deposit into a bank. The inflation inherent in the system finally went out of control in 1926. With buyers failing to keep up payments, banks went **bust** and were quickly followed by everyone else. A **hurricane** devastated Miami the same year – the city's house-builders never thought to protect the structures against tropical storms – and an even worse hurricane in 1928 caused Lake Okeechobee to burst its banks and flood surrounding communities.

With the Florida land boom well and truly over, the **Wall Street Crash** in 1929 proceeded to make paupers of the millionaires, such as Henry Flagler and Sarasota's **John Ringling**, whose considerable investments had helped to shape the state, and who would later found the **Ringling Brothers Barnum and Bailey Circus**.

The Depression and World War II

At the start of the Thirties, even the major railroads that had stimulated Florida's expansion were in receivership, and the state government only avoided bankruptcy with a constitutional escape clause. Due to the property crash, Florida had had a few extra years to adjust to grinding poverty before the whole country experienced the Depression, and a number of recovery measures – making the state more active in citizens' welfare – pre-empted the national New Deal legislation of President Roosevelt.

No single place was harder hit than **Key West**, which was not only suffering the Depression but hadn't been favored by the property boom either. With a population of 12,000, Key West was an incredible $5 million in debt, and had even lost its link to the mainland when the Overseas Railroad – running across the Florida Keys between Key West and Miami – was destroyed by the 1935 Labor Day hurricane.

What saved Key West, and indeed brought financial stability to all of Florida, was **World War II**. Once again, thousands of troops arrived to guard the coastline – off which there was an immense amount of German U-boat activity – while the flat inland areas made a perfect training venue for pilots. Empty tourist hotels provided ready-made barracks, and the soldiers, and their visiting families, got a taste of Florida that would bring many of them back.

In the immediate **postwar period**, the inability of the state to plan and provide for increased growth was resoundingly apparent, with public services – particularly in the field of education – woefully inadequate. Because of the massive profits being made through illegal gambling, corruption became endemic in public life. State governor **Fuller Warren**, implicated with the Al Capone crime syndicate in 1950, was by no means the only state official suspected of being in cahoots with criminals. A wave of attacks against blacks and Jews in 1951 caused Warren to speak out against the Ku Klux Klan, but the discovery that he himself had once been a Klan member only confirmed there was poison flowing through the heart of Florida's political system.

A rare upbeat development was a continued commitment to the conservation measures introduced in the Broward era, with $2 million allocated to buying the land that, in 1947, became **Everglades National Park**.

The 1950s and 1960s

Cattle, citrus, and tourism continued to be the major components of Florida's economy as, in the ten years from 1950, the state soared from being the twentieth to the tenth most populous in the country, home to some five million people. While its increased size raised Florida's profile in the federal government, the demographic changes within the state – most dramatically the shift from rural life in the north to urban living in the south – went unacknowledged, and **reapportionment** of representation in state government became a critical issue. It was only resolved by the **1968 constitution**, which provided for automatic reapportionment in line with population changes.

The fervent desire for growth and the need to present a wholesome public image prevented the state's conservative-dominated assembly from fighting as hard as their counterparts in the other Southern states against **desegregation**, following a ruling by the federal Supreme Court on the issue in 1956. Nonetheless, blacks continued to be banned from Miami Beach after dark and from swimming off the Palm Beach coast. In addition, they were subject to segregation in restaurants, buses, hotels, and schools – and barely represented at all in public office. As the **Civil Rights** movement gained strength during the early Sixties, bus boycotts and demonstrations took place in Tallahassee and Daytona Beach, and a march in St Augustine in 1964 resulted in the arrest of the movement's leader, Dr Martin Luther King Jr. The success of the Civil Rights movement in ending legalized discrimination did little to affect the deeply entrenched racist attitudes among much of Florida's longer-established population. Most of the state's blacks still lived and worked in conditions that would have been intolerable to whites: a fact that, in part, accounted for the **Liberty City riot** in August 1968, which was the first of several violent uprisings in Miami's depressed areas.

The ideological shift in Florida's near-neighbor, **Cuba** – declared a socialist state by its leader Fidel Castro in 1961 – came sharply into focus with the 1962 **missile crisis**, which triggered a tense game of cat and mouse between the US and the USSR over Soviet missile bases on the island. After world war was averted, Florida became the base of the US government's covert anti-Castro operations. Many engaged in these activities were among the 300,000 **Cuban immigrants** who had arrived following the Castro-led revolution. The Bay of Pigs fiasco in 1961 proved that there was to be no quick return to the homeland, and while not all of the new arrivals stayed in Florida, many went no further than Miami, where they were to change completely the social character – and eventually the power balance – of the city.

Another factor in Florida's expansion was the basing of the new civilian space administration, **NASA**, at the military long-range missile testing site at Cape Canaveral. The all-out drive to land a man on the moon brought an enormous influx of space industry personnel here in the early Sixties – quadrupling the population of the region soon to become known as the **Space Coast**.

The 1970s to 1990s

Florida's tourist boom truly began with the opening of **Walt Disney World** in 1971, which had actually been in development since the mid-Sixties. The state government bent over backwards to help the Disney Corporation turn a sizeable slice of central Florida into the biggest theme park complex ever known, even though throughout its construction debate raged over the commercial and ecological effects of such a major undertaking on the rest of the region. Undeterred, smaller businesses rushed to the area, eager to capitalize on the anticipated tourist influx, and the sleepy cow-town of **Orlando** suddenly found itself the hub of one of the state's fastest-growing population centers – soon to become one of the world's best-known holiday destinations.

Around the same time, Florida's other multi-billion dollar business – the **drug trade** – also began taking off. Indeed, Florida's proximity to various Latin and South American countries with large drug production operations perfectly positioned the state as a gateway for drug smuggling and money-laundering; estimates suggest that at least a quarter of the cocaine entering the US still arrives through the state. The inherent violence of the drug trade, along with lax Florida gun laws, helped Miami earn the unflattering designation "murder capital of the US" in the late Eighties, a label it has largely shaken off, though some incidents of **violence against tourists** in the early 1990s resullied its reputation.

Despite the social problems engendered, much money was being made by the US–Latin American trade, both legal and contraband, and poured into the coffers of a burgeoning **banking** industry, which set up shop in gleaming high towers just south of downtown Miami.

Time, plus Disney's success and Miami's rise to prominence, had only helped solidify Florida's place in the **international tourist market** by the Nineties. Directly or indirectly, one in five of the state's twelve million inhabitants was making a living from tourism. At the same time, the general swing from heavy to **hi-tech industries** had resulted in many American corporations forsaking their traditional northern bases in favor of Florida, bringing their white-collar workforces with them.

Increased protection of the state's **natural resources** was another positive feature of the Nineties. Impressive amounts of land were now under state control and, overall, wildlife was less threatened than at any time since white settlers first arrived. Most spectacular of all was the revival of the state's alligator population.

Behind the optimistic facade, however, lay many problems. For starters, much of southern Florida's resurgent landscape – and its dependent animals – could still be destroyed by south Florida's ever-increasing need for land and drinking water. And **nature** itself often posed a serious threat. In August 1992, **Hurricane Andrew** brought winds of 168mph tearing through the southern regions of Miami, blowing down the radar of the National Hurricane Center in the process and leaving an estimated $30 billion worth of damage in its wake. In the summer of 1999, another storm, **Hurricane Floyd**, came blowing through, leading to the evacuation of millions of residents all along the southeast US coast and causing considerable damage, though fortunately less than was feared.

The lack of state spending, due in part to low **taxes** intended to stimulate growth, reduced funding for public services, leaving the apparently booming state with appalling levels of adult illiteracy, infant mortality, and crime. Ironically, the switch in Florida's "war on drugs" from capturing dealers to clamping down on **money-laundering** began to threaten many of its financial institutions, built on – and it's an open secret – the drug trade.

The 2000 election and beyond

The political maneuvering by which **George W. Bush** became the 43rd president of the US in 2000 cast a shadow over the Sunshine State, as well as the entire country. The election itself was a virtual dead heat: **Al Gore**, the Democratic Party's nominee, won the country's **popular vote** by around half a million, but Bush led in the **electoral college** tally – with Florida too close to call. Bush's margin was so narrow – he led by less than 1000 votes out of a total of nearly six million cast – that a recount was called for. And although Bush's brother, **Governor Jeb Bush**, officially recused himself during the controversy, his Secretary of State – and Bush's campaign chairman for the state – **Katherine Harris** didn't. Instead, she disallowed a full count, shutting down normal recount operations while her man was leading by only a few hundred votes and calling him the winner. Thousands of Floridians protested amid accusations of illegal police roadblocks that kept African-Americans – who overwhelmingly supported Al Gore – from even getting to the polls. Attempts by the **Florida Supreme Court** to overturn the Harris decision were summarily quashed by the right-leaning **US Supreme Court**, which allowed the peremptory decision to stand. Although Florida quietly unloaded its outdated voting machines via online auctions in 2001, the replacements themselves proved less than successful, resulting in charges of electoral irregularities during the 2002 gubernatorial election that saw Jeb Bush returned for a second term.

Natural Florida

The biggest surprise for most people in Florida is the abundance of undeveloped, natural areas throughout the state and the extraordinary variety of wildlife and vegetation within them. From a rare hawk that eats only snails to a vine-like fig that strangles other trees, natural Florida possesses plenty that you've probably never seen before, and which – due to drainage, pressures from the agricultural lobby, and the constant need for new housing – may not be on view for very much longer.

Background

Many factors contribute to the unusual diversity of **ecosystems** found in Florida, the most obvious being **latitude**: the north of the state has vegetation common to temperate regions, which is quite distinct from the subtropical flora of the south. Another crucial element is **elevation**: while much of Florida is flat and low-lying, a change of a few inches in elevation drastically affects what grows, due in part to the enormous variety of soils.

The role of fire

Florida has more thunderstorms than any other part of the US, and the resulting lightning frequently ignites **fires**. Many Florida plants have adapted to fire by developing thick bark or the ability to regenerate from stumps. Others, such as cabbage palmetto and sawgrass, protect their growth bud with a sheath of green leaves. Fire is necessary to keep a natural balance of plant species – human attempts to control naturally ignited fires have contributed to the changing composition of Florida's remaining wild lands.

Human intervention was desperately needed in July 1998, when Florida suffered one of its most severe summer droughts. In an instant, devastating wildfires roared out of control in Volusia County, and raged on a head-on course for downtown Daytona and the beaches. Over 140,000 acres of forested lands were destroyed – approximately ten percent of the land in Volusia County. The total loss attributed to the fires was estimated at $379 million. Weary firefighters from across the country came to fight the fires, and due to billowing smoke, a long stretch of I-95 was shut down. For the first time in history, the Daytona International Speedway canceled a major race because of the close proximity of the fires, and turned its massive steel structure into a temporary shelter for displaced residents. The good thing is that there were very few casualties; what's more, the destruction of the underbrush will in fact promote a healthy rejuvenation of the forest floor.

Forests and woodlands

Forests and woodlands aren't the first thing people associate with Florida, but the state has an impressive assortment, ranging from the great tracts of upland pine common in the north to the mixed bag of tropical foliage found in the southern hammocks.

Pine flatwoods

Covering roughly half of Florida, **pine flatwoods** are most widespread on the southeastern coastal plain. These pine species – longleaf, slash, and pond – rise tall and straight like telegraph poles. The Spanish once harvested products such as turpentine and rosin from Florida's flatwood pines, a practice that continued during US settlement, and some trees still bear the scars on their trunks. Pine flatwoods are airy and open, with abundant light filtering through the upper canopy of leaves, allowing thickets of shrubs such as saw palmetto, evergreen oaks, gallberry, and fetterbrush to grow. **Inhabitants** of the pine flatwoods include white-tailed deer, cotton rats, brown-headed nuthatches, pine warblers, eastern diamondback rattlesnakes, and oak toads. Many of these creatures also inhabit other Florida ecosystems, but the **fox squirrel** – a large and noisy character with a rusty tinge to its undercoat – is one of the few mammalian denizens more or less restricted to the pine flatwoods.

Upland pine forests

As the name suggests, **upland pine forests** – or high pinelands – are found on the rolling sand ridges and sandhills of northeastern Florida and the Panhandle, conditions that tend to keep upland pine forests drier and therefore even more open than the flatwoods. Upland pine forests have a groundcover of wiregrass and an overstory of (mostly) longleaf pine trees, which creates a park-like appearance. Redheaded woodpeckers, eastern bluebirds, Florida mice, pocket gophers (locally called "salamanders," a distortion of "sand mounder"), and gopher tortoises (amiable creatures often sharing their burrows with gopher frogs) all make the high pine country their home. The latter two, together with scarab beetles, keep the forest healthy by mixing and aerating the soil. The now-endangered red-cockaded woodpecker is symbolic of old-growth upland pine forest; logging and repression of the natural fire process have contributed to its decline.

Hammocks

Wildlife tends to be more abundant in hardwood **hammocks** than in the associated pine forests and prairies (see below). Hammocks consist of narrow bands of (non-pine) hardwoods growing transitionally between pinelands and lower, wetter vegetation. The make-up of hammocks varies across the state: in the south, they chiefly comprised tropical hardwoods (see "The south Florida rocklands," opposite); in the north, they contain an overstory of oaks, magnolia, and beech, along with a few smaller plants. Red-bellied woodpeckers, red-tailed and red-shouldered hawks, and barred owls nest in them, while down below you can also find eastern wood rats, striped skunks, and white-tailed deer.

Scrubs and prairies

Scrub ecosystems once spread to the southern Rocky Mountains and northern Mexico, but climatic changes reduced their distribution and remnant stands are now found only in northern and central Florida. Like the high pines, scrub occurs in dry, hilly areas. The vegetation, which forms an impenetrable mass, consists of varied combinations of drought-adapted evergreen oaks, saw palmetto, Florida rosemary, and/or sand pine. The **Florida bonamia**, a morning glory with pale blue funnel-shaped blossoms, is one of the most attractive plants of the scrub, which has more than a dozen plant species officially listed as endangered. Scrub also harbors some unique animals, including the Florida mouse, the Florida scrub lizard, the sand skink, and the Florida **scrub jay**. The scrub jay has an unusual social system: pairs nest in cooperation with offspring of previous seasons, who help carry food to their younger siblings. Although not unique to scrub habitat, other inhabitants include black bear, white-tailed deer, bobcats, and gopher tortoises.

Some of Florida's inland areas are covered by **prairie**, characterized by love grass, broomsedge, and wiregrass – the best examples surround Lake Okeechobee. Settlers destroyed the bison that roamed here some two hundred years ago, but herds are now being reintroduced to some state parks. A more diminutive prairie denizen is the **burrowing owl**: while most owls are active at night, burrowing owls feed during the day and, equally unusually, live in underground dens and bow nervously when approached – earning them the nickname the "howdy owl." Eastern spotted skunks, cotton rats, black vultures, eastern meadowlarks, and box turtles are a few other prairie inhabitants. Nine-banded **armadillos** are also found in prairie habitats and in any non-swampy terrain. Recent invaders from Texas, the armadillos usually forage at night, feeding on insects. Due to poor eyesight, they often fail to notice a human's approach until the last minute, when they will leap up and bound away noisily.

The south Florida rocklands

Elevated areas around the state's southern tip – in the Everglades and along the Florida Keys – support either pines or tropical hardwood hammocks on limestone outcrops collectively known as the **south Florida rocklands**. More jungle-like than the temperate hardwood forests found in northern Florida, the **tropical hardwood hammocks** of the south tend to occur as "tree islands" surrounded by the sparser vegetation of wet prairies or mangroves. Royal palm, pigeon plum, gumbo-limbo (one of the most beautiful of the tropical hammock trees, with a distinctive smooth red bark), and ferns form dense thickets within the hammock. The **pine forests** of the south Florida rocklands largely consist of scraggly-looking slash pine and are similarly surrounded by mangroves and wet prairies.

Epiphytic plants

Tropical hammocks contain various forms of **epiphytic plant**, which use other plants for physical support but don't depend on them for nutrients. In southern Florida, epiphytes include orchids, ferns, bromeliads (**Spanish moss** is one of the most widespread bromeliads, hanging from tree branches throughout the state and forming the "canopy roads" in Tallahassee; see "The Panhandle," p.411). Seemingly the most aggressive of epiphytes, **strangler figs**, after germinating in the canopy of trees such as palms, cut off their host tree from sunlight. They then send out aerial roots that eventually reach the soil and then tightly enlace the host, preventing growth of the trunk. Finally, the fig produces so many leaves that it chokes out the host's greenery and the host dies leaving only the fig.

Other plants and vertebrates

The south Florida rocklands support over forty plants and a dozen vertebrates found nowhere else in the state. These include the crenulate lead plant, the Key tree cactus, the Florida mastiff bat, the Key deer, and the Miami black-headed snake. More common residents include **butterflies and spiders** – the black and yellow yeliconia butterflies, with their long paddle-shaped wings and a distinctive gliding flight pattern, are particularly elegant. Butterflies need to practice careful navigation as hammocks are laced with the foot-long webs of the banana spider. Other wildlife species include sixty types of land snail, green tree frogs, green anoles, cardinals, opossums, raccoons, and white-tailed deer. Most of these are native to the southeastern US, but a few West Indian bird species, such as the mangrove cuckoo, gray kingbird, and white-crowned pigeon, have colonized the south Florida rocklands.

Swamps and marshes

Although about half have been destroyed due to logging, peat removal, draining, or sewage outflow, swamps are still found all over Florida. Trees growing around swamps include pines, palms, cedars, oaks, black gum, willows, and bald cypress. Particularly adapted to aquatic conditions, the bald cypress is ringed by knobby "knees" or modified roots, providing oxygen to the tree, which would otherwise suffocate in the wet soil. Epiphytic orchids and bromeliads are common on cypresses, especially in the southern part of the state. Florida's official state tree, the sabal palm, is another swamp/hammock plant: "heart of palm" is the gourmet's name for the vegetable cut from its insides and used in salads.

Florida swamps also have many species of **insectivorous plants**; sticky pads or liquid-filled funnels trap small insects, which are then digested by the nitrogen-hungry plant. The area around the Apalachicola National Forest has the highest diversity of carnivorous plants in the world, among them pitcher plants, bladderworts, and sundews. Other swamp-dwellers include dragonflies, snails, clams, fish, bird-voiced tree frogs, limpkins, ibis, wood ducks, beavers, raccoons, and Florida panthers.

Wetlands with relatively few trees, **freshwater marshes** range from shallow wet prairies to deep-water cattail marshes. **The Everglades** form Florida's largest marsh, most of which is sawgrass. On higher ground with good soils, sawgrass (actually a sedge) grows densely; at lower elevations it's sparser, and often an algae mat covers the soil between its plants. Water beetles, tiny crustaceans such as amphipods, mosquitoes, crayfish, killifish, sunfish, gar, catfish, bullfrogs, herons, egrets, ibis, water rats, white-tailed deer, and Florida panthers can all be found. With luck, you might see a **snail kite**: a brown or black mottled hawk with a very specialized diet, entirely dependent on large apple snails. Snail and snail kite numbers have drastically fallen following the draining of marshes for agriculture and flood control, which so far has irreversibly drained over sixty percent of the Everglades.

Wetland denizens: alligators and wading birds

Alligators are one of the most widely known inhabitants of Florida's wetlands, lakes, and rivers. Look for them on sunny mornings when they bask on logs or banks. If you hear thunder rumbling on a clear day, it may in fact be the bellow of territorial males. Alligators can reach ten feet in length and primarily prey on fish, turtles, birds, crayfish, and crabs. Once overhunted for their hides and meat, alligators have made a strong comeback since protection was initiated in 1973; by 1987, Florida had up to half a million of them. They are not usually dangerous – only a handful of fatal attacks have been registered since 1973. Most at risk are people who swim at dusk and small children playing unattended near water. To many creatures, however, alligators are a life-saver: during the summer, when the marshes dry up, they use their snouts, legs, and tails to enlarge existing pools, creating a refuge for themselves and for other aquatic species. In these "gator holes," garfish stack up like cordwood, snakes search for frogs, and otters and anhingas forage for fish.

Wading birds are conspicuous in the wetlands. Egrets, herons, and ibis, usually clad in white or gray feathers, stalk frogs, mice, and small fish. Plume-hunters in the early 1900s decimated these birds to make fanciful hats, and during the last few decades habitat destruction has caused a ninety-percent reduction in their numbers. Nonetheless, many are still visible in swamps, marshes, and mangroves. Cattle egrets, invaders from South America, are a common sight on pastures, where they forage on insects disturbed by grazing livestock. Pink waders – roseate spoonbills and, to a much lesser extent, flamingoes – can also be found in southern Florida's wetlands.

Lakes, springs, and rivers

Florida has almost 8000 freshwater **lakes**. Game fish such as bass and bluegill are common, but the waters are too warm to support trout. Some native fish species are threatened by the introduction of the **walking catfish**, which has a specially adapted gill system enabling it to leave the water and take the fish equivalent of cross-country hikes. A native of India and Burma, the walking catfish was released into southern Florida canals in the early Sixties and within twenty years had "walked" across twenty counties, disturbing the indigenous food chain. A freeze eliminated a number of these exotic fish, though enough remain to cause concern.

Most Florida **springs** release cold fresh water, but some springs are warm and others emit sulfur, chloride, or salt-laden waters. Homosassa Springs (see "Tampa Bay and the Northwest," p.261), for example, has a high level of chloride, making it attractive to both freshwater and marine species of fish.

Besides fish, Florida's extensive **river** system supports snails, freshwater mussels, and crayfish. Southern river-dwellers also include the lovable **manatee**, or sea cow, which inhabits bays and shallow coastal waters. The only totally aquatic herbivorous mammal, manatees sometimes weigh almost a ton but only eat aquatic plants. Unable to tolerate cold conditions, manatees are partial to the warm water discharged by power plants, taking some of them as far north as North Carolina. In Florida during the winter, the large springs at Crystal River (see "Tampa Bay and the Northwest," p.261) attract manatees, some of which have become tame enough to allow divers to scratch their bellies. Although they have few natural enemies, manatees are on the decline, often due to powerboat propellers injuring their backs or heads when they feed at the surface.

The Coast

There's a lot more than sunbathing taking place around Florida's **coast**. The sandy beaches provide a habitat for many species, not least sea turtles. Where there isn't sand, you'll find the fascinating mangrove forests, or wildlife-filled salt marshes and estuaries. Offshore, coral reefs provide yet another exotic ecosystem, and one of the more pleasurable to explore by snorkeling or diving.

Sandy beaches

Waves bring many interesting creatures onto Florida's **sandy beaches**, such as sponges, horseshoe crabs, and the occasional sea horse. Florida's **shells** are justly famous – fig shells, moon snails, conches, whelks, olive shells, red and orange scallops, murex, cockles, and pen and turban shells are a few of the many varieties. As you beachcomb, beware of stepping barefoot on purplish fragments of **man-of-war** tentacles: these jellyfish have no means of locomotion, and their floating, sail-like bodies often cause them to be washed ashore – their tentacles, which sometimes reach to sixty feet in length, can deliver a painful sting. More innocuous beach inhabitants include wintering birds such as black-bellied plovers and sanderlings, and nesting black skimmers.

Of the seven species of **sea turtle**, five nest on Florida's sandy beaches: green, loggerhead, leatherback, hawksbill, and olive ridley. From February to August, the female turtles crawl ashore at night, excavate a beachside hole, and deposit a hundred-plus eggs inside. Not many of these will survive to adulthood:

Florida lobsters

Though the Maine coast may be the better-known source of **lobsters**, Florida boasts its share of these crustaceans, which differ from their northern counterparts by having a broad, flat tail, as opposed to the Maine variety's large, meaty claws. And while lobsters are prized by humans as a delicacy, they're vital to the ecosystem under the sea. As predators, lobsters are the custodians of the coral reefs: they gorge on the sea snails that aggressively graze the coral and keep the population in check. As prey, species like the spiny Florida lobster are a staple in the diet of many larger creatures – the jewfish, for example, feeds almost exclusively on them – and make a tasty treat for octopus, rays, and eels as well.

In recent years, **lobster fishing** has had a catastrophic effect on the underwater ecosystem around southern Florida, decimating the supplies of a key member of the food chain; while at the same time, **pollution** has diminished the oxygen content of the sea to such an extent that even hardy crustaceans suffer. To stem the losses, fishermen have agreed to take part in a government program that would reduce the number of **traps** left out each year. In recreational fishing, too, there are now **strict regulations** on the lobster's size (the carapace or body must be at least three inches long), the length of the season (Aug 6–March 31), and the number that can be caught (six lobsters per person per day). Meanwhile, locals grumble that opportunistic tourists have less respect for supplies than fishermen who rely on the lobsters for their livelihood, especially during the two-day **Sport Lobster season** (starting at 12.01am on the last Wednesday in July), when you're most likely to hear amateurs bragging about their sizeable catches with little regard for the environmental consequences. Only time will tell whether the government's actions are enough to bolster the lobster supplies, or whether the crustacean's fate will mirror that of the conch – once so abundant in the Keys but now mainly farmed in the Caribbean.

raccoons eat a lot of the eggs, and hatchlings are liable to be crushed by vehicles while attempting to cross the coastal highways. Programs to hatch the eggs artificially have helped offset some of the losses, however. The best time to view sea turtles is during June – peak nesting time – with one of the park-ranger-led walks offered along the southern portion of the northeast coast (see "The Northeast," p.369).

Mangroves

Found in brackish waters around the Florida Keys and the southwest coast, Florida has three species of **mangrove**. Unlike most plants, mangroves bear live young: the "seeds" or propagules germinate while still on the tree; after dropping from the parent, the young propagule floats for weeks or months until it washes up on a suitable site, where its sprouted condition allows it to put out roots rapidly. Like bald cypress, mangroves have difficulty extracting oxygen from their muddy environs and solve this problem with extensive aerial roots, which either dangle finger-like from branches or twist outwards from the lower trunk. **Mangrove inhabitants** include various fish species that depend on mangroves as a nursery, such as the mangrove snapper, as well as frogs, crocodiles, brown pelicans, wood storks, roseate spoonbills, river otters, mink, and raccoons.

Salt marshes and estuaries

Like the mangrove ecosystem, the **salt marsh and estuary habitat** provides a nursery for many fish species, which in turn serve as fodder for larger fish, herons, egrets, and the occasional dolphin. **Crocodiles**, which have narrower and more pointed snouts than alligators, are seldom sighted and are confined to saltwater at the state's southernmost tip. In a few southern Florida salt marshes, you might find a **great white heron**, a rare and handsome form of the more common great blue heron. Around Florida Bay, great white herons have learned to beg for fish from local residents, with each of these massive birds "working" a particular neighborhood – striding from household to household demanding fish by rattling window blinds with their bills or issuing guttural croaks. A less appealing salt marsh inhabitant is the **mosquito**: unfortunately, the more damaging methods of mosquito control, such as impounding salt water or spraying DDT, have inflicted extensive harm on the fragile salt marshes and estuaries.

The coral reef

A long band of living **coral reef** frames Florida's southeastern corner. Living coral comes in many colors: star coral is green, elkhorn coral orange, and brain coral red. Each piece of coral is actually a colony of hundreds or thousands of small, soft animals called polyps, related to sea anemones and jellyfish. The **polyps** secrete limestone to form their hard outer skeletons, and at night extend their feathery tentacles to filter seawater for microscopic food. The filtering process, however, provides only a fraction of the coral's nutrition – most is produced via the photosynthesis of algae that live within the polyps' cells. In recent years, influxes of warmer water, possibly associated with global warming, have killed off large numbers of the algae cells. The half-starved polyp then often succumbs to disease, a phenomenon known as "bleaching." Although this has been observed throughout the Pacific, the damage in Florida has so far been moderate; the impact of the tourist industry on the reef has been more pronounced, though reef destruction for souvenirs is now banned.

Coral reefs are home to a kaleidoscopic variety of brightly colored fish – beau gregories, porkfish, parrot fish, blennies, grunts, and wrasses – which swirl in dazzling schools or lurk between coral crevices. The **damselfish** is the farmer of the reef: after destroying a polyp patch, it feeds on the resultant algae growth, fiercely defending it from other fish. Thousands of other creatures live in the coral reef, among them sponges, feather-duster worms, sea fans, crabs, spiny lobsters, sea urchins, and conches.

Florida on film

The silver screen and the Sunshine State have one vital thing in common: escapism. Both on film and off, Florida has always represented the ultimate getaway. For nineteenth-century homesteaders, Cuban refugees, New York retirees, libido-laden college kids, or criminals on the lam, the state has always beckoned as some kind of paradise. Hollywood has also used Florida as an exotic backdrop for everything from light-hearted vacation flicks to black-hearted crime yarns, and the state has made the most of its movie-land charms. Henry Levin's phenomenally successful teen flick *Where the Boys Are* (1960), for instance, not only spawned a cinematic sub-genre, but also made Fort Lauderdale the country's top Spring Break resort. And Miami's rejuvenation in the Eighties can be attributed at least in part to the glamour imparted by filmmaker Michael Mann's TV series *Miami Vice*.

To immerse yourself in Florida's cinematic history, where images of palm trees, beaches, and luxury hotels predominate, is to take a virtual vacation. And though there are plenty of mediocre Florida flicks (most of them sun-addled Spring Break romps or Elvis Presley showcases), there are many that convey the unique and varied qualities of the state. Here are some of the best, of which those tagged with the ★ symbol are particularly recommended.

Drama and history

Any Given Sunday (Oliver Stone, 1999). Overblown football saga in which aging old-school coach Al Pacino wrestles with a cutthroat corporate owner played with surprising force by Cameron Diaz. They're battling for control of the fictional Miami Sharks, all while trying to win the big game with a cocky rookie quarterback ably played by Jamie Foxx.

Beneath the 12 Mile Reef (Robert Webb, 1953). In this beautiful travelogue, Greek sponge fishermen from Tarpon Springs venture south to fish the "Glades" and tangle with the Anglo "Conchs" of Key West. Robert Wagner plays a young Greek Romeo named Adonis, who dares to dive the "12 mile reef" for his sponge-worthy Juliet.

Distant Drums (Raoul Walsh, 1951). One of many movies that have focused on Florida's Seminole Indians (the first was made by Vitagraph in 1906), *Distant Drums*, set in the midst of the Seminole Wars in 1840, stars Gary Cooper as a legendary Indian fighter who finds himself and his men trapped in the Everglades. Cooper and his band encounter snakes, alligators, and hordes of Seminole braves as they attempt to reach dry land.

Reap the Wild Wind (Cecil B. De Mille, 1942). A stirring account of skulduggery in the Florida Keys of the 1840s. Spunky Paulette Goddard vacillates between sea salt John Wayne and landlubber Ray Milland while trying to outwit pirates, gangs, and a giant squid off the deadly coral reefs.

Ruby in Paradise (Victor Nunez, 1993). Ashley Judd plays Ruby, who leaves her home in the Tennessee mountains and hitches a ride south to taste life in the Florida Panhandle. Settling in Panama City, Ruby finds work in a tourist shop selling tacky souvenirs. She fends off the boss's son and finds herself along the way. The film was sensitively directed by Florida's own Victor Nunez, a true regional independent who has been making movies in northern Florida since 1970.

★ **Salesman** (Albert and David Maysles, 1968). The second half of this brilliant and moving documentary follows four Bible salesmen to Opa-Locka on the outskirts of Miami. It's not a tale of beaches and luxury hotels, but rather low-rent apartments, cheap motels, and the quiet desperation of four men trying to sell overpriced illustrated Bibles door to door.

Seminole (Budd Boetticher, 1953). Set five years before *Distant Drums* (see above) and far more sympathetic to the Seminoles' plight, Boetticher's Western stars Rock Hudson as a US dragoon and Anthony Quinn as his half-breed childhood friend who has become the Seminole chief Osceola. Attempting to claim even the swamps of Florida for white settlers, a power-hungry general sends a platoon into the Everglades to flush out the Seminole and drive them out west.

Stranger than Paradise (Jim Jarmusch, 1984). Jarmusch's austere indie masterpiece about two laconic hipsters and their Hungarian cousin. The trio travels from snow-bound Ohio to a lifeless, out-of-season Florida. The movie's Florida scenes consist of a cheap motel room and a deserted stretch of beach, proving the main characters' theory that everywhere starts to look the same after a while.

Sunshine State (John Sayles, 2002). Low-key but impressive ensemble piece featuring Edie Falco and Angela Bassett as two women facing disappointment over their unfulfilled dreams in small town Florida. Sayles highlights the power of real estate developers in the state, but doesn't neglect the quirky local details.

Ulee's Gold (Victor Nunez, 1997). Twenty-two years after *92 in the Shade*, Peter Fonda gave the best performance of his career as Florida beekeeper Ulee, a stoical Vietnam vet raising his granddaughters while his son is in jail. Local auteur Nunez (*Ruby in Paradise*) knows and captures northern Florida better than any filmmaker, and despite a strained plot about a couple of ne'er-do-wells and a stash of money, this meditative, measured movie is a triumph.

Vernon, Florida (Errol Morris, 1981). This documentary lovingly – if a little mockingly – captures every foible of the Florida eccentrics who fill the small town of Vernon in the Panhandle. Standout is the turkey hunter, memorable for his hushed and reverential attitude toward the birds he hunts and kills.

The Yearling (Clarence Brown, 1946). A Technicolor classic about a family struggling to eke out a living in the scrub country of northern Florida (in the vicinity of Lake George and Volusia) in 1878. Oscar-winner Claude Jarman Jr plays the son of Gregory Peck and Jane Wyman who adopts a mighty troublesome fawn. The movie was shot on location and based on Florida scribe Marjorie Kinnan Rawlings' Pulitzer Prize-winning novel of the same name.

Crime stories

Aileen Wuornos: The Selling of a Serial Killer (Nick Broomfield, 1993). British documentarian Broomfield, in his inimitably fearless, in-your-face style. stumbles into a swamp of avarice and exploitation in his search for the true story of Aileen Wuornos, America's first female serial killer. That a woman who was convicted of (and executed for) murdering seven men along a Florida Interstate comes across as more sympathetic than most of the people around her makes this portrait of backwoods Florida all the more chilling.

Bad Boys II (Michael Bay, 2003). Will Smith and Martin Lawrence return as a wisecracking, crime-busting duo in a movie packed with director Bay's trademark over-the-top action sequences. The plot – revolving around local drug dealers – may be skimpy, but the movie makes terrific use of locales in and around Miami, especially Coral Gables.

Black Sunday (John Frankenheimer, 1976). Palestinian terrorists, with the aid of disgruntled Vietnam vet Bruce Dern, plan to wipe out 80,000 football fans, including President Jimmy Carter, in the Orange Bowl on Super Bowl Sunday. Though the first half of the movie unfolds in Beirut and LA, the heart-stopping climax results in some fine aerial views of Miami.

Blood and Wine (Bob Rafelson, 1997). Jack Nicholson plays a dodgy Miami wine dealer with access to the cellars of southern Florida's rich and famous in this underrated thriller. He enlists a wheezy expat safe-breaker (Michael Caine) and a savvy Cuban nanny (Jennifer Lopez) in his scheme to snag a million-dollar necklace. When the jewels end up in the hands of his jilted wife (Judy Davis) and perpetually pissed-off stepson (Stephen Dorff) the action heads south to the Florida Keys.

Body Heat (Lawrence Kasdan, 1981). Filmed just south of Palm Beach in the small coastal town of Lake Worth, Kasdan's directorial debut makes the most of the sweaty potential of a southern Florida heat wave. Shady lawyer William Hurt falls for the charms of wealthy Kathleen Turner and plans to bump off her husband for the inheritance.

China Moon (John Bailey, 1994). Ed Harris plays a hard-boiled cop seduced into covering up a neglected wife's (Madeleine Stowe) murder of her philandering husband, only to find himself the prime suspect in this steamy, oddly satisfying B-movie.

Illtown (Nick Gomez, 1995). Depending on whom you ask, Nick Gomez's movie is either a stylish, strange, and ambitious achievement or a pretentious mess. Either way, it's hard to ignore: with Tony Danza as a gay mob boss, and a gaggle of familiar indie stars (Michael Rapaport, Adam Trese, Lili Taylor, and Kevin Corrigan) playing an unlikely bunch of Miami drug dealers.

Key Largo (John Huston, 1948). Though shot entirely on Hollywood sets, Huston's tense crime melodrama about an army veteran (Humphrey Bogart) and a mob boss (Edward G. Robinson) barricaded in a Key Largo hotel during a major hurricane has the credible feel of a muggy summer in the Florida Keys.

Miami Blues (George Armitage, 1990). Adapted from Charles Willeford's fiction, this quirky crime story about a home-loving psychopath (Alec Baldwin), the naive hooker he shacks up with (Jennifer Jason Leigh), and the burnt-out homicide detective who's on their trail (Fred Ward) is set in a seedy back-street Miami that glitters with terrific characters, gritty performances and delicious offbeat details.

Night Moves (Arthur Penn, 1975). In one of the great metaphysical thrillers of the post-Watergate Seventies, Gene Hackman plays a weary LA private eye with marital problems who is hired to track down a young and underdressed Melanie Griffith in the Florida Keys.

Out of Sight (Steven Soderbergh, 1998). Flip-flopping between past and present and between a jazzy, sun-drenched Florida and a snow-peppered Detroit, Soderbergh's movie is a hugely satisfying adaptation of Elmore Leonard's novel of the same name. The action is set in motion when George Clooney's urbane bank-robber tunnels out of a Pensacola penitentiary and into the life of Federal Marshal Jennifer Lopez.

Out of Time (Carl Franklin, 2003). Denzel Washington stars as the police chief of fictional Banyan Key, caught up in a formulaic but fun Floridian noir thriller. There are enough satisfying twists and pantomime baddies (like Dean Cain) to keep the story from getting too sluggish in the tropical heat.

Palmetto (Volker Schlondorff, 1998). Woody Harrelson returns from jail to the Sarasota beach town of Palmetto and becomes Florida's number one patsy when a bleach-blonde Elisabeth Shue walks into his life and proposes a little fake kidnapping. Perfectly exploiting Florida's sultry charms, *Palmetto* lapses into neo-noir cliché at times, but the twisty plot keeps things interesting.

★ **Scarface** (Brian De Palma, 1983). Small-time Cuban thug Tony Montana arrives in Miami during the 1980 Mariel boatlift and murders, bullies, and snorts his way to the top of his profession, becoming Miami's most powerful drug lord. One of the great Florida movies, De Palma's seductive and shocking paean to excess and the perversion of the American Dream stars Al Pacino in a legendary, go-for-broke performance.

The Specialist (Luis Llosa, 1994). A priapic, glossy portrait of Miami props up this otherwise dismal thriller featuring one of Miami's high profile former residents, Sylvester Stallone, as an ex-CIA agent hired by vengeful Sharon Stone to execute the Mafiosi who wiped out her family.

Tony Rome (Gordon Douglas, 1967). Wise-cracking, hard-living private eye Frank Sinatra tangles with pushers, strippers, gold diggers, and self-made millionaires on the wild side of Miami (the town love interest Jill St John calls "Twenty miles of beach looking for a city"). The movie is a run-of-the-mill detective yarn, but Frank was entertaining enough to warrant a sequel: *Lady in Cement*.

True Lies (James Cameron, 1994). Pulsing with action and peppered with one-liners, this schlocky thriller is still great fun, with Arnold Schwarzenegger just about managing to convince as a CIA agent with a double life and Jamie Lee Curtis as his trusting wife. The explosive set piece features the destruction of a significant chunk of Henry Flagler's old bridge in the Florida Keys.

Wild Things (John McNaughton, 1997). A convoluted, noirish thriller about handsome high-school counselors, lubricious schoolgirls, and wealthy widows in a well-heeled community in the Everglades. Beautifully shot and played to the hilt by Matt Dillon, Kevin Bacon, Denise Richards, and Neve Campbell, the plot corkscrews with twists until the final frame.

Comic capers

92 in the Shade (Thomas McGuane, 1975). A nutty, laidback comedy about rival fishing guides in Key West, starring a potpourri of Hollywood's greatest oddballs: Peter Fonda, Harry Dean Stanton, Warren Oates, Burgess Meredith, and William Hickey. Ripe with local color but somewhat lacking in affect, the movie was based on Thomas McGuane's acclaimed novel of the same name (see p.495).

Ace Ventura, Pet Detective (Tom Shadyac, 1994). The movie that launched Jim Carrey's thousand faces. Carrey stars as a bequiffed investigator on a quest to recover Snowflake, the Miami Dolphins' kidnapped mascot, on the eve of the Super Bowl. The Miami Dolphins and their quarterback Dan Marino appear as themselves.

Adaptation (Spike Jonze, 2002). Susan Orlean's bestseller (see p.492) serves as the springboard for this entertaining, fictionalized version, in which the film's screenwriter (Nicholas Cage) struggles to adapt the book, undermined all the while by his twin brother (also played by Cage). Meryl Streep's Orlean pursues orchid-poacher Chris Cooper to the Loxahatchee National Wildlife Refuge.

The Bellboy (Jerry Lewis, 1960). This movie was shot almost entirely within Miami Beach's ultra-kitsch pleasure palace *The Fontainebleau* (the same hotel where James Bond is meant to be sunbathing at the beginning of 1964's *Goldfinger*). Jerry Lewis, in his debut as writer-director, plays Stanley, the bellhop from hell, and cameos as vacationing movie star Jerry Lewis in one of the most site-specific movies ever made.

The Birdcage (Mike Nichols, 1996). Nichols' Miami remake of *La Cage Aux Folles* makes playful use of South Beach's burgeoning gay scene, portraying the rejuvenated Art Deco playground as a bright paradise of pecs, thongs, and drag queens – the opening scene plays as a love letter to Ocean Drive. Impresario Armand (Robin Williams) and reigning Birdcage diva Albert (Nathan Lane) are happily cohabiting in kitsch heaven until the day Armand's son brings his ultra-conservative future in-laws to dinner.

The Cocoanuts (Joseph Santley & Robert Florey, 1929). Set during Florida's real-estate boom, the Marx Brothers' first film stars Groucho as an impecunious hotel proprietor attempting to keep his business afloat by auctioning off land (with the usual interference from Chico and Harpo) in Cocoanut Grove, "the Palm Beach of tomorrow." Groucho expounds on Florida's climate while standing in what is really a sand-filled studio lot.

From Justin to Kelly (Robert Iscove, 2002). Witless, misguided attempt to resurrect the beach party movie genre of the Sixties, this cheesy musical – headlined by the winner and the runner up of the first season of talent contest *American Idol* – is most effective as an exhaustive showcase for every major Miami attraction, including an elaborate song and dance number in and around the Venetian Pool.

The Heartbreak Kid (Elaine May, 1972). An underrated comic masterpiece written by Neil Simon, in which Charles Grodin marries a nice Jewish girl, and then, on the honeymoon drive down to Florida, starts to regret it. His doubts are compounded when goddess Cybill Shepherd starts flirting with him on the beach while his sunburnt bride lies in bed.

Heartbreakers (David Mirkin, 2001). Mindless but enjoyable romp with mother-and-daughter scam duo Sigourney Weaver and Jennifer Love Hewitt homing in on Palm Beach tobacco baron Gene Hackman as their latest victim.

A Hole in the Head (Frank Capra, 1959). Frank Sinatra plays an irresponsible Miami Beach hotel owner who has dreams of striking it rich by turning South Beach into "Disneyland." The breezy opening titles in this musical comedy are pulled on airborne banners across the Miami Beach skyline.

Miami Rhapsody (David Frankel, 1995). Sarah Jessica Parker kvetches like a female Woody Allen in this disappointingly uneven comedy. Parker weighs commitment against the marital dissatisfaction and compulsive infidelity of her extended family in an otherwise picture-perfect, upscale Miami: "I guess I look at marriage the same way I look at Miami: it's hot and its stormy, and it's occasionally a little dangerous...but if it's really so awful why is there still so much traffic?"

Moon Over Miami (Walter Lang, 1941). Gold-digging, Texas-hamburger-stand waitress Betty Grable takes her sister and aunt to Miami, where "rich men are as plentiful as grapefruit, and millionaires hang from every palm tree." Grable has little trouble snagging herself a couple of ripe ones in this colorful, sappy musical comedy (the theme song "Oh Me, Oh Mi...ami!" sets the tone). On-location shooting took place in Winter Haven and Ocala, a few hundred miles north of Miami.

The Palm Beach Story (Preston Sturges, 1942). In this madcap masterpiece, Claudette Colbert takes a train from Penn Station to Palm Beach ("the best place to get a divorce," a cabbie tells her) to free herself from her penniless dreamer of a husband and find herself a good millionaire to marry.

Porky's (Bob Clark, 1981). The Citizen Kane of randy teen movies, the notorious (and Canadian) *Porky's* is set in fictional Angel Beach near Fort Lauderdale in the mid-Fifties. A group of high-school guys with only one thing on their minds venture into Florida's backcountry in the hopes of getting laid at *Porky's*, a licentious redneck bar.

★ **Some Like it Hot** (Billy Wilder, 1959). Wilder's classic farce starts in 1929 in Chicago. Jazz musicians Tony Curtis and Jack Lemmon escape retribution for witnessing the St Valentine's Day massacre by disguising themselves as women and joining an all-girl jazz band on a train to Miami. Though *Some Like it Hot* could be a candidate for the best movie ever set in Miami, it was actually shot at the *Hotel del Coronado* in San Diego.

There's Something About Mary (Peter and Bobby Farrelly, 1998). Years after a heinous pre-prom disaster (involving an unruly zipper), Rhode Island geek Ben Stiller tracks down Mary, the eponymous object of his affection, to her new home in Miami. Once there he finds he's not the only one suffering from obsessive tendencies. The Farrelly brothers have created a hysterical, gross-out masterpiece.

Fantasy lands

★ **Cocoon** (Ron Howard, 1985). Even extraterrestrials vacation in Florida. This charming, Spielberg-esque fantasy centers on residents of a Florida retirement community who discover a local swimming pool with alien powers of rejuvenation. Nearly half a century after he danced with Betty Grable in *Moon Over Miami*, Don Ameche won a Best Supporting Actor Oscar for this film.

Dumbo (Ben Sharpsteen, 1941). In the opening sequence of this Disney animated classic there is a wonderful stork's-eye view of the entire state of Florida, where the circus has hunkered down for the winter. Though the show eventually goes on the road, this eyeful of Florida seems prescient considering Disney's role in the state some quarter of a century later.

Revenge of the Creature (Jack Arnold, 1955). Transported comatose from the Upper Amazon, the Creature from the Black Lagoon is brought to Marinelands oceanarium to create the "greatest scientific stir since the explosion of the Atomic Bomb." He creates an even bigger stir when he cuts loose and heads for the beach, crashing a swing party at a seafront oyster house.

The Truman Show (Peter Weir, 1998). The picture-perfect, picket-fence community of Seahaven that Jim Carrey's Truman Burbank calls home turns out to be nothing more than a giant television studio, where

Truman is watched every minute of the day in the world's longest-running soap opera. The false paradise of Seahaven is actually the real, but equally artificial, Florida Gulf Coast town of Seaside, a planned vacation community (built in 1981) that looks like it's stuck in the Fifties.

Books

Florida's perennial state of social and political flux has always promised rich material for historians and journalists eager to pin the place down. Rarely have they managed this, though the picture of the region's unpredictable evolution that emerges can make for compulsive reading. Many established fiction writers spend their winters in Florida, but few have convincingly portrayed its characters, climate, and scenery. Those who have succeeded, however, have produced some of the most remarkable and gripping literature to emerge from any part of the US. Books tagged with the ★ symbol are particularly recommended. Publishers are listed after the title, US/UK if not published in both territories, and o/p denotes out of print.

History

Edward N. Akin *Flagler: Rockefeller Partner and Florida Baron* (Florida Atlantic University US). Solid biography of the man whose Standard Oil fortune helped build Florida's first hotels and railroads.

Charles R. Ewen and John H. Hann *Hernando de Soto Among the Apalachee* (University Press of Florida). A history and description of the archaeological site (located in downtown Tallahassee) believed to be a campsite used by Spanish explorer Hernando de Soto in the sixteenth century.

John T. Foster and Sarah Whitmer Foster *Beechers, Stowes, and Yankee Strangers* (University Press of Florida). An entertaining and relatively brief account about a group of Yankee reformers who lived in Florida at the end of the Civil War – including Harriet Beecher Stowe, author of *Uncle Tom's Cabin* – and their designs on a postwar Florida.

John J. Guthrie Jr, Philip Charels Lucas, and Gary Monroe *Cassadaga: The South's Oldest Spiritual Community* (University Press of Florida). A look at the history, people, and religious beliefs of the "metaphysical mecca" of Cassadaga – a small town between Orlando and Daytona Beach established more than a hundred years ago on the principle of continuous life.

★ **Carl Hiaasen** *Team Rodent* (Ballantine). A native of Florida, Hiaasen has been a firsthand witness to Disney's domination of Orlando, and this book is a scathing attack on the entertainment conglomerate, exposing Disney for what Hiaasen thinks it is: evil. "Disney is so good at being good that it manifests an evil," he writes, "so uniformly and courteous, so dependably clean and conscientious, so unfailingly entertaining that it's unreal, and therefore is an agent of pure wickedness." Like Hiaasen's fiction work (see p.494), the prose is a mix of sharp wit, informed research, and a lot of humor.

Stetson Kennedy *The Klan Unmasked* (Florida Atlantic University/University Press of Florida). A riveting history of the Klan's activity in the post-World War II era, including specific references to Florida.

Robert Kerstein *Politics and Growth in Twentieth Century Tampa* (University Press of Florida). A history of the politics and growth in Tampa from the coming of the railroads and cigar industry to the mid-1990s.

Howard Kleinberg *Miami: The Way We Were* (SeaSide Publications US). Oversized overview of Miami's history: colorful archival photos accompany text by a former editor-in-chief of the city's dominant newspaper, *The Miami News*.

Stuart B. McIver *Dreamers, Schemers, and Scalawags* (Pineapple Press). An intriguing mix of biography and storytelling that tells Florida's history through its mobsters and millionaires. This is volume one of a continuing series.

Jerald T. Milanich *Florida's Indians, from Ancient Times to the Present* (University Press of Florida). A comprehensive history spanning 12,000 years of Indian life in Florida.

Gary R. Mormino and George E. Pozzetta *The Immigrant World of Ybor City* (University Press of Florida). Flavorful accounts of the Cuban, Italian, and Spanish immigrants who built their lives around Ybor City's cigar industry at the turn of the twentieth century.

Helen Muir *Miami, USA* (University Press of Florida US). An insider's account of how Miami's first developers gave the place shape during the land boom of the Twenties: a little toothless, but a fair overview.

John Rothchild *Up for Grabs: A Trip Through Time and Space in the Sunshine State* (University Press of Florida). An irreverent look at Florida's checkered career as a vacation spa, tourist trap, and haven for scheming ne'er-do-wells.

Charlton W. Tebeau *A History of Florida* (University of Miami Press US). The definitive academic tome, but not for casual reading.

Victor Andres Triay *Fleeing Castro* (University Press of Florida). An emotional account of the plight of Cuba's children during the missile crisis. With their parents unable to obtain visas, 14,048 children were smuggled from the island; many never saw their families again.

Garcilaso de la Vega *The Florida of the Inca* (University of Texas Press). Comprehensive account of the sixteenth-century expedition led by Hernando de Soto through Florida's prairies, swamps, and aboriginal settlements. Extremely turgid in parts, but overall an excellent insight into the period.

David C. Weeks *Ringling* (University Press of Florida). An in-depth work chronicling the time spent in Florida by circus guru John Ringling.

Patsy West *The Enduring Seminoles* (University Press of Florida). A history of Florida's Seminole Indians, who, by embracing tourism, found a means to keep their vibrant cultural identity alive.

Lawrence E. Will *Swamp to Sugarbowl: Pioneer Days in Belle Glade* (Great Outdoors Publications o/p). A "cracker" account of early times in the state, written in first-person redneck vernacular. Variously oafish and offensive but never dull.

Natural history

Mark Derr *Some Kind of Paradise* (University Press of Florida). A cautionary history of Florida's penchant for mishandling its environmental assets, from spongers off the reefs to Miami's ruthless hotel contractors.

★ **Marjory Stoneman Douglas** *The Everglades: River of Grass* (Pineapple Press/Florida Classics). Concerned conservationist literature by one of the state's most respected historians, describing the nature and beauty of the Everglades from their beginnings. A superb work that contributed to the founding of the Everglades National Park. Douglas passed away in 1998 at the age of 108.

David McCally *The Everglades: An Environmental History* (University Press of Florida). For both general readers and environmentalists, this book examines the formation, development, and history of the Everglades – believed to be the most endangered ecosystem in North America.

National Geographic Society *Field Guide to the Birds of North America (4th ed)* (National Geographic). The best country-wide guide, with plenty on Florida, and excellent illustrations throughout.

Bill Pranty *A Birder's Guide to Florida* (American Birding Association). Detailed accounts of when and where to find Florida's birds, including maps and charts.

Aimed at the expert but excellent value for the novice bird-watcher.

Joe Schafer and George Tanner *Landscaping for Florida's Wildlife* (University Press of Florida). Step-by-step advice on how to replicate a sliver of Florida's wildlife in your own garden.

Glen Simmons with Laura Ogden *Gladesmen* (University Press of Florida). Entertaining accounts of the "swamp rats": rugged men and women who made a living wrestling alligators and trekking the "Glades."

Travel impressions

★ **William Bartram** *Travels* (University of Virginia Press/Peregrine Smith). The lively diary of an eighteenth-century naturalist rambling through the Deep South and on into Florida during the period of British rule. Outstanding accounts of the indigenous people and all kinds of wildlife.

Edna Buchanan *The Corpse Had a Familiar Face* (Diamond/Berkley Pub Group). Sometimes sharp, often sensationalist account of the author's years spent pounding the crime beat for the *Miami Herald*: five thousand corpses and gore galore. The subsequent *Vice* is more of the same.

Joan Didion *Miami* (Vintage). Didion's bony prose is hard going but it's worth persevering, at least in the early chapters, to understand the complex relationship between Cuban expats and the US government. Midway, though, she's derailed into musings on the minutiae of Washington politics, and the book rapidly loses focus.

Lynn Geldof *Cubans* (St Martins Press). Passionate and rambling interviews with Cubans in Cuba and Miami, which confirm the tight bond between them.

Henry James *The American Scene* (Penguin). Interesting waffle from the celebrated novelist, including written portraits of St Augustine and Palm Beach as they thronged with wintering socialites at the turn of the twentieth century.

Norman Mailer *Miami and the Siege of Chicago* (New American Library/Penguin). A rabid study of the American political conventions of 1968, the first part frothing over the Republican Party's shenanigans at Miami Beach when Nixon beat Reagan for the presidential ticket.

Kevin McCarthy *Alligator Tales* (Pineapple Press). This intriguing collection of both actual and slightly overblown encounters with alligators is illustrated with the photographs of John Moran.

Michele McPhee *Mob Over Miami* (Onyx Books). Gripping, exhaustively researched true crime tale, focusing on Staten Island mobster turned South Beach nightlife mogul Chris Paciello.

Susan Orlean *The Orchid Thief* (Ballantine). *New Yorker* staff writer Orlean immerses herself in the orchid-fancying subculture of South Florida, following an eccentric gardener on his illegal gathering trips in the wild. The basis for Spike Jonze's film *Adaptation* (see p.487).

Roxanne Pulitzer *The Prize Pulitzer: The Scandal that Rocked Palm Beach* (Ballantine). A small-town girl who married into the jet-set lifestyle of Palm Beach describes the mud-slinging in Florida's most moneyed community when she seeks a divorce.

Alexander Stuart *Life on Mars* (Black Swan). "Paradise with a lobotomy" is how a friend of the author described Florida. This is an often-amusing series of vignettes about the empty lives led by both the beautiful people of South Beach and the redneck "white trash" of upstate.

John Williams *Into the Badlands: A Journey through the American Dream* (HarperCollins/Flamingo). The author's trek across the US to interview the country's best crime writers begins in Miami, "the city that coke built," its compelling strangeness all too briefly reveled in.

Architecture

Barbara Baer Capitman *Deco Delights* (E.P. Dutton/Penguin). A tour of Miami Beach's Art Deco buildings by the woman who championed their preservation, with definitive photography.

Laura Cerwinske *Miami: Hot & Cool* (Three Rivers Press/Random House). Coffee-table tome with text on high-style south Florida living and glowing, color photos of Miami's beautiful homes and gardens. By the same author, *Tropical Deco: The Architecture & Design of Old Miami Beach* delivers a wealth of architectural detail.

Donald W. Curl *Mizner's Florida: American Resort Architecture* (MIT Press). An assessment of the life, career, and designs of Addison Mizner, the self-taught architect responsible for the "Bastard Spanish Moorish Romanesque Renaissance Bull Market Damn the Expense Style" structures of Palm Beach and Boca Raton.

★ **Hap Hatton** *Tropical Splendor: An Architectural History of Florida* (Knopf/Random House). A readable, informative, and well-illustrated account of the wild, weird, and wonderful buildings that have graced and disgraced the state over the years.

Nicholas N. Patricios *Building Marvelous Miami* (University Press of Florida) The architectural development of Florida's favorite city documented by 250 photos.

Art and photography

Todd Bertolaet *Crescent Rivers* (University Press of Florida). Ansel Adams-style photos of the dark, blackwater rivers that wind through Florida's Big Bend.

Anne Jeffrey and Aletta Dreller *Art Lover's Guide to Florida* (Pineapple Press). A comprehensive guidebook featuring 86 of the most dynamic and exciting art galleries in Florida, including museums and art centers.

Gary Monroe *Life in South Beach* (Forest and Trees US). A slim volume of black and white photos showing Miami Beach's South Beach before the restoration of the Art Deco district and the arrival of globetrotting trendies.

★ **Tom Shroder and John Barry** *Seeing the Light Wilderness and Salvation: A Photographer's Tale* (Random House). An attractive book describing the story of photographer Clyde Butcher's long connection with the Everglades and showcasing his wonderful pictures of the area.

Woody Walters *Visions of Florida* (University of Florida Press). Black-and-white photos, but ones that still convey the richness and beauty of Florida's terrain, from misty mornings in Tallahassee to bolts of lightning over the Everglades.

William Weber *Florida Nature Photography* (University of Florida Press US). A glossy, pictorial look at Florida's many state parks, recreation areas, and nature preserves.

Millard Wells *Florida Key Impressions* (Pineapple Press US). An illustrated journal describing a journey through the Florida Keys, highlighted by the author's original watercolor paintings.

Fiction

Pat Booth *Miami* (Ballantine UK). Miami's South Beach is used as a backdrop for this pot-boiling tale of seduction and desire.

Liza Cody *Backhand* (Doubleday/Bantam). London's finest female private investigator, Anna Lee, follows the clues from Kensington to the west coast of Florida – highly entertaining.

Harry Crews *Florida Frenzy* (University Press of Florida). A collection of tales relating macho outdoor pursuits like 'gator poaching and cockfighting.

Kate Di Camillo *Because of Winn-Dixie* (Candlewick Press). When a stray dog appears in the midst of the produce section of the Winn-Dixie grocery store, it leads 10-year-old India Opal Buloni from one new friend to the next in a small Florida town. The stories India gathers in this award-winning children's book help her to piece together a new definition of family.

Tim Dorsey *Triggerfish Twist* (HarperTorch). The latest novel in Dorsey's ongoing saga of psycho Florida eccentric Serge A. Storms takes in homicidal Little League parents, predatory real estate agents, and a mild-mannered corporate cog.

Edward Falco *Winter in Florida* (Soho Press/Bellow Pub Co.). Flawed but compulsive story of a cosseted New York boy seeking thrills on a central Florida horse farm.

Connie May Fowler *Before Women Had Wings* (Ivy Books). Set in and around Tampa in the Sixties, this powerful novel tells the story of the youngest daughter of a family crippled by poverty and the effects of alcohol, violence, and broken dreams.

James Hall *Under Cover of Daylight*; *Squall Line*; *Hard Aground* (W.W. Norton). Taut thrillers with a cast of crazies that make the most of the edge-of-the-world landscapes of the Florida Keys.

Ernest Hemingway *To Have and Have Not* (Scribner/Arrow). Hemingway lived and drank in Key West for years but set only this moderate tale in the town, describing the woes of fishermen brutalized by the Depression.

★ **Carl Hiaasen** *Double Whammy* (Warner). Ferociously funny fishing thriller that brings together a classic collection of warped but believable Florida characters, among them a hermit-like ex-state governor, a cynical Cuban cop, and a corrupt TV preacher. By the same author, *Skin Tight* explores the perils of unskilled plastic surgery in a Miami crawling with mutant hitmen, bought politicians, and police on gangsters' payrolls, and *Native Tongue* delves into the murky goings-on behind the scenes at a Florida theme park. Anyone with a passing interest in Florida should read at least one of these.

Carl Hiaasen (ed) *Naked Came the Manatee* (Ballantine/Fawcett). Thirteen of Miami's best-known novelists teamed up to pen this caper, which centers on the discovery of Fidel Castro's dismembered head. Full of in-jokes, this broad satire is good, if uneven, fun.

Zora Neale Hurston *Their Eyes Were Watching God* (Perennial/Virago Press). Florida-born Hurston became one of the bright lights of the Harlem Renaissance in the Twenties. This novel describes the founding of Eatonville – her home town and the state's first all-black town – and the laborer's lot in Belle Glade at the time of the 1928 hurricane. Equally hard to put down are *Jonah's Gourd Vine* and the autobiography, *Dust Tracks on a Road*.

Elmore Leonard *Stick* (HarperTorch); *La Brava* (HarperTorch/Avon); *Gold Coast* (HarperTorch/Penguin). The pick of this highly recommended author's Florida-set thrillers, respectively detailing the rise of an opportunist ex-con through the money, sex, and drugs of Latino Miami; lowlife on the seedy South Beach before the preservation of the Art Deco district; and the tribulations of a wealthy gangster-widow alone in a Fort Lauderdale mansion.

Peter Matthiessen *Killing Mister Watson* (Vintage). The first in a thoroughly researched trilogy on the early days of white settlement in the Everglades. Slow-paced but a strong insight into the Florida frontier mentality.

Thomas McGuane *Ninety-Two in the Shade* (Vintage). A strange, hallucinatory search for identity by a young man of shifting mental states who aspires to become a Key West fishing guide – and whose family and friends are equally warped. McGuane directed the film version; see p.486 for review.

Theodore Pratt *The Barefoot Mailman* (Florida Classics). A Forties' account of the long-distance postman who kept the far-flung settlements of pioneer-period Florida in mail by hiking the many miles of beach between them.

Marjorie Kinnan Rawlings *Short Stories* (University Press of Florida). A collection of 23 of Rawlings' most acclaimed short pieces, which draw heavily on Florida's natural surroundings for inspiration.

John Sayles *Los Gusanos* (Harper Perennial Library/HarperCollins). Absorbing if long-winded novel set around the lives of Cuban exiles in Miami at the time of the Mariel boatlift – written by the indie movie director.

Edmund Skellings *Collected Poems: 1958-1998* (University Press of Florida US). A "best of" collection of work by Florida's poet laureate.

Patrick D. Smith *A Land Remembered* (Pineapple Press US). This historical novel is an epic portrayal of the lives of an American pioneering family, set against the rich and rugged history of Florida.

Randy Wayne White *Sanibel Flats* (St Martins Press). First in a series of Doc Ford detective novels, this book tells the story of a murder committed on a deserted mangrove island on Florida's west coast.

Charles Willeford *Miami Blues* (Ballantine). Thanks to an uninspired movie, the best-known but not the best of a highly recommended crime fiction series starring Hoke Mosely, a cool and calculating, but very human, Miami cop. Superior titles in the series are *The Way We Die Now*, *Kiss Your Ass Goodbye*, and *Sideswipe*.

Cooking

Linda Gassenheimer *Keys Cuisine* (Atlantic Monthly Press/Avalon Travel Publications). A collection of recipes that captures the flavor of the Florida Keys.

Sue Mullin *Nuevo Cubano Cooking* (Book Sales). Easy-to-follow instructions and mouthwatering photographs of recipes fusing traditional Cuban cooking with *nouvelle cuisine*.

Dawn O'Brien and Becky Roper *Florida's Historic Restaurants and Their Recipes* (J.F. Blair US). Featuring a variety of cuisines, this book contains fifty recipes from Florida's best-known restaurants.

Ferdie Pacheco and Luisita Sevilla Pacheco *The Christmas Eve Cookbook* (University Press of Florida). A collection of over 200 holiday recipes and stories that illustrates the melting pot of immigrants that settled in Ybor City.

★ **Steven Raichleu** *Miami Spice* (Workman Publishing). Latin American and Caribbean cooking meets Florida and the Deep South, resulting in some of the tastiest dishes in America. Clear recipes and interesting background information.

Rough Guides

advertiser

...music & reference

Africa & Middle East
Cape Town
Egypt
The Gambia
Jerusalem
Jordan
Kenya
Morocco
South Africa, Lesotho & Swaziland
Syria
Tanzania
Tunisia
West Africa
Zanzibar
Zimbabwe

Travel Theme guides
First-Time Around the World
First-Time Asia
First-Time Europe
First-Time Latin America
Gay & Lesbian Australia
Skiing & Snowboarding in North America
Travel Online
Travel Health
Walks in London & SE England
Women Travel

Restaurant guides
French Hotels & Restaurants
London
New York
San Francisco

Maps
Algarve
Amsterdam
Andalucia & Costa del Sol
Argentina
Athens
Australia
Baja California
Barcelona
Boston
Brittany
Brussels
Chicago
Crete
Croatia
Cuba
Cyprus
Czech Republic
Dominican Republic
Dublin
Egypt
Florence & Siena
Frankfurt
Greece
Guatemala & Belize
Iceland
Ireland
Lisbon
London
Los Angeles
Mexico
Miami & Key West
Morocco
New York City
New Zealand
Northern Spain
Paris
Portugal
Prague
Rome
San Francisco
Sicily
South Africa
Sri Lanka
Tenerife
Thailand
Toronto
Trinidad & Tobago
Tuscany
Venice
Washington DC
Yucatán Peninsula

Dictionary Phrasebooks
Czech
Dutch
Egyptian Arabic
European
French
German
Greek
Hindi & Urdu
Hungarian
Indonesian
Italian
Japanese
Mandarin Chinese
Mexican Spanish
Polish
Portuguese
Russian
Spanish
Swahili
Thai
Turkish
Vietnamese

Music Guides
The Beatles
Cult Pop
Classical Music
Country Music
Cuban Music
Drum'n'bass
Elvis
House
Irish Music
Jazz
Music USA
Opera
Reggae
Rock
Techno
World Music (2 vols)

100 Essential CDs series
Country
Latin
Opera
Rock
Soul
World Music

History Guides
China
Egypt
England
France
Greece
India
Ireland
Islam
Italy
Spain
USA

Reference Guides
Books for Teenagers
Children's Books, 0–5
Children's Books, 5–11
Cult Football
Cult Movies
Cult TV
Digital Stuff
Formula 1
The Internet
Internet Radio
James Bond
Lord of the Rings
Man Utd
Personal Computers
Pregnancy & Birth
Shopping Online
Travel Health
Travel Online
Unexplained Phenomena
The Universe
Videogaming
Weather
Website Directory

Also! More than 120 Rough Guide music CDs are available from all good book and record stores. Listen in at www.worldmusic.net

Index

and small print

Index

Map entries are in color

F

G

H

I

J

K

L

M

N

INDEX

A Rough Guide to Rough Guides

In the summer of 1981, Mark Ellingham, a recent graduate from Bristol University, was traveling round Greece and couldn't find a guidebook that really met his needs. On the one hand there were the student guides, insistent on saving every last cent, and on the other the heavyweight cultural tomes whose authors seemed to have spent more time in a research library than lounging away the afternoon at a taverna or on the beach.

In a bid to avoid getting a job, Mark and a small group of writers set about creating their own guidebook. It was a guide to Greece that aimed to combine a journalistic approach to description with a thoroughly practical approach to travelers' needs – a guide that would incorporate culture, history, and contemporary insights with a critical edge, together with up-to-date, value-for-money listings. Back in London, Mark and the team finished their Rough Guide, as they called it, and talked Routledge into publishing the book.

That first *Rough Guide to Greece*, published in 1982, was a student scheme that became a publishing phenomenon. The immediate success of the book – with numerous reprints and a Thomas Cook prize shortlisting – spawned a series that rapidly covered dozens of destinations. Rough Guides had a ready market among low-budget backpackers, but soon also acquired a much broader and older readership that relished Rough Guides' wit and inquisitiveness as much as their enthusiastic, critical approach. Everyone wants value for money, but not at any price.

Rough Guides soon began supplementing the "rougher" information about hostels and low-budget listings with the kind of detail on restaurants and quality hotels that independent-minded visitors on any budget might expect, whether on business in New York or trekking in Thailand.

These days the guides – distributed worldwide by the Penguin group – offer recommendations from shoestring to luxury and cover more than 200 destinations around the globe, including almost every country in the Americas and Europe, more than half of Africa, and most of Asia and Australasia. Our ever-growing team of authors and photographers is spread all over the world, particularly in Europe, the USA, and Australia.

In 1994, we published the *Rough Guide to World Music* and *Rough Guide to Classical Music*, and a year later the *Rough Guide to the Internet*. All three books have become benchmark titles in their fields – which encouraged us to expand into other areas of publishing, mainly around popular culture. Rough Guides now publish:

- Travel guides to more than 200 worldwide destinations
- Dictionary phrasebooks to 22 major languages
- History guides ranging from Ireland to Islam
- Maps printed on rip-proof and waterproof Polyart™ paper
- Music guides running the gamut from Opera to Elvis
- Restaurant guides to London, New York, and San Francisco
- Reference books on topics as diverse as the Weather and Shakespeare
- Sports guides from Formula 1 to Man Utd
- Pop culture books from Lord of the Rings to Cult TV
- World Music CDs in association with World Music Network

Visit **www.roughguides.com** to see our latest publications.

Rough Guide credits

Text editor: Yuki Takagaki
Layout: Dan May
Cartography: Ed Wright
Picture research: Mark Thomas
Proofreader: Margaret Doyle

....

Editorial: London Martin Dunford, Kate Berens, Helena Smith, Claire Saunders, Geoff Howard, Ruth Blackmore, Ann-Marie Shaw, Gavin Thomas, Polly Thomas, Richard Lim, Lucy Ratcliffe, Clifton Wilkinson, Alison Murchie, Fran Sandham, Sally Schafer, Alexander Mark Rogers, Karoline Densley, Andy Turner, Ella O'Donnell, Andrew Lockett, Joe Staines, Duncan Clark, Peter Buckley, Matthew Milton; **New York** Andrew Rosenberg, Richard Koss, Yuki Takagaki, Hunter Slaton, Chris Barsanti, Thomas Kohnstamm, Steven Horak
Design & Layout: London Helen Prior, Dan May, Diana Jarvis; **Delhi** Madhulita Mohapatra, Umesh Aggarwal, Ajay Verma
Production: Julia Bovis, John McKay, Sophie Hewat
Cartography: **London** Maxine Repath, Ed Wright, Katie Lloyd-Jones; **Delhi** Manish Chandra, Rajesh Chhibber, Jai Prakesh Mishra, Ashutosh Bharti, Rajesh Mishra, Animesh Pathak
Cover art direction: Louise Boulton
Picture research: Sharon Martins, Mark Thomas, Jj Luck
Online: **New York** Jennifer Gold, Cree Lawson, Suzañne Welles; **Delhi** Manik Chauhan, Amarjyoti Dutta, Narender Kumar
Marketing & Publicity: **London** Richard Trillo, Niki Smith, David Wearn, Chloë Roberts, Demelza Dallow; **New York** Geoff Colquitt, David Wechsler, Megan Kennedy
Finance: Gary Singh
Manager India: Punita Singh
Series editor: Mark Ellingham
PA to Managing Director: Julie Sanderson
Managing Director: Kevin Fitzgerald

SMALL PRINT

Publishing information

This sixth edition published February 2004 by
Rough Guides Ltd,
80 Strand, London WC2R 0RL.
345 Hudson St, 4th Floor,
New York, NY 10014, USA.
Distributed by the Penguin Group
Penguin Books Ltd,
80 Strand, London WC2R 0RL
Penguin Putnam, Inc.
375 Hudson Street, NY 10014, USA
Penguin Books Australia Ltd,
487 Maroondah Highway, PO Box 257,
Ringwood, Victoria 3134, Australia
Penguin Books Canada Ltd,
10 Alcorn Avenue, Toronto, Ontario,
Canada M4V 1E4
Penguin Books (NZ) Ltd,
182–190 Wairau Road, Auckland 10,
New Zealand
Typeset in Bembo and Helvetica to an original design by Henry Iles.

Printed in Italy by LegoPrint S.p.A

This book originally written and researched by Mick Sinclair.

536pp includes index
A catalogue record for this book is available from the British Library
ISBN 1-84353-194-1
The publishers and authors have done their best to ensure the accuracy and currency of all the information in **The Rough Guide to Florida**; however, they can accept no responsibility for any loss, injury, or inconvenience sustained by any traveler as a result of information or advice contained in the guide.
1 3 5 7 9 8 6 4 2

Help us update

We've gone to a lot of effort to ensure that the sixth edition of **The Rough Guide to Florida** is accurate and up-to-date. However, things change – places get "discovered," opening hours are notoriously fickle, restaurants and rooms raise prices or lower standards. If you feel we've got it wrong or left something out, we'd like to know, and if you can remember the address, the price, the time, the phone number, so much the better.

We'll credit all contributions and send a copy of the next edition (or any other Rough Guide if you prefer) for the best letters. Everyone who writes to us and isn't already a subscriber will receive a copy of our full-color thrice-yearly newsletter. Please mark letters: "**Rough Guide Florida Update**" and send to: Rough Guides, 80 Strand, London WC2R 0RL, or Rough Guides, 4th Floor, 345 Hudson St, New York, NY 10014. Or send an email to **mail@roughguides.com**

Have your questions answered and tell others about your trip at **www.roughguides.atinfopop.com**

Acknowledgments

Mark In Miami, thanks to Erica Freshman and Jacquelynn D. Powers, who always keep me company till the early hours and up to date on the Next Big Thing. For smart insights and a friendly welcome, thanks to Jennifer Rubell, Lisa Treister, Herb Sosa, Katie Rhodes, Chad Oppenheim, Michael Capponi, Amelia Alonso, and Tara Solomon. I'm also grateful to Dindy Yokel, Norah Lawlor, Kristen Vigrass, and Brad Packer for making my visit as hassle-free as possible, and in the Florida Keys, to Carol O'Shaughnessy and Josie Gullicksen for scheduling my trip, and to Karen Peterson for road-tripping with me there. Thanks finally to Ben and Maureen for keeping the home fires burning in New York.

Ross would like to thank Yuki Takagaki for her careful editing, Ron and Juli Velton for their hospitality, and the following people for helping with the research for this guide: Debbie Bowen, Joe Lettelleir, Julie Fernandez, Dawn Grigsby, Bates Reed, Jason Lasecki, Camille Dudley, John Pricher, Cindy and Joe Montalto, Kelly Earnest, Wit Tuttell, Cindy Cockburn, Carol Lee Wallis, Starla Hayes, Jayna Leach, Stacy Garrett, and Amber Peterson.

Todd Huge thanks go out to: the power trio of Cindy Malin, Kathy Harper, and Jenny Martin; Patrick McSweeney; Jay Humphreys; Ann Margo Peart; Lee Rose; Andrew Rosenberg and Yuki Takagaki for their support and diligence; and Tina Musico for genuine northern Florida hospitality and enthusiasm. Also, gratitude to SuziQ for her sisterly assistance, and for all the DeRoses, Kellys, and Hazens: Hey ya!

Heartfelt thanks to Dan May for elegant production work, Ed Wright for sublime mapmaking, Margaret Doyle for assiduous proofreading, Mark Thomas for tireless picture research, Sheelah Kolhatkar for thoughtful indexing, Margaret Ross at Stanfords Map and Travel Bookshop for handy map information, and, as ever, to Andrew Rosenberg for his steady guidance.

Readers' letters

Thanks to all the readers who took the trouble to write in with their comments and suggestions (and apologies to anyone whose name we've misspelled or omitted):

Penny Campey, Sharon Gerrard, Rob Hammond, R. Keachie, John Knott, Dan Kriwitsky, Steve Lawlor, Cynthia Lindell, Rosemary Lovatt, Jutta Mistelbacher, Brian and Nan Morgan, Mike and Carol Shipley, Richard Thorley, Kevan Helen Tom, and Els van Ooijen.

Photo credits

Cover credits

main front: Miami Beach © Elan Fleisher
small front top picture: Car © Robert Harding
back lower picture: Epcot, Orlando © Robert Harding
back top picture: Ringling Museum of Art, Sarasota © Robert Harding
back lower picture: Everglades © Getty

Introduction

Sunbathers at Miami Beach © James L. Amos/Corbis p.i
Florida Oranges © Owaki-Kulla/Corbis p.iii
Golf Course © Tony Roberts/Corbis p.iv
Pine Glades Lake at Sunset © Galen Rowell/Corbis p.v
Biscayne Bay Pelicans © T. Why/Trip p.vi
Parasols and loungers © J. Miller/Alamy p.vi
St Augustine, Lightner Museum © Viesti Collection/Trip p.vii
Men playing dominoes, Little Havana © Neil Setchfield p.viii
Air plant, the Everglades © Picturesque /Trip p.ix
Coral reef and fish © Stephen Frink/Alamy p.ix
Mickey Mouse © James Morgan/Axiom p.x
Tarpon Springs sponge stall © Visit Florida p.xi

Things not to miss

01 Alligator encounters © Amanda Hall
02 Apalachicola National Forest © Visit Florida
03 Art Deco apartment © Tony Arruza/Corbis
04 Disney World, EPCOT Center © J. Greenberg/Trip
05 Boca Raton Resort © J. Greenberg /Trip
06 Starfish on Sanibel Island © Corbis
07 Canoeing in the Everglades © Richard Crawford /Axiom
08 Celebration town © John Miller/Robert Harding
09 Back to the Future ride, Universal Studios © Universal Studios
10 Gable and tower roof, Mount Dora © Dave G. Houser/Corbis
11 Sea turtle viewing © Robert Harding
12 Weathered shack on Cedar Key © Corbis
13 Flamenco Dancers in Tampa City © Tony Arruza/Corbis
14 Captain Tony's Saloon © Fraser Hall /Robert Harding
15 Venetian Pool, Coral Gables © Robert Holmes/Corbis
16 Corkscrew Swamp Sanctuary © Fraser Hall/Robert Harding
17 Bahamian Village house © Fraser Hall/Robert Harding
18 Fantasy Fest © Fantasy Fest Media
19 Fishing © Ann Curtis /Travel Ink
20 A pair of manatee © Douglas Faulkner/Corbis
21 Miami Art Museum logo © Richard Cummins/Corbis
22 Ocean Drive © F and M Hall
23 Ponce Inlet Lighthouse © J. Greenburg /Trip
24 Splendid China performance © Mark E. Gibson/Corbis
25 Chalet Suzanne © Chalet Suzanne
26 Cà d'Zan © Fraser Hall /Robert Harding
27 Space Shuttle launches, Cape Canaveral © Visit Florida
28 Statue of Pedro Menendez de Aviles © Lee Snider/Corbis
29 Conch fritters © Trevor Ward/Robert Harding

Black and whites

Miami Beach © Visit Florida p.58
Biscayne Bay © Visit Florida p.93
Palm trees, Key Largo © Corbis p.124
Ernest Hemingway House © Bob Krist/Corbis p.131
Egret © Visit Florida p.168
10,000 Islands © Visit Florida p.178
Fort Lauderdale © Visit Florida p.184
West Palm Beach © Visit Florida pp.193
Edison House © Visit Florida p.226
Horse Shoe Crabs, Ding Darling National Wildlife Reserve © Darrell Gulin/Corbis p.235
Tampa Skyline Bridge © John Sohm, ChromoSohm Inc/Corbis p.262
Cigar display at Ybor City State Museum © Richard Cummins/Corbis p.273
Walt Disney World © Peter Hammond/Network Aspen p.322
Sea World © M. MacKenzie/Trip p.333
Jacksonville Landing © Visit Florida p.370
NASCAR 2003, The Daytona 500 © George Tiedemann/New Sport/Corbis p.382
Dunes © Visit Florida p.412
The Panhandle © Visit Florida p.424